Introduction to Criminal Justice

EIGHTH EDITION

Introduction to Criminal Justice

EIGHTH EDITION

Lawrence F. Travis III
University of Cincinnati

Bradley D. Edwards
East Tennessee State University

Routledge
Taylor & Francis Group

LONDON AND NEW YORK

First published 2015 by Anderson Publishing

Published 2015 by Routledge
2 Park Square, Milton Park, Abingdon, Oxon OX14 4RN

and by Routledge
711 Third Avenue, New York, NY 10017, USA

Routledge is an imprint of the Taylor & Francis Group, an informa business

Acquiring Editor: Pamela Chester
Development Editor: Ellen S. Boyne
Project Manager: Punithavathy Govindaradjane
Designer: Russell Purdy

Library of Congress Cataloging-in-Publication Data

Travis, Lawrence F.
  Introduction to criminal justice / Lawrence F. Travis III and Bradley D. Edwards. – Eighth edition.
    pages cm
  ISBN 978-0-323-29071-5
  1. Criminal justice, Administration of–United States. I. Edwards, Bradley D. II. Title.
  HV9950.T7 2014
  364.973–dc23

2014014251

British Library Cataloguing in Publication Data
A catalogue record for this book is available from the British Library

ISBN 978-0-323-29071-5 (pbk)

Contents

Preface

This eighth edition maintains the same approach to criminal justice that characterized previous editions. The central purpose of this text is to provide students with a relatively brief, affordable, and comprehensive overview of the criminal justice system. As in earlier editions, the style and vocabulary are set at the reading level of the typical college freshman. I hope that reading this book is informative as well as exciting and entertaining for students.

Many introductory students do not realize that criminal justice is a science, with an ever increasing knowledge of the important topics covered in this text. As with previous editions, the most widespread changes in this edition of the text involve updating the references to reflect the most current knowledge available. There is increased discussion throughout the book of important topics such as terrorism and problem-oriented policing, which have become more prevalent over the past several years. Chapter 1, in particular, received a significant restructuring to include sections on criminal justice careers and a brief introduction to the academic side of criminal justice. Finally, this edition includes an increased number of graphs and transitions from a two-color to a four-color format to increase the visual appeal of the book. My hope is that these changes allow for a more pleasurable reading experience.

Those who have used previous editions will notice the addition of a new author. In fact, Lawrence Travis III did not participate in this edition of the book. I am grateful to Lawrence for creating the foundation for this book and its many successful editions. His mark will certainly be felt in this edition and any subsequent edition. I must also thank Steve Lab and John Whitehead, the authors of Chapter 14 on the juvenile justice system.

I am grateful to Michael Braswell for his support in general and on this book. I am also thankful to have worked with a wonderful staff at Elsevier, especially Ellen Boyne, the project editor. Her professionalism and dedication is unsurpassed. I also owe a thank-you to Kirsten Piatak for her help with the ancillary material. Finally, this edition would not have been completed without the love, support, and patience of my wife, Nyela. Thanks to you all.

Bradley D. Edwards

CHAPTER 1

Criminal Justice Perspectives

Imagine that you are standing on a busy street corner. You look at the people around you. What do you see?

> A woman drops a postcard in a mailbox.
> Across the street, a man carrying a small suitcase steps off a bus.
> Several feet away from you, a couple is arguing about something.
> A police car slowly passes through the intersection.
> Less than half a block away, someone is jaywalking while a small child nearby reads a street sign.
> A man deposits money in a nearby parking meter.
> A stranger approaches and asks that you sign a petition in support of banning cell phone use by drivers.

What you probably do not see is that the mix of pedestrian and vehicular traffic is orderly. You do not notice that almost everyone watches the police car, at least briefly. You do not realize that all of these strangers at the intersection are going about their own business, apparently unaware of each other. Yet, in a well-rehearsed routine, they stop and go on cue from the traffic light. You probably do not see a crime (with the possible exception of the jaywalker).

Without realizing it, you have observed the criminal justice system in action. What you did not know is that the postcard was a monthly report the woman was sending to her probation officer. Nor was it clear that the man with the suitcase just left the state penitentiary on parole. The arguing couple may be tonight's domestic disturbance (or last night's). The slow-moving police car is searching for the small child, who is reading the street signs because he is lost. The jaywalker crossed the street to avoid walking past a group of teens gathered on the sidewalk. The man at the parking meter wants to avoid a citation. The person with the petition hopes to ensure that motorists refrain from using cell phones by making it criminal to do so.

The workings of the criminal justice system affected the entire street corner scene just described, and all of the individuals in it. Interestingly, the individuals also directly affect the workings of that system. Should the argumentative couple become too boisterous, the shopper fail to deposit the correct coins in

Important Terms

closed system
community justice
crime control
    model
criminal justice
criminology
due process
    model
education
evidence-based
    policy
family model
federalism
formal social
    control
functions
informal social
    control
latent functions
local autonomy
manifest
    functions
open system
separation of
    powers
social control
system
theory
training

the parking meter, the woman not mail the postcard, and so on, you would expect some sort of official response from the justice system. Criminal justice is an integral part of our society and social living.

Sociologists often speak of the purposes of social institutions as "functions" (Parsons, 1966). **Functions** are the goals served by a social institution. For instance, schools serve the function of education. We can classify institutional functions as either manifest or latent. **Manifest functions** are the stated purposes of the institution, whereas **latent functions** are the unstated or hidden goals. Schools serve the manifest function of education through teaching students various academic subjects. They also meet the latent functions of providing child care and controlling the workforce by otherwise occupying millions of young people.

SOCIAL CONTROL

Cohen (1966:3) noted, "If human beings are to do business with one another, there must be rules, and people must be able to assume that, by and large, these rules will be observed." The making and enforcement of rules is a requirement for organized social living. **Social control** is the label given to the processes and structures that seek to limit rule-breaking behavior, or deviance.

There are a number of instruments of social control in any society, of which the law and criminal justice process are only one. Most discussions of social control attempt to classify the different means by which conformity is achieved (Black, 1976; Ross, 1926; Travis & Langworthy, 2008). These classifications focus on the procedures and processes that support conformity. The social control mechanisms in a society or a community can influence individual behavior by assigning "blame" and sanctions, or by prevention and education.

Types of Social Control

One of the most common ways of classifying social control processes is to distinguish between "formal" and "informal" social controls. **Formal social control** includes those sanctions applied by some authorized body after a public finding of fault. **Informal social control**, in contrast, refers to mechanisms that influence behavior without the need for a public finding of fault or the use of group-"authorized" sanctions. We can formally sanction a student who is disruptive in class by expulsion. In this case, the instructor, acting in his or her "official" (formal) capacity, or the educational institution itself, can apply the sanction of "banishment" on the offender. Alternatively, other members of the class can "hush" the offender by showing their disapproval without going through any formal process and punishment.

In the ideal, of course, the disruption would not have happened in the first place because the student would view the disruptive behavior as wrong or inappropriate. No matter how we achieve control over the behavior—formal sanctions, informal influence, or self-control—we stop or prevent the disruption.

The social business of the class can continue with relative order and predictability. The means of control vary, but the goal of social control remains the maintenance of order in social relations. Because the goal is uniform regardless of the means, the distinction among types of social control is often artificial. Rather than being completely distinct types of control, informal and formal mechanisms lie along a continuum of controls ranging from those that are internal to the individual to those imposed on the individual externally.

Suppose the student wishes to be disruptive, but refrains from doing so because of a fear of expulsion. The student has demonstrated self-control, but the impetus for control is the threat of a formal sanction. Has social control in this case been established by informal or formal methods? In general, if the use or threat of a formal sanction is the mechanism by which we maintain social order, we call the process "formal social control." If a formal sanction is not necessary (even if such a sanction exists), then we call it "informal social control."

Criminal Justice as Social Control

The primary function of criminal justice is social control. The components of the justice process are police, courts, and corrections. These components have the manifest function of controlling different kinds of deviance defined as crime. "Crime" is only a small part of the total activities and behaviors that are the targets of social control. Most social control works through "informal" mechanisms, such as shunning or ostracizing the person who is rude, insensitive, or bothersome. Other forms of deviance defined as mental illness are handled through the mental health system. Pound (1929:4) remarked, "Law does but a part of this whole task of social control; and the criminal law does but a part of that portion which belongs to the law."

Criminal justice is the formal social institution designed to respond to deviance defined as crime. Crime control is the primary purpose of the criminal justice system, but it also serves other latent functions. Police, courts, and corrections do much more than merely fight crime. Still, our examination of the criminal justice process cannot progress until we understand this central purpose. Whatever other functions it may serve, and whatever methods it may employ, we can judge or measure the justice system as an institution of formal social control.

Focusing on the social control function of criminal justice (specifically, the control of crime) makes it easier to study and understand criminal justice practices and policies. We assess the value of a policy and procedure, or proposed changes in them, by how well they meet the objective of crime control. Theoretically, it seems easy enough to maintain an "objectives" perspective, but it is often very difficult to do so in practice. Kellogg (1976:50) has observed that this perspective:

> has never made much of an impact on the administration of criminal justice, most likely because there is so little agreement as to the "objectives" of criminal justice, the purposes of punishment, and the most appropriate strategy to reduce crime.

The disagreement to which Kellogg refers concerns the means by which the justice system is expected to achieve crime control. It is not enough that criminal justice efforts control crime, those efforts must protect individual rights and otherwise be acceptable to our society. While it is true that criminal justice practices may be controversial in particular instances, the overriding interest in controlling crime is a constant goal. Although we may disagree over the use of the death penalty, wiretaps, plea bargaining, or probation, we can agree that what we want to do is reduce the incidence of crime. Unfortunately, criminal justice practices too often become focal points for debates stated in terms of the purposes of the justice system. The President's Commission on Law Enforcement and Administration of Justice (1967:70) aptly illustrated this confusion in its report:

> Any criminal justice system is an apparatus society uses to enforce the standards of conduct necessary to protect individuals and the community. It operates by apprehending, prosecuting, convicting, and sentencing those members of the community who violate the basic rules of group existence. The action taken against lawbreakers is designed to serve three purposes beyond the immediately punitive one. It removes dangerous people from the community; it deters others from criminal behavior; and it gives society an opportunity to attempt to transform lawbreakers into law-abiding citizens.

A debate may arise over whether deterring others from criminal behavior or transforming violators into law-abiding citizens is the best means of achieving the objective of social control, but no one questions the objective itself. This confusion of means and ends is not limited to disagreements over specific practices such as capital punishment but also includes ideological conflicts. People disagree not only over the appropriate forms of capital punishment (e.g., beheading, burning at the stake, electrocution, poison gas, lethal injection) but also over the appropriateness of capital punishment in general (e.g., the sanctity of life versus "an eye for an eye"). Yet, what would happen to these debates if the justice system could eliminate murder?

To further complicate an already complicated picture, the justice system is not the only social control institution in operation. The mental health system deals with many of the "rule violators" deemed inappropriate subjects for the justice system. Families, churches, schools, social organizations, and the media all serve social control purposes by informing us of what is acceptable behavior. The usefulness of the justice system must be understood within the total context of social control institutions. These other social control devices are often very effective (perhaps more effective than the criminal law), as illustrated in Box 1.1. Markowitz (2006:63) reported that when we lower the capacity of mental hospitals, the criminal justice system workload increases, writing, "In sum, public psychiatric hospital capacity is an important source of control of those whose behavior or public presence may at times threaten the social order."

BOX 1.1 SOCIAL CONTROL INSTITUTIONS IN AMERICA

Social control is achieved in many ways: through lessons learned by the individual about what is appropriate or inappropriate behavior, through structured opportunity that does not allow the individual the chance to deviate, through the exercise of coercive force to limit behavior. Nearly all social life affects social control, but the principal institutions in our society achieve social control in the following ways:

Lessons	Serve to teach us what behaviors are acceptable
Structures	Limit our opportunities for misbehavior
Coercion	Forces us to behave correctly, or prevents us from misbehaving

Lessons

The family	Children learn to respect others' property and opinions, and how to resolve conflict peacefully
Schools	Students learn appropriate behavior, work habits, and respect for others
Churches	Members learn rules for behavior (e.g., the Ten Commandments)
Social groups	Members learn tolerance and rules for personal relations and behavior (e.g., majority rule)
Recreation	Players learn rules and discipline, ways of behaving (e.g., fair play)
Employment	Workers learn discipline, work habits, "chain of command"
Mental health	Patients learn coping skills and ways of behaving (e.g., through token economies)
Law	Defendants and observers learn rules of behavior (laws) through their application

Structures

The family	Children are supervised, must abide by constraints on behavior (e.g., curfews)
Schools	Students follow fairly regimented academic schedules, are supervised by teachers
Churches	Members participate in legitimate activities (e.g., weekly services, sunday school, service projects)
Social groups	Members engage in activities (e.g., formal meetings)
Recreation	Players participate in organized activities and competitions
Employment	Workers engage in defined activities and meet performance standards (e.g., production quotas)
Mental health	Patients participate in organized activities (e.g., group meetings)
Law	Statutes require certain behaviors (e.g., providing care to children, maintenance of rental property)

Coercion

The family	Children are punished for wrongdoing (e.g., "grounding," spanking)
Schools	Students who misbehave are punished (e.g., detention, suspension from school, written assignments)

(Continued)

BOX 1.1 SOCIAL CONTROL INSTITUTIONS IN AMERICA—CONT'D

Churches	Offending members are penalized (e.g., excommunication, threat of eternal damnation)
Social groups	Offending members are sanctioned (e.g., ridicule, expulsion from the group, ostracism)
Recreation	Wrongdoers are punished (e.g., game forfeiture, penalties, loss of eligibility)
Employment	Misbehavior is penalized (e.g., loss of pay, dismissal, demotion)
Mental health	Behavioral problems are controlled (e.g., passive restraint, sedation, forcible restraint)
Law	Offenders are sanctioned (e.g., fines, incarceration, execution, assessment of damages)

That most of the pedestrians and vehicles in the illustration that opens this chapter obey the traffic lights and signs is evidence of social control. How are these individuals controlled? Some may be controlled by fear of a citation (justice system); others may react as a result of learning traffic safety at home, in school, or from the media. All of these sources of social control converge at this intersection to produce an orderly and predictable flow of traffic. How much credit for this level of conformity should go to the justice system?

In general, the criminal justice process is a formal social control mechanism. The basic social control tool available to agents of the criminal justice process is group-authorized punishment. The threat of coercive force is the ultimate sanction available for social control. The criminal justice process can be seen as the social control institution of last resort. Returning to our earlier idea of a continuum of social control, we can think of the criminal justice process as occupying the extreme end of the "formal" side of the continuum. Ideally, the individual will personally see some behavior (say, theft) as wrong, and avoid engaging in theft. If not, then the disapproval of others (family, friends, even strangers) may stop the individual from stealing. If not, then perhaps some more formal mechanism such as mental health counseling may prevent the theft. When all else fails, we can call on the criminal justice process to try to force the individual to stop stealing.

One need only consider two examples of traffic behavior to realize the complex interaction of the many sources of social control. First, compare the orderliness of most street traffic to the relative "free-for-all" chaos characteristic of most shopping mall parking lots. Second, think of the number of times you (as driver or passenger) have waited at a stoplight on a deserted street. It is clear that the presence or absence of others does not completely explain the differences in behavior. Rather, it may be the public nature of the road as opposed to the private nature of the parking lot. The criminal justice system addresses the issue of public social behavior, but it is not the only working mechanism of social control in those cases.

A number of factors influence people's behavior including personality, motivations, beliefs, peer pressure, and opportunities. Why people do or do not engage in crime is a complex question. Some of the explanation may be that the criminal justice process exists to punish criminal behavior, but that is not the complete answer. Gertz and Gould (1995) reported on a survey of college students that revealed that the chances of a student committing criminal acts were influenced more by the student's own personal beliefs that the acts were wrong than by their perceptions of being caught and punished. Similarly, Burton et al. (1995) found that parental discipline was an important factor in explaining why some juveniles committed delinquent acts while others did not. DeLisi and Berg (2006) suggested that people having low self-control share other personality characteristics (short tempered and generally unlikable) that might explain why they are more likely to be caught up in the criminal justice process. These studies and others indicate that social control is the product of both formal and informal processes, and they are interrelated. The existence of formal controls, such as the criminal law and criminal justice process, serves to "educate" people about what is right and wrong. In this way, the law supports informal social control mechanisms, even while the law itself is a formal social control mechanism (Bianchi, 1994).

During the past few decades, the criminal justice process in the United States has undergone substantial change. Increasingly, we define the function of the justice process more broadly than crime control. Karp and Clear (2000:324) described this change: "Among justice professionals there is growing interest in a new concept of justice more often referred to as 'community justice.'" **Community justice**, as an approach to social control, sees the criminal process as an integral part of other community institutions. Crime is a symptom of problems in communities, and criminal justice agents and organizations work with offenders, victims, community groups, and other governmental agencies to solve those problems. As Karp and Clear (2000:324) saw it, "these disparate approaches share a common core, in that they address community-level outcomes by focusing on short- and long-term problem solving … priority is given to the community, enhancing its responsibility for social control while building its capacity to achieve this and other outcomes relevant to the quality of community life."

In short, community justice entails recognizing that social control is an important requirement of community life, and that traditional criminal justice activities have often been ineffective at social control. As the social control institution of last resort, we have historically used the criminal process when all else had failed, and after crime had occurred. How much better would it be to prevent crimes from occurring in the first place? To prevent crime, the agents of the criminal process should work to strengthen and facilitate informal social control institutions.

Evidence of this shift in thinking abounds. Recent programs exemplify this new emphasis on proactive, preventive efforts that involve the criminal process with other services and institutions. In 1991, the U.S. Department of Justice launched "Operation Weed and Seed" in three pilot sites. The program supports local community efforts to arrest and remove drug and violent offenders. The traditional policing action (arrest) represents the "weeding out" of criminals from high crime areas. The program includes a second component where "community-focused human services programs and neighborhood improvement initiatives" are linked with the police action (Dunworth & Mills, 1999:1). The program seeks to rebuild communities and informal social control by removing lawbreakers and improving community services, organization, and institutions at the same time. The efforts to improve the community constitute the "seeding" with the capacity to maintain law-abiding behavior. Today, more than 250 high-crime neighborhoods are participating in Operation Weed and Seed (U.S. Department of Justice, 2010). See Figure 1.1.

Another initiative, the "Comprehensive Communities Program," was started in 1994. This initiative has goals very similar to those of Operation Weed and Seed. The Comprehensive Communities Program is based on the principles that communities must take a leadership role in combating crime and violence, and that state and local jurisdictions must establish coordinated, multidisciplinary approaches for dealing effectively with the issues of crime and violence (Kelling et al., 1998:2). Evaluation findings indicate that cities involved in the

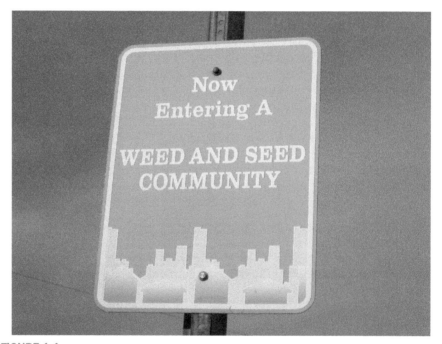

FIGURE 1.1
"Weed and Seed" programs attempt to weed out violent crime, gang activity, and drug use and trafficking in target areas, and then seed the target area by restoring the neighborhood through social and economic revitalization. The program is being implemented in communities across the country.
Ellen S. Boyne

Comprehensive Communities Program developed broad-based partnerships between police, courts, citizens, governmental agencies, and a variety of community agencies. The structure of service delivery among government and private agencies has also changed (Bureau of Justice Assistance, 2001).

Still more recently the Department of Justice instituted "Project Safe Neighborhoods." In 2001, the Department of Justice called on each of the 94 U.S. attorneys to cooperate with local officials to reduce gun and gang crime and violence. Each U.S. attorney developed a task force dedicated to gun and gang crime enforcement. This project also emphasizes community problem solving. Project Safe Neighborhoods relies on the traditional functions of the justice system. Local task forces work to identify, arrest, prosecute, and punish those guilty of gun and gang crimes (McGarrell et al., 2009).

Anyone studying criminal justice today will recognize the widespread use of words such as "community" and "partnership." After decades of evolution in which criminal justice professionals were increasingly isolated from the people they served, and where the "job" of criminal justice was defined narrowly as responding to crime, contemporary thinking holds that the best criminal justice is preventive, and that crime prevention is best accomplished by informal social control. As Friel (2000:15) explained, past efforts to improve public safety and reduce crime by professionalizing the criminal justice system had a downside. "The downside, however, has been growth in government bureaucracy, coupled with a tangle of laws, regulations, and red tape, which, although intended to restore the 'community,' instead has removed the government from that community." Building closer links between the criminal justice process and the broader community has complicated the criminal justice picture in the United States.

Supancic and Willis (1998) studied what they called "extralegal justice" and its relationship to the formal criminal justice process. They distinguish between the two, writing (1998:193), "Legal justice includes all formal responses to crime by the police, the court system, and the corrections system. On the other hand, extralegal justice is that form of informal collective action directed against deviant and criminal conduct which is administered outside the formalized legal authority and not legally sanctioned by such authority." Extralegal justice is, they contend, an important part of a total system of social control and justice. It relates to the quality and quantity of legal justice. They suggest that an understanding of criminal justice (legal justice) cannot exist without also paying attention to informal social control in the community (extralegal justice). Warner (2006) studied the use of formal and informal social control in neighborhoods, and her findings support this observation. Warner (2006:124) concluded that relying too much on the justice system may ultimately weaken informal social control but that using informal controls without support from the justice system can lead to vigilantism or some other abuse of power.

Criminal justice, as a topic of study, involves a high level of complexity. First, the study of the justice process involves the examination of social control, which itself is a complex topic. Furthermore, the justice process serves a number of conflicting—and often contradictory—purposes while achieving social control, and is characterized by a wide and expanding variety of agents, agencies, and structures. The immediate task is to develop a perspective that allows us to integrate these many components into a cohesive framework.

PERSPECTIVES ON CRIMINAL JUSTICE

As an academic field, criminal justice has frequently been accused of being "atheoretical," or lacking a unifying perspective or set of perspectives in which the operations of criminal justice agents and agencies can be understood (Hagan, 1989). As Marenin and Worrall (1998:465) noted, "Criminal justice, however, has not yet achieved theoretical integrity and coherence. There is little agreement on what criminal justice theory is or should be about, beyond the acknowledgment that criminal justice concepts and theories are to be drawn from a variety of established disciplines." They argue that criminal justice still has a way to go before it can claim independence as an academic discipline. Clear (2001:711) argued that, although still underdeveloped, criminal justice has come of age as an academic field.

Criminal justice should be distinguished from the related but distinct field of **criminology**. Criminology has been described as the scientific study of law breaking. For example, a criminologist would be interested in uncovering the nature, extent, and causes of crime (Vito & Maahs, 2012). Numerous criminological theories have been proposed through the years, becoming ever more sophisticated as time passes. The study of criminology is very important. In fact, many criminal justice academic programs require a course specializing in criminology. In contrast, criminal justice scholars focus primarily on the *response* to criminal behavior. The focus is on the progress of cases through the justice process. Which offenses and offenders are most likely to become subjects of criminal justice processing, and why? What explains why sometimes you get a traffic ticket, while at other times you receive a warning? How is it that some people get arrested, tried, convicted, and sent to prison, while others seem to "get away with murder"?

Criminal Justice Theory

A **theory** is a logical explanation of something. It is a statement about how things work to produce outcomes. Because we are interested in criminal justice, we might want to know why some places have lots of criminal justice, and others have little. Why do some cities experience high crime rates; employ many police, prosecutors, judges, and correctional personnel; and have high criminal justice caseloads? A theory of criminal justice would give us guidance in trying to understand differences in the size, structure, and operations of criminal justice processes in different places. Critics of criminal justice point to the lack of commonly held explanations and conclude that there is no theory in the field of criminal justice (Kraska, 2004).

Nonetheless, a number of theoretical works are aimed specifically at understanding the development and operation of the criminal justice process.

Gorecki (1979) and Duffee (1980) have proposed broad theories of criminal justice aimed at explaining the process as a whole. Others have written more narrow explanations or provided organizing perspectives designed to guide an understanding of criminal justice decisions and practices (Allen, 1964; Beccaria, 1764; Black, 1976; Chambliss & Seidman, 1971; Foucault, 1979; Kolonski & Mendelsohn, 1970; Packer, 1968). In reality, there are many theories of criminal justice. What is missing is a way of classifying and comparing those theories (Bernard & Engel, 2001; Kraska & Brent, 2011).

Unlike other areas of study, criminal justice researchers do not often test their theories. Rather, they examine topics and apply theories to explain their findings (Bernard & Engel, 2001). Physicists, for example, might test the theory of gravity, the theory of relativity, or chaos theory by studying the movement of planets or subatomic particles. Criminal justice scholars are more likely to study official decisions to arrest, levy charges, or impose sentences, and then apply a theory to explain what they have found (Zalman, 2007). Criminal justice has a large body of research on all sorts of topics, but lacks a structure in which to organize these findings (Kraska, 2006). Because of this, the study of criminal justice tends to be somewhat fragmented. Still, it is a mistake to conclude that there is no theory in criminal justice. In terms of criminal justice, Kraska (2004:9–10) argued, "It is impossible to conduct theory-less research. Theory influences the questions asked, the selection of the phenomenon under study, the way in which data are collected, the interpretation of those data, and the type of policies recommended." Kraska is saying that everything we do in relation to criminal justice is shaped by our "theory" (understandings and expectations). Although not formally stated as a theory, if someone believes hiring different people will change the way criminal justice is done, that person has a theory that criminal justice is a product of the officials making decisions.

Multidisciplinary Nature of Criminal Justice

Different aspects of the criminal justice process have been the topic of study in a variety of social science disciplines. Each discipline contains at least an implicit theory of what "causes" or explains criminal justice. How one views any particular decision in the process depends partly on whether the analyst is trained as a sociologist, psychologist, lawyer, political scientist, economist, or some other profession.

An arrest may be seen as an interpersonal interaction, the product of the police officer's perceptions, an exercise of legal authority, a power relation, a rational decision, or something different. In fact, most arrests probably result from a combination of these factors. The study of criminal justice operations in the United States is perhaps best described as multidisciplinary or interdisciplinary (Marenin & Worrall, 1998).

A discipline is a branch of study or learning. Thus, sociology and political science are branches of a more generic area of learning that could be called the study of "human behavior." In earlier years, the fact that programs in criminal

> ## BOX 1.2 DISCIPLINARY APPROACHES TO CRIMINAL JUSTICE
>
> Criminal justice professors (and researchers) come from a variety of disciplinary backgrounds. These backgrounds prepare them to approach justice topics and issues from different perspectives:
>
> - *Sociologists* look to the social organization of groups and interactions among people to explain how things occur.
> - *Historians* look to larger social and intellectual movements over time to explain how things occur.
> - *Psychologists* look to individual motivations and perceptions to explain how things occur.
> - *Political scientists* look to the processes of influence and the distribution of power to explain how things occur.
> - *Lawyers* look to established legal principles, statutes, and rules to explain how things occur.
> - *Economists* look to costs and benefits as an explanation of how things occur.

justice at colleges and universities tended to include courses in psychology, sociology, law, political science, social work, and other disciplines illustrated the multidisciplinary nature of criminal justice study. More recently, Southerland (2002) reported that criminal justice programs now rarely require supporting courses in sociology, psychology, political science, and law. Still, justice issues have been approached from a number of specialties. Box 1.2 briefly describes the approaches that analysts trained in different social science disciplines might prefer when studying justice topics.

A full understanding of arrests, criminal penalties, or other parts of the criminal justice system is achieved through the application of several disciplinary approaches. Thus, in studying the arrest decision, the analyst should be aware of the legal, political, rational, perceptual, organizational, and personal factors in operation.

Multidisciplinary approaches remind one of the old story about the blind men meeting an elephant. Each man feels a different part of the beast and concludes that it is something different. The man touching the trunk believes it is a snake; the one with the tail believes it is a horse; and the one at the leg believes he faces a tree. The result is that there are several interpretations of the same phenomenon, each shaped by the unique perspective of the observer. Critics of the interdisciplinary approach believe that the sighted observer would describe the elephant as a large gray or brown beast with a snake-like frontal appendage, a tail, and four large legs. In other words, he would be able to describe the elephant, but not know what it is.

SYSTEMS THEORY AND THE SYSTEMS APPROACH

This book relies on the systems approach of analyzing the criminal justice system. A **system** is a set or collection of interrelated parts working together to achieve a common goal. This perspective views the criminal justice process as a whole comprising the separate, but interrelated parts of law enforcement, courts, and corrections. These parts work together to achieve the goal of crime control in our society.

Walker (1992) observed that the systems perspective is the dominant scientific paradigm of criminal justice. That is, most people studying criminal justice use a systems model to understand the process. Walker suggested that this model came to dominate thinking about criminal justice because of the American Bar Foundation survey of criminal justice in the 1950s. Those who worked on that research project assumed leadership roles in the President's Commission on Law Enforcement and Administration of Justice in the mid-1960s. After intensive study of criminal justice operations, these researchers developed a paradigm (explanatory model) for understanding criminal justice. This paradigm was based on five general observations (Walker, 1992:66–70):

1. Criminal justice is complex, involving much more than law enforcement.
2. The role of the police, as a result, is also very complex, involving more than crime control.
3. The administration of justice is largely discretionary.
4. Discretionary decisions are not well controlled by law or formal rules.
5. The agencies of criminal justice are interrelated and form a system.

These observations have directed the development of criminal justice as a field of inquiry. The focus of criminal justice study became the decision-making processes of agents and agencies of the justice process. Rather than a simple question of law enforcement or the application of rules, each decision in the process was affected, or could be affected, by a variety of forces. Furthermore, the decisions made at one point in the process (e.g., arrest) have implications for later decisions.

What emerged from this orientation was a definition of criminal justice as a complex process of social control in which decisions reflected conflicting goals and expectations. The decisions themselves were variable. Contrary to expectations, an arrest was not solely or even primarily dependent on the existence of sufficient evidence of criminality. In addition, the separate decisions of criminal justice agents and agencies were linked in a sequential fashion, so that the choices of police officers constrained prosecutors, whose choices constrained judges, and so on. The goal of reforming criminal justice processing hinged on the ability to understand and thereby control the decision-making process. Understanding this process seemed to require viewing criminal justice as a system (Conley, 1994).

Types of Systems

Systems are identified and classified in a number of ways (Sutherland, 1975). For our purposes, we need only differentiate between "closed" and "open" systems. These terms refer to the sensitivity of a system to its environment. Closed systems are relatively impervious and insensitive to the environment, whereas those that more freely interact with their environments are open.

A **closed system** is often self-contained. One simplistic example of a closed system is an astronaut in a space suit. Whether standing on earth, conducting a spacewalk, or exploring another planet, the astronaut is insulated from the environment. To the degree that it functions regardless of surroundings, the life-support system of a space suit is a closed system.

An **open system** is sensitive to its environment, like a business. Among other things, changes in tax laws, wage rates, markets, environmental protection regulations, shipping rates, or costs of raw materials will affect profits. To remain profitable, a business must constantly adapt not only to internal pressures but also to external or environmental changes. Most organizations operate as open systems.

It is most accurate and useful to classify the justice system as an open system. Clearly, the justice process in American society must react to changes in the economy, population, and political components of its environment. Perhaps less clearly, it must also adapt to changes in social values, ideology, and information. We will see in later chapters how influential the environment of the justice system is in explaining the operations of the justice process. Finally, we must recognize that the criminal justice system influences the broader society.

THE ENVIRONMENT OF CRIMINAL JUSTICE

Having defined the criminal justice process as an open system, we must briefly examine the environmental factors that affect its operations. These factors have a direct impact on all aspects of criminal justice. The environment of criminal justice is both material and ideological. The material environment includes concrete resources such as money, personnel, equipment, and the like. The ideological environment comprises chiefly of values and beliefs about how the justice process should operate. Figure 1.2 illustrates the placement of criminal justice within this environment.

The Material Environment of Criminal Justice

In simple terms, each system has three stages: (1) input, (2) throughput, and (3) output. In manufacturing, for example, input is the reception of raw materials, throughput is the production process, and output is the final product. For the criminal justice system, criminal offenses are the input, the transformation of crime suspects into convicts is the throughput, and ex-convicts are the output.

As with manufacturing, the input stage of the criminal justice system involves labor, machinery, and capital. Law enforcement officers, prosecutors, judges, defense attorneys, correctional staff, police cars, courthouses, jails, and even paper clips for reports are parts of the justice system input. In addition, the output of the justice system is not limited to "ex-convicts." Some nonguilty suspects

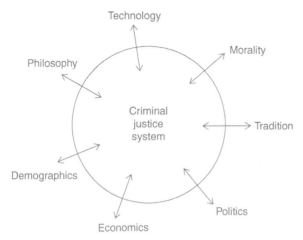

FIGURE 1.2
The environment of criminal justice.

are released at various stages in the process, as are some persons who are guilty yet not convicted of a crime. Many ex-convicts do not retain that label long before being arrested for a new crime. This illustration serves the purpose of identifying the principal material factors in the criminal justice system's environment: raw materials and the means of production.

RAW MATERIALS

The raw material of the criminal justice system consists of criminal offenses. Thus, the system is affected by changes in the nature and distribution of crime. Suppose our "petition-pusher" from the opening part of this chapter is successful and a law is passed that prohibits all drivers from using cell phones while driving. Use of cell phones while driving becomes a new source of "raw material" for the criminal justice system. However, if all criminal laws were repealed, there would be no raw materials for criminal justice.

Unlike the manufacturing firm, the justice system has little control over the volume of raw material it receives. Imagine the effects on a manufacturing plant of deliveries of materials that far exceed the plant's capacity to produce. For example, imagine the delivery of 1 million barrels of crude oil each day to a refinery that can process only 100,000 barrels every 24 hours. Similar situations have occurred in the justice process.

In cases of large crowds or demonstrations, police officers are often instructed to overlook minor violations and concentrate on the maintenance of order. In large measure, this is because large crowds are potentially dangerous, but it is also because there may be no capacity to handle mass arrests. In one massive demonstration in Washington, DC, resulting in thousands of arrests, suspects were held in RFK Stadium until they could be processed. Although this example is perhaps the exception, the abundance of raw material is a long-recognized problem for the justice system. Increasing demands on the justice system may result in lower levels of output. Decker, Varano, and Greene (2007) report that when faced with the demands of providing additional security and dealing with an influx of some 2 million visitors during the 2002 Winter Olympics, routine police enforcement activity by the Salt Lake City Police Department decreased significantly. After the Olympics had ended, police enforcement activity returned to its previous levels. We still do not know what will be the impact of contemporary concerns about the terrorist threat that arose during the 2000s. Unless we expand the size of police agencies, adding counterterrorism responsibility will most likely detract from other aspects of police work.

One response to the heavy caseloads of criminal justice agencies seeks to alter this aspect of the environment. Proponents of decriminalization would remove certain categories of criminal behavior from the justice system. They suggest that the justice system devotes too many resources to the control of essentially harmless or victimless crimes such as vagrancy, public intoxication, and disorderly conduct (see Luna, 2003). See Figure 1.3.

FIGURE 1.3
Boston police and emergency medical services personnel stand by during a political convention. In cases of large crowds or demonstrations, police officers are often instructed to overlook minor violations and concentrate on the maintenance of order.
Ellen S. Boyne

MEANS OF PRODUCTION

The means of production for the criminal justice system are the personnel, facilities, and equipment of the various justice agencies. Changes in the capacity to process criminal cases will have an effect on the entire justice system. Increases or decreases in the numbers of police, prosecutors, judges, prisons, or other components of the justice system will result in changes in the number of cases processed or in the manner in which cases are handled (Brandl, Chamlin, & Frank, 1995). Zhao, Scheider, and Thurman (2003) found that the increased number of police officers and improved police technology provided by the federal Office of Community Oriented Policing Services grants to local police agencies resulted in increased numbers of arrests over the years.

The actual outcome of changes in the means of production of the criminal justice system is not as important as the fact that the alterations will lead to adaptations in the system. For example, the recent problem of prison and jail crowding has meant that many offenders who would otherwise have been imprisoned have been released early or placed on probation instead of being sent to prison or jail. In addition, the recent trend toward "truth in sentencing" laws, which eliminate or reduce the opportunity for parole and good time credit, has been heralded as a way to "get tough" on crime and reduce sentencing discrepancies. However, these sentences also reduce the incentives for prisoners to obey prison rules, resulting in increased prisoner misconduct (Bales & Miller, 2012). Thus, a person considering reform in one part of the justice system (more or better police, prosecutors, judges, prisons, or what have you) must be sensitive to the fact that such changes will have a ripple effect on the remainder of the justice process. Indeed, systems theory suggests that fluctuations in the environment will be met with changes in the system to limit the disruption of equilibrium. One of the most salient characteristics of the criminal justice system (and one strongly supporting the use of a systems perspective) is that it is resistant to change (Travis, 1982).

The Ideological Environment of Criminal Justice

As a social institution, and particularly one of social control, perhaps the most important aspect of the environment in which the criminal justice system operates is ideological rather than material. The criminal justice system is rife with value conflicts, political and social controversy, and inefficient organization. These attributes of criminal justice reflect our deep ambivalence about social control.

VALUE CONFLICTS

Perhaps the most fundamental value conflict characteristic of criminal justice in the United States is that between individual freedom and social regularity. In his discussion of policing, Lundman (1980) determined that this conflict was one between liberty (freedom) and civility (order). As Culbertson (1984:vii) has observed:

> We demand that our police apprehend suspects, that our courts convict the accused, and that our correctional system, in some way, punish the convicted. We demand order. The tasks involved in insuring order would

be relatively straightforward were it not for our simultaneous demand that the police, courts and correctional agencies operate within the constraints placed upon them by the law.

Perhaps the best known analysis of this controversy is Packer's (1968) models of the criminal justice system, which he called crime control and due process (see Box 1.3). The **crime control model** of criminal justice would support efficiency with an emphasis on speedy case processing. We would expect an enhancement of police powers to search and arrest, and a relaxation in the rules of evidence to allow relevant information to be presented in court. The emphasis on speed would support plea bargaining, prosecutorial discretion, and mandatory sentences as methods for hastening the disposition of cases. Although consistent with the basic tenets of a democratic society (e.g., no coerced confessions), the crime control system would operate on a presumption of guilt. In contrast, the **due process model** would vigorously protect individual rights. It would put restrictions on searches and arrests without warrants, require full trials with strict rules of evidence, and support separate sentencing hearings to protect the interests of the individual offender.

With some degree of irony, we can say that America is constitutionally unsuited for criminal justice. Our emphasis on individual liberty and constrained governmental authority requires us to tolerate a certain level of inefficiency in criminal justice. We generally do not allow potentially effective crime control practices such as random wiretaps, warrantless searches, censorship of mail, or the use of "truth serum" during interrogation. We do provide defense counsel, pretrial release, and appellate review of trials and sentences in most cases. In an effort to preserve individual liberty, we not only constrain justice agencies from engaging

BOX 1.3 DUE PROCESS VERSUS CRIME CONTROL

New York City's stop-and-frisk policy is a prime example of the criminal justice system's conflicting goals. The policy allows the police to conduct a "pat-down" search on suspicious individuals in an attempt to find illegal weapons. Many critics of the policy view stop and frisk as a violation of one's rights and inherently discriminatory. In fact, statistics show that minorities are disproportionately targeted for these stops, and only 6% of these stops result in an arrest. Further, only half of those arrested following a frisk search are ultimately convicted of a crime and most of these convictions are for minor crimes such as graffiti and disorderly conduct (Schneiderman, 2013). New York mayor Michael Bloomberg defended the policy, claiming that it reduced crime through proactive policing. When asked about the large numbers of minorities stopped under the policy, the mayor's response was, "If we stopped people based on census numbers, we would stop many fewer criminals, recover many fewer weapons and allow many more violent crimes to take place" (Taylor, 2012).

Those individuals who advocate for a crime control model of criminal justice would likely favor the stop-and-frisk policy—as it might allow the police to effectively repress crime in a quick and efficient manner. Those favoring the due process model, however, would likely have concerns regarding the fairness of the searches.

in many activities, but we also actively impose barriers to the agencies' swift and simple operation. Spader (1987) remarked that criminal justice practice represents a "golden zigzag" between social protection and individual rights.

The criminal justice system is designed for crime control, but the control of crime must be consistent with our social and political heritage. The justice system must achieve a balance between competing values of federalism and uniformity, vengeance and assistance, and differing political persuasions, as well as between individual actors and social regularity. Balancing these opposing forces is part of what makes the justice system so complex.

The tension between our concerns for crime control (order or safety) and due process (limited governmental power or individual liberty) is clearly visible as we struggle to respond to the threat of terrorist attacks. As Lynch (2002:2) put it, "If one examines the history of the federal government's responses to terrorism, a disturbing pattern emerges. The federal government responds to terrorist attacks on U.S. soil—such as the Oklahoma City bombing in 1995—by rushing to restrict civil liberties." From expanded wiretap authority to increased surveillance of citizens, efforts to prevent terrorism often require (or produce) increases in governmental authority and limits on individual liberty.

Value conflicts are also evident as we try to determine what to do for, with, and about criminal offenders. We generally are not content with punishment for punishment's sake (Finckenauer, 1988). Rather, we expect some ultimate "good" to arise from governmental action.

In this vein, Griffiths (1970) suggested a third model of the justice system in opposition to those described by Packer. This third type is the **family model**. This model assumes that the interests of society and those of the offender are the same. The net effect of criminal justice processing of an offender should be beneficial to both the offender and the society.

The term "family model" is an apt description of the conflict between vengeance and assistance. While a parent may want or need to punish a child's misbehavior, the purpose of the punishment is to correct the child's error and to restore harmony in the family. Thus, actions taken by agents of the justice system are continually compared against two standards:

> Has punishment been administered?
> Has the offender been "helped"?

Albanese (1996) captured the essence of this conflict in his presidential address to the Academy of Criminal Justice Sciences. As have others before him, Albanese called for a merging of the choices between punishment and rehabilitation into a choice of punishment and rehabilitation. Still, despite decades of observations that we can both punish and help at the same time, current thinking is still dominated by the conception that the two are distinct and opposite.

Depending on the political persuasion of criminal justice policymakers (i.e., liberal or conservative), radically different strategies may be adopted to control crime (Reckless & Allen, 1979). The attitudes, perceptions, and tendencies of criminal justice agents and offenders are important factors in understanding the operations of the criminal justice system. The ability of individual actors to affect criminal justice decisions and processing is known as "discretion."

Individual Discretion

Glueck (1928:480) observed that the criminal justice system was a "clumsy admixture of the oil of discretion and the water of rule." By this he meant that the rule or "law" serves to place constraints on the actions of agents of the criminal justice system, but the system relies on discretion to process cases smoothly. Regardless of the specificity of applicable law, there is always room for "judgment calls."

Davis (1969) studied the pervasiveness of discretion in the justice process. He observed police, prosecutors, parole authorities, and judges, and noted their wide-ranging discretionary powers. In any specific instance, a decision to arrest, charge a suspect, impose a sentence, or grant release from prison is a judgment call. For example, the discretionary power of police officers is illustrated by our hope for a mere warning when we are caught exceeding the speed limit.

The fact of discretion in criminal justice decision making renders the explanation of specific case decisions very complex. However, an understanding of the forces at work in any given decision sheds light on the process. This chapter has attempted to illustrate these forces.

It is important to realize that discretion is not totally unfettered. Every discretionary decision is made within a context of forces operating at all levels of the justice system previously described. Therefore, the day-to-day workings of the justice system are structured by these larger and more distant factors, which must be kept in balance.

Federalism and Uniformity

One of the major criticisms of the systems approach to criminal justice is that the justice process is decentralized, disorganized, and lacks consistency. Yet, these limitations of the criminal justice system are congruent with two of our social and political values: federalism and the separation of powers.

The basic principle of governmental organization in the United States is that of **federalism**. Our nation is the result of a federation of sovereign states. The U.S. Constitution enumerates the rights and obligations of the federal government, and the Tenth Amendment includes the "reservation clause," which reads:

> The powers not delegated to the United States by the Constitution, nor prohibited by it to the states, are reserved to the states respectively, or to the people.

This amendment enables each state to pass and enforce its own criminal laws, and to create the offices and agencies necessary to perform these tasks. Thus, a federal justice system is created to deal with federal offenses (e.g., counterfeiting), and separate justice systems are created to enable each state to deal with state crimes (e.g., theft).

States, in turn, have constitutions under which they charter municipalities. These counties, cities, towns, and villages then provide for their own criminal offenses and operate offices and agencies to enforce local and state laws. This organizational structure of government ensures **local autonomy**, so that the citizens of each state and community have a fairly large degree of freedom from central control.

For the justice system, the result is thousands of police agencies at federal, state, and municipal levels; thousands of jails, courts, probation agencies, prosecutors, and defense offices; and scores of prison and parole agencies. It also results in differences in the definitions of crimes and the levels of punishments applicable to criminal behavior. Variety is central to criminal justice in the United States.

The Constitution of the United States also creates and maintains a **separation of powers** between the executive, judicial, and legislative branches of government. In simplistic terms, the legislature makes the law, the judiciary interprets the law, and the executive enforces the law. Each branch of government is checked and balanced by the other two branches. This tripartite governmental structure exists at the federal, state, and municipal levels of government.

This complex organization of the crime control function in America causes inefficiency. Yet, to preserve our interests in local autonomy and constrained governmental power, we must tolerate the inefficient organization of governmental service (Forst, 1977). Stolz (2002:52) observed:

> In the United States, governmental authority is constitutionally distributed among three levels of government—the federal, fifty state, and thousands of local governments.... Moreover, at each level of government, policy making authority is shared among three branches— the executive, legislative, and judicial.... These are the formal institutions of government and within these institutions the formal processes of government are carried out. In the criminal justice area, most policy making occurs at the local or state level but, particularly since the 1960s, the role of the federal government has expanded.

In short, a centralized, uniform system of criminal justice would be unconstitutional. Any efforts to understand the justice system and to promote consistency and simplicity in organization and in the processing of criminal cases must be sensitive to the values our society places on federalism. Effectiveness and efficiency of operation in the criminal justice system are not the only goals to be considered when analyzing its structure and operation.

CAREERS

The interdisciplinary nature of criminal justice, perhaps with the assistance of numerous crime-related television shows, has increased interest in the field of criminal justice. The ultimate goal of many reading this book will be to gain employment in the field of criminal justice. Luckily, the criminal justice field offers a great variety of employment opportunities. Employment options can be found in both the public and private sectors. Private-sector jobs include positions such as a loss prevention specialist, professional security specialist, or a fraud investigator (Tripp & Cobkit, 2013). However, most jobs within the criminal justice field exist under the umbrella of a local, state, or federal government agency. Job requirements and salaries typically vary widely depending upon the geographical location of the job as well as the particular level of government. In general, local- and state-level jobs within the criminal justice field will earn a lower salary than federal careers. However, federal agencies recruit from a much larger applicant pool and are thus much more selective. Employment opportunities are most often found within one of the three components of the justice system: (1) policing, (2) courts, and (3) corrections. Box 1.4 includes a sample of criminal justice employment opportunities.

Policing

Law enforcement is perhaps the most commonly cited career path among criminal justice college students. Johnson and White (2002) found that nearly 59% of college students indicated a preference for a law enforcement–type career. The overwhelming majority of these respondents desired a federal-level law enforcement career, such as the Drug Enforcement Agency; Central Intelligence Agency; Alcohol, Tobacco, Firearms, and Explosives (ATF); Federal Bureau of Investigation (FBI); and U.S. Customs. Only 5.3% of participants selected city,

---

BOX 1.4 SAMPLE OF CRIMINAL JUSTICE CAREER OPPORTUNITIES

Air Marshal	Detective
Arson and Fire Investigator	FBI Special Agent
ATF Agent	FBI Intelligence Analyst
Bailiff	Fish and Game Warden
Border Patrol Agent	Forensic Psychologist
Bounty Hunter	Forensic Science Technician
CIA Agent	Fraud Investigator
Correctional Treatment Specialist	Immigration Enforcement Agent
Corrections Officer	IRS Special Agent
Criminalist	Juvenile Probation Officer
Criminal Investigator	Loss Prevention Specialist
Crime Analyst	NSA Police Officer
Crime Laboratory Analyst	Park Ranger
Crime Prevention Specialist	Police Officer
Crime Scene Investigator	Private Security Officer
Crime Scene Technician	Probation Officer
Customs Agent	Secret Service Agent
DEA Agent	Security Officer

county, or state law enforcement as their preferred career path. Many local and state police agencies do not require applicants to possess a college degree, but most do require that applicants maintain a clean criminal record and often pass physical agility, psychological, and other preemployment screening. Applicants to federal law enforcement jobs typically have previous work experience and perhaps specialized experience or a proficiency in a foreign language. It is important to note that while the particular federal agencies listed above are the most popular, they are by no means the only opportunities. In fact, federal law enforcement officers are dispersed among approximately 100 federal departments, independent agencies, and subagencies (Walker, Burns, Bumgarner, & Bratina, 2008). See Figure 1.4.

Courts

Careers in the court system range from a bailiff (responsible for court security) to judgeships. Among the traditional faces of the court system are the various attorneys involved in each criminal case. As will be discussed in Chapter 8, criminal law is not one of the most desirable specializations among law school graduates. A primary reason for this lack of desirability is the relatively low income compared to other law specialties. For example, minimum entry-level salaries for assistant public defenders ranged from about $37,000–$58,000, with a median salary of $46,000 per year (Langton & Farole, 2010). The salary of a prosecutor

FIGURE 1.4
U.S. Immigration and Customs Enforcement agents inspecting marijuana and cocaine seized from a tunnel designed to smuggle drugs from Tijuana, Mexico, to San Diego. While federal law enforcement jobs like these appear to be the most preferred career path for students, there are a plethora of law enforcement jobs possible.
AP Photo/U.S. Immigration and Customs Enforcement, Paul Caffrey

is generally higher, but still not great in comparison to potential private practice earnings. The median salary for chief prosecutors in all jurisdictions in 2005 was $85,000. The salary is influenced by the size of the office; the median salary was $149,000 per year in the largest jurisdictions (Perry, 2006). Overall, only 37% of chief prosecutors earned more than $100,000 per year. Many offices also employ assistant prosecutors (also known as assistant district attorneys). Attorneys often seek these positions at the start of their careers to gain trial experience prior to starting their own practices (Rubin, 1984).

Judges typically earn the highest income of court employees. By mid-2009, the median salaries for judicial officials in state courts were $152,495 for chief justices of the highest court, $139,924 for intermediate appellate court justices, and $130,312 for general trial court judges (National Center for State Courts, 2010). State supreme court justices are paid an average of $122,400 per year, with intermediate and trial court judges earning average salaries of $117,000 and $109,800, respectively (*Sourcebook of Criminal Justice Statistics*, 2010). Compensation for federal judicial officers ranges from more than $15,200 per year for magistrates to more than $200,000 per year for the Chief Justice of the U.S. Supreme Court (*Sourcebook of Criminal Justice Statistics*, 2010).

Corrections

The corrections system of the criminal justice field has a wide variety of employment opportunities. Approximately 11% of Johnson and White's (2002) survey of college students indicated that they were interested in a career in corrections. Career opportunities include being a correctional officer, correctional counselor, or a probation/parole officer. Jails and prisons often recruit individuals to help supervise inmates. In fact, correctional officers are one of the largest classifications of state employees across the country. In 2012, the average annual salary for correctional officers was $43,550 (Bureau of Labor Statistics, 2013). Jail officers often are recruited in the same way as police officers, which is through local searches and civil service testing. Like jail officers, correctional officers in prisons are typically selected through civil service and are not particularly well paid. State and federal correctional facilities employed almost 450,000 personnel in 2005, with about two-thirds of these designated as custody or security staff (Stephan, 2008).

Unlike police or correctional officers, it is common for a probation officer to be required to have a college degree. Recruitment of probation officers tends to be local, consistent with the court's jurisdiction. In 2012, the Bureau of Labor Statistics (2013) reported that there were more than 86,000 probation officers and correctional treatment specialists in the United States. We can safely estimate that more than half this number is probation officers. The median salary for probation officers in 2012 was $52,380. A parole officer is often required to have a college education and to perform duties similar to those of a probation officer, except that a parole officer typically has a smaller caseload comprised of ex-inmates. Parole officers, on the average, receive slightly higher wages than do probation officers, and are selected from statewide pools through civil service procedures

ACADEMIC CRIMINAL JUSTICE

The study of criminal justice in an academic setting has evolved over time. Formal criminal justice education in the United States began in the 1920s and 1930s as an attempt to increase the professionalism of police departments. Many of these early criminal justice courses began and existed for many years as subspecialties of more established disciplines, such as sociology and law. These early courses resembled police academies. In fact, early criminal justice education was often much more focused on training than education (Finckenauer, 2005). As Eskridge (2003) pointed out, there are important distinctions between training and education. **Training** is job-specific, street-specific instruction that prepares a criminal justice professional to face his or her daily challenges. **Education**, on the other hand, is more of a long-term function aimed at developing a spirit of exploration, developing the academic tools (ability to read and write critically) and developing an introductory knowledge base of how the structure and process of the justice system works.

Criminal justice education began to expand and become more professional with the publication of the 1967 President's Commission on Law Enforcement and Administration of Justice. This report encouraged the increased education of criminal justice professionals as a way to improve the system. The recommendation led to government action in the form of a federal program which helped fund the education of students interested in a law enforcement field or to those currently working as a law enforcement officer but wanting to return to college (Flanagan, 2000). The increased student demand for criminal justice courses resulted in an expansion of class offerings; there were more than 53,000 criminal justice degrees awarded in the 2008/2009 academic year alone, representing a 74% increase over a 10-year period (Wrede & Featherstone, 2012).

Colleges and universities vary dramatically in the types of criminal justice programs offered. Many criminal justice programs still exist as subspecialties of other disciplines, most often sociology. However, contemporary criminal justice programs are often separate departments, with faculty specializing in distinct areas of the criminal justice system (Wrede & Featherstone, 2012). Some programs offer curriculums that are vocational-oriented, whereas others are more focused on theory and research (Birzer & Palmiotto, 2002). Regardless of the orientation of the specific program, the exposure to and application of social science research as it is relates to criminal justice has been increasing. This is evident in the movement toward **evidence-based policy**. Proponents of evidence-based crime policy (e.g., Walker, 2011) point to the American tradition of creating policy based on what is politically popular at the time. Unfortunately, these policies are often either ineffective or actually harmful to society and the criminal justice system. Scientific research helps policymakers better understand the criminal justice system and thus make more informed policy decisions. Academic scholars, government agencies, and even nonprofit groups conduct research that provides us a clearer picture of the criminal justice process and the effectiveness of our current crime prevention policies.

EXAMINING CRIMINAL JUSTICE

So far this chapter has served as a basic introduction to the study of criminal justice in the United States. The remainder of this book will explore criminal justice practices, agents, and agencies, building on what has been described here. Three themes emerging from this introduction will guide our examination of the U.S. system of criminal justice. The first is the notion of a systems approach to understanding the operations of the justice process. Criminal justice is part of the system of social control in American society, as well as part of the larger society. Changes in the environment (materials, ideas, values, etc.) will influence the justice process. A second theme is that there is a fundamental conflict between individual liberty and collective needs for predictability. The criminal justice system, each of its decision points, and all of the decision makers involved in the system must strike a balance between the interests of the individual citizen and the interests of the community. Finally, the existence of discretion in the justice system is the third theme in our approach to studying criminal justice. In most cases, criminal justice agents (police, prosecutors, judges, corrections officials, and others) have some latitude in deciding what to do about offenses and offenders. Much of our attention will be devoted to identifying what sorts of factors help us to understand the kinds of decisions that are made.

As we progress in our examination of criminal justice in the United States, we will describe the justice system and its structure, organizations, and agents. We will investigate the range of decisions that are made in cases at each stage of the justice process, and explore the factors that are associated with different decisions. Finally, we will try to place things into the larger context of seeking a balance between due process and crime control.

See Box 1.5 for a chart that seeks to present a simple yet comprehensive view of the movement of cases through the criminal justice system.

PREVIEW OF FORTHCOMING CHAPTERS

In the chapters to follow, we will examine the criminal justice system. The first four chapters set the stage for analyzing criminal justice operations. This chapter has provided a foundation of criminal justice perspectives. Chapter 2 presents an overview of the operations and structure of the criminal justice system of the United States. Chapter 3 includes a discussion of law and a description of some recent changes in criminal justice, and illustrates how the system reflects changes in our thinking about crime and criminals. In Chapter 4, sources of data on the nature and extent of crime are reviewed, and an overview of the way in which cases are "selected" for justice processing is provided. The next 10 chapters address the subsystems of the criminal justice system, from the detection of crime through investigation and arrest; to initial appearance in court; through formal charging, trial, and conviction; and finally to sentencing and the goals of criminal penalties. Incarceration and community-centered punishments are described and discussed, and the juvenile justice system is

BOX 1.5 THE CRIMINAL JUSTICE SYSTEM

Procedures in individual jurisdictions may vary from the pattern shown here. The differing weights of the lines indicate the relative volumes of cases disposed of at various points in the system. This information, however, is only suggestive because no nationwide data of this sort exist.

What is the sequence of events in the criminal justice system?

Note: This chart gives a simplified view of caseflow through the criminal justice system. Procedures vary among jurisdictions. The weights of the lines are not intended to show the actual size of caseloads.

1. May continue until trial.
2. Administrative record of arrest. First step at which temporary release on bail may be available.
3. Before magistrate, commissioner, or justice of peace. Formal notice of charge, advice of rights. Bail set. Summary trials for petty offenses usually conducted here without further processing.
4. Preliminary testing of evidence against defendant. Charge may be reduced. No separate preliminary hearing for misdemeanors in some systems.
5. Charge filed by prosecutor on basis of information submitted by police or citizens. Alternative to grand jury indictment; often used in felonies, almost always in misdemeanors.
6. Reviews whether government evidence sufficient to justify trial. Some states have no grand jury system; others seldom use it.
7. Appearance for plea; defendant elects trial by judge or jury (if available); counsel for indigent usually appointed here in felonies. Often not at all in other cases.
8. Charge may be reduced at any time prior to trial in return for plea of guilty or for other reasons.
9. Challenge on constitutional grounds to legality of detention. May be sought at any point in the process.
10. Police often hold informal hearings, dismiss or adjust many cases without further processing.
11. Probation officer decides desirability of further court action.
12. Welfare agency, social services, counseling, medical care, etc., for cases where adjudicatory handling not needed.

Source: President's Commission on Law Enforcement and Administration of Justice (1967) evaluated in a separate chapter. The last chapter presents a discussion of systemwide developments and issues and the future of criminal justice in the United States.

REVIEW QUESTIONS

1. What is the purpose of the criminal justice system?
2. What is social control?
3. What is a theory?
4. Define system and identify at least two types.
5. What components comprise the material and ideological environments of the criminal justice system?
6. What is the relationship between support for crime control and support for due process?
7. What is evidence-based policy?

References

Albanese, J. (1996). Presidential address: Five fundamental mistakes of criminal justice. *Justice Quarterly, 13*(4), 549–565.

Allen, F. (1964). *The borderland of criminal justice.* Chicago: University of Chicago Press.

Bales, W., & Miller, C. (2012). The impact of determinant sentencing on prisoner misconduct. *Journal of Criminal Justice, 40,* 394–403.

Beccaria, C. (1764). In R. Bellamy (Ed.), *On crimes and punishments and other writings.* Cambridge: Cambridge University Press (R. Davies, Trans., & V. Cox, 1995).

Bernard, T. J., & Engel, R. S. (2001). Conceptualizing criminal justice theory. *Justice Quarterly, 18*(1), 1–30.

Bianchi, H. (1994). *Justice as sanctuary: Toward a new system of crime control.* Bloomington, IN: Indiana University Press.

Birzer, M., & Palmiotto, M. (2002). Criminal justice education: Where have we been? And where are we heading? *The Justice Professional, 15*(3), 203–211.

Black, D. (1976). *The behavior of law.* New York: Academic Press.

Brandl, S., Chamlin, M., & Frank, J. (1995). Aggregation bias and the capacity for formal crime control: The determinants of total and disaggregated police force size in Milwaukee, 1934–1987. *Justice Quarterly, 12*(3), 543–562.

Bureau of Justice Assistance (2001). *Comprehensive communities program: Program account.* Washington, DC: Bureau of Justice Assistance.

Bureau of Labor Statistics (2013). *Occupational employment and wages—May 2012.* Washington, DC: U.S. Department of Labor.

Burton, V., Cullen, F., Evans, T., Dunaway, R., Kethineni, S., & Payne, G. (1995). The impact of parental controls on delinquency. *Journal of Criminal Justice, 23*(2), 111–126.

Chambliss, W., & Seidman, R. (1971). *Law, order, and power.* Reading, MA: Addison-Wesley.

Clear, T. R. (2001). Presidential address: Has academic criminal justice come of age? *Justice Quarterly, 18*(4), 709–726.

Cohen, A. (1966). *Deviance and control.* Englewood Cliffs, NJ: Prentice Hall.

Conley, J. (Ed). (1994). *The 1967 President's Crime Commission Report: Its impact 25 years later.* Cincinnati, OH: Anderson.

Culbertson, R. G. (Ed). (1984). *Order under law: Readings in criminal justice* (2nd ed.). Prospect Heights, IL: Waveland Press.

Davis, K. C. (1969). *Discretionary justice*. Baton Rouge: Louisiana State University Press.

Decker, S., Varano, S., & Greene, J. (2007). Routine crime in exceptional times: The impact of the 2002 winter Olympics on citizen demand for police services. *Journal of Criminal Justice, 35*(1), 89–101.

DeLisi, M., & Berg, M. (2006). Exploring theoretical linkages between self-control theory and criminal justice system processing. *Journal of Criminal Justice, 34*(2), 153–163.

Duffee, D. (1980). *Explaining criminal justice: Community theory and criminal justice reform*. Prospect Heights, IL: Waveland Press.

Dunworth, T., & Mills, G. (1999). *National evaluation of Weed and Seed*. Washington, DC: National Institute of Justice.

Eskridge, C. (2003). Criminal justice education and its potential impact on the sociopolitical-economic climate of central European nations: A short essay. *Journal of Criminal Justice Education, 14*(1), 105–118.

Finckenauer, J. O. (1988). Public support for the death penalty: Retribution as just deserts or retribution as revenge. *Justice Quarterly, 5*(1), 81–100.

Finckenauer, J. O. (2005). The quest for quality in criminal justice education. *Justice Quarterly, 22*(4), 413–426.

Flanagan, T. (2000). Liberal education and the criminal justice major. *Journal of Criminal Justice Education, 11*(1), 1–13.

Forst, M. L. (1977). To what extent should the criminal justice system be a system? *Crime & Delinquency, 23*(4), 403.

Foucault, M. (1979). *Discipline and punish: The birth of the prison*. New York: Vintage Books.

Friel, C. (2000). A century of changing boundaries. In C. Friel (Ed.), *Criminal justice 2000: Boundary changes in criminal justice organizations:* Vol. 2. (pp. 1–17). Washington, DC: National Institute of Justice.

Gertz, M., & Gould, L. (1995). Fear of punishment and the willingness to engage in criminal behavior: A research note. *Journal of Criminal Justice, 23*(4), 377–384.

Glueck, S. (1928). Principles of a rational penal code. *Harvard University Law Review, 41*, 453.

Gorecki, J. (1979). *A theory of criminal justice*. New York: Columbia University Press.

Griffiths, J. (1970). Ideology in criminal procedure or a third "model" of the criminal process. *Yale Law Journal, 79*, 359.

Hagan, J. (1989). Why is there so little criminal justice theory? Neglected macro- and micro-level links between organization and power. *Journal of Research in Crime and Delinquency, 26*(1), 116–135.

Johnson, K., & White, J. (2002). The use of multiple intelligences in criminal justice education. *Journal of Criminal Justice Education, 13*(2), 369–386.

Karp, D. R., & Clear, T. R. (2000). Community justice: A conceptual framework. In C. Friel (Ed.), *Criminal justice 2000: Boundary changes in criminal justice:* Vol. 2. (pp. 323–368). Washington, DC: National Institute of Justice.

Kelling, G., Hochberg, M. R., Kaminska, S. L., Rocheleau, A. M., Rosenbaum, D. P., Roth, J. A., et al. (1998). *The Bureau of Justice Assistance Comprehensive Communities Program: A preliminary report*. Washington, DC: National Institute of Justice.

Kellogg, F. R. (1976). Organizing the criminal justice system: A look at operative objectives. *Federal Probation, 40*(2), 9.

Kolonski, J., & Mendelsohn, R. (1970). *The politics of local justice*. Boston: Little, Brown.

Kraska, P. B. (2004). *Theorizing criminal justice: Eight essential orientations*. Long Grove, IL: Waveland Press.

Kraska, P. B. (2006). Criminal justice theory: Toward legitimacy and an infrastructure. *Justice Quarterly, 23*(2), 167–185.

Kraska, P. B., & Brent, J. J. (2011). *Theorizing criminal justice* (2nd ed.). Long Grove, IL: Waveland Press.

Langton, L., & Farole, D., Jr. (2010). *State public defender programs, 2007*. Washington, DC: Bureau of Justice Statistics.

Luna, E. (2003). Overextending the criminal law. *Cato Policy Report, 25*(6), 1, 15–16.

Lundman, R. A. (1980). *Police and policing: An introduction*. New York: Holt, Rinehart, & Winston.

Lynch, T. (2002). *Breaking the vicious cycle: Preserving our liberties while fighting terrorism: Executive summary. Policy Analysis, No. 443* (June). Washington, DC: CATO Institute.

Marenin, D., & Worrall, J. (1998). Criminal justice: Portrait of a discipline in process. *Journal of Criminal Justice, 26*(6), 465–480.

Markowitz, F. (2006). Psychiatric hospital capacity, homelessness, and crime and arrest rates. *Criminology, 44*(1), 45–72.

McGarrell, E., Hipple, N., Corsaro, N., Bynum, T., Perez, H., Zimmerman, C., et al. (2009). *Project safe neighborhoods—A national program to reduce gun crime: Final project report*. Retrieved 26.06.10, from http://www.ncjrs.gov/pdffiles1/nij/grants/226686.pdf.

National Center for State Courts (2010). *Survey of judicial salaries*. Retrieved 04.07.10, from http://www.ncsconline.org/D_KIS/Salary_Survey.

Packer, H. L. (1968). *The limits of the criminal sanction*. Stanford, CA: Stanford University Press.

Parsons, T. (1966). *Societies: Evolutionary and comparative perspectives*. Englewood Cliffs, NJ: Prentice Hall.

Perry, S. (2006). *Prosecutors in state courts, 2005*. Washington, DC: Bureau of Justice Statistics.

Pound, R. (1929). *Criminal justice in America*. New York: Henry Holt.

President's Commission on Law Enforcement and Administration of Justice (1967). *The challenge of crime in a free society*. New York: Avon.

Reckless, W. C., & Allen, H. E. (1979). Developing a national crime policy: The impact of politics on crime in America. In E. Sagarin (Ed.), *Criminology: New concerns*. Beverly Hills, CA: Sage.

Ross, E. A. (1926). *Social control: A survey of the foundations of order*. New York: Macmillan.

Rubin, H. T. (1984). *The courts: Fulcrum of the justice system* (2nd ed.). New York: Random House.

Schneiderman, E. (2013). *A report on arrests arising from the New York City Police Department's stop-and-frisk practices*. New York, NY: New York State Office of the Attorney General.

Sourcebook of Criminal Justice Statistics (2010). Retrieved 04.07.2010, from http://www.albany.edu/sourcebook.

Southerland, M. (2002). Presidential address: Criminal justice curricula in the United States: A decade of change. *Justice Quarterly, 19*(4), 589–601.

Spader, D. J. (1987). Individual rights vs. social utility: The search for the golden zigzag between conflicting fundamental values. *Journal of Criminal Justice, 15*(2), 121–136.

Stephan, J. (2008). *Census of state and federal correctional facilities, 2005*. Washington, DC: Bureau of Justice Statistics.

Stolz, B. A. (2002). The roles of interest groups in U.S. criminal justice policy making: Who, when, and how? *Criminal Justice, 2*(1), 69.

Supancic, M., & Willis, C. L. (1998). Extralegal justice and crime control. *Journal of Crime and Justice, 21*(2), 191–215.

Sutherland, J. W. (1975). *Systems: Analysis, administration and architecture*. New York: Van Nostrand Reinhold.

Taylor, K. (2012, June 10). Stop-and-frisk policy saves lives, mayor tells black congregation. *The New York Times*. Retrieved 19.12.13 from http://www.nytimes.com/2012/06/11/nyregion/at-black-church-in-brooklyn-bloomberg-defends-stop-and-frisk-policy.html.

Travis, L. F., III. (1982). The politics of sentencing reform. In M. L. Forst (Ed.), *Sentencing reform* (p. 59). Beverly Hills, CA: Sage.

Travis, L., & Langworthy, R. (2008). *Policing in America: A balance of forces* (4th ed.). Upper Saddle River, NJ: Prentice Hall.

Tripp, T., & Cobkit, S. (2013). Unexpected pathways: Criminal justice career options in the private sector. *Journal of Criminal Justice Education, 24*(4), 478–494.

U.S. Department of Justice (2010). *Weed and Seed.* Community Capacity Development Office. Retrieved 08.12.10 from http://www.ojp.usdoj.gov/ccdo/ws/welcome.html.

Vito, G.F., & Maahs, J.R. (2012). *Criminology: Theory, research, and policy* (3rd ed.). Sudbury, MA: Jones & Bartlett Learning.

Walker, S. (1992). Origins of the contemporary criminal justice paradigm: The American Bar Foundation survey, 1953–1969. *Justice Quarterly, 9*(1), 47–76.

Walker, S. (2011). *Sense and nonsense about crime, drugs, and communities* (7th ed.). Belmont, CA: Wadsworth.

Walker, J., Burns, R., Bumgarner, J., & Bratina, M. (2008). Federal law enforcement careers: Laying the groundwork. *Journal of Criminal Justice Education, 19*, 110–135.

Warner, B. (2006). Directly intervene or call the authorities? A study of forms of neighborhood social control within a social disorganization framework. *Criminology, 45*(1), 99–130.

Wrede, C., & Featherstone, R. (2012). Striking out on its own: The divergence of criminology and criminal justice from sociology. *The Journal of Criminal Justice Education, 23*(1), 103–125.

Zalman, M. (2007). The search for criminal justice theory: Reflections on Kraska's theorizing criminal justice. *Journal of Criminal Justice Education, 18*(1), 161–181.

Zhao, J., Scheider, M., & Thurman, Q. (2003). A national evaluation of the effect of COPS grants on police productivity (arrests) 1995–1999. *Police Quarterly, 6*(4), 387–409.

CHAPTER 2

The Justice Process

Cases move through the justice system from the first stage of detection by police through subsequent stages to final discharge from the system. Although there are some feedback mechanisms by which a case can move back to an earlier decision point, on the whole, cases flow in one direction through the system. This processing of cases represents the "total system" of criminal justice. It includes the subsystems of law enforcement, the courts, and corrections.

In this chapter, we trace the criminal justice system of the United States. In doing so, we skip many of the details and nuances of criminal justice processing in the interests of developing an understanding of the total justice system. In other words, to some extent we ignore the trees to get a better look at the forest. Later chapters will examine the subsystems of criminal justice in more detail.

Perhaps the greatest constant of criminal justice is variety. Even things as simple as titles differ among jurisdictions. For example, prosecutors are known as state's attorneys, district attorneys, U.S. attorneys, prosecutors, and other titles. In most states, the highest court is called the state supreme court; in New York, the supreme court is a trial court, and the highest court is the New York Court of Appeals. With an appreciation that what follows here is a sketch of the justice system, we are ready to proceed.

Important Terms

arraignment
arrest
circuits
conditional release
discharge
drug courts
initial appearance
investigation
preliminary hearing
private court
revocation
sentencing
trial
undetected crime
unfounded
unreported crime
unsolved

THE DECISION POINTS OF THE CRIMINAL JUSTICE SYSTEM

The criminal justice system begins with the detection of crime, proceeds through investigation, arrest, initial appearance before the court, charging (arraignment), trial, sentencing, and possible revocation, and ends with discharge. We will examine these decision points.

Detection

As the formal social institution charged with the control of deviance that is identified as criminal, the justice system is not mobilized until a criminal offense is detected. Crime that goes undetected does not influence the justice process directly. The process begins only when the justice system (usually through the police) notices a possible criminal offense.

Probably less than half of all crime is discovered by the justice system (Baumer & Lauritsen, 2010). Many crimes remain undetected because no one realizes that a crime was committed. Many others are detected but are not reported to the police, so that the justice system is not aware that criminal offenses have occurred.

Have you ever reached into your pocket or wallet for money you knew you had, only to discover that it was missing? Most of us at some time have experienced missing money. We cannot be certain that we did not spend it or lose it, but we also cannot remember when it was spent. Have we been the victims of theft? Do we report the money as stolen?

If we assume that we spent or lost the money and do not believe it was stolen, a theft may go undetected. Similarly, if we are convinced the money was stolen, we may still not report it because the sum is so small and the chance of recovery is so slim. In the latter case, a crime has gone unreported. **Undetected crime** is crime that is not known to the criminal justice system or to the victim—crimes that are not recognized as crimes. An **unreported crime** is one that victims recognize as law-breaking behavior but is not brought to the attention of authorities.

If a person has a fight with a friend or a relative and assumes it is "personal," an assault may go undetected or at least unreported. The first decision to influence the criminal justice process is determining whether a crime may have occurred. Citizens rather than criminal justice officials most often make this decision. A second decision is reporting a crime; again, someone other than a criminal justice official most often makes this decision (Avakame, Fyfe, & McCoy, 1999). Recent surveys of crime victims indicate that only about 50% of violent victimizations are reported to the police, compared to approximately 37% of property crimes (Truman & Planty, 2012).

In a study of reasons for reporting or not reporting domestic violence, Felson, Messner, Hoskin, and Deane (2002) found that victims do not report crime for reasons of privacy, protecting the offender, or fear of reprisal. They note that researchers have focused on reasons for not reporting, but have ignored reasons to report victimization. Felson and his colleagues found that victims of domestic violence were encouraged to report the crime for self-protection, because they viewed the offense as serious, and because they felt the police would take the offense seriously. Goudriaan, Lynch, and Nieuwbeerta (2004) studied crime reporting across several nations and found that the social and individual characteristics of the victims influence the likelihood of crime reporting.

Nonreporting of crime limits the ability of criminal justice agents and agencies to respond to crime. Table 2.1 presents the frequency with which different types of crimes are reported to the police, and Table 2.2 describes reasons typically given by people for not reporting violent crimes.

Table 2.1	Percent of Crimes Reported to Police by Type of Crime, 2011
Type of Crime	**Percent Reported**
Violent crimes	49
Rape/sexual assault	27
Robbery	66
Aggravated assault	67
Simple assault	43
Property crimes	37
Household burglary	52
Motor vehicle theft	83
Theft	30

Source: Truman and Planty (2012)

Table 2.2	Reasons Given for Not Reporting Violent Crimes, 2007
Reason	**Percent Giving Reason**
Reported to another official	15.1
Private or personal matter	20.4
Object recovered/offender unsuccessful	17.1
Not important enough	5.5
Lack of proof	2.6
Police would not want to be bothered	9.0
Police inefficient/ineffective or biased	3.8
Fear of reprisal	4.8
Too inconvenient or time consuming	5.8
Other reasons	15.9

Source: Bureau of Justice Statistics (2010)

When a crime or suspected crime is reported to the police, the justice system is mobilized. If agents of the justice system decide that a crime has occurred, they have made the detection decision. The police respond to the report of a crime. It is then that case decision making rests with official agents of the justice process. Once the police come to believe that a crime may have been committed, it is their decision whether and how to proceed. We can say that the criminal justice system starts when justice system officials (usually the police) believe a crime has occurred. At that point, the agents of the justice system take control over the official societal response to the crime.

Investigation

Upon deciding that a crime may have been committed, the next decision is whether to investigate, and if so, how thoroughly to investigate. An **investigation** is the search for evidence that links a specific person to a specific crime. It is a process in which the results of initial inquiries often determine the intensity of the investigation. If, for example, someone reports a prowler, the responding officers may make a visual check of doors and windows, find nothing suspicious, and leave. Alternatively, they may note footprints near a window or find scratch marks on a door or window frame, and then intensify their investigation.

At the conclusion of the investigation, three outcomes are possible. First, police may find no evidence of criminal activity and classify the possible crime as **unfounded**, or not real. Second, evidence of possible criminal activity may support the finding that a crime was committed or attempted, but there is not sufficient evidence for an arrest. In this case, the crime will be left **unsolved** (i.e., no offender is known), and the investigation, at least theoretically, will continue. Finally, the investigation may yield evidence of both a crime and a probable guilty party. In the last outcome, we reach the next decision stage: arrest.

Arrest

Despite expectations, media portrayals, or legal mandates, police officers do not have to arrest every violator of the criminal law. The police officer makes a decision whether to arrest a suspected offender. Many factors affect the arrest decision.

Perhaps the two most important factors that determine whether police make an **arrest**—that is, take a person into custody—are (1) the seriousness of the suspected offense and (2) the quality of the evidence against the suspect. The officer can exercise tremendous discretion in this decision, especially for less serious offenses. For example, if a traffic officer stops you for speeding, a citation is not the only possible outcome, even if you actually were speeding. How often does a person give the officer excuses for his or her violation of the traffic laws? How does a person feel about the officer who issues a citation when he or she knows that the officer could have instead opted for giving a warning?

Discretionary decisions not to arrest are often the result of an officer's attempts to achieve street justice. "Street justice" is a term used to describe attempts by police to deal with problems without formal processing. For example, an officer may counsel or warn loitering juveniles, rather than arresting them. In these cases, the officer tries to solve the problem in a way that avoids the negative consequences of formal processing. As we will see in our discussion of the police, much police work is problem solving, and arrest is one of many tools police use to solve problems. Many times, however, police officers do decide to arrest a suspect. If police make an arrest, the next decision stage is reached: initial appearance.

Initial appearance

Persons arrested for crimes are entitled to a hearing in court to determine whether they will be released pending further action. This **initial appearance** or hearing occurs relatively quickly after arrest, usually within a matter of hours. The hearing does not involve a determination of guilt, but rather an assessment of the defendant's likelihood of appearing at later proceedings. Arrested suspects are usually entitled to release before trial. With the exception of a few very serious crimes (murder, terrorism, kidnapping, etc.) specified in some statutes, arrested persons may be released while awaiting trial. Traditionally, this release happens by the posting of bail.

The primary purpose of bail is to ensure that the suspect will return to court for later hearings. The theory of bail is that a person will return to court if it would cost too much not to return. Traditional bail involves the defendant "posting bond," or leaving money on deposit at the court. If the defendant returns, the defendant gets the money back. If the defendant does not return for the next hearing, the court keeps the bail money and issues a warrant for his or her arrest.

Since the 1970s, criminal justice reforms have witnessed the rebirth of "release on recognizance" systems whereby suspects obtain pretrial release without posting bond as long as they have a job, house, family, and other ties to the community. If we expect a person to appear in court to avoid losing a few thousand dollars, it seems reasonable that he or she would also appear to keep a home, job, or family ties.

In many jurisdictions, it is possible for the prosecutor to ask for "preventive detention." In these cases, the prosecutor believes that, if released on bail, the defendant will present a danger of continued crime in the community. Upon a hearing that establishes that the defendant is indeed dangerous, the magistrate can deny pretrial release.

In many courts, bail schedules exist that link different bail amounts to different types of crime. For instance, the rate for burglary might be $5,000, but for robbery, $10,000. The bail decision, however, is not automatic. If the magistrate believes that the suspect will flee or fail to appear for later hearings, a higher bail may be set. In other cases, a lower bail than usual may be set to allow the defendant to keep his or her job or to maintain family contacts. In either case, after the initial appearance, the next decision relates to the justification for governmental (i.e., justice system) intervention in the life of the citizen.

Charging

Between the time of arrest and arraignment, the prosecutor reviews the evidence in the case and determines a formal criminal charge. The offense for which a person is arrested is not necessarily the one with which he or she will be charged. For example, the police may arrest someone for armed robbery, but be unable to prove that a weapon was used in the crime. The prosecutor may then formally charge the offender with traditional (unarmed) robbery.

Charges are brought in two principal ways: indictment by grand jury or by information. With an indictment, the prosecutor presents the case in secret to a grand jury, which decides whether the evidence is strong enough to warrant the issuance of an indictment. With an information, the prosecutor presents the case in open court before a magistrate, who determines if the evidence is sufficient to warrant a formal charge.

In the information process, a judge reviews the strength of the evidence against a suspect and decides if it is sufficient to have the defendant "bound over" to the felony court. Although not a determination of guilt or innocence, the **preliminary hearing** involves a judge ruling on the strength of the case against the defendant. Although the defendant ultimately may be found not guilty, if the available evidence supports probable cause to believe the defendant may be found guilty, the judge will typically order the case bound over to trial, allowing the state to continue.

About a quarter of felony arrests in large counties are dismissed before trial (Cohen & Kyckelhahn, 2010). The number of cases resulting in dismissal has been dropping during the past 2 decades. Earlier studies of criminal prosecution (Boland, Mahanna, & Sones, 1992) reported that nationally, 45% of felony arrests were dismissed before trial; nearly one-half were dismissed by the judge. The rates of dismissal of charges at preliminary hearings vary based on the procedures used to bring cases to court. In places where the prosecutor reviews evidence before appearing in court, the weakest cases are rejected before a preliminary hearing is held, and the number of cases dismissed by the judge is low. Where no such review occurs, the rate of dismissal at the preliminary hearing may exceed 40%.

Arraignment

At the **arraignment**, the judge notifies the defendant of the formal criminal charges against him or her and asks the defendant to plead to the charges. The arraignment is not a hearing on the facts of the case. The defendant may plead not guilty, guilty, or *nolo contendere* (no contest), or may stand silent. If the defendant pleads guilty or *nolo contendere*, the judge enters a finding of guilt. If the defendant remains silent, the judge enters a plea of not guilty and sets a trial date. The overwhelming majority of defendants plead guilty at arraignment, often as part of an agreement negotiated with the prosecutor (Devers, 2011; Durose, 2007). In the typical plea bargain, the prosecutor drops charges or otherwise changes the seriousness of the formal charge in exchange for the certain conviction without trial. See Figure 2.1.

Trial

Whereas most cases result in a guilty plea, those that receive the most media attention and publicity involve a trial at which the defense and prosecution contest the facts and law before a neutral decision maker. Most cases that go to trial are what Walker (2011:40) termed "celebrated cases." In these cases, defendants receive full-blown trials, very often trial by jury. Much of the public believes that the jury trial is the normal operating procedure of the justice system because these cases receive the most publicity.

At **trial**, the state (prosecutor) must prove, beyond a reasonable doubt, that the defendant committed the criminal offense with which he or she has been charged. The defense attorney seeks to discredit the state's case and, at a minimum, establish that there is some doubt as to whether the defendant committed the offense. Depending on the nature of the case, the defense can request one of two types of trials: a jury trial or a bench trial.

FIGURE 2.1
A defendant is shown on a monitor during his video arraignment on charges including arson and attempted murder. Video arraignment systems allow courts to conduct the requisite arraignment process without the need to transport the accused to the courtroom.
AP Photo/Times Herald, Mark R. Rummel

The jury trial is the ideal of the justice system. A panel of the defendant's peers hears all of the evidence and decides whether the defendant is guilty or not guilty. The bench trial is held before a judge alone, who hears all of the evidence and then decides whether the defendant is guilty or not guilty. If the verdict is not guilty, the justice process ends with the acquittal of the defendant. However, if the verdict is guilty (or if the defendant pleads guilty), the defendant stands convicted of the crime and reaches the next decision point in the justice system: sentencing.

Sentencing

Sentencing is the point at which officials select criminal punishments. The sentencing decision is bifurcated (i.e., has two parts). First, the judge decides the type of sentence. This can range from a fine to incarceration and covers a wide variety of alternatives, including probation, confinement in jail or prison, and combinations such as probation with a fine. In capital cases, such as murder, the type of sentence may be death. The second part of the decision involves the conditions of the sentence. These include the conditions of supervised release (probation), such as curfew, employment, and so on, as well as the length of prison term for those incarcerated. In states where offenders are convicted of capital crimes, this part of the decision may involve the method of execution (see Figure 2.2).

Sentencing power is shared among the three branches of the government. The legislative branch sets limits on penalties by establishing minimum and maximum prison terms and fine amounts, by declaring some offenses ineligible for probation, and by other similar actions. The judicial branch is where the sentencing judge selects the actual type and conditions of sentence from alternatives allowed by the legislature. The executive branch has the power to pardon,

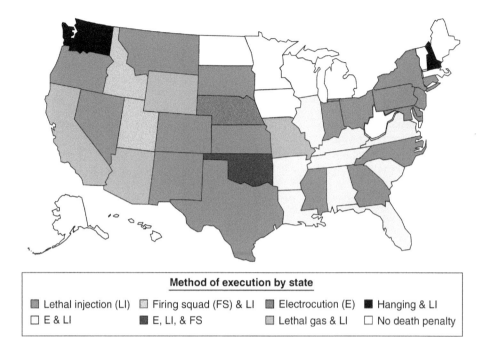

Method of execution by state

- Lethal injection (LI)
- Firing squad (FS) & LI
- Electrocution (E)
- Hanging & LI
- E & LI
- E, LI, & FS
- Lethal gas & LI
- No death penalty

FIGURE 2.2

Method of Execution. Note: Maryland abolished the death penalty in 2013, but the act was not retroactive and people remain on death row. New Mexico abolished the death penalty in 2009, but the act was not retroactive and people remain on death row. Lethal Injection (LI), Idaho, Louisiana, and Nebraska; Lethal Gas and LI, Maryland.

Source: Snell, T. L. (2010). Capital Punishment, 2011. Washington, DC: Bureau of Justice Statistics

to offer clemency, and, often, to authorize parole. Box 2.1 illustrates the sharing of sentencing power.

Most convicted offenders are sentenced to probation or a fine and are not incarcerated. Only about one-third of those convicted of felonies in 2006 were sentenced to prison (Cohen & Kyckelhahn, 2010). Those who are incarcerated most frequently gain release from prison through parole or mandatory release, and are required to live in the community under supervision and to obey conditions of release similar to those placed on probationers (Travis & Stacey, 2010). Failure to obey these conditions can lead to the next possible decision point in the justice process: revocation.

Revocation

The overwhelming majority of criminal offenders sentenced to correctional custody serve some portion of their sentence under community supervision on either probation or parole. Both of these sentences are a form of **conditional release**, where the offender remains in the community if he or she abides by certain conditions, such as reporting regularly to a supervising officer, observing a curfew, or refraining from further criminal activity. Violation of the conditions of release constitutes grounds for the **revocation** of liberty. For instance, a

BOX 2.1 DISTRIBUTION OF SENTENCING POWER AMONG BRANCHES OF GOVERNMENT

States vary in the degree of judicial and parole board discretion in sentencing and release decisions provided by law. Today, the range of state sentencing systems involves the following:

Indeterminate sentencing The judge has primary control over the type of sentence given (such as prison, probation or fine, and the upper and lower bounds of the length of prison sentences within statutory limits), but the actual time served is determined by the parole board.

Determinate sentencing The judge sets the type of sentence and the length of prison sentences within statutory limits, but the parole board may not release prisoners before their sentences have expired, minus time off for good behavior, or "good time."

Mandatory prison terms Legislation requires imposition of a prison sentence, often of specified length, for certain crimes and/or categories of offenders.

Presumptive sentencing The judge is required to impose a sentence whose length is set by law for each offense or class of offense. When there are mitigating or aggravating circumstances, however, the judge is allowed to shorten or lengthen the sentence within specified boundaries.

Some states have other practices that affect sentencing and the actual time served:

Sentencing guidelines The courts set sentences by using procedures designed to structure sentencing decisions, usually based on offense severity and criminal history.

Parole guidelines Parole boards use procedures designed to structure release decisions based on measurable offender criteria.

Good-time policies In nearly all states, legislation allows for reduction of a prison term based on the offender's behavior in prison.

Emergency crowding provisions These are policies that relieve prison crowding by systematically making certain inmates eligible for early release.

In recent years, many states have been moving away from sentencing systems that allow judges and parole boards wide discretion in sentences and time served. They are moving toward more certain and fixed punishments for crimes through mandatory sentences, sentences of fixed length (determinate sentencing), and the abolition of parole boards.

Source: Bureau of Justice Statistics (1989)

probationer ordered not to consume alcohol can lose his or her liberty if caught drinking. The revocation process is a miniature justice system in which the probation or parole officer detects and investigates violations of conditions, and arrests and prosecutes violators who are tried by the sentencing judge (if on probation) or parole authority (if on parole). Upon conviction of violating the conditions of release, the violator may be sentenced to incarceration or continued supervision. In 2011, more than 30% of all inmates admitted to state or federal prisons were parole violators (Carson & Sabol, 2012).

With the exception of the death penalty, incarceration in prison is this country's most severe penalty. Convicted offenders receive this sentence either directly from the court or, more circuitously, through the revocation of conditional liberty. In comparison to the total number of convicted offenders, less than 1% are sentenced to death or life imprisonment (Rosenmerkel, Durose, & Farole, 2009). Thus, for most offenders, a day comes when they are no longer under the control of the justice system. The last point in the justice process is discharge.

Discharge

Eventually, most criminal offenders receive a discharge from their sentences. **Discharge** is final release from criminal justice control or supervision. For some, this discharge will occur at the expiration of their term. For someone sentenced to a 10-year prison term, discharge will take place 10 years after the date of sentencing, whether the person was in prison for the full 10 years or received an earlier release by parole or reduction in term for good behavior.

Many states, however, have adopted procedures for early discharge. An offender serving a 10-year term may be paroled after serving 3 years, and then, after successfully completing 3 years (for example) under parole supervision, may receive an early discharge; thus, the offender may be released from sentence after serving only 6 years. Other jurisdictions in which no formal early discharge procedure exists may place similar offenders on unsupervised parole status after some time. In this case, the offender technically is still under sentence but is not supervised in the community and, for all practical purposes, has been discharged.

Upon discharge from sentence, the convicted offender becomes a member of free society again. In most cases, the record of conviction and collateral effects of conviction (limits on civil rights, employability, and the like) will haunt the ex-convict. Conviction of a crime, especially a felony, often disqualifies the offender from certain types of occupations, such as those requiring licensure or certification (teaching school, practicing law or medicine, and the like). In some cases, felony conviction leads to "civil death," that is, the offender has no rights to enter contracts (including marriage), borrow money, vote, or hold public office (Buckler & Travis, 2003; Burton, Cullen, & Travis, 1987).

Box 2.2 graphically portrays the decision points of the criminal justice system.

THE TOTAL CRIMINAL JUSTICE SYSTEM

As our brief description of the justice system illustrates, cases move through the various decision points on a contingency basis. If police detect a crime, an investigation may begin. If the investigation yields sufficient evidence, police may make an arrest. If police make an arrest, formal charges may be brought. The operative word is "if." Approaching this issue from the other direction, the sentence depends on the conviction, which depends on the charge, which depends on the investigation, which depends on the detection of crime. To paraphrase an old song about how bones are connected, we might say detection is connected

BOX 2.2 DECISION POINTS OF THE CRIMINAL JUSTICE SYSTEM

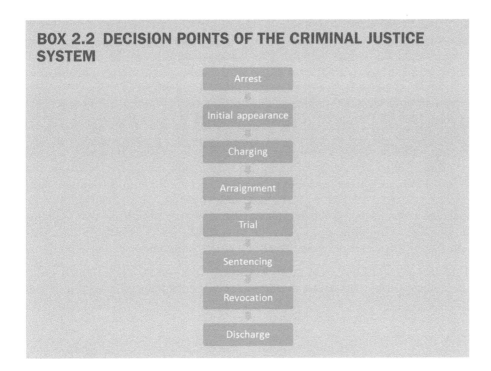

to investigation; investigation is connected to arrest; arrest is connected to charging; charging is connected to arraignment; arraignment is connected to trial; trial is connected to sentencing; sentencing is connected to correction; and correction is connected to discharge.

Each decision in the justice process is in large part determined by previous decisions. To a certain degree, earlier decisions depend on past practices in later points of the justice process. For example, if a county prosecutor routinely dismisses cases involving possession of minor amounts of marijuana, law enforcement officers are more inclined to stop arresting persons for possession of small amounts of that drug.

As the concept of a system implies, the components of the justice process (the decisions) are interdependent. As a result, the practices of all justice agencies affect those of every other agency to some extent. Similarly, environmental pressures will affect the operations of each justice agency to some degree. Some examples illustrate the manner in which environmental pressures and agency changes have systemwide effects: changing attitudes toward drunk driving, the focus on homeland security, the "war" on drugs, and the redefinition of domestic violence arrest policies.

Drunk Driving

In 2011, 765,635 arrests were made for driving under the influence, making drunk driving the fifth most common type of crime (FBI, 2011). Drunk driving, although a serious safety problem on the nation's highways, was not viewed as a particularly serious offense historically. In the 1980s, however, it became no longer acceptable to drink and drive, and the entertainment media replaced jokes about drunk drivers with dramas depicting the devastating effects of drunk driving. "In short, attitudes have changed. Today's drunk driver is a pariah. It is no longer socially acceptable to stagger out from a pub and sit behind the wheel" (Balko, 2003:9). During the past 3 decades all states have taken steps to control drunk driving, most often by redefining the offense as a more serious misdemeanor or felony, and by requiring mandatory incarceration of those convicted of drunk driving, regardless of harm. Every state and the District of Columbia now has defined a blood alcohol content (BAC) of 0.08 as a presumptive standard of intoxication. That is, if the BAC measures 0.08 or higher, the driver is assumed to be impaired. Table 2.3 describes statutory provisions that apply to driving under the influence (DUI). Persons convicted of driving while intoxicated accounted for more than 10% of all arrests nationally (see Table 2.4).

This shift in public attitude regarding drunk drivers—and the associated legislative changes—placed considerable strains on the criminal justice system. Police

Table 2.3	Statutory Provisions Concerning Driving under the Influence	
Statutory Provision	**Jurisdictions with Provision**	**Jurisdictions without Provision**
Felony DUI	46	5
Mandatory jail for second offense	47	4
Zero tolerance	51	0
Penalty for test refusal greater than for test failure	34	17
Vehicle confiscation	30	21
0.08 BAC per se intoxicated	51	0

Source: Mothers Against Drunk Driving (2007)

Table 2.4	Arrest in the United States, by Sex and Race
Offender Characteristic	**Percent**
Sex	
Male	11
Female	10
Race/ethnicity	
White	13
Black	4.4
Asian	13.7

Source: Snyder (2012)

arrested more persons for DUI of alcohol; more of those arrested refused to plead guilty; and many more of those found guilty received jail sentences.

With drunk driving defined and viewed as a more serious offense than in the past, police officers are more likely to investigate erratic drivers, to charge the offender with DUI rather than with reckless operation, to arrest rather than warn, and, generally, to process offenders. Cohen (1992) reported that between 1980 and 1989 the number of arrests for drunk driving rose by 22%, whereas the number of licensed drivers increased by only 14%. Prosecutors are more likely to charge drunk drivers and, with higher stakes (e.g., loss of driving privileges, stiff fines, mandatory incarceration), defendants are less likely to plead guilty (Meyer & Gray, 1997). As a result, the courts must hold more trials, and mandatory sentences create overcrowding in the jails. As seen in Box 2.3, all three components of the justice system had to adapt to the new emphasis on DUI enforcement.

The effort to control drinking and driving has continued and gotten more intense. Balko (2003) reported that more than 100 new pieces of drinking-and-driving legislation were considered in 31 states between 2002 and 2003. In 2000, the U.S. Congress passed a law creating a federal presumptive intoxication standard at a blood alcohol level of 0.08. This legislation tied federal highway money to adoption of the new standard. States that did not adopt the lower standard would not receive federal highway funds. Some states estimated that the increased costs of criminal justice processing of drivers found to have blood

BOX 2.3 EFFECTS OF MANDATORY JAIL TERMS FOR DRUNK DRIVING

To gage the impact of tougher sanctions on the criminal justice system, National Institute of Justice researchers examined the effects of mandatory confinement for drunk driving in jurisdictions in Washington, Tennessee, Ohio, and Minnesota. The findings revealed:

- When mandatory confinement is introduced and well publicized, drunk driver arrests usually increase.
- The introduction of mandatory confinement imposes new and heavy demands on courts, incarceration facilities, and probation services.
- The adoption of mandatory confinement is frequently accompanied by increased public concern about drunk driving and is associated with a decline in traffic fatalities.
- Mandatory confinement can be imposed either through legislation or through judicial policy.
- The implementation of mandatory confinement often requires additional resources for the criminal justice system.
- Appropriate systemwide planning can minimize dysfunction and substantially reduce the impact of mandatory confinement on criminal justice operation.

Source: National Institute of Justice (1985)

alcohol levels between 0.10 and 0.08 would exceed the amount of highway funds they received from the federal government. Those states initially chose not to adopt the new standard (Vartebedian, 2002), but all states now have this standard. The National Transportation Safety Board (NTSB) has recently recommended further reducing the blood alcohol limit that qualifies as drunken driving to 0.05 (Jansen, 2013).

A 1985 evaluation of changes in drunk driving enforcement revealed how justice agency policies can affect the total system as well. In Memphis, Tennessee, with little publicity about drunk driving, law enforcement attitudes did not change, and thus arrest rates, court loads, and jail populations of drunk drivers did not change. In Minnesota, however, even without new legislation, judges adopted a policy of mandatory incarceration; successfully anticipated problems for police, courts, and corrections; and took steps to minimize the problems.

Other analyses of drunk driving laws and enforcement practices show that organizational patterns of police agencies affect arrest decisions (Mastrofski, Ritti, & Hoffmaster, 1987). Individual officer characteristics also were found to be related to arrest decisions in drunk driving cases (Meyers, Heeren, Hingson, & Kovenock, 1987). These studies indicate that an understanding of the effect of justice reform is difficult. Knowledge of the changes in the law is only part of the answer. Organizational and individual characteristics of justice agencies and agents affect how a reform is implemented. The successful implementation of a reform, in turn, can be a critical determinant as to the success of reducing drunk driving behavior. Research shows that an anti-drunk driving enforcement campaign can be effective at reducing drunken driving, but only if the police enforcement and associated media campaigns are robust (Beck, 2009; Clapp et al., 2005). In other words, a half-hearted enforcement approach is unlikely to change public behavior. Even with a strong DUI enforcement program, deterrence might be particularly difficult to obtain among persons having an alcohol addiction or serious drinking problem (Yu, Evans, & Clark, 2006).

Homeland Security

In the wake of the terrorist attacks on the World Trade Center and the Pentagon on September 11, 2001, the United States began to wage a "war" on terror. The response of the United States to terrorism has been controversial, especially the response of local and state criminal justice agencies. Counterterrorism efforts in the United States illustrate the conflict between due process and crime control.

After the 2001 attacks the U.S. Congress took quick action to pass the USA PATRIOT Act, which broadened the powers of law enforcement and policing agencies to collect evidence and conduct surveillance on suspected terrorists, both domestic and international (see Box 2.4). In addition, billions of dollars of funding were allocated for counterterrorism activities. The federal government created a cabinet-level Department of Homeland Security that, as is described below, resulted in a major realignment of federal law enforcement organizations.

BOX 2.4 NATIONAL SECURITY LEAKS

Counterterrorism efforts since the September 11, 2001, attacks have included increased surveillance gathering within the United States and abroad. A series of recent information leaks have illustrated America's conflict between privacy and security.

In early 2010, Pfc. Bradley Manning leaked more than 700,000 classified documents to Wikileaks, a website devoted to publishing secret information. Manning had become increasingly disillusioned with the Iraq War during his service as an intelligence analyst (Leigh & Harding, 2011). The massive leak resulted in a large public outcry and ultimately led to Manning's conviction and sentence to 35 years in prison (Savage & Huetteman, 2013).

The most recent large-scale intelligence leak came when Edward Snowden revealed details of surveillance activities by the National Security Agency (NSA) to a British newspaper. Snowden has been charged with three federal crimes (Shane, 2013), but received temporary asylum by Russia (see Figure 2.3). The NSA has defended its surveillance programs, claiming that they have helped prevent numerous terrorist attacks since 9/11 (Savage, 2013).

FIGURE 2.3
Edward Snowden talks during a simulcast conversation during the SXSW Interactive Festival in March 2014, in Austin, Texas. Snowden talked with American Civil Liberties Union's principal technologist Christopher Soghoian, and answered tweeted questions.
Photo by Jack Plunkett/Invision/AP

Although some local criminal justice systems and agencies have made substantial investments in counterterrorism, most have not. Part of the reason for differences in response to the terrorist threat may be the size of most local criminal justice agencies. Schafer, Burruss, and Giblin (2009) reported that 6 years after the 9/11 attacks, most small municipal police agencies they studied had made few changes in response to terrorism. Smaller communities have fewer resources to devote to terrorism and typically do not perceive a major terrorist threat.

It is also not clear what we might expect local criminal justice agencies to do in terms of counterterrorism. The Federal Bureau of Investigation operates scores of Joint Terrorism Task Forces that involve federal, state, and local representatives. The goal of these task forces is to prevent and respond to terrorist acts in the United States. Much of the effort involved in fighting terrorism is aimed at intelligence gathering and data analysis. Most local criminal justice agencies do not have the skill or the resources to do this. Local police typically find themselves as information gatherers who report to regional or state data repositories or "fusion centers" where the information is analyzed.

Terrorist acts differ from "normal" crimes in terms of motivation. The 9/11 attacks involved kidnapping, murder, and arson. Local justice systems can respond to these offenses with existing policies, procedures, and law. Acts that fit federal definitions of terrorism, however, become federal offenses and typically are removed from local jurisdictions. Still, public concern, political pressure, the availability of additional federal funding, and other forces have made terrorism at least a nominal concern of local criminal justice agencies, especially police. At this point, the most important visible changes resulting from an emphasis on terrorism are greater cooperation between federal and local officials and increased pressure on local police to gather intelligence information. The counterterrorism tasks of local police complicate relations with the public, especially immigrants and minority group members (National Institute of Justice, 2008). Otherwise, almost a decade after the attacks, for most of American criminal justice, little has changed.

The War on Drugs

In 1973, the state of New York adopted legislation hailed as "the nation's toughest drug law" (U.S. Department of Justice, 1978). Although the most severe sanctions were finally eliminated by legislation in 2009, the law serves as a model for how the system responds to such a policy decision. The goal of this law was to "crack down" on those who sold heroin and other dangerous drugs. It had provisions for very stiff sentences and placed controls on plea bargaining. To cope with the anticipated increase in drug offense cases, it provided for the creation of more courts. The intent of the legislation was clear: to apprehend, convict, and punish those who sold heroin.

The effect of the law, however, is less clear. The officers and agencies of the justice system appear to have adapted to the changes to reduce the potentially disruptive effects on normal court operations that would result from the new law. Although there were no dramatic increases in arrests for the sale of heroin, fewer of those arrested were indicted, fewer of those indicted pleaded guilty, and fewer were convicted. For those convicted, both the rate of incarceration and the length of prison terms increased after the law took effect. However, in the final analysis, 3 years after the law was passed, the percentage of those arrested for heroin sale or possession going to prison remained stable at 11%, a figure identical to that occurring before the law was passed.

Several explanations are possible. First, a probable reason why the number of arrests did not increase was that most people already considered the sale and possession of large quantities of heroin to be serious offenses (even before the new law). The new law changed neither law enforcement nor public attitudes. The fact that fewer defendants pleaded guilty meant that prosecutors needed to be more certain of getting a guilty verdict before taking a case to trial. Indictments decreased as marginal cases were dismissed or downplayed. The increased number of trials created a backlog for the courts so that fewer cases were processed and acquittals were handed down in some cases in which previously a plea of guilty had ensured conviction.

The mandatory sentencing provisions of the legislation may account for the higher incarceration rate and more severe prison terms imposed under the new law. This suggests that there was no conscious effort to undermine the intent of the tough antidrug law, but rather, the court component of the justice process adapted to new pressures reflexively. As part of a system, the courts sought to maintain equilibrium and adapted to stresses and strains minimizing their impact.

In this example, the legislation initially and most specifically affected the criminal courts, and an effort was made to alleviate the strains through the creation of new courts. Had there been no new courts, it is likely that even more cases would have been dismissed or the backlog of cases would have been even greater. The law did not directly affect law enforcement. The effect of changes in prison sentences on corrections was not dramatic for two reasons. First, because heroin dealers are only a very small proportion of all those sentenced to prison, even large increases in their terms or rate of incarceration would not dramatically affect prisons. Second, the percentage of those arrested who were actually sentenced to prison did not change, and the effects of longer terms would not be felt until several years after those who received longer sentences had been imprisoned.

The war on drugs, having raged now for nearly 3 decades in its most recent form, has produced changes in the characteristics of prison populations. For many years, drug offenders accounted for the largest part of prison population growth (Cohen & Kyckelhahn, 2010; Harrison & Beck, 2003). This trend finally appears to have slowed and even might be reversing as the public attitude toward drug crime becomes more tolerant (Carson & Sabol, 2012; Newport, 2011). Nevertheless, the decades-long crackdown on drug crimes has contributed to the continued problem of prison and jail crowding and prompted the development of intermediate sanctions, specialized drug courts, and other adaptations in the criminal justice system. It has also had a disproportionately harsh impact on the poor, women, and members of minority groups (Welch, Wolff, & Bryan, 1998).

Domestic Violence Arrest Policies

The redefinition of domestic violence also illustrates the interdependency of the criminal justice system. The movement toward policies calling for mandatory arrests in cases of domestic violence has been complicated (Sherman, 1992). Some evaluators have noted that despite clear policy statements requiring arrest, police officers arrest domestic violence offenders in less than half of all cases (Belknap & McCall, 1994). This may be a result of the fact that the offender is not present when the police arrive (Feder, 1996), as well as because prosecutors and courts often still do not treat the offense as a serious matter (Kane, 1999). Whatever else has happened, there is some evidence that victims are increasingly likely to complain to the police, and that the police are increasingly likely to write formal reports, even if they make no arrests (Lanza-Kaduce, Greenleaf, & Donahue, 1995).

Johnson and Sigler (2000) compared public opinion about violence against women over a 10-year period and reported that public tolerance for violence has decreased as criminalization of such behavior has become more common. A more recent study indicates that the public is still intolerant of domestic violence, whether in the form of physical or verbal abuse (Boatwright-Horowitz, Olick, & Amaral, 2004). It is not possible to tell if opinion changes cause legal changes, or if the reverse is true. Still, domestic violence policy and law demonstrate the link between public opinion and criminal justice practice. Jones and Belknap (1999), studying the practices of the Boulder, Colorado, police, reported that the police response to domestic violence appears more formal and serious currently than it has in the past. Again, public perceptions of offense seriousness and the severity of justice system response are related.

One of the most important policy changes in the response to domestic violence has been a proliferation of preferred or mandatory arrest policies and laws. These reforms require the police to arrest offenders involved in domestic assaults. The impact of such policies is unclear. It appears that arrest generally reduces later instances of domestic violence, but the impact of arrest is different for white offenders and for black offenders, and may be different for people of different economic levels (Maxwell, Garner, & Fagan, 2002). There is also evidence that mandatory arrest policies have increased the arrests of domestic violence victims (Chesney-Lind, 2002). In most jurisdictions adopting these policies, the numbers and rates of arrests for both male and female parties to the incidents have increased dramatically. The unintended consequences of these policies, such as deterring victims from reporting offenses, increasing the number of victims subjected to arrest, and long-term effects on relationships and families, are still unknown (Humphries, 2002). Efforts to make prosecution of domestic violence easier may result in less effort by police to obtain victim cooperation, and ultimately in weaker cases and fewer convictions (Davis, Smith, & Taylor, 2003). A recent study even found that mandatory arrest laws might increase intimate partner homicides (Iyengar, 2009). What is clear is that the adoption and implementation of policy reforms in this area have been neither easy nor trouble free (Ostrom, 2003; Whitcomb, 2002).

All of these issues have proven to be difficult for criminal justice policymakers and reformers to manage. Experience with these efforts to change criminal justice practices in dealing with drunk drivers, counterterrorism, drug offenses, and domestic violence illustrates how the justice system interacts with its environment. In some cases, changes occur in all aspects of the justice process, such as drug enforcement, resulting in more arrests, convictions, and changes in the correctional population. In other cases, the system is able to adapt and minimize the impact of a reform by increasing rates of case dismissal or plea bargaining, or reducing the severity of sentences. All of these examples show that the criminal justice process operates as a system, adapting to change and pressure. They also indicate the complexity of evaluating the operations of the criminal justice process. This complexity becomes clearer when one examines the structure and organization of the agencies that comprise the system of criminal justice in the United States.

THE COMPONENTS OF CRIMINAL JUSTICE

It is common to divide the criminal justice system into three parts: law enforcement, courts, and corrections. Each of these three parts of the justice system itself comprises a multitude of separate agencies and actors. The organizations that make up the total criminal justice system are differently structured and funded, and draw from different personnel pools.

One of the most important distinctions among similar agencies is jurisdiction. Police departments, courts, and correctional agencies may be municipal (village, township, city, or county), state, or federal in nature. They may be specialized, like the U.S. postal inspectors, or they may have general duties, as does a typical police department. They may be public or private (such as security guards, many halfway houses, and other entities that provide crime control services). In this section, we examine the nature of criminal justice agencies in law enforcement, courts, and corrections.

Law Enforcement

There are so many agencies with law enforcement mandates that it is not possible to state their true number with confidence. In 1967, the President's Commission on Law Enforcement and Administration of Justice (1967) estimated that more than 40,000 police departments were in existence. Later, the U.S. Department of Justice (1980:24) reported that there were close to 20,000 state and local law enforcement agencies. This report, however, did not include townships with populations of less than 1,000 nor did it include federal or tribal law enforcement agencies. Most recently, the Bureau of Justice Statistics (Reaves, 2011) identified about 18,000 state and local police agencies.

FEDERAL LAW ENFORCEMENT

A number of federal law enforcement agencies exist. These agencies tend to be small with specific mandates, yet in total, federal law enforcement is very complex. We are all aware of the Federal Bureau of Investigation (FBI), and most of us have heard of the U.S. Marshals; the Postal Inspectors; the Drug Enforcement Administration (DEA); the Bureau of Alcohol, Tobacco, Firearms and Explosives (ATF); the Immigration and Customs Enforcement; Customs, and Border Protection; the Internal Revenue Service (IRS); and the Secret Service. Yet, many are unaware of the law enforcement duties of the National Park Service, the U.S. Supreme Court Police Department, the National Gallery of Art Protection Staff, and other federal police agencies. We seldom consider the military police, the tribal police departments on Native American reservations, or the investigative duties of auditors and staff of such organizations as the Federal Trade Commission (FTC) (Travis & Langworthy, 2008).

Reaves (2012) reported that in 2008, the federal government employed about 120,000 full-time officers with arrest powers who were authorized to carry firearms. The bulk of these employees worked for the U.S. Customs and Border Protection, and they included approximately 17,000 employees of the Federal Bureau of Prisons. Nineteen other federal agencies employed 500 or more such officers and agents. The most common duties performed by these federal officials were criminal investigations (37%), police response and patrol (23%), and inspections (15%). These federal employees do not include the officers of the Transportation Security Administration, created in the wake of the 9/11 terrorist attacks.

Creation of the Department of Homeland Security in 2002 resulted in organizational changes in federal law enforcement. The Department of Homeland Security is now the single largest employer of federal law enforcement officers, administering the U.S. Coast Guard, Secret Service, Federal Protective Service, and U.S. Customs and Border Protection (except for some revenue functions), and has taken over the responsibilities of the Immigration and Naturalization Service, which was abolished. With these changes, the Department of Homeland Security employs more than 45% of federal officers, and the Department of Justice employs about 33% (Reaves, 2012).

Because they serve the entire nation, these agencies recruit nationally and tend to have more stringent entry requirements than do most other police departments. The FBI, for example, requires a bachelor's degree in combination with investigatory experience or postgraduate training. Because federal law enforcement is funded at the federal level, salary and benefits for federal law enforcement officers are often higher than those paid to municipal police.

STATE LAW ENFORCEMENT

The most common form of state police agency is the highway patrol. The highway patrol enforces traffic laws on state and federal highways. Many states, however, also charge their state police with general law enforcement duties (International Association of Chiefs of Police, 1975). The New York State Police, for example, not only serve as traffic officers on that state's highways but also have as a primary duty the provision of general law enforcement service to residents in rural and unincorporated areas. In addition, several states have specialized state units to combat drug offenses, organized crime, liquor and cigarette tax violations, and the like. Finally, many states also charge their park services with law enforcement obligations. Reaves (2011) reported that state police agencies employed more than 93,000 full-time officers.

Like federal agencies, state agencies recruit from a pool of candidates that is considerably larger than that tapped by most local police departments. Entry requirements tend to be less stringent than federal law enforcement, but much more stringent than many local police departments. Moreover, in many states, the salary and benefits paid to state police officers are higher than those paid in most local departments.

MUNICIPAL LAW ENFORCEMENT

Municipal or local police departments provide the bulk of law enforcement services, as shown in Figure 2.4. These include the traditional city or township police department, as well as the county sheriff. The majority of police departments in the United States are local ones, and most police agencies are small. In fact, more than half of local police department employ fewer than 10 full-time officers (Reaves, 2011). Most police officers, however, work for large departments, because the relatively few large departments employ a great many officers. The largest 5% of police departments employ more than 60% of all local officers.

Municipal police departments rarely conduct national searches or recruitment drives, with the exception of a few, usually larger police departments. Most local police departments recruit locally and employ civil service testing to enlist new officers (Sanders, Hughes, & Langworthy, 1995). Sheriffs generally are elected, but many sheriff's deputies are recruited through civil service. It is common for police protection to comprise a major portion of a municipality's budget. In every state but Hawaii, law enforcement officers must first pass a required training curriculum before being sworn in, and new recruits must complete at least 600 hours of academy and field training. Recruits in the largest agencies complete about twice as many hours of training (nearly 1,600) as those employed in smaller ones (Reaves, 2009).

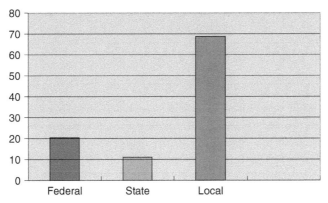

FIGURE 2.4
Percentage Distribution of Police Personnel and Costs by Level of Government
Source: Sourcebook of Criminal Justice Statistics (2010)

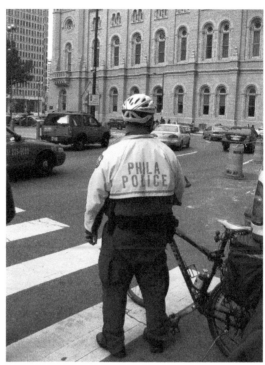

FIGURE 2.5
A Philadelphia bicycle cop observes the neighborhood. The bulk of law enforcement services are provided through municipal or local police departments.

On average, there are about two local police officers for every 1,000 residents. In 2007, local police agencies' costs were approximately $200 per resident per year (*Sourcebook of Criminal Justice Statistics*, 2010). The average starting salary for a full-time local police officer was $31,700 per year. As might be expected, departments serving smaller communities generally pay lower salaries than those serving larger communities (Hickman & Reaves, 2006). See Figure 2.5.

PRIVATE AND OTHER PUBLIC LAW ENFORCEMENT

In addition to the agencies described above, there are hundreds of special-purpose law enforcement agencies in cities and counties. Reaves (2011) identified more than 1,700 public, special-purpose police agencies including housing authority, school, airport, university, transit, and park police (see Figure 2.6). Furthermore, there are thousands of private and semipublic law enforcement agencies in the United States. For example, most factories, amusement parks, and hospitals have security staff, as do most retail chain stores. Many residential buildings and developments also have private security. Private police and private security personnel outnumber the public police by a ratio of at least three to one (Maahs & Hemmens, 1998). Additionally, the coroner or medical examiner is often considered to be a law enforcement official because of the investigative duties of that position.

FIGURE 2.6
The job of a park ranger is not always rural in nature; urban park rangers, like the ones in Boston Common, patrol city parks and park facilities.
Ellen S. Boyne

As we have seen, it may not be possible to speak accurately of law enforcement— or even of the police—in the United States. The diversity of agencies, standards, and duties is nearly mind-boggling. Because law enforcement is the largest (numerically) component of the justice process, a review of justice agencies in courts and corrections is less complicated, but only marginally so.

Courts

The picture that most Americans have of the court system is probably limited to that of a state felony court of general jurisdiction, where felony defendants are processed to determine guilt and innocence and proscribe a sentence that might include a lengthy prison term. In fact, the court system in the United States is fragmented and complicated (Rottman & Strickland, 2006). Each state has a different court system, as does the federal government. There are federal, state, and municipal courts. Thousands of courts of limited jurisdiction are also in operation. Ostrom, Kauder, and LaFountain (2003) reported that there are more than 15,550 state courts alone. These courts are divided further in terms of the types of cases they may hear and the types of decisions they may reach.

There are approximately 340 justices of the Supreme Court and other courts of last resort in the 50 states, District of Columbia, and federal systems. More than 960 additional justices serve in intermediate courts of appeal, with more than 26,000 judges serving in general trial courts (Langston & Cohen, 2007). The number of judges in general is on the increase as the caseloads of the court systems continue to rise.

FEDERAL COURTS

Federal judges and justices of the U.S. Supreme Court are nominated by the president and appointed with the advice and consent of the U.S. Senate. These judges have lifetime tenure. Federal magistrates are appointed to eight-year terms by federal district judges.

The federal courts are organized by **circuits**, with 12 regional circuits covering the entire nation and foreign possessions. Within the circuits, 94 district courts are trial courts. The circuit court is the appeals court for all trial courts in its region. In addition, more than 500 federal magistrates within these districts may hear minor offenses and conduct the early stages of felony trials and more serious civil trials. See Figure 2.7.

Federal courts decide cases of federal interest, for example, charges of federal law violation. Federal appeals courts also decide federal constitutional issues, even if such issues were raised during state trials or proceedings.

STATE COURTS

State judicial systems are similar to the federal judiciary in structure. They generally comprise trial courts, intermediate appellate courts, and a state supreme court. State judges and justices are either appointed (as is the federal judiciary) or elected. Members of most state judiciaries are in office for specified terms of office (unlike federal judges, who have lifetime tenure). Rhode Island's judges have lifetime tenure, and judges in Massachusetts and New Hampshire serve terms that do not expire until the judge reaches age 70 (Rottman & Strickland, 2006).

Federal judges are recruited nationally (although district court judges and circuit court judges are generally selected from among candidates residing in

FIGURE 2.7
U.S. District Court Building, Denver, Colorado.

the particular district or circuit). State court judges are elected statewide (or appointed) for statewide posts (e.g., the office of justice of the state supreme court), or from the jurisdiction of the lower court (e.g., the county of a specific county court). Although there may be no constitutional provision (Maine and Massachusetts do not require a law degree), as with U.S. judges, or statutory requirement that judges be members of the bar, most judges are attorneys.

LOCAL COURTS

There is a plethora of local courts in the United States. These are courts of limited jurisdiction because they are not allowed to decide felony cases, serious misdemeanors, or civil suits seeking damages above fairly low dollar amounts. Often these are known as justice of the peace courts. In many places, these limited-jurisdiction courts are known as police courts or mayor's courts. They usually decide traffic offense cases, hear violations of local ordinances and petty offenses, and make bail determinations.

Some of these judgeships are "ex officio." For example, on being elected mayor in Ohio, the new mayor becomes the judge of mayor's court. In states that retain the office of justice of the peace, often no formal legal training is required for this position. These limited-jurisdiction courts are not authorized to conduct jury trials, and their decisions may be appealed to courts of general jurisdiction, which are also known as trial courts.

Salaries for these local courts are usually not commensurate with what an attorney could earn in the private practice of law. However, many of these courts operate on a part-time basis, and members of the bar may serve as justices of the peace.

OTHER COURTS

Every court system has a number of special-jurisdiction courts. For example, the federal judiciary has a tax court, and states usually have a court of domestic relations and/or a juvenile court. Several jurisdictions also have bankruptcy courts and other special jurisdiction courts. A relatively recent innovation is what may be called a **private court**. In some places, offices or commissions for dispute resolution have been developed to divert cases away from the formal courts (Aaronson, Kittrie, Saari, & Cooper, 1977). Here, the parties to a dispute sit with a lay negotiator (or team of negotiators) and attempt to resolve their problem without resorting to the courts. Most of these private courts are staffed by volunteers or by paid staff whose salaries are lower than that of a judge. Examples of these types of private courts appear on television in shows like *The People's Court*, *Judge Judy*, or *Judge Roy Brown*. Court specialization within the criminal justice system has also increased with the development and spread of special **drug courts** dedicated to the processing and supervision of drug cases, as illustrated in Figure 2.8. Other special courts are increasingly common. Rottman and Casey (1999) described these as "problem-solving courts" where courts (judges, prosecutors, and the defense bar) work with offenders, victims, service providers, and the broader community to develop long-term solutions to the problems that bring cases to court.

FIGURE 2.8
Growth of drug courts.
Source: Huddleston and Marlowe (2011)

PROSECUTION

At all levels of courts, from local to federal, the prosecutor represents the interests of the state (not the victim). In the federal system, the prosecutor is the U.S. attorney or the deputy U.S. attorney. These are lawyers appointed by the nomination of the president with the consent of the Senate. Local prosecutors are common in most states; for the most part, they are lawyers elected at the county level. Prosecutors have many titles, including district attorney, state's attorney, county attorney, circuit attorney, commonwealth's attorney, and solicitor (Perry & Banks, 2011). The Bureau of Justice Statistics reported the existence of more than 2,300 prosecutor's offices responsible for felony cases in state criminal courts in 2007. The average prosecutor's office closes more than 1,248 cases per year. To handle the large caseloads, these offices employed about 78,000 people, including approximately 34,000 attorneys (Perry & Banks, 2011). Most often, a prosecutor's office will have a chief prosecutor along with one or more assistant prosecutors with a large support staff.

DEFENSE

There are three basic structures for the provision of defense counsel: private retention, public defenders, and assigned counsel. Private retention refers to the possibility of the defendant retaining his or her own attorney. Private retention is unusual because most criminal defendants cannot afford attorney fees. However, wealthy or notorious defendants often retain celebrated defense attorneys. Less than one-fifth of felony defendants in the largest counties and less than one-third of defendants in federal courts used privately retained counsel (Harlow, 2000:1). Public defenders usually have an appointed director or an administrator who hires a sufficient staff of attorneys to represent indigent clients in court (Goldberg & Lichtman, 1978). The most common form of criminal defense system is the public defender, but most criminal courts use two or more methods of providing defense counsel, including assigned counsel and contract systems. In the provision of assigned counsel, judges are presented either with a list of all attorneys practicing in their jurisdiction, or with a list of those attorneys willing to take on criminal defense cases. The judge then appoints an attorney for each indigent defendant from this list; he or she usually moves down the list from the first name to the last. The attorneys selected and assigned are then paid a set fee, which is usually on an hourly rate not to exceed some upper limit per case. In contract systems, the court enters an agreement with a law firm, bar association, or private attorney for indigent defense services for a specified period of time at a specified rate (Harlow, 2000).

Like prosecutors, defense attorneys employed in public defender offices (and most assigned counsel schemes) are not paid as well as judges, nor are they paid as much as they could earn in private practice as retained defense attorneys. Again, like prosecutors, young attorneys often seek this kind of work to gain trial experience.

Both prosecutors and defense attorneys recruit staff from local bar associations. Although the local nature of the recruitment is comparable to recruiting for most police officers and judges, the requirement of membership in the bar limits the pool of possible applicants.

WITNESSES AND JURORS

Many other persons are involved in the court process in addition to prosecutors, defense counsel, and judges. There are court support staff, such as court clerks, stenographers, bailiffs, and administrators; however, we will focus here on witnesses and jurors.

A variety of persons may serve as witnesses in a criminal case (Woodard & Anderson, 1984). Generally, the arresting officers and any investigators are called as witnesses in a criminal case. If any passersby saw the offense, they too may be called to testify. Sometimes the defendant (or a codefendant) is called to testify in criminal cases (but the defendant cannot be required to be a witness). Depending on the nature of the case, or of the defense, expert witnesses may be called. These individuals are first established as having special knowledge not commonly available to the average citizen. Experts in areas such as ballistics, forensic medicine, and psychology or psychiatry (for instance, when an insanity defense is raised) are asked to bring special knowledge to bear on issues at trial. The victim of a crime is useful only as a witness. Crimes are public wrongs; individual suffering is not at issue in criminal trials. In recent years, however, there has been an increased emphasis on using the criminal process to redress the harms suffered by individual victims. Balancing the interests of the victim with those of the defendant is a complicated task (Office for Victims of Crime, 2002).

Citizens participate directly and most strongly in the criminal justice process in the courts. Citizens make up the two types of juries used in the courts. Grand juries of citizens sit and listen to the prosecutor's case before deciding whether an indictment should be issued. Trial juries sit and listen to the criminal trial before deciding if the defendant should be convicted. In several states, and in death penalty cases, the jury also recommends a sentence to the judge after deciding to convict the defendant.

Jurors are selected from lists of residents in the court's jurisdiction. Often these lists are voter registration rolls, telephone books, or the billing records of utility companies. Trial jurors are then subjected to *voir dire*, a process by which the prosecutor and defense attorney seek to discover whether the jurors have any prejudices that could affect their decision in the trial. Attorneys may challenge a juror suspected of being unable to make an objective decision. The judge may dismiss a challenged juror.

Corrections

The general categories of incarceration and community supervision make up corrections. This general classification, however, grossly oversimplifies this complex component of the justice system. Incarceration includes both prisons and jails, whereas community supervision covers both probation and parole. With this dichotomy, it is not clear where such sanctions as halfway houses or "split sentences" fall.

INCARCERATION

The most frequent place of incarceration for criminal offenders and those suspected of criminal acts is the jail. There are more than 3,200 jails in the United States (Stephan & Walsh, 2011), most of which are municipal—either city or (more frequently) county jails. Most jails do not have treatment staffs of counselors, psychologists, and therapists. The major occupational group in jails is correctional officers. Many jail officers are minimally trained and low paid. Often, jail officers are members of the police department or the sheriff's department that is responsible for jail operation. Jail officers have traditionally earned less than patrol officers (Kerley & Ford, 1982).

The nation's jails supervise some 735,000 inmates on any given day, but because of the relatively short time most persons stay in jail, 11 million or more people may "do time" in jail each year (Minton, 2013). More than 60% of those held in jail are not yet convicted and are awaiting trial. It is not possible to determine how many jail admissions are of repeat offenders.

The nation's prisons house more inmates than do jails on any given day, but because of the longer terms, fewer people serve prison time each year than jail time. Whereas jails usually are municipal, the federal or state governments operate prisons. Prisons are more apt than jails to have counselors, therapists, industries, and educational programs, partly because prisons are larger and hold inmates longer, and partly because they have a larger resource base (state taxes) than do city and county jails. Still, the most common occupational category in prisons is that of correctional officers (Stephan, 2008).

NONINCARCERATION

The most common form of nonincarcerative sanction (after fines, perhaps) is probation. On any day approximately 4 million persons are under probation supervision (Maruschak & Parks, 2012). Probation officers supervise these persons in the community and also write presentence investigation reports and operate other programs, depending on the jurisdiction.

Probation departments operate either at the state or local (either city or county) level. State-level probation allows more consistency among probation services across the state, whereas local-level probation allows for flexibility based on local needs. States also differ in terms of into which branch of government probation falls. Most states administer probation under the executive branch, whereas other states prefer to place probation under the judicial branch.

Parole is similar to probation, except that parole is always a function of a state agency; parole officers are, therefore, state employees. At any given time, more than 850,000 persons are under parole supervision (Maruschak & Parks, 2012). These persons were released early from incarceration (mostly from prison) and are supervised by parole officers. Most states have parole boards in the executive branch of government that are responsible for deciding which inmates will be granted early release, as well as what should be the proper conduct of the prisoners' parole periods.

PRIVATE-SECTOR CORRECTIONS

As with law enforcement and the courts, there is private involvement in corrections as well. Traditionally, many correctional practices were the province of voluntary or private initiatives. Throughout the 1980s until the present, there has been a growing movement to privatize corrections, with private companies constructing and operating prisons and jails in addition to providing other services on a contract basis (Travis, Latessa, & Vito, 1985). In addition to these for-profit private correctional enterprises, volunteer service is relatively common in corrections. Volunteers write to and visit prison inmates, provide services to probation and parole offices and clients, and serve on a variety of boards and commissions. The boards and commissions range from those that govern halfway houses to citizen court-watching groups. Neighborhood Watch programs (see Figure 2.9), and other citizen crime-prevention projects have also increased the citizens' role in law enforcement. One of the most important trends in criminal justice during the past decade has been the resurgence of private initiative in the criminal justice system.

SYSTEMS AND CRIMINAL JUSTICE STRUCTURE

What this chapter has demonstrated is that the criminal justice system in the United States is extremely complex. The various agencies that comprise the system are organized at different levels of government, utilize different resource bases, and select differentially qualified personnel in different ways. In short,

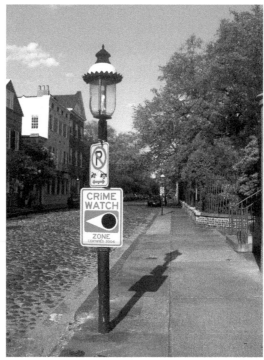

FIGURE 2.9
Neighborhood Watch programs exist across the country. Neighborhood Watch is an example of a crime prevention program that enlists the active participation of residents in cooperation with law enforcement to reduce crime.

although the justice system appears too diverse to be a system, the interdependence of its parts and its sensitivity to environmental changes support a systems approach.

There are at least 52 criminal justice systems in the United States: one for each state, the federal government, and the District of Columbia. This may be an underestimate of their numbers. If city police can arrest someone for violating a city ordinance, and we convict and punish them in a city court, do we have a city justice system? Although we can argue that there are many criminal justice systems in the United States, we will continue to examine and discuss the criminal justice system as a whole.

This systems approach to the study of criminal justice seems especially appropriate. Without a prevailing approach, we might be forced to throw up our hands in despair, unable to make sense of the confusion. Why do we have so many agencies? Why do these different agencies have conflicting and sometimes competing jurisdictions and goals? The answer is because they are part of an open system.

The large number of agencies and the various levels and branches of government involved are a manifestation of environmental impact on American criminal justice. Given our political and cultural values of federalism, local autonomy, and the separation of powers, we should not be surprised at the confusion in the justice system; it would be more surprising if there were no confusion. A single, well-organized, monolithic criminal justice system for the entire nation may well be "un-American."

REVIEW QUESTIONS

1. Identify the 10 decision points of the criminal justice process discussed in this chapter.
2. How does the justice process work as a directional flow of cases in the total system?
3. Give two examples of how the environment of the justice process affects the operations of all justice agencies.
4. What are the basic components of the justice process?
5. Describe the different types, levels, and staffing patterns of the components of the justice process.
6. Why is the systems approach especially appropriate to the study of American criminal justice?

References

Aaronson, D. E., Kittrie, N. N., Saari, D. J., & Cooper, C. S. (1977). *Alternatives to conventional criminal adjudication*. Washington, DC: U.S. Government Printing Office.

Avakame, E. F., Fyfe, J. J., & McCoy, C. (1999). "Did You Call the Police? What Did They Do?" An empirical assessment of Black's theory of the mobilization of law. *Justice Quarterly*, 16(4), 765–792.

Balko, R. (2003). *Back door to prohibition: The new war on social drinking*. CATO Policy Analysis, 501, 1–27.

Baumer, E., & Lauritsen, J. (2010). Reporting crime to the police, 1973–2005: A multivariate analysis of long-term trends in the National Crime Survey (NCS) and the National Crime Victimization Survey (NCVS). *Criminology*, 48(1), 131–186.

Beck, K. (2009). Lessons learned from evaluating Maryland's anti-drunk driving campaign: Assessing the evidence for cognitive, behavioral, and public health impact. *Health Promotion Practice*, 10, 370–377.

Belknap, J., & McCall, K. (1994). Woman battering and police referrals. *Journal of Criminal Justice*, 22(2), 223–236.

Boatwright-Horowitz, S., Olick, K., & Amaral, R. (2004). Calling 911 during episodes of domestic abuse: What justifies a call for help? *Journal of Criminal Justice*, 32(1), 89–92.

Boland, B., Mahanna, P., & Sones, R. (1992). *The prosecution of felony arrests, 1988*. Washington, DC: Bureau of Justice Statistics.

Buckler, K. G., & Travis, L. F. (2003). Reanalyzing the prevalence and social context of collateral consequence statutes. *Journal of Criminal Justice*, 31(5), 435–453.

Bureau of Justice Statistics (1989). *BJS Data Report, 1988*. Washington, DC: U.S. Department of Justice, pp. 20–21.

Bureau of Justice Statistics (2010). *Criminal victimization in the United States, 2007: Statistical tables.* Retrieved from http://bjs.ojp.usdoj.gov/content/pub/pdf/cvus0705.

Burton, V. S., Cullen, F. T., Travis, L. F., III (1987). The collateral consequences of a felony conviction: A national study of state statutes. *Federal Probation, 51*(3), 52–60.

Carson, E., & Sabol, W. (2012). *Prisoners in 2011.* Washington: DC. Bureau of Justice Statistics.

Chesney-Lind, M. (2002). Criminalizing victimization: The unintended consequences of pro-arrest policies for girls and women. *Criminology and Public Policy, 1*(2), 81–90.

Clapp, J., Johnson, M., Voas, R., Lange, J., Shillington, A., & Russell, C. (2005). Reducing DUI among US college students: Results of an environmental prevention trial. *Addiction, 100,* 327–334.

Cohen, R. (1992). *Drunk driving.* Washington, DC: Bureau of Justice Statistics.

Cohen, T., & Kyckelhahn, T. (2010). *Felony defendants in large urban counties, 2008.* Washington, DC: Bureau of Justice Statistics.

Davis, R., Smith, B., & Taylor, B. (2003). Increasing the proportion of domestic violence arrests that are prosecuted: A natural experiment in Milwaukee. *Criminology and Public Policy, 2*(2), 263–282.

Devers, L. (2011). *Plea and charge bargaining: Research summary.* Bureau of Justice Assistance: U.S. Department of Justice.

Durose, M. (2007). *State court sentencing of convicted felons, 2004—Statistical tables.* Washington, DC: Bureau of Justice Statistics.

Feder, L. (1996). Police handling of domestic calls: The importance of offender's presence in the arrest decision. *Journal of Criminal Justice, 24*(6), 481–490.

Federal Bureau of Investigation (2011). *Crime in the United States, 2011.* Ten-year arrest trends, 2002–2011. Washington, DC: U.S. Department of Justice.

Felson, R., Messner, S., Hoskin, A., & Deane, G. (2002). Reasons for reporting and not reporting domestic violence to the police. *Criminology, 40*(3), 617–648.

Goudriaan, H., Lynch, J., & Nieuwbeerta, P. (2004). Reporting to the police in western nations: A theoretical analysis of the effects of social context. *Justice Quarterly, 21*(4), 933–969.

Goldberg, N.A., & Lichtman, J.L. (1978). *Guide to Establishing a Defender System.* Washington, DC: U.S. Government Printing Office.

Harlow, C. (2000). *Defense counsel in criminal cases.* Washington, DC: Bureau of Justice Statistics.

Harrison, P. M., & Beck, A. J. (2003). *Prisoners in 2002.* Washington, DC: Bureau of Justice Statistics.

Hickman, M. J., & Reaves, B. A. (2006). *Local police departments, 2003.* Washington, DC: Bureau of Justice Statistics.

Huddleston, W., & Marlowe, D. (2011). *Painting the current picture: A national report on drug courts and other problem-solving court programs in the United States.* National Drug Court Institute: U.S. Department of Justice.

Humphries, D. (2002). No easy answers: Public policy, criminal justice, and domestic violence. *Criminology and Public Policy, 1*(2), 91–96.

International Association of Chiefs of Police, Division of State and Provincial Police (1975). *Comparative data report.* Gaithersburg, MD: IACP.

Iyengar, R. (2009). Does the certainty of arrest reduce domestic violence? Evidence from mandatory and recommended arrest laws. *Journal of Public Economics, 93,* 85–98.

Jansen, B. (2013). *Make DUI limit 0.05% blood-alcohol level, NTSB says.* USA Today. Retrieved from http://www.usatoday.com/story/news/nation/2013/05/14/national-transportation-safety-board-drunken-driving/2158107/.

Johnson, I., & Sigler, R. (2000). Public perceptions: The stability of the public's endorsements of the definition and criminalization of the abuse of women. *Journal of Criminal Justice, 28*(3), 165–179.

Jones, D., & Belknap, J. (1999). Police responses to battering in a progressive pro-hyphen arrest jurisdiction. *Justice Quarterly, 16*(2), 249–273.

Kane, R. (1999). Patterns of arrest in domestic violence encounters: Identifying a police decision-making model. *Journal of Criminal Justice, 27*(1), 65–79.

Kerley, K. E., & Ford, F. R. (1982). *The state of our nation's jails, 1982.* Washington, DC: National Sheriffs' Association.

Langston, L., & Cohen, T. (2007). *State court organization, 1987–2004.* Washington, DC: Bureau of Justice Statistics.

Lanza-Kaduce, L., Greenleaf, R., & Donahue, M. (1995). Trickle-up report writing: The impact of a proarrest policy for domestic disturbances. *Justice Quarterly, 12*(3), 525–542.

Leigh, D., & Harding, L. (2011). *Wikileaks: Inside Julian Assange's war on secrecy.* New York, NY: Public Affairs.

Maahs, J., & Hemmens, C. (1998). Guarding the public: A statutory analysis of state regulation of security guards. *Journal of Crime and Justice, 21*(1), 119–134.

Maruschak, L., & Parks, E. (2012). *Probation and parole in the United States, 2011.* Washington, DC: Bureau of Justice Statistics.

Mastrofski, S. D., Ritti, R. R., & Hoffmaster, D. (1987). Organizational determinants of police discretion: The case of drinking-driving. *Journal of Criminal Justice, 15*(5), 387–402.

Maxwell, C. D., Garner, J. H., & Fagan, J. A. (2002). The preventive effects of arrest on intimate partner violence: Research, policy and theory. *Criminology and Public Policy, 2*(1), 51–80.

Meyer, J., & Gray, T. (1997). Drunk drivers in the courts: Legal and extra-legal factors affecting pleas and sentences. *Journal of Crime and Justice, 25*(2), 155–163.

Meyers, A., Heeren, T., Hingson, R., & Kovenock, D. (1987). Cops and drivers: Police discretion and the enforcement of Maine's 1981 DUI law. *Journal of Criminal Justice, 15*(5), 361–368.

Minton, T. (2013). *Jail inmates at midyear 2012—Statistical tables.* Washington, DC: Bureau of Justice Statistics.

Mothers Against Drunk Driving. Retrieved July 7, 2007, from http://www.madd.org.

National Institute of Justice (1985). Jailing drunk drivers: Impact on the criminal justice system. *National Institute of Justice Reports,* 2 July.

National Institute of Justice (2008). *Policing in Arab-American communities after September 11.* Washington, DC: National Institute of Justice.

Newport, F. (2011). *Record-high 50% of Americans favor legalizing marijuana use.* Gallup Poll. Retrieved September 6, 2013 at http://www.gallup.com/poll/150149/record-high-americans-favor-legalizing-marijuana.aspx.

Office for Victims of Crime (2002). *The crime victim's right to be present. Legal series bulletin #3 (January).* Washington, DC: Office for Victims of Crime.

Ostrom, B. (2003). Domestic violence: Editorial introduction. *Criminology and Public Policy, 2*(2), 259–262.

Ostrom, B., Kauder, N., & LaFountain, R. (2003). *Examining the work of state courts 2002: A national perspective from the court statistics project.* Washington, DC: National Center for State Courts.

Perry, S., & Banks, D. (2011). *Prosecutors in state courts, 2007—Statistical tables.* Washington, DC: Bureau of Justice Statistics.

President's Commission on Law Enforcement and Administration of Justice (1967). *Task force report: The police.* Washington, DC: U.S. Government Printing Office.

Reaves, B. (2009). *State and local law enforcement training academies, 2006.* Washington, DC: Bureau of Justice Statistics.

Reaves, B. (2011). *Census of state and local law enforcement agencies, 2008.* Washington, DC: Bureau of Justice Statistics.

Reaves, B. (2012). *Federal law enforcement officers, 2008.* Washington, DC: Bureau of Justice Statistics.

Rosenmerkel, S., Durose, M., & Farole, D. (2009). *Felony sentences in state courts, 2006—Data tables.* Washington, DC: Bureau of Justice Statistics.

Rottman, D., & Casey, P. (1999). Therapeutic jurisprudence and the emergence of problem-solving courts. *National Institute of Justice Journal, 240,* 12–19 (July).

Rottman, D., & Strickland, S. (2006). *State court organization, 2004.* Washington, DC: Bureau of Justice Statistics.

Sanders, B., Hughes, T., & Langworthy, R. (1995). Police officer recruitment and selection: A survey of major police departments in the U.S. *Police Forum, 5*(4), 1–4.

Savage, C. (2013, June 18). N.S.A. chief says surveillance has stopped dozens of plots. *The New York Times.* Retrieved from http://www.nytimes.com/2013/06/19/us/politics/nsa-chief-says-surveillance-has-stopped-dozens-of-plots.html?pagewanted=all.

Savage, C. & Huetteman, E. (2013, August 21). Manning sentenced to 35 years for a pivotal leak of U.S. files. *The New York Times.* Retrieved from http://www.nytimes.com/2013/08/22/us/manning-sentenced-for-leaking-government-secrets.html?pagewanted=all.

Schafer, J., Burruss, G., & Giblin, M. (2009). Measuring Homeland Security in small municipal agencies: Policing in a post-9/11 world. *Police Quarterly, 12*(3), 263–288.

Shane, S. (2013, June 21). Ex-contractor is charged in leaks on N.S.A. surveillance. *The New York Times.* http://www.nytimes.com/2013/06/22/us/snowden-espionage-act.html?_r=0.

Sherman, L. (1992). *Policing domestic violence: Experiments and dilemmas.* New York: Free Press.

Snyder, H. (2012). *Arrest in the United States, 1990–2010.* Washington, DC: Bureau of Justice Statistics.

Sourcebook of Criminal Justice Statistics (2010). Retrieved July 4, 2010, from http://www.albany.edu/sourcebook.

Stephan, J. (2008). *Census of state and federal correctional facilities, 2005.* Washington, DC: Bureau of Justice Statistics.

Stephan, J., & Walsh, G. (2011). *Census of jail facilities.* Washington, DC: Bureau of Justice Statistics.

Travis, L. F., & Langworthy, R. H. (2008). *Policing in America: A balance of forces* (4th ed.). Englewood Cliffs, NJ: Prentice Hall.

Travis, L. F., Latessa, E. J., & Vito, G. F. (1985). Private enterprise in institutional corrections: A call for caution. *Federal Probation, 49*(4), 11–16.

Travis, L. F., & Stacey, J. (2010). A half century of parole rules: Conditions of parole in the United States, 2008. *Journal of Criminal Justice, 38*(4), 604–608.

Truman, J., & Planty, M. (2012). *Criminal victimization.* Washington, DC: Bureau of Justice Statistics.

U.S. Department of Justice (1978). *The nation's toughest drug law.* Washington, DC: U.S. Government Printing Office.

U.S. Department of Justice (1980). *Justice agencies in the United States.* Washington, DC: U.S. Government Printing Office.

Vartebedian, R. (2002, December 30). A spirited debate over DUI laws. *Los Angeles Times,* A1.

Woodard, P.L., & Anderson, J.R. (1984). *Victim/Witness Legislation: An Overview.* Washington, DC: U.S. Department of Justice.

Walker, S. (2011). *Sense and nonsense about crime and drugs: A policy guide* (7th ed.). Belmont, CA: Wadsworth.

Welch, M., Wolff, R., & Bryan, N. (1998). Decontextualizing the war on drugs: A content analysis of NIJ publications and their neglect of race and class. *Justice Quarterly, 15*(4), 719–742.

Whitcomb, D. (2002). Prosecutors, kids, and domestic violence cases. *National Institute of Justice Journal, 248,* 2–9 (March).

Yu, J., Evans, P., & Clark, L. (2006). Alcohol addiction and perceived sanction risks: Deterring drunk drivers. *Journal of Criminal Justice, 34*(2), 165–174.

CHAPTER 3
Crime and Crime Control

The business of the American criminal justice process is "crime"; yet, this does not explain much. One obstacle to the study of our system of criminal justice is our lack of precision in discussing the issue of crime. In short, what is crime?

Although it is relatively easy to provide examples of crime, it is not so easy to define it. We tend to assume a common meaning for the word "crime." The variety of actions and nuances of behavior that constitute crime is nearly infinite. If asked to name a crime, how many of us would say shoplifting, drunken driving, price fixing, or failure to register for the selective service? We are far more likely to mention murder, bank robbery, rape, or burglary. In that sense, we have a fairly clear common definition of crime, but one that is inadequate for the study of criminal justice.

These mental images of crime reflect those offenses that cause the most concern. Of the many different types of behaviors that we have defined as criminal, some types are more commonly agreed on to be criminal than others. There tends to be consensus among us about the criminality of the more serious offenses that involve actual physical harm or direct economic harm to individuals (Cullen, Link, & Polanzi, 1982). There is considerably less agreement about those offenses that do not cause such direct and potentially personal harm (Miethe, 1982; Newman & Trilling, 1975).

Similarly, we carry mental images of criminals about which there is general agreement. Most people would probably describe the average criminal as a relatively young, mean, menacing male. They seem to believe that the criminal knows—but does not care—that his or her behavior is wrong and harmful. The criminal is simply bad or lazy, preferring crime to some other more appropriate mode of earning a living or settling arguments. Yet, as with crimes, there is a wide variety of criminals. The hulking street offender, bullying rapist, calculating white-collar offender, college student selling drugs, and political terrorist are all criminals. Vogel (1998) reported on a study of perceptions of crime seriousness among African Americans. She gave respondents descriptions of six crimes that involved information about the actual behavior as well as the context of the offense. The context information included the motive of the offender, the amount of harm caused, and the actions of the victim. She found that there was

Important Terms

actus reus
career criminal
crime
deviance
felony
life-course
  criminality
mala in se
mala prohibita
mens rea
misdemeanor
problem-oriented
  policing
routine activities
situational crime
  prevention
strict liability
vertical
  prosecution
violation

little consensus about crime seriousness. Although we may be in widespread agreement about what behaviors are the most serious crimes in some abstract way, knowing the details about specific criminal behaviors produces less agreement among observers (Unnever, Cochran, Cullen, & Applegate, 2010).

Faced with the wide array of crimes and criminals, we need to organize our understanding of each in order to appreciate the demands placed on the justice system. Both crimes and criminals have been sorted into classes for ease of understanding. Before turning to these, however, we should try to answer the question, What is crime?

DEFINING CRIME

Crime refers in part to a set of behaviors that society deems to be wrong and in need of control. Most often, classifying a behavior as a crime includes a reference to the intent of the actor. In our society, the specification and definition of crimes are legislative functions. The legislature has the authority to declare certain behaviors criminal and describes the conditions under which a person may be said to have committed a crime. (Box 3.1 provides an example of a portion of a criminal statute.) Therefore, from a legalistic perspective, we

---

BOX 3.1 SEC: 2911.12 OHIO REVISED CODE: BURGLARY

A. No person, by force, stealth, or deception, shall do any of the following:
   1. Trespass in an occupied structure or in a separately secured or separately occupied portion of an occupied structure, when another person other than an accomplice of the offender is present, with purpose to commit in the structure or in the separately secured or separately occupied portion of the structure any criminal offense.
   2. Trespass in an occupied structure or in a separately secured or separately occupied portion of an occupied structure that is a permanent or a temporary habitation of any person when any person other than an accomplice of the offender is present or likely to be present, with purpose to commit in the habitation any criminal offense.
   3. Trespass in an occupied structure or in a separately secured or separately occupied portion of an occupied structure, with purpose to commit in the structure or separately occupied portion any criminal offense.
B. No person, by force, stealth, or deception, shall trespass in a permanent or temporary habitation of any person when any person other than an accomplice of the offender is present or likely to be present.
   Whoever violates division (A) in this section is guilty of burglary. A violation of division (A)(1) or (2) of this section is a felony of the second degree. A violation of division (A)(3) of this section is a felony of the third degree. Whoever violates division (B) of this section is guilty of trespass in a habitation when a person is present or likely to be present, a felony of the fourth degree.

Source: Ohio Revised Code (2010)

can conclude the cause of crime in America is the legislature. Without legislative action, there would be no conduct designated as crime. **Crime** is an act or omission in violation of a law punishable by the state. In the United States, the requirement that the behavior violates the law means we need legislative action to establish crime.

Of course, without the designation of certain conduct as crime, we would still have troublesome behavior, such as the taking of property or the infliction of injury. These actions would not be crimes, however, unless the legislature first defines them as such.

Although most of us do not think of legislative action as a necessary cause of crime, we understand the legislative role. If asked to define the cause of crime, most people will contend that bad companions, ignorance, poverty, psychological disturbance, or some other factor is what makes people break the law. Yet, when we see someone doing something that we believe is wrong, we are also apt to say, "There ought to be a law." This statement reflects an understanding of the role of the legislature. No matter how wrong the behavior in question, we cannot do anything about it unless there is a law against it.

This is an important concept for understanding the criminal justice system. The justice system is constrained by the law. We generally cannot use the justice process to control behavior that is unpleasant but not criminal. There are limits, then, to what level of control agents of the criminal process can assert. Of course, the power of the justice system to control behavior often leads people to pass laws. Luna (2003:15) has described the expansion of criminal law in the United States, noting that more than 3,000 offenses are punishable as federal crimes.

Criminologists have debated the definition of crime for many years (Schwendinger & Schwendinger, 1975). Some argue that only those behaviors identified in criminal laws are crimes. Others seek a broader definition that includes actions that are socially harmful or immoral. The issue of defining crime is somewhat different for these criminologists than it is for our purposes because they are trying to explain deviance, of which crime is one type. If the focus is on deviant behavior, there is no need to consider legal status. **Deviance** is behavior that violates socially accepted standards of proper conduct.

The approach we are using in this book requires a definition of crime that identifies those behaviors on which the criminal justice system focuses. Criminologists, however, are seeking to identify a set of behaviors explained by theories of criminal behavior (Tittle, 2000). Criminologists usually seek to explain the behavior of individuals (Willis, Evans, & LaGrange, 1999), whereas we wish to understand the criminal justice system and its parts as a social institution.

The definitions of most crimes contain two components. First, there is an action (or lack of action) known as *actus reus*. Second, there is the intent or mental condition of the offender known as *mens rea*. To be considered a criminal, it is usually not enough to do something illegal; one must also intend to do what is illegal to be convicted of a crime.

Most jurisdictions define the crime of burglary as the unlawful entry of a place with the intention of committing a crime therein. To be convicted of burglary, one must unlawfully enter a place (a home, business, storage building, etc.). Simply entering, however, does not make one a burglar. The entry is the *actus reus*. To be a burglar, it is also necessary that one enter with the intent to commit a crime while inside. This intent to commit a crime is the mental state of the offender, the *mens rea*.

Neither of the following two hypothetical persons is a burglar:

> P. was invited to a party at a neighbor's home. P. did not care much for these neighbors, but cared greatly for several of their possessions. P. accepted the invitation and attended the party for the express purpose of obtaining the property of the neighbors. P. is not a burglar, because the entry was lawful. In this case, P. is a thief.

> Q. was walking home from a party at which large quantities of alcoholic refreshments were consumed (the largest quantity by Q.). Passing a furrier, Q. blacks out from the combined effects of too many beverages and a long, tedious conversation with someone named P., a neighbor of the host. Q. falls over and crashes through the display window of the furrier's shop, landing in a huge pile of fur coats, on which Q. falls fast asleep. The police arrive within minutes, responding to the alarm, to discover the quietly resting Q., who is not a burglar, because there was no intent to commit a crime in the furrier shop. (Indeed, there was not even intent to enter.)

To obtain a criminal conviction, the state must prove all elements (both *actus reus* and *mens rea*) of an offense beyond a reasonable doubt. Television murder-mystery plots often include a missing victim when there is reason to believe that someone was murdered but the body cannot be found. The characters remark that it will be difficult to bring charges without the *corpus delicti*. Because of the plot, and the similarity between the words "corpus" and "corpse," audiences sometimes think that *corpus delicti* refers to the dead body. In fact, it refers to the body of the crime. The lack of a motive (also a frequent plot line) also hinders the filing of charges because, without a motive, it is difficult to establish intent, another part of the *corpus delicti*.

For some crimes, the job of the state in proving the guilt of an offender is somewhat easier. Some crimes, known as **strict liability** offenses, presume *mens rea* (Lilly & Ball, 1982). In these cases, if the prosecution proves that the defendant engaged in the prohibited behavior, a conviction will occur. Regardless of the intent of the offender, she or he is strictly liable for the consequences of the behavior.

Strict liability often applies to white-collar crimes. For example, the law may presume that the head of a company is responsible for the wrongdoing of his or her employees, even if the company head is unaware of the activity. Especially with strict liability offenses, the old adage "Ignorance of the law is no excuse" is true.

This brief explanation of the definition of crimes and of the elements of an offense helps us understand the nature of crime. However, this explanation alone does not help us to obtain a perspective on crime that will be useful to our examination of the criminal justice process. The legislatures in the various U.S. criminal jurisdictions have managed to define a large number of widely divergent behaviors and mental states as crimes. The justice system must respond to all of them with limited resources and ability. To better organize and deploy the limited resources for the control of crime, criminal justice officials must sort and rank this plethora of offenses.

CLASSIFICATION OF CRIMES AND CRIMINALS

We have already mentioned one simple classification of crimes as the difference between serious and less serious offenses. This same simplistic distinction is drawn between dangerous and normal crimes. Those offenses that are most threatening to individuals are usually defined as serious (or dangerous), whereas those that are less directly threatening are classed as less serious (or normal).

Sometimes this distinction between dangerous and normal crimes is explained as the difference between offenses that are wrong in themselves (*mala in se*) and those that are wrong because they are prohibited (*mala prohibita*). That is, certain crimes appear to be obviously criminal, whereas others are apparently criminal only because we say they are wrong.

Mala in se offenses encompass traditional or street crimes that seem wrong regardless of their legality. Purposely or carelessly causing physical harm or suffering to someone, or taking the property of others, is an act that most people believe to be simply wrong. One does not need a criminal law to realize that killing a person without cause (and often with cause) is wrong. These are the very offenses about which we have the most agreement and around which most of our mental images of crime focus. As Luna (2003:1) put it, "every U.S. jurisdiction has on its books a set of crimes and punishments that are incontrovertible, involving acts and attendant mental states that must be proscribed to constitute a just society—murder, rape, robbery, arson and the like."

Mala prohibita offenses, however, are those acts that are wrong because they are defined as wrong. The use of narcotics by adults within the confines of their own homes and the refusal to pay income taxes (especially if the money might be better spent on something else) are not behaviors that are necessarily wrong (at least in a secular perspective). What makes these behaviors criminal, and therefore wrong, is that society has prohibited them and defined them as crimes. We have the least agreement on these offenses, and they raise the most serious issues of individual liberty. Luna (2003:15) wrote, "These offenses are marked by the absence of violence or coercion, with parties engaged in voluntary transactions for desired goods or services."

A second major way in which we classify criminal offenses is into categories of felony, misdemeanor, or violation. These three levels of crime reflect the different seriousness of behaviors. Before explaining this difference, it is important to remember that there are exceptions to every rule. The following are merely rules of thumb.

A **felony** is the most serious level of offense and generally is punishable by a term of more than 1 year in a state prison. A **misdemeanor** is a less serious offense, generally punishable by a term of no more than 1 year in a local jail. A **violation** is the least serious offense and typically does not carry an incarceration penalty; the penalty is limited to a fine or loss of privilege. For example, in most states, a theft of $1,000 or more is a felony and can be punished by imprisonment for a number of years, whereas theft of $50 is a misdemeanor and can be punished by a jail term of up to several months. Exceeding the speed limit is a violation and punished by a fine of less than $500 (except for repeated offenses). As these examples illustrate, the classes of crimes reflect the amount of harm caused by the criminal behavior.

Still another distinction drawn between crimes is to label them as being either ordinary (normal) or aggravated (dangerous) (Newman, 1987:28–30). It is possible to rate crimes as being "better" or "worse" than each other, within the same crime type. A burglar may not do any more damage to a home than that required for entry and theft; this is an ordinary burglary. However, the burglar may vandalize the home in addition to breaking in and stealing; this might be an aggravated burglary. We will return to this type of classification system later when we discuss sentencing.

The ordinary-versus-aggravated distinction is generally used within some less precise classification (such as "robbery") to differentiate between the seriousness of several instances of the "same" behavior. As with the other classifications of crimes, the purpose of this distinction is to clarify the response the justice system should make. Typically, the agents and agencies of the justice system are more willing to expend resources in response to aggravated felonies than in response to ordinary violations. Indeed, many people express this rational choice when stopped for a traffic violation by wondering why the officer is not out "fighting crime" rather than focusing on trivial matters.

Ample evidence suggests that the type of crime is an important consideration in criminal justice decisions. Serious crimes are more likely to be reported by victims and witnesses, and are more likely to be investigated and processed by the police (Wilson & Ruback, 2003). Criminal justice officials at all points of the system devote more attention and resources to aggravated, *mala in se* felonies than to other, less serious crimes. When trying to understand criminal justice processing then, offense seriousness is an important consideration.

Gottfredson and Gottfredson reviewed the research on criminal justice processing. Across all types of criminal justice decisions from detection through parole, and even the crime victim's decision to report the offense to the police, three factors were most important predictors of decisions. Gottfredson and Gottfredson (1988:257–258) wrote, "from the host of offender, offense, victim, decision-maker, and situational factors that potentially influence individual decision making, three appear to play a persistent and major role throughout the system: the seriousness of the offense, the prior criminal record of the offender, and the personal relationship between the victim of the crime and the offender." Crime seriousness or the type of crime is an important influence on criminal justice processing.

When crimes are defined as felonies, they are more likely to be investigated than misdemeanors. Felonies result in incarceration sentences more often, and for longer periods of time, than less serious offenses. Jogerst, Daly, Brinig, and Bibas (2005) studied the relationship between crime seriousness and the reporting and investigation of those crimes. They found that in cases of elder abuse, the crime was more likely to be reported and more likely to be investigated in states that defined elder abuse as a more serious offense (criminal rather than civil; felony rather than misdemeanor).

DEFINING CRIMINALS

Like crimes themselves, the people who commit them are of an infinite variety. Assuming that there is a preventive component to the justice system's overall mission to control crime, knowledge of the type of offender is as important as knowledge about the type of crime (Holmes, 1989). We identify certain types of offenders as deserving specific types of justice system responses. A Bureau of Justice Statistics Report (1985:1) stated:

> Programs aimed at the serious, recidivistic offender require the capability to identify dangerous offenders at key decision points in the criminal justice system, such as pre-trial release and sentencing ...

> These programs are designed primarily to increase the effectiveness of criminal justice by targeting resources on offenders considered most likely to recidivate and on offenders whose detention is most likely to have an incapacitative or deterrent effect.

One common method of classifying offenders is by the crime they committed—someone guilty of murder is a murderer, someone guilty of robbery is a robber, someone guilty of burglary is a burglar, and so on. This is often how the media and correctional authorities identify offenders. Police frequently improve on this simple scheme by adding details of crimes, such as the time of the crime, type of weapon used, and characteristics of the victim. These added details comprise a *modus operandi* (M.O.) file. This type of classification is limited because it does not tell much about the offender. A study conducted by the RAND Corporation (Chaiken & Chaiken, 1982) showed that offenders often engage in a variety of criminal behavior. Today's robber may have been yesterday's thief and may be tomorrow's burglar. Recent research suggests that offenders may specialize at least in terms of types of crime. Deane, Armstrong, and Felson (2005) reported that some offenders are likely to commit crimes of violence, whereas others are unlikely to be violent. Offenders may not specialize along the lines of specific crimes as much as within violent or nonviolent crimes. Similarly, there are certain crime types that seem to "go together" and might represent something of a criminal lifestyle. Deane and his colleagues reported a link between armed robbery, other armed violence, selling drugs, and serious property crime. Criminals who engage in one of these crimes are also more likely to be involved in the others. Osgood and Schreck (2007) reported finding evidence of a specialization in violence among a sample of juvenile offenders, whereas Lo, Kim, and Cheng (2008) found modest support for specialization in violence among adults. These studies suggest that although it may not be accurate to speak of burglars or robbers, it may be accurate to classify offenders' crime types in terms of property offenders, violent offenders, or other types of offense such as drug offenders.

In contrast, Harris, Smallbone, Dennison, and Knight (2009) question the degree to which sex offenders specialize. A number of recent changes in criminal law, including such things as the Adam Walsh Child Protection and Safety Act and Megan's Law, which require sex offenders to register and limit where these offenders can live, are based on assumptions that these offenders specialize in sex offenses and will repeat their crimes. Harris and colleagues found that among a sample of sex offenders rapists were less specialized than those who committed incest or child molestation. Still, even these latter offenders were more likely to commit a range of crimes than to be limited only to their sexual offenses.

Another typical classification of offenders is similar to the ordinary/aggravated distinction applied to crimes. Here, offenders are identified as either "first-time" (ordinary) or "repeat" (more dangerous) offenders. Many jurisdictions have special procedures for the handling of repeat offenders, known as career criminals. The distinction drawn is one between periodic (or occasional) criminality and a criminal lifestyle. Those who lead a criminal life—that is, who routinely engage in criminal behavior—are responsible for a disproportionate share of crime committed (Greenwood, 1982).

Criminal Careers versus Career Criminals

Criminologists have studied criminal behavior through examination of the "criminal careers" of offenders (Gibbons, 1973; Nettler, 1982). These researchers seek to identify the paths followed by offenders throughout their lives that lead them into and out of crime. They recognize that criminality is not always central to the personality of an offender. The average person probably has committed (or will someday commit) a crime. Yet, few of us are (or will be) criminals. In contemporary parlance, this approach to the study of criminals is known as the study of **life-course criminality**—how people engage in or refrain from crime over the course of their lives (Farrington, 2003). We discuss life-course criminality in greater detail later.

The **career criminal** is someone for whom crime is a normal activity and for whom being a criminal is part of self-identification. This person is often called a "hardened criminal" or persistent offender. It has been suggested that these persistent offenders commit the majority of crimes (DeLisi, 2005). By attempting to focus attention on these individuals, justice officials hope to have the greatest impact on the crime rate.

For decades, some criminologists argued that the most useful classification of offenders would be one based on behavioral characteristics. They advanced several means of distinguishing among criminals based on the psychological or sociological traits of the offender. These have been used for prison classification (Bonta & Motiuk, 1992; Fox, 1983:59–62), probation and parole classification (Bonta, 1996; Clear & Gallagher, 1985; Warren, 1973), and prevention programs. Perhaps the most wide-ranging classification system that retained links to type of crime was suggested by Clinard, Quinney, and Wildeman (1994).

The principal goal of these criminologists is to understand why persons commit crimes or why certain persons commit certain crimes. For criminal justice agencies, this knowledge is useful only insofar as it can guide reactions to crime and criminals (Vito & Holmes, 1994). Clinard et al. (1994) classified offenders by the major forms of crime committed. They identified nine categories, ranging from violent personal criminal behavior through professional criminal behavior (see Table 3.1). Agents of the criminal justice system appear to use a similar classification scheme in their handling of offenders.

Table 3.1 Criminal Behavior Systems	
Classifications of Offenders	**Criminal Career of the Offender**
1. Violent personal criminal behavior	Crime is not part of the offenders' career. They usually do not conceive of themselves as criminal
2. Occasional property criminal behavior	Offenders have little or no criminal self-conception. The offenders do not identify with crime. They are able to rationalize their behavior
3. Public order criminal behavior	Most offenders do not regard their behavior as criminal. They do not have a clearly defined criminal career. Ambiguity in self-concept produced in continued contact with legal system
4. Conventional criminal behavior	Offenders begin their careers early in life, often in gang associations. Crime committed for economic gain. Vacillation in self-conception. Partial commitment to a criminal subculture
5. Political criminal behavior	Offenders do not usually conceive of themselves as criminals and do not identify with crime. They are defined as criminal because they are perceived as threatening to the status quo or they are criminal when they violate the laws that regulate the government itself (crime by government)

(Continued)

Table 3.1	Criminal Behavior Systems—Cont'd
Classifications of Offenders	**Criminal Career of the Offender**
6. Occupational criminal behavior	Offenders have little or no self-conception. They occasionally violate the law, accompanied by appropriate rationalizations. Violations tend to be a part of one's work. Offenders accept the conventional values in the society
7. Corporate criminal behavior	The violating corporate official and the corporation have high social status in society. Offenders are an integral part of corporate business operations. Violations are rationalized as being basic to business enterprise
8. Organized criminal behavior	Crime is pursued as a livelihood. There is a progression in crime and an increasing isolation from the larger society. A criminal self-conception develops
9. Professional criminal behavior	Offenders have established a highly developed criminal career. Professional offenders engage in specialized offenses, all of which are directed toward economic gain. They are committed to other professional criminals

Source: Clinard et al. (1994)

Typologies of crimes and criminals are used to plan and evaluate the uses to which criminal justice resources are put. Without such "shorthand" categorization of its basic types of business, the justice system would be overwhelmed by idiosyncrasies. Although by no means perfect, these classification schemes allow the justice system to be organized in a way that makes the system's operation more efficient.

For example, police officers may distinguish among burglars as juvenile burglars, average burglars, or cat burglars. The juvenile burglar, as the name implies, is a youth who commits an opportunistic burglary with little forethought and perhaps less care in the commission of the offense. The average burglar plans his or her crime and is careful to avoid detection. The cat burglar is someone who burglarizes a dwelling while the occupants are on the premises (Gibbons, 1973:14).

Although all of these are correctly labeled or categorized as "burglars," it is clear that they pose different levels of risk to citizens and that they require different responses by the police. The juvenile burglar is likely to grab whatever valuables can be quickly obtained and easily carried. The average burglar is unlikely to be discovered during the crime and generally will take more property. The cat burglar, although also unlikely to be detected, usually restricts his or her thefts to cash, jewels, or specific high-value items.

Agents and agencies of the justice system have organized to better combat the more serious offenses and offenders. The career criminal became the target of special crime control efforts and programs in the 1980s. "The concept of the career criminal has led to police and prosecutor programs that target resources on those offenders identified as the most persistent and frequent in their commission of serious crimes" (National Institute of Justice, 1986). Many police departments and prosecutor's offices have special repeat offender or career criminal bureaus. Some states have initiatives that support (or require) local justice agencies to focus attention on career criminals. The state of California supports a Career Criminal Prosecution Program with special state funding. In Virginia, the state supports the Serious or Habitual Offender Comprehensive Action Program (SHOCAP).

Criminologists have begun to focus (in some cases, refocus) on different dimensions of criminality. There has been a resurgence of "rational choice" theory, which treats criminals as economic decision makers who calculate the costs and benefits of crime before deciding to commit an offense (Tittle, 2000:62–67). Nagin (2007) argued that a focus on how offenders make choices about whether and which crimes to commit would expand our understanding of crime and our ability to control and prevent crime. He warned that rational choice approaches must be sensitive to the fact that decisions involve not only reason but also emotion. It may well be that certain decisions appear rational to us under some emotional circumstances such as when we are angry, afraid, or excited.

We hear less about career criminals today, and more about crime in the "life course" (Laub & Sampson, 1993; Thornberry, 1997). One of the best known theories of crime over the course of offenders' lives was suggested by Terrie Moffitt (1997). She suggested that some individuals engage in crime over their entire lives, whereas others experience certain periods (usually adolescence) when they have a greater risk of criminality. Life-course criminology is a subset of criminological theory that seeks to understand how people start, continue, and stop engaging in crime over the span of their lives.

Another theme relates to place, or environmental criminology. Cohen and Felson (1979) described a "**routine activities**" theory of crime. They suggested that crime occurs when a motivated offender and a suitable target (victim or property) come together in time and space in the absence of an effective guardian. That is, there are criminals and victims in society. At some times, and in certain locations, they come into contact. Unless someone is there to prevent it (the guardian), a crime will occur. Crime, then, depends on the interaction of offenders, targets, and guardians. This theory suggests a structural approach to crime. By increasing guardianship, for example, crime can be reduced. Criminologists also have focused attention on repeat victims—those people who are frequently the victims of crime (Pease & Laycock, 1996). A review of the research indicates that, in general, the available evidence supports the routine activities explanation of many crimes (Spano & Frelich, 2009).

CONTROLLING CRIME AND CRIMINALS

Francis A. Allen, professor of law and dean of the University of Michigan Law School, was one of the first observers of American criminal justice to identify the increasing burden placed on the justice system by expansions of the criminal sanction. Allen studied the tremendous growth of criminal laws and increasing use of the justice system to deal with social problems ranging from substance abuse to health care. He considered the most important task to be the definition of what reasonably could be expected from the criminal justice system. In 1964, he wrote

> The time has long been ripe for some sober questions to be asked. More and more it seems that the central issue may be this: What may we properly demand of a system of criminal justice? What functions may it properly serve? There is a related question: What are the obstacles and problems that must be confronted and overcome if a system of criminal justice is to be permitted to serve its own proper ends? These are broad and difficult questions, and the way in which they are answered will affect much that is important to the community at large.
>
> **(Allen, 1964:4)**

At base, Allen was attempting to set priorities for the use of the criminal law. His position was that the criminal law was increasingly being applied to social welfare problems (such as public intoxication) and regulatory needs. He decried the growing reliance on criminal law to solve social problems. He urged that we decide on those behaviors that would best be the objects of criminal law, and that we limit the activities of the justice system to the control of these particular behaviors.

Other observers of American criminal justice shared this sentiment (American Friends Service Committee, 1971; National Advisory Commission, 1973). During the 1970s, a growing number of scholars and practitioners came to agree that the most sensible approach to crime control required the identification of "serious" crimes and the focusing of enforcement resources on those crimes. As the National Advisory Commission on Criminal Justice Standards and Goals (1973:84) explained, "The empire of crime is too large and diverse to be attacked on all fronts simultaneously."

Observers and agents of the justice system have long recognized the fundamental truth of this comment. Traditionally, police officers, prosecutors, judges, correctional personnel, and parole boards have adopted ad hoc strategies to maximize the effectiveness of criminal justice processing in controlling crime. In this vein, Davis (1975:1) noted

> The police make policy about what law to enforce, how much to enforce it, against whom, and on what occasions. Some law is always or almost always enforced, some is never or almost never enforced, and some is sometimes enforced and sometimes not.

With a large number of criminal laws applied to a broad variety of behavior, agents of the justice system often must choose which laws to enforce and when to enforce them. Moreover, with the wide variety of offenders, it is similarly common to enforce laws differently against different types of individuals. We are not likely to ignore the dangerous, repeat offender, regardless of the violation. In a sense, this approach to the "rationing" of justice resources seeks to maximize effectiveness. Officials use the criminal law to control the most serious offenses and offenders.

Criminal justice officials historically have devoted most of their resources to the control of more dangerous crimes and criminals. For example, police investigate suspected felonies more thoroughly than misdemeanors, and prosecutors are less willing to negotiate for guilty pleas from repeat felons. For the most part, this focus of attention on serious crimes (such as felonies and violent acts) had not been a conscious policy decision.

In the recent past, this unconscious rationing of resources (by justice officials choosing cases on which to concentrate) was exposed and adopted as formal policy in many jurisdictions. Almost 30 years ago, Walker (1985:117) observed, "Career-criminal programs are the hottest fad in criminal justice these days." A brief review of the programs that flowed from these policies serves to illustrate the point and identify priorities in the justice system. Policies and programs directed at the control of serious offenses and offenders exist in law enforcement, courts, and corrections.

Law Enforcement Programs

Several types of police activities seek to control serious crime and criminals. In one, the police focus attention on identified serious offenders and carefully watch them for evidence of criminal conduct. In another, the police identify high-risk areas where serious crimes appear likely to occur, and devote increased patrol to those areas (see Figure 3.1). In yet another, the police identify likely victims and intervene to reduce the chances of crime by changing victim behavior or characteristics. In each case, officials decide that the best investment of police resources involves targeting specific individuals or locations. Often police departments have responded to "crime waves" by increasing police presence in a given area (Sherman, 1990).

Several police departments started programs that identified specific individuals as repeat offenders. In California, scores of police agencies developed repeat offender programs. Kansas City, Missouri, experimented with "perpetrator-oriented patrol." Minneapolis, Minnesota, instituted a "Target 8" program in which the police identified eight suspects as career criminals and all officers were expected to be alert for these suspects (Walker, 1985). The police in Washington, DC, perhaps attracted the most attention with a program called the "Repeat Offender Project" (ROP, pronounced "rope"), described in Box 3.2. This program assigned a special unit of more than 60 officers to focus attention on

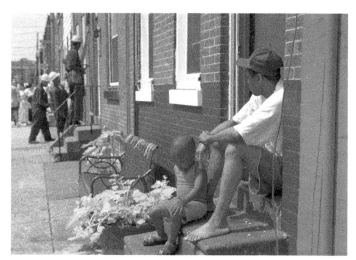

FIGURE 3.1
Citizens watch License and Inspection agents board up and condemn their neighbor's home in a troubled area of North Philadelphia's Kensington section. "Operation Sunrise," a landmark offensive aimed at the most crime-ridden square mile of the city, brought a brigade of police officers, street crews, and inspection workers to the area to make arrests and board up drug houses.
(AP Photo/Dan Loh)

BOX 3.2 CAREER CRIMINALS AND THE POLICE

The Washington, DC, repeat offender program (ROP) grabbed attention of many metropolitan police departments across the country after a 2-year evaluation of the program was completed by the Police Foundation, under a grant from the U.S. Justice Department's National Institute of Justice.

The study found that the ROP program achieved its goals in every area. For example, the program increased the likelihood of arrests of the target offenders and increased officer productivity (the officers actually made fewer arrests, but the arrests were for offenders with longer criminal histories). In addition, the program increased the likelihood that the offender would be prosecuted and increased the chances of a conviction.

The authors of the evaluation did urge some caution. The ROP program was costly to implement, and the trade-off for the focus in crime-fighting activities appeared to be reduced order maintenance activities by the police. Finally, the authors noted that without careful supervision, this program could lead to increased opportunities to violate a citizen's rights

Source: Martin and Sherman (1986)

persons thought to be committing at least five major offenses each week. A team of officers was given 48 hours to make an arrest. If, after that time, there was no arrest, the team was reassigned to another suspected repeat offender (Walker, 1985). "Operation Cease Fire" in Boston sought to reduce youth violence by targeting gang leaders for special enforcement (Kennedy, 1998). A search of the Internet for mentions of "repeat offender," "career criminal," or "habitual offender" will turn up scores of law enforcement agency websites describing police units and programs aimed at dangerous offenders.

In each of these programs, police administrators decided to devote resources to the control of specific crimes and criminals—or to the control of crime in areas where there was reason to believe that serious crime was most likely to occur. At the same time, regular police patrol and response to calls for service in the jurisdiction continued. In the departments mentioned, and in others with similar programs, police administrators have at least tacitly decided that some crimes or criminals are more deserving of police attention.

Court Programs

The repeat or career criminal is the subject of special treatment in at least two points of the court process: prosecution and sentencing. The goal of these special procedures is to ensure the conviction and punishment of offenders posing the greatest threat of future criminality.

Today, many trial jurisdictions have career criminal programs. In these programs, the prosecutor's office develops criteria to select cases involving repeat or career criminals. These cases become a priority in the system. Officials try to secure convictions in these cases even when, under normal circumstances, they may have dropped the case. Brosi (1979) explained the justification for these programs:

> Given the disproportionately large share of crime committed by repeat offenders, prosecutors seem justified in structuring their discretion so that an appropriate percentage of time and staff is focused on recidivists, even though this might mean that other cases with as much or more evidence and involving less frequent offenders would have to be rejected or pursued with less than normal intensity.

The organization of career criminal prosecution programs differs by jurisdiction. The theory behind the use of these programs is the same as that underlying the law enforcement programs described earlier. If identifiable individuals exist who will be continuing targets of prosecution, it is a wise investment of resources to devote attention to them in the present (INSLAW, 1977:8). That is, it makes sense to devote crime control resources to those cases that promise the greatest payoff in crime control. Several jurisdictions in Florida developed repeat offender courts in which the focus on repeat offenders means the court has a smaller caseload and is better able to ensure tough punishment.

Brosi (1979) described career criminal prosecution programs operating in the United States 35 years ago. In large, busy jurisdictions it was common for prosecutors to be assigned to specific decision points such as initial appearance, preliminary hearing, and arraignment. For career criminal prosecution programs, all but the District of Columbia used a procedure called **vertical prosecution** in which a single prosecutor was assigned to each career criminal case. That prosecutor stayed with the case from arrest through final disposition. The District of Columbia program used one prosecutor to stay with the case from arrest through indictment, and then the case became the responsibility of another prosecutor in the trial division. The idea was that the prosecutor would be more familiar with the case and the offender and less likely to accept a plea of guilty to a lesser charge or otherwise treat the offender leniently.

Each program established criteria for selecting cases for treatment in the career criminal program. In the District of Columbia, the program, which was known as "Operation Doorstop," took cases involving those arrested for a crime of violence or a felony while on probation or parole. Those arrested for a crime of violence who were possibly subject to pretrial detention also received special attention. The Prosecutor's Repeat Offender Bureau (PROB) in Detroit selected cases involving arrests for burglary or violent felonies by those having three prior felony convictions, and arrests of those having a combination of three prior convictions or pending charges. Other jurisdictions developed different methods of choosing cases. Worrall (2008) called these types of programs "strategic prosecution." He reviewed several programs across the country where prosecutors focus on specific crimes and offenders, such as gun crimes.

Career criminal prosecution programs in other jurisdictions have used a "point" system for selecting cases. Table 3.2 gives an example of one such scoring system. The Indianapolis program assigned points for previous violent and burglary convictions, any felony convictions or arrests, and pending cases. Milwaukee County employed a similar point system, assigning points for prior convictions, current status on bail, probation or parole, and current charges involving injury or weapons. Other jurisdictions target specific crimes, such as burglary or robbery.

In general, these career criminal prosecution programs have the effect of flagging specified cases for special treatment (Chaiken & Chaiken, 1991). This results in slightly higher rates of conviction and greatly increased rates of incarceration for those identified as career criminals. In most programs, career criminal cases are also disposed of more quickly than cases in the regular caseload. Again, prosecutors decide which cases deserve increased attention and investment of limited prosecutorial resources (Chaiken & Chaiken, 1991).

Increasingly prosecutors' offices have established specialized units devoted to particular crimes as well. It is not uncommon for a prosecutor's office to have a domestic violence unit or a drug unit. Here again, criminal justice agents have decided to focus effort and resources on particular types of crime or criminals. At the national level, the U.S. Department of Justice has implemented Project Safe Neighborhoods, which focuses criminal justice attention on firearms offenders. The U.S. Attorney (federal prosecutor) administers the program in each of the

Table 3.2	Scoring Criteria for Selection of Career Criminals for Special Attention by Federal Prosecutor	
Variable	**Points**	
Heavy use of alcohol	+5	
Heroin use	+10	
Age at time of instant arrest		
Less than 22	+21	
23–27	+14	
28–32	+7	
33–37	0	
38–42	−7	
43+	−14	
Length of criminal career		
0–5 years	0	
6–10	1	
11–15	2	
16–20	3	
21+	4	
Arrests during last 5 years		
Crimes of violence	4	Per arrest
Crimes against property	3	Per arrest
Sale of drugs	4	Per arrest
Other offenses	2	Per arrest
Longest time served, single term		
1–5 months	4	
6–12	9	
13–24	18	
25–36	27	
37–48	36	
49+	45	
Number of probation sentences	1.5	Per sentence
Instant offense was crime of violence[a]	7	
Instant offense was crime labeled "other"[b]	−18	
Critical value to label offender		
Career criminal	47	

[a]Violent crimes not only consist mostly of bank robberies but also include homicide, assault, sexual assault, and kidnapping.
[b]Other crimes include military violations, probation, parole, weapons, and all others except arson, burglary, larceny, auto theft, fraud, forgery, drug sale or possession, and violent crimes.

94 U.S. district courts. The project involves the creation of local task forces comprised of the U.S. Attorney and representatives from federal, state, and local law enforcement; prosecutors; other justice agencies; and other local leaders. The task forces identify gun crime problems and develop strategies to reduce gun crime, often involving federal prosecution for illegal gun possession and violent,

gang, and drug-related offenses involving a firearm (Bureau of Justice Assistance, 2004). Recent evidence suggests that these measures do in fact result in a modest decline in violent crime (McGarrell, Corsaro, Hipple, & Bynum, 2010).

Differential handling of career criminals at sentencing has long been a tradition in America. Most states have had habitual offender or recidivist sentencing statutes for decades. These statutes essentially make it criminal and thereby separately punishable for someone to have prior felony convictions. In many states, upon conviction of a third felony offense, one can be tried as a "habitual offender" and receive an extended prison term, even life imprisonment (Sigler & Culliver, 1990).

Other sentencing programs have been receiving increasing attention and support: selective incapacitation, mandatory sentencing, and "three strikes" laws. In each, the goal is to control the incidence of either specific crimes, or to lessen (through incarcerating offenders) the opportunity of specific criminals to commit crime in the future.

Selective incapacitation seeks to identify those offenders who are most likely to commit future crimes. This program reserves incarceration for these habitual offenders (Greenwood, 1982). Research showing the majority of crimes committed by a minority of offenders supports the idea that imprisoning those few would result in less crime. Selective incapacitation argues that because prison space is a scarce resource, reserving space for the most prolific offenders is a wise investment.

Mandatory sentencing is another strategy for controlling crime. In practice, mandatory sentencing really means mandatory incarceration. This approach relies on deterrence and does not target specific criminals, focusing instead on specific crimes. The examples discussed in Chapter 2 dealing with drunk driving and the New York State drug law illustrate the strategy of mandatory sentencing. By "ensuring" that those convicted of specific crimes we believe to be dangerous will be imprisoned, the hope is that the program will deter those who might consider committing the offense.

Finally, following in this tradition, the federal government and most states began passing three strikes laws starting in the mid-1980s. At the federal level, these laws began with the passage of the Armed Career Criminal Act in 1984, which subjected those who were convicted of certain gun crimes to a sentence of between 15 years and life if he or she had three prior qualifying convictions. Then, with the passage of the Violent Crime Control and Law Enforcement Act of 1994, offenders convicted of specific felonies for the third time were expected to be imprisoned for life (Saint-Germain & Calamia, 1996). Many states have passed three strikes laws with similar goals, although implementation of these laws varies widely by state (Schiraldi, Colburn, & Lotke, 2004; Turner, Sundt, Applegate, & Cullen, 1995). These laws seek to identify serious, repeat criminal offenders, and ensure that they receive sentences that result in long terms of imprisonment. With the help of federal incentives, states have also moved to ensure the imprisonment of those convicted of violent crimes under what is known as Violent Offender Incarceration/Truth in Sentencing programs (Ditton & Wilson, 1999).

As with law enforcement and criminal prosecution programs, sentencing programs either target criminals (selective incapacitation) or crimes (mandatory sentencing). In both cases, a decision has been made that resources (e.g., prison) should be targeted to specific cases of criminality.

Corrections Programs

Efforts to identify and provide special services and controls for repeat offenders in correctional settings are traditional. Correctional officials have given increased attention to classification of offenders, and have developed special "intensive supervision" programs for probationers and parolees. These efforts try to focus correctional resources on those offenders most in need of such attention.

Van Voorhis (1986) indicated the importance of classification for the organization and delivery of correctional services. She suggested that we get the greatest return on the correctional investment through matching the available services and programs with the needs of individual offenders. The implication of classification decisions for the effectiveness of correctional treatments is only one incentive for the increasing emphasis on this process (see Figure 3.2; Bonta, 1996; Bonta & Motiuk, 1992).

In an age of prison crowding (see Figure 3.3), classification became important as a check on the efficient use of correctional resources. Clear and Cole (1986:320) noted

> The prison crowding crisis and litigation challenging existing procedures have forced many correctional systems to reexamine their classification procedures. As space becomes a scarcer and more valuable resource, administrators feel pressured to ensure that it is used as efficiently as possible: that levels of custody are appropriate and that inmates are not held in "oversecure" facilities.

The other side of this, of course, is that we should not hold certain dangerous prisoners in "undersecure" facilities. Among other things (such as amenability to certain types of treatment or aptitude for certain job assignments), classification also reflects risk of future criminality. A large part of the classification decision in prisons, or within probation or parole caseloads, reflects a desire to identify and control the repeat offender.

A related development in corrections involves the use of "intensive supervision" with probationers and parolees. In these programs, officials classify offenders under community supervision by risk and need. Those posing the greatest risk of future crime and those presenting the greatest needs for service are assigned to special "intensive supervision" caseloads. These caseloads are smaller than the average probation or parole caseload, and the supervising officer is expected to make more contacts with his or her clients each month. Thus, the title "intensive supervision" reflects a greater concentration of traditional probation and parole resources on

FIGURE 3.2
Inmates at the Deuel Vocational Institute in Tracy, California, are seen housed in three-tier bunks, in what was once a multipurpose recreation room. In an age of prison crowding, classification has become an important check on the efficient use of prison resources.
(AP Photo/Rich Pedroncelli)

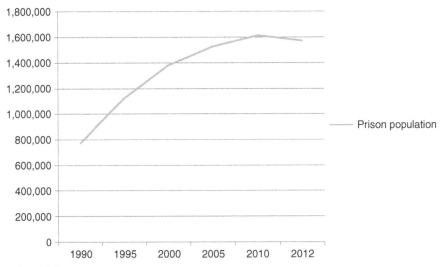

FIGURE 3.3
Prisoners under state or federal jurisdiction: 1990–2012.
Source: Beck and Harrison, 2001; Carson and Golineli, 2013

offenders who are selected because this greater investment is expected to produce higher returns in the control of future criminality (Latessa, 1985; Travis, 1984).

With many of the policies and programs being at least 20 years old, all of this discussion of career criminals and the justice system response to them may seem dated, until we realize that these programs and others like them continue today. They illustrate how criminal justice resources are devoted to those crimes and criminals defined as most serious, dangerous, or threatening. What has changed is the rate and number of persons sentenced to prison. During the past 20–30 years we have increasingly sentenced offenders to prison, leading to what some observers have called a policy of "mass incarceration" (Crutchfield, 2004). This suggests that the ability of the traditional criminal justice system to control or prevent crime is limited.

A NEW DIRECTION FOR CRIME CONTROL

Research into the causes of crime and the effectiveness of crime prevention practices during the past 30 years has produced some changes in how criminal justice system officials seek to control crime. Weisburd (1997) has suggested that crime control policy should shift from a focus on the causes of crime to a consideration of the context in which crime occurs. He wrote (1997:1), "This approach, which is often associated with **situational crime prevention**, looks to develop greater understanding of crime and more effective crime prevention strategies through concern with the physical, organizational, and social environments that make crime possible." That is, crime is more likely under some circumstances. Rather than viewing crime as a product of individual offenders and seeking crime prevention through control of those offenders, we should see crime as a product of a social context and seek to control crime by changing those contexts. Research into situational crime prevention has shown that crimes are more or less likely under different circumstances (Wilcox, Madensen, & Tillyer, 2007).

We have known for decades that crime is more likely to occur in some places than in others, and that some particular crimes are more likely to occur in certain places than in others. What Weisburd and others are suggesting is that we seek to understand the set of factors, or context, in which crimes are likely to occur and move to change the context to reduce the incidence of crime. Changes can take many forms. In some cases, changing the physical environment by better lighting, altering traffic patterns, installing locks and bars, removing bushes, and the like may reduce the chances of crime. In other cases, increased police patrol or organizing Neighborhood Watch groups can reduce the chances of crime. In still other instances, it may be that we need to identify and control specific high-rate offenders.

A new focus on the context of crime does not ignore offenders, but treats the criminal as only one of several factors that account for crime. The core logic of this argument is that offenders are only part of the crime problem, and focusing crime control efforts on offenders will then control only some of all crime. If the factors that account for crime vary, our crime control efforts should target various factors (Sherman et al., 1997; Worrall, 2008).

There is a noticeable movement today in the direction of addressing the context of crime. In the recent past, there has been increasing emphasis on the role of the community in crime control (Ward, 1997). Returning to our earlier discussion of social control, current strategies of crime control seek to strengthen informal social control by removing obstacles to informal control and strengthening mechanisms of control other than the criminal justice process. Changing traffic patterns by blocking streets, for example, reduces the number of strangers in a neighborhood, thereby making it easier for residents to recognize those who belong in the neighborhood and those who do not belong. Using civil laws to close bars, evict tenants who sell drugs, and similar efforts reduces the chances that crimes will occur. The use of curfews to remove juveniles from the streets in the late night hours also works to reduce the likelihood of crime and misbehavior. Rather than waiting for a fight or robbery to occur and then calling the police, these strategies work to prevent the fight or robbery in the first place.

In support of this more preventive approach to dealing with problems of crime, **problem-oriented policing** has developed as a widely accepted police strategy throughout the country. This method of policing uses the SARA model to problem-solve using a situational crime prevention approach (see Box 3.3). Problem-oriented policing focuses on individualized responses to specific local

BOX 3.3 SARA MODEL

A commonly used problem-solving method is the SARA model. The SARA model contains the following elements:

Scanning
- Identify recurring problems
- Prioritize the problems
- Develop goals

Analysis
- Identify and understand events and conditions that precede and accompany problem
- Research what is known about the problem type
- Narrow the scope of the problem
- Develop a working hypothesis about why the problem is occurring

Response
- Brainstorm for new interventions
- Search for what other communities with similar problems have done
- Outline a response plan
- Carry out the planned activities

Assessment
- Determine whether the plan was implemented properly
- Collect pre- and post-response data
- Determine whether the broad goals and specific objectives were attained

Adapted from http://www.popcenter.org

problems that may arise in a community. The Center for Problem-Oriented Policing (www.popcenter.org) has available more than 70 problem-specific guides and 10 response guides from which the police can find answers to their specific problems.

Scores of programs across the nation have been implemented and assessed. Box 3.4 highlights efforts to deal with the problem of youth violence in Boston (Office of Juvenile Justice and Delinquency Prevention, 1999). This effort involved a wide range of criminal justice and community agencies. It evolved over several years and gained national recognition as an exemplary project. Recognizing that homicide was an especially pressing problem among youths, the Boston Police Department organized a Youth Violence Strike Force. The police cooperated with the federal Bureau of Alcohol, Tobacco, Firearms, and Explosives, as well as the prosecutor's office (both local and federal) and the probation department, and implemented strategies for reducing homicides. The targets of these efforts were gun traffickers (including licensed gun dealers) and gang members. Enforcement strategies involved inspections of gun dealers and targeted investigations of gun traffickers. Police officers tried to obtain gun market information from offenders charged with serious nongun charges. Gang members were identified and warned that violence (especially gun violence) would no longer be tolerated. In cooperation with prosecutors and probation personnel, the police met with gang members and warned that any violence would receive swift, severe consequences. This illustrates a focused deterrence strategy often called "pulling levers," which has been shown to be more effective

BOX 3.4 A COORDINATED APPROACH TO YOUTH VIOLENCE IN BOSTON

Beginning in 1994, the Boston Police Department identified serious violence among youths as a major problem. During the next several years, a coordinated citywide strategy emerged that involved a combination of law enforcement and crime prevention programs. Criminal justice, local government, and private social service and commercial organizations combined their efforts to address the problem. Among others, the strategy involved:

Operation Cease Fire—A collaboration between the ATF (the U.S. Bureau of Alcohol, Tobacco, Firearms, and Explosives), the Boston Police Department, the U.S. Attorney, the local prosecutor, the state probation department, the State Department of Youth Services, clergy, schools, and social service agencies to identify gang members and to warn them that violence would be met with severe sanctions.

Boston Gun Project—A collaboration between the Boston Police, the ATF, the U.S. Attorney, and the local prosecutor to reduce the number of guns available to youths, and to disrupt the illegal gun market.

Operation Night Light—A collaboration between the Boston Police and the probation department to increase surveillance and supervision of youthful offenders on probation through increased unannounced visits to probationers in their homes, schools, and workplaces during nontraditional hours (7 P.M. to midnight).

than traditional unfocused policing strategies (Telep & Weisburd, 2012). In the end, these efforts seem to have reduced the incidence of homicide, and gang-related homicide in particular. The combined, coordinated efforts of police, courts, and corrections, at local, state, and federal levels, in conjunction with community service agencies, were brought to bear on the problem of juvenile homicides. One of the most remarkable things about the Boston project is not its results, but rather, the coordination of so many different agents and agencies to focus on one specific problem.

Recent research has confirmed the effectiveness of problem-oriented policing. For example, Weisburd, Telep, Hinkle, and Eck (2010) conducted an exhaustive review of the research involving problem-oriented policing. They found that among 45 studies that had compared crime data before and after a problem-oriented intervention, the average crime reduction was more than 40 percent. Studies that had used an experimental design showed a more modest but still significant reduction in crime. The most recent research available has confirmed the crime reduction effects for problem-oriented and focused deterrence techniques (Braga & Weisburd, 2012; Corsaro, Brunson, & McGarrell, 2013). Some researchers have even advocated for the elimination or reduction of standard policing tactics such as random preventive patrol to focus on solutions, including problem-oriented policing and focused deterrence programs (Telep & Weisburd, 2012).

A situational or contextual approach to crime prevention holds great promise of reducing the incidence of crime, but it is not without its limits. Recall our discussion of the central conflict between due process and crime control (see Box 3.5). A juvenile curfew may prevent much crime, but it is unlikely that the juveniles affected by the curfew appreciate the limits placed on their freedom. Blocking

BOX 3.5 DUE PROCESS VERSUS CRIME CONTROL: A DELICATE BALANCE

Individual Liberty versus Social Order
Costs versus Benefits
Rights versus Obligations

streets to reduce through traffic may prevent some offenders from entering a neighborhood, but it also inconveniences residents who live in the area (Lasley, 1998). The current effort to go beyond traditional criminal justice practices to achieve greater crime control poses the threat of expanding crime control at the cost to individual liberty or due process.

A final product of this broader view of crime control is the integration of criminal justice and community services. It is now common for interagency task forces to work toward the solution of crime problems. The Boston gun project is only one example. Across the country police, court, and correctional agencies are joining together in efforts to address crime and criminal justice problems (Sigmon, Nugent, Goerdt, & Wallace, 1999). Similar efforts include partnerships between criminal justice agencies and other governmental and community offices and groups not directly parts of the criminal justice system.

CRIME CONTROL IN GENERAL

This chapter began with a definition of crime and an explanation of the elements of criminal offenses. It then moved to a discussion of criminals and criminal types. We suggested throughout the discussion of these topics that the variety of behaviors and individuals included in the concepts of "crime" and "criminal," respectively, are exceedingly diverse. The justice system must respond to a large number of widely divergent instances and individuals.

To organize our perspective of this otherwise cumbersome task, we discussed the use of classes of crime or classes of offenders to allocate justice system resources. We provided descriptions of current efforts of police, court, and correctional agencies to focus attention and resources on the most serious crimes and criminals. It is important to establish priorities given the broad crime control mandate of the criminal justice system.

In practice, agents and agencies of criminal justice will respond to more serious crimes and offenders before responding to less serious incidents. For the most part, felonies and repeat offenders are more likely to attract the attention of the justice system and to receive full-scale justice processing than are misdemeanants and first offenders.

Our attention to the effect of the criminal justice process on rates and levels of crime in this chapter illustrates a core problem of criminal justice theory. Although our focus remains on the decisions in the system—how cases proceed from detection through the system—there is an equally important focus on the effect of the system on crime. Sometimes we find the explanation for why a case continues through the system is that officials expect a crime control payoff. The things that explain crime are not—and perhaps should not be—the same as those that explain criminal justice.

A redefinition of crime control that encompasses a broader range of social issues covering the context of crime promises to improve crime prevention but raises concerns about individual liberty. The task of the criminal justice system and criminal justice policymakers is to achieve a balance between crime control needs and due process requirements. Spader (1994) suggested that this balance involves weighing costs and benefits and competing values. The central questions that emerge in the conflict between due process and crime control in the American criminal justice system reflect these issues: Under what circumstances does the value of social control outweigh the value of individual liberty? How preventive should the agents and agencies of criminal justice be in their approach to crime control? How should we decide (and who should decide) which crimes and criminals deserve criminal justice attention? How much of our limited criminal justice resources should be devoted to "noncriminal" prevention activities versus detecting and apprehending criminals? We will return to these topics in later chapters.

REVIEW QUESTIONS

1. Define "crime."
2. What are the elements of a criminal offense?
3. Identify at least two ways we can classify crimes according to the level of their seriousness.
4. Define what is meant by the term "career criminal."
5. Give an example of career criminal programs in each segment of the criminal justice system (law enforcement, courts, and corrections).
6. What is the situational approach to crime control/prevention, and how does it differ from traditional approaches?
7. What key issues emerge when agents of the justice system choose crimes and criminals on which to focus attention?

References

Allen, F. A. (1964). *The borderland of criminal justice*. Chicago: University of Chicago Press.

American Friends Service Committee. (1971). *Struggle for justice*. New York: Hill & Wang.

Beck, A., & Harrison, P. (2001). *Prisoners in 2000*. Washington, DC: Bureau of Justice Statistics, U.S. Department of Justice.

Bonta, J. (1996). Risk-needs assessment and treatment. In A. Harland (Ed.), *Choosing correctional options that work* (pp. 18–32). Thousand Oaks, CA: Sage.

Bonta, J., & Motiuk, L. (1992). Inmate classification. *Journal of Criminal Justice, 20*(4), 343–352.

Braga, A., & Weisburd, D. (2012). The effects of focused deterrence strategies on crime: A systematic review and meta-analysis of the empirical evidence. *Journal of Research in Crime and Delinquency, 49*, 323–358.

Brosi, K. B. (1979). *A cross-city comparison of felony case processing*. Washington, DC: Institute for Law and Social Research.

Bureau of Justice Assistance (2004). *Program brief: Project safe neighborhoods: America's network against gun violence*. Washington, DC: Bureau of Justice Assistance.

Bureau of Justice Statistics (1985). *Special report: Crime control and criminal records*. Washington, DC: U.S. Department of Justice.

Carson, E., & Golinelli, D. (2013). *Prisoners in 2012—Advance counts*. Washington, DC: Bureau of Justice Statistics, U.S. Department of Justice.

Chaiken, J. M., & Chaiken, M. R. (1982). *Varieties of criminal behavior*. Santa Monica, CA: RAND.

Chaiken, M. R., & Chaiken, J. M. (1991). *Priority prosecution of high rate dangerous offenders*. Washington, DC: National Institute of Justice.

Clear, T. R., & Cole, G. F. (1986). *American corrections*. Monterey, CA: Brooks/Cole.

Clear, T. R., & Gallagher, K. (1985). Probation and parole supervision: A review of current classification practices. *Crime & Delinquency, 31*(3), 423–443.

Clinard, M. B., Quinney, R., & Wildeman, J. (1994). *Criminal behavior systems: A typology* (3rd ed.). Cincinnati, OH: Anderson.

Cohen, L., & Felson, M. (1979). Social change and crime rate trends: A routine activities approach. *American Sociology Review, 44*, 588–608.

Corsaro, N., Brunson, R., & McGarrell, E. (2013). Problem-oriented policing and open-air drug markets: Examining the Rockford pulling levers deterrence strategy. *Crime & Delinquency, 59*, 1085–1107.

Crutchfield, R. (2004). Commentary: Mass incarceration, editorial introduction. *Criminology and Public Policy, 3*(2), 265–266.

Cullen, F. T., Link, B. G., & Polanzi, C. W. (1982). The seriousness of crime revisited. *Criminology, 20*(1), 83–102.

Davis, K. C. (1975). *Police discretion*. St. Paul, MN: West.

Deane, G., Armstrong, D., & Felson, R. (2005). An examination of offense specialization using marginal logit models. *Criminology, 43*(4), 955–988.

DeLisi, M. (2005). *Career criminals in society*. Thousand Oaks, CA: Sage.

Ditton, P., & Wilson, J. (1999). *Truth in sentencing in state prisons*. Washington, DC: Bureau of Justice Statistics.

Farrington, D. (2003). Developmental and life-course criminology: Key theoretical and empirical issues—The 2002 Sutherland Award Address. *Criminology, 41*(2), 221–256.

Fox, V. (1983). *Correctional institutions*. Englewood Cliffs, NJ: Prentice Hall.

Gibbons, D. C. (1973). *Society, crime, and criminal careers* (2nd ed.). New York: Prentice Hall.

Gottfredson, M., & Gottfredson, D. (1988). *Decision making in criminal justice: Toward the rational exercise of discretion* (2nd ed.). New York: Plenum.

Greenwood, P. W. (1982). *Selective incapacitation*. Santa Monica, CA: RAND.

Harris, D., Smallbone, S., Dennison, S., & Knight, R. (2009). Specialization and versatility in sexual offenders referred for civil commitment. *Journal of Criminal Justice, 37*(1), 37–44.

Holmes, R. (1989). *Profiling violent crimes: An investigative tool*. Beverly Hills, CA: Sage.

INSLAW (1977). *Curbing the repeat offender: A strategy for prosecutors*. Washington, DC: U.S. Department of Justice.

Jogerst, G., Daly, J., Brinig, M., & Bibas, S. (2005). The association between statutory penalties and domestic elder abuse investigations. *Journal of Crime & Justice, 28*(2), 51–69.

Kennedy, D. (1998). Pulling levers: Getting deterrence right. *NIJ Journal, 236*, 2–13.

Lasley, J. (1998). *"Designing Out" gang homicides and street assaults*. Washington, DC: National Institute of Justice.

Latessa, E. J. (1985). Community supervision: Research, trends, and innovations. In L. F. Travis, M. D. Schwartz, & T. R. Clear (Eds.), *Corrections: An issues approach*. (pp. 159–167) (2nd ed.). Cincinnati, OH: Anderson.

Laub, J., & Sampson, R. (1993). Turning points in the lifecourse: Why change matters in the study of crime. *Criminology, 31*(3), 301–326.

Lilly, J. R., & Ball, R. A. (1982). A critical analysis of the changing concept of criminal responsibility. *Criminology, 20*(2), 169–184.

Lo, C., Kim, Y., & Cheng, T. (2008). Offense specialization of arrestees: An event history analysis. *Crime & Delinquency, 54,* 341–365.

Luna, E. (2003). Overextending the criminal law. *CATO Police Report, 25*(6), 15–16.

Martin, S. & Sherman, L. (1986). *Catching career criminals: The Washington, DC repeat offender program.* Police Foundation Report. U.S. Department of Justice.

McGarrell, E., Corsaro, N., Hipple, N., & Bynum, T. (2010). Project safe neighborhoods and violent crime trends in US cities: Assessing violent crime impact. *Journal of Quantitative Criminology, 26,* 165–190.

Miethe, T. D. (1982). Public consensus on crime seriousness. *Criminology, 20*(3–4), 515–526.

Moffitt, T. (1997). Adolescence-limited and life-course persistent offending: A complementary pair of developmental theories. In T. Thornberry (Ed.), *Developmental theories of crime and delinquency.* New Brunswick, NJ: Transaction.

Nagin, D. (2007). Moving choice to center state in criminological research and theory. *Criminology, 45*(2), 259–272.

National Advisory Commission on Criminal Justice Standards and Goals (1973). *A national strategy to reduce crime.* Washington, DC: U.S. Government Printing Office.

National Institute of Justice (1986). *Research program plan: Fiscal year 1987.* Washington, DC: U.S. Department of Justice.

Nettler, G. (1982). *Explaining criminals.* Cincinnati, OH: Anderson.

Newman, D. J. (1987). *Introduction to criminal justice* (3rd ed.). New York: Random House.

Newman, G. R., & Trilling, C. (1975). Public perceptions of criminal behavior. *Criminal Justice & Behavior, 2*(2), 217.

Office of Juvenile Justice (1999). *Promising strategies to reduce gun violence.* Washington, DC: Office of Juvenile Justice and Delinquency Prevention.

Osgood, D., & Schreck, C. (2007). A new method for studying the extent, stability, and predictors of individual specialization in violence. *Criminology, 45*(2), 273–312.

Pease, K., & Laycock, G. (1996). *Revictimization: Reducing the heat on hot victims.* Washington, DC: National Institute of Justice.

Saint-Germain, M., & Calamia, R. (1996). Three strikes and you're in: A streams and windows model of incremental policy change. *Journal of Criminal Justice, 24*(1), 57–70.

Schiraldi, V., Colburn, J., & Lotke, E. (2004). *Three strikes and you're out: An examination of the impact of 3-strikes laws 10 years after their enactment.* Washington, DC: Justice Policy Institute.

Schwendinger, H., & Schwendinger, J. (1975). Defenders of order or guardians of human rights? In I. Taylor, P. Walton, & J. Young (Eds.), *Critical criminology* (pp. 113–146). London: Routledge & Kegan Paul.

Sherman, L. (1990). *Police crackdowns.* Washington, DC: National Institute of Justice.

Sherman, L., Gottfredson, D., MacKenzie, D., Eck, J., Reuter, P., & Bushway, S. (1997). *Preventing crime: What works, what doesn't, what's promising?* Washington, DC: National Institute of Justice.

Sigler, R., & Culliver, C. (1990). Effectiveness of the Habitual Offender Act: An assessment of criminal histories. *American Journal of Criminal Justice, 15*(1), 105–121.

Sigmon, J., Nugent, M., Goerdt, J., & Wallace, S. (1999). *Key elements of successful adjudication partnerships.* Washington, DC: National Institute of Justice.

Spader, D. (1994). Teaching due process: A workable method of teaching the ethical and legal aspects. *Journal of Criminal Justice Education, 5*(1), 81–106.

Spano, R., & Frelich, J. (2009). An assessment of the empirical validity and conceptualization of individual level multivariate studies of lifestyle/routine activities theory published from 1995 to 2005. *Journal of Criminal Justice, 37*(3), 305–314.

Telep, C., & Weisburd, D. (2012). What is known about the effectiveness of police practices in reducing crime and disorder? *Police Quarterly, 15,* 331–357.

Thornberry, T. (1997). *Developmental theories of crime and delinquency*. New Brunswick, NJ: Transaction.

Tittle, C. (2000). Theoretical developments in criminology. In G. LaFree (Ed.), *The nature of crime: Continuity and change, criminology 2000: Vol. 1.* (pp. 51–101). Washington, DC: National Institute of Justice.

Travis, L. F. (1984). Intensive supervision in probation and parole. *Corrections Today, 46*(4), 36–38.

Turner, M., Sundt, J., Applegate, B., & Cullen, F. (1995). "Three strikes and you're out" legislation: A national assessment. *Federal Probation, 59*(3), 16–35.

Unnever, J., Cochran, J., Cullen, F., & Applegate, B. (2010). The pragmatic American: Attributions of crime and the hydraulic relation hypothesis. *Justice Quarterly, 27*(3), 431–457.

Van Voorhis, P. (1986). *The promise of confronting important gaps between knowledge and applications*. Paper presented at the First International Conference on Reaffirming Rehabilitation, Alexandria, VA, June, 1986.

Vito, G., & Holmes, R. (1994). *Criminology: Theory, research and policy*. Belmont, CA: Wadsworth.

Vogel, B. (1998). Perceptions of crime seriousness in the African American community: Exploring the presence of consensus. *Journal of Criminal Justice, 26*(3), 227–236.

Walker, S. (1985). *Sense and nonsense about crime: A policy guide*. Monterey, CA: Brooks/Cole.

Ward, C. (1997). Community crime prevention: Addressing background and foreground causes of criminal behavior. *Journal of Criminal Justice, 25*(1), 1–18.

Warren, M. Q. (1973). All things being equal. *Criminal Law Bulletin, 9*, 482.

Weisburd, D. (1997). *Reorienting crime prevention research and policy: From the causes of criminality to the context of crime*. Washington, DC: U.S. Department of Justice.

Weisburd, D., Telep, C., Hinkle, J., & Eck, J. (2010). Is problem-oriented policing effective in reducing crime and disorder? Findings from a Campbell systematic review. *Criminology & Public Policy, 9*(1), 139–172.

Wilcox, P., Madensen, T., & Tillyer, M. (2007). Guardianship in context: Implications for burglary risk and prevention. *Criminology, 45*(4), 771–804.

Willis, C., Evans, T., & LaGrange, R. (1999). "Down home" criminology: The place of indigenous theories of crime. *Journal of Criminal Justice, 27*(3), 239–247.

Wilson, M., & Ruback, R. (2003). Hate crimes in Pennsylvania, 1984–99: Case characteristics and police responses. *Justice Quarterly, 20*(2), 373–398.

Worrall, J. (2008). *Crime control in America: What works?* (2nd ed.). Boston: Pearson.

CHAPTER 4

Counting Crimes and Criminals

If we can consider the criminal justice system a business, it is a business run by people having no clear understanding of the market, the production and distribution process, or customer satisfaction. Not many commercial enterprises could succeed in such a state of ignorance. Yet, the criminal justice system does operate in ignorance.

Lack of knowledge about the types of crimes and criminals is not the only form of ignorance that hinders the criminal justice system in the United States. Not only do we not know very much about the nature of crimes and offenders, we also have difficulty determining their numbers. For decades, critics have written about the **"dark figure" of crime**; that is, the unknown amount of crime that occurs.

The dark figure represents the portion of crime about which we are ignorant. Like a half moon where part of the moon is in shadow and we can see only one-half of the lunar surface, current official crime statistics may reveal only one-half (more or less) of the actual amount of crime; the remainder is hidden in the "shadows." The dark figure is this crime in the shadows.

THE NEED FOR NUMBERS

At first we may ask, so what? How important can it be that we do not know how much crime there really is? Even when we cannot see the full moon, we know that it is there. Paradoxically, the problem is that without knowing what is in the shadows, we cannot know the importance of the crimes of which we are ignorant. Old sayings such as "Ignorance is bliss" and "What you don't know can't hurt you" do not always apply. This problem becomes clearer when we examine the uses to which we put criminal statistics.

Nettler (1984) listed four reasons for counting crime:

1. Description
2. Risk assessment
3. Program evaluation
4. Explanation

Important Terms

cohort studies
Crime Index
crime rate
"dark figure" of crime
defounding
forgetting
funnel effect
hierarchy rule
"hot spots" of crime
National Crime Victimization Survey (NCVS)
observations
official statistics
self-report studies
telescoping
unfounding
Uniform Crime Reports (UCR)
unofficial statistics
victimization data

Description is exactly what the term implies: painting an accurate picture of the number and distribution of criminal offenses. Such information is useful for the allocation of resources (Rich, 1995). We use knowledge of crime to determine where to concentrate police patrols and to estimate the number of prosecutors or judges needed. Descriptive measures of crime allow planners to detect changes in crime patterns over time and to adjust criminal justice operations accordingly.

Risk assessment was discussed earlier when we examined the differences between ordinary and dangerous criminals. Accurate data about crime allow us to make estimates about the risks of people becoming offenders and of people becoming victims of crime. Not knowing how much crime actually occurs makes it impossible to predict how much crime is likely to occur. To the degree that the justice process attempts to reduce criminality, lack of knowledge about the actual level of crime hinders our ability to affect future levels. Knowing what kinds of crimes occur, and where and when they occur, enables criminal justice agents to allocate resources more efficiently (Rich, 1996). This kind of knowledge also helps individuals to avoid becoming crime victims. Often the characteristics of victims link to the crimes they experience. If victims can change their behaviors, or be more careful given those characteristics, it is possible that crime can be avoided (Fisher, Daigle, & Cullen, 2010; Vandecar-Burdin & Payne, 2010).

Sherman, Gartin, and Buerger (1989) coined the term **"hot spots" of crime** to refer to locations where much more crime happens than at other places. The notion of a crime hot spot is useful when making decisions about where to assign police patrols. Several researchers have reported that focusing police efforts in places that have lots of crime is the most effective use of patrol in terms of crime prevention and control (Weisburd, Telep, Hinkle, & Eck, 2010). Similarly, if we know a certain location has more crime, we can try to avoid that place and reduce our chances of becoming a crime victim. Naturally, the effectiveness of these "strategies" depends on the accuracy of our identification of the hot spots.

Program evaluation is an effort that often relies on estimates of a program's effect on crime. In the previous chapter, we discussed several programs aimed at controlling career criminals. Evaluations of these programs attempted to compare the program's effects on the criminality of offenders with the effects of "normal" criminal justice processing. Should we continue or expand these programs? We do not know. Assuming a dark figure of crime, there is no way to tell what effect these programs have had on that figure. Each year researchers report scores of evaluations of criminal justice policies and programs. These evaluations usually include a test of impact on crime. It is difficult to determine the value of criminal justice programs and policies when our knowledge about crime is limited. We typically measure crime by counting arrests, but we know that the police do not know about all crimes and do not always arrest offenders. If the data about arrests is incomplete or wrong, we must have less confidence in the conclusions of our research (Krebs, Lattimore, Cowell, & Graham, 2010; Lilley & Boba, 2009; Worrall et al., 2009).

Explanation is the most troublesome of all the reasons why we need accurate numbers about crime and criminals. Why do some people break the law? Being unaware of many criminal offenses, we can offer only partial explanations. Many people believe that poverty causes crime, and most persons whom we know to have committed crimes are poor. However, a problem arises in that we do not know whether those who commit the dark figure of crime offenses are poor or wealthy. If these unknown offenders are not poor, then poverty explains only the criminality of those whom we can identify.

THE IMPACT OF IGNORANCE

One result of our ignorance about the nature and extent of crime is an inability to assess or predict the effects of policy changes on levels of crime. Changing our emphasis on enforcing laws against certain crimes also may have unintended and unpredictable effects. The war on drugs indicates the problem that the dark figure of crime poses for evaluations of criminal justice policy (see Box 4.1).

During the 1980s, beginning with the Reagan administration, the United States declared (or more accurately, redeclared) a war on drugs, and a national anti-drug campaign developed (Albanese & Pursley, 1993:265–270). Law enforcement agencies, prosecutors, and criminal courts increased their efforts to catch, convict, and punish drug law violators. Since that time, the number of drug cases and drug offenders has grown as a proportion of the criminal justice system's "business" far more rapidly than other types of offenses and offenders. Arrests, convictions, and prison sentences for drug offenders have increased dramatically, yet we do not appear any closer to winning the "war" than we were almost two decades ago.

One reason we may not be able to see any progress in terms of reducing the number of drug offenses and offenders is that for years many of these crimes have been a part of the dark figure. With increased emphasis on drug crimes,

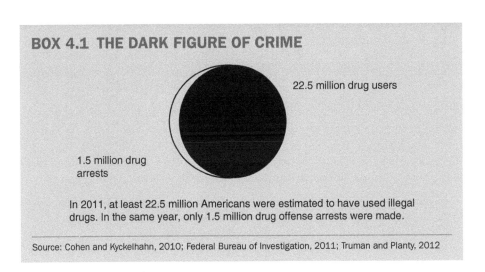

BOX 4.1 THE DARK FIGURE OF CRIME

22.5 million drug users

1.5 million drug arrests

In 2011, at least 22.5 million Americans were estimated to have used illegal drugs. In the same year, only 1.5 million drug offense arrests were made.

Source: Cohen and Kyckelhahn, 2010; Federal Bureau of Investigation, 2011; Truman and Planty, 2012 agents and agencies of the justice system have uncovered offenses that have been present for years. Because drug offenses have gone unreported in the past, Zeisel (1982) noted that they present an almost limitless supply of business for the police. Changing public perceptions of the seriousness of drug offenses has supported increased drug enforcement efforts. If police ignored large numbers of casual or "small-time" drug users in the past, vast increases in arrests, convictions, and imprisonment may signal small increases in the proportion of drug offenders caught and processed.

Kraska (1992:524) observed that with drug offenders, police "can seek actively to detect drug crimes, as opposed to violent and property crimes, for which they have little choice but to react to complaints." Thus, the volume of drug offenders entering the justice system is more a product of police activity than is that of violent or property offenders. Political pressure to treat drug offenses more seriously (Linnemann, 2013), coupled with giving incentives such as profit from seizing the property of drug offenders (Baumer, 2008; Holden, 1993; Worrall & Kovandzic, 2008), spurs more aggressive police action. When applied to offenses that are largely underenforced, these activities can produce dramatic increases in criminal justice caseloads without affecting basic levels of offense behavior.

Assuming available data are accurate, arrests for drug law violations in 2011 affected less than 7% of the population reporting use of illegal drugs that year. Doubling the number of arrests for drug violations would still leave more than 85% of users untouched. In terms of assessing the impact of doubling enforcement efforts, an evaluator would conclude that doubling efforts (and costs) would not have a significant impact on actual drug use. Indeed, between 2002 and 2008, the number of arrests for drug offenses increased by more than 15% whereas the estimated number of persons using illegal drugs increased by about 8% (Substance Abuse and Mental Health Services Administration, 2010). By 2011, the number of arrests for drug offenses had decreased by more than 30% from their 2008 levels, but changes in arrests do not make much change in the number of persons using drugs. In 2011, 8.7% of those aged 12 or older reported using drugs, compared to 8.1% in 2008 (Substance Abuse and Mental Health Services Administration, 2012). For comparison, consider the case of gambling. If we were to declare a war on gambling, how could we know what effect criminal justice efforts were having on the scope of the problem? What commitment of resources would it take to stamp out gambling?

We have long recognized the inadequacies of our data about crimes and criminals. Yet, with repeated calls for improvement in the collection and use of statistics on crime, how is it that we have made so little progress? The answer lies within the complex nature of criminal justice in the United States.

Thousands of agencies in thousands of separate jurisdictions collect information. These agencies often use their own definitions of crimes and criminals, and report their data to national centers on a voluntary basis. Each agency needs different types of information for its own planning and operation. It is very difficult to follow cases through the justice process, because the police, prosecutor, criminal court, and correctional agencies use their own forms to collect the information that is useful to them, with little regard to a systemwide need for information.

Much data are available concerning the number of crimes and criminals, justice agencies, and operations of the justice system. However, we do not know exactly how much crime exists and where it occurs. The crime problem is one without clearly marked boundaries. The sources of information about crime and criminal justice are of two basic types: official statistics and unofficial statistics.

OFFICIAL STATISTICS

Official statistics are statistics provided by criminal justice agencies as official records of their activities. The most familiar of all official crime statistics is the **Uniform Crime Reports (UCRs)**, published annually by the Federal Bureau of Investigation (FBI) from reports received by the nation's police departments. These data describe the volume of business handled by the law enforcement agencies of the country. The basic statistic of the UCR is "crimes known to the police."

Only those offenses detected by the police are crimes known to the police. If someone steals your wallet and you do not report the theft to the police, the crime is unknown to the police and not counted in the UCR. If you report the theft, or a police officer witnesses the crime, then the offense will be "known to the police." In addition, the police officer decides whether a crime has occurred and, if so, what crime it was.

In the aforementioned example, suppose you report the theft to a police officer, but the officer decides that you are not telling the truth. The process of **unfounding** occurs if the officer decides that your criminal complaint is "unfounded"; that is, the officer believes that the crime you reported is not supported by available evidence and, therefore, has reason to believe that no crime occurred. In this instance, the theft will remain "unknown" to the police because the officer considers your report untrustworthy.

A similar decision is **defounding** a crime, which occurs when a police officer decides that an offense was less serious than reported. If the criminal stole your wallet by threatening to harm you with a knife, an armed robbery occurred. If the police officer does not believe that you were actually threatened, he or she may simply record a theft of your wallet. In this instance, the police know about the crime, but the crime is reported as less serious than it actually was.

An English economist, Sir Josiah Stamp, warned of the dangers of official statistics. He stated, "The government is very keen on amassing statistics. They collect them, raise them to the nth power, take the cube root and prepare wonderful diagrams. But you must never forget that every one of these figures comes in the first instance from the village watchman, who just puts down what he damn pleases" (quoted in Platt, 1999).

The Uniform Crime Reports

The UCRs cover 29 different crimes, including eight crimes that, when totaled, are known as the **Crime Index**. We can use this total to compare levels of crime over time. The eight Crime Index offenses are homicide, forcible rape, robbery, aggravated assault, burglary, larceny-theft, auto theft, and arson. Table 4.1 illustrates the Crime Index for 2011. The remaining UCR crimes are considered Part II offenses and include crimes such as drug abuse violations and simple assault.

Participating police agencies voluntarily report data to the FBI. Most (but not all) police departments report to the FBI. The UCR has been published since 1930 (U.S. Department of Justice, 2004), and thus has provided information on the rate and level of crime in the United States for more than 70 years. Nonetheless, criminologists question the value of the UCR on several grounds (Kleinman & Lukoff, 1981; Menard, 1987, 1991).

Many criminologists warn that UCR data must be used cautiously (Maltz, 1999). The data are voluntarily reported and may reflect different definitions of offenses employed by the multitude of police departments participating. Moreover, the UCR counts only non-Index crimes (simple assault, etc.) if an arrest is made in the case. As shown in Table 4.1, less than half of Index crimes are cleared by an arrest. Thus, there is reason to believe that requiring an arrest to be made for non-Index crimes is a major limitation to the data. The data also mask the actual numbers of offenses and offenders through a reporting procedure often referred to as the **hierarchy rule**. For example, if a number of crimes are committed during a single criminal episode (say a bank robber kills a teller, kidnaps a hostage, steals a car for the escape, and flees across state lines), only the most serious offense is counted (in this case, the homicide). Finally, Geis (1986) noted that changes in UCR data may reflect police efficiency more than changes in crime. A city with an aggressive police department that proactively fights crime and clears a large percent of known crimes with an arrest will have a higher official crime rate than a city with a weaker or more passive police department, even if the true level of crime is the same for both cities.

Other criticisms have been leveled about the reporting of crimes as the crime rate in which the amount of crime is "adjusted" for population size. Using the **crime rate** formula, the number of crimes is reported as a function of population such that:

$$\frac{(\text{Crime} \times 100)}{\text{Total population}} = \text{Crime rate}$$

In this way, the Crime Index treats crimes such as homicide and theft as equal. In addition, for many years the FBI used the decennial (10-year) census for the population total. As a result, the UCR based the 1969 crime rate on the same population as it did the 1960 rate. This caused an artificial inflation of the crime rate because the formula did not reflect the actual increase in the population (Eck & Riccio, 1979).

Table 4.1   Estimated Number and Rate (per 100,000 Inhabitants) of Criminal Offenses, 2011, by Offense and Percent Cleared by Arrest or Exceptional Means

| Area | Population[a] | Violent Crime | | | | | | Property Crime | | | |
		Total	Murder and Non-negligent Man-slaughter	Forcible Rape	Robbery	Aggravated Assault	Total	Burglary	Larceny-Theft	Motor Vehicle Theft
United States, total	311,519,917	1,203.564	14,612	83,425	354,396	751,131	9,063.173	2,188,005	6,159,795	715,373
Rate per 100,000 inhabitants		386.3	4.7	26.8	11,307	241.1	2,908.7	702.2	1,976.9	229.6
Percent cleared by arrest or by exceptional means		47.7	64.8	41.2	28.7	56.9	18.6	12.7	21.5	11.9

Note: Although arson is an Index crime, the FBI does not include arson data in rate statistics owing to insufficient data.
[a]*Populations are U.S. Census Bureau provisional estimates as of July 1, 2011, and are subject to change.*
Source: Federal Bureau of Investigation (2011), Tables 2 and 25 [Online]

The purpose of the crime rate is to make fairer comparisons between jurisdictions. If we have a city with 100,000 people where 20 murders occurred last year, and a town of 5,000 people where one murder occurred last year, which is safest? The raw numbers indicate that murder is 20 times as likely to occur in the city as in the town. In fact, however, if you reside in either community, your chances of being a homicide victim are equal. The city has a homicide rate of 20 per 100,000 populations. The town has a homicide rate of 1 per 5,000 (or 20 per 100,000), which is equal to the homicide rate in the city, because the city is 20 times larger than the town in population. Nolan (2004) has shown that the level of crime increases with city size so that larger cities have higher crime rates than smaller cities. This means using the crime rate to make comparisons between different-sized cities more fair is only partly successful.

Despite the problems with UCR data, it is still an important indicator of the nature and extent of crime in the nation. Rosenfeld and Decker (1999) tested the accuracy of official arrest reports as a measure of substance abuse. In comparison to public health and drug test data, they found that the arrest data were quite similar to other measures for drugs such as heroin and cocaine, but that the various measures differed for marijuana. The UCR also releases separate publications that provide some detail on the numbers of hate crimes committed in the country each year and on the numbers of police officers killed and assaulted in the line of duty. These publications are available at http://www.fbi.gov/stats-services/crimestats. As long as the user is aware of the limitations of the UCR and is cautious in its interpretation, it is an important source of information.

IMPROVING THE UCR

In late 1982, a task force composed of representatives of the U.S. Bureau of Justice Statistics and the FBI began to study ways of improving the UCRs (Bureau of Justice Statistics & Federal Bureau of Investigation, 1985). Although there was broad support for this revision of the crime-reporting program, the task is not yet completed. The new reporting system is the National Incident-Based Reporting System (NIBRS). In comparison to the traditional UCR, the NIBRS gathers information about crimes known to the police that are much more detailed (see Table 4.2).

The NIBRS format asks police to record information for each incident of crime, as opposed to recording information about only the most serious crime. Instead of eight Index offenses, the NIBRS has 22 Group A offense categories and 11 Group B offenses. Some crime definitions have changed. For example, the UCR defines rape as a crime by a male against a female, whereas the NIBRS uses a sexually neutral definition. Finally, NIBRS records information for each incident in six segments representing data about the case (administrative), crime (offense), property, victim, offender, and arrestee. The result is a much richer and more detailed set of information about crimes known to the police.

This information enables analysts to study relationships among offenders and victims, characteristics of places and times offenses occur, and other topics

Table 4.2	Comparing the Uniform Crime Reports and National Incident-Based Reporting System
Uniform Crime Reports (UCR)	**National Incident-Based Reporting System (NIBRS)**
Tracks eight crimes	Tracks 46 crimes
Does not report arrests in specific incidents	Contains information about arrests in each incident
Gives a tally of the incidents; does not contain information on each reported incident	Contains information on each incident reported to police, including: Characteristics of victims and offenders Relationship between victims and offenders Crimes committed Injuries at the incident scene Weapons used Arrests made
Does not provide information about simple assault, which is the most commonly reported domestic violence offense	Provides information about simple assault
Reports only the most serious crime committed in a single incident	Requires officers to report multiple offenses, victims, and offenders

Source: Hirschel (2009:1)

(Reaves, 1993). The new reporting format, however, results in higher numbers of crimes reported as known to police. It is likely to be some time before the new reporting format will achieve widespread use. As of 2010, well under half of the nation's law enforcement agencies report data in the NIBRS format (Friedmann, Rosenfeld, & Borissova, 2010). If the NIBRS format ever becomes a true national level measure of crime, it has been suggested that the changes will go a long way toward fixing most of the problems identified with the UCR (Hirschel, 2009).

Other Official Statistics

Other criminal justice and governmental agencies collect and publish data that are relevant to measuring crime and criminals in the United States. Increasingly during the past three decades, the U.S. Bureau of Justice Statistics has gathered and published information about the operations of criminal justice agencies by surveying law enforcement, court, and correctional organizations. There are periodic censuses of the nation's jails and data on case filings in the courts of the United States. Other data are available regarding the numbers and distribution of juvenile offenders, operations of pretrial release programs, and other aspects of justice processing. Some of the more common and more important sources of official information about criminal justice operations in the United States include the Law Enforcement Management and Administrative Statistics, National Pretrial Reporting, National Judicial Reporting, and National

Corrections Reporting programs. The Bureau of Justice Statistics administers all these programs (http://www.ojp.usdoj.gov/bjs).

UNOFFICIAL STATISTICS

Recognizing that official statistics tell only part of the story of crime in the United States, criminologists have developed other ways of estimating how much crime occurs and who commits criminal offenses. **Unofficial statistics** are those measures of the rate and nature of crime that do not rely on the reporting of official agencies and agents of criminal justice. Two basic sources of crime data (collected without relying on the official reports of justice agencies) are victim surveys and self-report. These data reveal that official statistics cover only about half of all crime. They also show that persons arrested for criminal offenses are not representative of all those who commit crimes. To avoid the problems and limitations of official statistics, particularly the UCR, researchers developed these other methods of counting crimes and criminals (National Research Council, 2008; Salas & Surette, 1984). Each gives a slightly different view of the overall crime picture and thus serves as an aid to understanding the true nature and extent of crime in the United States.

Victim Surveys

In 1965, the National Opinion Research Center (NORC) of the University of Chicago conducted the first survey of crime victims. The researchers used the results to estimate the nature and extent of crime. The President's Commission on Law Enforcement and Administration of Justice (1967:96) instructed the NORC to conduct a survey of 10,000 households. The survey results indicated that crimes known to the police were only a fraction of all crimes committed.

The NORC survey contacted a spokesperson for each household surveyed and asked that person if anyone residing in the household had been the victim of certain crimes in the past year. Interviewers asked respondents whether the crime had been reported to the police and, if not, why it had not been reported. Beginning in 1971, the U.S. Bureau of the Census began collecting similar data through the **National Crime Victimization Survey (NCVS)**.

Results of the survey over the years continue to indicate that the UCR data are incomplete. Respondents to victim surveys report that many crimes, especially less serious property crimes and violent crimes among friends and acquaintances remain unreported to the police. Box 4.2 compares the victim surveys of the NCVS with the UCR. **Victimization data** provide information about the nature and extent of crime as understood by those reporting that they have been crime victims.

The NCVS asks about the number of times that members of the responding household have been the victims of assault, personal larceny, robbery, and forcible rape. It also counts automobile theft, burglary, and household larceny as crimes against households. The data are not directly comparable to the UCR.

Nonetheless, the wide gap (see Box 4.2) between the number of victimizations reported in the surveys and the number of crimes reported in the UCR indicates that much more crimes occur than are brought to the attention of the justice system. However, victim survey reports reveal that the UCR accurately portrays types of crimes and their relative numbers (Booth, Johnson, & Choldin, 1977; Cohen & Lichbach, 1982; Hindelang, 1978; O'Brien, 1990). Figure 4.1 shows a sample NCVS incident report.

Although victim surveys and the UCR differ over the absolute number of crimes committed, their respective findings are similar in other regards. Both show similar relative proportions of crime that consist of burglaries or robberies,

BOX 4.2 COMPARISON OF THE NCVS AND THE UCR

The National Crime Victimization Survey (NCVS)

Using stable data collection methods since 1973, the NCVS has the following strengths:

- It measures both reported and unreported crimes.
- It is not affected by changes in the extent to which people report crime to police or improvements in police record-keeping technology.
- It collects information that was not available when the initial police report was made including contacts the victim has with the criminal justice system after the crime, extent and costs of medical treatment, and recovery of property.
- It collects detailed information about victims and characteristics of the victimization including who the victims are, what their relationship is to the offender, whether the crime was a part of a series of crimes occurring over a 6-month period, what self-protective measures were used and how the victims assess their effectiveness, and what the victim was doing when victimized.
- On occasion, it includes special supplements about particular topics such as school crime and the severity of crime.

The Uniform Crime Reports

The UCR program measures police workload and activity. Local police departments voluntarily report information to the FBI including the numbers of crimes reported to police, arrests made by police, and other administrative information. The UCR program has the following strengths:

- It can provide local data about states, counties, cities, and towns.
- It measures crimes affecting children under age 12, a segment of the population that experts agree cannot be reliably interviewed by the NCVS.
- It includes crimes against commercial establishments.
- It collects information about the number of arrests and who was arrested.
- It counts the number of homicides (murders and nonnegligent manslaughters), crimes that cannot be counted in a survey that interviews victims. UCR also collects detailed information about the circumstances surrounding homicides and the characteristics of homicide victims.

Source: Bureau of Justice Statistics (1992)

and both have similar findings as to the location of crimes (urban areas, lower classes, etc.). Thus, UCR data may underestimate the amount of crime, but may accurately reflect the types of crimes committed, and where and when criminal offenses are likely to occur.

In addition to the NCVS, researchers have adopted the victim survey to measure the level and extent of crime for other purposes. Although the NCVS allows us to compare national victim survey results with the UCR, the technique of surveying crime victims is useful for any measure of changes in crime. In addition to official police reports, researchers have conducted victim surveys in evaluations of several programs. The victim survey has become an important tool in studying crime (Cantor & Lynch, 2000).

Victim surveys also have their limitations (O'Brien, 1986). The victim survey's major problems may revolve around the phenomena known as "telescoping" and "forgetting." The interviewer asks the respondent if anyone has been the victim of a particular crime in the past 6 months. In **telescoping**, the respondent errs by including an offense that may have occurred, say, 7 months earlier, thereby "telescoping" it into the covered period. **Forgetting** occurs when the respondent forgets about a crime that did occur in the period under study (Schneider & Sumi, 1981). Moreover, it is always possible when interviewing a person that (for whatever reason) the person is not telling the truth in answering the questions.

Another limitation of victim surveys is that many crimes may have gone unnoticed by the respondent. The NCVS interviewer relies on one individual to have knowledge of the criminal victimizations experienced by the entire household. Finally, victim surveys do not cover some offenses (Cantor & Lynch, 2000). For example, the NCVS asks about only a small number of offenses, and it is not possible to gather data about homicide, for example, from the victims of the crime. During the past 30 years, the increasing cost of collecting data has meant that the size of the victimization sample and the scope of the interview have been reduced. The combination of a smaller sample size and crime rates at their lowest levels in decades during the recent past means that it is difficult to detect significant changes in rates of victimization from year to year (Catalano, 2006; National Research Council, 2008).

IMPROVING THE NCVS

In 1992, responding to many of the problems identified with the NCVS, the Bureau of Justice Statistics changed the interview used to gather victimization information. Among other changes, the survey now interviews all persons aged 12 or older residing in households included in the sample. The redesign changed some offense classifications, such as classifying all thefts as household victimizations. Interviewers now specifically ask respondents about their experiences as victims of rape or sexual assault, and the interview gathers more detailed information about victimization and some offenses such as assault (Bureau of Justice Statistics, 1996). The changes in the interview were phased into use over several

OMB No. 1121-0111: Approval Expires 09/30/94

NOTICE — Your report to the Census Bureau is **confidential** by law (U.S. Code 42, Sections 3789g and 3735). All identifiable information will be used only by persons engaged in and for the purposes of the survey, and may not be disclosed or released to others for any purpose.	Sample	Control number				HH No.
	J ____	PSU	Segment	CK	Serial	

FORM NCVS-2(X)
(10-13-92)

U.S. DEPARTMENT OF COMMERCE
BUREAU OF THE CENSUS

ACTING AS COLLECTING AGENT FOR THE
BUREAU OF JUSTICE STATISTICS
U.S. DEPARTMENT OF JUSTICE

Notes

CRIME INCIDENT REPORT
REDESIGN PHASE III
NATIONAL CRIME VICTIMIZATION SURVEY

N C V S   2 (X)   I N C I D E N T   R E P O R T

PGM 6

1a. LINE NUMBER OF RESPONDENT ⟶ [601] _____ Line number

1b. SCREEN QUESTION NUMBER ⟶ [602] _____ Screen question number

1c. INCIDENT NUMBER ⟶ [603] _____ Incident number

CHECK ITEM A See item 33a on the NCVS-1(X). Has the respondent lived at this address for more than 6 months? *(If not sure, ask.)*

☐ Yes (more than 6 months) – **SKIP** to 3
☐ No (6 months or less) – Ask 2

2. You said that during the last 6 months — *(Refer to appropriate screen question for description of crime.)* **Did (this/the first) incident happen while you were living here or before you moved to this address?**

[605] 1 ☐ While living at this address
2 ☐ Before moving to this address

3. (You said that during the last 6 months — *Refer to appropriate screen question for description of crime.)* **In what month did (this/the first) incident happen?** *(Show calendar if necessary. Encourage respondent to give exact month.)*

[606] ☐☐ ☐☐ Month   Year

4. *If known, mark without asking. If not sure, ASK —* **Altogether, how many times did this type of incident happen during the last 6 months?**

[607] _____ Number of Incidents

CHECK ITEM B Refer to 4. How many incidents?

[608] 1 ☐ 1–5 incidents (not a "series") — **SKIP** to 5b
2 ☐ 6 or more incidents — *Fill Check Item C*

CHECK ITEM C Are these incidents similar to each other in detail, or are they for different types of crimes? *(If not sure, ask.)*

[609] 1 ☐ Similar — *Fill Check Item D*
2 ☐ Different (not a "series") — **SKIP** to 5b

CHECK ITEM D Can you (respondent) recall enough details of each incident to distinguish them from each other? *(If not sure, ask.)*

[610] 1 ☐ Yes (not a "series") — **SKIP** to 5b
2 ☐ No (is a "series") — *Reduce entry in screen question if necessary — Ask 5a*

5a. The following questions refer only to the most recent incident.

5b. Was it daylight or dark outside when (this/the most recent) incident happened?

[611] 1 ☐ Light — Ask 6
2 ☐ Dark — Ask 6
3 ☐ Dawn, almost light, dusk, twilight — Ask 6
4 ☐ Don't know — **SKIP** to 7

6. About what time did (this/the most recent) incident happen?

During day
[612] 1 ☐ After 6 a.m. – 12 noon
2 ☐ After 12 noon – 6 p.m.
3 ☐ Don't know what time of day

At night
4 ☐ After 6 p.m. – 12 midnight
5 ☐ After 12 midnight – 6 a.m.
6 ☐ Don't know what time of night

Or
7 ☐ Don't know whether day or night

FIGURE 4.1
Sample NCVS incident report.

years, with the final form of the new survey implemented between 1992 and 1993. The results of the changes in interview format and content included finding much higher rates of victimization. The greatest changes occurred in estimates of rape and assault (Rand, Lynch, & Cantor, 1997). In 2003, changes in federal regulations allowed survey participants to choose more than one racial category, making it difficult to compare recent victims with past victims in terms of race. Finally, the Bureau of Justice Statistics added questions over the years to collect information on emerging topics such as cybercrime and identity theft.

Self-Reports

Both the UCR and victim surveys attempt to describe criminal offenders. The FBI reports the characteristics of persons arrested for crimes, providing descriptions of those persons officially recognized as probably having committed crimes. The respondents to victim surveys describe the offenders involved, if possible. These data provide a description of criminal offenders as seen by the victims of crime. Both efforts at describing criminal offenders are severely limited. Moreover, although there is a fair degree of agreement between victim surveys and UCR data, it is possible that neither measure accurately reflects all crime. Thus, researchers also use a third method of counting crimes: surveys of criminal offenders.

Self-report studies attempt to measure the amount of crime committed and describe the characteristics of criminal offenders by asking people if they have committed offenses. In these studies, researchers ask a sample of the public if they have committed any crimes (Thornberry & Krohn, 2000). This crime measure yields information on the types of persons likely to commit crimes as well as another estimate of the amount of crime that is committed each year.

Traditionally, self-report studies involved juvenile populations. As such, the studies frequently included questions about behaviors that would not necessarily be crimes if committed by adults. For example, disobeying teachers or parents and skipping classes are "delinquent" acts for those with the status of juvenile, but such acts are not crimes for adults. Such "status offenses" included in self-report surveys cloud the issue of how much crime is committed and by whom (Hood & Sparks, 1970).

These studies also have other limitations. They share the problems of telescoping and forgetting that afflict victim surveys, and it is difficult to determine whether respondents are telling the truth. There is reason to believe that some may exaggerate to make themselves appear to be notorious and that some will be reticent, fearing that disclosure of their criminality will lead to punishment. When researchers have compared reported crimes and arrests with official records, however, they find respondents tell the truth (Cantner, 1982; but also see Nettler, 1984). For example, Golub, Johnson, Taylor, and Liberty (2002) found that arrestees provided relatively truthful responses to questions of their past behavior. However, they also reported that rates of truthful responses varied among type of question asked. For example, 81% of respondents truthfully disclosed recent marijuana use, but the respondents were less likely to answer questions honestly about more serious drugs such as cocaine or heroin. In addition, respondents were unlikely to disclose a prior arrest for an Index crime, especially violent Index crimes. Other research has found that the degree of truthful reporting depends on many factors, including the types of people. McElrath, Dunham, and Cromwell (1995) reported the rates of truthful responses varied by jurisdiction, race, types of people interviewed, the characteristics of the interviewer, and the type of charge for which the offender had been arrested.

Nonetheless, self-report studies indicate that almost everyone will admit to having violated some criminal law. The most important finding of self-report studies is not who does or does not break the law, but rather how often crimes are committed and how serious are those violations. Institutionalized populations of delinquents or adult criminals report more frequent and more serious law violations than do "free citizens." Males report more criminal activity than females; African Americans report more frequent and more serious offenses than Caucasians do. In general, with the exception that self-reports indicate that everyone probably breaks some law, the findings of these studies echo those of victim surveys and official reports.

Other Measures of Crime and Criminal Justice

Researchers have used several other methods to measure crime and study the criminal justice process. Information gathered from cohort studies and observations helps to better describe and explain the operations of the criminal justice process and the nature and extent of crime.

Cohort studies begin with an identifiable group (or "cohort") and trace the group's interaction with the justice system over time. The individuals studied in such research are members of a cohort. The cohort is a collection of all persons sharing a common selection characteristic. Thus, a cohort might include all entering freshmen at a university or all persons married in a given year. For criminal justice research, the selection criterion normally relates to a justice system decision (such as all those arrested in a given time period) or to an age limit (such as all those born in a specified year).

The most famous cohort study selected cases by specifying all males born in Philadelphia in the year 1948. *Delinquency in a Birth Cohort* (Wolfgang, Figlio, & Sellin, 1978) was the report of a study designed to examine the criminal careers of youths. Researchers tracked all males born in Philadelphia in 1948 for a 20-year period to determine which of them were arrested, tried, and sentenced for delinquent behavior. Additionally, they studied the distribution of delinquent offenses among the cohort and characteristics of individuals most often involved in delinquent behavior.

This study allowed the researchers to estimate the proportion of youths that would become entangled in the juvenile justice process, how serious the youths' misbehavior would be, and who among them were most likely to be delinquent.

Wolfgang has been involved in at least two additional cohort studies of delinquency (Navares, Wolfgang, & Tracy, 1990; Tracy, Wolfgang, & Figlio, 1990). Similar cohort analyses of persons arrested for crime could be used to estimate how the justice system processes cases from arrest to final disposition. Such data would be invaluable to an understanding of the justice process. The problem with cohort studies is one of expense. By definition, most cohort studies must be extensive; that is, they involve large numbers of cases followed over a period of several years.

For *Delinquency in a Birth Cohort*, the researchers actually identified their cohort in 1976 and backtracked through official records to estimate the subjects' involvement in juvenile delinquency. A similar study of those born this year would take 20 years to complete. Despite this limitation, cohort studies allow us to examine the operations of criminal justice agencies in a broader context than is normally possible. Cohort studies provide an estimate of the distribution of crime across an entire population over time.

Observations, as the term implies, involve researchers watching the behavior of criminals, agents of the justice system, or other samples of people. The American Bar Foundation (ABF) series mentioned in Chapter 1 is one example of an observation study. The ABF study reported observations of police, prosecutors, judges, and correctional personnel during investigation, arrest, conviction, and sentencing. Other observation studies have been conducted that seek to determine when people break the law, when they report lawbreaking, what factors justice system agents consider in their decision making, and how cases move from one stage of the justice process to the next.

Like cohort studies, observational methods can be expensive to use and, thus, often result in limited data confined to one location, or in a few decisions rather than national, systemwide descriptions. There is concern that criminal justice officials, recognizing they are being watched, will change their behavior. Spano (2007) assessed the likely effect of observers on police behavior and found that police officers do seem to react to the presence of researchers. He found that officer reactions varied and depended on characteristics of the observer and other situational factors.

Interest in and use of geographic data in the analysis of crime has increased in recent years (Anselin, Cohen, Cook, Gore, & Tita, 2000). Geographic data provide a different perspective from which to view crime and criminal justice, giving us a better feel for the reasons behind decisions and behaviors. Increasingly, police departments use sophisticated analyses of large databases to predict or understand the nature and distribution of crime, especially large police departments. Called "intelligence-led policing," analysts link crime data and offender information with a variety of other information about communities to identify links and predict how best to intervene to prevent crime (Bureau of Justice Assistance, 2005; Ratcliffe, 2008). These initiatives, of course, depend on accuracy and timeliness of the data used.

SUMMARY OF CRIME STATISTICS

While each of these methods of counting crimes and criminals uses different means of gathering data and collects information from different sources, in total, the "picture" each gives us of crime is generally consistent (Nettler, 1984:98–156). Absolute numbers may vary (for instance, victim surveys may show much more crime than police reports), but the relative frequency of crimes (e.g., more thefts than robberies, more robberies than assaults, more assaults than rapes) reported by all three procedures is similar.

Where these three research methods differ is in the picture they paint of offenders. In a comparison of self-report, victim survey, and arrest data, Hindelang (1978) noted that self-report studies show little difference between race and offense behavior, whereas the other two measures are in general agreement that African Americans are more likely to be offenders. Self-report studies also show little difference between social classes in the likelihood of engaging in crime. Both upper- and lower-class respondents admit to committing criminal offenses. However, lower-class youths are more likely to commit crimes more frequently, and to commit more serious crimes than middle- or upper-class youths (Williams & Gold, 1972).

One point that is apparent (assuming that victim and self-report measures are accurate) is that persons arrested, and therefore subjected to justice system processing, are not representative of the general population (O'Brien, 1985). Poor, urban dwellers and minority group members are far more likely to be arrested and processed than their numbers in the population suggest. In addition, females are less likely to become involved in the justice process than their numbers in the population would indicate. One exception here is the juvenile justice system, where girls are often subjected to more justice processing than boys (Kempf-Leonard & Sample, 2000).

One of the questions raised in response to these findings concerns the fairness of the justice process. If nearly everyone admits to committing some crimes, why is it that minorities and the poor are most often arrested, convicted, and incarcerated? Why are women less likely to be arrested and convicted for crimes than are men? Is the justice system racist, sexist, and prejudiced against the poor? In short, the evidence of differential treatment of certain classes of the population has led some observers to suggest that the justice system is discriminatory.

DISCRIMINATION IN THE JUSTICE SYSTEM

The data suggest that the justice process appears to identify and select certain offenders for processing in a manner that reflects their relative involvement in crime. Yet some have argued that the justice process is discriminatory and repressive because it differentially selects and processes members of disadvantaged groups, such as youth, minorities, the poor, and urban residents (Petersilia, 1983). Others have suggested that the justice system is sexist because it does not subject females to equal treatment as offenders (Visher, 1983). Based on the data presented in Figure 4.2, these criticisms seem accurate. Yet, there are some other possible explanations.

Recall that the justice system exists in an ideological environment that contains our society's values and biases. Differences are more understandable between victim and self-report surveys' conclusions as to who commits crimes and whom we arrest and process through the justice system. Females are less likely to engage in most crimes than are males, partly because of socially defined opportunities

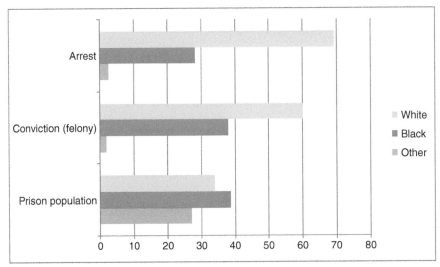

FIGURE 4.2
Characteristics of persons processed in the criminal justice system (by percent).
Source: Carson and Sabol, 2012; Federal Bureau of Investigation, 2012; Rosenmerkel et al., 2009

for women (both criminal and noncriminal). Additionally, the types of offenses women commit and for which police arrest women were traditionally less serious and less threatening than crimes common to males (Lauritsen, Heimer, & Lynch, 2009). We are far more likely to fully process robbers, rapists, and assaulters than we are prostitutes, thieves, and drug users. Even if they are aware of the relatively large number of female offenders, agents of the justice system are likely to concentrate their resources on the more serious offenses.

Until there are greater numbers of female offenders engaged in homicide, rape, and robbery, it is not possible to assess accurately the extent of the sexism and paternalism operating in the justice system. Some observers think that these changes are afoot and that females are becoming more involved in traditional crimes, and taking a more active role in the crimes they commit (Schwartz & Rookey, 2008). Others suggest that changes in how we treat certain crimes (e.g., drug crimes and domestic assault) have resulted in a greater likelihood of arrest for women (Schwartz, Steffensmeier, Zhong, & Ackerman, 2009). In a study of incarcerated female offenders, however, Alarid, Marquart, Burton, Cullen, and Cuvelier (1996) reported that less than one-half of these women said they were leaders or even equal partners in their crimes. Thus, in this study at least, even among women subjected to full justice system processing, the majority reported that the crime, and their role in it, was not their idea. There is some evidence too, that not only are the crimes committed by females less likely to be reported, those committed by black offenders are more likely to be reported (Mastrofski, Reisig, & McCluskey, 2002). If the behaviors of males and minorities are socially defined as more serious, the justice system will be activated more frequently to deal with those offenders.

As for the disparities among those arrested for crime and those who report having committed crimes (or whom victims report having seen commit crimes), the explanation is equally plausible. Research has documented that minority group members commit more serious crimes over a longer period than do white offenders. Thus, the arrest statistics reflect the increased probability of being caught, which is a result of the greater frequency of criminal conduct. The concentration of justice system resources on the more serious offenses also produces disproportionate numbers of arrests of minority group members as compared to the numbers of whites arrested. Still, data from observational studies and reviews of arrests, as well as the outcomes of arrest (charges dropped/trial/conviction), indicate that, as Weitzer (1996:312) noted, "police are involved in at least some discrimination against members of racial and ethnic minorities...." Research into the effect of a driver's race on police decisions to stop motorists indicates that minority drivers are more likely to be stopped than whites when police are engaged in law enforcement and order maintenance activities than when the police are focused on traffic enforcement (Warren, Tomaskovic-Devey, Smith, Zingraff, & Mason, 2006). Once stopped, automobiles driven by African Americans are more likely to be searched by police than the cars of Caucasians (Engel, 2008). There is additional evidence to suggest that cultural differences between white and minority citizens influence police officer development of suspicion. Johnson (2006) reported that African American and Hispanic citizens were less likely to maintain eye contact with police officers and were also likely to speak and smile differently than Caucasian citizens. These differences in behavior while dealing with police tended to make the officers more suspicious of African American and Hispanic citizens.

The greater number of youths in arrest statistics reflects the fact that crime tends to be a young person's game. The idleness, good physical condition, and lack of responsibilities that many youths enjoy may create special opportunities for them to commit crime. As one who engages in crime grows older, she or he generally risks longer prison terms as a habitual offender. Giving longer terms to older offenders means they are less likely to have the opportunities to commit the crimes that are available to the young. Finally, in a catch-22 fashion, the police actually are more likely to look for crimes among the young precisely because so many of the young have been found to be engaged in crime.

Similar reasoning applies to members of minority groups. Idleness (even if forced by unemployment) allows more time for crime and subjects people to greater police scrutiny. However, the greatest factor appears to be urbanism. Most arrests are of young, urban offenders. Minority groups tend to be concentrated most greatly in the cities of the United States. Simply put, both the police and young, minority males are overrepresented in the cities (Akins, 2003; Swanson, 1981). The justice system statistics reflect the organization, both social and geographical, of our society. Nelson (1992) observed that discriminatory handling of minorities may not be recognizable in statewide statistics, but is visible in county-level analyses. Thus, when minority populations are concentrated in a few urban counties, checks of statewide conviction or incarceration data will not reveal discriminatory patterns. Neighborhood disadvantage, living in poverty in places with few social services, and the presence of little informal social control all lead to greater levels of crime and greater reliance on the justice system. In the United States, African Americans are disproportionately found in the most disadvantaged neighborhoods (McNulty, 2001; Schaefer, Huebner, & Bynum, 2003; Velez, 2001). Brennan (2006) found that sentences imposed on female misdemeanants in New York City reflected social class and not race. However, because African American and other minority women were more likely to be from the lower class, they were more likely to receive jail sentences than were Caucasian women.

In rural and suburban areas, the population is more dispersed, and there are fewer police officers. It is more difficult for police to observe crimes and respond quickly to reports of crime. In addition, smaller communities have available more informal mechanisms of social control. People are less frequently strangers to one another and can resolve differences more easily without involving the police. It is more likely that people define disputes as "personal" and not demanding of police intervention. In the future, however, differences between rural and urban areas in terms of crime are likely to diminish. As urban sprawl continues, and with the increasing importance of a global economy and improved communications, many of the problems of cities are likely to also affect rural areas (Lee & Thomas, 2010; Weisheit & Wells, 1999).

We will return to the question of discrimination in the justice system a little later. For now, it is enough to say that the presence or absence of discrimination in criminal justice processing, the degree to which discrimination exists, and the effects of possible discrimination in the justice system are complex questions. In a review of the discrimination literature, Weitzer (1996) concluded that discrimination appears to exist in the justice system, but not to the extent we might expect.

UNDERSTANDING THE JUSTICE SYSTEM

Counting the number of crimes and criminals yields an estimate of the volume of "business" conducted by the criminal justice system. Other data are available that lend insight into the complex operations of criminal justice in the United States. Statistics that detail the numbers of persons arrested, prosecuted, tried, convicted, sentenced, incarcerated, or placed under community supervision, released, and discharged describe the working of the justice system.

Ideally, data obtained from all the methods discussed above would be available for answering whatever questions we might have about crime and criminal justice. Unfortunately, such data (at least on a national level) are not always available, and the student of criminal justice must rely on limited information or make inferences from what information can be obtained. Yet another problem is that the periodic revisions of how we collect information, like the development of the NIBRS and revised NCVS, often mean that it is not possible to make direct comparisons of data collected before and after the changes.

One fact readily apparent in an overview of these data is that the criminal justice system operates like a giant sieve. It continuously filters the huge volume of crimes and criminals down to the relatively small number of offenders found in the nation's prisons. By beginning with crimes known to the police and then using different data sources to track arrests, prosecutions, convictions, and sentences, it is possible (as is illustrated in Box 4.3) to observe this "**funnel effect.**"

As one moves through the criminal justice system, from the crime itself through police, courts, and correctional processing, to discharge, the volume of cases becomes progressively smaller. At each successive stage, the less serious offenses and less dangerous offenders are diverted from the justice system. "Weak cases"—those in which the evidence against the offender is less complete or less compelling—are also dropped. Some accused offenders who are innocent are removed from the process. In the end, a very select group is subjected to the full force of the criminal law.

From this perspective, it is clear that crime does indeed pay, at least in the case of an individual offense. Wilson and Abrahamse (1992:375) noted, "To someone contemplating the commission of any given crime, the answer is that it pays

BOX 4.3 "FUNNEL EFFECT" OF THE CRIMINAL JUSTICE SYSTEM

Crime = 100%

Reported to police = 50%

Cleared by arrest = 22%

Convicted = 68%

Sentenced to prison = 24%

Fewer than 4% to prison

reasonably well." They go on, however, to observe that a career in crime does not pay. Of course, this conclusion about a criminal career's costs and benefits was based on a study of unsuccessful criminals: inmates in three state prisons. The chances of going to prison for a criminal act are slim (except regarding certain criminal acts, such as homicide, which have higher risks of imprisonment). It may be that we have too many criminals for the justice system to accommodate and that this selection process is required so that the entire justice system does not collapse under the number of cases. This is the argument most commonly raised in support of such practices as plea bargaining: that the courts could not handle the volume of criminal trials if bargaining were abolished. It is in the close observation of the filtering process that we begin to understand our society's crime control priorities. It is here, too, that we most clearly see the systemic nature of the criminal justice process. Our task is to develop an understanding of how the criminal justice system in the United States works the way it does.

Recalling our earlier discussion of systems theory, the total system of criminal justice exists within the whole "system" of American society. As an open system, criminal justice is sensitive to a variety of social values and social forces. That is, we cannot understand criminal justice processing in isolation from its place within American society. Although a comprehensive study of society is beyond our scope (and may be impossible), certain aspects of American society are relevant to our understanding of criminal justice operations. One of the most important of these is the emphasis we place on democratic values.

Criminal Justice in a Democracy

At its base, the criminal justice system is a legal system, or more accurately, part of a legal system. Black (1980) observed that legal systems can be characterized as being more or less democratic. Further, the degree of democracy shown in a legal system has implications for how the law develops, how it is applied, and what it accomplishes (Meehan & Ponder, 2002). Black concluded that more democracy in a legal system means that the law is mobilized (or applied) by the citizens more so than by governmental agents. Thus, "crimes" are brought to the attention of authorities more by citizen complaints than by police investigation. In democratic societies, the law is reactive-responsive to citizens. As a result, the law will reflect existing patterns of social stratification, and will be more responsive to changes in social morals and social structure. Thus, one effect of the high value Americans place on democracy is the creation of a legal system (criminal justice system) that reflects society in the United States.

Democracy also leads to the development of constraints on the powers of government and the ability of the criminal justice system to affect crime. Packer (1960) identified "due process" and "crime control" models of criminal justice. In the first, concerns about individual rights and liberty dominate a justice system's actions. In the latter, concerns for crime control and social order dominate. Similarly, Lundman (1980) noted that the police in American society reflect a "dynamic tension" between liberty (individual freedom) and civility (social order). Similarly, O'Leary and Duffee (1971) characterized correctional policies as variously emphasizing concern for the individual or concern for the community.

Each of these views suggests that the criminal justice system must achieve a balance between the rights of the individual and society's need for order. This balance may change over time, but the essential conflict between individual interests and social interests is central to criminal justice in the United States. How this conflict is resolved is the product of the thousands of individual decisions made in the criminal justice system each day. These decisions, in turn, reflect how that balance exists throughout American society.

With regard to the question of discrimination in the criminal justice system, the effect of democracy on the workings of the criminal justice process is evident. Wilbanks (1987) and Mann (1987) debated the existence of racial discrimination in U.S. criminal justice processing. Relying on empirical studies of official decision making, Wilbanks concluded that differential treatment of minority group members at arrest, bail, trial, and sentencing does not represent discrimination based on race. Rather, he concluded that minority group members commit more serious offenses. It is their behavior, not their race or ethnicity, that explains justice decisions. Mann argued, to the contrary, that data (especially the greater prior arrest/conviction records of minorities) represent racial discrimination. Moreover, she suggested that some of the strongest evidence of discrimination is not "quantified," like arrest statistics, but exists in the qualitative experiences of minority group members.

Who is correct? It is entirely likely that both Wilbanks and Mann are correct in their assertions about the existence of discrimination in criminal justice processing. Wilbanks is essentially saying that the data do not indicate, for example, that criminal justice officials consciously apply more severe treatment to minority group members. Thus, it would appear that most police, prosecutors, judges, juries, and correctional officials are not racist in their individual decisions. Mann is suggesting that minority group members are more often the targets of justice system processing because of their minority status. The aggregate data clearly indicate that this is the case. Zatz (1987), for instance, suggested that relatively high rates of case dismissal for racial minorities may be evidence of discrimination in arrest. That is, minorities are arrested on the basis of less evidence than whites (Barnes & Kingsnorth, 1996). Others have suggested that different outcomes of criminal justice processing may be the product of different choices made by members of minority groups. For example, Meyer and Gray (1997) reported that minority defendants charged with driving under the influence were more likely to plead guilty to the charge than were white defendants.

An alternative resolution of the question might be that whereas agents of the justice system are generally "color-blind" in their decision making, society in the United States is structured so that minority group members are more likely to come under justice system control. Society may grant minority group members less access to adequate education, resulting in less employment and fewer resources. These citizens then may be less able to defend themselves from criminal charges (unable to afford bail, private defense counsel, fines, etc.) and may be less suitable for leniency in treatment (e.g., probation sentences) because of a lack of community resources such as stable residence, job, family ties, and so on. As Black's thesis would suggest, if the society in which a legal system exists is discriminatory, a democratic legal system will also discriminate. Avakame, Fyfe, and McCoy (1999) studied the characteristics of who calls the police, as well as what the police do when called. Among other things, they observed that minorities and the poor are more likely to call the police to deal with problems. Perhaps because they lack access to other resources, poor people and members of minority groups are likely to have greater exposure to the police, and thus a greater chance of being involved in the criminal justice process (Mastrofski et al., 2002).

The enforcement of drug laws provides an example of institutional or systemic discrimination. Barnes and Kingsnorth (1996) examined sentences imposed on persons convicted of drug law violations in a California court. Among other things, their findings suggested that possession of drugs favored by minority ethnic groups (crack cocaine and heroin) was defined in the law as a more serious offense (a felony) than possession of drugs favored by whites (marijuana and methamphetamines), which was more likely to be defined as a misdemeanor offense. Defining some drugs as more dangerous than others coupled with the tendency of the police to focus on street drug markets led to disproportionate arrests of minorities. A combination of forces—including ethnic differences in drugs of choice and "drug marketing," police availability and strategies, and court decisions based on statutory definitions—together produce disproportionate rates of arrest, conviction, and incarceration for minority group members.

Beckett, Nyrop, and Pfingst (2006) studied drug enforcement in Seattle, Washington, and found that the drug crimes of minority group members and poor people were more likely to be the targets of police enforcement efforts than were the crimes of whites. For example, the police were more likely to investigate and arrest crack cocaine offenses than those involving powder cocaine, and to focus on crime in the downtown area than in suburban or other neighborhoods. In these cases, African Americans and other minorities were more at risk for arrest than were Caucasians. This has great implications in terms of sentencing, where crack cocaine has traditionally carried a more severe punishment than powder cocaine. Until 2010, the federal sentencing disparity between minimum sentences for crack and powder cocaine was 100:1. In other words, someone who had just 5 g of crack cocaine would receive a similar punishment as someone who had 500 g of powder cocaine. In 2010, Congress passed the Fair Sentencing Act, which reduced this disparity to 18:1 (Cratty, 2011).

This is not to say that discrimination is acceptable or inevitable. However, this observation has important implications for those who would seek to change the system. If the discrimination that exists in the justice process is rooted in the social system, changes in the justice process alone will have limited impact on levels of discrimination (Meehan & Ponder, 2002). Geis (1990) suggested that if the roots of crime are found in the society, the ability of the justice system to control crime is limited. Changes in the social system would be required to achieve either a reduction in discrimination or crime. In a democratic society, the criminal justice system is a part of—and a reflection of—the society in which it exists.

On a more positive note, some research has failed to discover evidence of racial discrimination. Kingsnorth, Lopez, Wentworth, and Cummings (1998) investigated race effects on prosecutions of sexual assault cases. They found that no combination of offender and victim race was any more important in understanding charging or plea bargaining. Similarly, DeLisi and Regoli (1999) tested five hypotheses based on an assumption of racial discrimination in criminal justice decision making. Based on their research, DeLisi and Regoli concluded that the available evidence does not support the notion that overt racial discrimination explains criminal justice operations. This does not mean that discrimination does not exist in the system, but rather that discrimination, where it exists, is only one of many factors that explains criminal justice operations.

The next chapters of this book are dedicated to an in-depth examination of the practices and decisions of the agents and agencies of the criminal justice system. In this examination, we will identify the factors that seem to be most important in determining which cases remain in the system and which are diverted. Our focus will be on the decisions made in the criminal justice system and on the identification of explanations for those decisions.

REVIEW QUESTIONS

1. What is the "dark figure" of crime?
2. Give four reasons for counting crime.
3. What are official statistics? Give an example.
4. Define the terms "unfounding" and "defounding."
5. Explain how to calculate a crime rate. What does the term mean?
6. Describe two types of unofficial crime statistics.
7. What do the data reveal about discrimination in the criminal justice system?
8. Describe cohort and observation studies of crime and criminal justice.
9. Explain how the criminal justice system operates like a funnel.
10. What is the effect of democratic values on the criminal justice system?

References

Akins, S. (2003). Racial segregation and property crime: Examining the mediating effect of police strength. *Justice Quarterly, 20*(4), 675–695.

Alarid, L., Marquart, J., Burton, V., Cullen, F., & Cuvelier, S. (1996). Women's roles in serious offenses: A study of adult felons. *Justice Quarterly, 13*(3), 431–454.

Albanese, J., & Pursley, R. (1993). *Crime in America: Some existing and emerging issues.* Englewood Cliffs, NJ: Prentice Hall.

Anselin, L., Cohen, J., Cook, D., Gore, W., & Tita, G. (2000). Spatial analysis of crime. In D. Duffee (Ed.), *Criminal justice 2000: Measurement and analysis of crime and justice; Vol. 4.* (pp. 85–138). Washington, DC: National Institute of Justice.

Avakame, E., Fyfe, J., & McCoy, C. (1999). Did you call the police? What did they do? An empirical assessment of Black's theory of mobilization of law. *Justice Quarterly, 16*(4), 765–792.

Barnes, C., & Kingsnorth, R. (1996). Race, drug, and criminal sentencing: Hidden effects of the criminal law. *Journal of Criminal Justice, 24*(1), 39–56.

Baumer, E. (2008). Evaluating the balance sheet of asset forfeiture laws: Toward evidence-based policy assessments. *Criminology and Public Policy, 7*(2), 245–256.

Beckett, K., Nyrop, K., & Pfingst, L. (2006). Race, drugs, and policing: Understanding disparities in drug delivery arrests. *Criminology, 44*(1), 105–137.

Black, D. (1980). *The manners and customs of the police.* New York: Academic Press.

Booth, A., Johnson, D. R., & Choldin, H. M. (1977). Correlates of city crime rates: Victimization surveys versus official statistics. *Social Problems, 25,* 187–197.

Brennan, P. (2006). Sentencing female misdemeanants: An examination of the direct and indirect effects of race/ethnicity. *Justice Quarterly, 23*(1), 60–95.

Bureau of Justice Assistance (2005). *Intelligence-led policing: The new intelligence architecture.* Washington, DC: Author.

Bureau of Justice Statistics (1992). *Criminal victimization in the United States, 1991.* Washington, DC: U.S. Department of Justice.

Bureau of Justice Statistics (1996). *Criminal victimization in the United States, 1994.* Washington, DC: U.S. Department of Justice.

Bureau of Justice Statistics & Federal Bureau of Investigation (1985). *Blueprint for the future of the uniform crime reporting program.* Washington, DC: U.S. Department of Justice.

Cantner, R. J. (1982). Sex differences in self-report delinquency. *Criminology, 20*(3–4), 373–393.

Cantor, D., & Lynch, J. (2000). Self-report surveys as measures of crime and criminal victimization. In D. Duffee (Ed.), In *Criminal justice 2000: Measurement and analysis of crime and justice: Vol. 4.* (pp. 85–138). Washington, DC: National Institute of Justice.

Carson, E., & Sabol, W. (2012). *Prisoners in 2011*. Washington, DC: U.S. Department of Justice.

Catalano, S. (2006). *Criminal victimization, 2005*. Washington, DC: Bureau of Justice Statistics.

Cohen, T., & Kyckelhahn, T. (2010). *Felony defendants in large urban counties, 2006*. Washington, DC: U.S. Department of Justice.

Cohen, L. J., & Lichbach, M. (1982). Alternative measures of crime: A statistical evaluation. *Sociological Quarterly, 23*, 253–266.

Cratty, C. (2011). *New rules slashing crack cocaine sentences go into effect.* CNN, Retrieved from: http://cnn.com/2011/11/01/justice/crack-cocaine-sentencing/Index.html.

DeLisi, M., & Regoli, R. (1999). Race, conventional crime, and criminal justice: The declining importance of skin color. *Journal of Criminal Justice, 27*(6), 549–557.

Eck, J. E., & Riccio, L. J. (1979). Relationship between reported crime rates and victimization survey results: An empirical and analytical study. *Journal of Criminal Justice, 7*(4), 293–308.

Engel, R. (2008). A critique of the "outcome test" in racial profiling research. *Justice Quarterly, 25*(1), 1–36.

Federal Bureau of Investigation (2011). *Crime in the United States, 2011*. Retrieved from: http://www.fbi.gov/about-us/cjis/ucr/crime-in-the-u.s/2011/crime-in-the-u.s.-2011.

Federal Bureau of Investigation (2012). *Crime in the United States, 2012*. Retrieved from: http://www.fbi.gov/about-us/cjis/ucr/crime-in-the-u.s/2012/crime-in-the-u.s.-2012.

Fisher, B., Daigle, L., & Cullen, F. (2010). What distinguishes single from recurrent sexual victims: The role of lifestyle-routine activities and first-incident characteristics. *Justice Quarterly, 27*(1), 102–129.

Friedmann, R., Rosenfeld, R., & Borissova, N. (2010). *Improving crime data project.* Atlanta, GA: The Statistical Analysis Bureau at Georgia State University.

Geis, G. (1986). On the declining crime rate: An exegetic conference report. *Criminal Justice Policy Review, 1*(1), 16–36.

Geis, G. (1990). Crime and criminal justice: Where have we been, where are we going? *Journal of Contemporary Criminal Justice, 6*, 254–263.

Golub, A., Johnson, B., Taylor, A., & Liberty, H. (2002). The validity of arrestees' self-reports: Variations across questions and persons. *Justice Quarterly, 19*(3), 477–502.

Hindelang, M. J. (1978). Race and involvement in crimes. *American Sociological Review, 43*(1), 93–109.

Hirschel, D. (2009). *Expanding police ability to report crime: The National Incident-Based Reporting System.* Washington, DC: National Institute of Justice.

Holden, R. (1993). Police and the profit-motive: A new look at asset forfeiture. *ACJS Today, 12*(2), 1, 3, 24–25.

Hood, R., & Sparks, R. (1970). *Key issues in criminology.* London: World University Library.

Johnson, R. (2006). Confounding influences on police detection of suspiciousness. *Journal of Criminal Justice, 34*(4), 435–442.

Kempf-Leonard, K., & Sample, L. (2000). Disparity based on sex: The interaction of formal and informal social controls. *Justice Quarterly, 17*(1), 89–128.

Kingsnorth, R., Lopez, J., Wentworth, J., & Cummings, D. (1998). Adult sexual assault: The role of racial/ethnic composition on prosecution and sentencing. *Journal of Criminal Justice, 26*(5), 359–371.

Kleinman, P. H., & Lukoff, I. F. (1981). Official crime data: Lag in recording time as a threat to validity. *Criminology, 20*(2), 169–184.

Kraska, P. (1992). The processing of drug arrestees: Questioning the assumption of an ambivalent reaction. *Journal of Criminal Justice, 20*(6), 517–525.

Krebs, C., Lattimore, P., Cowell, A., & Graham, P. (2010). Evaluating the juvenile breaking the cycle program's impact on recidivism. *Journal of Criminal Justice, 38*(2), 109–117.

Lauritsen, J., Heimer, K., & Lynch, J. (2009). Trends in the gender gap in violent offending: New evidence from the National Crime Victimization Survey. *Criminology, 47*(2), 361–400.

Lee, M., & Thomas, S. (2010). Civic community, population change, and violent crime in rural communities. *Journal of Research in Crime and Delinquency, 47*, 118–147.

Lilley, D., & Boba, R. (2009). Crime reduction outcomes associated with the state criminal alien assistance program. *Journal of Criminal Justice, 37*(3), 217–224.

Linnemann, T. (2013). Governing through meth: Local politics, drug control and the drift toward securitization. *Crime, Media, Culture, 9*, 39–61.

Lundman, R. (1980). *Police and policing: An introduction.* New York: Holt, Rinehart & Winston.

Maltz, M. (1999). *Bridging gaps in police crime data.* Washington, DC: Bureau of Justice Statistics.

Mann, C. R. (1987). Racism in the criminal justice system: Two sides of a controversy. *Criminal Justice Research Bulletin, 3*(5), 1–5.

Mastrofski, S., Reisig, M., & McCluskey, J. (2002). Police disrespect toward the public: An encounter-based analysis. *Criminology, 40*(3), 519–552.

McElrath, K., Dunham, R., & Cromwell, P. (1995). Validity of self-reported cocaine and opiate use among arrestees in five cities. *Journal of Criminal Justice, 23*(6), 531–540.

McNulty, T. (2001). Assessing the race–violence relationship at the macro level: The assumption of racial invariance and the problem of restricted distributions. *Criminology, 39*(2), 467–490.

Meehan, A., & Ponder, M. (2002). Race and place: The ecology of racial profiling African American motorists. *Justice Quarterly, 19*(3), 399–430.

Menard, S. (1987). Short-term trends in crime and delinquency: A comparison of UCR, NCVS and self-report data. *Justice Quarterly, 4*(3), 455–474.

Menard, S. (1991). Encouraging news for criminologists (in the year 2050)? A comment on O'Brien (1990). *Journal of Criminal Justice, 19*(6), 563–567.

Meyer, J., & Gray, T. (1997). Drunk drivers in the courts: Legal and extra-legal factors affecting pleas and sentences. *Journal of Criminal Justice, 25*(2), 155–164.

National Research Council (2008). *Surveying victims: Options for conducting the National Crime Victimization Survey.* Washington, DC: The National Academies Press.

Navares, D., Wolfgang, M., & Tracy, P. (1990). *Delinquency in Puerto Rico: The 1970 Birth Cohort Study.* New York: Greenwood Press.

Nelson, J. (1992). Hidden disparities in case processing: New York State, 1985–1986. *Journal of Criminal Justice, 20*(3), 181–200.

Nettler, G. (1984). *Explaining crime* (3rd ed.). New York: McGraw-Hill.

Nolan, J. (2004). Establishing the statistical relationship between population size and UCR crime rate: Its impact and implications. *Journal of Criminal Justice, 32*(6), 547–556.

O'Brien, R. (1985). *Crime and victimization data.* Beverly Hills, CA: Sage.

O'Brien, R. (1986). Rare events, sample size, and statistical problems in the analysis of NCS city surveys. *Journal of Criminal Justice, 14*(5), 441–448.

O'Brien, R. (1990). Comparing detrended UCR and NCS crime rates over time: 1973–1986. *Journal of Criminal Justice, 18*(3), 229–238.

O'Leary, V., & Duffee, D. (1971). Correctional policy: A classification of goals designed for change. *Crime & Delinquency, 18*(3), 379.

Packer, H. (1960). *The limits of the criminal sanction.* Englewood Cliffs, NJ: Prentice Hall.

Petersilia, J. (1983). *Racial disparities in the criminal justice system.* Santa Monica, CA: RAND.

Platt, S. (Ed.), (1999). *Respectfully quoted: A dictionary of quotations. Requested from the Congressional Research Service*. http://www.Bartleby.com/73, Retrieved 26.01.2005.

President's Commission on Law Enforcement and Administration of Justice (1967). *The challenge of crime in a free society*. Washington, DC: U.S. Government Printing Office.

Rand, M., Lynch, J., & Cantor, D. (1997). *Criminal victimization, 1973–95*. Washington, DC: Bureau of Justice Statistics.

Ratcliffe, J. (2008). *Intelligence-led policing*. Cullompton, Devon, UK: Willan.

Reaves, B. (1993). *Using NIBRS data to analyze violent crime*. Washington, DC: Bureau of Justice Statistics.

Rich, T. (1995). *The use of computerized mapping in crime control and prevention programs*. Washington, DC: National Institute of Justice.

Rich, T. (1996). *The Chicago Police Department's Information Collection for Automated Mapping (ICAM) program*. Washington, DC: National Institute of Justice.

Rosenfeld, R., & Decker, S. (1999). Are arrest statistics a valid measure of illicit drug use? The relationship between criminal justice, and public health indicators of cocaine, heroin, and marijuana use. *Justice Quarterly, 16*(3), 685–699.

Rosenmerkel, S., Durose, M., & Farole, D. (2009). *Felony sentences in state courts, 2006—Statistical tables*. Washington, DC: U.S. Department of Justice.

Salas, L., & Surette, R. (1984). The historical roots and development of criminological statistics. *Journal of Criminal Justice, 12*(5), 457–466.

Schaefer, J., Huebner, B., & Bynum, T. (2003). Citizen perceptions of police services: Race, neighborhood context, and community policing. *Police Quarterly, 6*(4), 440–468.

Schneider, A. L., & Sumi, D. (1981). Patterns of forgetting and telescoping: An analysis of LEAA survey victimization data. *Criminology, 23*(1), 41–50.

Schwartz, J., & Rookey, B. (2008). The narrowing gender gap in arrests: Assessing competing explanations using self-report, traffic fatality, and official data on drunk driving, 1980-2004. *Criminology, 46*(3), 637–671.

Schwartz, J., Steffensmeier, D., Zhong, J., & Ackerman, J. (2009). Trends in the gender gap in violence: Reevaluating NCVS and other evidence. *Criminology, 47*(2), 401–426.

Sherman, L., Gartin, P., & Buerger, M. (1989). Hot spots of predatory crime: Routine activities and the criminology of place. *Criminology, 27*(1), 27–55.

Spano, R. (2007). How does reactivity affect police behavior? Describing and quantifying the impact of reactivity as behavioral change in a large-scale observational study of police. *Journal of Criminal Justice, 35*(4), 453–465.

Substance Abuse and Mental Health Services Administration (2010). *Results of the 2008 National Survey on Drug Use and Health: National findings*. Rockville, MD: Author. Retrieved from: http://www.oas.samhsa.gov/p0000016.htm#2k5.

Substance Abuse and Mental Health Services Administration (2012). *Results of the 2011 National Survey on Drug Use and Health: National findings*. Rockville, MD: Substance Abuse and Mental Health Services Administration. Retrieved from: http://www.samhsa.gov/data/nsduh/2k11results/nsduhresults2011.pdf.

Swanson, C. R. (1981). Rural and agricultural crime. *Journal of Criminal Justice, 9*(1), 19–28.

Thornberry, T., & Krohn, M. (2000). The self-report method for measuring delinquency and crime. In D. Duffee (Ed.), *Criminal Justice 2000: Measurement and analysis of crime and justice: Vol. 4*. (pp. 33-84). Washington, DC: National Institute of Justice.

Tracy, P., Wolfgang, M., & Figlio, R. (1990). *Delinquency careers in two birth cohorts*. New York: Plenum Press.

Truman, J., & Planty, M. (2012). *Criminal victimization, 2011*. Washington, DC: U.S. Department of Justice.

U.S. Department of Justice (2004). *The nation's two crime measures*. Washington, DC: Author.

Vandecar-Burdin, T., & Payne, B. (2010). Risk factors for victimization of younger and older persons: Assessing differences in isolation, intra-individual characteristics, and health factors. *Journal of Criminal Justice, 38*(2), 109–117.

Velez, M. (2001). The role of public social control in urban neighborhoods: A multilevel analysis of victimization risk. *Criminology, 39*(4), 837–864.

Visher, C. A. (1983). Gender, police arrest decisions and notions of chivalry. *Criminology, 21*(1), 5–28.

Warren, P., Tomaskovic-Devey, D., Smith, W., Zingraff, M., & Mason, M. (2006). Driving while black: Bias processes and racial disparity in police stops. *Criminology, 44*(3), 709–738.

Weisburd, D., Telep, C., Hinkle, J., & Eck, J. (2010). Is problem-oriented policing effective in reducing crime and disorder? Findings from a Campbell systematic review. *Criminology and Public Policy, 9*(1), 139–172.

Weisheit, R., & Wells, L. (1999). The future of crime in rural America. *Journal of Crime and Justice, 22*(1), 1–26.

Weitzer, R. (1996). Racial discrimination in the criminal justice system: Findings and problems in the literature. *Journal of Criminal Justice, 24*(4), 309–322.

Wilbanks, W. (1987). Racism in the criminal justice system: Two sides of a controversy. *Criminal Justice Research Bulletin, 3*(5), 1–5.

Williams, J., & Gold, M. (1972). From delinquent behavior to official delinquency. *Social Problems, 20*, 209–228.

Wilson, J., & Abrahamse, A. (1992). Does crime pay? *Justice Quarterly, 9*(3), 359–377.

Wolfgang, M. E., Figlio, R. M., & Sellin, T. (1978). *Delinquency in a birth cohort*. Chicago: University of Chicago Press.

Worrall, J., Hiromoto, S., Merritt, N., Du, D., Jacobson, J., & Iguchi, M. (2009). Crime trends and the effect of mandated drug treatment: Evidence from California's Substance Abuse and Crime Prevention Act. *Journal of Criminal Justice, 37*(2), 109–113.

Worrall, J., & Kovandzic, T. (2008). Is policing for profit? Answers from asset forfeiture. *Criminology & Public policy, 7*(2), 219–244.

Zatz, M. (1987). The changing forms of racial/ethnic biases in sentencing. *Journal of Research in Crime and Delinquency, 24*(1), 69–92.

Zeisel, H. (1982). *The limits of law enforcement*. Chicago: University of Chicago Press.

CHAPTER 5
Police and Policing

The most visible image of the formal control applied by the criminal justice system comes in the form of the various police agencies across the United States. A variety of federal, state, municipal, special jurisdiction (housing authority, transit authority, etc.), and private agencies provide law enforcement services. The Bureau of Justice Statistics identified roughly 16,000 local and state police agencies. Combined with federal law enforcement, these agencies combine to employ approximately 885,000 sworn law enforcement officers across the country (Burch, 2012; Reaves, 2011).

Approximately 73% of the law enforcement agencies are relatively small, employing 24 or fewer officers (see Figure 5.1). The largest police agencies, however, employ the most officers, meaning that although the typical police organization is small, the typical police officer works in a large agency. Regardless of agency size, most sworn police personnel are assigned to patrol and similar field operations duties. Patrol officers do the bulk of police work in the United States, and the work of patrol officers is varied.

Police agencies provide a variety of services to the communities they serve, ranging from travelers' aid through ambulance service. Yet, we continue to think of them as law enforcement. Indeed, enforcing criminal laws is, at most, a part-time activity for most police departments and police officers. The police are what Wilson (1968) called the "agency of last resort." Although we focus here on the law-enforcing duties of police agencies because of our interest in criminal justice, it is also important to remember that other demands are placed on police.

Because police are available 24 hours each day, are mobile, and carry authority, we call on them to resolve many issues and problems (Goldstein, 1990). Most of these problems are not, strictly speaking, law enforcement oriented in nature (Kennedy, 1983). The principal task of a police agency is best described as "order maintenance." The peacekeeping function of police is far more important than the law enforcement function. Law enforcement is a small part of order maintenance (Eck & Spelman, 1987).

The criminal law is only one of many tools available to police officers and police agencies in their efforts to keep peace in our communities. The police

Important Terms

community-
  oriented policing
constable
cynicism
intelligence-led
  policing
legalistic style
order
  maintenance
paramilitary
  structure
police
  specialization
proactive
quality-of-life
  policing
reactive
service style
shire reeve
watchman style

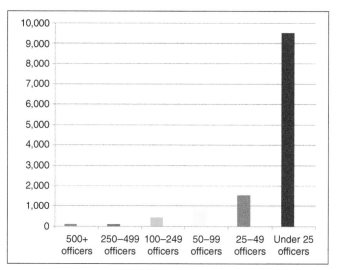

FIGURE 5.1
Distribution of police departments, by size of department.

are responsible for dealing with stray children and dogs, lost travelers, injured persons, stranded motorists, traffic accidents, parades, domestic disputes, and crime. It seems that almost any disruptive event can be resolved by "calling the cops" (Bittner, 1970). In many cases, people have reported fires to the police first, rather than to the fire department. The police are often called to deal with abandoned cars, but the reason they are called is not because the car may have been involved in a crime. People call the police because the police are the first agency that comes to mind.

People also call the police because they have come to know that the police can (and probably will) do something about the problem. Bittner (1970) observed that the police have a monopoly on the legitimate use of coercive force. The ability to use force and to make people behave in certain ways defines the police role in society. The police are called to deal with a variety of problems that may require force (Klockars, 1985). For example, the police may be called to intervene with a mentally disturbed person because, if all else fails, they can arrest and remove the individual (Lurigio & Swartz, 2000). This action may not cure the mental disorder, but it will solve the immediate problem.

Given the scope of police responsibilities (some assigned, some assumed, and some simply evolved), it is clear that law enforcement is only a small part of police duties. Studies of police tasks have revealed that actual crimes consume a small portion of police resources and comprise a small percentage of police tasks (Liederbach & Frank, 2006; Webster, 1970; Wilson, 1968). Depending on the definitions used by researchers, the majority of police time is devoted to general patrol, service calls, and paperwork (Mastrofski, Parks, Reiss, & Worden, 1999a; Mastrofski, Parks, Reiss, & Worden, 1999b; Parks, Mastrofski, DeJone,

& Gray, 1999). Nonetheless, the public, the media, and the police themselves continue to define policing principally as crime fighting (Manning, 1978). This conception of the police as "crime fighters" developed historically as a response to difficulties encountered in the police role.

THE DEVELOPMENT OF AMERICAN POLICING

The idea of police controlling the behavior of individuals is a relatively recent addition to society. The American colonists did not employ police, and no police forces were created in the United States until the 1840s. In colonial times, law enforcement was the duty of every citizen, and no specialized occupational group had responsibility to ensure public order. As with so much of our justice system, we can trace the origins of public police to our English tradition.

Law Enforcement in England

Most of England had no specialized police force or public office charged with maintaining public order until after the Norman Conquest in 1066 (Critchley, 1972; Stewart-Brown, 1936). At that time, the Normans, having gained control over England and occupying a hostile population, created a centralized governmental structure based on feudalism. High-ranking officers and nobles of William the Conqueror's army received control of large parcels of England. In return, these nobles were to provide a percentage of the production from these lands to the king as taxes, and to supply soldiers in time of war. They also were required to obey the commands of the king and to ensure the "king's peace" in their lands.

To accomplish this administrative task, these nobles further subdivided their lands to lesser officers and nobles, and required them to remit a portion of their profits and to supply a number of soldiers when necessary. The subdivision continued, with each successive rank being required to pay a larger portion of taxes but supply a smaller number of soldiers. The increased taxes represented the need to meet the demands of the king and the higher nobility for income. The lower number of soldiers reflected the increased number of officers who were granted lands. If a duke promised to provide 10,000 soldiers and 5% of profits to the king, he could do it by dividing the land among 10 barons. Each baron might be required to provide 1,000 soldiers (10,000 total) and 8% of profits (5% for the king; 3% for the duke). Feudalism provided a structure for government in medieval times.

Essentially rural and agrarian, England was divided into 10 family units called tythings. Each tything was responsible for its own tax collection and order maintenance. With the advent of Norman control, new units of 100 families, called shires, were created. Being an occupied country, maintenance of the Norman king's law was problematic, and tax collection was difficult. The office of shire reeve emerged.

The **shire reeve** was responsible for the collection of taxes and the mainte-nance of the king's peace within the shire, which was usually an area similar to a county or parish in the United States today. The reeve was elected from a list of candidates approved by the lord of the manor. Over time, the shire reeve became known as the sheriff. We can see the resistance of the English to this new structure in the tales of Robin Hood, whose nemesis was the Sheriff of Nottingham.

Each manor also operated a manorial court. To assist in the day-to-day opera-tion of the court functions, they created the office of constable. The lord of the manor selected the **constable** from among qualified property holders. The con-stable performed the clerical duties of the court and housed prisoners awaiting trial. Over time, these functions expanded to include general peacekeeping.

As villages and towns developed, this rural order-maintenance apparatus proved to be inadequate to the task of law enforcement in congested areas. Traditionally, every citizen was responsible for order maintenance. Drawing on this tradition, town constables were empowered to draft citizens for a watch system. In this system, citizens were required to provide unpaid watch service (typically at night) to patrol for fires and breaches of the peace. As towns grew larger and cities developed, it became increasingly difficult to find either adequate watchmen or persons willing to take the role of constable.

By the early 1800s, English towns and cities were crowded and unruly. The nobility and wealthy citizens traveled with hired guards (footmen) and avoided the more dangerous sections of town. Several experiments with paid watches, "private" law enforcement, and rejuvenated constabulary offices had all failed to provide adequately for order maintenance. One of the most famous of these experiments was the organization of the Bow Street Runners by Henry Fielding. Also known as "thief-takers," this group of men was orga-nized to provide police protection in the Bow Street area of London. There was clearly a need to create a specialized body charged with maintaining the peace. See Figure 5.2.

During the 1820s, Sir Robert Peel, British home secretary, proposed the cre-ation of a police force for England (see Figure 5.3). This force would com-prise paid, uniformed, armed, and disciplined officers whose job would be the enforcement of the law, the maintenance of order, and the prevention of crime. Crime prevention was expected to result from the presence of police on the streets. Patrolling police officers would act to deter criminal offend-ers. Parliament, fearing the effects of such an armed force on the "rights of Englishmen," resisted Peel's idea. In democratic societies, and especially in the Anglo-American tradition, there has always been a tension or conflict between liberty and civility (Lundman, 1980). Our need for order (civil-ity) is in direct conflict with our desire for personal freedom (liberty). The English Parliament had to be convinced that the new police would not unduly threaten English liberty. Peel revised his proposal and, in 1829, Parliament

FIGURE 5.2
Great Scotland Yard. Scotland Yard is internationally famous as a symbol of policing. The name of the headquarters is derived from its original location on Great Scotland Yard, the buildings used to accommodate Scottish kings when they visited English royalty.

FIGURE 5.3
A member of the professional police force organized by Sir Robert Peel. Initially referred to as "Peelers," they later came to be known as "Bobbies."
Metropolitan Police, New Scotland Yard, London

agreed to "experiment" with a Metropolitan Police Force in London. This force would be unarmed, but in every other respect, it would mirror Peel's original plan. If it worked in London, the idea might be expanded. The Metropolitan Police Force of London, created in 1829, was the first modern police force.

The Colonial and Early American Experience

As in many other areas of social life, the American colonists relied on their traditions and experiences from England in developing a social control system. Colonial villages and towns normally had the offices of constable and/or sheriff. The duties of each were similar to those of its English counterpart (Jones & Johnstone, 2012). As towns and cities grew, the Americans experimented with watch systems. In time, it became clear that these less formal systems for order maintenance were inadequate.

Unlike England, however, there was no strong central government in America, and weapons and violence were more commonplace in the New World. Although the American police followed the same general pattern of development, these differences resulted in a modification of the English police structure to suit the situation in America. If anything, Americans were more strongly concerned with liberty, and distrust of centralized governmental power meant that any police would be limited.

By the 1840s, waves of immigrants began arriving on the shores of America, and industrialization was beginning. The population of American cities swelled, and the cities became unruly and dangerous places. The upper and middle classes viewed the urban poor, especially immigrants, as prerevolutionary. It became common to speak of the immigrant poor in America's congested cities as the "dangerous classes."

To control these "dangerous" people, and to bring order and stability to the cities, Americans began to consider the creation of police forces. On many occasions, the militia or the army was used to quell riots or to break strikes (and would still be used for these purposes in the future), but these were extraordinary circumstances. Many people believed a more permanent solution to the problems of day-to-day disorder was required. The importance of ethnic and cultural conflict to the emergence and development of policing in America cannot be overstated (Barlow & Barlow, 2000).

Knowing about the English experiments and developments, many reformers began to advocate the creation of police forces for the cities. In 1845, New York City created a police force modeled after the Metropolitan Police Force of London, but with several significant differences (Jones & Johnstone, 2012:233–236). The mayor appointed police officers from among candidates recommended by political ward leaders. A Board of Police Commissioners administered the police force. Each officer was to be a resident of the ward in which he would work. Officers objected to wearing uniforms and wanted to be armed.

The New York City Police were created and funded locally. This new American police department had a weak central administration, a municipal organization, and direct political involvement. Over the years, the issues of uniforms and arms were resolved, so that municipal police were both armed and uniformed. Each city created its own police force and organizational structure. In the next 10 years, the New York City Police were followed by the creation of police in most major American cities (see Box 5.1). Monkonnen (1981) noted that local police in America were first modeled on the police of London, but that American police agencies quickly grew independent of this original model. It is important to note that the police in America developed in specific cities and towns, with no effort to create a national police force. This ensured that the American police would be under local control and direction.

The American Police

Similar to New York's, most early police departments in America were not centrally organized and did not have strong leadership. This was in response to a fear of the effect of police on the exercise of rights by individuals (similar to the English Parliament's fears regarding the Metropolitan Police). It was common to employ a "police commission" to govern the department so that no single individual could gain too much power. With the growth of political machines in the cities, however, this weak administrative structure left city police forces open to manipulation and corruption.

BOX 5.1 MILESTONES IN AMERICAN LAW ENFORCEMENT

1748	Bow Street Runners organized by Henry Fielding
1829	Metropolitan police force created in London, England
1838	Boston police created with nine officers
1844	New York City police created with 800 officers
1852	Cincinnati and New Orleans police created
1854	Philadelphia and Boston police establish formal patrol
1855	Chicago police created
1857	Baltimore police created
1893	Organization of the National Chiefs of Police Union
1905	August Vollmer elected marshal of Berkeley, California
1908	Bureau of Investigation (later FBI) created; Berkeley Police School started
1924	J. Edgar Hoover named director of FBI
1930	*Uniform Crime Reports* first published
1931	Police science program started at San Jose State University
1935	FBI National Police Academy opened
1960	O. W. Wilson named Chicago police commissioner
1974	Kansas City preventive patrol experiment initiated
1982	Broken windows theory appears.
1994	Violent Crime Control and Law Enforcement Act passed (created the Office of Community Policing Services)
2001	Terrorists attack the World Trade Center and Pentagon on September 11

Initially, the principal duty of the police was to maintain order. The success of a police officer was most easily established by the absence of disorder on the patrol beat. The fact that officers were recruited from the neighborhoods they were to patrol and were sometimes unwilling to arrest their friends and acquaintances meant that officers tolerated much "deviance," which the upper and middle classes found frightening. Drinking of alcohol, for example, was viewed with suspicion by many city leaders, yet tolerated (even shared) by many officers. The failure of the police to remain free of political influence and corruption, coupled with neighborhood enforcement styles, led to an early call to reform the police.

In the latter part of the nineteenth century, a reform effort to enhance police accountability and to professionalize the police emerged (Fogelson, 1977; Travis & Langworthy, 2008; Walker, 1977). Vollmer, perhaps the foremost proponent of police professionalism, led the reform. Vollmer sought higher personnel standards and stronger police leadership. The push for police professionalism continued well into the twentieth century and is still felt (Vogel & Adams, 1983). The police were given strong central administration and a clear crime control mandate. The focus on law enforcement was supposed to circumvent the difficulties that accompanied the more general role of maintaining order (Johnson, 1981). According to many policing historians, the movement to professionalize the police was an effort by middle-class, native-born citizens to gain control over the police and to restrain the growing immigrant population (Toch, 1997).

With the crime control mandate came an equally important definition of the police as serving a crime prevention function. The police were not only expected to detect and apprehend offenders, but police presence on the streets of a city was expected to deter others from committing crimes. From this came the tradition of preventive patrol. The uniformed officer on patrol would not only be better able to detect crime, but the patrol presence would prevent crime as well. Although the technology may have changed from foot patrol to motorized patrol (and perhaps back again), the idea is essentially the same.

The tradition of police as peacekeepers (order maintenance), however, has also remained (Kappeler, 1996). Inasmuch as the definition of the police became (and remains) one of a crime control force, the functions of a modern police department are far broader. The police are the most visible representatives of government in a community, and they represent the legitimate authority of the law. Because they are always (theoretically) present and available, the police have become ombudsmen for all social and legal problems.

THE FUNCTIONS OF POLICE

The role of the police has been broadly classified into three categories. Wilson (1968) suggested that the police are responsible for law enforcement, order maintenance, and service. Further, he argued that, of the three, order maintenance is at once both the most important and the most troublesome. Order maintenance is the main purpose of police. If they do nothing else, the police must ensure that the citizens can go about their daily business safely and efficiently.

Order maintenance activities include settling disputes, dispersing crowds, keeping sidewalks and streets clear and traffic flowing smoothly, and other important activities. These are troublesome responsibilities because the officer often must operate in the "gray areas" of the law and must choose whether to intervene and, if so, how and with whom (Eck & Spelman, 1987).

The service functions of police have evolved over time out of necessity. Citizens ask police to provide a variety of services, from giving directions to travelers to finding missing children. Partly because of a potential link to criminal behavior, police also investigate traffic accidents, provide first aid to victims, and, often, transport the injured to medical facilities. Whatever the reasons, modern police provide a wide variety of services that do not strictly conform to the role of crime control (Bittner, 1970; Das, 1987; Rossler & Terrill, 2012; Trojanowicz, Kappeler, Gaines, & Bucqueroux, 1998).

Law enforcement activities are those that relate directly to the detection and apprehension of criminal offenders. Responding to alarms and citizen complaints of crime, investigating suspicious persons and circumstances, and arresting suspected offenders are all law enforcement activities. Our focus is on the crime control function of police, although it does not comprise the bulk of police tasks. Before turning our attention to the crime control activities of the police, however, we must more fully explore the diverse obligations of contemporary police.

The Police as a Human Services Agency

To understand the role of the police, it is helpful to describe what it is that the police do. Ideally, perhaps, it would be possible to determine what it is that police are supposed to do and, from that, develop a definition of the police role. The problem is that it is not clear what it is that we want the police to do. Historically, the police acquired responsibilities because no other agency existed to perform particular tasks. Today, a variety of social, political, legal, and administrative factors shape the police role.

Whatever it is that the police do, research shows that most of what they do is not criminal law enforcement. Figure 5.4 displays the results of several analyses of police work. Although the exact percentages for each category differ, in no case did the police devote the majority of resources on enforcing the criminal laws. Rather, administrative tasks and service provision appear to be important components of the police task, and thus, the police role. Based on observations of police officers in Indianapolis, Indiana, Mastrofski et al. (1999a) concluded that police spent about one-quarter of their time interacting with citizens, and only one-half of that (less than 13% of total time) involved with potentially criminal matters. Christine Famega (2004) reviewed studies of police officer activity and concluded that only about one-quarter of a patrol officer's time is spent responding to calls for service or dispatches.

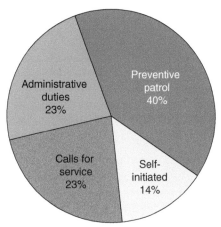

FIGURE 5.4
Workload analysis of police patrol officers' time.
Source: Gay, Schell, and Schack (1977)

Table 5.1	Public Safety Functions of Local Police: Percent of Departments
Search and rescue	21
Emergency medical	26
Civil defense	19
Animal control	65
Fire services	10
Underwater recovery	4
Bomb disposal	3

Source: Hickman and Reaves (2006)

If you think of your own interactions with the police over the course of your lifetime, how often have you dealt with police officers in nonlaw-enforcement situations? The investigation of traffic accidents and crowd control at parades, demonstrations, sporting events, and the like are important, nonlaw-enforcement services provided by the police. Table 5.1 shows that many local police departments have primary responsibility for safety functions such as search and rescue, animal control, and civil defense. Other police departments that do not have primary responsibility for these functions still must often respond to calls about such safety problems.

Despite the fact that most police activities do not involve enforcing criminal laws, the view of the police as crime fighters persists. The entertainment media, politicians, and the police themselves reinforce this view of the police (Goldstein, 1978; Graber, 1979; Van Maanen, 1978). One reason for the continuation of such a narrow and distorted image of the police is the historical rationale behind giving priority to the crime control mandate. There is agreement that the police ought to enforce the criminal laws. In comparison to all other police tasks, crime control is the least controversial. Order maintenance and service activities present the greatest role definition problems for police in the United States.

Kennedy (1983) argued that the police qualify as a human services agency. After reviewing the literature on human services, Kennedy concluded that five characteristics identify human services agencies: (1) systemic integration of services, (2) comprehensiveness and accessibility, (3) client troubles defined as problems in living, (4) generic helping activities, and (5) service provider accountability. In an overview of police activities, Kennedy established that each of these factors applies to contemporary police work, although the public (and often the police themselves) object to the use of "human services" as a description.

The police serve as a referral center for people in trouble, linking victims, the ill, and others in need of service with available community resources (e.g., hospitals, mental health clinics, travelers' aid societies). The police are available all day and every day throughout their jurisdiction. Whether crime, injury, illness, or disputes cause the police to intervene, police problems generally represent problems in living. The sheer scope and variety of situations for which people call the police are evidence of their generic helping activities. Finally, the police, like all governmental agencies, are ultimately responsible to the public (their clients) and the courts.

Historically, as a human services agency, the most important role of the police was that of first aid. Whether, the problem is a lost child, domestic disturbance, landlord/tenant dispute, public intoxication, or traffic accident, the police are normally first on the scene. In this role, the police provide first aid by taking charge of the situation, providing immediate help and counseling, and giving referrals for further care (Fritsch, Caeti, Tobolowsky, & Taylor, 2004). It is common, especially in larger police departments, to give officers a directory of social service agencies to which the officers can refer citizens. The fact that the police do not always provide complete human services to resolve the living problems of those with whom they come into contact does not negate the important role of the police in the first stages of human service (Das, 1987).

The Police as a Crime Control Agency

The police control crime in one of two basic ways: reactively or proactively (Black, 1972). These types of policing represent ideal types. A **reactive** police department would only respond (or react) to crime. A **proactive** police department would use its own initiative in aggressively seeking out crimes and criminals. The strictest type of reactive police department would remain at the police station, watching television, cleaning cruisers, and the like, until a complaint of a crime was received or an alarm sounded, when the officers would rush to their cruisers and speed to the scene of the crime. Having investigated or made an arrest, the officers then would return to the station to await their next call.

In contrast, a fully proactive police department would resemble the vice squad. All officers would be in the field seeking out crime. Undercover officers would perform much police work because marked cars and uniforms would forewarn offenders. Traffic officers would establish speed traps rather than patrol stretches of highway. Decoy teams and sting operations would be prevalent.

In reality, of course, one does not find either ideal type. Rather, it is possible to classify police departments as being more or less proactive or reactive. The democratic nature of our society and the municipal organization of the majority of our police forces make police in the United States more reactive than proactive (Travis & Langworthy, 2008). As a society, we prefer to set policing priorities through our complaints and calls. The alternative is for the police to set priorities through deciding how and when to combat crime. Proactive police seeking to prevent crime are required to act on their own initiative to avoid citizen complaints about crime. In a study of proactive police efforts in two cities, Sun (2003) concluded that officers in the study were less proactive than had been expected, engaging in relatively few problem-focused or aggressive preventive patrol activities.

The Police as a Peacekeeping Agency

In television and motion picture Westerns, the marshal has responsibility for keeping the peace. At base, peacekeeping means the maintenance of order. The police control disruptions such as fights and riots. They maintain traffic flow and ensure a general level of satisfaction with living in the community. Police protect and enhance orderly social interactions. Wilson (1968:16) argued that order maintenance is at the core of the police task. He wrote

> The patrolman's role is defined more by his responsibility for maintaining order than by his responsibility for enforcing the law. By "order" is meant the absence of disorder, and by disorder is meant behavior that either disturbs or threatens to disturb the public peace or that involves face-to-face conflict among two or more persons. Disorder, in short, involves a dispute over what is "right" or "seemly" conduct or over who is to blame for conduct that is agreed to be wrong or unseemly.

As Wilson's explanation implies, disorder is often noncriminal. Order-maintenance problems usually involve questions of propriety rather than questions of legality. Youths loitering on a street corner, a neighbor who plays her stereo too loudly, homeless persons congregating in a park, and other noncriminal events are frequently the basis for order-maintenance calls to the police. In these situations, people expect the responding officer to resolve the conflict and thereby restore order.

Most order-maintenance problems fall into a gray area of the law where frequently the officer has no clear legal authority to act. As a matter of practicality, the officer is compelled to do something. Order maintenance is the most common activity of police officers. These tasks often expose officers to physical danger and involve the exercise of discretion by the officer. Order maintenance is the least "consensual" part of the police task (Wilson, 1968). For these reasons, order maintenance is perhaps the most difficult aspect of policing. Jiao (1998) suggested that different communities hold different expectations of their police. He urges police to develop policies and practices based, in large part, on the expectations of the community. Other research has indicated that some police decisions reflect community characteristics. Jackson and Wade (2005) observed that the police are more proactive in their enforcement efforts in neighborhoods characterized by high rates of crime than in low-crime areas. It seems the likelihood of criminal activity influences the decisions of officers to intervene with citizens.

Although there may be a consensus that robbery is intolerable, that police should arrest robbers, that accident victims deserve help, and that the police should help them, there often is no such consensus for order-maintenance questions. In the case of the neighbor with the loud stereo, it is clear that dissension or disagreement exists; one party believes that the stereo is too loud and the other thinks that it is set at an acceptable level. Into this conflict steps the officer. Regardless of the outcome, at least one (if not all) of the parties will be dissatisfied.

Difficult as it is, order maintenance is a critical component of policing. Left unattended, minor disputes can escalate into criminal acts (such as assault or vandalism if the complaining neighbor takes the matter of the loud stereo into his or her own hands). Further, the police and the entire justice system must serve the major function of social control. We should be able to go about our daily lives in a relatively smooth and predictable fashion. More than any other police function, order maintenance ensures the routine functioning of society.

Despite all this, Moore, Trojanowicz, and Kelling (1988:1) observed that crime control is the core mission of the police in the United States. The police can work to control crime by enforcement of laws and by prevention. Police efforts to maintain order and provide services often have the effect of preventing crime. There is growing evidence that citizens appreciate and support police efforts at crime control, even when those efforts involve tactics such as aggressive traffic enforcement (Chermak, McGarrell, & Weiss, 2001; Hawdon, Ryan, & Griffin, 2003). In contrast, efforts to engage citizens in community development and order-maintenance activities are not associated with improved citizen perceptions of the police. Further, as we will discuss in more detail later, the police can (and do) use criminal law to achieve order maintenance and service functions.

COMMUNITY POLICING: A REVISED ROLE FOR THE POLICE

Throughout the past 30 years, the role of the police has been redefined as that of crime control through order maintenance. Wilson and Kelling (1982) published an article in which they argued that signs of neighborhood decay and disorder led to increased crime. Coined the broken windows theory, Wilson and Kelling's contention was that signs of disorder, including broken windows, graffiti, and litter, indicate that no one is in charge of a neighborhood. In these "chaotic" neighborhoods, criminals feel safe from apprehension because no one appears to be responsible for maintaining order. Thus, crime is higher in disorganized neighborhoods.

The logic of the argument supports the idea that if we are to prevent and control crime, we must strengthen and improve neighborhoods. Because disorder is linked to crime, preventing disorder through strengthening neighborhoods will ultimately prevent crime. With other developments, including the suggestion by Goldstein (1990) that police should view crime as a symptom of larger problems that they should seek to solve, the broken windows theory led to a revised view of the police role. Worrall (2006) reported enforcement against minor offenses does seem to be associated with reductions in more serious crimes. The focus on minor crimes as a means of preventing serious crime also is called **quality-of-life policing** because police efforts are focused on day-to-day issues such as loitering, littering, loud noises, and the like. This type of policing has been shown to be the most effective in neighborhoods with lower levels of informal social control by residents (Kane & Cronin, 2013). Improving the quality of life in these neighborhoods through the formal actions of police can act as a supplement for the lower informal social controls and, ultimately, lead to less serious crime.

Whereas quality-of-life policing primarily views crime reduction as a police-initiated solution, another policing trend seeks to actively engage the public, ultimately leading to more effective informal social controls. **Community-oriented policing** is an approach to policing that relies on community definitions of police functions and a partnership between the police and the community in the production of public safety. As Fielding (2005b) described, community policing is a "style of policing in which the police are close to the public, know their concerns from regular everyday contacts, and act on them in accord with the community's wishes" (p. 460). Community-oriented policing, however, is still elusive of definition. Many agencies report that they practice community-oriented policing, but each agency seems to describe something different with this term. Still, community-oriented policing involves an expansion of the police role from reactive crime fighters to proactive problem solvers. In partnership with the community, the police identify community problems that contribute to crime and seek solutions designed to alleviate those problems. Community policing is now a topic of basic police training in most police academies in the United States (Reaves, 2009). See Table 5.2 for some statistics on community policing activities.

The rapid acceptance of this new role definition of policing has led some commentators to suggest that community-oriented policing is the new "orthodoxy," or commonly accepted purpose for the police. The police, under community-oriented philosophies, are supposed to be more closely tied to the communities

Table 5.2	Percent of Local Police Departments Engaging in Community Policing Activities	
	2003 (%)	2007 (%)
Community-oriented police officers	58	47
Partnerships	60	38
Citizen feedback	37	15
Citizen police academy	17	15
Formal agency plan	14	16

Source: Hickman and Reaves (2006), Reaves (2010)

they police, more accessible to the public, and less bureaucratic. The range of issues that are now defined as legitimate police problems is enormous, including street lighting, sanitation removal, recreational and health programming, housing, and almost every other public problem (Fielding, 2005a).

In practice, community-oriented policing has supported decentralized organization in police agencies, alternative patrol strategies and resource allocation, and increased police involvement in civic issues. In theory, the police should be involved in this wide range of problems because they are broadly responsible for public order, and because they are perhaps best organized (jurisdiction-wide, 24-hour availability) to learn about problems, develop solutions, and monitor outcomes. In most places adopting formal community-oriented policing programs, departments assign at least one neighborhood officer to each neighborhood. Permanent assignment to a specific beat is expected to help the officers develop a better understanding of the area and its residents, and to take greater responsibility for public safety and problem solving in the beat. See Figure 5.5.

Kane (2000) examined the effect of permanent assignments on how officers worked in their beats. He concluded that within a few weeks, officers permanently assigned to an area "took ownership" of the beat and began to engage in more proactive, problem-solving efforts. Residents quickly come to appreciate having their own officer. Evidence suggests that community-oriented policing improves citizens' satisfaction with local government and reduces fear of crime.

Evaluations of community policing to date have been largely positive. For example, Connell, Miggans, and McGloin (2008) conducted an 8-year evaluation and found significant and permanent reductions in both property and violent crime. However, the implementation of community policing has not been easy in all departments. Chappell (2009) identified three primary obstacles to the implementation of community policing: (1) lack of resources, (2) time constraints, and (3) cultural resistance from within the police department. Likewise, Liederbach, Fritsch, Carter, and Bannister (2007) found that whereas citizens valued the community policing in their neighborhoods, many officers still resisted the movement. Smaller police departments seem to have a particularly difficult transition to community policing, as the low turnover rates and infrequent hiring

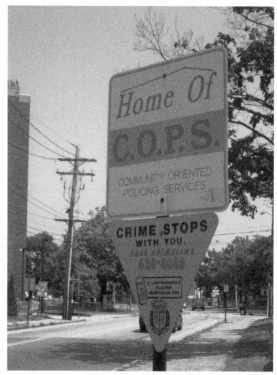

FIGURE 5.5
The Manchester, New Hampshire, Police Department touts its commitment to community-oriented policing (C.O.P.S.) with signs posted around the city.
Ellen S. Boyne

of new officers creates an environment that tends to value traditional techniques over more radical changes (Morabito, 2010). The central question for community policing remains largely unanswered (Duffee, Fluellen, & Renauer, 1999). If successful, community policing will support the development of nonpolice social controls in communities so that crime and disorder are prevented (Buerger & Mazerolle, 1998; Skogan, 2008) and communities are strengthened.

COUNTERTERRORISM AND HOMELAND SECURITY

In the aftermath of the terrorist attacks of September 11, 2001, there has been some concern that the increased expectations in terms of security would overshadow the emphasis on community policing. In fact, the use of community policing did decline in the years after the terrorist attacks (see Box 5.2). However, recent research shows that many police agencies view community policing and homeland security as complementary strategies (Chappell & Gibson, 2009; Roberts, Roberts, & Liedka, 2012). Community policing

BOX 5.2 COMMUNITY-ORIENTED POLICING

Programmatic elements

- Foot patrol
- Bicycle patrol
- Mounted (horse) patrol
- Neighborhood ministations
- Citizen police academies
- Neighborhood Watch
- School resource officers
- D.A.R.E. programs
- Citizen ride-along programs
- Neighborhood police officers
- Prioritizing calls for service
- Geographic mapping

Although community-oriented policing is often discussed as a fundamental philosophical shift in the way police agencies do business, departments reporting the existence of community policing initiatives often point to the implementation of special programs such as these as evidence that they are "doing community policing."

Source: Hickman and Reaves (2006:19, 21)

can improve community relations, which in turn can improve security. Even so, community policing and terrorism preparedness do at least compete for resources (Lee, 2010).

Several federal and state initiatives involve police in counterterrorism activities. The roles of police and law enforcement agencies in counterterrorism differ by size and type of agency. Many federal law enforcement agencies now operate within the Department of Homeland Security. Some local police departments, especially the largest ones, have counterterrorism units or include counterterrorism efforts within expanding intelligence units. Many observers argue that the most important role of local police in counterterrorism efforts is as producers and consumers of intelligence (O'Connell, 2008). See Figure 5.6.

Perhaps the biggest change in policing since 9/11 has been the growth of **intelligence-led policing**—the idea of basing police activity on criminal intelligence. Great effort has been directed to increase intelligence gathering and information sharing among police departments at various levels. Much of this effort has been directed toward the increased use of FBI-sponsored Joint Terrorism Task Forces (JTTFs), which allow state and local police agencies to collaborate with federal agencies. Approximately one-third of local law enforcement agencies collaborate with these task forces (Riley, Treverton, Wilson, & Davis, 2005). The creation of state-level fusion centers has perhaps

FIGURE 5.6
Police at the Los Angeles crime analysis center assist with investigations, suspect information, and geographic profiling by sifting through data such as 911 calls, the location of GPS-monitored parolees, and up-to-the-minute developments at crime scenes.

been a more significant development. These centers serve as a clearinghouse of information for the Department of Homeland Security and provide opportunities for agencies at all levels to share information about terrorist or other criminal threats (Chermak, Carter, Carter, McGarrell, & Drew, 2013).

The role of police agencies in counterterrorism preparedness largely depends on the size of the agency. Schafer, Burruss, and Giblineagues (2009) reported on a study of small municipal police agencies in Illinois. They found that smaller agencies had done relatively little in response to concerns about terrorism. Agencies located close to Chicago or other large cities and larger police departments had done more preparation. Those police chiefs who had done more preparation naturally felt more prepared to respond to acts of terror. Finally, those agencies that perceived a terrorist threat were more likely to prepare to respond.

William Pelfrey (2007) reported a case study of early responses in South Carolina. His research indicated, again, that most local police agencies had done relatively little specifically to prepare for a terrorist attack. Pelfrey found that factors such as the size of the police agency, its technological capacity, and whether it had a SWAT team predicted its level of preparation. He noted that perhaps not every police agency needed to prepare to combat terrorism.

The small size and limited jurisdiction of most local police departments militate against their having a major role in counterterrorism. It is not clear what we can reasonably expect of the local police concerning terrorism. Reaves (2009) reported that more than 90% of law enforcement training academies provided some basic training on terrorism to new police recruits. Although there is widespread concern about homeland security in the United States, it has never been a core part of the local police role. The structure of American police reflects their predominantly local focus.

THE STRUCTURE OF AMERICAN POLICING

The structure and organization of law enforcement agencies in the United States show the influences of historical development and the conflicting tasks expected of them. Unlike the police agencies of other countries, most American police agencies exist at a local level. This fragmentation of police service supports the value we place on federalism and local autonomy. Americans do not want national police, and we insist on maintaining a civilian police force that is distinct from the military (Kraska, 1994; Moore, 1987).

The focus of police organization and administration is to standardize the use of civil force (Alpert & Dunham, 1988). The police must weigh the mandate to control behavior against the requirement that they respect individual rights. This double responsibility places a premium on controlling and directing the actions of individual police officers.

Organizational options were limited when police departments came into being in the mid-1800s. The only organizational model available that allowed control of large groups of personnel was the military model. For this reason above any other, the police often adopted a **paramilitary structure** with ranks and a chain of command. The trappings of a military organization are still a part of American policing in most places (King, 2003).

In the military model, information flows up the chain of command from the street officers to the police administrator. Orders and commands flow down the chain to the street officers. In theory, the police administrator controls the actions of the officers on the street. Organizationally, this structure enables the police to meet their conflicting functions in a routine manner.

In practice, the structure of policing is different from the military model. Wilson (1968) noted that, unlike other organizations, street officers have more discretion than administrators do. The reality of police work is that officers on the street must react to a variety of situations. It is not practical for police officers to report every call and await instructions from their superiors.

The fear of a strong, centralized police force was one cause of decentralization. The variety of calls for service received by the police further supported allowing individual initiative among officers. Most police departments did not closely supervise street officers (Kelling, 1988). Rather, patrol officers were generalists expected to deal appropriately with the majority of calls for assistance without guidance from higher ranks.

As policing entered the twentieth century, the advent of the automobile as well as changes in American cities affected the structure of police departments. Although the paramilitary model remained, policing became increasingly bureaucratic. The radio and the telephone allowed more communication between officers and supervisors. In addition, the new communication tools increased demand for police service because a citizen only had to pick up a telephone to request help. However, these changes also served to alienate the officer from the community (Sherman, 1988).

The separation of the police from the community led to increased concern about controlling police behavior. The bureaucratic response to this concern was the creation of rules and procedures for officers to follow. These departmental policies, or standard operating procedures (SOPs), became a factor determining the actions of individual officers. Although not perfect, the rules affect how officers decide to handle cases (Fyfe, 1979; Mastrofski, Ritti, & Hoffmaster, 1987). Like other organizations, police agencies change slowly in response to external pressures (King, 1999).

Early police officers were sworn into office, issued uniforms and weapons, and sent to the streets. Most states now require training and certification of recruits prior to being assigned to patrol. Beginning in 1972, many police agencies developed field-training programs to evaluate how well new officers apply laws and departmental policies to field situations (McCampbell, 1986). These programs help ensure that police officers know and follow the rules of the police bureaucracy. Today field training is a component of basic police training in the overwhelming majority of American police departments, with a third of all police academies requiring it. When not part of the basic academy training, the agency that hired the recruit usually provides field training (Reaves, 2009).

Another development in policing during the twentieth century was specialization. Large police departments, especially those in our biggest cities, use task specialization to assign officers. **Police specialization** divides tasks into special units or divisions. Whereas departments differ among themselves in how they separate and name tasks, Alpert and Dunham (1988:59) identified four basic elements: (1) administration, (2) communication, (3) patrol, and (4) internal review. They observed that many police agencies use divisions that are more precise. Patrol and investigation are two units that include the crime control function of the police. A traffic division and community relations unit may combine with the patrol unit to provide service and order maintenance. Administrative services and internal affairs units assist police administrators in running and controlling the department.

A typical large police department may have several divisions. The investigation unit, for example, may be further divided into homicide, robbery, fraud, vice, and other squads. Similarly, departments organize patrol units by geography into precincts or districts. Regardless of the complexity of the police bureaucracy, most retain the military ranks and chain of command. Figure 5.7 presents a model organizational chart for a specialized police department. This chart shows an organization that has a well-defined hierarchy—there are many steps between the individual patrol officer and the chief of police. Most police departments, however, are small and do not have such a detailed and specialized organization. Still, even the smallest of police departments has a chief of police. An alternative organization, depicted in Figure 5.8, "flattens" this hierarchy, giving patrol officers easier input into policy development and shortened lines of communication. This flatter organizational structure is more consistent with contemporary calls for community-oriented policing (Maguire, Shin, Zhao, & Hassell, 2003; Zhao, Ren, & Lovrich, 2010).

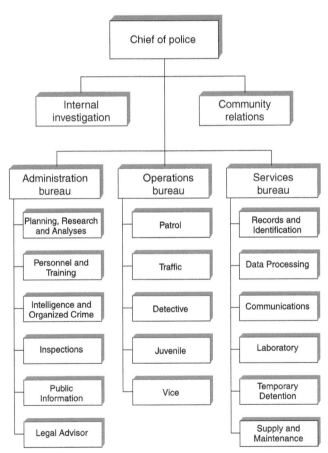

FIGURE 5.7
Organizational chart for a police department.
Source: President's Commission on Law Enforcement and Administration of Justice (1967), Task Force Report: Police (Washington, DC: U.S. Government Printing Office):47

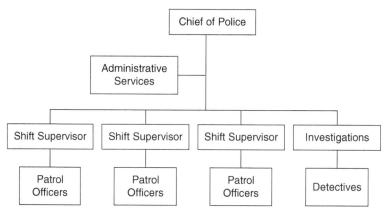

FIGURE 5.8
A flattened organizational structure.

The movement toward community-oriented policing promised to "flatten" the organizational hierarchy of police agencies (Greene, 2000). If a community-oriented policing philosophy is implemented departmentwide, each police officer is expected to have responsibility for his or her beat area. The officers work with residents to identify problems and implement solutions. This direct link between the officer and the community naturally lessens the bureaucratic control and "chain of command" characteristic of the more formal, specialized police agency. So far, most police organizations have not shown substantial change in their organizational structure. King (2005) suggested that a rigid rank structure is only one part of police hierarchy and that if officers have discretion to make decisions, the police organization can operate in a decentralized fashion while keeping the traditional rank structure.

We must remember that even in the most specialized city police department, patrol officers are generalists. Observers have called patrol the "backbone of policing." Patrol officers still provide the majority of police services. Nearly 70% of officers in local police departments have assignments to patrol (Reaves, 2010). It is unlikely that the decentralized performance of police service by patrol officers will change in the future. What may change is the amount of direction and supervision these generalist patrol officers receive from the central administration.

The degree of specialization in any police department is at least partly the result of the size of the department (Langworthy, 1985). Larger departments are more likely to be specialized than are smaller ones. Additionally, the police in larger departments are less likely to reflect neighborhood values in police activities (Alpert & Dunham, 1988). This is a result of specialization and bureaucracy. The varying sizes of American police departments influence how the tasks of police are accomplished and how the public perceives the police.

Recall that the majority of police officers work in large, bureaucratic departments, but that most departments are small. This fact of police organization means duplication and inefficiency are part of American policing. Our police serve communities as much as (or more than) they serve in the enforcement of the criminal law. The price we pay for local control of police is inefficiency. To ensure that we have police who are responsive to local needs, we must be willing to tolerate multiple jurisdictions and thousands of separate police agencies. However, the existence of many police agencies in a relatively small area does not necessarily translate into a large amount of overlap and wasted effort. Ostrom, Parks, and Whitaker (1978) noted that in metropolitan areas the norm is cooperation among police agencies, not conflict and duplication in service delivery.

UNDERSTANDING POLICE

Because we are examining the criminal justice system, we will proceed to discuss policing almost exclusively in terms of law enforcement. In doing so, it is easy to forget the other complex demands placed on the police. The purpose of the previous discussion was to recognize and highlight the fact that enforcing the criminal law is only one part of the police function. In dealing with many social problems, the police must develop workable, immediate responses. King and Dunn (2004) reported on police "dumping." Dumping involves transporting people who are mentally ill or those who are or otherwise troublesome out of the local jurisdictions. This may not solve the long-term problem of mental illness, homelessness, or substance abuse, but it does solve the immediate problem of what to do with a disorderly person.

Requiring our police to provide services, to maintain order, and to serve crime control ends means that police do not devote their full resources to law enforcement. It also means that law enforcement is not entirely occupied with detecting and apprehending serious criminal offenders. On occasion, police officers use the criminal law to achieve order-maintenance or service ends. Police in some large cities frequently employ "mercy bookings" to provide shelter and medical care for the poor (Finn & Sullivan, 1988; Gelman & Huck, 1987:48). Panzarella and Alicea (1997) reported a survey of officers assigned to a special unit having responsibility for dealing with people who are emotionally disturbed. These officers noted that they were unlikely to arrest such persons, but often took them into custody and delivered them to medical or psychiatric services. Bittner (1990) noted that police officers seek to control disturbances on the street, and will use arrest as a means to achieve order even when the circumstances of the event would not otherwise justify arresting the citizen. Teplin (2000) suggested that officers may arrest people who are mentally ill when the lack of mental health resources leaves them with no other alternative. In contrast, Engel and Silver (2001) reported that officers often resort to informal dispositions when mental health treatment is unavailable and the criminal law is inappropriate. Cooper, McLearen, and Zapf (2004) reported that police officers recognize a responsibility to deal with people who are mentally ill, but often complain that the community resources available for these people are inadequate.

These examples illustrate how the multiple goals of policing complicate an analysis of the crime control actions of police departments. Nonetheless, we shall endeavor to focus on the role of the police in the criminal justice system—and that role includes crime control. Several factors influence the practice of policing, but three of the most important are the characteristics of the community, the police organization, and those of the police officer.

Police and Communities

Most policing in the United States happens at a local level. The police serve their various communities. As Wilson (1968) reported, there are varieties of police behavior. It is our goal to understand and explain police behavior as it relates to crime control. We cannot accomplish that goal if we ignore the contributions of community to the decisions of police officers.

Wilson (1968) used the frequency and formality with which officers intervened in the lives of citizens to classify police department styles. Formality refers to the use of the criminal law, whereas frequency refers to the rate at which police interact with citizens. He identified three basic styles of policing: (1) legalistic, (2) service, and (3) watchman. The **legalistic style** involved relatively frequent and formal interventions. In the **service style**, police intervened frequently, but informally (there was little law enforcement). In contrast, in the **watchman style**, police intervened infrequently. For example, in the case of a curfew violation, legalistic policing would involve the police stopping and issuing a citation (formal intervention); the service style would involve a stop followed by a warning (informal intervention); and the watchman style would predict that the officers were likely to ignore the violation (no intervention).

Because these are ideal types, we can expect variety in practice. Sometimes officers in a legalistic-style department will ignore the violation, those in a service-style department will issue a citation, and those in a watchman-style department will stop the citizen. However, the police department as a whole develops a style of policing that is generally characteristic of the organization. Wilson (1968) suggested that these different styles reflect differences in the communities served by the police. Thus, police departments develop policing styles that are appropriate to the desires and needs of the communities in which they work. Although it is difficult to determine exactly what characteristics of communities explain variation in police department styles, it seems clear that local police do exhibit different styles (Liederbach & Travis, 2008). It is also true that neighborhood or community characteristics help explain public perceptions of the police. Schuck, Rosenbaum, and Hawkins (2008) reported that neighborhood disadvantage and problems explain residents' attitudes toward the police.

Other research has shown that police react to neighborhood or community characteristics. Varano, Schafer, Cancino, and Swatt (2009) found that police were likely to discount the seriousness of several types of crimes depending on the neighborhood in which they occurred. Although police usually report some crimes, such as robbery, as serious crimes, police in lower-class and crime-ridden neighborhoods did not record other crimes, including drug offenses and some assaults. Police tend to identify more problems in disadvantaged neighborhoods and see more crime problems there than do the residents (Sun & Triplett, 2008). Similarly, Sun, Payne, and Wu (2008) reported that police are more likely to use aggressive tactics and force in disorganized and disadvantaged neighborhoods than in other neighborhoods.

A long tradition of policing research has reported community and neighborhood effects on police actions. It is clear that community characteristics are an important part of the police equation and that explanations of police behavior must include reference to community and neighborhood factors. These community influences are likely to resist change. Zhao and colleagues (2010) found that "incrementalism" best explains community financial support for local police. A tradition of high or low support is a better explanation of current support than is any other. Communities that have supported the police in the past are likely to continue to do so, whereas those that were less supportive will continue to be less supportive. The link between communities and their police is traditional and enduring.

Police Organizations

Beyond recognizing the multiple functions served by police, we must also remain aware of the structure and organization of policing. The actions of police officers and police departments reflect different patterns of organization (Holmes, 1997). Departmental policies and procedures, as well as recruit training, serve as boundaries on police behavior. The diversity of organizational sizes, structures, and policies ensures variety in the practice of policing.

Wilson's (1968) model of police styles explains differences in police organizations resulting from different community characteristics. These organizational differences produce different officer behaviors. In this model, the organization mediates (or transmits) community characteristics to officer behavior. The greatest influence on what officers do is the product of the police organization.

Morabito (2008) reported that police organizational characteristics are important factors explaining the adoption of community policing. Different police departments were more or less likely to adopt community policing based on such things as organizational size, available resources, and other organizational factors. Although community variables were important, the organization was also critically important.

Phillips and Varano (2008) reported that police officer charging decisions reflect organizational influences. The number and types of charges made in domestic violence cases by local police officers differed from those of state police. The local police decisions reflected their awareness of conditions in the local courts that affected case prosecutions. Wilson and Zhao (2008) found assaults against police officers related to police organizations. Officers in departments that focused on more proactive and aggressive crime control experienced more assaults.

Not surprisingly, the police organization can control and direct the decisions of police officers. Training, regulations, supervision, and discipline all work to constrain the behavior of officers. Beyond these direct controls, much evidence supports the notion that informal understandings and rules exist that structure the decisions and behaviors of officers. Even though individual officers still exercise discretion, their choices are constrained by the organization for which they work.

Selection of Police Officers

The police officer is a very important component of the justice process. In some ways, he or she is the most important component: Police officers decide whom to subject to justice processing, what crimes to investigate, and how vigorously to enforce laws. As the most numerous and most visible agents of criminal justice, police officers are disproportionately responsible for citizens' opinions about the entire justice system. Ultimately, police officers are ordinary people entrusted with extraordinary powers, and they are charged with what some have called "an impossible mandate" (Manning, 1978).

The discretionary nature of the decisions officers make concerning the criminal justice system means that the forces that influence their decisions also influence the workings of the justice system (Brooks, 1989). If a police officer is prejudiced, the system will be prejudiced to some extent. Thus, the characteristics of officers, as well as their relationship to the organization and the citizenry, are important influences on criminal justice system operations. The characteristics of individual officers, including demographic factors (age, gender, race, ethnicity) and experience (education, rank, years on the job, etc.), have been linked to officer decisions (Bayley & Garafalo, 1989; Fridell & Binder, 1992; Harris, 2009; Hassell & Brandl, 2009; Riksheim & Chermak, 1993).

Because it is believed that individual officer characteristics influence police decisions, the selection and training of police officers is an important topic. Police selection typically involves a number of steps that are designed to produce the best qualified police officers. Research into the police selection process, however, indicates that it is not always effective. Metchik (1999) suggested that our reliance on a "screening out" model aimed at dismissing unsuitable candidates is not as effective as one that seeks to identify and retain good candidates. Similarly, Gaines and Falkenberg (1998) argued that traditional written examinations may not adequately identify the best candidates, and may have the negative effect of excluding female and minority candidates. Henson, Reyns, Klahm, and Frank (2010) reported that selection tests and performance in the academy may be unrelated to performance as a police officer. Likewise, selecting police officers largely based on their education might not have as substantial of an impact as once assumed. Although officers who have a college education might be less likely to resort to the use of force than less educated officers, education does not seem to have an impact on other key discretionary decisions (Rydberg & Terrill, 2010). Only 14% of state and local law enforcement agencies specifically target recruits with a 4-year college degree (Reaves, 2012).

One of the recent changes in American policing has been the increased hiring of women and minority group members. Some observers feared that women would be unable to endure the danger and rigors of police work (Hale & Wyland, 1993; Potts, 1983). Others believed that the inclusion of women and minorities would improve community relations. Analyses of the effects and effectiveness of these new police officers remain incomplete. Thus far, however, the data show that female and minority group members make good police officers (Burke, Richardsen, & Martinussen, 2006; Lundman, 2009; Poteyeva & Sun, 2009). However, only about 12% of sworn officers are female, and about 25% are members of ethnic minority groups (see Figure 5.9). Haar (1997) studied the integration of female and minority police officers into one police department. She noted that minority and female officers faced several problems in their interpersonal interactions with white, male officers. In part, this is because efforts by the organization to assist integration, such as vigorous support of affirmative action, served to drive a wedge between the patrol officers, dividing them by race and sex.

Challenges to affirmative action policies threaten to limit diversity among police personnel. Moore (2001) contended that the solution to challenges to affirmative action policies in police agencies involves careful planning and research to determine and justify the goals of the policy. At the same time, there is evidence that traditional officer selection practices such as physical ability testing still work to exclude qualified female and minority candidates (Cordner & Cordner, 2011; Lonsway, 2003). In contrast, Jordan, Fridell, Gaggiani, and Kubu (2009) reported that recruitment strategies targeted to attract women and minority candidates are effective. Overall, only 21% of law enforcement agencies have such recruitment efforts targeting females and minorities (Reaves, 2012).

Beyond selecting police officers, training and experience also produce differences among officers, and training frequently is used as a vehicle to change

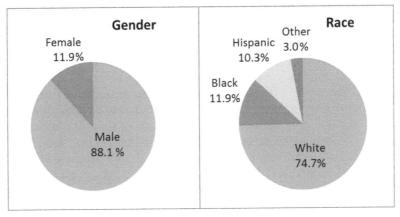

FIGURE 5.9
Gender and race of full-time police officers.

officer attitudes and practices (Buerger, 1998). Hoath, Schneider, and Starr (1998) and Travis and Winston (1998) have suggested that officer attitudes are related to job satisfaction. Johnson (2012) found that officers reported lower job satisfaction when they experienced role conflict, defined as discomfort when the required job-related behaviors are inconsistent with the officer's personal beliefs. In short, part of the task in police officer selection and training is to develop a good match between the skills and orientations of officers and the tasks and goals of the police organization.

Police Personalities and Subculture

Many observers have identified what they have termed the "police personality" (Evans, Coman, & Stanley, 1992; Niederhoffer, 1967; Skolnick, 1966). Some have suggested that policing as a career attracts people who are more cynical, authoritarian, suspicious, brutal, and so on. Others argue that the nature of the job changes an average person into the police personality. Whatever causes the police officer to have this unique personality, it is important to understand the complex set of forces that affects the policing activities of the individual officer.

Just as Wilson (1968) suggested that there are types of police organizations, others have suggested that there are types of police officers. Muir (1977), for example, argued that officers differ in terms of their willingness to use coercive force and their ability to empathize with or understand citizens. These differences result in four distinct types of officers differing in the ways they do policing. Muir used the term "enforcers" to describe those officers who are willing to use force but unable to empathize with citizens. Those comfortable with force and able to empathize he called "professionals." Officers who were unwilling to use force were either "reciprocators," who could empathize with citizens, or "avoiders," who did not understand citizens. Although many anecdotal and qualitative data are available to support the notion that police officer types exist, attitudinal surveys of officers have not identified these types (Hochstedler, 1981). Nonetheless, it is reasonable to conclude that police officers probably differ among themselves, and that these differences are relevant to an understanding of their criminal justice decisions (Travis & Langworthy, 2008).

The complexity of the job facing the individual officer is multiplied several times when we analyze the complexity of policing in society on an organizational level. The police officer is a member of an organization and, as such, must be careful to serve the ends of the organization. She or he is also a bureaucrat, and must abide by the rules and regulations of the bureaucracy. Finally, the officer is a member of an occupational group that is larger than his or her individual department. Thus, in any given situation, the behavior of the officer reflects the limits imposed by (1) the department, (2) the goals of the organization, and (3) the prestige of the occupational group. The officer is (at least subliminally) aware that his or her actions will be judged against all of these criteria. Indeed, Bazemore and Senjo (1997) reported that officers assigned as neighborhood police interacted with juveniles differently than officers with traditional assignments. They noted that the neighborhood officers engaged in more preventive and coalition-building activities, and displayed a more positive attitude toward youths (1997:77).

To this mix of standards, we must add the social context of the situation in which the officer is operating (Worden, 1989). Many times the goals or expectations of the audiences of a police department conflict with each other and with those of the department. The victim/witness has a set of expectations about how the officer will behave. The officer has expectations about himself or herself and about the victim/witness. Finally, onlookers also have their expectations. The officer is aware of many of these expectations, and they affect his or her behavior. Although not all calls to which the police respond are dangerous or difficult, there are no simple calls. As we discovered when we examined the arrest decision, the law is only one influence on police officer decisions. Other "contextual" factors that may influence the decisions of officers include characteristics of the citizens (Chermak, 1998; Mastrofski, Parks, & Worden, 1998). The presence of witnesses and bystanders can also influence the officer's decisions (Connolly, Huzurbazar, & Routh-McGee, 2000).

Studies of the police show that officers frequently act as if they are cynical (Regoli, Crouch, Culbertson, & Poole, 1987). **Cynicism** entails distrust or suspicion. In terms of police, the term refers to a perception or belief that citizens, department leaders, politicians, and other criminal justice officials are not truthful and honest in their dealings with officers. From a police officer's perspective, laws are often created by legislatures who have no background in criminal justice. Further, the officer's job is criticized by a public who have no understanding of the nature of police work (Caplan, 2003). In this sense, cynicism can create a barrier between the officer and the public for which they serve. Part of the explanation for police cynicism may also be the stress of the job (Terry, 1985; Travis & Vukovich, 1990).

Police Officer Stress

The existence and nature of police officer stress has been an important but elusive topic of research for several decades. The evidence about the level of stress experienced by police officers in comparison to those in other occupations is unclear. Policing, as an occupation, contains some unique stressors, such as the chance of killing someone, the threat of attack, and the need to deal with human misery and crime. Police officers also face many of the same stressors faced by other workers, such as rotating shifts, organizational insensitivity, red tape, and the like (Vila & Kenney, 2002). Recent investigations of police stress indicate that causes and levels of stress may differ among officers (Gachter, Savage, & Torgler, 2011). Contemporary reforms aimed at implementing community-oriented policing appear to be stressful for some officers, especially for police supervisors (Lord, 1996). Research reveals that officers experience stress differently and develop different coping patterns based on their gender, race, level of family support, and length of service (Hassell &

Brandl, 2009; Kurtz, 2008; Morash, Kwak, & Haar, 2006). Although police may experience stress as do other people, neither all police experience it to the same degree, nor cope with it as well. Some officers respond to stress by leaving the profession (Wood, 2001, 2002). Burnout and turnover represent costly problems for police organizations, because replacing officers requires extensive and expensive selection and training processes.

POLICING IN THE WHOLE SYSTEM

Returning to our discussion of the location of the criminal justice system within the whole system of American society, Wilson's observations about the police indicate the influence of environmental factors. He saw police agency styles as related to community characteristics. The size, structure, and composition of the community, Wilson (1968) argued, created a "political culture" in which the police exist. Part of this culture defined the limits of police actions that were acceptable in the community. Service-style agencies existed in suburban, middle-class communities. Watchman-style and legalistic agencies operated in heterogeneous (mixed population in terms of social class and ethnicity) cities. The distinction between whether the police would demonstrate a watchman or legalistic style seemed to be related to the type of government in the cities. Those with "professional" governments (city managers) were legalistic; those in "political" governments (strong mayor) were watchman style.

Wilson (1968) did not contend that city governments directly influenced policing practices, but that differences in communities created different environments and that police styles reflected those environments. Thus, the job the police do and the way in which they do it reflects the values and structure of the community in which they exist (Travis & Langworthy, 2008). As a subsystem of the criminal justice and social systems, the police department adapts to its environment, supporting the existing equilibrium. Consider the likely public reaction to a watchman style of policing in a homogeneous, middle-class, suburban community. It is likely that citizens would complain about the failure of the police to enforce the laws, and would demand police reform. On the other hand, a legalistic style would also generate complaints about overzealous enforcement. The service style is most likely to fit the desires and expectations of the citizens in such a community.

Finally, given the essentially democratic nature of government (and policing in particular) in the United States, it is logical that the police reflect the desires of the citizens. After all, if citizens define the police job through their calls for service, the citizens direct the police. The spread of community-oriented policing promises to increase variety in policing. Each large police department can potentially become composed of a large number of distinct "neighborhood" or "community" police. The types of issues that attract police attention, and the ways in which police react to problems, may begin to vary not just between departments but within departments between neighborhoods.

The next chapter examines the law enforcement role in the criminal justice system. It continues our discussion of the forces that affect discretionary decisions by police officers. The final part of the chapter examines some contemporary issues in law enforcement. Each of these topics must be understood within the context of police history, functions, and organization.

REVIEW QUESTIONS

1. What is meant by calling the police the "agency of last resort"?
2. Briefly trace the development of policing in the United States.
3. Describe how the police can be considered to be a human services agency.
4. How can community policing be considered a revised role for the police?
5. Differentiate between reactive and proactive policing.
6. How do the multiple tasks expected of the police affect them as part of the justice system?
7. What factors influence the decisions and behavior of police officers?

References

Alpert, G., & Dunham, R. (1988). *Policing urban America*. Prospect Heights, IL: Waveland.

Barlow, D., & Barlow, M. (2000). *Police in a multicultural society: An American story*. Prospect Heights, IL: Waveland.

Bayley, D., & Garafalo, J. (1989). The management of violence by police patrol officers. *Criminology, 27*(1), 1–25.

Bazemore, G., & Senjo, S. (1997). Police encounters with juveniles revisited: An exploratory study of themes and styles in community policing. *Policing, 20*(1), 60–82.

Bittner, E. (1970). *The functions of police in modern society*. Rockville, MD: National Institute of Mental Health.

Bittner, E. (1990). *Aspects of police work*. Boston: Northeastern University Press.

Black, D. J. (1972). The mobilization of law. *Journal of Legal Studies, 2*(1), 125–149.

Brooks, L. (1989). Police discretionary behavior: A study of style. In R. Dunham & G. Alpert (Eds.), *Critical issues in policing: Contemporary readings* (pp. 121–145). Prospect Heights, IL: Waveland.

Buerger, M. (1998). Police training as Pentecost: Using tools singularly ill-suited to the purpose of reform. *Police Quarterly, 1*(1), 27–64.

Buerger, M., & Mazerolle, L. (1998). Third-party policing: A theoretical analysis of an emerging trend. *Justice Quarterly, 15*(2), 301–327.

Burch, A. (2012). *Sheriff's offices, 2007—Statistical tables*. Washington, DC: Bureau of Justice Statistics.

Burke, R., Richardsen, A., & Martinussen, M. (2006). Gender differences in policing: Reasons for optimism? *Policing: An International Journal of Police Strategies and Management, 29*(3), 513–523.

Caplan, J. (2003). Police cynicism: Police survival tool? *The Police Journal, 7*, 304–313.

Chappell, A. (2009). The philosophical versus actual adoption of community policing: A case study. *Criminal Justice Review, 34*, 5–38.

Chappell, A., & Gibson, S. (2009). Community policing and homeland security policing: Friend or foe? *Criminal Justice Policy Review, 20*(3), 326–343.

Chermak, S. (1998). Predicting crime story salience: The effects of crime, victim, and defendant characteristics. *Journal of Criminal Justice, 26*(1), 61–70.

Chermak, S., Carter, J., Carter, D., McGarrell, E., & Drew, J. (2013). Law enforcement's information sharing infrastructure: A national assessment. *Police Quarterly, 16*(2), 211–244.

Chermak, S., McGarrell, E., & Weiss, A. (2001). Citizens' perceptions of aggressive traffic enforcement strategies. *Justice Quarterly, 18*(2), 365–391.

Connell, N., Miggans, K., & McGloin, J. (2008). Can a community policing initiative reduce serious crime? A local evaluation. *Police Quarterly, 11*, 127–150.

Connolly, C., Huzurbazar, S., & Routh-McGee, T. (2000). Multiple parties in domestic violence situations and arrest. *Journal of Criminal Justice, 28*(3), 181–188.

Cooper, V., McLearen, A., & Zapf, P. (2004). Dispositional decisions with mentally ill: Police perceptions and characteristics. *Police Quarterly, 7*(3), 295–310.

Cordner, G., & Cordner, A. (2011). Stuck on a plateau? Obstacles to recruitment, selection, and retention of women police. *Police Quarterly, 14*(3), 207–226.

Critchley, T. (1972). *A history of police in England and Wales* (2nd ed.). Montclair, NJ: Patterson Smith.

Das, D. (1987). *Understanding police human relations.* Metuchen, NJ: Scarecrow Press.

Duffee, D., Fluellen, R., & Renauer, B. (1999). Community variables in community policing. *Police Quarterly, 2*(1), 5–35.

Eck, J., & Spelman, W. (1987). Who you gonna call? The police as problem busters. *Crime & Delinquency, 33*(1), 31–52.

Engel, R., & Silver, E. (2001). Policing mentally disordered suspects: A reexamination of the criminalization hypothesis. *Criminology, 39*(2), 225–252.

Evans, B., Coman, G., & Stanley, R. (1992). The police personality: Type A behavior and trait anxiety. *Journal of Criminal Justice, 20*(5), 429–442.

Famega, C. (2004). Variation in officer downtime: A review of the research. *Policing: An International Journal of Police Strategies and Management, 28*(3), 388–414.

Fielding, N. (2005a). *The police and social conflict* (2nd ed.). London: Glasshouse Press.

Fielding, N. (2005b). Concepts and theory in community policing. *The Howard Journal, 44*(5), 460–472.

Finn, P. E., & Sullivan, M. (1988). Police respond to special populations. *National Institute of Justice Reports, 209*, 2–8 (May/June).

Fogelson, R. (1977). *Big-city police.* Cambridge, MA: Harvard University Press.

Fridell, L., & Binder, A. (1992). Police officer decision making in potentially violent confrontations. *Journal of Criminal Justice, 20*(5), 385–399.

Fritsch, E., Caeti, T., Tobolowsky, P., & Taylor, R. (2004). Police referrals of crime victims to compensation sources: An empirical analysis of attitudinal and structural impediments. *Police Quarterly, 7*(3), 372–393.

Fyfe, J. J. (1979). Administrative intervention on police shooting discretion: An empirical examination. *Journal of Criminal Justice, 7*(4), 309–324.

Gaines, L., & Falkenberg, S. (1998). An evaluation of the written selection test: Effectiveness and alternatives. *Journal of Criminal Justice, 26*(2), 175–183.

Gay, W., Schell, T., & Schack, S. (1977). *Improving patrol productivity, volume 1: Routing patrol.* Washington, DC: U.S. Department of Justice, 3.

Gelman, D., & Huck, J. (1987, November 9). Forcing the mentally ill to get help. *Newsweek, 110*(19), 47–48.

Goldstein, H. (1978). *Policing a free society.* Cambridge, MA: Ballinger.

Goldstein, H. (1990). *Problem-oriented policing.* New York: McGraw-Hill.

Graber, D. (1979). Evaluating crime-fighting policies: Media images and public perspective. In R. Baker, & F. Meyer (Eds.), *Evaluating alternative law-enforcement polices* (pp. 179–199). Lexington, MA: Lexington Books.

Greene, J. (2000). Community policing in America: Changing the nature, structure, and function of the police. In J. Horney (Ed.), *Criminal Justice 2000: Policies, procedures, and decisions of the criminal justice system*: Vol. 3. (pp. 299–370). National Institute of Justice: Washington, DC.

Gachter, M., Savage, D., & Torgler, B. (2011). Gender variations of physiological strain amongst police officers. *Gender Issues, 28*, 66–93.

Haar, R. (1997). Patterns of interaction in a police patrol bureau. Race and gender barriers to integration. *Justice Quarterly, 14*(1), 53–85.

Hale, D., & Wyland, S. (1993). Dragons and dinosaurs: The plight of patrol women. *Police Forum, 3*(2), 1–6.

Harris, C. (2009). Exploring the relationship between experience and problem behaviors: A longitudinal analysis of officers from a large cohort. *Police Quarterly, 12*(2), 192–213.

Hassell, K., & Brandl, S. (2009). An examination of the workplace experiences of police patrol officers: The role of race, sex, and sexual orientation. *Police Quarterly, 12*(4), 408–430.

Hawdon, J., Ryan, J., & Griffin, S. (2003). Policing tactics and perceptions of police legitimacy. *Police Quarterly, 6*(4), 469–491.

Henson, B., Reyns, B., Klahm, C., & Frank, J. (2010). Do good recruits make good cops? Problems predicting and measuring academy and street-level success. *Police Quarterly, 13*(1), 5–26.

Hickman, M., & Reaves, B. (2006). *Local police departments, 2003*. Washington, DC: Bureau of Justice Statistics.

Hoath, D., Schneider, F., & Starr, M. (1998). Police job satisfaction as a function of career orientation and position tenure: Implications for selection and community policing. *Journal of Criminal Justice, 26*(4), 337–348.

Hochstedler, E. (1981). Testing types: A review and test of police types. *Journal of Criminal Justice, 9*(6), 451–466.

Holmes, S. (1997). *The occupational definition of police use of excessive force* (Unpublished doctoral dissertation). Cincinnati, OH: University of Cincinnati Division of Criminal Justice.

Jackson, A., & Wade, J. (2005). Police perceptions of social capital and responsibility: An explanation of proactive policing. *Policing: An International Journal of Police Strategies and Management, 28*(1), 49–68.

Jiao, A. (1998). Community-oriented policing and policing-oriented community. *Journal of Crime and Justice, 20*(1), 135–158.

Johnson, D. R. (1981). *American law enforcement: A history*. St. Louis, MO: Forum Press.

Johnson, R. (2012). Police officer job satisfaction: A multidimensional analysis. *Police Quarterly, 15*(2), 157–176.

Jones, M., & Johnstone, P. (2012). *History of criminal justice* (5th ed.). Boston: Elsevier (Anderson Publishing).

Jordan, W., Fridell, L., Gaggiani, D., & Kubu, B. (2009). Attracting females and racial/ethnic minorities to law enforcement. *Journal of Criminal Justice, 37*(4), 333–341.

Kane, R. (2000). Permanent beat assignments in association with community policing: Assessing the impact on police officers' field activity. *Justice Quarterly, 17*(2), 259–280.

Kane, R., & Cronin, S. (2013). Associations between order maintenance policing and violent crime: Considering the mediating effects of residential context. *Crime & Delinquency, 59*, 910–929.

Kappeler, V. (1996). Making police history in light of modernity: A sign of the times? *Police Forum, 6*(3), 1–6.

Kelling, G. (1988). *Foot patrol. Crime file study guide*. Washington, DC: National Institute of Justice.

Kennedy, D. B. (1983). Toward a clarification of the police role as a human services agency. *Criminal Justice Review, 8*(2), 41–45.

King, W. (1999). Time, constancy, and change in American Municipal Police Organizations. *Police Quarterly, 2*(3), 338–364.

King, W. (2003). Bending granite revisited: The command rank structure of American police organizations. *Policing: An International Journal of Police Strategies and Management, 26*(2), 208–230.

King, W. (2005). Toward a better understanding of the hierarchical nature of police organizations: Conception and measurement. *Journal of Criminal Justice, 33*(1), 97–109.

King, W., & Dunn, T. (2004). Dumping: Police initiated transjurisdictional transport of troublesome persons. *Police Quarterly, 7*(3), 339–358.

Klockars, C. (1985). *The idea of police.* Beverly Hills, CA: Sage.

Kraska, P. (1994). The police and the military in the post–cold war era: Streamlining the state's use of force entities in the drug war. *Police Forum, 4*(1), 1–8.

Kurtz, D. (2008). Controlled burn: The gendering of stress and burnout in modern policing. *Feminist Criminology, 3*(3), 216–238.

Langworthy, R. H. (1985). Police department size and agency structure. *Journal of Criminal Justice, 13*(1), 15–28.

Lee, J. (2010). Policing after 9/11: Community policing in an age of homeland security. *Police Quarterly, 13*(4), 347–366.

Liederbach, J., & Frank, J. (2006). Policing the big beat: An observational study of county level patrol and comparisons to local small town and rural officers. *Journal of Crime and Justice, 29*(1), 21–44.

Liederbach, J., Fritsch, E., Carter, D., & Bannister, A. (2007). Exploring the limits of collaboration in community policing: A direct comparison of police and citizen views. *Policing: An International Journal of Police Strategies & Management, 31*(2), 271–291.

Liederbach, J., & Travis, L. (2008). Wilson redux: Another look at varieties of police behavior. *Police Quarterly, 11*(4), 447–467.

Lonsway, K. (2003). Tearing down the wall: Problems with consistency, validity, and adverse impact of physical agility testing in police selection. *Police Quarterly, 6*(3), 237–277.

Lord, V. (1996). An impact of community policing: Reported stressors, social support, and strain among police officers in a changing police department. *Journal of Criminal Justice, 24*(6), 503–522.

Lundman, R. (1980). *Police and policing: An introduction.* New York: Holt, Rinehart & Winston.

Lundman, R. (2009). Officer gender and traffic ticket decisions: Police blue or women too? *Journal of Criminal Justice, 37*(4), 342–352.

Lurigio, A., & Swartz, J. (2000). Changing the contours of the criminal justice system to meet the needs of persons with serious mental illness. In J. Horney (Ed.), *Criminal Justice 2000: Policies, processes, and decisions of the criminal justice system*: Vol. 3. (pp. 45–108). Washington, DC: National Institute of Justice.

Maguire, E., Shin, Y., Zhao, J., & Hassell, K. (2003). Structural change in large police agencies during the 1990s. *Policing: An International Journal of Police Strategies and Management, 26*(2), 251–275.

Manning, P. K. (1978). The police: Mandate, strategies and appearances. In P. K. Manning, & J. Van Maanen (Eds.), *Policing: A view from the street* (pp. 7–31). Santa Monica, CA: Goodyear.

Mastrofski, S., Parks, R., Reiss, A., & Worden, R. (1999a). *Policing neighborhoods: A report from Indianapolis.* Washington, DC: National Institute of Justice.

Mastrofski, S., Parks, R., Reiss, A., & Worden, R. (1999b). *Policing neighborhoods: A report from St. Petersburg.* Washington, DC: National Institute of Justice.

Mastrofski, S., Parks, R., & Worden, R. (1998). *Community policing in action: Lessons from an observational study.* Washington, DC: National Institute of Justice.

Mastrofski, S. D., Ritti, R. R., & Hoffmaster, D. (1987). Organizational determinants of police discretion: The case of drinking-driving. *Journal of Criminal Justice, 15*(5), 387–402.

McCampbell, M. S. (1986). *Field training for police: State of the art.* Washington, DC: National Institute of Justice.

Metchik, E. (1999). An analysis of the "screening out" model of police officer selection. *Police Quarterly, 2*(1), 79–95.

Monkonnen, E. (1981). *Police in urban America: 1860–1920.* Cambridge, UK: Cambridge University Press.

Moore, E. (2001). Emerging legal constraints on affirmative action in police agencies and how to adapt to them. *Journal of Criminal Justice, 29*(1), 11–19.

Moore, M., Trojanowicz, R., & Kelling, G. (1988). *Crime and policing.* Washington, DC: U.S. Department of Justice.

Moore, R. (1987). *Posse comitatus* revisited: The use of the military in civil law enforcement. *Journal of Criminal Justice, 15*(5), 375–386.

Morabito, M. (2008). The adoption of police innovation: The role of the political environment. *Policing: An International Journal of Police Strategies and Management, 31*(3), 466–484.

Morabito, M. (2010). Understanding community policing as an innovation: Patterns of adoption. *Crime & Delinquency, 56*(4), 564–587.

Morash, M., Kwak, D., & Haar, R. (2006). Gender differences in the predictors of police stress. *Policing: An International Journal of Police Strategies and Management, 29*(3), 541–563.

Muir, W. (1977). *Police: Streetcorner politicians.* Chicago: University of Chicago Press.

Niederhoffer, A. (1967). *Behind the shield: The police in urban society.* Garden City, NJ: Anchor Books.

O'Connell, P. (2008). The chess master's game: A model for incorporating local police agencies in the fight against global terrorism. *Policing: An International Journal of Police Strategies and Management, 31*(3), 456–465.

Ostrom, E., Parks, R., & Whitaker, G. (1978). *Patterns of metropolitan policing.* Cambridge, MA: Ballinger.

Panzarella, R., & Alicea, J. (1997). Police tactics in incidents with mentally disturbed persons. *Policing: An International Journal of Police Strategies and Management, 20*(2), 326–338.

Parks, R., Mastrofski, S., DeJone, C., & Gray, M. (1999). How officers spend their time with the community. *Justice Quarterly, 16*(3), 483–518.

Pelfrey, W. (2007). Local law enforcement terrorism efforts: A state level case study. *Journal of Criminal Justice, 35*(3), 313–321.

Phillips, S., & Varano, S. (2008). Police criminal charging decisions: An examination of post-arrest decision-making. *Journal of Criminal Justice, 36*(4), 307–315.

Poteyeva, M., & Sun, I. (2009). Gender differences in police officers' attitudes: Assessing current empirical evidence. *Journal of Criminal Justice, 37*(5), 512–522.

Potts, L. (1983). Equal employment opportunity and female employment in police agencies. *Journal of Criminal Justice, 11*(6), 505–524.

Reaves, B. (2009). *State and local law enforcement training academies, 2006.* Washington, DC: Bureau of Justice Statistics.

Reaves, B. (2010). *Local police departments, 2007.* Washington, DC: Bureau of Justice Statistics.

Reaves, B. (2011). *Census of state and local law enforcement agencies, 2008.* Washington, DC: Bureau of Justice Statistics.

Reaves, B. (2012). *Hiring and retention of state and local law enforcement officers, 2008—Statistical tables.* Washington, DC: Bureau of Justice Statistics.

Regoli, R. M., Crouch, J. P., Culbertson, R. G., & Poole, E. D. (1987). Police professionalism and cynicism reconsidered: An assessment of measurement issues. *Justice Quarterly, 4*(2), 257–275.

Riksheim, E., & Chermak, S. (1993). Causes of police behavior revisited. *Journal of Criminal Justice, 21*(4), 353–382.

Riley, J. K., Treverton, G., Wilson, J., & Davis, L. (2005). *State and local intelligence in the war on terrorism.* Santa Monica, CA: Rand Corporation.

Roberts, A., Roberts, J., & Liedka, R. (2012). Elements of terrorism preparedness in local police agencies, 2003–2007: Impact of vulnerability, organizational characteristics, and contagion in the post-9/11 era. *Crime & Delinquency, 58*, 720–747.

Rossler, M., & Terrill, W. (2012). Police responsiveness to service-related requests. *Police Quarterly, 15*, 3–24.

Rydberg, J., & Terrill, W. (2010). The effect of higher education on police behavior. *Police Quarterly, 13*, 92–120.

Schafer, J., Burruss, G., & Giblin, M. (2009). Measuring homeland security innovation in small municipal agencies: policing in a post-9/11 world. *Police Quarterly, 12*(3), 263–288.

Schuck, A., Rosenbaum, D., & Hawkins, D. (2008). The influence of race/ethnicity, social class, and neighborhood context on residents' attitudes toward the police. *Police Quarterly, 11*(4), 496–519.

Sherman, L. (1988). *Neighborhood safety, crime file study guide.* Washington, DC: National Institute of Justice.

Skogan, W. (2008). Broken windows: Why—and how—we should take them seriously. *Criminology and Public Policy, 7*(2), 195–201.

Skolnick, J. (1966). *Justice without trial.* New York: John Wiley.

Stewart-Brown, R. (1936). *The serjeants of the peace in medieval England and Wales.* Manchester, UK: Manchester University Press.

Sun, I. (2003). Officer proactivity: A comparison between police field training officers and non-field training officers. *Journal of Criminal Justice, 31*(3), 265–277.

Sun, I., Payne, B., & Wu, Y. (2008). The impact of situational factors, officer characteristics, and neighborhood context on police behavior: A multilevel analysis. *Journal of Criminal Justice, 36*(1), 22–32.

Sun, I., & Triplett, R. (2008). Differential perceptions of neighborhood problems by police and residents: The impact of neighborhood-level characteristics. *Policing: An International Journal of Police Strategies and Management, 31*(3), 435–455.

Teplin, L. (2000). Police discretion and mentally ill persons. *National Institute of Justice Journal, 244*, 8–15.

Terry, W. C. (1985). Police stress as a professional self-image. *Journal of Criminal Justice, 13*(6), 501–512.

Toch, H. (1997). The democratization of policing in the United States: 1895–1973. *Police Forum, 7*(2), 1–8.

Travis, L., & Langworthy, R. (2008). *Policing in America: A balance of forces* (4th ed.). Englewood Cliffs, NJ: Prentice Hall.

Travis, L. F., III, & Vukovich, R. (1990). Cynicism and job satisfaction in policing: Muddying the waters. *American Journal of Criminal Justice, 15*(1), 90–104.

Travis, L. F., III, & Winston, C. (1998). Dissension in the ranks: Officer resistance to community policing, cynicism, and support for the organization. *Journal of Crime and Justice, 21*(2), 139–156.

Trojanowicz, R., Kappeler, V., Gaines, L., & Bucqueroux, B. (1998). *Community policing: A contemporary perspective* (2nd ed.). Cincinnati, OH: Anderson.

Van Maanen, J. (1978). Observations on the making of policemen. In P. K. Manning, & J. Van Maanen (Eds.), *Policing: A view from the street* (pp. 292–308). Santa Monica, CA: Goodyear.

Varano, S., Schafer, J., Cancino, J., & Swatt, M. (2009). Constructing crime: Neighborhood characteristics and police recording behavior. *Journal of Criminal Justice, 37*(6), 533–563.

Vila, B., & Kenney, D. (2002). Tired cops: The prevalence and potential consequences of police fatigue. *National Institute of Justice Journal, 248*, 16–221.

Vogel, R., & Adams, R. (1983). Police professionalism: A longitudinal cohort study. *Journal of Police Science and Administration, 11*(4), 474–484.

Walker, S. (1977). *A critical history of police reform: The emergence of professionalism.* Lexington, MA: Lexington Books.

Webster, J. A. (1970). Police task and time study. *Journal of Criminal Law, Criminology, and Police Science, 60*(1), 94–100.

Wilson, J. Q. (1968). *Varieties of police behavior.* Cambridge, MA: Harvard University Press.

Wilson, J., & Kelling, G. (1982). Broken windows: Police and neighborhood safety. *Atlantic Monthly, 249*, 29–38 (March).

Wilson, S., & Zhao, J. (2008). Determining the correlates of police victimization: An analysis of organizational level factors on injurious assaults. *Journal of Criminal Justice, 36*(5), 461–468.

Wood, D. (2001). Rural Alaskan police face high turnover. *National Institute of Justice Journal, 30*(3), 16–23.

Wood, D. (2002). Explanations of employment turnover among Alaska village public safety officers. *Journal of Criminal Justice, 30*(3), 197–216.

Worden, R. (1989). Situational and attitudinal explanations of police behavior: A theoretical reappraisal and empirical assessment. *Law & Society Review, 23*(4), 667–711.

Worrall, J. (2006). Does targeting minor offenses reduce serious crime? A provisional, affirmative answer based on an analysis of county-level data. *Police Quarterly, 9*(1), 47–72.

Zhao, J., Ren, L., & Lovrich, N. (2010). Police organizational structures during the 1990s: An application of contingency theory. *Police Quarterly, 13*(2), 209–232.

CHAPTER 6

Law Enforcement in the Criminal Justice System

Three principal decision points of the criminal justice system occur in the law enforcement segment of the process: (1) detection of crime, (2) investigation, and (3) arrest. As decisions, the police have choices about what, when, how, and whom to detect, investigate, or arrest. The existence of choices means that the police have discretion in these decisions. These activities comprise the scope of police crime control, with the exception of preventive practices such as uniformed patrol and proactive problem-solving efforts. It is these three decision points to which we will devote most of our attention in this chapter.

DETECTION

Detection is the discovery of crime or probable crime by the police. Once the police come to believe that a crime has been committed, the justice process begins. Detection hinges on many factors, ranging from the seriousness of the alleged crime and the observation powers of the officer, to the credibility of the complainant or witness. As indicated by our earlier discussion of "unfounding," sometimes the officer decides that a reported crime did not actually occur. In this case, she or he would label the complaint "unfounded," and would proceed as if nothing out of the ordinary had happened (Sudnow, 1964).

Detection of crime by police takes place in two major ways, as described in Chapter 5: reactively or proactively. The most common way in which police come to learn about crime is reactively, through the receipt of citizen complaints. Most crimes are brought to the attention of the police rather than discovered by them (Tiffany, McIntyre, & Rotenberg, 1967). Some, however, are detected proactively, through undercover operations or through the observations of officers on patrol. Still other crimes are discovered through the actions of related agents, such as investigative grand juries, legislative committees, and the like. These latter means of detection can best be categorized under the heading of "reactive detection," because in these cases police gain knowledge of the existence of crimes from complaints.

We refer to detection as a decision process because often what appears to be a quick decision, made on the spur of the moment, is actually the culmination of

Important Terms

arrest
automobile
 search
booking
cold case squads
consent search
crackdown
custodial
 investigation
decoy operation
detection
entrapment
exclusionary rule
frisk
good faith
 exception
hot pursuit
interrogation
inventory search
investigation
lineups
low visibility
Miranda warnings
plain view
 doctrine
probable cause
procedural justice
search
search incident to
 lawful arrest
sting operation
street sense
throw-downs
working rules

months or years of training or effort. This is particularly true of many of those crimes discovered by the police. What seems to be a nearly arbitrary decision to stop and question someone, or to check the license of a particular automobile, is in fact the result of a long process of learning and intelligence gathering. What the officer does is decide that further investigation is warranted. Stroshine, Alpert, and Dunham (2008) found that officers develop "working rules" that guide their detection decisions. **Working rules** are guidelines for behavior that identify the circumstances that justify different police actions. Such rules might have the officer check cars parked in business areas during nonbusiness hours.

Smith, Makarios, and Alpert (2006) reported on a study of police officer decision making in Miami. The results suggested that police officers form suspicion based on prior experience. For instance, if the officer has primarily encountered crime among males, the officer will be more suspicious of men. In the end, this means officers will be more observant of males, more likely to search and question males, and more likely to arrest males. The researchers noted that this may lead to a sort of "self-fulfilling prophecy" over time because police will look for crime where they expect to find it—among males, for example. In turn, they will find more crime among males because that is where they look, and that will encourage them to continue to be more suspicious of men than of women. Of course, other data (self-report and victimization) suggest that men are more likely to be criminal, so increased police suspicion of males may simply be reasonable.

Sacks (1978) described **street sense**, which he called an "incongruity procedure." Street sense is the ability of experienced police officers to "know" who is likely to be a criminal or to be dangerous. Sacks's term is appropriate because what the police officer relies on is that something about the individual or circumstances is incongruous or "not right"; that is, something does not fit. What appears normal to the average citizen may appear strange to the experienced officer. Police officers learn to observe clues, such as overcoats worn on warm days, mud splatters on rear license plates, and the like. The average citizen either does not notice such things or does not interpret them as possibly being crime related. After several years of experience, most officers become quite adept at the use of the incongruity procedure. The detection of crime then often rests on the police officer's perception or interpretation of the incongruous circumstances. Stroshine et al. (2008) reported that one common "working rule" focused on people or things that were "out of place."

Over time, and with training, police officers become sensitive to crime and potentially criminal circumstances. Police officers see (and seek) evidence of potential crime in circumstances that the typical citizen would not view as suspicious. Several efforts have been made to improve officer accuracy in identifying criminal situations. One of the most controversial of these has been the use of profiles in the enforcement of drug laws. Based on data taken from arrests, some jurisdictions developed "profiles" of people who are likely to be engaged in certain types of crimes. For example, young, male, minority group members driving late-model automobiles are targeted for traffic stops and preliminary investigations as potential drug couriers. These profiles understandably antagonize law-abiding citizens whom they target and contribute to poor public relations with the police (Reitzel & Piquero, 2006).

INVESTIGATION

Investigation is a process that continues throughout the law enforcement segment of the criminal justice system, and that often continues into the court segment as well. The decision involved in investigation has two parts: (1) whether to investigate a suspected crime and (2) how best to proceed with the investigation if one is initiated. Figure 6.1 presents a model of police activity in responding to crime.

An investigation is the accumulation of information and evidence that links a particular person or group of persons to a particular crime or set of crimes (Blair & Rossmo, 2010). It is the process by which formal criminal charges can be brought against identified individuals. As an evidence-gathering activity, the principal tools of investigation are search and interrogation. Other tools and skills employed depend on the nature of the offense and the resources that are available to the police, for example, forensic analyses, lineups, and surveillance (Palmiotto, 1984).

Search

Search involves the seeking out of evidence of a crime or the location of a suspect. It entails the physical inspection of papers, premises, and possessions by the police. The U.S. Constitution provides that searches be conducted only on the issuance of a warrant based on probable cause. In practice, however, the warrant requirement has proven impractical and problematic. The U.S. Supreme Court has recognized a number of exceptions to the warrant requirement. Most of these depend on a determination of reasonable behavior by the police under the circumstances. If the police have behaved reasonably, the Court rules the search to be valid.

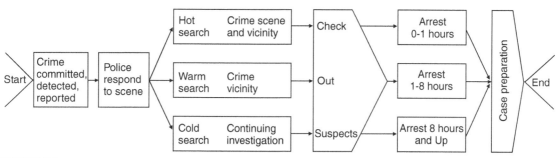

FIGURE 6.1
The criminal apprehension process.
Source: Weston and Wells (1986)

Police can obtain a search warrant from a judge or magistrate if they provide the court with information that establishes the existence of **probable cause** (evidence that leads a reasonable person to conclude that a crime has occurred and evidence of the crime may be found) to support the search. In this case, the court has the chance to review the police decision and protect the right of the suspect to be free from unreasonable intervention by the police.

To control unreasonable or improper police behavior in searches, the Supreme Court has adopted the **exclusionary rule**. This rule states that police cannot use illegally or improperly obtained evidence in a trial. The logic of the rule is that the police conduct a search to obtain evidence of criminal behavior, and excluding this evidence from trial defeats the purpose of the search. Thus, theoretically, if the police cannot conduct a legal search, they will not conduct any search.

The Supreme Court developed and imposed an exclusionary rule on federal law enforcement in 1914, in *Weeks v. United States*, but refused to apply it to the states, hoping instead that the various state systems would arrive at a better solution to the problem of illegal searches. Finally, in 1961, the Court applied the rule to the states in the case of *Mapp v. Ohio*.

Acting on a tip that a suspect (wanted in connection with a bombing) and gambling equipment were at the home of Dolree Mapp, Cleveland police went there and asked for admission, which Mapp refused. Three hours later, more officers arrived and again the police asked to enter. When Mapp refused, one of the officers displayed papers that he claimed to be a search warrant and the officers entered the home, searched the premises, and discovered pornographic materials in a trunk in the basement of the house. The police arrested Mapp, charging her with possession of obscene materials.

The Supreme Court ruled that the police behavior in this case was unacceptable and ordered the exclusion of evidence (the obscene materials) from any future trial of Mapp. Weighing heavily in the Court's decision were the facts that the police had time to secure a warrant but did not do so, that the officers claimed to have had a warrant (but never introduced one in Mapp's trial), and that Mapp was apparently not guilty of the crimes of which she was suspected. In the end, the Court held that the exclusionary rule used to support the Fourth Amendment of the U.S. Constitution was applicable to state cases through the due process clause of the Fourteenth Amendment.

The *Mapp* case and the *Miranda* decision (discussed below) led to charges that the Supreme Court was "handcuffing" the police. Critics of the Court launched virulent attacks on this interpretation of the Constitution. They believed that an "overly liberal" stance characterized these and similar decisions of the Court (Leo & Thomas, 1998). Nonetheless, the Supreme Court had interpreted the Constitution, and the exclusionary rule became the law of the land (Wilson, 1988).

Given that the Court would distinguish between the types of searches that would yield admissible evidence and those that would not, it was possible to determine exceptions to the warrant requirement by learning the circumstances under which the Court had ruled evidence was admissible in warrantless searches. Generally, the Court has identified the following circumstances to be exempt from the warrant requirement:

- Limited protective searches (frisks)
- Searches incident to lawful arrest
- Searches conducted in emergency situations or in hot pursuit of a suspect
- Border searches, on the consent of the person being subjected to the search
- Searches of automobiles
- Inventory searches
- Seizure of evidence "in plain view" of the officer

The **frisk** is a traditional police practice that the Supreme Court has upheld when conducted under specific circumstances. The Court outlined the requirements for a valid frisk in 1968 when it decided the case of *Terry v. Ohio*. In this case, an experienced Cleveland police officer conducted a limited "pat down" of the outer garments of suspected robbers to ensure his own safety as well as that of innocent bystanders.

In the *Terry* case, a 39-year veteran officer observed two suspects repeatedly walk past and look into a store. The officer concluded that the men were "casing" the store for a robbery, and he approached them to investigate. When the two stopped to confer with another man, the officer approached and asked for their names. When they mumbled in response, he turned one of them around and patted him down, finding a revolver. He frisked the other man, found another gun, and placed both men under arrest.

The Supreme Court ruled that the officer had acted reasonably under the circumstances and that he took the evidence (guns) in a reasonable search. Therefore, they allowed the use of the evidence at trial. If an officer has a reasonable suspicion that criminal activity is occurring, the officer has the authority to stop persons and to request identification and information. Moreover, if the officer has a reasonable belief that these individuals may be armed, and if nothing in the initial investigation dispels this reasonable fear, an officer may conduct a "frisk" to protect him- or herself and others.

The ability for the police to conduct a frisk is not without limits. For example, a federal judge has recently rejected a long-standing "stop and frisk" policy by the New York Police Department, calling it a form of indirect racial profiling (Goldstein, 2013). Critics of the policy had accused the police department of disproportionately stopping young minority men, the overwhelming majority of which were not involved in any criminal activity (see Figure 6.2). This will undoubtedly be the source of debate and future legal decisions.

The frisk is a protective search limited in scope to only that which is required to ensure that the person with whom the officer is dealing is not capable of injuring the officer. Upon a lawful arrest, however, the officer's authority to search is broader. Whereas frisking is limited to a "pat down" of the outer garments

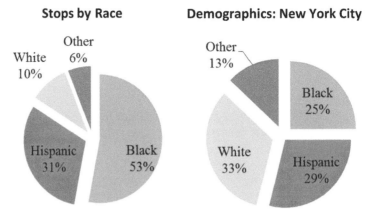

FIGURE 6.2
Stop and frisk: New York City demographics compared to police frisk stops.
Source: Office of the Public Advocate, 2013

to discover weapons, a full search by the officer is permissible in the case of an arrested person. The Court allowed **search incident to lawful arrest** to protect officers through discovery of any weapons, and to secure any evidence of the crime that the offender might otherwise be able to destroy. This type of search is limited to the area within the immediate control of the offender (*Chimel v. California*, 1969). In April 2009, the U.S. Supreme Court decided *Arizona v. Gant*. Police stopped Gant for a traffic violation and arrested him for driving with a suspended license. After handcuffing Gant and placing him in the police cruiser, the officer searched Gant's car and found drugs. The Court ruled the police could not introduce the drugs at trial because there was no reason to search the car once Gant was in custody. In these circumstances, there was no chance Gant could obtain a weapon or destroy evidence in the car. Search incident to lawful arrest only applies to the area immediately in the reach or control of the suspect.

The Supreme Court recognized a **hot pursuit** exception to the warrant requirement in the case of *Warden v. Hayden* (1967). While the Court generally prefers that police officers obtain warrants before conducting a search, it recognizes that at times this is impractical. In the *Hayden* case, the police learned of the crime (a robbery) from a cab driver who followed the suspect to a building. The police arrived at the scene within minutes after the suspect entered the building and the cab driver stated that the suspect had gone inside. The police entered the building and searched the premises for evidence of the robbery and for the suspect described to them by the cab driver. The Court decided that, under the circumstances, although the police could have cordoned off the building and awaited a warrant, the time lag involved might have allowed the suspect to destroy the evidence of the crime or to escape. Thus, when in hot pursuit, officers may follow and search for the suspect. Likewise, officers can conduct a search in an emergency situation without obtaining a search warrant. For example, police can enter a home to protect an occupant from imminent injury.

The law regarding search at international borders is different from the law of searching residences, according to the Court. Given the volume of traffic that crosses our borders and faces the U.S. Customs and Border Protection Service, as well as the potential for smuggling, the Court allows searches of persons and possessions at the nation's borders without the requirement of warrants. Indeed, the U.S. Customs and Border Protection Service periodically conducts random searches at border points.

It is possible for a competent adult to waive his or her right of protection from unreasonable searches. In a **consent search**, the suspect consents or agrees to the search so any evidence found will be admissible. In the *Mapp* case, for example, if Mapp had voluntarily allowed the police to enter her home and search for the bombing suspect, she would not have been successful in her efforts to have the evidence excluded from trial. Anyone with a right to grant consent may do so. In *United States v. Matlock* (1974), the Court ruled that a co-occupant of an apartment could grant consent to a search. In a later case, *Georgia v. Randolph* (2006), the court ruled that police must observe the objections of an occupant even if a co-occupant has given consent for the search.

Because of the mobility of automobiles, the Court treats **automobile searches** differently from searches of houses or buildings. In *United States v. Ross* (1982), the Court ruled that police officers could conduct a full search of an automobile that the officers had legitimately stopped, as long as they had probable cause to believe that the automobile contained contraband. The Court has applied the warrant standard of probable cause to the search of automobiles. Thus, as long as the police have probable cause to believe that an automobile contains contraband or evidence, they may search the vehicle and any containers in it. In 2011, the Supreme Court expanded the definition of an automobile search to include Global Positioning System (GPS) tracking devices in the case of *United States v. Jones*. These devices have been used by law enforcement to track the movement of suspected criminals, and the decision clarifies that the police must obtain a search warrant before GPS tracking is authorized.

A related issue surrounding automobiles in particular is the **inventory search**. If the police seize an automobile or other item, they generally search it to determine the contents for the purpose of inventory. They do not want the owner to claim that valuable property is missing after retrieving the car. In *Chambers v. Maroney* (1970), the Court ruled that a search of an automobile shortly after it was seized was permissible. In *Coolidge v. New Hampshire* (1981), however, the Court held that a search of an automobile required that the officers first obtain a warrant. The fact that the police had held the car for a long period before the search negated the possibility that the *Coolidge* case involved an inventory search. Because the car was in police custody and could not be moved, the probable cause standard of *Ross* was inapplicable because the officers could have obtained a warrant.

Not only may officers search an automobile they have legitimately stopped, they can also order the driver and passengers from the car and frisk those individuals

(*Maryland v. Wilson*, 1997). Beyond this, in the event the police legitimately arrest the driver, they are authorized to search the passenger compartment of the automobile (*Thornton v. United States*, 2004).

The **plain view doctrine** does not pertain to a type of search. What it means is that if an officer sees criminal evidence in plain view (i.e., the evidence did not have to be searched for), the officer may seize that evidence. Thus, if you approach an officer for directions, and you are openly carrying a controlled substance, the officer may seize the substance with no other justification than that it was in plain view. In *New York v. Class* (1986), an officer trying to read the VIN (vehicle identification numbers) through the windshield of a stopped automobile reached into the car to clear material from the number. While doing so, the officer saw a gun under the seat. The Court ruled that the officer had a right to check the VIN and thus the discovery of the gun "in plain view" was not violation of the warrant requirement. A related issue is that of "open fields": the issue of whether or when police can search for evidence of crime in fields that are fenced but visible. The Supreme Court has ruled that police may make special arrangements to fly over these areas to look for evidence and as long as the police view the evidence from publicly accessible areas, the search and seizure is acceptable (*Florida v. Riley*, 1989).

The legal authority to conduct a search often requires an understanding of the exceptions above and can be complex, as evidenced by the case of *Kentucky v. King* (2011). In this case, the police were involved in a chase of a suspected drug trafficker. The police lost sight of the suspect, but knew that the suspect had entered either of two adjacent apartments. As the police came to the apartments, a strong smell of marijuana coming from one of the doors led police to believe that the suspect was in that particular apartment. After knocking on the door and yelling "police, police, police," the officers heard noises behind the door that led them to believe that evidence was being destroyed. At this point, the police knocked down the door and arrested three people who were using drugs in plain view of the officers. Interestingly, the three defendants were not the initial suspect; the police later found the trafficker in the adjacent apartment. The Court ruled that the police acted properly. The officers had only entered the property after reasonable belief that evidence was being destroyed. Once the officers were inside the apartment, the drugs were in plain view.

The purpose of the exclusionary rule and the general requirement of a warrant are to protect the liberty of the individual citizen. The fact that there are exceptions indicates a consideration for order and crime control. The police must walk a fine line between what is necessary for the protection of the public and the control of crime, and what the protection of individual liberties requires. The warrant process, whereby a magistrate reviews the evidence and either confirms the judgment of the police (issues a warrant) or rejects it, and court rulings as to the admissibility of evidence are examples of how the justice system attempts to check the discretionary powers of the police.

Decisions whether to search, how to search, and what to search are governed by evidentiary standards such as "reasonable suspicion" or "probable cause," but in practice are discretionary in nature. The officer on the street must decide whether to take investigatory steps. Although this decision reflects the evidentiary standards of the courts, many other factors come into play when making the decision.

Rubinstein (1973) wrote that the decision to pursue an investigation hinges on the seriousness of the crime reported, the credibility of the witness/complainant, and the circumstances of the event. The less serious the crime, the less likely the police are to invest scarce investigation resources in solving it. Jogerst, Daly, Brinig, and Bibas (2005) reported that the police are more likely to devote resources to investigating allegations of elder abuse when the offense is defined as more serious (e.g., a felony rather than a misdemeanor). The less believable or sympathetic the witness/complainant, the less likely the police are to investigate. Finally, the busier the police are, the less likely they are to take the time to investigate a given complaint. Brandl (1993) reported evidence sufficiency has perhaps the greatest influence on investigation decisions. If there is enough evidence to suggest that the case can be solved, detectives are likely to devote time to its investigation (Roberts, 2008). Given equal probabilities of solving cases, however, other concerns exert an effect, including the seriousness of the crime. As with other criminal justice decisions, police exert more effort responding to cases that are seen as more serious (involving physical harm, threats, or substantial property loss). Wilson and Ruback (2003) found that in "hate crime" cases, police responses were determined in large part by the seriousness of the offense—how much harm was done.

Other factors also can affect the decisions of police officers when detecting crime. A rash of crimes, negative press pressure, the importance or status of the victim, political interference, and similar factors all can play roles in the decision to investigate. Increasingly, police agencies are instituting what are known as "**cold case squads**." These are teams of detectives dedicated to pursuing unsolved cases lacking significant leads. Turner and Kosa (2003) noted that such squads can effectively reduce the backlog of unsolved cases. As cold case squads proliferate, the traditional wisdom that police devote attention to new cases with the greatest chance for successful resolution may have to change. Here too detectives select cases based on the availability of evidence. They most often select cases having DNA, ballistic, or fingerprint evidence easily searched by computer.

Interrogation

Interrogation of suspects and witnesses has long been a mainstay of criminal investigation. We are all familiar with entertainment-media portrayals of police investigations in which detectives "grill" the suspect or continually return to the witness to extract details of the crime. Interrogation is a "search" for evidence through seeking testimony or responses to questions put to the suspect.

Just as the Fourth Amendment to the U.S. Constitution protects the homes, papers, and possessions of the citizenry from unreasonable searches, the Fifth Amendment protects citizens from overzealous interrogation by the police. The Fifth Amendment states that no one can be compelled to give testimony against oneself. *Miranda v. Arizona* (1966), perhaps the most famous of the Court's exclusionary rule cases, involved the Fifth Amendment.

In the *Miranda* case, as in many other cases preceding it, the police arrested the suspect and held him in custody for several hours while questioning him about the crime. At the conclusion of the interrogation, the suspect had confessed to the crime. Miranda's attorneys appealed the conviction stating Miranda was not aware that he did not have to speak during the interrogation and that he had a right to an attorney during questioning. Thus, the attorneys contended that police obtained the confession improperly and it should not have been allowed as evidence at the trial. The Supreme Court agreed, ruling that when police have a suspect in custody, they must advise the suspect that he or she may remain silent, that what is said may be used against the suspect in court, and that the suspect has the right to either a retained (hired) or appointed attorney during questioning (see Box 6.1).

The *Miranda* decision revolutionized police interrogation practices. One of the reasons the case is so well known is that the Court required that police provide suspects with warnings as to their rights at interrogation, and these required warnings became known as the **Miranda warnings**. Traditional practices of "incommunicado" (not permitting the suspect to see or speak with anyone except the investigating officers), as well as the psychological advantage held by the police in such interrogations, were abolished.

Within 2 years of the decision, the U.S. Congress included language in the Omnibus Crime Control Act of 1968 that redefined the conditions making a confession voluntary. The U.S. Department of Justice, however, never sought to implement that statute (*Dickerson v. United States*, 2000). As long as the confession was voluntary, the statute did not require that the police give the *Miranda* warning. In 2000, the U.S. Supreme Court reviewed this issue and held that the requirements of the *Miranda* ruling still apply. Essentially, the Court ruled that absent the warnings it would not be possible to conclude that a suspect voluntarily confessed because the warnings ensure that the suspect knows his or her rights and that he or she need not cooperate with the police.

BOX 6.1 MIRANDA WARNINGS

- You have the right to remain silent.
- Anything you say can and will be used against you in a court of law.
- You have the right to an attorney during questioning.
- If you cannot afford an attorney, one will be appointed for you by the court.

Since the original *Miranda* decision, numerous cases have been heard by the Court regarding interrogation, particularly regarding the issue of a time lapse between interrogation sessions. The Court has generally been consistent in ruling that when a suspect requests the assistance of counsel during an interrogation, any future waiver of *Miranda* rights is invalid (Ross & Myers, 2010). Finally, in 2010 the Supreme Court held that a break in custody of two or more weeks is all that is needed to allow police to attempt to question a suspect again. In *Maryland v. Shatzer* (2010), Shatzer, who was in prison, refused to answer questions about alleged child sexual abuse. More than 2 years later, the police reopened the case and interrogated Shatzer. This time he answered questions, and the police used his statements to convict him of the child abuse crime. The court ruled that although Shatzer originally invoked his Fifth Amendment privilege, the long break in custody meant that the second questioning did not violate Shatzer's original refusal. Because he was warned again before the second questioning, Shatzer's testimony was admissible.

The *Miranda* decision, most of all, led some commentators to charge that the Supreme Court was "handcuffing the police." These critics expressed fears that, because of this decision, the police would be unable to obtain confessions, and thereby convict far fewer offenders (Cassell, 1996). However, most evaluations of the effects of the *Miranda* warnings on conviction rates and the recovery of stolen property have failed to support these earlier criticisms. Leo (2001) concluded that the *Miranda* decision has had very little impact on the criminal justice system. As Leo pointed out, most offenders in modern society have knowledge of these rights through exposure to popular television programs. In addition, the overwhelming majority of suspects voluntarily waive their *Miranda* rights, thus not creating a problem for law enforcement personnel. These arguments have been backed up by recent surveys of police chiefs. Only 1% of police chiefs nationwide believe that too many offenders get off easy as a result of *Miranda* warnings (Zalman & Smith, 2007). In fact, many police chiefs report that one outcome of the *Miranda* ruling has been a proliferation of more professional and effective police officers (Time & Payne, 2002). In part, the critics were wrong in their contention because they probably did not consider the system qualities of the justice process and the ability of systems to resist change and to maintain equilibrium. Several practices developed that may have served to blunt the effect of *Miranda*.

A practice that enabled police to get around the *Miranda* requirement was "psychological warfare." One effect of the *Miranda* decision may have been to increase the skill of police interrogators. Davis (2008) called the modern interrogation process an extended "anti-Miranda warning," where the interrogator works to "convince the suspect that everything he says—preferably including a detailed confession to the crime at hand—can and will work to his benefit, whereas denial or failure to talk to his interrogator can and will be held against him" (p. 1). Suspects can be motivated to confess either by (1) increasing stress and discomfort to motivate confession as a method of escaping the situation or (2) leading the suspect to the rational conclusion that confessing is in his or her best interests. Interrogators have developed many tactics to facilitate confessions through one or both of these paths (Davis, 2008). One such interrogation technique involves officers telling suspects that they have physical evidence or witnesses when no such evidence exists. Officers believe guilty suspects will confess when told the police have other evidence (Alpert & Noble, 2009). Other techniques include role playing, exaggerating, or minimizing the severity of the crime, and the use of implied promises of leniency (Ellwanger, 2012).

It is important to note that *Miranda* warnings are only necessary whenever there is a **custodial interrogation** (Ellwanger, 2012). In other words, a suspect is only entitled to the warning in situations where they are under arrest *and* being interrogated by officers. Therefore, officers can arrest a suspect and simply listen to him or her talk. If the suspect provides any incriminating statements, these are generally allowable in court. Likewise, the warnings are not required when an officer is engaged in a simple interview, which is often conducted by the police at the early stages of an investigation when they do not have a particular suspect and are primarily concerned with gaining general information about the crime. An interrogation begins when, for example, the officers ask accusatory questions to a specific individual.

THE "GOOD FAITH" EXCEPTION

In 1967, the U.S. Supreme Court decided the case of *Katz v. United States*. In this case, federal investigators who suspected Katz of involvement in gambling placed an electronic eavesdropping device on the exterior of a telephone booth they believed Katz used to transmit betting information. Katz was convicted of transmitting betting information by telephone in violation of a federal law. He appealed, stating that the federal agents had violated the Fourth Amendment by not securing a warrant for the eavesdropping. Prior to this case, the Court interpreted the Fourth Amendment as designed to protect places. By locating the device on the exterior of a public telephone booth, the agents believed they had not violated Katz's rights. The Supreme Court, however, reversed the conviction, ruling that the Fourth Amendment protected people, not places. The decision turned on Katz's expectation of privacy. In this case, although law enforcement officials took pains to comply with the Constitution and believed they were behaving appropriately, a guilty defendant was set free.

The *Katz* case illustrates one problem with the exclusionary rule. The rule seeks to deter police officials from violating citizens' rights. What happens when the police believe they are obeying the law? If the police make an honest mistake, their behavior cannot be deterred. What we need, many observers believed, was a "good faith" exception to the exclusionary rule. If the police work in good faith in the belief that they are not violating the Constitution, then any evidence they obtain should be admissible.

In 1984, the Court established a good faith exception in the case of *United States v. Leon*. In this case, officers relied on information from a confidential informant to obtain a search warrant. At trial, Leon's attorneys argued that the information on which the warrant was based was insufficient to establish probable cause, and thus the evidence from the search should be suppressed (excluded). The judge agreed. Here, officers sought and obtained a warrant, executed the search, found large quantities of drugs, and yet the evidence was still suppressed because of an error by the magistrate issuing the warrant. The Supreme Court ruled that because the exclusionary rule seeks to deter police misconduct rather than punish errors of judges or magistrates, the state could use the evidence. If the police conduct a search believing in good faith that the search is permissible, then the evidence can be used at trial, making a **good faith exception**.

Since then, the Court has expanded on the good faith exception. In *Arizona v. Evans* (1995), the Court ruled that a police search of Evans based on a mistaken belief that he was a fugitive was legal. Police stopped Evans for a traffic violation, and the subsequent computer check revealed an outstanding arrest warrant. The officer arrested Evans based on the warrant, and then searched the car, finding marijuana. The arrest warrant, however, had been removed 2 weeks earlier. There was no warrant for Evans's arrest at the time of the search. Still, the officer believed, in good faith, that Evans was wanted and that the arrest and subsequent search were constitutional. The Supreme Court ruled that the exclusionary rule is not designed to prevent clerical errors (the computer record of the warrant had not been updated), and thus the officer was acting reasonably and the evidence was admissible. In 1995, the U.S. Congress considered legislative action to curtail the exclusionary rule. In separate bills, both the House of Representatives and the Senate considered legislation that would have statutorily instituted and defined a good faith exception to the exclusionary rule (Davis, 1997). Neither house's version of exclusionary rule reform passed, but the exclusionary rule remains a topic of intense debate in criminal justice.

The USA PATRIOT (Uniting and Strengthening America by Providing Appropriate Tools Required to Intercept and Obstruct Terrorism) Act of 2001 has raised concerns about potential governmental intrusion on individual rights. The act allows investigators to execute search warrants without notifying the owner or occupant of the location. It has eased restrictions on the use of wiretaps and other electronic surveillance. Although aimed at counterterrorism and national security, the powers given law enforcement officers to detect and prevent terrorism can and will also be used to detect and apprehend more traditional criminal offenders.

Other Investigatory Practices

In addition to search and interrogation, police obtain evidence in a number of ways. The offender's age, race, sex, and size can be determined from hairs found at the scene of the crime. Police can identify clothes worn by the offender from fibers collected at the crime scene. The police can ascertain the weapon used in the crime from ballistics examinations. All these techniques are staples of a forensic scientist's investigation. While rarely employed because of costs and a lack of necessity, the techniques of a forensic scientist sometimes provide the answers to investigators (Peterson, 1987). Forensic science is becoming increasingly important in criminal investigations, as can be seen in the increased attention paid to DNA typing. The Combined DNA Index System (CODIS) serves as a database allowing for comparisons between crime scene DNA samples and existing profiles of convicted offenders. While still relatively rarely used, the application of DNA analysis has experienced amazing advances in the past several years (Dale, Greenspan, & Orokos, 2006). Still, despite television dramas, forensic examinations are not common to most investigations, and DNA evidence is rarely used to solve cases (Schroeder & White, 2009). Television dramas based on crime scene investigators have popularized forensic science and crime scene analysts, often leading to unrealistic public expectations (Ley, Jankowski, & Brewer, 2012).

IDENTIFICATION TECHNIQUES: THROW-DOWNS AND LINEUPS

More common is the identification of offenders through throw-downs and lineups, whereby the police seek the identity of a suspect from a pool of possibilities by having witnesses examine photographs (**throw-downs**) or observe possible offenders (**lineups**). The major concern of the courts regarding these practices is that the police not be too suggestive in their behavior (Cutler, Duaherty, Babu, Hodges, & Wallendael, 2009). For example, the identification of a white male suspect from a lineup comprised of the man and six black females would be too suggestive. To protect against the possibility that the police would encourage a false identification, the Supreme Court has held that suspects in custody have the right to have an attorney present during lineups (*United States v. Wade*, 1967). Unless the victim or witness knows the offender, it is unlikely that these procedures by themselves will yield the offender. More often, police use these procedures after they have enough evidence to conclude that the suspect is probably guilty of the offense. Thus, these identifications tend to constitute supporting evidence and are not the heart of the case.

SURVEILLANCE

Still another investigation tool is surveillance. Police use both physical and electronic surveillance techniques to gather evidence of criminal activity. Wiretaps, hidden microphones, cameras, and other forms of surreptitious surveillance such as GPS tracking devices generally require warrants and are therefore used infrequently. The point of most surveillance is to gather evidence on persons suspected of crimes, but against whom insufficient evidence exists to obtain a search warrant. Usually, surveillance does not involve tapping telephone lines or watching individual residences. The bulk of surveillance conducted by police agencies is physical surveillance, by which officers watch a certain location or follow a suspect to gather evidence (Nunn, Quinet, Rowe, & Christ, 2006). One exception is the use of video surveillance of public areas. The British have been using video surveillance of public areas for years, and the practice is becoming more common in the United States (see Table 6.1). British research suggests that the use of surveillance cameras has a modest effect in reducing crime (Welsh & Farrington, 2002). Surette (2006) reported the results of video surveillance in an American city. He concluded that the evidence suggests that cameras produce a deterrent effect on crime.

Table 6.1	Percent of U.S. Local Police Departments Regularly Using Video Surveillance in 2007
Any use	66
In patrol cars	61
Fixed site	13
Mobile surveillance	9

Source: Reaves (2010)

Surveillance techniques yield evidence of specific criminality and information (or "intelligence") on suspicious persons and places. In the former case, officers generally have reason to believe that a particular person is engaged in criminal activity, or that crimes are occurring at a particular place, and the surveillance seeks to provide evidence about those specific offenses. In intelligence gathering, police suspect an individual or location and conduct surveillance in hopes of obtaining further evidence or information to confirm or reject their suspicions.

Technological advances are constantly improving the intelligence potential of surveillance methods. Police use license plate readers, both at static locations and mounted on police vehicles, to help locate stolen cars or suspect vehicles. Police can review computerized records of the license plate scanning effort later to determine if a particular vehicle was at the scene. Face-recognition technology coupled with video surveillance helps police to determine if a particular person was observed at some place. We will discuss technology more in Chapter 15. It is enough to recognize that technological advances greatly increase the surveillance capabilities of the police.

INFORMANTS

Informants are another investigation tool used by the police. To some, the use of informants seems inappropriate because it frequently requires the police to join forces with criminals to enforce the law. Nonetheless, informants are extremely useful to police in intelligence gathering. Usually neither criminals nor the police respect the informant, in keeping with a norm that one should not be a "rat." However, informants are often able to learn and observe things that an undercover officer would find difficult to discover even after months of work—and that a uniformed officer would find impossible to obtain. Police can use information from informants, even anonymous tips, but they must be able to convince the magistrate that the informant's information is credible. In *Illinois v. Gates* (1983), the Supreme Court allowed police to rely on an anonymous tip about Gates's involvement in drug trafficking as long as the police had taken reasonable steps to verify the accuracy of the tip.

Informants do not make particularly good witnesses. Typically, their credibility is questioned either because of their own criminal pasts, or because their information is provided with the expectation of a reward and not as a matter of civic responsibility. Add to this the fact that many informants are not willing to testify in open court, and this valuable source of information for police becomes less than ideal for solving crimes. To combat these weaknesses, many police departments employ undercover police officers. These officers are assigned to work in "plain clothes" and are directed to mix with the general public so that their identities as police officers will not be readily apparent.

CRACKDOWNS

Yet another police response to crime that combines investigation with detection and arrest is the **crackdown** (Sherman, 1990a). In crackdowns, the police devote increased attention and resources to either specific types of crime (drug sales, prostitution, street robberies, etc.) or to crime in particular places (downtown areas, parking lots, schools, etc.). Crackdowns are temporary in nature and often involve practices of saturation patrol, in which a large number of uniformed officers are used to flood a locale with police, or policy directives, in which officers are directed to arrest in certain crime situations whenever possible. Crackdowns allow the police to show that they are "doing something" about crime, and tend, at least in the short run, to depress levels of criminal activity in the affected areas. Crackdowns affect general levels of disorder, drug trafficking, serious crime, prostitution, and drunk driving (Mazerolle, Soole, & Rombouts, 2007; Sherman, 1990b).

In more sophisticated applications, the notion of a crackdown has evolved into a specific policing strategy for preventing crime in areas known as "hot spots" of crime (see Figure 6.3). Sherman, Gartin, and Buerger (1989) reported that some places have much higher rates of crime (or citizen complaints of crime) than do

FIGURE 6.3
St. Louis police officers increase their presence in College Hill in February 2013 after four shootings killed three people in the neighborhood. The second phase of an effort to turn around the crime-ridden neighborhood involves several city departments working together to secure vacant houses, clean debris, and ensure that streetlights are working.
AP Photo/St. Louis Post-Dispatch, Robert Cohen

others. They labeled these high-rate locations as hot spots of crime. Once hot spots are located, the police must determine how to respond. A typical response is to increase police presence in these areas, or crack down on the hot spot. A number of studies have shown that such efforts have at least short-term effects of reducing crime and disorder (Koper, 1995; Telep & Weisburd, 2012; Weisburd, 2005). Lawton, Taylor, and Luongo (2005:449) had this to say about a crack-down effort in Philadelphia, "Crackdowns respond to current crises. Because they are 'out of the ordinary,' they cost a lot, they attract attention, and as we show here, they get results. But they are rarely sustainable because of high costs."

UNDERCOVER OPERATIONS

Certain types of crimes, such as the "victimless" offenses associated with vice enforcement, are not likely to yield complainants. The customer who solic-its a prostitute or purchases drugs is unlikely to complain to the police. In so doing, of course, the complainant would implicate himself or herself in crimi-nal behavior. Thus, the police must aggressively (proactively) seek evidence of these crimes. Almost every major police department has a vice unit comprised of officers who attempt to uncover instances of victimless crimes. These officers pose as either potential consumers or potential providers of the illicit goods and services, and then wait for would-be offenders to approach them.

Police approach other crimes in a proactive manner in some places. They detect robberies, especially street robberies, using plainclothes "decoys." Areas of high incidence of specific crimes are determined through reviews of police reports. Police then conduct a **decoy operation**, in which officers are disguised as poten-tial victims in those areas, with other officers serving as "backups" (Halpher & Ku, 1976). When the criminal strikes, the backup officers close in and make an arrest. These types of undercover operations have proven to be very successful with specific types of crimes.

The "sting" is an additional form of undercover operation used to detect and arrest burglars and other forms of criminal offenders. The **sting operation** gets its name from the slang of confidence artists. These "con artists" gain the trust of their victims and then take the victim's money. The actual taking of the money is the "sting." Because the police pretend to be criminals to gain the trust of offenders until they have sufficient evidence to make an arrest, the undercover operations also are called stings. One of the most famous sting operations was the Federal Bureau of Investigation's ABSCAM operation, in which FBI agents posed as wealthy foreign representatives and attempted to uncover bribery activ-ity among members of Congress and other governmental officials (Coleman, 1985:104–106; *Time*, 1980).

The most common police sting involves the establishment of a "fencing" opera-tion; that is, police officers pose as dealers of stolen goods. Police photograph burglars and thieves when they come to sell (fence) goods they have stolen. Later, police arrest these offenders based on the evidence obtained in the fake fence operation.

There are two commonly raised criticisms of undercover operations. First, there are those who argue that these operations, especially sting operations, create crime because they provide an easily identifiable outlet for stolen property, which encourages people to steal (Langworthy, 1989; Langworthy & LeBeau, 1992, 1993). Second, and perhaps more important, there are those who suggest that such operations ensnare the innocent through entrapment.

The **entrapment** defense to criminal charges is applicable when the entrapped offender did not have the inclination to commit a crime absent police entice-ment. If the police entice an otherwise innocent individual to commit a crime, that individual may have a defense of entrapment (Park, 1976). Assuming that you would not generally think of committing a crime, how would you respond if I offered you $1 million to transport some drugs across town for me?

For many people, this offer is too good to refuse. If you were to say yes to my offer and I then wished to arrest you for transporting drugs, you could say you were entrapped. You only committed the crime because I came to you with the idea and offered you an inducement too great to refuse. The same logic applies if an officer suggests a price and activity to a suspected prostitute. This is true regardless of the price offered; the law does not question judgment and worth as much as it does motive.

It is important to distinguish between entrapment and encouragement. Unlike entrapment, it is permissible for the police to "encourage" someone to complete a crime the person is already contemplating. An officer who approaches a pros-titute and offers to pay for a service may be placing the idea in the mind of the prostitute. Someone contemplating an act of prostitution, however, already has the criminal idea. The fact that an officer allows a person to make a proposition is not entrapment; it is encouragement.

The investigation of crimes, through whatever means the police employ, pro-vides a basis for the next decision of importance in the law enforcement seg-ment of the justice process: arrest. When police have probable cause to believe that an individual has committed a crime, we expect them to place that person under arrest. Yet, as with investigation and detection, arrest is a decision process that depends on a number of factors.

ARREST

Arrest is the act of taking a person into custody. Once arrested, a person is no longer free to leave. The authority to arrest offenders is but one of a number of tools available to the police officer in his or her efforts to maintain order. There are times when this authority is the best or most appropriate tool; at other times it is inappropriate. The decision regarding the appropriateness of arrest is often a discretionary one for the officer.

Goldstein (1960) discussed police discretion in deciding whether to employ the criminal law. He identified the decision not to arrest as "noninvocation discretion" (decision not to invoke the law). He termed the process "low-visibility decision making." If an officer decides not to make an arrest when an arrest is justified, who has knowledge about the decision? Generally, only the officer and the offender are aware of the failure to arrest. Thus, this decision has **low visibility**, meaning that most people (including the police administration) do not see it. If an officer decides not to issue a traffic citation to you, no one will know unless the officer or you report this decision. How many times have you reported to the police station that an officer did not issue a citation to you?

The other face of noninvocation discretion is, logically, "invocation discretion" (the decision to invoke the law). This decision is more visible, because the officer must report the arrest, the suspect will most likely have legal counsel, and eventually the case may get into the courts. Yet, the decision to arrest someone is often as discretionary as the decision not to arrest. Officers or departments follow rules of thumb when deciding to invoke the criminal law. Occasionally, an officer will opt to enforce the law when the rule of thumb would suggest noninvocation. Exemplifying this are "tolerance limits" regarding excessive speed. Most departments attempt to avoid bad public relations (and close court decisions) in traffic cases by suggesting that offenders not be cited if they are traveling at a rate within a specified difference from the speed limit. If the speed limit is 55 mph, we might expect traffic officers to cite only those motorists traveling in excess of 60 mph. However, a motorist stopped for traveling 58 mph could be cited instead of warned (regardless of the tolerance limit) if the officer feels the motorist's behavior is inappropriate. Schafer and Mastrofski (2005) described traffic enforcement in one community in which the policy of the department supported leniency by officers, but also noted that citizen behavior was associated with the use of more formal and more severe sanctions. Sun, Payne, and Wu (2008) reported that a number of situational and neighborhood factors influence officer decisions.

A responding officer might decide that arrest is necessary to separate combatants in a dispute, or that such an arrest might prove more harmful than beneficial in a given situation. An officer might arrest an ill child to secure needed medical treatment in the absence of parents, or might fail to arrest a known offender in return for information about other offenses or offenders. In all these situations, it is apparent that arrest is a tool for the officers involved, or a means to an end. To understand the exercise of the arrest power in a particular instance, one must understand the intent of the officer involved.

A number of researchers have investigated the arrest decision by police officers. Many would be surprised at how often the police do not make an arrest. In fact, Terrill and Paoline (2007) found that police failed to make an arrest in the vast majority of the cases that they examined. Factors predicting arrest included the seriousness of the crime, the suspect's demeanor, and signs of alcohol and other drug abuse. In addition, officers arrested suspects more often if they had been called on by the public than those cases for which the officer initiated the contact. Interestingly, the amount of evidence did not impact an officer's likelihood of making an arrest. In domestic violence cases where many agencies have mandatory or preferred arrest policies, police still often fail to make arrests (Phillips & Sobol, 2010). Circumstances that influence arrest in intimate partner violence include the race, age, and marital status of the victim and the offender, as well as the type of violence involved (Dichter, Marcus, Morabito, & Rhodes, 2011). Clearly, the available research indicates that police officers decide between arrest and nonarrest in many cases.

When police do make an arrest, the justice process becomes fully involved. The arresting officer must file reports, and the offender/suspect must be transported to a detention facility and booked (where police make an official record of the arrest). Shortly after the arrest, the suspect must be given the opportunity to contact an attorney. The suspect has the right to be considered for pretrial release. These procedures quickly move the case from the law enforcement segment of the justice system into the courts.

As is evident in the *Miranda* ruling, the behavior of police officers is much more tightly controlled after arrest than before it. Once the suspect is in custody, the procedures designed to protect the liberty of individuals are initiated. Police officers often complain that suspects are returned to freedom on the streets through bail before the officers have completed their paperwork. Typically, these officers are expressing frustration with the justice system because it seems to be "stacked" in favor of the suspect. In fact, they are correct. The criminal justice system is intentionally constrained by the Constitution to protect the due process rights of the accused who are facing a potential punishment from the criminal justice system.

Booking, the official public recording of an arrest, seeks to prevent the police from holding an offender/suspect incommunicado; anyone can check the booking records to determine whether a person is in police custody. Bail or pretrial release is a provision of the Eighth Amendment of the U.S. Constitution, which is designed to prevent a suspect from unnecessary confinement prior to conviction and to allow the defendant to be free to cooperate in his or her own defense. A third stage, the preliminary hearing (which will be discussed in Chapter 7), is a review of the evidence and the arrest decision by a magistrate or judge. The hearing is held to determine whether the police had sufficient grounds for placing a person in custody. All these procedures illustrate the care with which we protect the rights of the individual in conformity with the presumption of innocence. Frustration arises because, although the law requires police and other actors in the justice system (at least theoretically) to presume that the suspect is innocent, to do their jobs, they often have to believe in the probable guilt of suspects.

DUE PROCESS, CRIME CONTROL, AND THE POLICE

Even if the core mission of the police is crime control, crime control is not the only criterion on which we assess the police and police actions. The police must not only strive to reduce, prevent, and respond to crime, they must do so in a constrained fashion. We require the police to enforce the law and protect the public, but to observe and protect individual rights in the process (Bayley, 2002). Our discussion of entrapment illustrates the tension that exists between due process and crime control in policing. It is not enough for the police to establish that someone broke the law; they must do so without unduly influencing the person to engage in crime. The requirements of due process support a reactive style of policing by restricting what police can do to detect and arrest potential criminals.

The exclusionary rule also illustrates the tension between due process and crime control. The exclusionary rule applies to only those cases in which the police find evidence that crime has occurred. If the police search a home without a warrant and find no criminal evidence, there is no evidence to exclude. The exclusionary rule applies only when there is evidence that someone is guilty of a crime. The exclusionary rule works to release the guilty. In doing so, the rule implies that due process concerns outweigh crime control concerns. The courts would rather let a criminal go free than allow the police to violate constitutional rights.

The Supreme Court wrestled with this question of balance in the case of *United States v. Leon*, when it defined a good faith exception to the exclusionary rule. In *Leon* (and later cases), the police took all reasonable steps to protect the rights of the accused, but still made a technical error. The Court noted that the police believed the warrant they had obtained was valid and conducted a search based on that warrant. It later turned out that the warrant was issued erroneously. The Court ruled that if police obtain evidence of crime based on what they, in good faith, believe to be a valid warrant, the evidence need not be excluded even if the warrant is invalid.

Rather than view the exclusionary rule as universal, the Court recognized a circumstantial test of police behavior. The purpose of the exclusionary rule is to deter or prevent police misconduct. The Court suggested that in cases in which the police believe they are obeying procedural law, there is no police behavior to deter. Thus, if the exclusionary rule would not be working to protect individual rights (due process), the social cost of letting the guilty go free is unjustified. Crime control proponents applaud this decision because it allows the police and justice system to avoid ignoring crime based on legal technicalities. Due process proponents worry that the *Leon* decision signals a shift in the balance between due process and crime control away from an emphasis on individual liberty.

The good faith exception to the exclusionary rule represents the balancing act that characterizes the entire American system of criminal justice. It seeks to define when, and under what conditions, our interests in individual liberty outweigh our interests in crime control. When do we trust the police to act in our best interests, and when are we suspicious of police powers?

The movement toward community-oriented or problem-oriented policing also demonstrates this balance. As the police become more proactive in seeking to prevent and control crime, the ability of citizens to control police behavior through calls for service is reduced. When the police are encouraged to identify and select problems that seem to produce crime, and when they are urged to focus on disorder at least as much as crime, the role of the police expands. Rather than responding to citizen calls for service, the police themselves determine when and how they will intervene.

This discretion can cause problems between the police and the community. If there is disagreement among members of the community about what is acceptable behavior, the police end up taking sides when they decide whether to act to control such behavior (Kelling, 1999). As important, when the behavior in question relates to order more than crime, the authority of the police to act is unclear. If citizens believe that they are not violating any laws, they may be resistant to police efforts to control them. Facing resistance, the officers often must rely on force, or the threat of force, to make citizens obey. This, in turn, leads to citizen views of the police as brutal and authoritarian. Many researchers have studied citizen attitudes toward the police (e.g., Cao, Stack, & Sun, 1998; Frank, Smith, & Novak, 2005; Warren, 2011). In general, citizens who have had negative experiences with the police, or who have friends, family, and acquaintances who report negative experiences with the police, are less likely to report positive feelings toward the police themselves. This negative opinion of the police can, in turn, affect the suspect's demeanor in subsequent encounters with the police (Rosenbaum, Schuck, Costello, Hawkins, & Ring, 2005). In a sense, citizen attitudes toward police can be a self-fulfilled prophecy. If the citizen expects a negative interaction with the police, their disrespectful demeanor will result in a negative reaction by the officer, which then serves to reinforce the suspect's original view of the police (Dunham & Alpert, 2009). This raises several important questions. When, and for what types of disorder, should the police direct citizen behavior? If a behavior is not criminal in itself, should the police be able to intervene to prevent future crime?

These issues have become even more important as local law enforcement has been called on to take a more active role in homeland security. Recent federal legislation and growing public concern about the threat of terrorist attacks have resulted in increased demands that police take steps to prevent terrorist activity (DeLone, 2007). Preventive actions, of course, are in some sense less democratic than reactive, enforcement actions, because the police work under their own initiative. Critics of our reaction to the terrorist threat point out that efforts to prevent future terrorist acts that negate our freedoms are, in the end, proof that the terrorist attacks have been successful (Lynch, 2002). To the extent that concerns about the harm of terrorist attacks outweigh our concerns about individual liberty, we can expect a shift in police practice toward a greater emphasis on crime control and a reduced concern with due process.

See Table 6.2 for a brief summary of some important cases in law enforcement.

Table 6.2	Selected Court Cases in Law Enforcement
Weeks v. United States 232 U.S. 383 (1914)	Evidence illegally obtained by law enforcement officers is not admissible in federal criminal prosecutions. This is referred to as the "exclusionary rule"
Mapp v. Ohio 367 U.S. 643 (1961)	The exclusionary rule, which prohibits the use of evidence obtained as the result of unreasonable searches and seizures, is applicable in state criminal proceedings (See *Weeks v. United States* for the exclusionary rule)
Miranda v. Arizona 384 U.S. 436 (1966)	Police must advise a suspect in custody of his or her right to remain silent, the fact that what is said may be used against him or her in court, and of the right to the counsel of a hired or appointed attorney during questioning
United States v. Wade 388 U.S. 218 (1967)	A suspect in custody has the right to an attorney during postindictment lineups
Warden v. Hayden 387 U.S. 294 (1967)	A warrantless search may be valid under circumstances of "hot pursuit"
Terry v. Ohio 392 U.S. 1 (1968)	Stop and frisk is valid on "reasonable suspicion" in order to ensure the safety of police and bystanders
Chimel v. California 395 U.S. 752 (1969)	When making a valid arrest, police may search the area of the arrestee's "immediate control," whether the arrest is with or without a warrant
Chambers v. Maroney 453 U.S. 42 (1970)	Police may perform a warrantless search of an automobile shortly after it is seized
Brewer v. Williams 430 U.S. 387 (1977)	Conversations with or appeals to a suspect that may induce a confession constitute an interrogation that requires both *Miranda* warnings and the right to counsel
Coolidge v. New Hampshire 403 U.S. 443 (1981)	A search is valid only if the warrant is issued by a neutral and detached magistrate. Search of a car after it is in police possession for a period of time does not constitute a valid inventory search
United States v. Ross 456 U.S. 798 (1982)	Police can conduct a full search of an automobile as long as they have probable cause to believe that the automobile contains contraband

(Continued)

Table 6.2	Selected Court Cases in Law Enforcement—Cont'd
Illinois v. Gates 462 U.S. 213 (1983)	The two-pronged test established under *Aguilar* and *Spinelli* is abandoned in favor of a "totality of circumstances" approach. The task of an issuing magistrate is to make a practical decision whether, given all the circumstances, there is a fair probability that the evidence of a crime will be found in a particular place
United States v. Leon 484 U.S. 897 (1984)	Even if the warrant relied on is eventually found invalid, the exclusionary rule allows the use of evidence obtained by officers acting in reasonable reliance on the validity of the warrant
Dickerson v. United States 530 U.S. 428 (2000)	*Miranda* waivers are still required when police officers are interrogating suspects who are in custody. This supersedes the provision of the Omnibus Crime Control Act of 1968, which provides that a defendant's statement is admissible in federal court if given voluntarily, regardless of whether *Miranda* rights have been waived
Arizona v. Gant 556 U.S. 332 (2009)	The Fourth Amendment requires law enforcement officers to demonstrate an actual and continuing threat to their safety posed by an arrestee, or a need to preserve evidence related to the crime of arrest from tampering by the arrestee, to justify a warrantless vehicular search incident to arrest conducted after the vehicle's recent occupants have been arrested and secured
Maryland v. Shatzer 559 U.S. 98 (2010)	Police may reopen questioning of a suspect who previously asked for counsel if there has been a 14-day or more break in custody
United States v. Jones 132 S. Ct. 945 (2012)	Installing a GPS tracking device on a vehicle constitutes a search under the Fourth Amendment, requiring the police to obtain a search warrant

Source: Portions of this table were adapted from del Carmen and Walker (2012)

ISSUES IN LAW ENFORCEMENT

It is difficult to identify a limited set of important issues in contemporary policing. Almost everything about the police is problematic, and given the dilemma inherent in policing a free society, all these problems are important. For instance, the increasing tendency of civilians to sue the police is evidence of a conflict between police practice and citizen expectancies (Kappeler, Kappeler, & del Carmen, 1993). However, it is necessary to narrow the field and examine only a few of the problems. Corruption, for example, is a traditional problem in policing, and people often suspect that the police are corrupt. Additionally, the use of force—especially deadly force—has been an issue in policing since the first use of force by police. The relationship between the police and the community also has traditionally been a source of conflict. Finally, the role of the police in controlling crime remains unclear.

Corruption

In terms of corruption, police in the United States have a flawed tradition. From the beginning, when police were loosely controlled, political patronage and the influence of politicians and criminals on police operations contributed to a perception among the general public of the police as corruptible at least, if not actually corrupt (Sherman, 1974). The public, aware of past practices, tends to believe that police will treat their friends and political leaders differently than they do the average citizen (Dowler & Zawilski, 2007). This perception of favoritism supports a view of the police as corrupt.

Periodic scandals exposing police acceptance of bribes further reinforce this perception. Corruption is an issue not simply because it means the police are criminal, but because it raises the question of who controls the police. Public fears of police corruption are based more on the fact that a corrupt police department is out of control than on the belief that graft is, in itself, morally wrong. In recent years, concern about police corruption has again risen to prominence. Renewed interest in police corruption is partly a product of the recent war on drugs. Revelations of widespread and serious police misconduct in New York, Miami, Los Angeles, and other cities have attracted attention.

The police have broad powers, and yet they operate with decentralized patrols. The discretionary authority of police officers is generally well known (i.e., we all hope for a "break," even if we do not get it). This combination of power and lack of accountability is what makes corruption possible. In fact, given the nature of American policing, it might be more surprising that there is so little widespread corruption than that there is so much of it. In the end, police corruption is difficult to define. Withrow and Dailey (2004) suggested that corruption lies on a continuum that includes lawful and proper activity. Police behavior is corrupt, they said, when the police officer comes to expect or demand special treatment or reward.

Carter (1990a, 1990b) classified police officer corruption associated with drug enforcement. He characterized the opportunities for corruption as being of two basic types: (1) for personal benefit and (2) for organizational gain. Personal benefit corruption exists when police officers take bribes, convert seized evidence (drugs) and property to personal use, or similarly use their position to advance their individual well-being. Organizational gain characterizes police corruption that involves lying or perjury to secure convictions of drug offenders, undercover officers engaging in criminality to gain access to higher levels of drug organizations, and similar practices designed, not for personal benefit, but to achieve the goals of the organization in drug enforcement. Some commentators (Holden, 1993; Skolnick, 2008) have suggested that statutes allowing police seizure of the property of drug offenders may work to corrupt the police agency by instilling a profit motive into law enforcement, and by reducing the ability of the government to control police through the budgetary process. What makes corruption such an important issue is this concern about the negative effects of police that are beyond citizen control.

"Police corruption" is a term that almost everyone understands, but that has a variety of meanings to different people. Clearly, most people see taking bribes not to enforce the law, stealing from crime scenes, and similar acts of crime as corrupt. There is less agreement about other actions in which police officers may engage. Officers who conduct background checks on persons for their friends, or who use their access to criminal and driving records for personal information, may be corrupt. Often, what people call police corruption is something that is "not right," but is not a violation of the law. Some police corruption consists of violations of departmental regulations and can be sanctioned, whereas other improper police behavior is not covered by any rules. In an exploratory study of police officer sexual violence, Maher (2003) discovered a continuum of police misbehavior with regard to sexual behavior. This continuum ranged from nonsexual contacts, such as making a traffic stop for the purpose of getting a closer look at the driver, viewing unsuspecting lovers having sex in their car, and unnecessary callbacks or visits with an attractive crime victim, to serious criminal acts such as rape and sexual shakedowns. The continuum illustrates one problem with police corruption: Some misbehavior is clearly illegal (rape), whereas other behavior is inappropriate but not yet defined as a punishable wrong.

Police misconduct is an especially vexing problem. Rabe-Hemp and Braithwaite (2012) found that nearly 40% of officers involved in sexual misconduct investigations are repeat offenders, averaging four victims over a 3-year span of offending. This raises the question, who polices the police? Perceived police misconduct is often at the root of tension between the police and citizens, especially minority citizens (Jesilow & Mayer, 2001; Lersch, 1998; Weitzer, 2002). Walker and Graham (1998) studied citizen perceptions of police misconduct. They found that most incidents that generate complaints involve relatively minor forms of misconduct and perceptions that the police failed to provide service. They also found that, faced with perceived police misconduct, the majority of citizens did not report the incident. Figure 6.4 presents the reasons citizens gave for not reporting police misconduct. Concern about excessive force, brutality, and bullying are core to public perceptions of police misconduct. It is to this topic that we turn next.

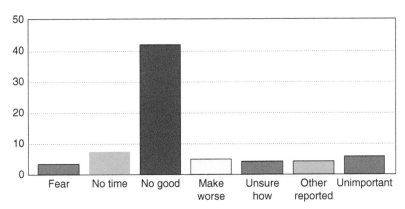

FIGURE 6.4
Reasons for not reporting police misconduct.
Source: Walker and Graham (1998:78)

Use of Force

Similar fears surround the issue of justified use of force by the police. Among all police powers, the ability to employ physical force legitimately to secure compliance with police orders, or with the law, is one of the most problematic issues in law enforcement (Bittner, 1970). Police officers resent having their decisions to employ force second-guessed by civilians or by the internal affairs unit of the department. Citizens fear the unbridled use of force by the police. The issue revolves around the definition of excessive force, that is, force that is greater than what would be required to achieve the lawful aims of the officer.

Fears of excessive police force are particularly clear in cases of the use of deadly force. Few people seriously question an officer's ability and duty to use deadly force to protect self or others from death or serious harm. Most observers (e.g., Bazley, Lersch, & Mieczkowski, 2007; Brandl & Stroshine, 2003) reported that assaults on police officers are, statistically speaking, relatively rare events and most police use of force is of a minor nature. Nevertheless, as Figure 6.5 illustrates, the need for self-defense by police officers is real. Remember, however, that officers are also at great risk of injury through accident (Brandl, 1996). Many believe that we should allow police officers to use deadly force to prevent the escape of dangerous offenders who are likely to injure people again. Questions arise, however, when a police officer strikes an offender "too many times" or when an officer shoots and kills an innocent or unarmed person.

The Bureau of Justice Statistics (Hickman, 2006) reported that citizen complaints about excessive force by police officers are quite common in large local law enforcement agencies employing 100 or more officers. In those departments, there were 6.6 complaints for every 100 full-time sworn officers. The complaint rate was higher in the largest departments. Fewer than 10% of these

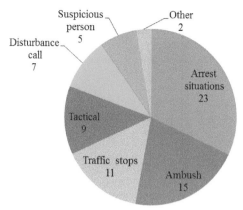

FIGURE 6.5
Number of officers killed, 2011: by circumstance.

citizen complaints were sustained on review. However, in agencies that allowed citizens to appeal decisions about use-of-force complaints, the percentage of complaints sustained was more than twice as great as in those not allowing appeals.

Illustrating this concern are police use-of-force cases such as that of Rodney King in Los Angeles in the 1990s, as well as more recent instances of police excessive force against citizens in New York City and similar cases involving allegations of excessive force in many other cities. One recent case that received public attention is the shooting of Oscar Grant by a police officer employed by the Oakland-area transit system BART. Grant was an unarmed African American man who was being restrained facedown when he was fatally shot by the BART officer. The officer in this case was convicted of involuntary manslaughter and sentenced to 2 years in prison. To some, the BART shooting was a clear case of police brutality and drew comparisons to the Rodney King case (Egelko, 2009) (see Figure 6.6). African Americans are not the only targets of police use of force, of course, but they are subjected to police assaults disproportionately. Because of the discretionary nature of decisions to employ force, citizens are suspicious of officer motives in these cases. Many people believe that the King and Grant cases would not have occurred if the victims had been white. Although there is no way to know the real impact of race in these cases, knowledge that the use of force is discretionary to some degree makes racial prejudice a viable explanation.

In a review of the processing of excessive force complaints against the Chicago police, Kerstetter, Rasinski, and Heiert (1996) found that the investigators generally took complaints by citizens of a different race than the officer accused of excessive force seriously. So too, Son, Davis, and Rome (1998) found that police officers did not consider the race of the citizen involved when they were asked to assess the seriousness of police misconduct by other officers. On the other hand, Barkan and Cohn (1998) reported that whites who displayed racially prejudiced

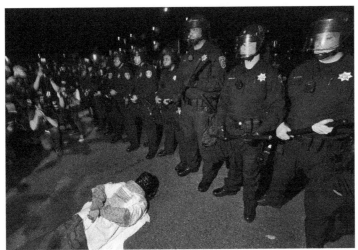

FIGURE 6.6
A demonstrator lies on the ground in protest after the sentencing of former Bay Area Rapid Transit police officer Johannes Mehserle. Mehserle was convicted of involuntary manslaughter for the fatal shooting of Oscar Grant at a BART station in 2009.
AP Photo/Noah Berger

FIGURE 6.7
A Taser is a type of electric stun gun used as a "pain compliance" device by law enforcement. Taser use has been the subject of controversy in several lawsuits, and at least one appeals court has ruled that using a Taser can constitute excessive force.

attitudes were more likely to support police use of force against citizens than non-prejudiced persons. Johnson and Kuhns (2009) found that African Americans tended to be less supportive of police use of force than whites. Whereas Gau, Mosher, and Pratt (2010) reported that suspect behavior was a more important explanation for use of Tasers (stun guns) than suspect race, there were still some race effects in the use of Tasers (see Figure 6.7).

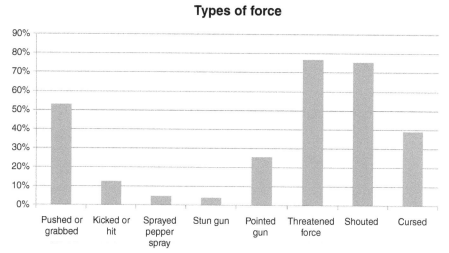

FIGURE 6.8
Types of force used or threatened by police, among residents who reported force used.

The actual use of substantial force by police officers against citizens is a relatively rare event. Approximately 2% of residents who have contact with the police experience the use or threat of force by police (Eith & Durose, 2011). It appears that most police officer use of force is at a lower level, such as threatening force or shouting (see Figure 6.8). Garner, Maxwell, and Heraux (2002) concluded that police use of force is dependent on suspect/citizen resistance. Suspects tended to report more instances of officers using force at low levels (hitting or pushing) than did officers, but less instances of force at the highest level (threat or use of a weapon). MacDonald, Alpert, and Tennenbaum (1999) noted that police use of deadly force is linked to the level of violent crime that exists in a community. That is, the police are most likely to use force in places and at times when violent crime is also most likely to occur. They suggest that knowledge of the risk of violence influences officers' decisions to use deadly force. However, it appears that the police are more likely to threaten force or be disrespectful to certain citizens, including minorities and youths (Mastrofski, Reisig, & McCluskey, 2002). The appearance of officers, complete with baton, firearm, and uniform, coupled with officers' issuance of commands, creates a perception of the police as threatening in the minds of many citizens.

Police officers and citizens may hold different views toward those incidences in which force is used. In a given interaction, the police might justify the use of force based on a threat to officer safety, whereas a suspect might focus on claims of procedural injustice or having their actions misinterpreted (Rojek, Alpert, & Smith, 2012). Perceptions of excessive force by police translate into lower citizen satisfaction with the police and a greater reluctance to cooperate with the police (Browning, Cullen, Cao, Kopache, & Stevenson, 1994; Son, Tsang, Rome, & Davis, 1997). Table 6.3 reports the conduct of those residents who report police use of force.

Table 6.3	Conduct of Residents during Police Contacts in Which Force Was Used or Threatened
Behavior in Which Resident Engaged	**Percent**
Argued with, cursed at, insulted, or verbally threatened the police	21.9
Disobeyed or interfered with officers	11.6
Resisted being handcuffed, arrested, or searched	4.8
Tried to get away from the police	3.4
Pushed, grabbed, or hit officers	0.6

Source: Eith and Durose (2011)

The core of the problem is that we have granted our police the power to inflict death and injury without a clear understanding of the fact that the officer must decide when to use this power. The decisional aspect of police use of force is what troubles us most (Terrill, 2005). When the evidence reveals that force is not applied randomly and that certain people are more likely to be victims than others, we fear discrimination based on factors other than the threat posed to the officer or to the law. In addition, recent research has also found that a small proportion of officers are responsible for a disproportionate number of incidents involving force (Brandl & Stroshine, 2013). If we could control the decisions of officers to employ force, we would be less troubled by the issue. Griswold (1994:218) investigated complaints against police in one sheriff's office. He found that one-fifth of complaints involved allegations of excessive force, consistent with earlier studies. Further, he found that complaints of excessive force were least likely to be upheld by the complaint review board. Griswold speculated that the low rate of sustained complaints may be explained by several facts. Complaints about use of force are serious, as are the consequences for accused officers. It might be that the evidentiary standard used by the review board for such serious complaints is higher than that applied to less serious complaints. It may be that persons accusing officers of excessive force are not credible witnesses because they tend to have been subjects of arrest. It also may be that the combination of higher evidentiary standards and less credible complainants combines to produce a low rate of sustained complaints. Whatever the reason, the fact that it is difficult to lodge a complaint of excessive use of force successfully contributes to citizen suspicion of police use of force.

Most police agencies attempt to constrain the use of force by officers through training and policy (Alpert & Smith, 1994; Morrison, 2006). Terrill and Paoline (2013) reported wide variation in the comprehensiveness and thoroughness of use-of-force policies. Most agencies used a use-of-force continuum, but policies varied widely by department. For example, some agencies instructed their officers to use chemical sprays and conducted energy devices (stun guns) at earlier stages in the progression of force than other agencies. Moreover, some departments take factors such as the level of resistance by suspects into consideration, whereas others do not give explicit guidance to officers relative to the level of resistance encountered. Increasingly, police agencies are turning to technological solutions such as less lethal weapons as a means to overcome concerns about the use of force. While there is still some concern about the safety of electronic control devices (e.g., stun guns like the Taser), many police departments are issuing less lethal weapons to their officers (White & Ready, 2007).

COMMUNITY RELATIONS

Community relations is an issue of long standing that became an important topic of the civil protests and riots of the late 1960s. However, the problem of police and community relations has always plagued the police departments of the United States. To what extent should the community determine policing policy and priorities? In the early days of American policing, police officers served in their own neighborhoods, and the officers very clearly reflected community standards and norms in the enforcement of the laws. Later, policing became more centralized and more impersonal. Communities now desire closer control of their police departments and more input in the setting of police policy. The problem arises when we define the police as experts about policing matters but still want them to observe our wishes. The police oppose what they term "political interference," but must maintain community support.

Less than one-fifth of U.S. residents aged 16 or older had a face-to-face contact with the police in 2008 (Eith & Durose, 2011). Police and citizen contact is most common among younger, white, male citizens and most typically occurs during traffic stops. This limited amount of citizen contact with the police contributes to strained relations between the police and the community. Not only is there little interaction, most of it takes place in stressful circumstances. Police officers typically assume a professional, detached role in dealing with citizens, suggesting that the police are separate from the communities they serve.

In reality, the police are dependent on, and responsible to, the community. At the same time, the community has charged the police with controlling the behaviors of community members while complaining about the fact that the police control behavior. The dilemma is that the community has hired the police to do many things, and some of these are things that the community does not really want to see done. Community relations problems center on those issues in which it is not clear who (the police or the community) should directly define the police role (Radelet & Carter, 1994).

The movement to community-oriented policing sought to increase the role of citizens in setting police policy. The police work with the community to identify problems and select solutions. The community defines problems, suggests and/or approves solutions, and cooperates in police efforts to improve the quality of life in the community. A problem arises when the community and the police disagree about which police actions are appropriate. Webb and Katz (1997) reported that citizens do not believe that the preventive activities of police officers are as legitimate and important as more traditional enforcement activities. Satisfaction with the police and support for police appear linked to feelings of personal safety. Those who feel safest in their communities are most likely to be supportive of the police and of community policing initiatives (Dietz, 1997). Those persons least in need of police assistance are most happy with police service. The very people the police most need to engage—those living in high-crime neighborhoods—are the ones least likely to trust the police or be satisfied with police service. As police seek to prevent disorder in these neighborhoods so as to improve community conditions and prevent serious crime, the targets of disorder control are community members the police are seeking to assist. When the police crack down on loitering, for example, the persons confronted by the police tend to be those living in the neighborhood (Sun et al., 2008). The attempt to improve community conditions has the effect of undermining police and community relations (Reibstein, 1997).

POLICE CRIME CONTROL

A final issue for our consideration is the role of the police in the control of crime. The police do not define what behaviors are criminal, do not control their own budget, and do not control the social and psychological forces that lead individuals to commit crimes, yet they are responsible for the control and prevention of crime. Manning (1978) called crime control an "impossible mandate" for police. The police are responsible for the control of something over which they have no control.

To control crime, police have adopted a number of strategies throughout the years that theoretically appear to serve the function of crime control. Many of these, however, are of questionable value (Worrall, 2008). Rapid response and preventive patrol are but two of these strategies.

For decades, police leaders distributed the typical police force over the entire jurisdiction for which it is responsible. They based this distribution on the belief that officers would be able to respond more quickly to calls for aid, and that quicker responses would prove more successful in apprehending offenders. Research indicates that this is not true, at least insofar as complainants often do not notify the police soon enough that an offense has occurred. By the time most victims call the police, responding within a minute of the call normally is not important (Cordner, Greene, & Bynum, 1983).

Another reason for placing officers out in the community is to provide a "police presence" to deter potential violators and reassure law-abiding citizens. When they are not responding to calls for help, we expect the police to patrol and to prevent crime. Research on police questions the assumption that patrolling prevents crime. There is little reason to believe that preventive patrol is the crime-reduction strategy it is thought to be (Kelling, Pate, Dieckman, & Brown, 1974; Sherman, 1997). While the effectiveness of preventive patrol requires further study, the general effectiveness of the police in controlling crime has come into question.

The primary issue involved in the question of police effectiveness appears to be one of preventing crime. While there is interest in how to improve police efficiency in apprehending and processing offenders, and there is hope of success in this area, the greatest questions revolve around the ability of the police to prevent crimes. Suggestions range from increased technological adaptations to community crime watch to environmental design (Fleissner & Heinzelmann, 1996; Lab, 1990). In each of these prevention strategies, the role of the police in actual crime prevention is minimal. Perhaps we must reconsider the long-held view that police can prevent most crime (Kelling & Coles, 1996). The question to be decided is whether the police role should continue to cover the dual mandates of crime control and crime prevention.

As an outgrowth of the recognition that police efforts to control crime are limited and that police relationships with citizens are strained, there has been a call to reform policing in the United States. Many police experts, administrators, and observers support the movement toward crime prevention as the major purpose of policing. Indeed, some called the shift to a greater cooperation between the police and the community a "quiet revolution" (Kelling, 1988). The revolution involved is a restructuring of the relationship between the police and the community, and a redefinition of the police task. The central idea is that if the police, working with the community, can minimize disorder, more serious crime will also decline.

There is the emerging notion that whereas the police cannot do much to control actual levels of crime, police can have an effect on levels of disorder and the fear of crime (Wilson & Kelling, 1982). To be successful, the police must take direction from the community to determine which important community problems are relating to crime and fear of crime. The police then work with community leaders to develop necessary resources to solve those problems from within both the private and public sectors. To do this, the police must decentralize decision making to the level of the patrol officer as well as take policy direction from the community. These changes reflect very different arrangements than were evident in the policing of the past (Skolnick & Bayley, 1986).

Community policing, in theory at least, suggests a model in which the police can organize a reactive form of crime prevention (Travis & Langworthy, 2008). Thus, the police are still reactive (democratic), whereas crime control becomes proactive through community organizations. While supporters of community policing believe this will result in stronger communities with more effective informal social controls, others are skeptical (Sampson, 2002). See Figure 6.9.

Skeptics believe that this task will prove to be impossible for a variety of reasons. Some have suggested that early police were closely tied to the community, and point out that this close link led to corruption (Strecher, 1991; Travis, 1992). They fear that a return to decentralized policing may produce increased amounts of ethnic discrimination and disparity in law enforcement. Others (Williams & Wagoner, 1992) have argued that the reality of police crime prevention efforts is that they must be antidemocratic in the sense that the police will not be able to simply enact the wishes of the community. Still others have argued that as the police emphasize order maintenance in an attempt to prevent serious crime, they will lose legitimacy in the eyes of the public. This loss of legitimacy will be

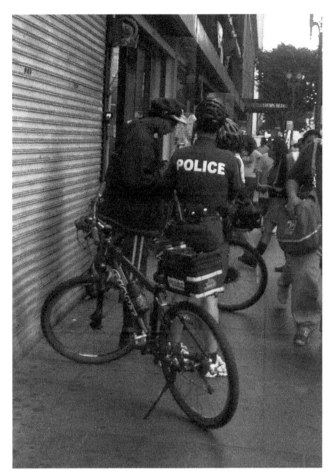

FIGURE 6.9
Police bike patrols are often developed as a facet of a department's proactive approach to law enforcement and community service.
Ellen S. Boyne

manifest in increased resentment and resistance by citizens (Piquero & Bouffard, 2003; Taylor, Turner, Esbensen, & Winfree, 2001). In response to this resistance, the police will increasingly rely on force, leading to further resistance and poisoning the relationship between the police and the public.

The increasing emphasis on proactive, problem-solving approaches to crime raises questions about citizen support for the police (Davis, Mateu-Gelabert, & Miller, 2005). Overly zealous enforcement efforts may cause citizens to question whether the police are concerned about helping citizens (Tyler, 2005). If people believe they are simply the targets of police enforcement and that police are not concerned about their welfare, they may begin to question the legitimacy of the police, and of the law more generally. In the end, public perceptions of unjust and uncaring enforcement can lead to "rebellion," with higher rates of crime and less citizen cooperation with police. The control and prevention of crime by the police requires a balance between the needs for crime control and requirements of due process.

The perspective of **procedural justice** suggests that people oppose rules when they believe their treatment is unfair. An outcome (whether the officer writes a ticket or arrests us) is less important than how the officer treats us in terms of our assessment of the legitimacy of the officer's actions. If we believe the process is fair, we tend to support it regardless of outcomes (Sunshine & Tyler, 2003). The reverse of this, of course, is that we resist police authority if we think our treatment is unfair. We are less likely to obey the law, cooperate with the police, or report crime when we see police treatment of us as unfair. Preventive efforts lead to police intervention in minor disturbances or before crimes occur. Citizens subjected to police control in these "noncriminal" situations can question the fairness of police action. Balancing prevention with procedural justice is a difficult task (Gau & Brunson, 2010).

THEORY AND THE POLICE

How can we explain the actions of police? Why do the police arrest some people and not others? How is it that police decide to use force against some individuals and the types of force they will use? What explains the decision of police officers to defound a reported crime, or to conduct an investigation? Theories of criminal justice can explain these questions.

We have seen that the law explains much police behavior. The more serious the crime or suspected crime, the more seriously the police respond. The characteristics of the community in which the police work are also important explanatory factors. The police are asked to do different things, and do the same things differently, based on community characteristics. The police organization, its rules, supervision, size, resources, and other characteristics explain much officer behavior. So too, the characteristics of individual officers are related to what they do and how they do it.

As we explored the police, we identified many explanations for police behavior reported in the research literature. We will see that similar explanations exist for court and correctional decisions. We may not have well-established "grand theories" of criminal justice, but we do have a great deal of consistency in what research we find to be important explanations of criminal justice decisions.

REVIEW QUESTIONS

1. Identify and explain the three principal justice system decision points contained in the law enforcement component of the system.
2. Under what circumstances has the U.S. Supreme Court ruled that police need not obtain a warrant prior to conducting a search?
3. What is meant by the "exclusionary rule," and how does it reflect the conflict between due process and crime control?

4. What is the significance of the *Miranda* ruling, and what does it require of the police?
5. What is the good faith exception to the exclusionary rule?
6. Define what is meant by the term "entrapment."
7. What pressures influence the decisions and behavior of police officers?
8. Identify three contemporary issues in American law enforcement.

References

Alpert, G., & Noble, J. (2009). Lies, true lies, and conscious deception: Police officers and the truth. *Police Quarterly, 13*(2), 237–254.

Alpert, G., & Smith, W. (1994). How reasonable is the reasonable man?: Police and excessive force. *Journal of Criminal Law and Criminology, 85*(2), 481–501.

Barkan, S., & Cohn, S. (1998). Racial prejudice and support by whites for police use of force: A research note. *Justice Quarterly, 15*(4), 743–753.

Bayley, D. (2002). Law enforcement and the rule of law: Is there a tradeoff? *Criminology & Public Policy, 2*(1), 133–154.

Bazley, T., Lersch, K., & Mieczkowski, T. (2007). Officer force versus suspect resistance: A gendered analysis of patrol officers in an urban police department. *Journal of Criminal Justice, 35*(2), 183–192.

Bittner, E. (1970). *The functions of police in modern society.* Rockville, MD: National Institute of Mental Health.

Blair, J., & Rossmo, K. (2010). Evidence in context: Bayes' theorem and investigation. *Police Quarterly, 13*(2), 123–135.

Brandl, S. (1993). The impact of case characteristics on detectives' decision making. *Justice Quarterly, 10*(3), 395–415.

Brandl, S. (1996). In the line of duty: A descriptive analysis of police assaults and accidents. *Journal of Criminal Justice, 24*(3), 255–264.

Brandl, S., & Stroshine, M. (2003). Toward an understanding of the physical hazards of police work. *Police Quarterly, 6*(2), 172–191.

Brandl, S., & Stroshine, M. (2013). The role of officer attributes, job characteristics, and arrest activity in explaining police use of force. *Criminal Justice Policy Review, 24*(5), 551–572.

Browning, S., Cullen, F. T., Cao, L., Kopache, R., & Stevenson, T. J. (1994). Race and getting hassled by the police: A research note. *Police Studies, 17*(1), 1–10.

Cao, L., Stack, S., & Sun, Y. (1998). Public attitudes toward the police: A comparative study between Japan and America. *Journal of Criminal Justice, 26*(4), 279–289.

Carter, D. (1990a). Drug-related corruption of police officers: A contemporary typology. *Journal of Criminal Justice, 18*(2), 85–98.

Carter, D. (1990b). An overview of drug-related misconduct of police officers: Drug abuse and narcotic corruption. In R. Weisheit (Ed.), *Drugs and the criminal justice system* (pp. 79–109). Cincinnati, OH: Anderson.

Cassell, P. (1996). Miranda's social costs: An empirical reassessment. *Northwestern University Law Review, 90,* 387–499.

Coleman, J. W. (1985). *The criminal elite.* New York: St. Martin's.

Cordner, G. W., Greene, J. R., & Bynum, T. S. (1983). The sooner the better: Some effects of police response time. In R. R. Bennett (Ed.), *Police at work: Policy issues and analysis* (pp. 145–164). Beverly Hills, CA: Sage.

Cutler, B., Duaherty, B., Babu, S., Hodges, L., & Wallendael, L. (2009). Creating blind photo arrays using virtual human technology: A feasibility test. *Police Quarterly, 12*(3), 289–300.

Dale, W., Greenspan, W.M., & Orokos, D. (2006). *DNA forensics: Expanding uses and information sharing.* SEARCH: National Consortium for Justice Information and Statistics.

Davis, R. (1997). What Fourth Amendment? HR666 and the satanic expansion of the good faith exception. *Policing, 20*(1), 101–112.

Davis, D. (2008). Selling confession: The interrogator, the con man, and their weapons of influence. *Wisconsin Defender, 16*(1), 1–16.

Davis, R., Mateu-Gelabert, P., & Miller, J. (2005). Can effective policing also be respectful? Two examples in the South Bronx. *Police Quarterly, 8*(2), 229–247.

del Carmen, R. V., & Walker, J. T. (2012). *Briefs of leading cases in law enforcement* (8th ed.). Boston: Elsevier (Anderson Publishing).

DeLone, G. (2007). Law enforcement mission statements post–September 11th. *Police Quarterly, 10*(2), 218–235.

Dichter, M., Marcus, S., Morabito, M., & Rhodes, K. (2011). Explaining the IPV arrest decision: Incident, agency, and community factors. *Criminal Justice Review, 36*, 22–39.

Dietz, A. (1997). Evaluating community policing: Quality police service and fear of crime. *Policing, 20*(1), 83–100.

Dowler, K., & Zawilski, V. (2007). Public perceptions of police misconduct and discrimination: Examining the impact of media consumption. *Journal of Criminal Justice, 35*(2), 193–203.

Dunham, R., & Alpert, G. (2009). Officer and suspect demeanor: A qualitative analysis of change. *Police Quarterly, 12*, 6–21.

Egelko, B. (2009). BART shooting draws Rodney King case parallels. *San Francisco Chronicle.* Retrieved from http://www.sfgate.com/bayarea/article/BART-shooting-draws-Rodney-King-case-parallels-3176756.php.

Eith, C., & Durose, M. (2011). *Contacts between police and the public, 2008.* Washington, DC: Bureau of Justice Statistics.

Ellwanger, S. (2012). Deception in police interrogation. In M. Braswell, B. McCarthy, & B. McCarthy (Eds.), *Justice, crime and ethics* (7th ed.). Burlington, MA: Elsevier.

Fleissner, D., & Heinzelmann, F. (1996). *Crime prevention through environmental design and community policing.* Washington, DC: National Institute of Justice.

Frank, J., Smith, B., & Novak, K. (2005). Exploring the basis of citizens' attitudes toward the police. *Police Quarterly, 8*(2), 206–228.

Garner, J., Maxwell, C., & Heraux, C. (2002). Characteristics associated with the prevalence and severity of force used by the police. *Justice Quarterly, 19*(4), 705–746.

Gau, J., & Brunson, R. (2010). Procedural justice and order maintenance policing: A study of inner-city young men's perceptions of police legitimacy. *Justice Quarterly, 27*(2), 255–279.

Gau, J., Mosher, C., & Pratt, T. (2010). An inquiry into the impact of suspect race on police use of Tasers. *Police Quarterly, 13*(1), 27–48.

Goldstein, J. (1960). Police discretion not to invoke the criminal process: Low visibility decisions in the administration of justice. *Yale Law Journal, 69*, 543–594 (March).

Goldstein, J. (2013). Judge rejects New York's stop-and frisk policy. *The New York Times.* Retrieved 10.13.2013 from http://www.nytimes.com/2013/08/13/nyregion/stop-and-frisk-practice-violated-rights-judge-rules.html?_r=0.

Griswold, D. (1994). Complaints against the police: Predicting dispositions. *Journal of Criminal Justice, 22*(3), 215–222.

Halpher, A., & Ku, R. (1976). *An exemplary project: New York police department street crime unit.* Washington, DC: U.S. Government Printing Office.

Hickman, M. (2006). *Citizen complaints about police use of force.* Washington, DC: Bureau of Justice Statistics.

Holden, R. N. (1993). Police and the profit motive: A new look at asset forfeiture. *ACJS Today, 12*(2), 1.

Jesilow, P., & Mayer, J. (2001). The effects of police misconduct on public attitudes. *Journal of Crime & Justice, 24*(1), 109–121.

Jogerst, G., Daly, J., Brinig, M., & Bibas, S. (2005). The association between statutory penalties and domestic elder abuse investigations. *Journal of Crime and Justice, 28*(2), 51–69.

Johnson, D., & Kuhns, J. (2009). Striking out: Race and support for police use of force. *Justice Quarterly, 26*(3), 592–623.

Kappeler, V. E., Kappeler, S. F., & del Carmen, R. V. (1993). A content analysis of police civil liability cases: Decisions of the federal district courts, 1978–1990. *Journal of Criminal Justice, 21*(4), 339–352.

Kelling, G. (1988). *Police and communities: The quiet revolution.* Washington, DC: U.S. Department of Justice.

Kelling, G. (1999). *Broken windows and police discretion.* Washington, DC: National Institute of Justice.

Kelling, G., & Coles, C. (1996). *Fixing broken windows.* New York: Free Press.

Kelling, G., Pate, T., Dieckman, D., & Brown, C. E. (1974). *The Kansas City preventive patrol experiment: A summary report.* Washington, DC: The Police Foundation.

Kerstetter, W., Rasinski, K., & Heiert, C. (1996). The impact of race on the investigation of excessive force allegations against police. *Journal of Criminal Justice, 24*(1), 1–15.

Koper, C. (1995). Just enough police presence: Reducing crime and disorderly behavior by optimizing patrol time in crime hot spots. *Justice Quarterly, 12*(4), 649–672.

Lab, S. (1990). Citizen crime prevention: Domains and participation. *Justice Quarterly, 7*(3), 467–492.

Langworthy, R. H. (1989). Do stings control crime? An evaluation of a police fencing operation. *Justice Quarterly, 6*(1), 27–45.

Langworthy, R. H., & LeBeau, J. (1992). The spatial distribution of sting targets. *Journal of Criminal Justice, 20*(6), 541–551.

Langworthy, R. H., & LeBeau, J. (1993). Spatial evolution of a sting clientele. *Journal of Criminal Justice, 20*(2), 135–146.

Lawton, B., Taylor, R., & Luongo, A. (2005). Police officers on drug corners in Philadelphia, drug crime, and violent crime: Intended, diffusion, and displacement impacts. *Justice Quarterly, 22*(4), 427–451.

Leo, R. (2001). Questioning the relevance of Miranda in the twenty-first century. *University of Michigan Law Review, 99*, 1000–1029.

Leo, R. & Thomas, G. (Eds.). (1998). *The Miranda debate: Law, justice, and policing.* Boston: Northeastern University Press.

Lersch, K. (1998). Predicting citizen race in allegations of misconduct against the police. *Journal of Criminal Justice, 26*(2), 87–97.

Ley, B., Jankowski, N., & Brewer, P. (2012). Investigating CSI: Portrayals of DNA testing on a forensic crime show and their potential effects. *Public Understanding of Science, 21*, 51–67.

Lynch, T. (2002). *Policy analysis: Breaking the vicious cycle: Preserving our liberties while fighting terrorism.* Washington, DC: CATO Institute.

MacDonald, J., Alpert, G., & Tennenbaum, A. (1999). Justifiable homicide by police and criminal homicide: A research note. *Journal of Crime and Justice, 22*(1), 153–166.

Maher, T. (2003). Police sexual misconduct: Officers perceptions of its extent and causality. *Criminal Justice Review, 28*, 355–381.

Manning, P. K. (1978). The police: Mandate, strategies and appearances. In P. K. Manning, & J. Van Maanen (Eds.), *Policing: A view from the street* (pp. 7–31). Santa Monica, CA: Goodyear.

Mastrofski, S., Reisig, M., & McCluskey, J. (2002). Police disrespect toward the public: An encounter-based analysis. *Criminology, 40*(3), 519–552.

Mazerolle, L., Soole, D., & Rombouts, S. (2007). Drug law enforcement: A review of the evaluation literature. *Police Quarterly, 10*(2), 115–153.

Morrison, G. (2006). Deadly force programs among larger U.S. police departments. *Police Quarterly, 9*(3), 331–360.

Nunn, S., Quinet, K., Rowe, K., & Christ, D. (2006). Interdiction day: Cover surveillance operations, drugs, and serious crime in an inner-city neighborhood. *Police Quarterly, 9*(1), 73–99.

Office of the Public Advocate (2013). *Stop and frisk and the urgent need for meaningful reforms.* Office of Bill de Blasio, New York: Public Advocate for the City of New York.

Palmiotto, M. (Ed.), (1984). *Critical issues in criminal investigation.* Cincinnati, OH: Anderson.

Park, R. (1976). The entrapment controversy. *Minnesota Law Review, 60*, 163–274.

Peterson, J. L. (1987). *Use of forensic evidence by the police and courts.* Washington, DC: National Institute of Justice.

Phillips, S., & Sobol, J. (2010). Twenty years of mandatory arrest: Police decision making in the face of legal requirements. *Criminal Justice Policy Review, 21*, 98–118.

Piquero, N., & Bouffard, L. (2003). A preliminary and partial test of specific defiance. *Journal of Crime and Justice, 26*(1), 1–22.

Rabe-Hemp, C., & Braithwaite, J. (2012). An exploration of recidivism and the officer shuffle in police sexual violence. *Police Quarterly, 16*(2), 127–147.

Radelet, L., & Carter, D. (1994). *The police and the community* (5th ed.). New York: Macmillan.

Reaves, B. (2010). *Local police departments, 2007.* Washington, DC: Bureau of Justice Statistics.

Reibstein, L. (1997). NYPD black and blue. *Newsweek, 129*, 66 (June 2).

Reitzel, J., & Piquero, A. (2006). Does it exist? Studying citizens' attitudes of racial profiling. *Police Quarterly, 9*(3), 161–183.

Roberts, A. (2008). The influence of incident and contextual characteristics on crime clearance of nonlethal violence: A multilevel event history analysis. *Journal of Criminal Justice, 36*(1), 61–71.

Rojek, J., Alpert, G., & Smith, H. (2012). Examining officer and citizen accounts of police use-of-force incidents. *Crime & Delinquency, 58*, 301–327.

Rosenbaum, D., Schuck, A., Costello, S., Hawkins, D., & Ring, M. (2005). Attitudes toward the police: The effects of direct and vicarious experience. *Police Quarterly, 8*(3), 343–365.

Ross, D., & Myers, J. (2010). Recent legal developments: *Maryland v. Shatzer*: Revisiting reinterviewing after invoking Miranda's right to counsel. *Criminal Justice Review, 35*(3), 371–385.

Rubinstein, J. (1973). *City police.* New York: Farrar, Straus & Giroux.

Sacks, H. (1978). Notes on police assessment of moral character. In P. K. Manning & J. Van Maanen (Eds.), *Policing: A view from the street* (pp. 187–202). Santa Monica, CA: Goodyear.

Sampson, R. (2002). Transcending tradition: New directions in community research, Chicago style—The American Society of Criminology 2001 Sutherland Address. *Criminology, 40*(2), 213–230.

Schafer, J., & Mastrofski, S. (2005). Police leniency in traffic enforcement encounters: Exploratory findings from observations and interviews. *Journal of Criminal Justice, 33*(3), 225–238.

Schroeder, D., & White, M. (2009). Exploring the use of DNA evidence in homicide investigations: Implications for detective work and case clearance. *Police Quarterly, 12*(3), 319–342.

Sherman, L. W. (Ed.). (1974). *Police corruption: A sociological perspective.* Garden City, NJ: Anchor Books.

Sherman, L. W. (1990a). Police crackdowns. In C. Klockars, & S. Mastrofski (Eds.), *Thinking about police: Contemporary readings* (pp. 188–211). New York: McGraw-Hill.

Sherman, L. W. (1990b). Police crackdowns. *National Institute of Justice Reports, 219*, 2–6 (March/April).

Sherman, L. (1997). Policing for crime prevention. In L. Sherman, D. Gottfredson, D. MacKenzie, J. Eck, P. Reuter, & S. Bushway (Eds.), *Preventing crime: What works, what doesn't, what's promising?* Washington, DC: National Institute of Justice.

Sherman, L., Gartin, P., & Buerger, M. (1989). Hot spots of predatory crime: Routine activities and the criminology of place. *Criminology, 27*(1), 27–55.

Skolnick, J. (2008). Policing should not be for profit. *Criminology & Public Policy, 7*(2), 257–262.

Skolnick, J., & Bayley, D. (1986). *The new blue line: Police innovation in six American cities.* New York: Free Press.

Smith, M., Makarios, M., & Alpert, G. (2006). Differential suspicion: Theory specification and gender effects in the traffic stop context. *Justice Quarterly, 23*(2), 271–295.

Son, I., Davis, M., & Rome, D. (1998). Race and its effect on police officers' perceptions of misconduct. *Journal of Criminal Justice, 26*(1), 21–28.

Son, I., Tsang, C., Rome, D., & Davis, M. (1997). Citizen's observations of police use of excessive force and their evaluation of police performance. *Policing, 20*(1), 149–159.

Strecher, V. (1991). Histories and futures of policing: Readings and misreadings of a pivotal present. *Police Forum, 1*(1), 1–9.

Stroshine, M., Alpert, G., & Dunham, R. (2008). The influence of "working rules" on police suspicion and discretionary decision making. *Police Quarterly, 11*(3), 315–337.

Sudnow, D. (1964). Normal crimes: Sociological features of the penal code in the public defender's office. *Social Problems, 12*, 81.

Sun, I., Payne, B., & Wu, Y. (2008). The impact of situational factors, officer characteristics, and neighborhood context on police behavior: A multilevel analysis. *Journal of Criminal Justice, 36*(1), 22–31.

Sunshine, J., & Tyler, T. (2003). The role of procedural justice and legitimacy in shaping public support for policing. *Law & Society Review, 37*, 103–135.

Surette, R. (2006). CCTV and citizen guardianship suppression: A questionable proposition. *Police Quarterly, 9*(1), 100–125.

Taylor, T., Turner, K., Esbensen, F., & Winfree, L. (2001). Coppin' an attitude: Attitudinal differences among juveniles toward the police. *Journal of Criminal Justice, 29*(4), 295–306.

Telep, C., & Weisburd, D. (2012). What is known about the effectiveness of police practices in reducing crime and disorder? *Police Quarterly, 15*(4), 331–357.

Terrill, W. (2005). Police use of force: A transactional approach. *Justice Quarterly, 22*(1), 107–138.

Terrill, W., & Paoline, I. I. I. (2007). Nonarrest decision making in police-citizen encounters. *Police Quarterly, 10*, 308–331.

Terrill, W., & Paoline, I. I. I. (2013). Examining less lethal force policy and the force continuum: Results from a national use-of-force study. *Police Quarterly, 16*, 38–65.

Tiffany, L. P., McIntyre, D. M., & Rotenberg, D. J. (1967). *Detection of crime: Stopping and questioning, search and seizure, encouragement and entrapment.* Boston: Little, Brown.

Time, V., & Payne, B. (2002). Police chiefs' perceptions about Miranda: An analysis of survey data. *Journal of Criminal Justice, 30*(1), 77–86.

Time (1980, February 18). The F.B.I. stings congress. *Time.* 10–14, 18–21.

Travis, L. F., III (1992). Making history: Explaining the development of the police. *Police Forum, 2*(2), 6–10.

Travis, L. F., & Langworthy, R. H. (2008). *Policing in America: A balance of forces* (4th ed.). Upper Saddle River, NJ: Prentice Hall.

Turner, R., & Kosa, R. (2003). *Cold case squads: Leaving no stone unturned.* BJA Bulletin, Washington, DC: Bureau of Justice Assistance (July).

Tyler, T. (2005). Policing in black and white: Ethnic group differences in trust and confidence in the police. *Police Quarterly, 8*(3), 322–342.

Walker, S., & Graham, N. (1998). Citizen complaints in response to police misconduct: The results of a victimization survey. *Police Quarterly, 1*(1), 65–89.

Warren, P. (2011). Perceptions of police disrespect during vehicle stops: A race-based analysis. *Crime & Delinquency, 57*(3), 356–376.

Webb, V., & Katz, C. (1997). Citizen ratings of the importance of community policing activities. *Policing, 20*(1), 7–23.

Weisburd, D. (2005). Hot spot policing experiments and criminal justice research: Lessons from the field. *Annals of the American Academy of Political and Social Science, 599,* 220–245.

Weitzer, R. (2002). Incidents of police misconduct and public opinion. *Journal of Criminal Justice, 30*(5), 397–408.

Welsh, B., & Farrington, D. (2002). *Crime prevention effects of closed-circuit television: A systematic review.* London: Home Office Research, Development, and Statistics Directorate.

Weston, P., & Wells, K. (1986). *Criminal investigation: Basic perspectives* (4th ed.). Englewood Cliffs, NJ: Prentice Hall, 3. Reprinted by permission of Prentice Hall, Inc., Upper Saddle River, NJ.

White, M., & Ready, J. (2007). The TASER as a less lethal force alternative: Findings on use and effectiveness in a large metropolitan police agency. *Police Quarterly, 10*(2), 170–191.

Williams, R., & Wagoner, C. (1992). Making the police proactive: An impossible task for improbable reasons. *Police Forum, 2*(2), 1–15.

Wilson, J. Q. (1988). *The exclusionary rule: Crime file study guide.* Washington, DC: U.S. Department of Justice.

Wilson, J. Q., & Kelling, G. (1982). Broken windows: Police and neighborhood safety. *Atlantic Monthly, 249,* 29–38 (March).

Wilson, M., & Ruback, R. (2003). Hate crimes in Pennsylvania, 1984–99: Case characteristics and police responses. *Justice Quarterly, 20*(2), 373–398.

Withrow, B., & Dailey, J. (2004). A model of circumstantial corruptibility. *Police Quarterly, 7*(2), 159–178.

Worrall, J. (2008). *Crime control in America: What works?* (2nd ed.). New York: Pearson.

Zalman, M., & Smith, B. (2007). The attitudes of police executives toward Miranda and interrogation policies. *Journal of Criminal Law & Criminology, 97*(3), 873–942.

Important Cases

Arizona v. Evans, 115 S. Ct. 1185 (1995).

Arizona v. Gant, 556 U.S. 332 (2009).

Brewer v. Williams, 430 U.S. 387 (1977).

Chambers v. Maroney, 453 U.S. 42 (1970).

Chimel v. California, 395 U.S. 752 (1969).

Coolidge v. New Hampshire, 403 U.S. 443 (1981).

Dickerson v. United States, 530 U.S. 428 (2000).

Florida v. Riley, 488 U.S. 455 (1989).

Georgia v. Randolph, 547 U.S. 103 (2006).

Illinois v. Gates, 462 U.S. 213 (1983).

Katz v. United States, 389 U.S. 347 (1967).

Kentucky v. King, 131 S. Ct. 1849 (2011).

Mapp v. Ohio, 367 U.S. 643 (1961).

Maryland v. Shatzer, 559 U.S. 98 (2010).

Maryland v. Wilson, 519 U.S. 408 (1997).

Miranda v. Arizona, 384 U.S. 436 (1966).

New York v. Class, 475 U.S. 106 (1986).

Terry v. Ohio, 392 U.S. 1 (1968).

Thornton v. United States, 541 U.S. 615 (2004).

United States v. Jones, 132 S. Ct. 99 (2012).

United States v. Leon, 484 U.S. 897 (1984).

United State v. Matlock, 415 U.S. 164 (1974).

United States v. Ross, 456 U.S. 798 (1982).

United States v. Wade, 388 U.S. 218 (1967).

Warden v. Hayden, 387 U.S. 294 (1967).

Weeks v. United States, 232 U.S. 383 (1914).

CHAPTER 7

The Criminal Courts

There are more than 16,000 courts in operation in the United States (Rottman & Strickland, 2006). Most of these are at the local level in cities and counties across the country, and they employ more than 30,000 justices, judges, magistrates, or other judicial officers (Schauffler, LaFountain, Strickland, & Raftery, 2006). As with police agencies, the large number of individual courts in the United States reflects our belief in local autonomy. Justice agents filed more than 20 million criminal cases (excluding traffic cases) in American state courts in 2010 (LaFountain, Schauffler, Strickland, & Holt, 2012). Another 55 million traffic cases also arose that year. In addition, courts process cases involving domestic relations (e.g., divorce) and civil disputes each year. Thus, crime is a part-time function for our courts. Figure 7.1 describes the workload of America's courts.

Every county is served by a felony court (sometimes a court serves more than one county), but most cases arise in the few populous counties. The 42 largest jurisdictions (in terms of population) accounted for more than one-quarter of criminal

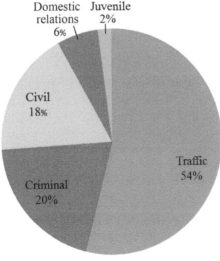

FIGURE 7.1
Types of cases filed in state courts, 2010.

cases closed in 2005 (Perry, 2006). In 2001, slightly fewer than 5% of prosecutors' offices serving jurisdictions having 500,000 or more persons represented 45% of the nation's population and accounted for nearly one-half of all felony case closures (DeFrances, 2001). In terms of crime control, then, American courts mirror the police. Crime control activities are a relatively small part of the total workload of the courts, and criminal cases are concentrated in a few populous areas.

The basic purpose of the courts is to resolve disputes (Neely, 1983; Stumpf, 1988). As our society becomes increasingly complex, we not only encounter more disputes, but informal mechanisms of dispute resolution become less effective. Added to this is the fact that the large and increasing number of attorneys in our society makes it easier for people to obtain legal counsel and to use the courts. Thus, more people are bringing their disputes to the courts each year. Each of these individuals is seeking justice. In discussing the purpose of the courts, Rubin (1984:4) noted

> If we try to describe the purpose of the courts, someone will usually first suggest that their purpose is to "do justice," to provide individualized justice in individual cases. This is true, but whether justice is done depends typically upon the interests or viewpoints of the affected or interested parties. We are confident that some guilty people have been found innocent in our courts, and that innocent persons have been found guilty. These trials may have been conducted fairly, but was justice done?

The point here is that justice is elusive of definition. Indeed, the courts are like jugglers attempting to keep many divergent interests in motion without dropping anything. The courts must strike a balance between the rights of disputing parties. In the criminal courts, the principal balance is between the rights of an individual (and by extension, all individuals) and the rights of the state. The resolution of criminal cases more often entails compromise than competition. Perhaps the best example of this "juggling act" quality of the criminal courts is seen in the practice of plea bargaining.

In plea bargaining, the state and the individual defendant compromise, with neither side getting all that it would hope to achieve. The judge serves as the juggler, balancing the interests of the state (in securing a conviction and punishing a criminal) against the interests of the individual (in protecting his or her liberty and constitutional rights). The alternative to plea bargaining is trial. Trial is the epitome of competition filled with costs and uncertainties for both parties involved in the dispute. Either side may "win" the trial, but both sides will have to expend time and money, experience aggravation, and risk losing to the competition. In plea bargaining, the accused is convicted but avoids the full measure of punishment for the offense of which he or she is accused. Neither side is completely satisfied with the outcome, but both can accept it.

We must understand these compromises, which characterize the workings of the criminal courts, within the organizational context of the courts. They involve not only a defendant and a prosecutor as two competing parties but also a defense attorney (or defender's office), a prosecutor's office, a judge, witnesses, other court staff, the police, possibly jurors, and others. Each actor or set of actors in every criminal case affects the outcome (Panzarella & Shapiro, 1988). However complicated the issues involved in any case are, the complexity of the court process matches or exceeds the complexity of the issues (Mays & Taggart, 1986).

THE ORGANIZATION OF AMERICAN COURTS

The term "courts" covers a wide range of decision-making bodies, ranging from part-time justice of the peace (or mayor's) courts, in which the "judge" often is not trained in the law, to the nine-member U.S. Supreme Court. There are many different types of courts organized on two basic levels: federal courts and state courts. The existence of two sets of courts in the United States, one federal and the other state, has led observers to speak of a **dual system** of courts. Box 7.1 provides a diagram of the American court process.

Court systems contain two basic types of courts: trial courts and appellate courts. **Trial courts** are fact-finding bodies whose job it is to determine the facts of a case (i.e., did the defendant commit the crime?). **Appellate courts** are law-interpreting bodies whose job it is to determine if the laws were correctly applied and followed (i.e., should the defendant have been provided defense counsel at trial?).

Within trial courts, distinctions exist based on **jurisdiction**, which is the definition of a court's authority. Determination of a court's jurisdiction typically involves both geography (a county court hears cases arising in its county) and type of case. A court of **general jurisdiction** can hear civil and criminal cases of all sorts. A court of **limited jurisdiction** typically is constrained to hearing only minor cases, or conducting the early parts of more serious cases. **Special jurisdiction** courts are also created to deal with specific types of cases, such as family matters (court of domestic relations) or wills and estates (probate court).

Federal Courts

The federal judicial system comprises the U.S. Supreme Court, 12 U.S. courts of appeals, 94 district courts, more than 400 magistrates assigned to the district courts, and a number of special courts for tax, patent, customs, and contract cases. In comparison to most state court systems, the federal courts are relatively simply organized. U.S. magistrates, appointed by district court judges, are empowered to issue warrants, hear petty cases, and conduct the preliminary stages of more serious criminal cases.

District courts exist in each of the 50 states, the District of Columbia, and the federal territories. District courts are trial courts of the federal system and, combined with magistrates, they comprise the lower courts in the federal system. They hear both civil and criminal cases involving the federal government or violations of federal laws. The workload of the federal district courts is described in Figure 7.2.

U.S. courts of appeals represent the 50 states, the District of Columbia, and the federal territories. Numbers identify 11 of these courts; the twelfth is the Court of Appeals for the District of Columbia. These courts receive appeals from the decisions of the district courts and decide appeals from the decisions of many federal administrative agencies. Their decisions become binding on all federal district courts under their jurisdiction.

BOX 7.1 THE STRUCTURE OF AMERICAN COURTS

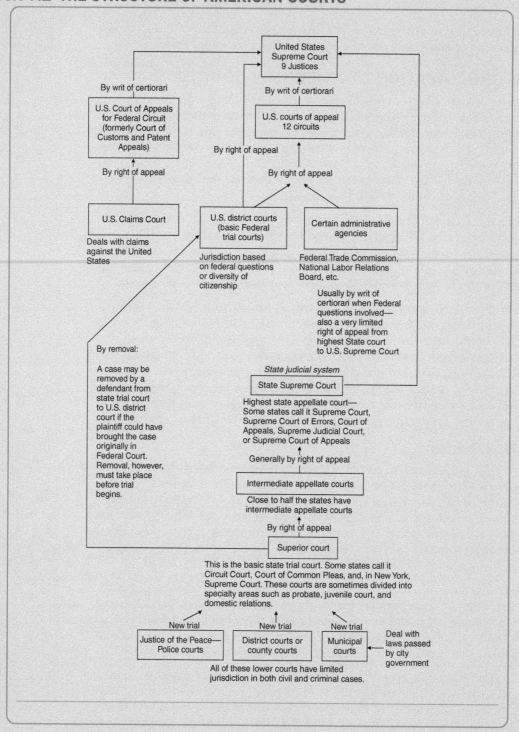

Source: Bureau of Justice Statistics (1988)

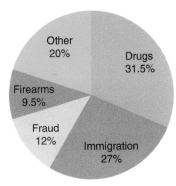

FIGURE 7.2
U.S. district courts: nature of offense.

The U.S. Supreme Court is the nation's highest court (see Figure 7.3). Its nine justices hear appeals from the U.S. courts of appeals as well as those from state courts of last resort (usually state supreme courts) that involve questions of federal law or the U.S. Constitution. In most cases, the Supreme Court is not obligated to decide a case and only elects to do so by granting a **writ of certiorari**. This writ is an order to the lower court to send its records of the case so that the Supreme Court can review them. The Court receives thousands of applications

FIGURE 7.3
The U.S. Supreme Court is the nation's highest court. It is located in Washington, DC.

for certiorari each year, but agrees to hear only around 80 cases per term (Owens & Simon, 2012).

State Courts

In terms of general organization, state court systems mirror the federal courts. They are divided into triers of limited or special jurisdiction, general jurisdiction courts, and a court of last resort. Boxes 7.2 and 7.3 illustrate two state court systems that differ in terms of their complexity. From state to state, the courts vary greatly in name, number, administration, and power. General jurisdiction trial courts are commonly referred to as: circuit, district, superior, chancery, common pleas, supreme, county, or simply trial courts. Several court systems have multiple court names, such as circuit courts and district courts. Courts at this level employ nearly 10,000 judges, ranging from 16 in Maine to more than 2,000 in Texas (Rottman & Strickland, 2006).

State court systems take one of two basic organizational structures. A traditional court structure involves separate general jurisdiction and limited jurisdiction courts. A **unified court system** combines the two types of courts into one. The numbers and names of state courts and their organization are diverse. Rubin (1984:11) observed

> At the state level, courts are created by state constitutions and legislative enactments, and by municipal and county-level legislation. In too many jurisdictions the proliferation of courts has left the citizen unsure of what court to go to for a particular cause of action (divorce, contract dispute, crime, etc.), and for that matter attorneys are not always sure of where to file a particular suit. Some actions can be filed in two or three different courts, and appeals can be taken to several forums.

Indeed, very often the greatest service an attorney can provide a client is to ensure that the proper papers are filed with the appropriate court. Jackson (1974) described the structure of American courts as one that would "make a chart-maker collapse in despair." He described the organizational chart of courts in the United States as "a bewildering maze of parallel, perpendicular, crisscrossing, and overlapping lines." It is frequently difficult to determine whether, how, and where to enter the courts with any given case.

Suppose that you have a disagreement with a neighbor about parking spaces on the street. For the moment (because your car is already parked in front of the neighbor's house), you have won. The next morning, you awaken to discover four flat tires. What should you do? The options are many. First, you may "grin and bear it." Not knowing for sure who did you wrong, you may opt to repair the tires and try to forget the incident (although you may spend several nights monitoring your car, or you may be more selective in deciding where you park). Second, you may confront your neighbor because you surmise that he is the guilty party. (If relations between you and your neighbor were better, you would have had an informal mechanism to avoid this incident in the first place.) Third, you may seek revenge by slashing your neighbor's tires that evening. Fourth, you

BOX 7.2 TEXAS COURT STRUCTURE

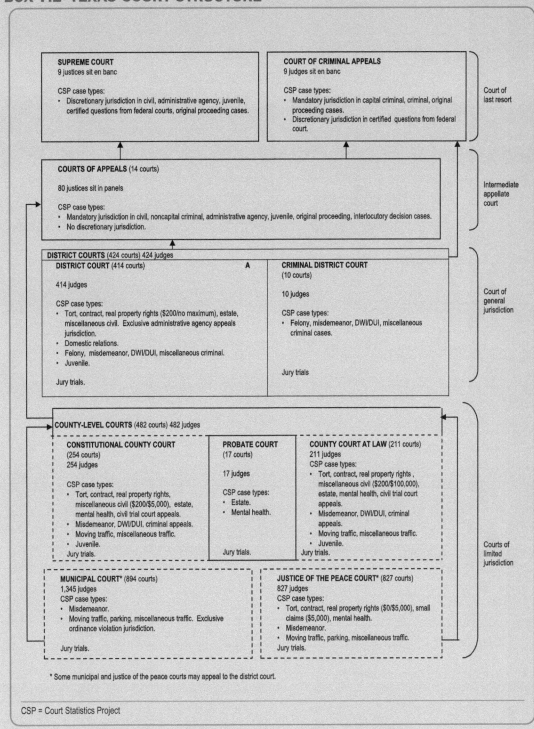

SUPREME COURT
9 justices sit en banc

CSP case types:
- Discretionary jurisdiction in civil, administrative agency, juvenile, certified questions from federal courts, original proceeding cases.

COURT OF CRIMINAL APPEALS
9 judges sit en banc

CSP case types:
- Mandatory jurisdiction in capital criminal, criminal, original proceeding cases.
- Discretionary jurisdiction in certified questions from federal court.

Court of last resort

COURTS OF APPEALS (14 courts)

80 justices sit in panels

CSP case types:
- Mandatory jurisdiction in civil, noncapital criminal, administrative agency, juvenile, original proceeding, interlocutory decision cases.
- No discretionary jurisdiction.

Intermediate appellate court

DISTRICT COURTS (424 courts) 424 judges

DISTRICT COURT (414 courts)   A

414 judges

CSP case types:
- Tort, contract, real property rights ($200/no maximum), estate, miscellaneous civil. Exclusive administrative agency appeals jurisdiction.
- Domestic relations.
- Felony, misdemeanor, DWI/DUI, miscellaneous criminal.
- Juvenile.

Jury trials.

CRIMINAL DISTRICT COURT
(10 courts)

10 judges

CSP case types:
- Felony, misdemeanor, DWI/DUI, miscellaneous criminal cases.

Jury trials

Court of general jurisdiction

COUNTY-LEVEL COURTS (482 courts) 482 judges

CONSTITUTIONAL COUNTY COURT
(254 courts)
254 judges

CSP case types:
- Tort, contract, real property rights, miscellaneous civil ($200/$5,000), estate, mental health, civil trial court appeals.
- Misdemeanor, DWI/DUI, criminal appeals.
- Moving traffic, miscellaneous traffic.
- Juvenile.
Jury trials.

PROBATE COURT
(17 courts)

17 judges

CSP case types:
- Estate.
- Mental health.

Jury trials.

COUNTY COURT AT LAW (211 courts)
211 judges
CSP case types:
- Tort, contract, real property rights, miscellaneous civil ($200/$100,000), estate, mental health, civil trial court appeals.
- Misdemeanor, DWI/DUI, criminal appeals.
- Moving traffic, miscellaneous traffic.
- Juvenile.
Jury trials.

MUNICIPAL COURT* (894 courts)
1,345 judges
CSP case types:
- Misdemeanor.
- Moving traffic, parking, miscellaneous traffic. Exclusive ordinance violation jurisdiction.

Jury trials.

JUSTICE OF THE PEACE COURT* (827 courts)
827 judges
CSP case types:
- Tort, contract, real property rights ($0/$5,000), small claims ($5,000), mental health.
- Misdemeanor.
- Moving traffic, parking, miscellaneous traffic.
Jury trials.

Courts of limited jurisdiction

* Some municipal and justice of the peace courts may appeal to the district court.

CSP = Court Statistics Project

Source: Rottman and Strickland (2006:312)

BOX 7.3 INDIANA COURT STRUCTURE

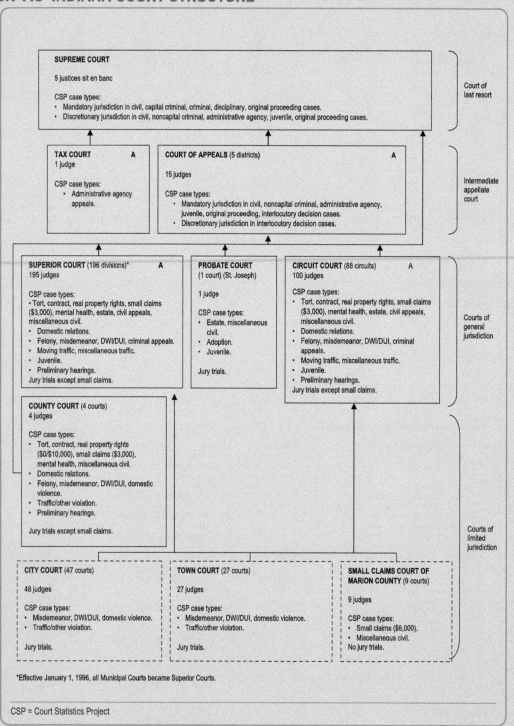

SUPREME COURT

5 justices sit en banc

CSP case types:
- Mandatory jurisdiction in civil, capital criminal, criminal, disciplinary, original proceeding cases.
- Discretionary jurisdiction in civil, noncapital criminal, administrative agency, juvenile, original proceeding cases.

Court of last resort

TAX COURT   A
1 judge

CSP case types:
- Administrative agency appeals.

COURT OF APPEALS (5 districts)   A

15 judges

CSP case types:
- Mandatory jurisdiction in civil, noncapital criminal, administrative agency, juvenile, original proceeding, interlocutory decision cases.
- Discretionary jurisdiction in interlocutory decision cases.

Intermediate appellate court

SUPERIOR COURT (196 divisions)*   A
195 judges

CSP case types:
- Tort, contract, real property rights, small claims ($3,000), mental health, estate, civil appeals, miscellaneous civil.
- Domestic relations.
- Felony, misdemeanor, DWI/DUI, criminal appeals.
- Moving traffic, miscellaneous traffic.
- Juvenile.
- Preliminary hearings.
Jury trials except small claims.

PROBATE COURT
(1 court) (St. Joseph)

1 judge

CSP case types:
- Estate, miscellaneous civil.
- Adoption.
- Juvenile.

Jury trials.

CIRCUIT COURT (88 circuits)   A
100 judges

CSP case types:
- Tort, contract, real property rights, small claims ($3,000), mental health, estate, civil appeals, miscellaneous civil.
- Domestic relations.
- Felony, misdemeanor, DWI/DUI, criminal appeals.
- Moving traffic, miscellaneous traffic.
- Juvenile.
- Preliminary hearings.
Jury trials except small claims.

Courts of general jurisdiction

COUNTY COURT (4 courts)
4 judges

CSP case types:
- Tort, contract, real property rights ($0/$10,000), small claims ($3,000), mental health, miscellaneous civil.
- Domestic relations.
- Felony, misdemeanor, DWI/DUI, domestic violence.
- Traffic/other violation.
- Preliminary hearings.

Jury trials except small claims.

Courts of limited jurisdiction

CITY COURT (47 courts)

48 judges

CSP case types:
- Misdemeanor, DWI/DUI, domestic violence.
- Traffic/other violation.

Jury trials.

TOWN COURT (27 courts)

27 judges

CSP case types:
- Misdemeanor, DWI/DUI, domestic violence.
- Traffic/other violation.

Jury trials.

SMALL CLAIMS COURT OF MARION COUNTY (9 courts)

9 judges

CSP case types:
- Small claims ($6,000).
- Miscellaneous civil.
No jury trials.

*Effective January 1, 1996, all Municipal Courts became Superior Courts.

CSP = Court Statistics Project

Source: Rottman and Strickland (2006:282)

may decide to call the police and report the vandalism. Calling the police could lead to a court appearance. There may be other options, but these four appear to be the most likely.

If you find the first three options unacceptable, in all probability you would call the police. This allows you to collect insurance payments for damages, and it transfers the decision of what to do to the responding officer. The dispute then may reach the courts as a criminal complaint, but deciding whether, where, and how to enter the courts would be someone else's problem. Unless you have extraordinarily expensive tires, you could take your case to small claims court and sue your neighbor for damages. You could also secure counsel by hiring an attorney or by contacting a legal aid office.

This hypothetical case resulted from a dispute among neighbors about parking privileges. It could go to a number of different courts as a **tort** (a dispute between private parties over a wrongful injury suffered; that is, damaged tires), a crime (willful destruction of property by your neighbor), or both. Given this complexity, how can the average citizen know how and where to file a court case?

The general structure of state courts includes courts of limited jurisdiction that are empowered to hear petty cases such as traffic violations, and to conduct the preliminary stages of more serious cases (much like federal magistrates). These limited jurisdiction courts include misdemeanor courts that hear cases involving less serious crimes. Commentators have frequently criticized misdemeanor courts, often including traffic courts, for their practices.

Feeley (1979) wrote a book on the misdemeanor courts arguing, "the process is the punishment." Feeley explained that sentences in these courts tend to be very lenient because the inconvenience and disruption defendants experience in the court process is sufficient penalty for most of the minor crimes tried in misdemeanor courts. Feeley described practices in the New Haven, Connecticut, misdemeanor courts 40 years ago that are remarkably similar to those of the current day. The National Association of Criminal Defense Lawyers (NACDL) described practices in misdemeanor courts in 26 jurisdictions (Boruchowitz, Brink, & Dimino, 2009). The NACDL report described an informal process in which conditions encouraged defendants to waive rights, decline counsel and trials, and move to complete the process as quickly as possible. The NACDL made many recommendations for changes to make the process more adversarial and better protect the rights of defendants.

At a second level of courts are those of general jurisdiction, which conduct trials for civil and criminal cases. Most states also have a juvenile or family court. This court is a special jurisdiction trial court empowered to hear juvenile delinquency cases, but is not otherwise involved with criminal matters. Such courts also hear divorce, child custody, and related domestic relations cases. Finally, there are frequently other special-purpose courts, such as probate and surrogate's courts.

Specialized criminal courts, such as drug courts, are also on the rise (see Figure 7.4). Another trend is imposing specialized caseloads so that one judge hears most or

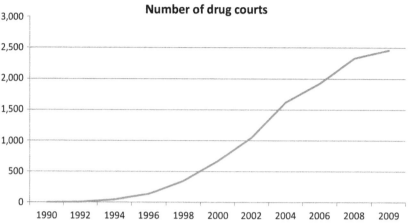

FIGURE 7.4
Growth of drug courts in the United States.

all of certain types of offenses, such as domestic violence, gun crimes, or violent crimes. By 2009, there were more than 2,400 drug courts in the United States (Huddleston & Marlowe, 2011). Drug courts focus on delivering drug treatment services to substance-abusing offenders, using the criminal process to ensure that needed treatment is available (Wenzel, Longshore, Turner, & Ridgely, 2001). Other specialized courts include teen courts (Butts & Buck, 2000) and dispute resolution programs. We can call all of these types of courts the "lower courts" because they are the first courts in the hierarchy of tribunals to receive cases. Lower courts decide issues of fact. They conduct trials, receive evidence, and establish guilt or innocence. Lower-court judges preside over trials and impose criminal sentences on convicted offenders.

In most states, a third level of appellate courts exists, at which the courts operate like the U.S. courts of appeals (i.e., they hear appeals from the lower courts). Some states have more than one intermediate appeal level, so that a case may go through two or more appeals before reaching the third level of courts. Each state has a court of last resort or a supreme court, which receives appeals from all lower courts in the state and from the intermediate appellate courts (see Figure 7.5). The decisions of these courts are binding on all other courts in the state.

Appellate courts do not decide issues of fact; rather, appellate courts serve to interpret the law. Appellate courts accept the findings of fact from the lower courts, and then decide whether the lower-court judges interpreted and applied the law correctly. They resolve questions of law raised by those who lost in the lower courts. Decisions of higher courts on the interpretation and application of the law are binding on all the courts beneath them. Thus, when the U.S. Supreme Court decides on an interpretation of the U.S. Constitution, that interpretation is binding on all other courts in the nation.

FIGURE 7.5
The Supreme Court of South Carolina is located in the state capital of Columbia.
Ellen S. Boyne

Problem-Solving Courts

As indicated, in the past 2 decades, a growing emphasis has been placed on specialized courts aimed at solving specific types of problems. These courts range from drug courts that deal exclusively with offenders who have substance abuse problems to domestic violence courts and reentry courts that specialize in returning prisoners to productive lives in the community. As is occurring in policing, there is a growing movement to develop and implement community courts in the United States. **Community courts** attempt to resolve problems and disputes in ways that address all concerned, including the community at large (Quinn, 1998). The courts connect to community resources and seek to solve problems rather than simply find facts. Thus, the court tries not only to resolve a conflict but also to understand its underlying causes and secure necessary community services to prevent the conflict from happening again (Rottman & Casey, 1999). Some community courts are actually diversion programs or mediation centers that focus on less serious disputes. In some places, however, actual community courts exist. They tend to practice **restorative justice**, a form of negotiation and discussion between the parties involved in a case designed to create or improve understanding. Kuo, Longmire, and Cuvelier (2010:327) stated, "Restorative justice aims to heal victims and offender through dialog, which is the essence of the restorative justice process." After discussing the crime, its causes, and effects, the parties agree to what they believe is a fair settlement of their differences.

Rottman (1996) described the movement to community courts. His description of the development and spread of community courts mirrors similar accounts of the development of community policing. Initially, courts represented the community and served as forums for dispute resolution in which the resolution process reflected community life. As the courts became more professional and centralized, courts became divorced from the communities they served, in part to reduce the impact of "politics" on court processing. The community court movement seeks to reestablish the link between courts and communities. The community courts generally have a greater range of sentencing options than traditional courts, including community service, substance abuse treatment, and requirements to obtain attend GED classes. In addition, community courts often provide defendants with referrals for job training and housing assistance (Frazer, 2006). A key component of community courts is citizen involvement (Terry, 2000). A part of this general movement involves **community prosecution**, in which the prosecutor is assigned to the case from initial appearance through disposition and works with the police, community, and other agencies not just to secure conviction, but also to solve the problems that led to the criminal behavior (Jansen & Dague, 2006).

Although not yet well evaluated, community courts hold promise for improving justice for less serious disputes and crimes that often find their way into the lower courts of the criminal justice system. Henry and Kralstein (2011) reported that the limited evaluations to date indicate that community courts (1) rely on community service sentencing, (2) are viewed favorably by both the public and defendant, (3) decrease jail sentences, (4) increased compliance with court conditions, and (5) conclude cases more quickly than traditional criminal courts. However, studies are less conclusive regarding other goals of community courts. Specifically, evidence of a reduction in crime for defendants processed through a community court is mixed. Evidence is also mixed regarding whether the community courts result in a cost savings to the jurisdiction.

Community courts are one type of problem-solving court designed to address not just specific instances of criminal behavior, but community problems that lead to crime (Casey & Rottman, 2003). As with community and problem-solving policing, the emergence of problem-solving courts raises a number of important questions. It remains to be seen how a proliferation of community and other problem-solving courts will affect case processing and outcomes across communities. It is not clear what will happen if one party to a dispute is not a member of the community. The questions revolve around the issue of how community courts will affect the balance between individual liberty and community interests.

THE DEVELOPMENT OF AMERICAN COURTS

During the colonial period, most political power was in the hands of the colonial governor (Neubauer, 1984:36). The colonists generally adopted the existing English system of courts and government but modified the system to fit the less complicated nature of colonial life. They did not fully transplant the many specialized courts that had evolved in Britain. Rather, they established a county court as the basic forum for adjudication. Appeals from rulings of the county court went directly to the governor. Although it was possible to appeal a gubernatorial decision to the English courts, it was seldom done (Glick, 1983:35).

As the colonies grew and commerce developed, the county courts became increasingly less able to handle the number and intricacy of cases that arose. Each colony created special courts to expedite the handling of cases. They developed new courts of general jurisdiction to reduce the need for litigants to travel great distances to have their cases heard in county courts. The addition and creation of new courts took place on a haphazard basis. New courts were created to resolve specific problems, not with any grand scheme of court structure in mind. Furthermore, court development occurred independently in each colony (Stumpf, 1988:70–73). One result of this method of development is that courts performing the same functions often have different names.

After the American Revolution, the greatest issues facing the courts were those surrounding the balance between federal and state powers. The nature of the U.S. Constitution, with its limitations on federal powers and reservation of certain governmental powers to the states, ensured the continuation of state judicial systems. The Federal Judiciary Act of 1789, designed to create a court system for the resolution of cases arising from federal laws, was a compromise between the federalists (who favored a strong central government) and the antifederalists (who championed states' rights and feared the results of a strong central government). The compromise was that they created federal courts, but that these courts would not cross state lines. To this day, no U.S. district court has more than one state within its jurisdiction.

State judges were required to swear an oath of allegiance to the U.S. Constitution. The Judiciary Act of 1789 gave the Supreme Court of the United States authority to review state decisions involving questions of a constitutional or federal nature. Although this fact gave the appearance that state courts were subservient to the federal courts (Jacob, 1984:162), state courts retained tremendous powers. The federal courts did not gain significantly in authority until social changes in the United States caused state courts to become ineffective.

Throughout the nineteenth century, the development of industry, the completion of the transcontinental railroad, and the growth in interstate commerce combined to create conditions in which state courts were not capable of resolving a large number of cases. In time, citizens increasingly called on federal courts to resolve disputes. As Jacob (1984:163) noted

> Just as state governments in general became less important to national policymaking, so state courts, to a somewhat lesser degree, lost their pre-eminent position in the judicial system and increasingly concentrated on private law cases, which enforce existing norms and affect only the immediate parties to a case.

THE FUNCTIONS OF COURTS

In describing the role of the courts, one of the first goals of the process is likely to be "justice" (Rubin, 1984). That is, the purpose of the courts is to do justice. However, we are not able to agree on exactly what is "just." Alan Dershowitz

(1982:xvi) suggested that, in fact, "nobody wants justice." Rather, parties to a suit are only interested in winning.

It is not possible to understand the operations of the criminal courts without having an appreciation for the complexity of the job performed by the courts. Addressing this issue, Neely (1983:16) noted

> As long as we are talking only about criminal courts, the questions are relatively simple. As soon, however, as civil courts enter the picture, all bets are off. For while improved funding of the criminal courts would return economic dividends to the public, improved funding of the civil courts has mixed income effects.

Neely cited New York City increasing funds to courts of general jurisdiction to help alleviate caseload backlogs as an example where the creation of more courts and the appointment of more judges opened more opportunities for people to press civil lawsuits. In many of these accelerated cases, the defendant in the civil suit was the city of New York. In effect, the citizens of New York City had paid more money to create more courts that could then be used by plaintiffs to sue the city for still more money in damages.

Because most courts empowered to hear criminal cases also hear civil cases (as is true in New York City), it is not possible to enhance court capacities selectively. Creating new judgeships and courts to accelerate criminal trials, for example, will necessarily also serve to speed civil trials. In fact, the civil docket may be so crowded that increasing the number of courts or judges will not substantially affect the outcome of criminal cases. Whereas our focus is on the criminal courts for the remainder of this chapter and the next, we must remember that the civil caseload lurks in the background and represents the largest portion of court workload (with the exception of traffic cases).

The functions of the criminal courts are twofold: the repression of crime and the protection of the rights of individuals accused of crimes. Courts serve these goals within an environmental context that includes many factors. These factors include the characteristics of the various actors (defendants, witnesses, juries, judges, prosecutors, defense attorneys, etc.), the organizational goals of involved agencies, the political climate, present social forces, and the like. The law is only one of several factors that impinge on judicial outcomes. As Glick (1983:18) stated, "Most cases also are settled through informal negotiation, not trials. Personal decision making and compromise are the keys to understanding how disputes are settled."

THE CRIMINAL COURT PROCESS

The basic dispute addressed in criminal courts is that between the need to control criminal behavior and the desire to protect individual rights and liberties. This dispute is at the core of each decision in the court segment of the justice system. After arrest, the suspect proceeds to the court stage of the criminal justice process and moves along a series of hearings and decisions that result in either conviction and punishment, or release from custody. The principal decision points in the courts are initial appearance (bail determination), formal charging, preliminary hearing, arraignment on charges, and trial. Sentencing, or punishment, is the subject of Chapter 9.

Initial Appearance

Shortly after arrest, the suspect comes before a magistrate for the setting of bail. **Bail** is a security posted by the defendant to ensure appearance at later court proceedings. The Eighth Amendment to the U.S. Constitution provides that "excessive bail shall not be required." There is some controversy as to whether this provision creates a right to bail for criminal defendants, or whether it merely protects them from facing an excessive bail. The leading U.S. Supreme Court decision on bail was rendered in the case of *Stack v. Boyle* (1951). Under federal law, defendants in noncapital cases are entitled to bail. The issue in this case was whether bail set at $50,000 was excessive, given the defendant's inability to post that amount. The Court decided that the purpose of bail is to ensure appearance at later proceedings and, absent evidence to support an exception, bail that is not reasonably calculated—or that is higher than that normally fixed for a similar offense—is excessive.

Neubauer (1984:213) reported that federal law and the constitutions of most states expressly provide a right to bail in most cases. In the latter part of the 1960s and in the early 1970s, bail was the subject of great scrutiny and debate (Wice, 1974). The Vera Institute of New York City conducted an experiment on the effects of bail on criminal defendants that demonstrated that many of those accused of crimes were unable to meet even relatively low bail amounts, and that those who were unable to make bail suffered with higher rates of conviction and incarceration (Ares, Rankin, & Sturz, 1963). Because of this report, and because of the general interest in bail reform in the United States, a number of bail projects developed across the country. The ways in which a defendant could "make bail" expanded. In addition to monetary bail, in which the defendant posts cash in the amount specified by the court, a number of alternatives were developed. These emerged largely in response to perceived problems with the role of the bail bond agents.

Bail bond agents are often small business owners who provide bail for criminal defendants for a fee. Usually, the bond agent charges 10% of the bail amount, which is not refundable. Thus, if you face a bail of $2,500, the bond agent will charge you $250 and post the full bond to secure your release. If you appear at the later stages of your trial, the court refunds the bail to the bond agent, but you are out the $250. Should you fail to appear at later hearings, the bond agent will seek you out and return you to court to protect his or her investment (Burns, Kinkade, & Leone, 2005). Some observers of the bail process were uncomfortable with several factors: profit as the motive behind pretrial release; the lack of regulation of bail agents; the errors made by bond agents in apprehending those who "skipped" bail; and irregularities in the posting of bond (using the same assets to secure release for several defendants) (Bradford, 2012; Goldfarb, 1965; Goldkamp, 1980; Johnson & Stevens, 2013). See Figure 7.6.

Approximately 58% of state-level felony defendants are released before trial (Cohen & Kyckelhahn, 2010). The average amount of bail set for defendants is largely influenced by the type of crime that the defendant is accused of committing (see Table 7.1). As a result, defendants who are facing serious charges are least likely to obtain pretrial release (see Table 7.2). The ability to obtain bail has been shown to have significant effects to the outcome of a defendant's case, as research has shown that defendants who do not secure release prior to trial are convicted at higher rates and are punished more severely (Cohen & Reaves, 2006; Reaves & Perez, 1994; Sacks & Ackerman, 2014).

In reaction to its findings, the Vera Institute and other programs initiated **release on recognizance (ROR)**, whereby a defendant with ties to the community (a job, family, stable residence, etc.) would be released on his or her own recognizance without posting bail if there was reason to believe that he or she would not flee the jurisdiction (Maxwell, 1999). In other places, courts allowed defendants to post only 10% of the full amount, because 10% was the percentage risked by a defendant when a bond agent posts bail or to post surety (such as property deeds or automobile titles) rather than cash. Another innovation was the use of issuing citations in lieu of arrest (Kalmanoff, 1976). Here, defendants are issued a summons to appear in court (much like a traffic citation), rather than being arrested. Baumer and Adams (2006) investigated the effects of a county's summons in lieu of arrest policy for seven nonviolent misdemeanor offenses. The policy was put into place primarily to reduce overcrowding in the county jail. They found that the policy did in fact reduce the population of the county jail, but effects were minimized by the fact that the county was often not arresting these low-level

FIGURE 7.6
A bail bond office near a jail and courthouse. Bail bond agents often seek to attract clients by conspicuously locating their offices close to county and municipal jails.
Ellen S. Boyne

Table 7.1	Mean Bail Amount, by Most Serious Charge
Most Serious Charge	**Bail Amount ($)**
Violent offense	112,000
Property offense	29,300
Drug offense	43,100
Public-order offense	37,600

Source: Cohen and Kyckelhahn (2010)

Table 7.2	Pretrial Release Status of Felony Defendants and Percent Convicted, 2006	
Case Characteristic	**Released (%)**	**Not Released (%)**
Total of all cases	58	42
Violent offense charged	52	48
Property offense charged	59	41
Drug offense charged	60	40
Public-order offense charged	62	38

Source: Cohen and Kyckelhahn (2010)

offenders even before the formal policy was put into place. In addition, persons issued citations were more likely to miss their initial court appearances. Overall, 33% of defendants obtain release by means of financial bail, 25% obtain release by means of nonfinancial bail, 37% are unable to post bail successfully, and 5% of defendants are denied bail (Cohen & Kyckelhahn, 2010). Box 7.4 summarizes the major forms of pretrial release that are available to defendants.

A central question in bail determinations is to what extent the setting of a bail amount should reflect concern for protecting public safety. Although the only constitutionally recognized purpose of bail is to ensure appearance by the defendant at later court proceedings, a common concern of police, prosecutors, and magistrates (not to mention the public) is to keep suspected offenders off the streets until they can be convicted and punished. To accomplish this goal, some persons advocate **preventive detention**, in which the court denies pretrial release for defendants suspected of being dangerous (Sorin, 1988).

The federal Bail Reform Act of 1984 authorizes the pretrial detention of categories of offenses or offenders. In 1987, the U.S. Supreme Court ruled that pretrial detention of defendants was permissible under the Eighth Amendment. In *United States v. Salerno* (1987), the court held that when using adversarial procedures in open court to determine that a defendant poses a risk of pretrial crime, it is permissible to deny pretrial release. Reaves (1994) reported that federal defendants who had a record of failing to appear in court or who were charged with serious crimes were likely to be denied bail. Similarly, those who had criminal records or who were under criminal justice custody at the time of their new

BOX 7.4 PRETRIAL RELEASE PROCEDURE

Financial bond	Alternative release options
Fully secured bail: The defendant posts the full amount of bail with the court	**ROR:** The court releases the defendant on the promise that he or she will appear in court as required
Privately secured bail: A bondsman signs a promissory note to the court for the bail amount and charges the defendant a fee for the service (usually 10% of the bail amount). If the defendant fails to appear, the bondsman must pay the court the full amount. Frequently, the bondsman requires the defendant to post collateral in addition to the fee	**Conditional release:** The court releases the defendant subject to his or her following specific conditions set by the court, such as attendance at drug treatment therapy or staying away from the complaining witness
Deposit bail: The courts allow the defendant to deposit a percentage (usually 10%) of the full bail with the court. The full amount of the bail is required if the defendant fails to appear. The percentage bail is returned after disposition of the case, but the court often retains 1% for administrative costs	**Third-party custody:** The defendant is released into the custody of an individual or agency that promises to assure his or her appearance in court. No monetary transactions are involved in this type of release
Unsecured bail: The defendant pays no money to the court but is liable for the full amount of bail should he or she fail to appear	**Citation release:** Arrestees are released pending their first court appearance on a written order issued by law enforcement personnel

Source: Bureau of Justice Statistics (1983:59), Bureau of Justice Statistics (1988:76)

crime were also likely to be denied bail. Cohen and Kyckelhahn (2010) reported that fewer than half of felony defendants in large jurisdictions who had a prior criminal record were able to secure pretrial release.

There have been many cases in which persons released on bail committed several crimes while on pretrial release—crimes that could have been avoided if the defendant had not been released (Ervin, 1971). Cohen and Kyckelhahn (2010) reported that about 18% of released defendants in 75 large urban counties were arrested for new offenses, and fully one-third engaged in some sort of misconduct with about 80% making all scheduled court appearances.

In practice, this dilemma is resolved through the establishment of bail schedules and the criteria employed to determine whether a defendant is suitable for ROR. Those with prior criminal records, who have no visible means of support, who are accused of serious offenses, or are otherwise thought to be dangerous usually do not qualify for ROR or low-amount bail. Most jurisdictions have enacted preventive detention statutes that establish the criteria and procedures followed in establishing the dangerousness of a defendant and deciding whether to deny pretrial release (Kennedy, 1980). Nonetheless, problems remain with the bail decision. Maxwell (1999:129) observed, "Criteria used in making pretrial release decisions in many jurisdictions, are often arbitrary and laws guiding pretrial release are vague with no clear policies for judges to follow, nor are judges required to note reasons for their decisions to release, set bail, or detain a defendant prior to trial."

With the exception of preventive detention hearings, the bail decision is usually not concerned with assessing evidence. For defendants arrested without a warrant, the U.S. Supreme Court has held that there must be a "prompt" judicial determination of probable cause. In those cases, the magistrate or judge must assess the adequacy of the evidence on which the arrest was based. This assessment occurs at the initial appearance for defendants arrested without warrants. In *County of Riverside v. McLaughlin* (1991), the Supreme Court ruled that such a review must occur within 48 hours of the arrest.

Preliminary Hearing

Whether the defendant makes bail or secures other pretrial release, the next decision point in the court process is the **preliminary hearing**. At this stage, the case against the accused is reviewed by a neutral magistrate to determine whether the evidence is sufficient to justify binding the defendant over for trial (Chen, 1991). The preliminary hearing is not a full trial of the case but is an open court process in which the strength of the state's case against the defendant is tested. The prosecution must establish that there is sufficient evidence to show probable cause that the defendant committed a crime. The defense may cross-examine witnesses, testify, and call witnesses on his or her behalf. The "information" or presentment method of charging occurs at this point.

If the magistrate decides that there is sufficient evidence to justify further action, the defendant may be "bound over" for trial. In many states, this action means that the case will go to the grand jury for a decision about formal criminal charges. In other states, the preliminary hearing serves as a charging process. The purpose of the hearing, however, is to ensure that the state is justified in continuing to proceed against the defendant.

Formal Charging

At some point in the pretrial segment of the court process, the state must file **formal charges** against a defendant. These charges are allegations of the specific crimes for which the defendant will stand trial. They are termed "formal charges" to distinguish them from the arrest charge, which may not actually reflect the offense for which the state will try the accused. In **charging**, the prosecutor (or state's attorney or district attorney) applies the criminal law to the facts of the case and identifies which provisions of the criminal code the offender violated.

For example, the police may arrest someone who is holding a screwdriver while standing on the porch of a home and charge him or her (in the arrest report) with attempted burglary. Upon reviewing the case and the law, the prosecutor may decide that the evidence will not support so serious a charge and opt instead to charge criminal trespassing and possession of burglar's tools. Similarly, the police may arrest someone for first-degree murder, but use the formal charge of manslaughter.

The evidentiary standard for charging is the same as that for arrest: probable cause. However, there is a subtle difference in interpretation of probable cause among police and prosecutors. Police tend to be "backward looking" in attempting to justify an arrest, whereas the prosecutor is "forward looking" in attempting to predict the likelihood of successful prosecution (Newman, 1978). That is, the police require probable cause to believe the suspect has committed a crime, whereas the prosecutor requires probable cause to believe it is possible to convict the suspect (now defendant) of the crime (Adams, 1983; Boland & Forst, 1985).

The state can file formal charges by either of two methods. One is by the information process through the preliminary hearing. The second is **indictment** by the grand jury. In about one-third of the states and in the federal jurisdiction, the grand jury indictment is the normal method of charging. In the remaining states, the information process is the routine manner of formal charging. Grand jury charging for felony offenses is required in only 17 states, the District of Columbia, and the federal system. Some states require grand jury indictments in capital (death penalty) cases. In most instances, the defendant can waive the right to a grand jury indictment (Rottman & Strickland, 2006:215–217).

The grand jury is a part of the court processes of all but two American criminal jurisdictions. Connecticut and Pennsylvania abolished the indicting grand jury, and Wisconsin has not convened a grand jury in decades, though the state still has a grand jury statute on the books. The **grand jury** is a panel of citizens (often sitting for a month or longer) that reviews evidence in criminal cases to determine whether sufficient evidence exists to justify trial of an individual (Acker & Brody, 2004). Grand juries are usually larger than trial juries (sizes range from a minimum of 5 jurors in Virginia, to 23 jurors in the federal, District of Columbia, and 11 state jurisdictions). In addition to this charging function, grand juries also have investigative powers and occasionally investigate suspected criminality and can issue formal charges based on the results of that investigation (Alpert & Petersen, 1985; Rottman & Strickland, 2006).

In *United States v. R. Enterprises* (1991:292, 299), the Supreme Court had this to say about the grand jury: "A grand jury may compel the production of evidence or the testimony of witnesses as it considers appropriate, and its operation is unrestrained by the technical procedural and evidentiary rules governing the conduct of criminal trials." This virtually unrestrained investigatory power is open to abuse both by the grand jury itself and by the prosecutor. Some critics of the grand jury argue that police and prosecutors use it to obtain evidence by subpoena that they could not secure by search warrant (Dillard, Johnson, & Lynch, 2003) wrongly use its investigation powers.

Some have criticized the grand jury as a "rubber stamp" of the prosecutor. The prosecutor in secret proceedings without a magistrate or judge to instruct the jury presents cases to the grand jury. Dillard et al. (2003:3) stated, "As a practical matter, the prosecutor calls the shots and dominates the entire grand jury process." In about 95% of cases, the grand jury issues a "true bill" or indictment, a formal document that lists the specific violation of the criminal code of which the defendant is accused. In cases in which the defendant is accused of more than one crime, each violation of the law identified in the indictment is a **count**. In only about 5% of cases does the grand jury go against the wishes of the prosecutor and issue a "no bill," or fail to indict. Thus, it appears that the grand jury does not perform its function of checking the discretion of the prosecutor. The problem with this type of analysis, however, is that it assumes that the prosecutor wants an indictment in every case presented to the grand jury, and that a 5% rejection rate is evidence of inefficiency. Critics suggest that prosecutors probably have insufficient evidence for charging in more than the 5% of cases that grand juries reject.

In contrast, the **information process** occurs in open court and the defendant and his or her attorney are present and allowed to examine witnesses. The proceedings of the preliminary hearing become part of an official record, and the hearing takes place before a magistrate or judge who ensures that rules of evidence are followed. The result of both processes is the same: Either the defendant is held for trial on formal charges or the evidence is found to be insufficient to support the charges and the case is dismissed. The choice of charging process often depends on jurisdictional tradition and laws and is at the discretion of the prosecutor. In some places, it is the prosecutor's choice regarding which process to follow.

The grand jury is more under the control of the prosecutor, but it does not allow a test of evidence sufficiency at trial (i.e., how well witnesses will "hold up" under cross-examination), and it yields no evidence that can be entered into the trial record directly. The U.S. Supreme Court has consistently held that the grand jury process is not subject to the same due process requirements as other decision points. In *United States v. Williams* (1992), the court held that the prosecutor is not required to disclose exculpatory evidence to the grand jury. **Exculpatory evidence** is evidence that tends to establish the innocence of the accused or defendant. Normally at trial, prosecutors are bound to disclose such evidence to the defense. The Supreme Court reasoned that such issues are dealt with at trial, and requiring strict due process protections at the grand jury stage would only delay proceedings and not add to trial fairness.

The grand jury also has the advantage of not disclosing the nature of the case or evidence to the defense attorney. The preliminary hearing, however, allows the state to test the strength of its case and, because the defendant faces his or her accusers and to cross-examine witnesses, testimony presented at this hearing can be used at trial if necessary. The disadvantage to the prosecution is that it must follow rules of evidence more strictly and, therefore, the defense gets a good indication of the nature and strength of the case against the defendant. For the defendant, the information process is preferred because of the stricter rules of evidence and the chance to preview the prosecution's case.

Traditionally, the prosecutor has had broad, almost uncontrolled discretion in charging decisions. Prosecutors have the ability to "nol pros" cases, meaning they can decide not to press formal charges regardless of the available evidence. The term comes from the Latin *nolle prosequi*, which means "I do not prosecute." Many observers—especially proponents of more serious criminal treatment of domestic violence—have criticized the broad charging discretion of prosecutors. In response, some prosecutors' offices have adopted "mandatory filing" policies by which the prosecutor files charges against every suspect arrested for domestic violence. Evaluations of this policy report no substantial benefit from mandatory filing over discretionary practices (Davis, O'Sullivan, Farole, & Rempel, 2008; Peterson & Dixon, 2005). Among other things, it appears that prosecutors exercise their charging discretion so as to reduce the number of charges filed in cases that are unlikely to result in conviction.

The broad discretion of the prosecutor in deciding criminal charges raises questions about fairness. The criminal code represents "the arsenal of the prosecutor." The prosecutor can use the criminal law as a weapon to reward, punish, and motivate the defendant. A bigoted prosecutor can level charges that are more serious against minority group members, or refuse to reduce charges in plea agreements. The prosecutor can withdraw charges or recommend sentencing leniency for defendants who cooperate with an investigation or testify for the state. The charging discretion of the prosecutor is not only broad, but it is also almost completely free from review. The lack of controls on prosecutor charging raises important questions about the fairness of charging. There has been little research on charging to date. What research findings exist are mixed. Spohn and Fornango (2009) found differences between federal prosecutors regarding their use of certain procedures. Whether a federal prosecutor recommended leniency for a defendant who assisted the case depended, in large measure, on the prosecutor. Frederick and Stemen (2012) found that whereas strength of evidence was the most important factor, characteristics of both the victims and offender also impacted the prosecutor's decision making. In contrast, Shermer and Johnson (2010) reported they found little evidence of discrimination in prosecutor decisions to reduce criminal charges. The grand jury or the magistrates at the initial appearance have responsibility for controlling prosecutorial charging discretion.

Regardless of the method of filing formal charges, once charged courts hold defendants for trial, the next decision point is conviction. The popular media generally depict this decision as being the result of a jury trial characterized by calculated strategy and dignified, formal courtroom demeanor and drama. In reality, most criminal cases end at the next stage of the court process, the arraignment. This is the point at which courts ask the defendant to plead to the charges.

Arraignment

Once formally charged with a crime, the defendant is called into court to be notified of the charges against him or her, and is asked to plead to the charges. In most criminal cases, the defendant will enter a plea of guilty at this point, and avoid a trial of the case on the facts. This high percentage of guilty pleas clearly illustrates the "compromise" nature of the court process. It is most often the result of what is known as plea bargaining.

At **arraignment**, the formal charges are read and the defendant is asked, "How do you plead?" The defendant (usually it is the defense attorney who speaks at this point) can answer in one of five ways: (1) not guilty, (2) not guilty by reason of some defense (i.e., a special, affirmative defense such as insanity or self-defense), (3) guilty, (4) *nolo contendere*, or (5) the defendant can stand silent. If the defendant is silent, the judge will enter a plea of "not guilty" for the defendant.

The only plea a judge must accept at this point is "not guilty." The plea of *nolo contendere* means that the defendant does not contest the charge and will be convicted of the offense. The difference is that the conviction cannot be used against the defendant in other proceedings, especially civil actions. This can be very important, depending on the nature of the offense. It is a relatively common plea in white-collar offenses.

Suppose you drank too much at a party, and while driving home, struck and injured a pedestrian. The responding officer who investigates the accident will probably discover that you are drunk, and charge you with driving under the influence. At arraignment, you plead *nolo contendere* and stand convicted, with all that the conviction entails (such as loss of driving privileges, mandatory jail term, a fine, and the like). The pedestrian you injured files a tort suit against you for pain and suffering, alleging negligence on your part. Conviction of drunken driving would establish your blame for the civil case in itself. By pleading *nolo contendere*, the pedestrian must establish your negligence at the civil trial, without reference to the outcome of your criminal trial.

Certain affirmative defenses involve special pleadings in which the defense states the reason for asserting innocence (e.g., "not guilty by reason of insanity"). In these cases, the defense generally is not contesting the facts of the case regarding the criminal act (*actus reus*), but rather is asserting that the requisite mental state (*mens rea*, or intention to commit a crime) does not exist for the act to be a crime. This special plea gives notice to the state that the defense will use an affirmative defense, and shifts the burden of proof from the state to the defense. As we will see, the state generally is required to prove all elements of a criminal offense beyond a reasonable doubt. Failure to do so results in an acquittal. With affirmative defenses, the defense is required to raise a question about the case; for example, the defense may give evidence that the defendant might have been legally "insane" at the time of the crime (Klofas & Weisheit, 1987). Box 7.5 summarizes the common defenses available to defendants.

BOX 7.5 COMMON DEFENSES TO CRIMINAL LIABILITY

Justification: Defendants admit they were responsible for their acts but argue that what they did was right under the circumstances.

Examples:
- Self-defense
- Choice of evils
- Consent

Excuses: Defendants admit what they did was wrong but argue that they were not responsible for their acts.

Examples:
- Insanity
- Diminished capacity
- Age
- Duress
- Intoxication
- Entrapment

Source: Samaha (2014)

Conceivably, the defense could remain silent throughout an entire trial and, after the state enters all its evidence, move for a directed verdict (dismissal) because the state failed to meet the burden of proof beyond a reasonable doubt. If the state's case is indeed not strong enough, the court dismisses the charges, acquitting the defendant. With most affirmative defenses, the defendant admits the act but denies some element crucial to the mental aspect of the crime, such as intent. The burden then falls on the defense to raise a reasonable doubt about that element, which the state must then prove (beyond a reasonable doubt) actually existed at the time of the offense.

The "not guilty" plea results in setting a trial date and subsequent moving for trial. This stage includes jury selection and the filing of pretrial motions for disclosure of evidence, suppression of evidence, and the like, in preparation for the trial itself. Although this is a typical outcome of arraignment on television and in the movies, it is very rare in the actual operations of the criminal courts. Cohen and Kyckelhahn (2010) reported that 95% of felons convicted in large jurisdictions were convicted by a guilty plea. Ostrom, Kauder, and LaFountain (2004:61) reported that in 2001, only about 3% of all criminal cases (including misdemeanors and DWI offenses) went to trial.

The "guilty" plea is an admission of the offense and obviates the need for a trial. It is left to the judge's discretion whether to accept a plea of guilty, for it entails a waiver of the right to trial. In many states, it is also a waiver of the right to appeal rulings on the admissibility of the evidence and other controversies. The Federal Rules of Criminal Procedure (see Box 7.6) instruct the judge to investigate the factual nature of the plea, the voluntariness of the plea, and the defendant's awareness of the effects of the plea before accepting a guilty plea.

> ### BOX 7.6 FEDERAL RULES OF CRIMINAL PROCEDURE, RULE 11—PLEAS
>
> A defendant may plead not guilty, guilty, or, with the consent of the court, *nolo contendere*. The court may refuse to accept a plea of guilty, and shall not accept such plea or a plea of *nolo contendere* without first addressing the defendant personally and determining that the plea is made voluntarily with understanding of the nature of the charge and the consequences of the plea. If a defendant refuses to plead or fails to appear, the court shall enter a plea of not guilty. The court shall not enter a judgment upon a plea of guilty unless it is satisfied that there is a factual basis for the plea.

If the defendant does not plead guilty, the next stage of the court process is trial. This is the point at which the court decides about conviction. Here, the state presents the case against the defendant and the defense attempts to discredit or otherwise cast doubt on the case presented by the prosecutor. The act of pleading guilty means that the state's case will go uncontested. Although contested trials are the exception in criminal law (if not all law), it is at trial that the full strength of the value placed on individual liberty is evident.

Trial

Although not often used, the jury trial is the "balance wheel" (Neubauer, 1984:284) of the court process. It is the possibility of the jury trial that serves to ensure "justice" in the more common event of plea bargaining. As Jacob (1984:207) explained

> Although critics focus on plea bargains, bench and jury trials continue to constitute an essential part of the criminal justice process. It is true that only a very small proportion of cases go to trial, and an especially small proportion go to trial by jury. But the possibility of going to trial constrains the plea bargaining process. No one has to accept a bargain that is worse than the decision that could be obtained at a jury trial. Doubtful cases can be brought to a jury or bench trial, even when the prosecutor would rather close the case with a lenient bargain.

Only the more "celebrated" cases (Walker, 2011:39–44) tend to receive the full panoply of rights, including jury trial, but the full justice process is available to all. Trials occur in approximately 10% of felony cases in the United States. These trials are of two types: bench trials and jury trials.

A common form of criminal trial is the **bench trial**, held before a judge sitting alone, with no jury. These trials are routine for petty offenses for which the maximum penalty does not exceed incarceration for 6 months. Defendants in more serious cases often accept a bench trial in lieu of the more costly and time-consuming jury trials. The **jury trial** involves a panel of citizens who have the task of determining the facts of the case. In these trials, the judge rules on questions of law and presides over the trial, but the jury is responsible for questions of fact, how much weight to give the testimony of a witness, and the final decision about guilt or innocence. Criminal trials are almost evenly split between jury trials and bench trials. For persons charged with felonies in the largest jurisdictions, only 5% of cases went to trial, and of them, 40% were jury trials. The more serious the offense charged, the greater the likelihood that the defendant would choose to go to trial (Cohen & Reaves, 2006).

The right to trial by jury is rooted in our legal tradition and firmly established in the U.S. Constitution. The U.S. Supreme Court ruled that any criminal defendant facing a punishment of incarceration of more than 6 months had the right to trial by jury in the case of *Baldwin v. New York* (1970). Individual states may grant the right to trial by jury for those facing less serious charges if they desire, but the U.S. Constitution does not require them to do so.

Most of us envision the jury as a body of 12 members who come to a unanimous decision about whether the defendant is guilty. To some, the phrase "jury of one's peers" connotes that the members of the jury should be representative of the defendant in terms of age, sex, education, place of residence, race, and other factors. "Peers," however, has been determined to refer to fellow citizens, and thus the jury does not need to reflect the characteristics of the defendant. Moreover, the jury does not have to consist of 12 members, and does not have to reach a unanimous verdict in all states. Box 7.7 shows state requirements of jury size for felony and misdemeanor cases.

The U.S. Supreme Court has addressed the unanimity of jury verdicts and the size of the jury. Although some questions remain, the Court decided that it was permissible to use a jury of six members in a robbery trial in the case of *Williams v. Florida* (1970). The Court further decided that nonunanimous verdicts are permissible. It has upheld convictions based on juror votes of 9–3 (*Johnson v. Louisiana*, 1972) and 10–2 (*Apodaca v. Oregon*, 1972). Nonetheless, only two states and Puerto Rico allow nonunanimous verdicts (Rottman, Flango, Cantrell, Hansen, & LaFountain, 2000). The Court has not ruled on how close a jury vote could be and still be valid, nor has it ruled on the effect of a split vote on a jury of fewer than 12 members. In 2013, the Supreme Court declined to hear a legal challenge to nonunanimous juries. The Court has ruled that cases heard by juries of fewer than six members are unconstitutional (*Ballew v. Georgia*, 1978), and that in serious criminal cases, a jury of six must render a unanimous verdict (*Burch v. Louisiana*, 1979). Because most states and the federal system require unanimous verdicts, the failure of the jury to reach consensus means there is no decision. A jury that cannot reach consensus about the verdict is a **hung jury**. The actual rate of hung juries is very low (about 6% of jury trials), but it varies widely from court to court (Mott, Kauder, Ostrom, & Hannaford-Agor, 2003).

At trial, the burden of proving guilt rests with the state, and the rights of the offender are strictly protected. In the case of *In re Winship* (1970), the U.S. Supreme Court ruled that the prosecution must prove every element of the offense "beyond a reasonable doubt." In *Gideon v. Wainwright* (1963), the Court

---

BOX 7.7 STATE REQUIREMENTS FOR JURY SIZE, FELONY, AND MISDEMEANOR TRIALS

All states with capital punishment require a 12-member jury in capital cases
Nine states allow fewer than 12 members in at least some felony cases
Fewer than 12 members

Arizona	Louisiana
Arkansas	Massachusetts
Connecticut	Pennsylvania
Florida	Utah
Indiana	

Thirty-seven states authorize juries of fewer than 12 members for at least some misdemeanor cases

Alaska	Iowa	New Mexico
Arizona	Kansas	New York
Arkansas	Kentucky	North Dakota
California	Louisiana	Ohio
Colorado	Massachusetts	Oklahoma
Connecticut	Michigan	Oregon
Florida	Minnesota	Pennsylvania
Georgia	Montana	South Carolina
Hawaii	Nebraska	Texas
Idaho	Nevada	Utah
Illinois	New Hampshire	Virginia
Indiana	New Jersey	West Virginia
		Wyoming

Source: Rottman and Strickland (2006:233–237)

---

held that the state must provide an accused with defense counsel at state expense if he or she is unable to provide for his or her own defense. This case involved a convicted felon who had asked for the assistance of a defense attorney at trial and was denied. The Court ruled that the right to counsel at trial applied to felony cases. In a later case, *Argersinger v. Hamlin* (1972), the Court extended the right to any criminal prosecution in which the possible penalty included incarceration. Thus, not only does the defendant have a right to contest the state at trial, but if he or she is unable to retain an attorney, the defendant has a right to counsel provided by the state.

Although relatively rare, the full jury trial is the center of the court process. As such, the trial is what we most often think of when we consider the courts. The jury trial epitomizes our adversary system of justice, in which we expect truth to emerge from the arguments of two sides of a question. If acquitted, the defendant is set free and generally cannot be tried again for the offense.

The U.S. Constitution protects criminal defendants from double jeopardy. **Double jeopardy** occurs when a defendant faces trial or punishment more than once for a single offense. The case of Byron de la Beckwith, who was convicted of the murder of civil rights leader Medgar Evers, illustrates the point. Although some believe that the double jeopardy protection should support a defendant's right to achieve finality—to put the case behind him or her (Hickey, 1995), double jeopardy applies only if the original jeopardy terminates. In the de la Beckwith case, the defendant was tried twice in 1964, with both trials resulting in hung juries. In 1969, the prosecutor entered a *nolle prosequi* order for this case but did not terminate the case. In 1990, de la Beckwith was indicted, and his subsequent trial resulted in a conviction. In reviewing the double jeopardy issues, the Mississippi Supreme Court ruled (*Beckwith v. State*, 1992) that de la Beckwith was not entitled to double jeopardy protection because his jeopardy (risk of conviction) had never been terminated.

If convicted, the case proceeds to the next decision point of the justice system: sentencing. Sentencing and punishment are the focus of Chapter 9.

THEORY AND THE COURTS

How can we explain the workings of the criminal courts? Why do some cases result in trials whereas others result in dismissing criminal charges? How is it that prosecutors pursue some cases but decline to prosecute others? What explains differences in rates or outcomes of plea bargaining? Which defendants are likely to secure pretrial release?

In this chapter (and the next), we see that the law controls or explains a great deal of court practices. The seriousness of criminal charges and the risk the defendant poses influence pretrial release, bail, charging, and conviction decisions. At the same time, the characteristics of the defendant and those of the justice system officials frequently explain at least some outcomes. At a minimum, we have two sets of theories that seem to apply. First, a legal theory suggests that changing the law will change court outcomes. Second, an "interaction" theory suggests that changing the people involved (judge, prosecutor, defense attorney, and defendant) can change outcomes. Of course, changing the structure or organization of courts will also produce change.

In Chapter 8, we examine issues in the courts. As we review these issues, we can see how they relate to "explanations" or theories of the courts. Commentators actually present theories of the courts each time they suggest causes of these issues. We need to pay particular attention to how explanations for courts compare to explanations for police or corrections. If we can find explanations that apply to all three subsystems, we can identify theories of criminal justice.

DUE PROCESS, CRIME CONTROL, AND THE COURTS

If, as we suggest, the primary purpose of the courts is to resolve conflicts, it should not be surprising that the conflict between due process and crime control comes into high relief in the criminal courts. As the core issue in the criminal justice system, the conflicting interests in liberty and order are a common theme in court procedures. Our entire system of adversary trial illustrates a "combat" between the individual and the society. The procedures and decisions of the courts reflect the difficulty of resolving this conflict. Referring to the problems in bail decisions, Maxwell summarized this conflict between due process and crime control. She wrote (1999:127), "The difficulty arises in balancing the rights of defendants on the one hand, who are presumed innocent before conviction and should not be unnecessarily detained, and ensuring future court appearances and community safety, on the other."

Those who champion individual rights over public safety tend to support practices that increase the numbers of defendants who secure pretrial release through bail or other programs. They endorse practices such as the preliminary hearing and grand jury process, in which a neutral magistrate or panel of citizens reviews the government's justification for proceeding against a citizen. The provision of defense counsel, the requirement of high evidentiary standards for conviction, and the use of juries to decide criminal matters all promise to protect the rights of individuals. On the other hand, those who wish to protect public safety and control crime tend to support preventive detention of dangerous offenders. They encourage speedy resolution of criminal cases through guilty pleas, less-than-unanimous jury verdicts, and a generally streamlined decision process in the courts.

Community courts and other specialized courts (e.g., drug courts) aim to improve the workings of the judicial component of the justice system. Dissatisfaction with current procedures underlies these reform movements. Drug courts seek to use the justice system and its coercive control to ensure that drug offenders receive the treatment necessary to prevent future crime. Community courts try to restore harmony in the community by both resolving minor disputes and attacking the causes of community conflicts. In both of these cases, we use the criminal justice system to solve individual or community problems that manifest themselves in crime, but that are not limited to criminal behavior. It remains to be seen if these efforts represent an expansion of state power over individuals (crime control), or a focusing of state power for the benefit of individuals (due process). At present, the hope is to achieve a balance between the two that best serves the interests of the individual and of the community.

Each of the criminal justice system decision points discussed in this chapter revolves around the conflict between due process and crime control. Specific practices in pretrial and trial proceedings represent efforts to achieve a balance between concerns for individual liberties and social needs for order. In later stages of the justice process (sentencing and corrections), the guilt of the defendant has been established. Although concerns about the rights and interests of offenders continue, the fact of guilt renders crime control interests more salient.

See Box 7.8 for selected court cases on criminal procedure.

BOX 7.8 SELECTED COURT CASES ON CRIMINAL PROCEDURE

Stack v. Boyle 342 U.S. 1 (1951)	The right to bail established in noncapital cases. Noted the purpose of bail is to secure appearance at later court proceedings
Gideon v. Wainwright 372 U.S. 335 (1963)	An accused must be provided with defense counsel at state expense if he or she is unable to provide for his or her own defense
Baldwin v. New York 399 U.S. 66 (1970)	Any criminal defendant facing a punishment of more than 6 months of incarceration has the right to trial by jury
In re Winship 397 U.S. 358 (1970)	In deciding the burden of proof required for a juvenile adjudication, the Court held that "the Due Process Clause protects the accused against conviction except upon proof beyond a reasonable doubt of every fact necessary to constitute the crime…"
Williams v. Florida 399 U.S. 78 (1970)	In a robbery case it is permissible to use a jury of six members
Apodaca v. Oregon 406 U.S. 404 (1972)	Nonunanimous verdicts are permissible. Court upheld a jury's vote of 10–2
Argersinger v. Hamlin 407 U.S. 25 (1972)	A defendant has a right to counsel at trial (either hired or appointed) if the possible penalty for the offense includes incarceration
Johnson v. Louisiana 406 U.S. 356 (1972)	Nonunanimous verdicts are permissible. Court upheld a jury's vote of 9–3
United States v. Selerno 481 U.S. 739 (1987)	Defendants can be detained prior to trial without bail if the government is able to establish that the defendant is dangerous to the community

REVIEW QUESTIONS

1. Briefly describe how the courts in the United States are organized. Explain how this particular court structure developed.
2. Distinguish between lower and higher courts.
3. Identify the principal decision points in the criminal court process.
4. What is bail, and what is its constitutional purpose?
5. What is meant by preventive detention?
6. Describe two ways in which formal criminal charges are brought against defendants.
7. What are community courts?
8. Differentiate between a bench trial and a jury trial.

References

Acker, J., & Brody, D. (2004). *Criminal procedure: A contemporary perspective* (2nd ed.). Sudbury, MA: Jones & Bartlett.

Adams, K. (1983). The effect of evidentiary factors on charge reduction. *Journal of Criminal Justice, 11*(6), 525–538.

Alpert, G., & Petersen, T. K. (1985). The grand jury report: A magic lantern or an agent of social control? *Justice Quarterly, 2*(1), 23–50.

Ares, C. E., Rankin, A., & Sturz, H. (1963). The Manhattan Bail Project: An interim report on the use of pre-trial parole. *New York University Law Review, 38*, 71–92 (January).

Baumer, T., & Adams, K. (2006). Controlling a jail population by partially closing the front door: An evaluation of a "summons in lieu of arrest" policy. *The Prison Journal, 86*(3), 386–402.

Boland, B., & Forst, B. (1985). Prosecutors don't always aim to pleas. *Federal Probation, 54*(2), 10–15.

Boruchowitz, R., Brink, M., & Dimino, M. (2009). *Minor crimes, massive waste: The terrible toll of America's broken misdemeanor courts*. Washington, DC: National Association of Criminal Defense Lawyers.

Bradford, S. (2012). *For better or for profit: How the bail bonding industry stands in the way of fair and effective pretrial justice*. Washington, DC: Justice Policy Institute.

Bureau of Justice Statistics (1983). *Report to the nation on crime and justice: The data (p. 59)*. Washington, DC: U.S. Department of Justice.

Bureau of Justice Statistics (1988). *Report to the nation on crime and justice* (2nd ed.). Washington, DC: U.S. Department of Justice.

Burns, R., Kinkade, P., & Leone, M. (2005). Bounty hunters: A look behind the hype. *Policing: An International Journal of Police Strategies and Management, 28*(1), 118–138.

Butts, J., & Buck, J. (2000). *Teen courts: A focus on research*. Washington, DC: Office of Juvenile Justice and Delinquency Prevention.

Casey, P., & Rottman, D. (2003). *Problem-solving courts: Models and trends*. Washington, DC: National Center for State Courts.

Chen, H. (1991). Dropping in and dropping out: Judicial decision making in the disposition of felony arrests. *Journal of Criminal Justice, 19*(1), 1–17.

Cohen, T., & Kyckelhahn, T. (2010). *Felony defendants in large urban counties, 2006*. Washington, DC: Bureau of Justice Statistics.

Cohen, T., & Reaves, B. (2006). *Felony defendants in large urban counties, 2002*. Washington, DC: Bureau of Justice Statistics.

Davis, R., O'Sullivan, C., Farole, D., & Rempel, M. (2008). A comparison of two prosecution policies in cases of intimate partner violence: Mandatory case filing versus following the victim's lead. *Criminology and Public Policy, 7*(4), 633–662.

DeFrances, C. (2001). *State court prosecutors in large districts, 2001*. Washington, DC: Bureau of Justice Statistics.

Dershowitz, A. M. (1982). *The best defense*. New York: Vintage Books.

Dillard, W., Johnson, S., & Lynch, T. (2003). A grand facade: How the grand jury was captured by government. In Policy analysis. Washington, DC: CATO Institute (May 13).

Ervin, S. J. (1971). *Preventive detention*. Chicago: Urban Research Corporation.

Feeley, M. (1979). *The process is the punishment*. New York: Russell Sage Foundation.

Frazer, M. S. (2006). *The impact of the community court model on defendant perceptions of fairness: A case study at the Red Hook Community Justice Center*. New York, NY: Center for Court Innovation.

Frederick, B., & Stemen, D. (2012). *The anatomy of discretion: An analysis of prosecutorial decision making*. New York, NY: Vera Institute of Justice.

Glick, H. R. (1983). *Courts, politics and justice*. New York: McGraw-Hill.

Goldfarb, R. (1965). *Ransom: A critique of the American bail system*. New York: Harper & Row.

Goldkamp, J. (1980). *Two classes of accused*. Lexington, MA: Lexington Books.

Henry, K., & Kralstein, D. (2011). *Community courts: The research literature*. New York, NY: Center for Court Innovation.

Hickey, T. (1995). A double jeopardy analysis of the Medgar Evers murder case. *Journal of Criminal Justice, 23*(1), 41–51.

Huddleston, W., & Marlowe, D. (2011). *Painting the current picture: A national report on drug courts and other problem-solving court programs in the United States*. Alexandria, VA: National Drug Court Institute.

Jackson, D. D. (1974). *Judges*. New York: Atheneum.

Jacob, H. (1984). *Justice in America*. Boston: Little, Brown.

Jansen, S., & Dague, E. (2006). Working with a neighborhood community prosecutor. *The Police Chief, 73*(7), 40–44. Retrieved July 16, 2007, from http://policechiefmagazine.org.

Johnson, B., & Stevens, R. (2013). The regulation and control of bail recovery agents: An exploratory study. *Criminal Justice Review, 38*(2), 190–206.

Kalmanoff, A. (1976). *Criminal justice: Enforcement and administration*. Boston: Little, Brown.

Kennedy, E. (1980). A new approach to bail release: The proposed federal code and bail reform. *Fordham Law Review, 48*, 6.

Klofas, J., & Weisheit, R. (1987). Guilty but mentally ill: Reform of the insanity defense in Illinois. *Justice Quarterly, 4*(1), 39–50.

Kuo, S. Y., Longmire, D., & Cuvelier, S. (2010). An empirical assessment of the process of restorative justice. *Journal of Criminal Justice, 38*(3), 318–328.

LaFountain, R., Schauffler, R., Strickland, S., & Holt, K. (2012). *Examining the work of state courts: An analysis of 2010 state court caseloads*. Williamsburg, VA: National Center for State Courts.

Maxwell, S. (1999). Examining the congruence between predictors of ROR and failures to appear. *Journal of Criminal Justice, 27*(2), 127–141.

Mays, G. L., & Taggart, W. A. (1986). Court clerks, court administrators and judges: Conflict in managing the courts. *Journal of Criminal Justice, 14*(1), 1–8.

Mott, N., Kauder, N., Ostrom, B., & Hannaford-Agor, H. (2003). *A profile of hung juries*. Williamsburg, VA: National Center for State Courts.

Neely, R. (1983). *Why courts don't work*. New York: McGraw-Hill.

Neubauer, D. W. (1984). *America's courts and the criminal justice system*. Monterey, CA: Brooks/Cole.

Newman, D. J. (1978). *Introduction to criminal justice* (2nd ed.). Philadelphia: J.B. Lippincott.

Ostrom, B., Kauder, N., & LaFountain, N. (2004). *Examining the work of state courts, 2003*. Williamsburg, VA: National Center for State Courts.

Owens, R., & Simon, D. (2012). Explaining the Supreme Court's shrinking docket. *William and Mary Law Review, 53*(4), 1219–1285.

Panzarella, R., & Shapiro, I. (1988). Policy, job practices, and personal values in decision making by court officers. *Journal of Criminal Justice, 16*(2), 111–120.

Perry, S. (2006). *Prosecutors in state courts, 2005*. Washington, DC: Bureau of Justice Statistics.

Peterson, R., & Dixon, J. (2005). Court oversight and conviction under mandatory and nonmandatory domestic violence case filing policies. *Criminology & Public Policy, 4*(3), 535–558.

Quinn, T. (1998). Restorative justice: An interview with visiting fellow Thomas Quinn. *National Institute of Justice Journal, 235,* 10–16 (March).

Reaves, B. (1994). *Pretrial release of federal felony defendants.* Washington, DC: U.S. Department of Justice.

Reaves, B., & Perez, J. (1994). *Pretrial release of felony defendants, 1992.* Washington, DC: Bureau of Justice Statistics.

Rottman, D. (1996). Community courts: Prospects and limits. *National Institute of Justice Journal, 231,* 46–51 (August).

Rottman, D., & Casey, P. (1999). A new role for courts? *National Institute of Justice Journal, 240,* 12–19 (July).

Rottman, D., Flango, C., Cantrell, M., Hansen, R., & LaFountain, N. (2000). *State court organization, 1998.* Washington, DC: Bureau of Justice Statistics.

Rottman, D., & Strickland, S. (2006). *State court organization 2004.* Washington, DC: Bureau of Justice Statistics.

Rubin, H. T. (1984). *The courts: Fulcrum of the justice system* (2nd ed.). New York: Random House.

Sacks, M., & Ackerman, A. (2014). Bail and sentencing: Does pretrial detention lead to harsher punishments? *Criminal Justice Policy Review, 25,* 59–77.

Samaha, J. (2014). *Criminal law* (11th ed.). Belmont, CA: Wadsworth, Cengage Learning.

Schauffler, R., LaFountain, R., Strickland, S., & Raftery, W. (2006). *Examining the work of state courts, 2005. A national perspective from the court statistics project.* Washington, DC: National Center for State Courts.

Shermer, L., & Johnson, B. (2010). Criminal prosecutions: Examining prosecutorial discretion and charge reductions in U.S. federal district courts. *Justice Quarterly, 27*(3), 394–430.

Sorin, M. D. (1988). *Out on bail: Crime file study guide.* Washington, DC: National Institute of Justice.

Spohn, C., & Fornango, R. (2009). U.S. attorneys and substantial assistance departures: Testing for interprosecutor disparity. *Criminology, 47*(3), 813–846.

Stumpf, H. P. (1988). *American judicial politics.* New York: Harcourt, Brace, Jovanovich.

Terry, W. (2000). *Opening the courts to the community: Volunteers in Wisconsin's courts.* Washington, DC: Bureau of Justice Assistance Bulletin.

Walker, S. (2011). *Sense and nonsense about crime, drugs and communities* (7th ed.). Belmont, CA: Wadsworth.

Wenzel, S., Longshore, D., Turner, S., & Ridgely, M. (2001). Drug courts: A bridge between criminal justice and health services. *Journal of Criminal Justice, 29*(3), 255–267.

Wice, P. B. (1974). *Freedom for sale.* Lexington, MA: Lexington Books.

Important Cases

Apodaca v. Oregon, 406 U.S. 404. (1972).

Argersinger v. Hamlin, 407 U.S. 25. (1972).

Baldwin v. New York, 399 U.S. 66. (1970).

Ballew v. Georgia, 435 U.S. 223. (1978).

Beckwith v. State, 615 So. 2d. 1134. (1992).

Burch v. Louisiana, 441 U.S. 130. (1979).

County of Riverside v. McLaughlin, 500 U.S. 44. (1991).

Gideon v. Wainwright, 372 U.S. 335. (1963).

In re Winship, 397 U.S. 358. (1970).

Johnson v. Louisiana, 406 U.S. 356. (1972).

Stack v. Boyle, 342 U.S. 1. (1951).

United States v. R. Enterprises, 498 U.S. 292. (1991).

United States v. Salerno, 481 U.S. 739. (1987).

United States v. Williams, 504 U.S. 36. (1992).

Williams v. Florida, 399 U.S. 78. (1970).

CHAPTER 8

People and Problems in the Courts

Four sets of people play major roles in the court segment of the justice system: (1) defense attorneys, (2) prosecutors, (3) judges, and (4) jurors. These people have a direct effect on decisions in the criminal courts. With the exception of jurors, who are usually typical citizens, all are trained in the law and therefore share a common culture (Glick, 1983:2–3; Holten & Lamar, 1991:115–119). In many ways, prosecutors and defense attorneys are similar, except for the fact that they are adversaries at trial. Very often, judges are recruited from the ranks of prosecutors and (to a lesser extent) defense attorneys. As a result, judges not only share a common training and educational experience, they often share common career paths.

DEFENSE ATTORNEYS

In the field of law, criminal law is not a particularly well-respected specialty (Neubauer, 1984:156). Wice (1978) studied defense attorneys across the country and reported that defense counsel generally were solo practitioners or attorneys working in small offices (with two or three associates). They usually began their private practices late in life, and many obtained their criminal law experience and training in prosecutors' offices. Most were not graduates of the nation's best law schools, and their salaries were generally on the lower end of the earnings scale for the legal profession. As Neubauer and Fradella (2014:184) observe, "Most lawyers view criminal cases as unsavory." Of the hundreds of thousands of attorneys in the United States, relatively few will take criminal cases. The number of criminal law specialists is quite low (Bartollas, Miller, & Wice, 1983; Glick, 1983; Neubauer & Fradella, 2014).

Of those attorneys who routinely take criminal cases, many do so on a part-time basis to supplement their earnings from a general law practice. Criminal defense services typically are provided by young, inexperienced attorneys, or by older, somewhat less successful attorneys. As Holten and Lamar (1991:124) observed, "The field (criminal defense law) does seem to attract more than its share of marginal practitioners." Among several reasons given to explain the attraction of marginal practitioners is that much of criminal defense work is mundane and uncomplicated. One result of the *Gideon* and *Argersinger* decisions

Important Terms

assigned counsel
community justice
contract systems
courtroom work
   group
indigent
innocence projects
jury
jury nullification
Missouri Plan
panel attorneys
peremptory
   challenges
plea bargaining
privately retained
   counsel
pro se defense
prosecutorial
   case
   management
public defender
special
   prosecutor
Speedy Trial Act
venire
vertical
   prosecution
voir dire
wrongful conviction

(see Chapter 7) has been an increase in criminal defense work for attorneys. By requiring that defense counsel be appointed for indigent (i.e., poor) defendants, these decisions place the burden of paying for defense on the government when the defendant is poor. Nationally, the annual cost of providing defense counsel to indigent defendants exceeds $3 billion.

Traditional defense services were available to a defendant only if he or she could afford to retain the services of an attorney. Privately retained counsel is still an option for criminal defendants today, and involves the defendant hiring his or her own attorney, who for a fee then represents the defendant at trial and in all other stages of the court process. For those unable to pay an attorney, however, the effect of the Supreme Court's decisions on the right to counsel has been the development of alternative systems for the provision of defense services. The most common are the creation of a public defender's office and the use of assigned counsel. About half of all criminal jurisdictions use a combination of indigent defense services (Harlow, 2000).

Privately retained counsel, public defenders, and assigned counsel comprise the three major methods of securing representation for criminal defendants. A fourth method, contract systems (those in which defense services for the poor are secured by contract with a private attorney, the local bar association, or a private law firm), is used in relatively few counties (Harlow, 2000:4). In most states, the county is responsible for providing indigent defense services. County governments pay almost 60% of indigent defense costs in the most populous counties (DeFrances & Litras, 2000).

In terms of the volume of cases handled, the most common of these forms is the public defender's office (Rubin, 1984:201). Larger jurisdictions (those having the heaviest caseloads) are likely to operate a public defender's office that mirrors the prosecutor's office. In many jurisdictions, the public defender is elected and authorized to employ a number of assistant public defenders to serve all indigent defendants. In these systems, the defense attorneys work for the municipality on salary. Young attorneys often seek these positions to develop trial experience prior to beginning their own private practices. Some older attorneys, weary of the rigors of private practice, also take positions with the public defender's office.

Langton and Farole (2009) reported on 957 public defender offices operated in 49 states and the District of Columbia in 2007. Only Maine did not report any public defender offices. Twenty-two states operated state defender offices, with the other 27 having county-level organizations. Of these systems, states and counties funded 13 jointly. In 14 states, counties alone paid for public defender offices (see Figure 8.1).

The majority of criminal jurisdictions use an assigned counsel system (often in conjunction with some other form of defense, e.g., a public defender), but this system serves fewer than half of all indigent criminal defendants. In jurisdictions in which criminal caseloads usually are not large enough to justify the

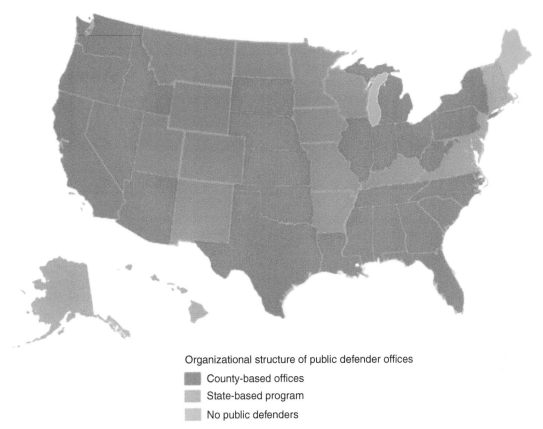

Organizational structure of public defender offices

■ County-based offices
■ State-based program
■ No public defenders

FIGURE 8.1
Counties or local jurisdictions funded and administered public defender offices in 27 states and the District of Columbia in 2007.
Source: Farole and Langton (2010b:1)

expense of developing and operating public defenders' offices, assigned counsel are used. In this system, attorneys voluntarily enter their names to be considered for criminal defense work or, in some places, all members of the local bar are enrolled on the defenders' list. As indigents come before the court, the judge appoints an attorney from the list, moving down the list of attorney names as needed. In this system, the assigned counsel generally receives a fee based on an hourly rate, but with a maximum. The fee paid generally is less than an attorney would charge a private client (especially when all members of the bar appear on the list). Again, because of the relatively low fees available under this system, only younger, less established attorneys tend to seek out assigned counsel appointments. In the federal system, assigned counsel are referred to as panel attorneys because defense counsel are assigned from a list or panel of approved lawyers. Similarly, the public defender system in the federal district courts consists of the federal defender organizations, which include both the federal public defender's office and community defender organizations where applicable.

There is great variation in the cost of publicly provided defense counsel (Stevens, Sheppard, Spangenberg, Wickman, & Gould, 2010). Costs vary from state to state, within states by county or judicial district, and, often, by type of case. In general, death penalty cases are more expensive than noncapital felonies, which are often more expensive than misdemeanor cases. The costs for providing defense counsel ranged from approximately $5 million in North Dakota to more than $444 million in New York. The federal rate of compensation ranges from $94/hour for noncapital cases to a maximum of $170/hour in capital cases. In fiscal year 2008, the state and federal governments spent more than $5 billion for indigent defense (see Figure 8.2).

There has been some debate regarding which of these systems provides the best defense services to the accused. In 2007, an average of 370 cases was assigned to each attorney employed by a public defender office (Farole & Langton, 2010a). These large caseloads have led some scholars to suggest that public defenders are overworked and cannot provide any meaningful defense for their clients (Baxter, 2012). However, analyses comparing privately retained counsel with publicly appointed attorneys have not demonstrated any significant differences in the quality of service provided (Hartley, Miller, & Spohn, 2010; Rattner, Turjeman, & Fishman, 2008). Cohen (2014) found that although public defenders perform as well as privately retained attorneys, defendants represented by assigned counsel were convicted and sentenced to prison at higher rates than those with other forms of representation.

Harlow (2000) reported that public defenders or assigned counsel represented about 80% of defendants in the largest counties, and that about 74% of prison inmates had been represented by public defenders or assigned counsel, indicating that type of counsel makes no difference in terms of imprisonment. Just over three-quarters of defendants were convicted regardless of form of representation.

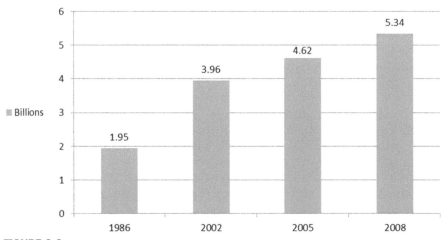

FIGURE 8.2
U.S. indigent defense spending.
Source: Stevens et al. (2010)

Defendants represented by publicly paid defense attorneys were more likely to receive a sentence to jail or prison, but for shorter terms than those represented by privately retained counsel. Keep in mind that most cases never go to trial, but instead most defendants plead guilty in exchange for a reduced sentence. Public defenders have regular working relationships with the prosecutors and the judge, which might allow them to negotiate more favorable sentences than privately retained attorneys. Table 8.1 compares experiences with defense counsel as reported by prison inmates.

A final option for defendants in criminal cases is to defend themselves. Fewer than 1% of felony defendants in the largest counties represented themselves in 1996 (Harlow, 2000:5). Given the adage that "a lawyer who represents himself has a fool for a client," do defendants have the right to make fools of themselves? The U.S. Supreme Court has decided that they do. In *People v. Faretta* (1975), the defendant, Faretta, sought self-representation, but the trial judge denied his request, insisting that Faretta accept the assistance of appointed defense counsel. Faretta appealed, arguing that it was his right to represent himself at trial. The Supreme Court agreed with Faretta that self-representation (*pro se* defense) is a constitutional right of the defendant. In *McKaskle v. Wiggins* (1984), the Supreme Court ruled that states are allowed to appoint a standby counsel over the objections of a defendant who is representing themselves. The Court further clarified the right to self-representation in

Table 8.1	State Prison Inmate Reports of Court Experiences by Type of Defense Counsel	
	Type of Counsel	
Experience	**Private (%)**	**Public (%)**
Contact with counsel		
Within a day of arrest	8.8	26.3
Within a week of arrest	27.7	33.9
More than a week before trial	32.8	29.6
Within a week of trial	12.6	4.8
At trial	13.6	3.5
None	4.5	1.9
Number of contacts with counsel		
0	4.6	2.0
1	24.6	9.6
2–3	44.5	30.6
4–5	13.4	20.7
6 or more	12.9	37.2
Type of plea		
Not guilty	24.3	31.4
Guilty	60.6	54.7
No contest	11.1	10.3
Other	6.7	7.0

Source: Harlow (2000:8)

Indiana v. Edwards (2008). In this case, the defendant suffered from a mental illness and was determined to be competent to stand trial but not competent to represent himself. Upon appeal, the Supreme Court held that the defendant could not carry out the basic tasks needed to present his own defense. Therefore, the Court permitted the state to deny the defendant's request for self-representation.

Although relatively rare, *pro se* defenses do occur. Reasons that a defendant would insist on self-representation include a desire to communicate his or her motives to the jury, disagreement with his or her counsel's strategy, the desire to avoid paying legal fees (in nonindigent cases), or little faith in the fairness of the legal system. Conversely, the defendant might have too much faith in the legal system and believe that his or her innocence will be clear to the jury (Homiak, 1976). An article in *Time* magazine (1977) described some of the pitfalls that can upset a *pro se* defense. Among them are cases in which defendants make incriminating statements (e.g., asking a witness how, because the perpetrator was wearing a mask, she could be so sure he was the offender), fail to follow proper procedure, or underestimate the strength of the state's case.

PROSECUTORS

Unlike defense services, there is no privately retained prosecutor. Rather, prosecutors, usually elected officials, have the duty to provide legal counsel for the state in criminal trials. Only three states (Alaska, Connecticut, and New Jersey) have appointed prosecutors. Depending on the size of the jurisdiction and the size of its criminal caseload, prosecutors may be either full time or part time. Nationally, about 85% of chief prosecutors are full time, and often hire a large staff of assistant prosecutors, supervisory attorneys, victim advocates, investigators, and support staff (Perry & Banks, 2011). Depending on the size of the prosecutor's office, the prosecutor (frequently called the county attorney, state's attorney, or district attorney) may actually serve as a manager, rarely engaging in trial preparation or courtroom appearances. Table 8.2 describes the distribution of staff in prosecutors' offices in the United States.

Prosecutors are usually locally elected for a specified term, usually about 4 years (Dawson, 1992:2). In 2007, the average chief prosecutor had been in office for almost 10 years (Perry & Banks, 2011). In the largest jurisdictions, prosecutors work full time and hire assistants who provide the bulk of legal services for the office. These assistants are salaried employees of the municipality. The overwhelming majority of assistant prosecutor positions are full-time appointments. These positions are most attractive to young attorneys seeking trial experience and to older attorneys who do not wish to engage in private practice or who have not been able to secure a position with a larger law firm. The average entry-level salary for an assistant prosecutor ranges from approximately $42,000 to $64,000, depending on the population of the jurisdiction. Chief prosecutors earn a salary ranging from approximately $100,000 to $165,000, depending on location (Perry & Banks, 2011).

Table 8.2	Personnel Categories in Prosecutor's Officers
Position	**Percent of Personnel**
Chief prosecutor	3
Assistant prosecutor	32
Support staff	33
Staff investigators	9
Managers/supervisors	7
Legal services (clerks/paralegals)	5
Civil attorneys	2
Victim advocates	6
Other	2
Total	100
Estimated personnel: 77,927	

Source: Perry and Banks (2011)

At the federal level, U.S. attorneys provide prosecutorial services. U.S. attorneys are presidential appointees who are empowered to employ assistants to handle federal criminal cases. In addition, the federal government (as well as some state and municipal governments) sometimes creates an Office of the Special Prosecutor, where an attorney is employed to investigate and prosecute cases arising out of some special circumstance, such as the Watergate investigation during the Nixon administration or the Whitewater investigation during the Clinton administration. Jurisdictions hire a special prosecutor when there is concern about possible conflicts of interest, or when a case is so complex that the need to perform the ordinary duties of the prosecutor's office would render it impossible for that office to pursue the case adequately. In the Watergate and Whitewater examples, because the president appoints U.S. attorneys, it might be difficult for one of them to investigate criminal allegations against the president.

Although similar in many respects, one major difference between the prosecutor's office and the public defender's office is that the prosecutor's office traditionally has been a stepping-stone for political careers. Partly because of its elective nature, and partly because the prosecutor can garner considerable media coverage by tackling certain cases (sex crimes, white-collar crime, child abuse, etc.), the office of prosecutor enables incumbents to prepare for political advancement. An attorney who is interested in a political career as a judge or other elected official often begins in the prosecutor's office (Stumpf, 1988:179–181). Unlike the prosecutor, the public defender generally does not gain voter support, mostly because he or she earns a living by defending the accused (who may be sex offenders, child abusers, or other unsavory characters).

JUDGES

In 2011, there were almost 29,000 judgeships, including appellate courts and courts of limited jurisdiction (Malega & Cohen, 2013). Judgeships are prestigious positions. To many attorneys, becoming a judge represents the pinnacle of a legal career (Neely, 1983). Compared to the general practice of law, being a judge is more prestigious, more secure, and less stressful. The overwhelming majority of the nation's judges achieve their offices through election. Unfortunately, judicial elections—at least as measured by voter turnout—generally do not provoke much citizen interest. Yet, the selection of judges is important because it is the judge's decisions on matters such as the admissibility of evidence and objections from the prosecutor and defense attorney during a trial that can ultimately influence the nature of evidence presented to the jury. The judge holds the responsibility of ensuring that both the prosecutor and defense attorneys follow proper procedures to determine guilt or innocence.

Two basic methods are used to select judges in the United States: election and appointment. In the case of elections, states determine whether judicial races will be partisan or whether they must be nonpartisan in nature. In elections, judges run for office in much the same way as mayors or state legislators. In states having appointment processes, the governor or state legislature is empowered to appoint judges to office. For many years, there has been debate about how best to ensure that those selected for judicial positions have the requisite qualifications for the job (Reddick, 2010). Generally, the debate has focused either on the election of judges or on the Missouri Plan.

In the Missouri Plan (so named because it originated in the state of Missouri), a judicial nominating commission rates the qualifications of candidates and identifies qualified candidates or recommends appointment to the governor (Reddick, 2002). The governor appoints someone from the list of qualified/ recommended candidates. The appointed judge must then periodically face an uncontested "retention election," in which the sole question before the voters is whether the judge should be retained in office. Should the voters decide to oust the judge, the governor appoints another from a list of qualified candidates, and the process repeats. Supporters of this system of judicial selection argue that it provides the best of all worlds; that is, the system includes direct voter input in the selection of judges through the retention election, yet it ensures that only qualified candidates become judges and insulates those judges, at least somewhat, from political pressure and from partisan politics. However, the evidence is not clear that this method of choosing judges is better than direct election (Webster, 1995). Recently, Reddick (2010) reported that judges selected on merit were less likely to receive judicial discipline than those elected to office. Figure 8.3 shows the methods by which judges are selected in the United States.

The federal judicial system operates differently with federal judges appointed for life terms by the president of the United States. The president generally accepts nominations from the senators of the state in which the district court judge will serve, but is not required to do so. The president then nominates the candidate, whose final appointment is subject to the advice and consent of the Senate. Controversy about the appointment of Supreme Court justices during the Reagan administration illustrated the hazards of Senate confirmation faced by federal judicial nominees.

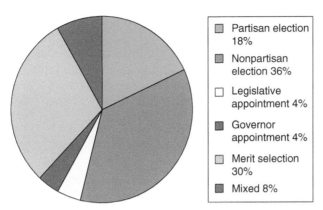

FIGURE 8.3
Methods of judicial selection for judges of state general jurisdiction courts.
Source: American Judicature Society, http://www.ajs.com

In the autumn of 1987, President Reagan nominated three candidates before he was able to obtain the consent of the Senate. Seeking conservative justices who would be strict constructionists in their interpretation of constitutional issues, the president nominated Judge Robert Bork, followed by Judge Douglas Ginsburg and Judge Anthony M. Kennedy. An active senatorial committee dominated by Democrats closely investigated all three candidates. Judge Bork was found unacceptable because of his record on equal rights issues. Judge Ginsburg removed his name from consideration after acknowledging that he had experimented with marijuana in his youth (*Criminal Justice Newsletter*, 1987). The third nominee, Judge Kennedy, won Senate approval. The controversy surrounding the confirmation hearings on the appointment of Justice Clarence Thomas (President George H. W. Bush's nominee) also illustrates the confirmation process. The Senate eventually confirmed Justice Thomas, despite great controversy regarding charges of sexual harassment. President Barack Obama's nomination of Elena Kagan to the U.S. Supreme Court in 2010 led to several days of rancorous Senate hearings.

The principal difference between the federal and state judiciaries is the tenure of judicial office in each. State judges (except those in Rhode Island), no matter how selected, undergo periodic review and face possible removal without impeachment. Judges in Rhode Island, like federal judges, receive lifetime tenure upon appointment to the bench. Lifetime tenure insulates the judge from improper political or other influence, but it also means that it is difficult to remove incompetent or corrupt judges from office. For example, removal of federal judges requires impeachment in the U.S. Senate.

JURORS

The last important set of decision makers in the criminal courts is the jury. The jury is a panel of citizens, selected through the process of *voir dire* (literally, "to speak the truth"), who are charged with hearing cases and determining guilt or innocence. Although rarely used, the criminal trial jury is symbolically important as evidence that the citizenry reigns. The U.S. Constitution guarantees the right to a jury trial. Regardless of the testimony and other evidence presented at trial, the verdict of the jury is almost totally within its discretion, and it is binding on the court. Only in very rare instances can the defense attorney succeed in convincing the judge to order a directed verdict of acquittal. This occurs when, at the conclusion of presenting its case, the prosecution has failed to provide enough evidence about some important element of the offense. In such cases, the defense counsel requests the court to dismiss charges because the prosecution has failed to establish its case. Juries also play a role in sentencing. In 35 states, the jury must agree on the death penalty before the judge can order execution. In six states, the jury has a role in determining sentences for noncapital crimes.

Because of the tremendous discretionary power of the jury, prosecutors and defense attorneys are very careful in the jury selection (*voir dire*) process. Each side receives a number of peremptory challenges, which allow them to remove otherwise qualified jurors from service. In addition, each side may challenge any number of prospective jurors for cause. Thus, during the selection process, prospective jurors may be asked how they feel about the defendant, whether they know about the case, and other such questions. Any answer may be cause for a challenge. Attorneys use peremptory challenges when they cannot establish a just cause for keeping someone off the jury, yet they believe that the individual will not be receptive to their case.

Both the prosecution and the defense seek to seat jurors whom they believe will support their respective presentations of the case. In many ways, jury selection is the most important part of the trial process (Fried, Kaplan, & Klein, 1975). Just as judicial decisions reflect the characteristics of the judge, jury decisions reflect the characteristics of the jury (Kalven & Zeisel, 1966; Simon, 1980). A juror's background, experience, personality type, and values all serve as a filter through which evidence and legal arguments are viewed (Frederick, 2012).

Prospective jurors usually are selected randomly from the population within a court's jurisdiction. These prospective jurors form a panel (called the venire) from which the attorneys select (through the *voir dire* process) members who will serve on the jury. The representativeness of the panel of jurors is a thorny issue.

To ensure that juries reflect the characteristics of the community, courts select prospective juror names from voter registration lists, driver's license records, public utility customer records, city/county directories, tax rolls, and other lists that are likely to include all potential jurors (Rottman & Strickland, 2006). The court then randomly selects members of the venire from the list. Still, this process frequently fails to produce a representative sample (Fukurai, Butler, & Krooth, 1991). Not only do juries frequently lack proportionate representation of minorities, those minorities selected for jury duty tend to come from higher social class standings than might be desired.

Jury selection seems to discriminate against minorities in general, and lower-class minorities in particular (Fukurai, 1996). Taylor, Ratcliffe, Dote, and Lawton (2007) reported that neighborhood characteristics are linked to the likelihood that those summoned for jury duty actually show up at the courthouse. People in poorer, less stable neighborhoods and those from minority neighborhoods are less likely to respond to a jury summons. The relationships are complex, but part of the explanation may be that people in these neighborhoods do not receive the summonses.

Some persons are exempt from jury duty (Rottman & Strickland, 2006). The list of exemptions varies from state to state but typically includes certain professions (attorneys, physicians, etc.), public safety and active military members, and those with health problems. Half the states do not identify any exemptions from jury duty, but the judge can choose to dismiss a prospective juror. Most states require that jurors speak English and disqualify those who do not speak the language.

During the *voir dire* process, both prosecution and defense seek to identify possible biases in the potential jurors through their responses to questions. At best, this is an imprecise process. As Judge Peter O'Connell (1988:183) stated, the process of asking a potential juror whether he or she can be impartial "is a little like asking a practicing alcoholic if he has his drinking under control; we are asking the person who has the prejudice to determine if the prejudice will affect his decision." Seltzer, Venuti, and Lopes (1991) reported that nearly 40% of jurors were untruthful during the *voir dire*. Many lawyers have begun conducting Internet searches during the *voir dire* process to research the background of potential jurors (Lundberg, 2012).

The selection of jury members is important in part because the jury is empowered to decide the ultimate fate of a case. The tradition of English and American law is that the jury can nullify a law by voting to acquit even if the evidence supports conviction. Jury nullification occurs when jurors refuse to convict a guilty defendant because of their belief that the law or the government's use of the law in that case is unjust (Simon, 1992). Reviewing the verdict in the Marion Barry trial, Simon argued that the decision to acquit Barry on the felony perjury charges was an example of jury nullification. She suggested that the six African American jurors refused to convict the defendant because they saw the case as an example of government injustice in which police entrapped the mayor. (Barry was the mayor of Washington, DC. He was videotaped using cocaine with an alleged prostitute and charged with a drug offense.) Controversy about jury nullification has escalated in recent years, especially as crime control policies such as the "war on drugs" are seen to have disproportionate effects on minority group members. Some observers cite the highly publicized murder trial of retired football star O. J. Simpson as a case in which the jury ignored the facts and thereby nullified the law (Zatz, 2000). In fact, several jurors believed that the Los Angeles police planted the evidence against Simpson. In their view, the police "framed" Simpson and the evidence was not believable.

ISSUES IN THE CRIMINAL COURTS

As with every stage of the justice system, the court process is plagued with problems and issues that defy easy resolution. We touched on some issues earlier in this chapter, such as the best mechanism for the provision of defense counsel, the effects of judicial selection, and the process of jury selection. We will assess four additional issues in this section: (1) speedy trial, (2) the role of the press in the trial process, (3) court specialization, and (4) plea bargaining. With severe overcrowding in the nation's jails and hundreds of persons accused of terrorist connections or plans, the right to a speedy trial is again an important practical and constitutional issue. Court delay contributes to jail crowding as defendants wait for hearings and trials. There is also a debate about whether suspects arrested after the September 11, 2001, terrorist attacks and as a result of ongoing antiterror investigations should be tried in criminal or military courts, and how long the government can hold these persons without trial (McCarthy, 2014). The role of the press in trials is also still unresolved. This issue, which was particularly important during the political trials of the student antiwar and civil rights activists in the early 1970s, has resurfaced and again gained prominence with the war on terror. Additional issues involve the role of the courts and the impact of technology on court operations.

Speedy Trial

We most often consider the issue embodied in the phrase "speedy trial" as court delay. Speedy trial is the solution to the problem of what some perceive as unacceptable delays in the processing of criminal cases from arrest to disposition. Supporters of speedy trial argue one of three positions: (1) speedy trials protect the rights of the defendant; (2) speedy trials are fairer to crime victims; or (3) speedy trials assist crime control (Bureau of Justice Statistics, 1986; Thompson, 2011).

The Sixth Amendment to the U.S. Constitution guarantees defendants the right to a speedy and public trial. Lengthy delays between arrest and trial (or between charging and trial) can be to the disadvantage of criminal defendants. Especially in those cases in which the defendant is unable to make bail, denial of a speedy trial amounts to incarceration prior to conviction. By virtue of their inability to obtain pretrial release, defendants awaiting trial for long periods of time are likely to suffer further losses, such as loss of income (if not loss of job), possible loss of residence, separation from family and friends, and, upon conviction, higher rates of incarceration.

The determination of when the right to a speedy trial has been violated is rarely a matter of simple objective fact. In *Barker v. Wingo*, the Supreme Court spelled out four factors for courts to weigh in determining if a defendant's constitutional right to a speedy trial has been denied. The length of the delay is the most important consideration, but it must be judged in light of the reasons for the delay. Deliberate attempts to delay by the government weigh heavily in favor of the defendant. Certain reasons, such as the absence of a key witness, are considered valid. The court must also determine if the defendant asserted his or her rights to a speedy trial and if the delay prejudiced the case against the defendant. Federal criminal proceedings are guided by the Speedy Trial Act of 1974. This federal law outlined specific time limits for which the indictment and trial must begin after an arrest. Charges are dismissed if the time limits are exceeded, unless an approved delay is requested in compliance with the provisions of the Speedy Trial Act. These delays are common, which has limited the actual effects of the Speedy Trial Act in terms of processing criminal actions (Bridges, 1982). Many states have also enacted similar laws which provide procedural guidance ensuring defendants the right to a speedy trial.

Delays in the prosecution of defendants arrested as terror suspects have raised a number of issues about the right to a speedy trial. An example is the case of José Padilla, an American citizen arrested in Chicago and charged with terrorism. Police arrested Padilla as an "enemy combatant" and held him for more than 2 years without formal criminal charges. In 2004, the U.S. Supreme Court avoided ruling in the case when it noted that Padilla's *habeas corpus* appeal against Defense Secretary Donald Rumsfeld was mistaken and needed to be filed against the commander of the military prison in which he was housed (*Rumsfeld v. Padilla*, 2004). The courts have generally ruled that a period of military detention does not start the clock on a defendant's right to a speedy trial (Kuhn, 2012). Although the court has allowed continued detention without trial of foreign combatants, as formal hostilities end, the question of speedy trial rights will come to the fore.

The Obama administration decided to proceed with criminal trials of the detainees from Guantanamo Bay. They planned to hold trials in U.S. District Court in New York City. In the first case to come forward, *United States v. Ghailani* (2010), the Second Circuit Court of Appeals denied a claim by the defendant that his lengthy detention violated the Sixth Amendment. The court held that his detention as an enemy combatant was not a criminal punishment and that the detention did not justify a dismissal of criminal charges. It is still too early to tell what will ultimately happen as future cases are tried and make their way through the appeals process. A serious question involves characterizing individuals as enemy combatants. In the war on terror, enemy combatants do not wear uniforms and we do not capture them on a conventional battlefield. We can hold prisoners of war until the end of hostilities without trial. If we wrongly identify someone as an enemy combatant, lengthy detention violates due process protections. What we need is a way to ensure that our identification of enemy combatants is accurate.

Many people believe that the justice system frequently ignores crime victims. Indeed, the role of the victim in the justice process, if anything, is generally that of witness. The justice system is not designed to alleviate the suffering of crime victims. Lengthy court proceedings, especially those in which the victim is involved as a witness, result in lost work days, mental anguish while awaiting resolution of the case, delays in recouping stolen property, and other costs to the victim. Although speedy trials act to the advantage of the accused (especially the innocent accused), it has been suggested that the crime victim has a stake in the early resolution of a criminal case (Walker, 2011). In the past two decades, concern for the plight of crime victims has led to the development of victim and witness service programs across the country (Smith & Huff, 1992). Speedy trial, some argue, provides quick closure to crime victims and minimizes the inconvenience of cooperating with the prosecution or simply watching for the outcome of the criminal process.

Yet another reason for speedy trials is the desire to control crime. Critics blame pretrial delays for high rates of plea bargaining. They blame plea bargaining, in turn, for the lack of deterrent effect of the criminal law. A more quantifiable effect of case-processing delays on crime, however, may be the amount of crime committed by criminal defendants who are free on bail and at large in the community. Cohen and Kyckelhahn (2010:9) reported that police rearrested 18% of felons granted pretrial release while awaiting trial. The longer a defendant is at liberty on bail, the greater the likelihood that he or she will commit a new crime while awaiting trial. Speedier trials and convictions (especially those resulting in incarceration) would reduce at least this one aspect of crime (Walker, 2011). Finally, the longer the period is between when a crime occurs and trial, the more difficult it is to secure a conviction. Witnesses sometimes move or die, memories fail, outrage at the offense lessens, and general interest in the case wanes. Indeed, defense attorneys often use delay strategies to win cases; that is, they seek repeated continuances in the hope that witnesses eventually will fail to appear. Table 8.3 presents information on case-processing time.

In spite of the relatively widespread support for speedy trial, it is not easily realized. Speedy trials are neither in the best interest of the guilty defendant, nor

Table 8.3	Felony Case-Processing Times
Average Elapsed Time from Arrest to Sentencing by Type of Offense	
Offense Charged	**Elapsed Time in Days**
All offenses	265
Murder	505
Sexual assault (including rape)	348
Robbery	282
Aggravated assault	279
Other violent offenses	244
Burglary	234
Larceny	220
Fraud	261
Drug possession	257
Drug trafficking	282
Weapons offenses	253

Source: Rosenmerkel, Durose, and Farole (2009)

always in the best interest of the prosecutor. Especially when the defendant is incarcerated and awaiting trial, the length of time between arrest and trial serves as an inducement to the defendant to engage in plea bargaining, thereby assuring conviction. Also important is the fact that the general workload of the courts is constantly increasing.

The most promising development in reducing delay involves changes in prosecutorial case management (Jacoby, Ratledge, & Gramckow, 1992). This involves policies and procedures to expedite case processing, including moves toward early screening of cases to plan for later processing; assignment of cases to tracks that anticipate trial, plea, diversion, and so on; and continuous monitoring of case progress (Cooper, 1994). Jurisdictions implementing such case management systems have experienced dramatic reductions in case-processing time. In general, these changes reflect recognition of "typical" cases so that prosecutors have better guidance concerning how to proceed and what to expect in a given case. Terry Baumer (2007) reported on an evaluation of an expedited case screening process that provided case reviews "24/7" and resulted in significant reductions in detention time and quicker releases of cases being discharged. Steelman, Goerdt, and McMillan (2000) described **differentiated case management** programs in operation in the United States. In these programs, prosecutors select certain types of cases that can proceed quickly through the court system. These simple cases are distinguished from those cases that have contested facts or involve complex legal issues. Rather than treating each case as unique, screening classifies cases into types that typically receive different treatments (e.g., diversion, plea bargaining, trial). Based on this, prosecutors can know what to expect in each case and better plan and manage the total caseload.

Many prosecutors' offices operate diversion programs or deferred prosecution for first offenders. Diversion programs quickly identify and refer these offenders to community-based social services, job training, or community service. Diversion programs are particularly useful for offenders suffering from mental illness or drug addiction (Sirotich, 2009; Sung, 2006). The goal is for the treatment to reduce future criminal behavior, while saving valuable time and money within the traditional criminal justice system. Most often, offenders are either not charged with a crime or the crime is expunged upon successful completion of the treatment.

Prosecutors have also adopted vertical prosecution for specific types of cases. In large prosecutors' offices, the tradition was to assign different assistant prosecutors to different stages of the court process. Thus, one assistant would handle bail hearings, another charging, yet another arraignment, and so forth. No single prosecutor followed a case from the initial appearance up through sentencing. Vertical prosecution, on the other hand, refers to the practice of assigning the responsibility of a case to a single prosecutor who then follows that same case throughout the entire court process. DeFrances, Smith, and van der Does (1996:2) reported that more than 40% of prosecutors' offices use vertical prosecution for all cases. Some offices use this management technique for specific types of crimes such as sexual assault, drug offenses, homicide, and child abuse. One potential benefit of vertical prosecution is that with specialization, prosecutors develop greater consistency in their handling of cases so that defendants and victims receive fairer treatment (Kingsnorth, MacIntosh, & Wentworth, 1999).

Klemm (1986) reported that case-processing time in five cities was more dependent on the type of plea than on other factors. Thus, defendants who plead not guilty and go to trial experience longer court delays than those who plead guilty. A report from the Bureau of Justice Statistics (1986), based on courts in 12 jurisdictions, echoed Klemm's findings. In addition, Langan and Brown (1997) reported that the time from arrest to sentencing for felony cases differed by type of conviction. Although the cases of those convicted at trial took about 9 months, cases in which the offender pleaded guilty took only about 6 months from arrest to sentencing. Moreover, as Feeley (1983) recognized, reforms that aim to promote speedy trials are subject to the desires of the courtroom work group. The judges, prosecutors, and defense attorneys who regularly work in U.S. courts realize that speedy trials will disrupt their operations and, therefore, generally oppose such reform (even if they do not knowingly and openly voice their opposition). This opposition is usually enough to render the reform ineffective. Case-processing delays, in fact, are more likely to be products of this work group and the legal culture of a community than the result of caseload pressures, trial rates, or other factors (Klemm, 1986). In support of this conclusion, a comparison of case-processing time in nine courts concluded that court "culture" was the most important factor in explaining differences in case-processing time (Ostrom & Hanson, 2000). In courts where judges, prosecutors, and defense counsel understand and share goals for case-processing time, cases are resolved more quickly. More than types of charges, rates of trial, or other factors, the courtroom work group determined court operations.

The Courtroom Work Group

Eisenstein and Jacob (1977) and other observers of the criminal courts have identified what has come to be called the courtroom work group. This designation refers to the "regular" players in U.S. criminal courts: judges, prosecutors, and defense attorneys. This group, through close working relationships that develop over time, comes to a shared understanding of what are appropriate and inappropriate court procedures and outcomes. The shared norms and definitions among this informal group have real consequences for case outcomes and attempts at court reform. The work group often determines the "going rate" for crimes. For example, the group may define a suitable penalty for breaking and entering as a 6-month jail sentence. Having this shared understanding, all parties are likely to agree to a negotiated plea in which a defendant accused of breaking and entering receives a 6-month jail term (e.g., criminal trespass).

Because all members of the group are responsible for the orderly processing of cases, the development of shared understandings is useful to each of them. Rather than treat every case as unique, it becomes possible to classify cases as typical (i.e., deserving the going rate) or unusual (i.e., requiring alternative processing). Once they develop this informal understanding, it is exceptionally difficult to change. Myers and Reid (1995) studied efforts to change sentencing outcomes in three Florida county courts. They discovered that sentences imposed on defendants differed across counties, but were quite similar within each county. Thus, they concluded that prosecutors and defense attorneys, as well as judges, were important to efforts to change sentencing. Their research confirms that the courtroom work group is alive and important in those courts.

Harris and Jesilow (2000) studied the implementation of the three-strikes sentencing law in California. The law passed as a public initiative, with more than 80% of state voters supporting the law. It requires prosecutors to charge defendants who have prior convictions, and it enhances sentences for those who have prior convictions, so that each prior conviction (strike) results in a longer prison term. It also means that what would be misdemeanor offenses for persons with no prior convictions are sometimes elevated to felonies if the defendant has prior "strikes." In general, Harris and Jesilow found that the effect of the three-strikes law was to destabilize the courtroom work group. The law greatly enhances the importance of the prosecutor's charging decisions (to allege prior strikes), but its popularity with voters prevents prosecutors from avoiding the law in many cases. Harris and Jesilow found some evidence that the work group had already adjusted to reduce the impact of the law, but that new norms for plea negotiations had not yet emerged. They wrote (2000:202), "Despite the obvious need to establish norms within the courtroom workgroup for negotiations concerning strike priors, we find little evidence that such norms will be established in the near future. The situation is clouded further by uncertainty stemming from defendants' willingness to go to trial and by juries' inclination to nullify the law and find defendants not guilty." They suggested that one result of the law is that case outcomes are less predictable, and thus trials are more likely. For this reason, the court process is becoming less efficient, and cases are beginning to backlog. We can expect similar outcomes whenever efforts are made to treat cases more severely than had been traditional practice.

Free Press and Fair Trial

The circumstance of media coverage compromising the trial process, although relatively rare, is an important concern (Duncan, 2008; Loges & Bruschke, 2005). This deals with a balance of rights—the right of the defendant to a fair and impartial hearing, and the right of the press to report on operations of the government (or, as might be stated by members of the news media, the public's "right to know"). Press coverage of criminal trials may affect court processes in two significant ways. First, the effects of pretrial publicity may make it difficult, if not impossible, to select a jury not exposed to prejudicial coverage of the case (Brady, 1983). This rationale applied in two famous trials of the 1990s: the trial of the Los Angeles police officers accused of beating Rodney King and the trial of Timothy McVeigh, the individual accused of bombing the Oklahoma City Federal Building in 1995. Second, in cases in which members of the press are allowed into the courtroom, it is possible that the entire trial will take on a circuslike atmosphere. Not only will the behavior of reporters disrupt the court proceedings, the very presence of reporters may alter the behavior of the judge, prosecutor, defendant, jury, and others (Giglio, 1982; Hannaford-Agor, 2008).

The 2013 trial of George Zimmerman for the shooting of Trayvon Martin demonstrates how the media can have substantial effects on the criminal justice process. The case garnered national attention and created intense pressure on the police and prosecutors to make an arrest. After weeks of nonstop media attention, a resignation from the city's police chief, and the appointment of a special prosecutor, Zimmerman was arrested and charged for the killing of Martin. By that time, Zimmerman had been portrayed as a racist, paranoid vigilante who was the aggressor against an unarmed innocent teenager who had been the victim of racial profiling (Aizenman, 2012). Though Zimmerman was ultimately acquitted, the pretrial media attention had created many potential issues for Zimmerman's defense team during the trial. Further, Zimmerman's subsequent encounters with the police have received far more media attention than the same crimes would have received if committed by someone less notorious. See Figure 8.4.

Because this issue involves two constitutional guarantees, the right to a fair trial and the right to a free press, the courts generally have adopted a "totality of circumstances" test, wherein they attempt to balance the rights of the media to cover trials against the rights of the state and the accused to proceed in an orderly fashion. The issue becomes important only in those cases that receive the lion's share of media attention—those cases that involve particularly gruesome offenses or are otherwise newsworthy (involving well-known victims or defendants). Surette (1989) concluded that most "media trials" focus on specific types of themes that are typical of entertainment media. These types of trials dominate news coverage of the courts and, Surette argued, distort public understanding and possibly affect future cases. He noted (1989:300), "The significance is that media trials, while publicizing only a single case, probably influence the handling of a large number of defendants, including those who receive no coverage." This influence works in a number of ways, one of which is by sensitizing justice officials to public concern about types of crimes.

It is instructive to compare the American method of handling news media coverage of criminal trials with that of England (Brandonwood, 2000). English law forbids the press from reporting on pending criminal cases, under penalty of contempt of court. Once a criminal case has been opened, the British press is banned from commenting on it. Violation of this ban can (and usually does) result in jailing the offending reporter for contempt of court. In the United States, such a ban on reporting would violate the First Amendment's prohibition against "prior restraint" (censoring free speech before it occurs). Rather, U.S. courts have relied on posttrial remedies, such as declaring convictions invalid and ordering new trials, as in *Sheppard v. Maxwell* (1966) and *Estes v. Texas* (1965).

FIGURE 8.4
Recording artists Beyoncé, left, and Jay-Z, second left, join Trayvon Martin's mother, Sybrina Fulton, and Rev. Al Sharpton at a "Justice for Trayvon" vigil in New York. One week after a jury found George Zimmerman not guilty in the death of Trayvon Martin, people gathered for nationwide rallies to press for changes to self-defense laws and for federal civil rights charges against the former neighborhood watch leader.
AP Photo/Noerdlinger Media. Rachel Noerdlinger

The strong American value placed on individual rights, such as free speech, and the nation's commitment to the sovereignty of the citizen prevent us from banning press coverage of trials. The U.S. Supreme Court has ruled that criminal trials must remain public (*Richmond Newspapers, Inc. v. Virginia*, 1980). The other side of the dilemma is the commitment to fairness and recognition that media coverage of criminal cases can bias juries and result in unfair verdicts. The American solution of posttrial remedies and the British use of prior restraint reflect the different values of the two societies. As Giglio (1982:349) stated, "The British emphasis, therefore, is on justice being done, rather than witnessed." Conversely, the American emphasis is on justice being witnessed, to ensure that justice is done.

In practice, much of the problem of balancing the rights to free press and fair trial has been resolved in U.S. courts through the development of norms of doing business. Occasionally, judges, attorneys, and the press reach agreement on explicit policies. More often, understandings of what constitutes appropriate or inappropriate reporting develop tacitly. The reliance on posttrial remedies for prejudicial media coverage of criminal cases allows the courts and the press to learn from experience and develop policies that will avoid future controversies. Thirty-eight states allow cameras and/or audio recording in criminal courts (Rottman & Strickland, 2006). In most states, the judge can deny the use of cameras and audio recorders.

Aside from specific cases, the attention of the media does appear to have effects on the operation of courts. Surette (1999) examined the effect of a well-publicized case on the overall work of courts. Comparing cases processed before and after a highly publicized case of child molestation in a day-care facility, he found that court practices changed in response to the attention. The basic change was that more molestation cases went to court. It appeared that one effect of media exposure was to make law enforcement and prosecutors more sensitive to those cases. Prosecutors were less likely to dismiss charges. Of course, this meant that "weaker" cases came to trial, resulting in acquittal of those defendants. Other than increasing the number of such cases brought to court, the effects of the publicized case seemed to cancel each other out (more cases, but more acquittals). Loges and Bruschke (2005) reported that publicity seemed to make no difference in terms of trial outcomes (i.e., convictions), but high-profile cases seem to result in stiffer sentences. What is important is that the media seems to influence prosecutors (and other justice system actors).

The question of fair trial versus free press is complex because the coverage of criminal cases by the media, although sometimes misleading (e.g., by presenting the jury trial as the norm), contributes to better understanding of criminal justice processes for the citizenry. Media coverage of criminal cases supports the ultimate accountability of justice system officers to the public. On the other hand, we cannot ignore the possible biasing effects of media commentary about criminal cases. In comparing American and British practices, Giglio concluded that one result of freer press coverage of criminal cases in the United States is that American citizens have a better understanding of their system of justice than do citizens of Britain. The inherent difficulty in balancing the good against the bad of media coverage of criminal cases ensures that this issue will remain relevant for some time to come.

The issue of fair trial versus free press has been complicated since the terrorist attacks of September 11, 2001. In response to terrorism, the United States has embarked on a number of practices that raise issues about fair trials. It is not so much media access to trials but rather public access in general. In late 2001, Thomas and Isikoff wrote an article in *Newsweek* entitled "Justice Kept in the Dark." The article examined new policies on the treatment of noncitizen terror suspects, including the use of military tribunals for secret trials, holding suspects and witnesses "incognito," and not notifying defendants of the charges against them. Whereas the rights of U.S. citizens are protected, even legal resident aliens could be subjected to secret investigations and trials. The dilemma involves protecting the interests of the defendants in maintaining their freedom while trying to prevent terrorist attacks and not providing terrorists with important information concerning the whereabouts of their personnel.

Court Specialization

In Chapter 7 we briefly discussed the development of specialty courts, including such focused tribunals as drug courts, domestic violence courts, and reentry courts. In combination, these have been called "problem-solving courts" (Casey & Rottman, 2003) because the role of the court has been redefined as that of responding to specific problems such as drug abuse or domestic violence. Huddleston and Marlowe (2011) found more than 3,600 problem-solving courts operating in 2009. Wolf (2007) outlined six principles that guide the development of problem-solving courts:

Enhanced information: Problem-solving courts are equipped with better staff training and specialized knowledge regarding the particular problem. This allows judges to make more informed decisions about the treatment needs and risks of an individual defendant.

Community engagement: Courts can engage the community to discuss topics of interest such as local "hot spots" of crime. Courts have used a variety of methods to engage the community, ranging from mailed surveys to community gatherings.

Collaboration: Courts can improve interagency communication by bringing together multiple parties such as judges, prosecutors, probation officers, social service partners, victims groups, and so on. This increased communication can foster new sentencing options to address problems.

Individualized justice: Courts can sentence offenders to individually tailored community-based services that can reduce recidivism, improve community safety, and enhance confidence in the system.

Accountability: The courts can improve the accountability of offenders by sending the message that all criminal behavior, even low-level crime, has an impact on community safety and has consequences.

Outcomes: The courts can analyze the outcomes, costs, and benefits of the court's operations. By doing so, the courts become more accountable to the public.

Table 8.4 describes the range of problem-solving courts. The most common of these courts are drug courts, where the caseload comprises drug-involved offenders and the court focuses on solving the substance abuse problems of offenders.

Another common problem-solving court involves domestic violence cases. Domestic violence courts allow the criminal justice system to address the core problems that might be influencing the offender's behavior. These courts often require offenders to receive alcohol or other substance abuse treatment, mental health counseling, anger management classes, or a variety of other programs (see Table 8.5). It is important to note that these courts do not always substitute these programs in lieu of traditional criminal justice punishment. In fact, only 10% of courts report dismissing the criminal case when offenders successfully complete a required program (Labriola et al., 2009). Some specialty courts focus on offenders with mental health problems, or those returning to the community after imprisonment (reentry courts). There is a large variety of problem-solving courts. One relatively recent development is to specialize "drug courts" to deal specifically with alcohol problems, particularly offenders convicted of driving under the influence of alcohol (Bouffard, Richardson, & Franklin, 2010). There

Table 8.4	Types of Problem-Solving Courts in the United States, 2009	
Court Type	**Number Reported**	**Percent**
Drug	2,459	67.4
Truancy	352	9.7
Domestic violence	288	7.9
Mental health	206	5.6
Reentry	26	0.7
Community	25	0.7
Homeless	25	0.7
All other	221	6.1
Total	3,648	100

Source: Huddleston and Marlowe (2011)

Table 8.5	Types of Programs Defendants in Domestic Violence Courts Are Required to Attend
Type of Program	**Percent of Courts Reporting This Program Type**
Alcohol or other substance abuse treatment	94
Mental health treatment/counseling	86
Parenting class	64
Anger management for other domestic violence cases	49
Anger management for intimate partner violence	44
Supervised visitation	37
Couples counseling	11
Mediation	5
None	2

Source: Labriola, Bradley, Rempel, and Moore (2009)

are courts devoted to truancy, child abuse, and a range of other narrowly defined problems.

At the same time, some courts have broadened the problem-solving approach to community problems. "Community courts" have developed and spread to deal with a range of community problems through the application of the criminal law (and less formal adjudication options). The proliferation of community courts has occurred in conjunction with the development of "community prosecution" and the expectation that the prosecutor's office will develop working partnerships with a range of community agencies. Most prosecutors' offices report engaging in at least some community prosecution activities, such as regularly meeting with advocacy groups, school groups, and so on (Perry, 2006).

Community prosecution, according to DeFrances (2002:9), "has been defined by prosecutors as a way to involve the community to solve crime and coordinate their office, law enforcement, local residents, and organizations to improve public safety and quality of life."

Community courts and community prosecution represent an expansion of the role of criminal courts and prosecutors. We no longer expect prosecutors simply to seek conviction of criminal offenders, or courts to simply determine guilt and assign penalties. Rather, prosecutors and judges are to be community advocates and use the resources and power of their offices to solve recurrent community problems. It is not enough to process cases. Community courts and community prosecution seek to address the underlying factors that cause criminal cases to develop. Much like community and problem-solving policing, the philosophy of community courts is that justice system agents must become more proactive in preventing crime and should be more responsive to members of the community in selecting cases for prosecution and court attention (Goldkamp, Irons-Guynn, & Weiland, 2003).

Feinblatt and Berman (2001) note that community courts seek to produce "community justice." They say (2001:1) community justice "takes many forms, but at its core are partnership and problem solving. Community justice is about creating new relationships both within the justice system and with stakeholders in the community, such as residents, merchants, churches, and schools, and testing new and aggressive approaches to public safety rather than merely responding to crime." Among other things, community courts maintain supervision over offenders and use the criminal sanction to reward treatment progress or punish failure. Court or justice services, such as training and employment assistance, are available to all members of the community to prevent future problems.

One central question that applies to these efforts (and to problem-solving policing as well) is how a proactive stance toward crime prevention may alter the traditional definition of criminal justice. In the past, a reactive criminal justice process responded to persons who had violated the law, but until there was evidence that someone broke the law, the justice system did not intervene. More proactive stances by criminal justice officials often call for intervention with citizens based on the likelihood that someone who has not yet broken the law may do so in the future. This pits individual interests in being free from government intervention against community interests in solving problems and preventing crime.

Plea Bargaining

As shown in Figure 8.5, the overwhelming majority of criminal convictions come as a result of a negotiated plea of guilty. The Bureau of Justice Statistics (Cohen & Kyckelhahn, 2010) reported that 95% of felony convictions resulted from guilty pleas. Plea bargaining refers to the process in which the state (through the

FIGURE 8.5
Methods of conviction for felons in the United States.
Source: Durose and Langan (2004)

prosecutor) and the defendant negotiate the terms under which the defendant will enter a plea of guilty. The importance of plea bargaining in the court process cannot be denied. There are divided opinions, however, as to the appropriateness of pleading guilty for considerations (Abrams, 2011; Bar-Gill & Ben-Shahar, 2009).

On the one hand, there are those who argue that plea bargaining violates the rights of the accused. Some believe the incentives to plead guilty are too enticing, especially in cases in which possible penalties are very severe, or in which the defendant is in jail awaiting trial. In most jurisdictions, by pleading guilty, the defendant has not only waived his or her right to a jury trial, but also to appeal questions of evidence admissibility. On the other hand, there are those who suggest that plea negotiations are unfair to the state and to the victim. These critics argue that plea bargains serve to let the guilty off without sufficient punishment. They contend that negotiated guilty pleas serve to lessen the deterrent effect of the law because offenders avoid their due penalties. Further, the idea that justice is open to negotiation is repugnant to the critics of plea bargaining.

Plea negotiations, however, do have some supporters. Some observers argue that the criminal justice system could not possibly provide the number of trials required if every criminal defendant were to demand one. The justice system would collapse under the burden of so many trials. The plea bargain results in a sure conviction of the offender, whereas a jury trial may not, and the defendant who pleads guilty is entitled to a sentence concession as a result of his or her honesty in admitting guilt, his or her demonstration of remorse in pleading guilty, or his or her cooperation with the state (Champion, 1987). Deciding the case of *Santobello v. New York* (1966), the U.S. Supreme Court declared that plea bargaining, when properly carried out, is something to be encouraged.

There are several competing views of the reality and purposes of plea bargaining. Some believe that plea bargaining is the effect of better representation of defendants. Feeley (1982) argued that plea bargaining is a product of increased adversariness. Prior to the twentieth century and the court reforms that added protections to defendants, trials were perfunctory. Plea bargaining occurs because the defendant now has an advocate, someone who can negotiate for him or her. Others have noted that one desired outcome of plea bargaining is case dispositions that are seen as just or fair (Douglas, 1988; Garafalo, 1991). That is, when the defense and prosecution engage in bargaining, they settle on a case outcome that seems fair. Plea bargaining can thus allow for the individualization of justice.

In an ideal world, perhaps it would be best if every criminal defendant were given a trial and plea bargaining were not allowed. In reality, however, this is unlikely to occur. Empirical research does not support the caseload-pressure argument, which explains high levels of plea bargaining as necessary (Klemm, 1986; Parnas, 1980). The abolition of plea bargaining in some jurisdictions (e.g., Alaska) has not resulted in a tremendous decrease in the number of cases concluded by guilty pleas (Call, England, & Talarico, 1983; Rubinstein & White, 1979). Thus, not only does it appear that plea bargaining is not associated with limited ability to provide trials, it further appears that plea bargaining is not a practice that can be easily abolished. Similar results were obtained in an analysis of the abolition of plea bargaining in trials within the U.S. Coast Guard (Call et al., 1983).

The National Association of Criminal Defense Lawyers (NACDL) (Boruchowitz, Brink, & Dimino, 2009) criticized the process of misdemeanor courts that encouraged high rates of guilty pleas. They reported that in many misdemeanor court systems up to 70% of cases were resolved at the initial appearance. Prosecutors offer limited-time plea deals to encourage defendants to waive their right to counsel and to plead guilty immediately. Even those cases that proceed beyond the initial appearance, the NACDL argues, most often result in guilty pleas. A lack of time and resources, coupled with low compensation to defense counsel, encourages plea bargaining.

Whatever else we may say about plea bargaining, it appears to be a functional practice. Again, the concept of a courtroom work group is important. Whether or not pleas of guilty result from formal negotiations between the prosecution and defense, the negotiations will continue, as will the pleas of guilty. Failure to recognize the informal structure of the courthouse—and the professional relationships that exist among the prosecutors, judges, and defense attorneys—leads reformers to believe that plea negotiations are somehow aberrant. Instead, given that the purpose of the court is to resolve disputes, it is only natural that a certain amount of compromise develops among the actors that engage in dispute resolution daily. Indeed, the history of plea bargaining indicates that it is a useful and traditional practice (Sanborn, 1986). Plea bargaining is a good example of the effect of people on the justice system. In assessing the operations of the justice process, it is important to remember that people make up the system and the system operates through people (Champion, 1989).

Additional Issues in the Courts

We discussed "community courts." These new courts try to increase the involvement of citizens in the court process. For at least the past 100 years, the role of average citizens in the court process has been shrinking. Citizen involvement in the courts has been limited to jury service and service as witnesses. Citizens have often tried to avoid jury duty, and the crime victim had a role only as a witness. In recent decades, however, there has been an effort to expand the role of citizens in the courts and to increase the voice of victims in court proceedings. The reasons for increasing citizen involvement in the courts are both practical and philosophical.

On the practical side, lack of citizen cooperation hinders the orderly process of court cases. When victims and other witnesses refuse to testify, it is impossible for agents of the justice system to gain convictions of guilty offenders. A perception of increased witness and victim intimidation, especially in relation to crimes associated with gang drug activity, spurred efforts to improve witness and juror protection. Healey (1995) reported that more than 50% of prosecutors in large jurisdictions identified victim and witness intimidation as a major problem, whereas more than 80% reported intimidation to be at least a moderate problem. Responding to this problem, courts developed a number of solutions to victim and witness intimidation. Courts implemented emergency relocation and support, requests for higher bail or denial of release, increased pretrial and courtroom security, protective custody for victims and witnesses, and community outreach programs seeking to better educate the public and gain the cooperation of community service organizations in assisting victims and witnesses.

The voice of the victim has been amplified in criminal court proceedings throughout the past several decades. Prosecutors often consult with crime victims before accepting a negotiated plea (Dawson, Smith, & DeFrances, 1993), and most jurisdictions have provisions for victim input into the sentencing decision. Judges, too, will usually thank citizens who serve on juries and recognize their contribution to the workings of the court. One reason for this concern with citizens' experiences in courts, of course, is that most prosecutors and judges are elected officials and thus need to serve the citizenry. A more important reason, however, is the growing recognition that victims, witnesses, and jurors deserve better treatment than they have traditionally received.

In response to this shift in our thinking about what kinds of consideration are owed to victims, witnesses, and jurors, courts have improved the jury selection process, streamlined jury service terms, and improved the physical facilities in which jurors convene. Similar changes have improved conditions for witnesses and victims. In the case of victims, legislation in most states requires the courts (generally the prosecutor's office) to provide services to crime victims. These services include notification about case progress; providing help with and information about restitution, compensation, and victim impact statements; and offering an orientation to the court process. Some jurisdictions require the prosecutor's office to provide escort services for victims and witnesses and to assist with referral to community services, the provision of counseling, and the return of property held as evidence. Box 8.1 describes the rights available to victims of federal crimes.

A second development affecting the operations of criminal courts consists of the availability of new technologies and the improvement of existing ones. These technological changes include the increasing use of forensic evidence such as DNA testing, videotape evidence, 911 emergency system audiotapes, polygraph evidence, and expert witness testimony. Popular dramas such as the *CSI* television shows create an expectation of sophisticated forensic investigations. The "CSI effect" is a term that summarizes the expected impact of these shows on citizen expectations (Kim, Barak, & Shelton, 2009).

These improvements in technology, especially DNA testing and information system technology, have raised new issues about the fairness and accuracy of our courts. Improved evidence and information have increased the recognition of wrongful convictions, cases in which courts convict innocent persons of criminal acts. When asked, justice officials estimate wrongful conviction occurs in as many as 3% of felony cases (Zalman, Smith, & Kiger, 2008). The number of convicted offenders later exonerated has increased dramatically in recent years. Gross, Jacoby, Matheson, Montgomery, and Patil (2004) reported that there are more than 40 "innocence projects" in existence in more than 30 states.

BOX 8.1 VICTIMS' RIGHTS IN FEDERAL CRIMINAL CASES

1. The right to be reasonably protected from the accused.
2. The right to reasonable, accurate, and timely notice of any public court proceeding or any parole proceeding involving the crime, or of any release or escape of the accused.
3. The right not to be excluded from any such public court proceeding, unless the court, after receiving clear and convincing evidence, determines that testimony by the victim would be materially altered if the victim heard other testimony at that proceeding.
4. The right to be reasonably heard at any public proceeding in the district court involving release, plea, sentencing, or any parole proceeding.
5. The reasonable right to confer with the attorney for the government in the case.
6. The right to full and timely restitution as provided in law.
7. The right to proceedings free from unreasonable delay.
8. The right to be treated with fairness and with respect for the victim's dignity and privacy.

Source: Office for Victims of Crime, http://www.ovc.gov/rights/legislation.html

Innocence projects are efforts to investigate claims of innocence maintained by persons convicted of criminal offenses (see http://www.innocenceproject.org). The growth of these projects and the rate of exonerations suggest that courts convict many thousands of innocent persons each year in the United States (Gross et al., 2004:11). Although most of these convictions are for less serious offenses, for which the convicted person serves a relatively short sentence, the likelihood that innocent defendants are convicted of crimes raises questions about the quality of justice. Huff (2002:3) summed up the problem: "Most people can readily understand that convicting an innocent person is unjust, even though they might express more concern with the guilty who go free. A society that views itself as just and fair simply cannot afford to ignore this problem."

Krieger (2011) surveyed the most common reasons that innocent persons are convicted. His analysis showed that the most common reasons for wrongful convictions are:

Inaccuracy of eyewitnesses: The most common cause of wrongful convictions. Eyewitness errors often take the form of live lineups, photos spreads, etc.

Perjured testimony: Knowingly false testimony by witnesses at trial.

Availability of DNA testimony: Although DNA has helped exonerate many wrongful conviction cases, the availability of DNA is relatively rare and is often not preserved for postconviction appeals.

Accuracy of DNA testing and scientific evidence: Many types of forensic science is very subjective, and methods of analyzing scientific evidence that were acceptable in the past are now considered inaccurate.

Prosecutorial misconduct: Prosecutors often do not assist in postconviction reviews of the evidence regardless of the merits of the appeal.

Ineffective defense representation: In general, defense attorneys have far fewer resources than prosecutors.

Ineffective capital representation: Defense representation in capital punishment cases have been the source of many legal challenges.

Police misconduct: A false confession obtained by the police is very strong evidence against the defendant.

Pretrial criminal procedure processes: Many procedural processes are aimed at efficiency but can hamper the defense's efforts to find witnesses, view evidence, etc.

A recent study shows that the plea bargaining process might also play an important role in wrongful convictions, as innocent defendants might falsely admit guilt in return for a reduced sentence (Dervan & Edkins, 2013).

Each instance of a wrongful conviction threatens public confidence in the fairness and accuracy of the courts. On the other hand, that we eventually recognize innocence and punish official misbehavior is a positive. Although not downplaying the seriousness of wrongful conviction, it remains true that exonerations have occurred in only a small percentage of cases. Even counting the thousands of cases in which wrongful convictions might occur, these are in relation to the millions of convictions each year. As with perhaps no other issue, the problem of wrongful convictions highlights the tension between due process and crime control. How do we ensure that we convict and punish guilty persons and prevent the conviction of an innocent person?

THE CRIMINAL COURTS IN THE WHOLE SYSTEM

Like the police, the criminal courts are a subsystem of the criminal justice system, which itself exists within the whole system of American society. This context can be understood when we consider the fact that those courts that hear criminal cases do so on a part-time basis. Most cases are civil in nature, and criminal cases are a part-time responsibility for the courts. Thus, we cannot easily resolve delay in criminal case processing by merely hiring more court personnel and building more courtrooms, because these changes will have the effect of accelerating both civil and criminal cases.

Black's (1976) theory of the sociology of law suggests that as a society becomes more diverse and larger, the use of the law will expand. In the criminal courts, we find the majority of cases and court personnel in a few very large jurisdictions. Moreover, the practice of plea bargaining represents, at some level, a less formal means of social control than trial and conviction. Even as we see proposals to reduce or eliminate plea bargaining and make formal trials more common, we also see a movement to develop less formal, problem-solving courts. We should not be surprised that the majority of cases are disposed of by plea bargaining. Trials seem to be reserved for those cases in which less formal resolutions are unworkable.

As our thinking about the role of citizens in the courts has changed, the courts themselves have become more sensitive to the needs and desires of victims, witnesses, and jurors. With the advent of community-based justice, we see the development of community courts. As communications technology improves, issues emerge surrounding media coverage, especially television coverage, of courts. The courts themselves adopt, and adapt to, new technologies to improve operations.

The courts reflect changes in the larger society and, in turn, the courts affect the larger society (Calvi & Coleman, 1989). Many of the conflicts and controversies existing in the courts represent efforts to manage the relationship between the courts and social forces. The role of juries and the selection of judges and prosecutors are evidence of the commitment of the United States to a legal system that is sensitive to our perceptions of what is right and what is wrong. As perceptions change (e.g., drug offenses are seen as more serious than in the past), there is pressure for the courts to change. Yet, we want the courts to be predictable and fair as well as free from improper outside influence. Thus, we want to know what the courts are doing, but we do not want court decisions to be biased by pre-conceived notions. As with achieving a balance between due process and crime control, the courts must seek a balance between responsiveness to social change and the commitment to impartiality.

REVIEW QUESTIONS

1. Identify three ways in which defendants in criminal cases may obtain defense counsel.
2. Compare criminal defense attorneys with prosecutors. In what ways are their jobs similar?
3. Decide which method of judicial selection you think is most likely to yield competent judges who are responsive to the public. Explain how the system you select will accomplish this goal.
4. Describe the *voir dire* process and explain how it allows attorneys to protect the interests of their clients.
5. How can the right to a speedy trial be expected to reduce strains in other areas of the justice system?
6. The conflict between a free press and a fair trial reflects one of the ideological dilemmas of American criminal justice. Explain this conflict and propose a solution.
7. Take a position on the issue of plea bargaining (i.e., either support or oppose the practice) and give arguments against those who take the opposing position to yours.
8. What are "problem-solving courts"?
9. How do the courts reflect changes in the larger American society?

References

Abrams, D. (2011). Is pleading really a bargain? *Journal of Legal Studies, 8,* 200–221.

Aizenman, H. (2012). *Pretrial publicity in a post-Trayvon Martin world. Criminal Justice, 27*(3), 12–17.

Bar-Gill, O., & Ben-Shahar, O. (2009). The prisoners' (plea bargain) dilemma. *Journal of Legal Analysis, 1*(2), 737–773.

Bartollas, C., Miller, S., & Wice, P. (1983). *Participants in American criminal justice: The promise and the performance.* Englewood Cliffs, NJ: Prentice Hall.

Baumer, T. (2007). Reducing lockup crowding with expedited initial processing of minor offenders. *Journal of Criminal Justice, 35*(3), 273–281.

Baxter, H. (2012). Too many clients, too little time: How states are forcing public defenders to violate their ethical obligations. *Federal Sentencing Reporter, 25*(2), 91–102.

Black, D. (1976). *The behavior of law.* New York: Academic Press.

Boruchowitz, R., Brink, M., & Dimino, M. (2009). *Minor crimes, massive waste: The terrible toll of America's broken misdemeanor courts.* Washington, DC: National Association of Criminal Defense Lawyers.

Bouffard, J., Richardson, K., & Franklin, T. (2010). Drug courts for DWI offenders? The effectiveness of two hybrid drug courts on DWI offenders. *Journal of Criminal Justice, 38*(1), 25–33.

Brady, J. (1983). Fair and impartial railroad: The jury, the media, and political trials. *Journal of Criminal Justice, 11*(3), 241–264.

Brandonwood, J. (2000). You say "fair trial" and I say "free press": British and American approaches to protecting defendants' rights in high profile trials. *New York University Law Review, 75,* 1412–1451.

Bridges, G. (1982). The Speedy Trial Act of 1974: Effects on delays in federal criminal litigation. *Journal of Criminal Law and Criminology, 73,* 50–73.

Bureau of Justice Statistics. (1986). *Felony case-processing time.* Washington, DC: U.S. Department of Justice.

Call, J., England, D., & Talarico, S. (1983). The abolition of plea bargaining in the Coast Guard. *Journal of Criminal Justice, 11*(4), 351–358.

Calvi, J., & Coleman, S. (1989). *American law and legal systems.* Englewood Cliffs, NJ: Prentice Hall.

Casey, P., & Rottman, D. (2003). *Problem-solving courts: Models and trends.* Williamsburg, VA: National Center for State Courts.

Champion, D. (1987). Felony offenders, plea bargaining, and probation: A case of extra-legal exigencies in sentencing practices. *Justice Professional, 2*(2), 1–18.

Champion, D. (1989). Private counsels and public defenders: A look at weak cases, prior records, and leniency in plea bargaining. *Journal of Criminal Justice, 17*(4), 253–263.

Cohen, T. (2014). Who is better at defending criminals? Does type of defense attorney matter in terms of producing favorable case outcomes? *Criminal Justice Policy Review, 25,* 29–58.

Cohen, T., & Kyckelhahn, T. (2010). *Felony defendants in large urban counties, 2006.* Washington, DC: Bureau of Justice Statistics.

Cooper, C. (1994). *Expedited drug case management.* Washington, DC: Bureau of Justice Assistance.

Criminal Justice Newsletter. (1987). President cites crime issue in choosing Kennedy for high court. *Criminal Justice Newsletter, 18*(22), 4.

Dawson, J. (1992). *Prosecutors in state courts, 1990.* Washington, DC: U.S. Department of Justice.

Dawson, J., Smith, S., & DeFrances, C. (1993). *Prosecutors in state courts, 1992.* Washington, DC: Bureau of Justice Statistics.

DeFrances, C. (2002). *Prosecutors in state courts, 2001.* Washington, DC: Bureau of Justice Statistics.

DeFrances, C., & Litras, M. (2000). *Indigent defense services in large counties, 1999.* Washington, DC: Bureau of Justice Statistics.

DeFrances, C., Smith, S., & van der Does, L. (1996). *Prosecutors in state courts, 1994.* Washington, DC: Bureau of Justice Statistics.

Dervan, L., & Edkins, V. (2013). The innocent defendant's dilemma: An innovative empirical study of plea bargaining's innocence problem. *The Journal of Criminal Law & Criminology, 103,* 1–48.

Douglas, R. (1988). Tolerated contests? Plea and sentence in the Victorian magistrate's courts. *Journal of Criminal Justice, 16*(4), 269–290.

Duncan, S. (2008). Pretrial publicity in high profile trials: An integrated approach to protecting the right to a fair trial and the right to privacy. *Ohio Northern University Law Review, 34,* 755–795.

Durose, M., & Langan, P. (2004). *Felony sentences in state courts, 2002.* Washington, DC: Bureau of Justice Statistics.

Eisenstein, J., & Jacob, H. (1977). *Felony justice.* Boston: Little, Brown.

Farole, D., & Langton, L. (2010a). A national assessment of public defender office caseloads. *Judicature, 94*(2), 87–90.

Farole, D., & Langton, L. (2010b). *Count-based and local public defender offices, 2007.* Washington, DC: Bureau of Justice Statistcs.

Feeley, M. (1982). Plea bargaining and the structure of the criminal process. *Justice System Journal, 7*(Winter), 338–355.

Feeley, M. (1983). *Court reform on trial.* New York: Basic Books.

Feinblatt, J., & Berman, G. (2001). *Responding to the community: Principles for planning and creating a community court*. Washington, DC: Bureau of Justice Assistance.

Frederick, J. (2012). *Mastering voir dire and jury selection: Gaining an edge in questioning and selecting your jury*. Chicago, IL: ABA Publishing.

Fried, M., Kaplan, K., & Klein, K. (1975). Juror selection: An analysis of voir dire. In R. Simon (Ed.), *The jury system in America*. Beverly Hills, CA: Sage.

Fukurai, H. (1996). Race, social class, and jury participation: New dimensions for evaluating discrimination in jury service and jury selection. *Journal of Criminal Justice, 24*(1), 71–88.

Fukurai, H., Butler, E., & Krooth, R. (1991). Cross-sectional jury representation or systematic jury representation? Simple random and cluster sampling strategies in jury selection. *Journal of Criminal Justice, 19*(1), 31–48.

Garafalo, J. (1991). Police, prosecutors, and felony case attrition. *Journal of Criminal Justice, 19*(5), 439–449.

Giglio, E. (1982). Free press—Fair trial in Britain and America. *Journal of Criminal Justice, 10*(5), 341–358.

Glick, H. (1983). *Courts, politics and justice*. New York: McGraw-Hill.

Goldkamp, J., Irons-Guynn, C., & Weiland, D. (2003). *Community prosecution strategies*. Washington, DC: National Institute of Justice.

Gross, S., Jacoby, K., Matheson, D., Montgomery, N., & Patil, S. (2004). *Exonerations in the United States: 1989 through 2003*. Chicago: American Judicature Society.

Hannaford-Agor, P. (2008). When all eyes are watching: Trial characteristics and practices in notorious trials. *Judicature, 91*(4), 197–201.

Harlow, C. (2000). *Defense counsel in criminal cases*. Washington, DC: Bureau of Justice Statistics, 4, 8.

Harris, J., & Jesilow, P. (2000). It's not the old ball game: Three strikes and the courtroom workgroup. *Justice Quarterly, 17*(1), 186–203.

Hartley, R., Miller, H., & Spohn, C. (2010). Do you get what you pay for? Type of counsel and its effect on criminal court outcomes. *Journal of Criminal Justice, 38*, 1063–1070.

Healey, K. (1995). *Victim and witness intimidation: New developments and emerging responses*. Washington, DC: National Institute of Justice.

Holten, N. G., & Lamar, L. (1991). *The criminal courts: Structures, personnel, and processes*. New York: McGraw-Hill.

Homiak, R. (1976). *Faretta v. California* and the pro se defense: The constitutional right of self-representation. *The American University Law Review, 25*, 897–937.

Huddleston, W., & Marlowe, D. (2011). *Painting the current picture: A national report on drug courts and other problem-solving court programs in the United States*. Alexandria, VA: National Drug Court Institute.

Huff, C. R. (2002). Wrongful conviction and public policy: The American Society of Criminology presidential address. *Criminology, 40*(1), 1–18.

Jacoby, J., Ratledge, E., & Gramckow, H. (1992). *Expedited drug case management programs: Issues for program development*. Washington, DC: U.S. Department of Justice.

Kalven, H., & Zeisel, H. (1966). *The American jury*. Boston: Little, Brown.

Kim, Y., Barak, G., & Shelton, D. (2009). Examining the "CSI-Effect" in the cases of circumstantial evidence and eyewitness testimony: Multivariate and path analyses. *Journal of Criminal Justice, 37*(5), 452–460.

Kingsnorth, R., MacIntosh, R., & Wentworth, J. (1999). Sexual assault: The role of prior relationship and victim characteristics in case processing. *Justice Quarterly, 16*(2), 275–302.

Klemm, M. (1986). A look at case processing time in five cities. *Journal of Criminal Justice, 14*(1), 9–23.

Krieger, S. (2011). Why our justice system convicts innocent people, and the challenges faced by innocent projects trying to exonerate them. *New Criminal Law Review, 14*(3), 333–402.

Kuhn, W. (2012). The speedy trial rights of military detainees. *Syracuse Law Review, 62,* 209–253.

Labriola, M., Bradley, S., Rempel, C., & Moore, S. (2009). *A national portrait of domestic violence courts.* New York, NY: Center for Court Innovation.

Langan, P., & Brown, J. (1997). *Felony sentences in state courts, 1994.* Washington, DC: Bureau of Justice Statistics.

Langton, L., & Farole, D. (2009). *Public defender officers, 2007—Statistical tables.* Washington, DC: Bureau of Justice Statistics.

Loges, W., & Bruschke, J. (2005). *Free press vs. fair trials: Examining publicity's role in trial outcomes.* Oxford: Routledge.

Lundberg, J. C. (2012). Googling jurors to conduct voir dire. *Washington Journal of Law, Technology & Arts, 8*(2), 123–136.

Malega, R., & Cohen, T. (2013). *State court organization, 2011.* Washington, DC: Bureau of Justice Statistics.

McCarthy, B. (2014). Terrorism and ethics. In M. Braswell, B. McCarthy, & M. McCarthy (Eds.), *Justice, crime, and ethics (8th ed.).* Burlington, MA: Anderson Publishing.

Myers, L., & Reid, S. (1995). The importance of county context in the measurement of sentence disparity: The search for routinization. *Journal of Criminal Justice, 23*(3), 223–241.

Neely, R. (1983). *Why courts don't work.* New York: McGraw-Hill.

Neubauer, D. (1984). *America's courts and the criminal justice system.* Monterey, CA: Brooks/Cole.

Neubauer, D., & Fradella, H. (2014). *America's courts and the criminal justice system* (11th ed.). Belmont, CA: Wadsworth Cengage Learning.

O'Connell, P. (1988). Pretrial publicity, change of venue, public opinion polls—A theory of procedural justice. *University of Detroit Law Review, 65*(2), 169–197.

Ostrom, B., & Hanson, R. (2000). *Efficiency, timeliness, and quality: A new perspective from nine state criminal trial courts.* Washington, DC: National Institute of Justice.

Parnas, R. (1980). Empirical data, tentative conclusions, and difficult questions about plea bargaining in three California counties. *Federal Probation, 44*(2), 12.

Perry, S. (2006). *Prosecutors in state courts, 2005.* Washington, DC: Bureau of Justice Statistics, 2.

Perry, S., & Banks, D. (2011). *Prosecutors in state courts, 2007—Statistical tables.* Washington, DC: Bureau of Justice Statistics.

Rattner, A., Turjeman, H., & Fishman, G. (2008). Public versus private defense: Can money buy justice? *Journal of Criminal Justice, 36*(1), 43–49.

Reddick, M. (2002). Merit selection: A review of the social scientific literature. *Dickinson Law Review, 106,* 729–744.

Reddick, M. (2010). *Judging the quality of judicial selection methods: Merit selection, elections, and judicial discipline.* Chicago: American Judicature Society. Retrieved July 18, 2010, from, http://www.acjs.org.

Rosenmerkel, S., Durose, M., & Farole, D. (2009). *Felony sentences in state courts, 2006—Statistical tables.* Washington, DC: Bureau of Justice Statistics.

Rottman, D., & Strickland, S. (2006). *State court organization, 2004.* Washington, DC: Bureau of Justice Statistics.

Rubin, H. (1984). *The Courts: Fulcrum of the justice system* (2nd ed.). New York: Random House.

Rubinstein, M. L., & White, T. J. (1979). Plea bargaining: Can Alaska live without it? *Judicature, 62,* 266.

Sanborn, J. B. (1986). A historical sketch of plea bargaining. *Justice Quarterly, 3*(2), 111–138.

Seltzer, R., Venuti, M., & Lopes, G. (1991). Juror honesty during the voir dire. *Journal of Criminal Justice, 19*(5), 451–462.

Simon, R. (1980). *The jury: Its role in American society.* Lexington, MA: Lexington Books.

Simon, R. (1992). Jury nullification, or prejudice and ignorance in the Marion Barry trial. *Journal of Criminal Justice, 20*(3), 261–266.

Sirotich, F. (2009). The criminal justice outcomes of jail diversion programs for persons with mental illness: A review of the evidence. *The Journal of the American Academy of Psychiatry and the Law, 37*(4), 461–472.

Smith, B., & Huff, C. R. (1992). From victim to political activist: An empirical examination of a state-wide victim's rights movement. *Journal of Criminal Justice, 20*(3), 201–215.

Steelman, D., Goerdt, J., & McMillan, J. (2000). *Caseflow management: The heart of court management in the new millennium.* Williamsburg, VA: National Center for State Courts.

Stevens, H., Sheppard, C., Spangenberg, R., Wickman, A., & Gould, J. (2010). *State, county and local expenditures for indigent defense services: Fiscal year 2008.* The Spangenberg Project. Retrieved December 16, 2013 from http://www.americanbar.org/content/dam/aba/administrative/legal_aid_indigent_defendants/ls_sclaid_def_expenditures_fy08.authcheckdam.pdf.

Stumpf, H. (1988). *American judicial politics.* New York: Harcourt, Brace, Jovanovich.

Sung, H. (2006). From diversion experiment to policy movement: A case study of prosecutorial innovation. *Journal of Contemporary Criminal Justice, 22*(3), 220–240.

Surette, R. (1989). Media trials. *Journal of Criminal Justice, 17*(4), 293–308.

Surette, R. (1999). Media echoes: Systemic effects of news coverage. *Justice Quarterly, 16*(3), 601–631.

Taylor, R., Ratcliffe, J., Dote, L., & Lawton, B. (2007). Roles of neighborhood race and status in the middle stages of juror selection. *Journal of Criminal Justice, 35*(4), 391–404.

Thomas, E., & Isikoff, M. (2001). Justice kept in the dark. *Newsweek,* 36–43 (Dec. 10, 2001).

Thompson, C. (2011). A shooting suspect's release revives the right to a speedy trial in Missouri. *Missouri Law Review, 76,* 971–998.

Time (1977, May). *Fools in court.* 45.

Walker, S. (2011). *Sense and nonsense about crime, drugs, and communities.* Monterey, CA: Brooks-Cole.

Webster, P. (1995). Selection and retention of judges: Is there one "best" method? *Florida State University Law Review, 23,* 1–34.

Wice, P. (1978). *Criminal lawyers: An endangered species.* Beverly Hills, CA: Sage.

Wolf, R. (2007). *Principles of problem-solving justice.* New York, NY: Center for Court Innovation.

Zalman, M., Smith, B., & Kiger, A. (2008). Officials' estimates of the frequency of "actual innocence" convictions. *Justice Quarterly, 25*(1), 72–100.

Zatz, M. (2000). The convergence of race, ethnicity, gender, and class on court decision making: Looking toward the 21st century. In J. Horney (Ed.), *Criminal Justice 2000: Policies, processes, and decisions of the criminal justice system: Vol. 3.* (pp. 503–552). Washington, DC: National Institute of Justice.

Important Cases

Argersinger v. Hamlin, 407 U.S. 25 (1972).

Barker v. Wingo, 407 U.S. 514 (1972).

Estes v. Texas, 381 U.S. 532 (1965).

Gideon v. Wainwright, 372 U.S. 335 (1963).

Indiana v. Edwards, 554 U.S. 164 (2008).

McKaskle v. Wiggins, 465 U.S. 168 (1984).

Richmond Newspapers, Inc. v. Virginia, 448 U.S. 555 (1980).

People v. Faretta, 422 U.S. 806 (1975).

Rumsfeld v. Padilla, 542 U.S. 426 (2004).

Santobello v. New York, 404 U.S. 257 (1966).

Sheppard v. Maxwell, 384 U.S. 333 (1966).

United States v. Ghailani, S10 98 Crim. 1023 (2010).

CHAPTER 9

Sentencing: The Goals and Process of Punishment

After conviction, the next major decision point in the criminal justice system is **sentencing**, the decision about punishment. In many ways, the sentencing decision represents the crux of the justice system, for it is at this point that we determine what to do to, for, with, or about the criminal offender.

Criminal sentences may involve the imposition of fines, community supervision, or incarceration. In some cases, a criminal sentence includes a combination of all of these. Excluding fines and short-term incarceration in a local jail, millions of people each year receive criminal sentences of probation or imprisonment. If we include punishments for all sorts of offenses, including traffic citations, we sentence more than 15 million people each year. In 2006, of more than 1.1 million people convicted of felonies in state courts, only 41% received a sentence to prison (Rosenmerkel, Durose, & Farole, 2009).

To understand how the distinction is drawn between who is incarcerated and who is allowed to remain in the community under supervision, we need to understand the purposes of punishment and the motivations of the people who make the punishment decision. This chapter examines these factors.

THE PURPOSES OF PUNISHMENT

Traditionally, four purposes or justifications for criminal penalties have been advanced: (1) deterrence, (2) incapacitation, (3) treatment (or rehabilitation), and (4) just deserts (or retribution). These theories of punishment answer the question "Why punish at all?" The average citizen does not often hear this question in the context of criminal law. Yet, most of us have heard the expression that "two wrongs do not make a right." Applied to the criminal law, this suggests that imposing a punishment on someone who has broken the law is a "second wrong," which does not make it right. If I steal your television and am sent to prison for a year because of it, have things turned out right? You are deprived of your television, I am deprived of a year of my life, and all of us pay the costs of trial and imprisonment.

From this point of view, the punishment of crime seems useless, if not wasteful. However, we usually do not think of it this way. Rather, it seems almost automatic that we punish someone who breaks the law (von Hirsch, 1976). What

Important Terms

boot camp
concurrent term
consecutive term
determinate
  sentencing
deterrence
disparity
false negative
false positive
focal concerns
general deterrence
good time
habitual offender
  statutes
incapacitation
indeterminate
  sentencing
intermediate
  sanctions
just deserts
mandatory
  minimum
  sentences
parole eligibility
partial disclosure
presentence
  investigation
  (PSI)
presumptive
  sentencing
rehabilitation
retribution
sentencing
sentencing
  commissions
specific deterrence
split sentences
three-strikes laws
treatment
truth in sentencing

can justify a system of penalties that we can argue involves nothing but costs to everyone affected?

Deterrence is a purpose of punishment based on the idea that punishment of the individual offender produces benefits for the future by making the crime less attractive. Deterrence has two parts: **specific deterrence**, in which the object of the deterrent effect is the specific offender, and **general deterrence**, in which the object of the deterrent effect is a wider audience (the general public). According to deterrence theory, punishment is an example of what awaits law violators and serves to educate would-be offenders, so that they will weigh the costs of crime against its benefits (Paternoster, 1987).

With specific deterrence, after release from prison, I will think twice before I steal another television because I now know that I will face a year in prison if the police catch me stealing again. With general deterrence, after seeing what happened to me, you will rethink your plan to replace your missing television by stealing your neighbor's set. In both cases, the punishment serves to prevent future crimes. If society does not punish, there may be no reason for us to obey the law.

Deterrence has a certain intuitive appeal. On the surface, it makes sense that deterrence will work. Unfortunately, the evidence of its effectiveness is not very clear (Newman, 1983:101–105). Few (if any) criminals believe they will be caught and punished (indeed, if they expected to be caught, they most probably would not commit the offense). Although we have used the term "educate," deterrence really operates on fear. Would-be offenders must fear the penalty, and thus we are left with a society in which "proper" behavior is based on fear—a basis that most of us do not favor. Finally, when someone has thought about it and decided not to commit a crime, it is unclear whether the person made the decision based on fear of punishment, fear of public ridicule, fear of eternal damnation, or some other factor entirely.

Deterrence has strong appeal, but it is difficult to prove. Following a long tradition of research into the workings of deterrence, Gertz and Gould (1995) studied a sample of college students and found that the likelihood of students engaging in crime was affected more by their personal perceptions that the behavior was wrong than by fear of arrest and punishment. Others have studied criminal offenders and found that their perceptions of being caught and the likely penalty if caught influence their decisions about engaging in crime (Shover, 1996; Wright & Decker, 1994). In a study of 15 active residential burglars, Piquero and Rengert (1999) found that although burglars considered the risk of arrest and punishment, the potential payoff of the burglary was a more important factor in their decision to commit a crime. Nagin and Pogarsky (2001) came to similar conclusions in a study of deterrence in which they found that offender preferences for risk-taking influenced the deterrent effects of punishments. These studies and others (Pogarsky, 2002) suggest that different people view the risk of penalty differently so that it may not be possible to deter all potential offenders with a single penalty.

The theory of deterrence assumes that humans are rational beings guided by a pleasure principle. That is, humans do things that please them and avoid things that hurt them. Further, it holds that we are able to assess the likely effects of our behavior and guide ourselves according to these assessments. As rational beings, we will avoid bad behaviors, such as committing crimes, when the behaviors will produce unpleasant results (punishments). Rationality, of course, is difficult to establish. Indeed, many crimes, especially violent offenses among friends and family, are more emotional than rational.

For a punishment to deter a would-be offender, it must meet two conditions. First, the penalty must be severe enough that the pain of the punishment will outweigh the pleasure of the criminal act. Using an economic example, if the penalty for theft were a $100 fine, it may be severe enough to stop someone from stealing $50. Given the opportunity to steal $500, however, the rational person may take the money and pay the fine, keeping a $400 profit. Thus, deterrence depends in part on the severity of the punishment.

The second condition is that the offender must believe we will impose the penalty. Not only must the punishment be severe enough to outweigh the gain realized by crime, but also the likelihood of punishment must be high enough that the offender takes the threat seriously. If the punishment for theft were 10 years in prison, but the chance of punishment were only one in a million, the threat of punishment probably would not deter. Deterrence theory suggests that the lower the risk of punishment, the higher the likelihood that a crime will be committed.

Research indicates that, of these two conditions, certainty of punishment is the more important aspect of deterrence. Given a rational offender, uncertainty of punishment makes deterrence even more troublesome. The offender will assess the likelihood of capture, and then take steps to reduce the chance of detection before committing an offense. Deterrence may best serve to make offenders more cautious rather than less criminal. In a review of the deterrence literature, Paternoster (2010) suggested that criminals do appear to be rational actors, but that because of the delays in administering punishment, the criminal justice system is not able to exploit this rationality.

In a study of the specific deterrent effects of punishment for DUI offenses, Kingsnorth, Alvis, and Gavia (1993) suggested that offenders have different perceptions of sanction severity. Thus, some offenders may not view a sanction or set of sanctions as very severe by some, or may allow others to minimize the severity of the penalty. Would-be offenders must also perceive that the crime is likely to result in arrest and punishment (Schoepfer, Carmichael, & Piquero, 2007). As Bruce Jacobs (2010) put it, it may be impossible to deter some offenders because they do not consider the consequences of their actions. Finally, some researchers have found that the experience of being incarcerated actually increases the likelihood of future crime in some offenders (Wood, 2007). Whereas this might seem counterintuitive, one must realize that the incarcerated offender is isolated from conventional society, placed in an environment where they are in constant contact with other offenders, and face significant stigma along with difficulty finding housing upon release.

Incapacitation, like deterrence, suggests that punishment serves to prevent future crime, but not by education or fear. An incapacitative punishment prevents future crimes by removing opportunities for crime. One good reason to imprison a criminal is to ensure that he or she does not have the chance to commit a crime in society again. I cannot steal your television if I am in prison. Probably the most effective incapacitative penalty is capital punishment. Not only do the dead tell no tales but they also commit no crimes. See Figure 9.1.

Incapacitation has two major drawbacks. First, it is expensive to incapacitate most offenders. Second, it is difficult to predict who is likely to commit an offense in the future. At the current level of sophistication, it is not possible to identify precisely those persons likely to pose a threat of serious crime in the future (Visher, 1987). The prediction problem is simply too complex.

In any attempt to predict "dangerousness" among a population of criminal offenders (not to mention the general population), one runs a risk of making two types of errors: false positives and false negatives. A **false positive** refers to someone who is predicted to be dangerous (positive on danger), but who turns out not to be a threat (false). A **false negative** refers to someone who is predicted to be safe (negative on danger), but who turns out to be dangerous (false). We incapacitate false positives as if they were dangerous, wasting prison resources and needlessly infringing on individual freedoms. We fail to incapacitate false negatives leaving them free to victimize others. Every crime prediction scheme

FIGURE 9.1
The traditional cagelike appearance of the prison or jail cell, shown here at the Old Salem Jail, is symbolic of incapacitation as a purpose of sentencing. The Old Salem Jail in Salem, Massachusetts, was operational from 1813 until 1991.
Ellen S. Boyne

available makes both types of errors. Under the best of circumstances, roughly eight false positives will be incapacitated for each truly dangerous offender imprisoned, and nearly one-half of the dangerous offenders will be classified as posing little danger and released (Wenk, Robison, & Smith, 1972). In addition, most predictive models do not account for the possibility that offenders change over time and that their risk of new crime increases or decreases based on life experiences after a sentence is imposed (LeClair & Guarino-Ghezzi, 1991). Given these limitations, policymakers must decide how much error they are willing to tolerate (Smith & Smith, 1998), balancing concerns about due process (false positives) with concerns about crime control (false negatives).

Largely because of the numerous false positives, incapacitation entails a significant increase in prison space (Greenwood, 1982; Van Dine, Conrad, & Dinitz, 1979). If we work with the eight-to-one ratio of false positives to "true positives" (actual dangerous offenders), for us to incapacitate 100 more dangerous offenders each year, we will also need to incarcerate 800 more nondangerous offenders. The prison populations increase nine times as fast as the population of dangerous offenders. To provide sufficient prison capacity for these larger populations, we must build four to six times as many more prisons. Incapacitation is ultimately rational, but a determination of its effectiveness must await the development of accurate prediction devices. Upon reviewing the available evidence about incapacitation, Cullen, Jonson, and Nagin (2011:605) concluded, "[W]e need to take a giant collective step backward and understand that imprisonment is not a panacea for the crime problem."

Treatment (also called **rehabilitation**) is another rationale based on a reduction of future crime. Unlike deterrence or incapacitation, treatment is concerned with the offender as an individual (Cullen & Gilbert, 1982, 2013). Here, the punishment imposed is one that fits the individual and is most likely to result in a change in the individual's desire to commit crime. Treatment suggests that individuals commit crimes for a variety of reasons and that the solution to the problem of crime will be achieved through changing individuals so that they will not wish to engage in crime, and by having other options available to them that will allow them to avoid criminality.

As with prediction, the behavioral sciences do not yet have a level of sophistication that allows treatment programs imposed as criminal sentences to be entirely successful. Partly because of pragmatic need, the treatment options available for criminal offenders are limited. Generally, we provide some type of counseling to a wide range of offenders. Although designed to deal with individuals, the realities of large numbers of offenders and limited treatment resources mean that treatment is applied to groups and tailored (often not very well) to individuals. Many early studies of the effects of treatment suggested that treatments for criminal offenders generally were not effective (Bailey, 1966; Martinson, 1974). Even though many perceive treatment as an ineffective and lenient punishment, the public continues to support rehabilitative efforts, particularly for juvenile offenders (Piquero, Cullen, Unnever, Piquero, & Gordon, 2010).

Despite discouraging results from many attempts at rehabilitation, efforts to treat criminal offenders continue, and many show reason for hope (Lipsey & Cullen, 2007). Many treatment programs show promise of being effective answers to the criminality of specific populations of offenders. Completing a review of the evidence on rehabilitation effectiveness, Lipsey and Cullen argued that we do have successful programs, but that there is large variation in success rates. What is lacking, they contended, is an understanding of what works best, for whom, and under what circumstances. Reviewing the research on correctional treatment, Mackenzie (1997:9–16) noted, "The important issue is not whether something works but what works for whom." Like incapacitation, treatment is eminently plausible, but must await greater sophistication in the design and delivery of services to offenders, as well as in the investment of sufficient resources, before it meets in practice what we expect in theory (Flores, Russell, Latessa, & Travis, 2005).

What appears from the research on treatment effectiveness is that we have not been very sophisticated in our application of treatments. Gendreau (1996) maintained that we must focus treatments on high-risk offenders. He suggested that one of the reasons why studies of treatment effectiveness show low impact is because we have "wasted" treatment on those who do not need it. Today, treatment as a part of sentencing has experienced a resurgence as we seek to prevent future crime (Harland, 1996). The problem-solving courts, such as drug courts and domestic violence courts, attempt to use the threat or application of criminal sanctions to support treatment programs and ensure that the offender participates in treatment (Casey & Rottman, 2003).

Just deserts (also called **retribution** or desert) is the only justification for criminal punishment that is not "forward looking." It does not offer a reduction in future crime as the principal justification for the imposition of a punishment. Rather, the idea of "just deserts" operates from the belief that whoever breaks the law "deserves" to be punished. Breaking the law in itself is justification for punishment, whether that punishment reduces, increases, or has no effect on future levels of crime. The criminal law is a promise wherein we (the state) promise to punish anyone who violates the law, and in the desert rationale, we must keep our promise.

Just deserts places limits on the degree to which we can punish someone. Punishment is expected to be commensurate with (or proportionate to) the severity of the crime committed. For example, public torture and execution of parking violators would deter most of us from parking illegally (if not from driving altogether), and these methods would be acceptable in a purely deterrent system of punishment. In contrast, these extreme forms of punishment for parking violations would be unthinkable in a desert scheme. Although a purely deterrent system of punishment does not require that the person punished be convicted first, the just deserts rationale holds that only convicted offenders should be punished.

Supporters of deterrence often engage in "penalty escalation" because it is easier to alter the severity of punishment than its certainty (Newman, 1983). In this case, the penalty for a given offense—for example, 5 years of imprisonment for theft—is increased (perhaps to 10 years). It is easier to increase penalty severity than to become more efficient at catching and punishing thieves. Furthermore, deterrence rests on an argument that the good of the penalty (in terms of crimes prevented) must outweigh its harm in terms of injury to the punished. It is possible, then, to impose a deterrent penalty on an innocent person, as long as the social good outweighs the individual harm.

We can argue that incapacitative penalties have the effect of punishing the innocent. The determination of how severe a penalty should be for incapacitation does not rest on the seriousness of the crime committed but on a prediction that the offender will commit another crime. Like the queen in *Alice in Wonderland*, proponents of incapacitation invoke the penalty first, and the crime comes later, after the penalty. If there in fact is no crime, so much the better.

Treatment penalties assume an "identity of interest" between the state and the offender. The state wants what is best for the offender, that is, to improve his or her chances in life and to reduce the offender's desire to commit crimes. The offender either wants the same thing or would want it if he or she were competent. Thus, the imposition of a punishment is for the offender's own good. A sanction that seems disproportionate to the seriousness of the offense is not a problem, as long as it is "good" for the offender.

People often state the just deserts justification for punishment in biblical terms as "an eye for an eye." It fits rather well with our beliefs that, regardless of the reason, those who break the law should be punished (Johnson & Sigler, 1995). The difficulty with desert is that we cannot yet precisely measure levels of crime severity, or of punishment severity (Durham, 1988). Additionally, we are uncomfortable with the idea that punishment can (or should) be imposed simply for the sake of punishment. Retribution is also difficult to achieve in practice. There tends to be widespread disagreement about how much punishment those convicted of different kinds of crimes deserve (Griset, 1995). Furthermore, as Wonders (1996) observed, sentencing is located in the middle of the criminal justice system. Attempts to make sentencing "fair" must contend with both earlier (investigation, arrest, charging) and later (correctional placements, parole release) decisions. Finally, as Myers and Reid (1995) observed, statewide legislation is implemented in different localities, and each of these has its own courtroom work group and definition of appropriate penalties.

These four rationales for the imposition of criminal punishment—deterrence, incapacitation, treatment, and just deserts—have been presented separately and analyzed as if they were required to stand alone. In practice, however, sentencing systems support many purposes. The sentencing judge may "throw the book" at a defendant for deterrent purposes, whereas correctional authorities seek to "treat" the offender's problems and rehabilitate him or her, only to have a paroling authority refuse to release the offender because of a fear that the offender will commit a new crime and, therefore, must be incapacitated.

Not only do most sentencing systems expressly serve all four of these functions, the decision makers in those sentencing systems (judges, parole authority members, correctional workers, and administrators) favor different justifications for punishment. To complicate matters even more, these different actors favor different rationales for punishment of different offenders at different points in time. Furthermore, each criminal jurisdiction has its own structure for the determination and implementation of criminal sentences.

SENTENCING STRUCTURES IN THE UNITED STATES

Substantial differences exist among the states regarding how they go about the sentencing of criminals. As the Bureau of Justice Statistics (1984:1) reported:

> It requires more than 200 pages to describe the basic features of the sentencing laws in each state. In addition to the different laws that govern sentencing, there are differences in how specific offenses are defined and classified by the criminal code in each state.

Criminal sentencing has been the topic of a great deal of interest and debate (Clear, 1994; Tonry, 1996; Travis, 2012; Ulmer, 1997; Zalman, 1987). Since 1975, many states have adopted changes in the structures used for criminal sentencing. The result has been the addition of a number of innovative formats for sentencing. If anything, criminal sentencing in the United States has become even more complicated in the past three decades. Tonry (1999:1) observed, "There are now many approaches to sentencing and corrections in this country. Some states have guidelines with parole release, and some without. Some three-strikes states have adopted truth in sentencing; some have not. And so on, through the litany of changes in recent decades." Nonetheless, the traditional distinction made between determinate and indeterminate sentencing is useful.

Determinate sentencing structures are those in which at the time of sentencing the offender knows the exact length and nature of his or her punishment. **Indeterminate sentencing** structures are those in which the precise length of the penalty is unknown until some time has passed since the imposition of the penalty. Within each of these classes are several types of sentencing structures that represent a balance of power among the legislative, judicial, and executive branches of government. The structure of sentencing reflects varying degrees of emphasis on each of the goals of criminal sentencing, and it affects how sentencing is conducted.

Box 9.1 depicts sentencing structures found across the United States. The majority of sentencing authority rests with the legislature, which establishes criminal penalties and defines crimes. There has traditionally been a certain level of sentencing power vested in the executive branch in the form of clemency. The governor of a state or the president of the United States can grant pardons, commutations, reprieves, and other forms of mercy. Legislatures usually delegate sentencing power to parole authorities and sentencing judges.

In indeterminate sentencing systems, the legislature establishes a range of penalties (minimum to maximum), and the sentencing judge is then authorized

---

BOX 9.1 BASIC SENTENCING STRUCTURES IN THE UNITED STATES

Indeterminate sentencing—The judge specifies minimum and maximum sentence lengths. These set upper and lower bounds on the time to be served. The actual release date (and therefore the time actually served) is determined later by parole authorities within those limits.

Partially indeterminate sentencing—A variation of indeterminate sentencing in which the judge specifies only the maximum sentence length. An associated minimum sentence automatically is implied but is not within the judge's discretion. The implied minimum may be a fixed time (such as 1 year) for all sentences or a fixed proportion of the maximum. In some states the implied minimum is zero; thus, the parole board is empowered to release the prisoner at any time.

Determinate sentencing—The judge specifies a fixed term of incarceration, which must be served in full (less any "good time" earned in prison). There is no discretionary parole release.

Mandatory minimum sentencing—A minimum sentence that is specified by statute for all offenders convicted of a particular crime with special circumstances (e.g., robbery with a firearm). Mandatory minimum sentences can be used in both determinate and indeterminate sentencing structures.

Presumptive sentencing guidelines—The appropriate sentence for an offender in a specific case is presumed to fall within a range authorized by sentencing guidelines that are adopted by a sentencing body such as a sentencing commission. Judges are expected to sentence within this range or provide written justification for departure. These guidelines often provide for some appellate review for a departure.

Voluntary sentencing guidelines—Recommended sentencing policies that are not required by law and are based on past sentencing practices.

Source: Bureau of Justice Assistance (1998:1-2); Bureau of Justice Statistics (1988:91)

---

to impose a sentence that is not less than the minimum and not more than the maximum. In some cases, the legislature establishes a minimum term and then allows the judge to set a maximum within some absolute outer limit. In other cases, the legislature sets a minimum term that is some fraction of the maximum term decreed by the judge. In any indeterminate sentencing system, a paroling authority has power to grant release sometime between the end of the minimum term and the end of the maximum term. Thus, the judge has powers delegated by the legislature, and the paroling authority has power that is limited both by the legislature and by the decision of the judge.

In determinate sentencing systems, the legislature generally reserves most of the sentencing power for itself. In some cases, the legislature will actually determine the sentence for persons convicted of a specific offense. Here, the judge and parole authority have no sentencing power. More common is the model in which the legislature describes the expected or normal penalty for an offense, and then allows the sentencing judge to modify it (with reasons given). This is

presumptive sentencing. The law establishes what the legislature "presumes" will be the sentence, and then requires the judge to explain any case in which the judge does not impose the presumed penalty. In determinate sentencing systems, the parole authority typically has no sentencing power.

In most cases, the legislature grants the sentencing judge the ability to choose between a sentence of incarceration and one of community supervision. This is considerable sentencing power, even in a system in which the judge's power to determine the length of a prison sentence has been strictly curtailed. The decision as to which decision maker receives how much sentencing power reflects a different emphasis on each of the four purposes of criminal sentencing.

Anspach and Monsen (1989) observed that the sentencing process and the achievement of sentencing purposes are complex. In a study of the effects of sentencing reform in Maine, they noted that adoption of determinate sentencing alone does not ensure rational sentencing. In abolishing indeterminate sentencing and parole, the legislature in Maine provided sentencing judges with a list of eight purposes of penalties that were themselves contradictory. Anspach and Monsen (1989) concluded that failing to provide a consistent rationale for the imposition of sentences promotes unfair and/or irrational punishments. Even though sentencing structures are differently suited to achieving or promoting a specific purpose of punishment, structural reform alone is not enough. The structure of the sentencing process requires a clear statement about the relative importance of particular sentencing purposes. Kramer and Ulmer (1996) found that even within a sentencing structure designed to promote equality in sentencing, judges still imposed different sentences in cases that were similar to each other.

Griset (2002) examined the development of sentencing policy in Florida over 20 years, as the general sentencing structure in the state moved from essentially indeterminate to determinate sentencing. She observed that sentencing policy is the product of many different decision makers, including the legislature, judiciary, and various executive branch officials. With regard to Florida, Griset (2002:299) observed, "Like a dysfunctional family, the three branches of government in different places and at different times, have employed a variety of pathological adaptations in exercising their punishment powers, often resulting in muddled or destructive punishment policy." Whereas one branch might be trying to lengthen terms, another might be seeking to reduce them. One set of decision makers might be trying to increase the use of imprisonment, and another sought to increase diversion from prison. In short, the shared nature of sentencing power, coupled with the political importance of crime and punishment, often led to inconsistent and contradictory sentencing actions.

Deterrent sentences are best defined and imposed by the legislature, so that it is clear to everyone beforehand that a specific punishment will follow a certain criminal conviction. This is the rationale behind **mandatory minimum sentences**. In these sentences, the legislature decrees that anyone convicted of a particular offense (say, use of a handgun in the commission of a crime or drunk driving) receives a minimum number of days or years of incarceration. The prison sentence is mandatory and legislators expect it will deter offenders. Rottman and Strickland (2006) reported 44 states and the District of Columbia have mandatory minimum prison sentences for offenders convicted of committing at least some felonies while armed with a deadly weapon. However, as states continue to face challenges in funding the large prison population, many have begun to relax their mandatory minimum sentences on certain offenses (Porter, 2013).

Just deserts, or retributive, sentencing is perhaps best accomplished by granting limited sentencing power to the judge. The legislature sets an expectation or limit on how severe a penalty may be imposed for a particular criminal act, but the judge is expected to "fine-tune" the sentence so that the severity of the sentence matches the severity of the offense.

Rehabilitative (treatment) and incapacitative sentences work best by granting substantial control in sentencing to the paroling authority. This authority can then determine when the offender is safe for release (that is, cured of criminal tendencies) and can adjust the sentence accordingly. The legislature and sentencing judge are ill suited to this task because either they do not deal directly with the offender or their roles occur too early in the process. Both of these rationales require that someone continually monitor the offender for progress.

Alternatively, for the purpose of incapacitation, the legislature can develop **habitual offender statutes** that allow for increased penalties for repeat offenders. One such law is the California "three strikes and you're out" law. This law was enacted as a result of a voter initiative (referendum) and provides for a doubling of the sentence upon a second felony conviction "strike," and a tripling of the sentence (or 25-year term, whichever is longer) on the third "strike" (Harris & Jesilow, 2000). The problem with such laws is that they seek to imprison all offenders meeting the criteria (e.g., a third felony conviction) and risk relatively high rates of false positives (Saint-Germain & Calamia, 1996; Turner, Sundt, Applegate, & Cullen, 1995) (see Figure 9.2). Most contemporary **three-strikes laws** increase prison terms for offenders having prior convictions but have been written so they are applied only to the most violent repeat offenders, reducing their likely impact on overall prison populations (Clark, Austin, & Henry, 1997).

Chen (2008) assessed the impacts of California's three-strikes law compared to the more modest habitual offender laws existing in other states. She found that, although crime did decrease in California after the implementation of the three-strikes law, this law was not dramatically more effective at reducing crime than laws existing in other states. She concluded "the narrowly constructed and seldom-used habitual offender policies adopted in many states appear to produce results comparable to those observed in California" (Chen, 2008:363). The policy question, of course, is whether the increased costs in terms of incarceration are justified by the modest reductions in future crime.

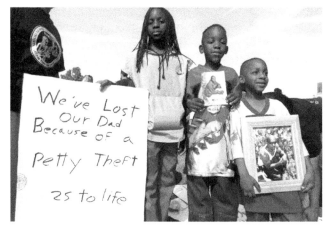

FIGURE 9.2
Children display photos of their father, who was jailed for a term of 25 years to life, during a protest against California's three-strikes law.
AP Photo/Damian Dovarganes

SENTENCING IN THE JUSTICE SYSTEM

Criminal sentencing is the final decision point in the court segment of the criminal justice system (with the possible exception of probation revocation, which we discuss in Chapter 12). It represents a transitional decision point at which judicial and correctional officials jointly determine the fate of the offender. In cases of negotiated pleas of guilty, the prosecutor also plays a large role in determining the sentence (Alschuler, 1978). In noncapital cases in three states (Kentucky, Missouri, and Virginia), the jury sentences those convicted of felonies, and in three more (Arkansas, Indiana, and Texas), the jury recommends a sentence to the judge in felony cases. In these states, however, the judge can alter a jury sentence or recommendation (Rottman & Strickland, 2006).

In capital cases (18 states do not have the death penalty), the jury will either determine the sentence or recommend a sentence to the judge. In one state (Nebraska), a panel of judges makes the sentencing decision. In Pennsylvania, either a judge or jury can decide the sentence.

The decision about sentence is bifurcated (Wilkins, Kress, Gottfredson, Calpin, & Gelman, 1976), having two stages. First, the sentencing judge decides whether to incarcerate the convicted offender. Next, the conditions of sentence are determined. These conditions range from the restrictions and obligations placed on those who receive probation to the length of term for those incarcerated.

Historically, sentencing judges had a greater voice in setting the conditions of prison confinement for sentenced offenders. The judge used to be able to specify the institution to which an offender would be sent, or to require that the sentence be served "at hard labor." Today, most jurisdictions restrict the judge to setting the term of confinement, and leave to the correctional authorities the discretionary power to establish the place and conditions of confinement.

Especially in indeterminate sentencing systems based on a rehabilitative rationale, the sentencing decision is expected to be based on the results of a **presentence investigation (PSI)** conducted by a probation officer. The PSI report describes the offense and offender and, in many jurisdictions, includes a recommendation of sentence from the reporting officer (Czajkoski, 1973). PSIs are common in most felony cases across the nation, thereby involving probation officers in the sentencing decision.

Presentence Investigation

After conviction, the judge generally sets a date for sentencing that is delayed long enough to allow the probation department to conclude a PSI. This investigation includes a detailed assessment of the offense and the offender's criminal and social background. The probation department prepares and submits the PSI report to the sentencing judge for use in arriving at an appropriate sentence. In addition to its usefulness at the sentencing stage, the PSI serves many other purposes. It is a basic information source for the correctional programming used in developing probation plans and institutional classifications; it provides background data used by parole boards in their decisions; and it serves as a basic resource document for research on correctional authorities, offenders, and corrections (U.S. Division of Probation, 1974).

The typical PSI report includes a face sheet, which contains basic offense and offender demographic information. The textual part of the report generally covers (1) the offense giving the official (police) version and the offender's version of the facts (occasionally the victim's version is also added); (2) the social history of the defendant (describing his or her childhood) and current family, employment, economic, and educational situations; and (3) the prior criminal record of the offender. The probation officer obtains much of this information through interviews with the offender, members of the offender's family, and others who know the offender. The material in the report need not meet the strict evidentiary standards of trial. Weinrath (1999) assessed the accuracy of narrative presentence reports and found that the traditional descriptive report was not an accurate means of predicting whether the offender would successfully complete probation. He urged that we discontinue narrative reports and move to the use of more objective risk assessments for judicial sentencing. To this day almost all jurisdictions still use narrative reports although many now include objective risk-assessment scores.

Traditionally, the court need not disclose the PSI report to the defendant. In 1949, the U.S. Supreme Court decided the case of *Williams v. New York*, which dealt with the issue of disclosure of the PSI report. Williams was convicted of capital murder, but the jury had recommended leniency. After reviewing the PSI report, the judge imposed the death penalty. Williams's attorney was not allowed to see the report and verify its accuracy. The Court ruled that there was no constitutional right to review the report. However, in 1977, the Court ruled in *Gardner v. Florida* that when the death penalty is imposed because of information contained in a PSI report, the defense has a right to review that report. Therefore, at least in a capital case, the court must disclose the contents of the PSI report to defense counsel.

In jurisdictions where probation officers make recommendations to the sentencing judge, sentencing judges concur with these recommendations in the great majority of cases (Leifker & Sample, 2011). This is one reason why some argue for disclosure to the defendant. Disclosure of the PSI report, however, is opposed by others, who argue that letting the defendant see the report will cause those interviewed to withhold information, or that disclosure might jeopardize the rehabilitation of the offender, should he or she learn things from the report that would be detrimental to rehabilitative programming.

In many jurisdictions, this issue has been resolved, either through disclosure of the entire report (Dubois, 1981) or, more frequently, through partial disclosure. In **partial disclosure**, the judge either summarizes the facts and the reasons for sentence, allowing the defense to contest any errors, or provides a copy of the body of the report to the defense. In jurisdictions where the court provides a copy to the defendant, it does not disclose a confidential addendum.

The Sentencing Hearing

There is no constitutional right to a separate hearing for sentencing, but generally, a sentencing hearing is held for felony defendants. Many states have statutory provisions for sentencing hearings (Rottman, Flango, Cantrell, Hansen, & LaFountain, 2000). In jurisdictions or cases in which there is no PSI, sentencing typically follows conviction. Although there is not a separate hearing, the defendant is afforded the opportunity to speak on his or her own behalf (usually through counsel), and the state (prosecutor) is asked to comment on sentencing. Sometimes the victim is present and allowed to speak or submit a written statement for consideration at sentencing.

At the point of sentencing, whether there is a separate hearing for that purpose, the defendant has the right to counsel. In 1967, in *Mempa v. Rhay*, the U.S. Supreme Court ruled that sentencing was a "critical stage" of the justice system, at which the defendant stands to lose protected rights and interests. The Court held that the offender had the right to representation by counsel at sentencing.

The Parole Hearing

In cases where the offender receives a sentence to incarceration in prison under an indeterminate sentence model, a parole authority usually makes the final sentencing decision. In these cases, the judge imposes a sentence that has a minimum and maximum term, but the actual duration of the penalty is unknown. The paroling authority has the power to grant release (i.e., limit the duration of confinement) at some point between the end of the minimum term and the end of the maximum term. The entire board or a panel of board members usually makes the decision after a hearing with the inmate. In Oklahoma, the parole board advises the governor, but the governor holds the authority to grant parole. Only about one-third of the states continue to use parole as the primary means of release for prison inmates. In those states in particular, the parole release decision is an important part of the sentencing process.

Parole eligibility defines which types of inmates the parole board can release at what points in their sentence. The legislature determines parole eligibility. For example, the legislature might require that the offender serves a minimum term before release is authorized. Similarly, the legislature can define certain offenses (or offenders) as ineligible for parole. In cases in which states use the "life without parole" sentence for murder, the legislature has defined murderers as "ineligible" for parole. Given eligibility, the parole authority can grant release to a prison inmate.

At the parole hearing, the paroling authority reviews the criminal and social history of the offender, assesses his or her adjustment to prison, and evaluates the offender's potential for success under parole supervision. The inmate can speak at this hearing and present whatever evidence he or she thinks is relevant. There is no right to counsel at the parole release hearing. Many have criticized discretionary release on parole for failing to protect the community by releasing dangerous offenders early as well as for violating individual rights through discriminatory decisions. Bennett (1995) argued that although these are real problems with traditional parole release systems, the development of guidelines for release decisions and better policies for supervision of parolees can overcome the most serious problems. In contrast, Turpin-Petrosino (1999) studied parole in New Jersey and concluded that changes in the law intended to control parole board discretion had no effect on parole decision making. In another study of parole in Nebraska, Proctor (1999) concluded that parole decisions were routine and based primarily on eligibility. He did not find much evidence of discretionary decision making in release determinations. In a study of parole decisions with sex offenders, Huebner and Bynum (2006) reported that parole decisions demonstrate effects of both legal and extralegal factors and that protection of public safety is a primary concern. A later study (Huebner & Bynum, 2008) revealed that inmate race was not as important in explaining release to parole as were legally relevant factors such as offense seriousness and length of sentence. Morgan and Smith (2008) reported legally relevant factors had the greatest influence on parole decisions in Alabama. Morgan and Smith also noted that institutional factors such as prison crowding and fiscal pressures influenced overall rates of parole.

CONDITIONS OF SENTENCE

Whether the judge chooses probation or incarceration, the second decision in sentencing relates to the conditions of sentence. In cases of probation, the judge retains broad discretionary power to set the conditions of supervision.

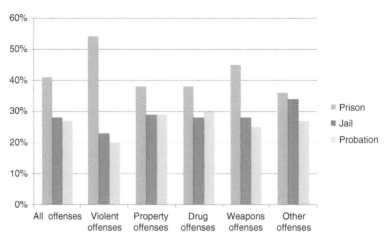

FIGURE 9.3
Types of felony sentences imposed by state courts, by offense type.
Source: Rosenmerkel et al. (2009)

With incarceration sentences, the legislature shares sentencing power with correctional authorities. Figure 9.3 describes the basic sentences imposed on those convicted of felonies in 2006.

Probation

Probation, as a punishment for criminal behavior, is conditional liberty. The convicted offender can remain in the community under the supervision of a probation officer, provided he or she abides by certain conditions of conduct established by the judge. Should the probationer violate the conditions of release, he or she may be taken before the court for a hearing, at which time probation may be revoked and the probationer sentenced to prison.

Both the public and offenders generally regard probation sentences as leniency (Gibbs, 1985; Israel & Dawes, 2002; Newman, 1983). Probation may be imposed in a variety of ways. The most common way in which probation is imposed is when a pronounced prison sentence is ordered suspended; that is, when the execution of a sentence (the taking of an offender to prison) is suspended. Another very common practice is suspended sentencing, in which the offender is placed on probation before a sentence (prison term) is actually pronounced. A third method entails a direct sentence to probation, in which the sentence is a probation term. However, surprisingly few jurisdictions actually have statutes that specifically recognize and authorize probation as a criminal sentence. Other, less formal mechanisms for probation may also be used, but these more closely mirror "diversion" programs than criminal sentences. In diversion cases, the court does not enter or record the conviction if the defendant successfully completes the probation term. Spohn, DeLone, and Spears (1998) describe one such practice as a "decision to withhold adjudication" in Miami, Florida.

A probation officer who works for the court supervises the offender on probation, but the probationer is responsible to the judge. The judge establishes the conditions of release, including such things as "punish lessons," curfews, partial incarceration, and community service (Parisi, 1980; Umbreit, 1981). Because of the large number of judges, and their individual discretion, probation conditions include a wide variety of restrictions and prescriptions (Jaffe, 1979). We discuss these more fully in Chapter 12.

Incarceration

Although we examine incarceration in detail in Chapter 10, the conditions of a sentence of incarceration involve two dimensions: the type of facility and the length of term. In any jurisdiction with more than one correctional facility, there will be differences in the experience of being imprisoned depending on where the offender is incarcerated. Prisons differ in terms of population (hardened, dangerous criminals, or first offenders), type of programs offered (educational/vocational or industrial), and level of custody (maximum, medium, or minimum security). As an example of the variance in prison experiences, serving 3 years by working outside on a prison farm for half of the day and attending school for the other half is qualitatively different from spending the same amount of time locked inside a huge maximum-security prison making automobile tags all day.

Sometimes statute controls the decision as to where an offender will serve his or her sentence, so that offenders older than a certain age or those convicted of a specified crime must be incarcerated in a maximum-security prison. What the offender will do while incarcerated, and where he or she will be incarcerated, however, are questions that often are left to the discretion of correctional authorities.

The length of sentence is controlled by statutory provisions that define parole eligibility (minimum term) and by the **good time** (reductions in length of prison sentence for good behavior while incarcerated) policies and laws of the jurisdiction. Most states shorten an offender's prison term for good behavior while incarcerated (Rottman et al., 2000). Some states only credit good time against the maximum term, which serves to advance the date of mandatory release. In others, it counts against the minimum term, advancing the date of parole eligibility. Still others apply good time credit against both the minimum and maximum terms. Thus, the legislature, judge, and parole board all have some power regarding sentence length, but correctional administrators who award and revoke good time also share in this decision.

ISSUES IN SENTENCING

Like the rest of the justice system, sentencing is fraught with questions and unresolved issues. The sentencing process is constantly emerging and evolving, sometimes returning to earlier practices and procedures previously abandoned as inappropriate. Today sentencing is undergoing considerable scrutiny and reform. In the latter part of the nineteenth century, we began to abandon corporal and capital penalties and long, harsh prison terms in favor of rehabilitative strategies that included more flexible prison sentences. In the last quarter of the twentieth century, we abandoned rehabilitative, indeterminate sentences in favor of more retributive fixed terms. Today, we are moving away from retributive sentences toward an unclear future.

We will examine four core issues that allow us to understand better the complex problems of criminal sentencing. Disparity is a central issue today and is the concern at the base of many efforts to change criminal sentencing. Corporal and capital punishment have reemerged (perhaps continued) as issues in sentencing. The calculation of prison time and "truth in sentencing" are still points of contention, and, finally, we continue to grapple with the development of intermediate or alternative sanctions.

Disparity

Disparity refers to the unequal treatment of similar offenders at sentencing (Gottfredson, 1979). Most of us would agree that offenders with similar criminal histories convicted of the same offense ought to receive similar penalties. When differences in sentences appear among similar offenders, the differences generally are termed "disparity." Yet, disparity actually refers to *unwarranted* differences (Gottfredson, Cosgrove, Wilkins, Wallerstein, & Rauh, 1978).

For example, if a jurisdiction follows an incapacitation sentencing rationale and has two first-offender burglars, it would not be disparity if one offender who was determined to pose a great risk of further crime receives a prison sentence, when the other, thought to pose little risk, receives probation. Under the concerns of incapacitation, these offenders are not similar. The current debate over disparity hinges, in large measure, on the definition of "similar" (Vining, 1983).

Since 1976, several states and the federal government have enacted legislation that alters their sentencing structures. In large measure, these changes seek to increase equity (reducing disparity) in criminal sentences (Anspach & Monsen, 1989; Goodstein & Hepburn, 1983; LaGoy, Hussey, & Kramer, 1978; Ulmer, 1997; von Hirsch & Hanrahan, 1979). Several states have implemented presumptive or determinate sentencing to ensure that similarly situated offenders receive similar sanctions. The results of these reforms are still unclear and evaluations continue (Wooldredge, 2009).

One type of determinate sentencing that states and the federal government have adopted in hopes of controlling disparity and ensuring more certainty in punishment is the use of sentencing guidelines. Sentencing guidelines identify the factors that judges should consider in sentencing and give an indication of what would be an acceptable penalty for each of many different types of cases. By 2005, 18 states and the federal government had developed sentencing guidelines. As shown in Figure 9.4, in five jurisdictions, the guidelines are mandatory;

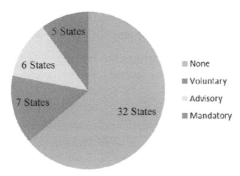

FIGURE 9.4
Sentencing guidelines, by number of states.
Source: Rottman and Strickland (2006)

in seven, they are voluntary. In the remaining jurisdictions, the guidelines are advisory, in that the judge may deviate from the guidelines. Most jurisdictions use decision matrices in which offense seriousness and risk or prior criminal record determine appropriate sentences. A few states use other types of guidelines in which general principles guide the sentencing judge in selecting an appropriate punishment (Griffin & Katz, 2002).

Commentators identify the individual whims of justice system officials (judges, parole board members, etc.) that come out in the exercise of discretionary authority as the culprit for sentencing disparity. This concern reflects perceptions that sentencing decisions demonstrate ethnic and sex discrimination more than differences in crimes and risk of new crimes (Anderson & Spohn, 2010; Wellford, 2007). To combat the disparity in decisions, reformers have moved to give legislatures tighter control over sentencing power by more closely defining sentences and the factors relied on in determining punishments (Bureau of Justice Assistance, 1996). The effects of reform are unclear, and may involve changes in incarceration rates, the types of crimes for which offenders are imprisoned, and the lengths of terms (Tonry, 1999). Twenty-one states have created **sentencing commissions**, formal bodies assigned to assess and oversee criminal sentencing and recommend reforms (Kauder & Ostrom, 2008).

In the spring of 2004, the U.S. Supreme Court decided the case of *Blakely v. Washington*. The sentencing guidelines of the state of Washington allowed the judge to increase a prison term if the judge found that the offense or offender represented an aggravated or more serious case than normal. The Supreme Court ruled that relying only on a judicial determination of facts in this instance violates a constitutional right to have facts determined by a jury. It is still unclear what might be the full effects of this decision. Although some commentators feared the decision spelled the end to sentencing guidelines, a more cautious and restrained assessment of the decision suggests that sentencing guidelines, especially in most state systems, can survive constitutional challenge (Frase, 2007; Skove, 2004). The next year the Court decided *United States v. Booker* (2005), in which it ruled that even though federal judges must consider the federal sentencing guidelines, they can alter sentences for other factors.

Defendant race and sex seem to influence sentencing. A large body of research reports that the age and sex of the defendant explain at least some variation in criminal sentences (Daly & Bordt, 1995; Spohn, 1994; Steffensmeier & Demuth, 2006). Women generally receive less severe sentences than men do. This difference not only reflects differences in the types of offenses and prior records of men and women but also probably reflects the justice system's recognition of the sex differences that exist in society. There are similar persistent differences in the sentencing of African Americans as compared to Caucasians. African American defendants generally receive more severe sentences than Caucasians do, but again the picture is complicated by differences in rates of conviction for certain types of offenses and in prior criminal records of Caucasians and African Americans. It may be that these differences in offenses and criminal records explain some of the differences in sentencing, yet it is also likely that criminal sentencing reflects the disadvantaged status of minority group members in American society (Zatz, 2000).

Steffensmeier, Ulmer, and Kramer (1998) identified the **"focal concerns"** of judges at sentencing. These are public protection, blameworthiness, and practical considerations. Judges base sentences on how "bad" and how dangerous the defendant is, as well as the effect of decisions on families, communities, and the justice system. Gainey, Steen, and Engen (2005) found that offender characteristics such as sex, race, and the decision to go to trial versus enter a guilty plea explained the use of alternatives to incarceration with drug offenders. Griffin and Wooldredge (2006) reported that the adoption of sentencing guidelines in Ohio had mixed effects on the sentencing of female offenders, but that females might benefit from some "chivalrous" treatment in sentencing. Doerner and Demuth (2010) observed that the race and sex of defendants interact and combine with earlier decisions (arrest, charging, etc.) to complicate an understanding of criminal sentences. Finally, Cano and Spohn (2012) reported that "sympathetic" or "salvageable" offenders received lower sentences in federal courts. For example, offenders who were employed, educated, female, and had dependent children often received sentences below the federal mandatory minimum sentence.

Corporal and Capital Punishment

In America, from colonial times through the early part of the nineteenth century, most punishments for serious offenses involved physical pain, such as branding, maiming, flogging, and death. In recent history, we have abandoned those forms of punishment in favor of the more humane alternative of incarceration. Yet there has been a rebirth of support for physical punishment (Bloom, 1995). In 2011, 43 inmates were executed, and more than 3,000 inmates were on death row. Between 1977 and 2011, there were more than 1,200 executions in 35 states and the federal system (Snell, 2013). However, the number of death penalty sentences has significantly declined since the peak in the mid-1990s.

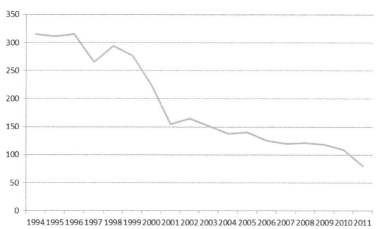

FIGURE 9.5
Number of prisoners sentenced to death, by year of sentencing.
Source: Snell (2013)

Figure 9.5 shows the trend in death penalty sentences. Figure 9.6 describes the offenders who were on death rows around the country in 2011.

Flogging or whipping as a sanction for offenses was finally abandoned in this country in the 1970s, when the state of Delaware removed the whipping post from its penitentiary. In a review of case law through the year 2000, Maddan and Hallahan (2002) concluded that it is possible we could revive corporal

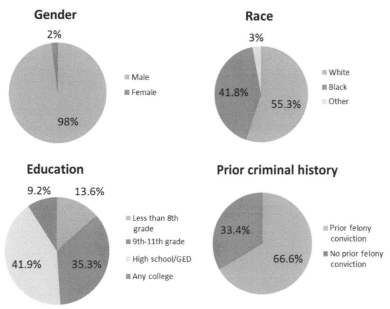

FIGURE 9.6
Selected characteristics of death row population.
Source: Snell (2013)

punishment, in the form of whipping, in the United States. The constitutionality of corporal and capital punishment is always subject to question. The U.S. Supreme Court has not ruled the death penalty to be cruel and unusual punishment or to be otherwise unconstitutional. Moreover, in the 1976 case of *Gregg v. Georgia*, the Court held that the death penalty, per se, is not unconstitutional. Earlier, in *Furman v. Georgia* (1972), the Court focused on the procedures by which states imposed the death penalty. Having found the existing procedures too vague and unstructured, the Court did not address the issue of the death penalty itself. The *Gregg* decision was the first of several in which the Court reviewed revised procedures for imposing the death penalty. Given an acceptable procedure (jury recommendation based on a presentation of aggravating and mitigating factors identified in the statute), the Court also addressed the constitutionality of the death penalty itself.

Some support the death penalty as an incapacitative sanction, saying that murderers pose too great a risk to society. Vito and Wilson (1988) addressed this issue and found that most prisoners sentenced to death in their sample were not particularly dangerous. Fewer than 25% of death row inmates who were released committed new crimes, and none committed a new homicide. Others suggest that an alternative to capital punishment is to impose life sentences without possibility of parole (Cheatwood, 1988).

The debate over capital punishment continues. The public, it appears, is in the midst of a shift regarding its view of capital punishment. An annual Gallup public opinion survey revealed that in 2013, 60% of Americans favored the death penalty for an offender who had been convicted of murder. However, this was the lowest level of support for capital punishment since 1972. Not surprisingly, political affiliation is a strong predictor of one's views of the death penalty. Whereas 81% of Republicans currently favor capital punishment, only 47% of Democrats support the punishment. It is important to note that support among all political parties has declined in the last 25 years (Jones, 2013).

Those supporting corporal punishment argue that physical pain, properly administered, is less destructive, less costly, and more effective than lengthy incarceration (Newman, 1983). Those who are opposed to corporal punishment suggest that such penalties will continue to be considered cruel and unusual and, therefore, unconstitutional. If someone brought the issue to the U.S. Supreme Court, it is not clear how the Court would decide the question. A principal rationale in support of corporal punishment is that our current practices are not effective in controlling crime, and that our prisons and jails are too crowded to accommodate many more prisoners. Added to this is the reasoning that as we allow death as a penalty for crime, penalties less than death should also not be considered too severe.

To date, no state has reinstituted corporal punishment, but there are continuing calls for physical punishments, including "chain gang" service. Among intermediate penalties are programs of community service in which convicted offenders are required to perform some labor, often physical, as part of their sentence. It is difficult to predict how the system will respond to suggestions for a return to corporal punishment. On one hand, some see it as a practical alternative to incarceration for those convicted of serious offenses for which probation seems too lenient. On the other hand, it is entirely likely that, if accepted, corporal punishment would be added to current penalties, resulting in sentences to prison with corporal punishment, or bodily punishment as a condition of probation. Whatever the result, the resurgence of this once-discredited response to criminality illustrates the intractable nature of the issues involved in sentencing.

The importance of pain as a component of criminal punishments, however, has regained prominence. Clear (1994) has written about how the imposition of harm (pain) for harm has become a central component of contemporary sentencing and correctional practice. The renewed emphasis on the imposition of physical suffering on criminal offenders is illustrated by the popularity of **boot camp** or shock incarceration programs in prisons (Lutze, 1998). Boot camps are relatively short-term programs modeled after the military's basic training. Through a regimen of physical training and discipline, these programs aim to establish self-discipline, respect for authority, and fear of the criminal justice system in the offender (Whitehead, Dodson, & Edwards, 2013).

Supporters expect the programs to be more physically demanding than traditional imprisonment and of shorter duration than most prison sentences. In essence, the increase in physical pain involved in the boot camp experience balances a shorter length of confinement. Even though we may not adopt electric shock or return to flogging offenders, the spread of the use of boot camps indicates that we are not opposed to using some forms of corporal sanctions.

Using Time as a Penalty: Truth in Sentencing

We already have seen how provisions for good time affect sentencing decisions by adding correctional administrators to the list of officials who exercise authority in sentencing decisions. What is not as clear is the complexity of using time as a penalty. Although most states allow the death penalty for heinous murders, the basic limitation on criminal penalties in the United States is time. Although conditions of confinement vary, for the individual offender the length of term is critical. How long an offender serves is dependent on several factors, each of which has importance for the severity of punishment and the operation of correctional institutions.

We typically measure prison time in days, although we impose sentences in months and years. Most states with provisions for good time award reductions of sentence on a "per days served" basis. Good time is to be an incentive to encourage inmates to obey prison rules. Emshoff and Davidson (1987) recognized that sentence reductions may affect inmate behavior, but contended that other factors are at least as important. A typical model awards 1 day of good time for every 2 served, so that after serving 20 days, officials add 10 days to complete the month. This model reduces a 6-year sentence to 4 years (one-third reduction). Some states award good time on a sliding scale so the longer the sentence, or the longer the term served, the more good time days received. An inmate could earn 10 days for every 30 for the first 3 years, and 15 days for every 30 for the next 3 years, and so on, "sliding" up the scale of good time award. To this sentence may be added "meritorious" good time, earned by the inmate for special accomplishments such as exceptional industry, donating blood, and the like. Reductions for good behavior, then, can be substantial.

Whatever the reductions for good behavior, other factors complicate time calculations. For an offender unable to secure pretrial release on bail, what part of his or her pretrial time counts as time served? The time spent in jail after conviction but before going to prison generally counts toward a prison sentence. The decision whether to count the time spent in jail prior to conviction is discretionary with the judge or correctional authorities. Thus, an offender who is in jail for 6 months prior to conviction and 3 months after conviction, prior to transport to the prison, may be granted 9 months off his or her sentence, and generally must be granted 3 months. A question remains, however, as to whether the offender also receives good time for time served before going to prison. Generally, prisoners do not receive good time for time spent in jail.

A final consideration is the ability of the judge to impose terms for multiple convictions to run either consecutively or concurrently. **A consecutive term** is one in which each sentence must be served in order, one following the other. **A concurrent term** is one in which all the sentences run at the same time. Two 5-year terms imposed consecutively total 10 years; the same terms imposed concurrently total 5 years.

The unresolved problem in the calculation of prison time is that the imposed sentence generally is not the same as the actual term served, as can be seen in Table 9.1. Von Hirsch and Hanrahan (1979) suggested that one of the major difficulties faced in sentencing reform is that we do not sentence offenders in "real time." The public sees the sentence imposed as being the maximum term ordered by the judge, without reference to good time or to the fact that judges frequently impose concurrent terms. If an offender sentenced to three concurrent 5-year terms is released in 2 years, the public may begin to believe that the law

Table 9.1	Estimated Percentage of Sentence to Be Served in State Prison by Conviction Offense		
Conviction Offense	**Mean Sentence (months)**	**Time to Be Served (months)**	**Percent of Sentence**
All offenses	53	27	51
Violent offenses	84	52	62
Property offenses	41	20	49
Drug offenses	48	20	43
Weapon offenses	38	24	63
Other offenses	39	19	50

Source: Durose and Langan (2004:5)

does not mean what it says. Felons sentenced to prison in state courts typically serve only half of their sentences before release.

Concern about the gap between the length of sentence imposed by the court and that actually served by convicted offenders spurred a call for "truth in sentencing." In 1995, Congress passed legislation calling for states to develop **truth in sentencing** so that those convicted of violent offenses will serve at least 85% of the term they receive. Federal aid was made available to states that adopt such truth in sentencing laws, and many states changed their sentencing laws to achieve sentences that are more truthful (see Box 9.2). Thus far, the solutions sought by the states involve reserving prison space for those convicted of violent crimes by reducing the rate of imprisonment and length of terms for nonviolent offenders. Of course, one solution to the problem would be the imposition of prison sentences in real time. However, most legislators are unwilling to admit to the public that violent offenders, on average, will serve a little more than 4 years instead of the 10 years to which they are sentenced.

The impact of truth in sentencing is likely to be the diversion of repeat, nonviolent offenders to community sanctions such as probation. The effects of these changes on both community corrections and prison populations are difficult to

BOX 9.2 THE "TRUTH IN SENTENCING" REFORM

Highlights
Three decades of sentencing reform—1970s through 1990s

- *Indeterminate sentencing:* Common in the early 1970s, parole boards have the authority to release offenders from prison.
- *Determinate sentencing:* States introduced fixed prison terms that could be reduced by good time or earned time credits.
- *Mandatory minimum sentences:* States added statutes requiring offenders to be sentenced to a specified amount of prison time.
- *Truth in sentencing (TIS):* First enacted in 1984, TIS laws require offenders to serve a substantial portion of their prison sentence. Parole eligibility and good time credits are restricted or eliminated.
- Violent offenders released from prison in 1996 were sentenced to serve an average of 85 months in prison. Prior to release they served about half of their prison sentence or 45 months.
- Under TIS laws requiring 85% of the sentence, violent offenders would serve an average of 88 months in prison based on the average sentence for violent offenders admitted to prison in 1996.
- Nearly 7 in 10 state prison admissions for a violent offense in 1997 were in states requiring offenders to serve at least 85% of their sentence.
- By 1998, states and the District of Columbia met the federal Truth in Sentencing Incentive Grant Program eligibility criteria. Eleven states adopted TIS laws in 1995, a year after the 1994 Crime Act.

Source: Ditton and Wilson (1999:1)

estimate. It is clear, however, that truth in sentencing affects both prison and community corrections populations. Turner, Greenwood, Fain, and Chiesa (2006) reviewed the impact of truth in sentencing laws, noting that whereas many states did in fact pass legislation to ensure that violent offenders would serve at least 85% of their sentence, most of the states would have done so without the federal aid. Instead, public concern over crime was a key factor influencing legislation. In addition, many states complied with the 85% threshold by reducing the average sentence length, making it easier for offenders to serve the required 85% of their sentence without significantly impacting actual time served. This finding was confirmed by Durose and Langan (2007), who reported that violent felons now receive shorter sentences but serve a greater percentage of their sentence.

Owens (2011) reported that truth in sentencing laws might have a broader impact than first envisioned. Specifically, offenders arrested for violent felonies but convicted on lesser charges are treated more punitively in states that have adopted truth in sentencing laws. Judges in these cases seem to honor the spirit of the truth in sentencing laws, showing yet again how a punishment targeting a specific group of defendants can have impact on the system as a whole.

Intermediate Sanctions

Throughout the past two decades, there has been increasing interest in the development and implementation of **intermediate sanctions** for crime or punishments that fall somewhere between imprisonment and traditional probation. Historically, sentencing judges chose between community supervision and confinement in prison or jail as the primary sanctions for crime. Especially as the numbers of people convicted of crime have increased, and prison and jail populations have exceeded the capacity of institutions, these choices have been seen as inadequate. DuPont (1985) called for the development of a meaningful continuum of sanctions ranging from no restriction to maximum-security incarceration. Others echoed the call (Klein, 1997; Morris & Tonry, 1990; Petersilia, 1987).

In response to the perceived need for a wider variety of sanctions, a number of innovative practices emerged. These include various combinations of incarceration and community supervision dispositions. We discuss specific forms of these sanctions in more detail in Chapters 12 and 13, but a brief listing is in order. Sanctions combining incarceration with supervision have emerged, including shock probation, shock parole, placement in community residential facilities, home incarceration, and **split sentences** (sentences combining a period of incarceration with a period of probation supervision) (Petersilia, Lurigio, & Byrne, 1992). So, too, penalties have been developed that make the experience of community supervision more severe. These include day reporting, intensive supervision, electronic monitoring, and community service orders.

The growth of these penalties blurs the traditional distinction between incarceration and community supervision. Prison boot camps involve a short, intense incarceration. The offender goes to prison, but for a much shorter period.

Observers note that these sanctions allow gradations in punishment along a continuum (Holsinger & Latessa, 1999; McCarthy, 1987; Schwartz & Travis, 1996). Thus, penalties can escalate from traditional probation supervision through intensive supervision to day reporting (offenders report to the probation office daily). If we desire more restrictive punishments, the offender could be placed under house arrest (restricted to his or her home), sent to a residential facility (halfway house), or sent to prison. As Table 9.2 shows, judges often impose multiple penalties on convicted offenders.

Recalling our discussion of sentencing disparity, the development of a range of punishments is potentially troublesome. If we suspect sentencing decisions of reflecting prejudice when only a few choices were available, the provision of more choices increases the chances of disparate treatment. The more things the judge can do to punish an offender, the greater the judicial discretion. Conversely,

Table 9.2	Additional Penalties Imposed on Felons by Conviction Offense, 2006				

	Percent of Felons with an Additional Penalty of:				
Most Serious Conviction Offense	Fine	Restitution	Treatment	Community Service	Other
All offenses	38	18	11	11	2
Violent offenses	36	18	11	12	2
Murder	28	13	8	7	1
Sexual assault	37	18	15	13	2
Rape	38	24	21	19	2
Other sexual assault	36	14	11	9	2
Robbery	26	18	10	9	1
Aggravated assault	40	18	10	12	1
Other violent	36	17	13	15	3
Property offenses	37	27	11	12	2
Burglary	34	27	11	12	2
Larceny	35	26	11	13	3
Motor vehicle theft	34	28	20	22	3
Fraud/forgery	42	29	10	11	3
Drug offenses	41	14	13	11	2
Possession	36	19	23	20	2
Trafficking	45	11	5	4	2
Weapon offenses	27	8	5	7	1
Other offenses	40	13	9	10	2

Source: Rosenmerkel et al. (2009:8)

intermediate sanctions may reduce the relative degree of disparity. Rather than a simple "either/or" issue of incarceration, disparate sentences may be closer in degree of restrictiveness. The difference between intensive supervision and day reporting is not as great as that between probation and prison. The Sentencing Project reports that faced with financial emergencies, many states are changing sentences and developing alternatives to incarceration (Porter, 2010). O'Hara (2005) questioned the ability of alternative sanctions or processes to ensure uniformity in sentencing. Specifically regarding restorative justice, O'Hara argued that if we seek equivalent sentencing outcomes, we probably need to reduce, rather than increase, sentencing choices.

See Table 9.3 for a table of selected court cases on sentencing.

THEORY AND SENTENCING

What explains criminal punishments? How is it that persons convicted of the same offense are often given different penalties? If we want to change criminal sentencing, how can we best accomplish it? Do changes in the law or changes in the characteristics of sentencing officials lead to changes in sentencing?

As with other aspects of the justice system, our answers to these questions reveal our theoretical understanding of the issue. Our review of sentencing identified several factors that can, and do, influence sentencing. The seriousness of the crime, the risk posed by the offender, and the characteristics of both defendants and officials influence the sentencing outcome. Research indicates that the characteristics of the court, its organization and culture, also affect sentencing decisions. It is important to recall that sentencing decisions also reflect the

Table 9.3	Selected Court Cases on Sentencing
Williams v. New York 377 U.S. 241 (1949)	There is no constitutional right to review a presentence investigation (PSI) report. See later controlling case, *Gardner v. Florida* (1977)
Mempa v. Rhay 389 U.S. 128 (1967)	An offender has the right to representation by counsel at the point of sentencing
Furman v. Georgia 408 U.S. 238 (1972)	Current procedures for imposing the death penalty violate the equal protection clause of the Fourteenth Amendment and the prohibition against cruel and unusual punishment
Gregg v. Georgia 428 U.S. 153 (1976)	Death penalty statutes that contain sufficient safeguards against arbitrary and capricious imposition are constitutional
Gardner v. Florida 430 U.S. 349 (1977)	When the death penalty is imposed as a result of information contained in a presentence investigation (PSI) report, the defense has a right to review that report

Source: Portions of this table were adapted from del Carmen, Ritter, and Witt (2008)

directional flow of decisions in the process. Earlier decisions about investigation, arrest, bail, and charging exert influence on sentence outcomes.

Although there are some specific sentencing theories such as focal concerns, theory has not guided much of the research in this area. The same kinds of factors that appear to explain police decisions and earlier court outcomes also relate to sentencing decisions. It is useful to remember these explanations as we proceed. In the end, we may be able to identify some broad categories of criminal justice theory.

DUE PROCESS, CRIME CONTROL, AND SENTENCING IN THE WHOLE SYSTEM

The sentencing decision links the court subsystem to the correctional subsystem of the justice process. Sentencing decisions reflect the demands and stresses placed on corrections, and indicate how the justice process reacts to social change. For example, with the emergence of drug abuse as a serious criminal problem, the sentencing of those convicted of drug-related offenses has changed. Many more drug offenders now receive prison sentences than in the past, and their sentences to prison are longer than before. As society has come to see drug offenders as more serious criminals, the increased seriousness has been reflected in more severe sentences. These sentences have changed the composition of correctional (especially prison) populations (Barnes & Kingsnorth, 1996; Beck, 1997; Kraska, 1992).

Perhaps the most contemporary wave of social change that has influenced criminal justice sentencing pertains to sex offenders. Partly as a result of increased media attention, sex offenders are currently among the country's most hated criminals. As a result, the public has demanded the implementation and enforcement of specialized punishments for those convicted of sex offenses (Sample & Kadleck, 2008). These laws often include increased prison time, sex offender registrations, housing restrictions, and electronic monitoring. The interplay between the public's perceptions, the legislator's actions, and the correctional officials who are tasked with enforcing these specialized punishments illustrates the systematic nature of the justice process.

Remember that one of the primary motivations for reform of criminal sentencing and the development of alternative sanctions is a desire for fairness. Not only do we seek punitive and incapacitative alternatives to prison for crime control reasons, we seek equitable sanctions for diverse individuals. The sentencing decision is the point at which the full weight of state power bears on the individual. The challenge for sentencing is to achieve crime control goals while respecting the rights of the individual offender. Yet, available evidence suggests that criminal sentences reflect differences in sex, race, and age. If we seek equal treatment of persons at sentencing, it is likely that we will first have to develop equal treatment of persons in the broader society.

Perhaps the major obstacle to reforming criminal sentencing in the United States lies not in sentencing's considerable complexity of operation and calculation, but more in the lack of effort among our citizens to achieve understanding of the sentencing process. To achieve a rational and workable system of sentencing, it may first be necessary to be more open and honest about the meaning of criminal sentences—and more consistent in our purposes served by criminal sanctions.

REVIEW QUESTIONS

1. Identify the four traditional purposes of criminal penalties.
2. What types of errors are involved in the prediction of dangerousness at sentencing?
3. Distinguish between determinate and indeterminate criminal sentencing structures.
4. What is the presentence investigation, and what purposes does it serve?
5. What is the sentencing hearing, and what takes place at one?
6. Identify two principal types of sanctions imposed on serious criminal offenders.
7. What is meant by "parole eligibility"?
8. What is a sentencing disparity?
9. Besides sentencing disparity, identify two other current issues in criminal sentencing.

References

Alschuler, A. W. (1978). Sentencing reform and prosecutorial power: A critique of recent proposals for "fixed" and "presumptive" sentencing. In *Determinate sentencing: Reform or regression?* Washington, DC: U.S. Government Printing Office. (pp. 59–88).

Anderson, A., & Spohn, C. (2010). Lawlessness in the federal sentencing process: A test for uniformity and consistency in sentence outcomes. *Justice Quarterly, 27*(3), 362–391.

Anspach, D., & Monsen, S. (1989). Determinate sentencing, formal rationality, and khadi justice in Maine: An application of Weber's typology. *Journal of Criminal Justice, 17*(6), 471–485.

Bailey, W. (1966). Correctional outcome: An evaluation of 100 reports. *Journal of Criminal Law, Criminology & Police Science, 57,* 153–160.

Barnes, C., & Kingsnorth, R. (1996). Race, drug, and criminal sentencing: Hidden effects of the criminal law. *Journal of Criminal Justice, 24*(1), 39–55.

Beck, A. (1997). Growth, change, and stability in the U.S. prison population, 1980–1995. *Corrections Management Quarterly, 1*(2), 1–14.

Bennett, L. (1995). In defense of parole—Is it worth the effort? *Perspectives, 19*(3), 14–17.

Bloom, S. (1995). Spare the rod, spoil the child? A legal framework for recent corporal punishment proposals. *Golden Gate University Law Review, 25*(2), 361–389.

Bureau of Justice Assistance (1996). *National assessment of structured sentencing.* Washington, DC: Bureau of Justice Assistance.

Bureau of Justice Assistance (1998). *1996 national survey of state sentencing structures.* Washington, DC: Bureau of Justice Assistance.

Bureau of Justice Statistics (1984). *Sentencing practices in 13 states.* Washington, DC: U.S. Department of Justice.

Bureau of Justice Statistics (1988). *Report to the nation on crime and justice* (2nd ed.). Washington, DC: U.S. Department of Justice.

Cano, M., & Spohn, C. (2012). Circumventing the penalty for offenders facing mandatory minimums: Revisiting the dynamics of "sympathetic" and "salvageable" offenders. *Criminal Justice and Behavior, 39*(3), 308–332.

Casey, P., & Rottman, D. (2003). *Problem-solving courts: Models and trends.* Williamsburg, VA: National Center for State Courts.

Cheatwood, D. (1988). The life-without-parole sanction: Its current status and a research agenda. *Crime and Delinquency, 34*(1), 43–59.

Chen, E. (2008). Impacts of "three strikes and you're out" on crime trends in California and throughout the United States. *Journal of Contemporary Criminal Justice, 24*(4), 345–370.

Clark, J., Austin, J., & Henry, D. (1997). *"Three strikes and you're out": A review of state legislation.* Washington, DC: National Institute of Justice.

Clear, T. (1994). *Harm in American penology: Offenders, victims, and their communities.* Albany, NY: SUNY Press.

Cullen, F. T., & Gilbert, K. E. (1982). *Reaffirming rehabilitation.* Cincinnati, OH: Anderson.

Cullen, F. T., & Gilbert, K. E. (2013). *Reaffirming rehabilitation.* Boston: Elsevier (Anderson Publishing).

Cullen, F. T., Jonson, C. L., & Nagin, D. S. (2011). Prisons do not reduce recidivism: The high cost of ignoring science. *The Prison Journal, 9*(3), 48S–65S.

Czajkoski, E. H. (1973). Exposing the quasi-judicial role of the probation officer. *Federal Probation, 37*, 9.

Daly, K., & Bordt, R. (1995). Sex effects and sentencing: An analysis of the statistical literature. *Justice Quarterly, 12*(1), 141–175.

del Carmen, R. V., Ritter, S. E., & Witt, B. A. (2008). *Briefs of leading cases in corrections* (5th ed). Newark, NJ: LexisNexis Matthew Bender (Anderson Publishing).

Ditton, P., & Wilson, D. (1999). *Truth in sentencing in state prisons.* Washington, DC: Bureau of Justice Statistics.

Doerner, J., & Demuth, S. (2010). The independent and joint effects of race/ethnicity, gender, and age on sentencing outcomes in U.S. federal courts. *Justice Quarterly, 27*(1), 1–27.

Dubois, P. L. (1981). Disclosure of presentence reports in the United States district courts. *Federal Probation, 45*(1), 3–9.

DuPont, P. (1985). *Expanding sentencing options: A governor's perspective.* Washington, DC: U.S. Department of Justice.

Durham, A. M. (1988). Crime seriousness and punitive severity: An assessment of social attitudes. *Justice Quarterly, 5*(1), 131–153.

Durose, M., & Langan, P. (2004). *Felony sentences in state courts, 2003.* Washington, DC: Bureau of Justice Statistics.

Durose, M., & Langan, P. (2007). *Felony sentences in state courts, 2004.* Washington, DC: Bureau of Justice Statistics.

Emshoff, J. G., & Davidson, W. S. (1987). The effect of "good time" credit on inmate behavior: A quasi-experiment. *Criminal Justice and Behavior, 14*(3), 335–351.

Flores, A., Russell, A., Latessa, E., & Travis, L. (2005). Evidence of professionalism or quackery: Measuring practitioner awareness of risk/need factors and effective treatment strategies. *Federal Probation, 69*(2), 9–14.

Frase, R. (2007). The Apprendi-Blakely cases: Sentencing reform counter-revolutions? *Criminology & Public Policy, 6*(3), 403–432.

Gainey, R., Steen, S., & Engen, R. (2005). Exercising options: An assessment of the use of alternative sanctions for drug offenders. *Justice Quarterly, 22*(4), 488–520.

Gendreau, P. (1996). The principles of effective interventions with offenders. In A. Harland (Ed.), *Choosing correctional options that work: Defining the demand and evaluating the supply.* Thousand Oaks, CA: Sage.

Gertz, M., & Gould, L. (1995). Fear of punishment and the willingness to engage in criminal behavior: A research note. *Journal of Criminal Justice, 23*(4), 377–384.

Gibbs, J. J. (1985). Clients' views of community corrections. In L. F. Travis (Ed.), *Probation, parole, and community corrections.* Waveland: Prospect Heights, IL.

Goodstein, L., & Hepburn, J. (1983). *Determinate sentencing and imprisonment.* Cincinnati, OH: Anderson.

Gottfredson, M. R. (1979). Parole guidelines and the reduction of sentencing disparity: A preliminary study. *Journal of Research in Crime and Delinquency, 16*(2), 218–231.

Gottfredson, D. M., Cosgrove, C. A., Wilkins, L. T., Wallerstein, J., & Rauh, C. (1978). *Classification for parole decision policy.* Washington, DC: U.S. Government Printing Office.

Greenwood, P. (1982). *Selective incapacitation.* Santa Monica, CA: RAND.

Griffin, B., & Katz, L. (2002). Sentencing consistency: Basic principles instead of numerical grids: The Ohio Plan. *Case Western Reserve Law Review, 53*(1), 1–75.

Griffin, T., & Wooldredge, J. (2006). Sex-based disparities in felony dispositions before and after sentencing reform in Ohio. *Criminology, 44*(4), 893–923.

Griset, P. (1995). Determinate sentencing and agenda building: A case study of the failure of a reform. *Journal of Criminal Justice, 23*(4), 349–362.

Griset, P. (2002). New sentencing laws follow old patterns: A Florida case study. *Journal of Criminal Justice, 30*(4), 287–301.

Harland, A. (Ed.) (1996). *Choosing correctional options that work: Defining the demand and evaluating the supply.* Thousand Oaks, CA: Sage.

Harris, J., & Jesilow, P. (2000). It's not the old ball game: Three strikes and the courtroom workgroup. *Justice Quarterly, 17*(1), 185–203.

Holsinger, A., & Latessa, E. (1999). An empirical evaluation of a sanction continuum: Pathways through the juvenile justice system. *Journal of Criminal Justice, 27*(2), 155–172.

Huebner, B., & Bynum, T. (2006). An analysis of parole decision making using a sample of sex offenders: A focal concerns perspective. *Criminology, 44*(4), 961–992.

Huebner, B., & Bynum, T. (2008). The role of race and ethnicity in parole decisions. *Criminology, 46*(4), 907–938.

Israel, M., & Dawes, J. (2002). "Something from nothing": Shifting credibility in community correctional programmes in Australia. *Criminal Justice, 2*(1), 5–25.

Jacobs, B. (2010). Deterrence and deterrability. *Criminology, 48*(2), 417–442.

Jaffe, H. J. (1979). Probation with a flair: A look at some out-of-the ordinary conditions. *Federal Probation, 43*(1), 25–36.

Johnson, I., & Sigler, R. (1995). Community attitudes: A study of definitions and punishment of spouse abusers and child abusers. *Journal of Criminal Justice, 23*(5), 477–487.

Jones, J. (2013). U.S. death penalty support lowest in more than 40 years. Gallup.com. Retrieved December 28, 2013 at http://www.gallup.com/poll/165626/death-penalty-support-lowest-years.aspx.

Kauder, N., & Ostrom, B. (2008). *State sentencing guidelines: Profiles and continuum.* Williamsburg, VA: National Center for State Courts.

Kingsnorth, R., Alvis, L., & Gavia, G. (1993). Specific deterrence and the DUI offender: The impact of a decade of reform. *Justice Quarterly, 10*(2), 265–288.

Klein, A. R. (1997). *Alternative sentencing, intermediate sanctions and probation* (2nd ed.). Cincinnati, OH: Anderson.

Kramer, J., & Ulmer, J. (1996). Sentencing disparity and departures from guidelines. *Justice Quarterly, 13*(1), 81–106.

Kraska, P. (1992). The processing of drug arrestees: Questioning the assumption of an ambivalent reaction. *Journal of Criminal Justice, 20*(6), 517–525.

LaGoy, S. P., Hussey, F. A., & Kramer, J. H. (1978). A comparative assessment of determinate sentencing in the four pioneer states. *Crime & Delinquency, 24,* 385–400.

LeClair, D., & Guarino-Ghezzi, S. (1991). Does incapacitation guarantee public safety: Lessons from Massachusetts' furlough and prerelease programs. *Justice Quarterly, 8*(1), 9–36.

Leifker, D., & Sample, L. (2011). Probation recommendations and sentences received: The association between the two and the factors that affect recommendations. *Criminal Justice Policy Review, 22*(4), 494–517.

Lipsey, M., & Cullen, F. (2007). The effectiveness of correctional rehabilitation: A review of systematic reviews. *Annual Review of Law and Social Science, 3,* 297–320.

Lutze, F. (1998). Are shock incarceration programs more rehabilitative than traditional prisons? A survey of inmates. *Justice Quarterly, 15*(3), 547–566.

Mackenzie, D. (1997). Criminal justice and crime prevention. In L. Sherman, D. Gottfredson, J. Eck, P. Reuter, & S. Bushway (Eds.), *Preventing crime: What works, what doesn't, what's promising.* Washington, DC: U.S. Department of Justice pp. 9-1-9-76.

Maddan, S., & Hallahan, W. (2002). Corporal punishment in the 21st century: An examination of Supreme Court decisions in the 1990s to predict the reemergence of flagellance. *Journal of Crime and Justice, 25*(2), 97–120.

Martinson, R. (1974). What works? Questions and answers about prison reform. *The Public Interest, 35,* 22–54.

McCarthy, B. (Ed.), (1987). *Intermediate punishments.* Monsey, NY: Criminal Justice Press.

Morgan, K., & Smith, B. (2008). The impact of race on parole decision-making. *Justice Quarterly, 25*(2), 411–435.

Morris, N., & Tonry, M. (1990). *Between prison and probation: Intermediate punishments in a rational sentencing system.* Oxford, UK: Oxford University Press.

Myers, L., & Reid, S. (1995). The importance of county context in the measurement of sentence disparity: The search for routinization. *Journal of Criminal Justice, 23*(3), 223–241.

Nagin, D., & Pogarsky, G. (2001). Integrating celerity, impulsivity, and extralegal sanction threats into a model of general deterrence: Theory and evidence. *Criminology, 39*(4), 865–892.

Newman, G. R. (1983). *Just and painful.* New York: Macmillan.

O'Hara, M. (2005). Is restorative justice compatible with sentencing uniformity? *Marquette Law Review, 89,* 305–325.

Owens, E. (2011). Truthiness in punishment: The far reach of truth-in-sentencing laws in state courts. *Journal of Empirical Legal Studies, 8,* 239–261.

Parisi, N. (1980). Combining incarceration and probation. *Federal Probation, 44*(2), 3–12.

Paternoster, R. (1987). The deterrent effect of the perceived certainty and severity of punishment: A review of the evidence and issues. *Justice Quarterly, 4*(2), 173–217.

Paternoster, R. (2010). How much do we really know about criminal deterrence? *The Journal of Criminal Law and Criminology, 100*(3), 765–823.

Petersilia, J. (1987). *Expanding options for criminal sentencing.* Santa Monica, CA: RAND.

Petersilia, J., Lurigio, A., & Byrne, J. (1992). Introduction: The emergence of intermediate sanctions. In J. Byrne, A. Lurigio, & J. Petersilia (Eds.), *Smart sentencing: The emergence of intermediate sanctions* (pp. ix–xv). Beverly Hills, CA: Sage.

Piquero, A., Cullen, F., Unnever, J., Piquero, N., & Gordon, J. (2010). Never too late: Public optimism about juvenile rehabilitation. *Punishment & Society, 12*(2), 187–207.

Piquero, A., & Rengert, G. (1999). Studying deterrence with active residential burglars. *Justice Quarterly, 16*(2), 451–471.

Pogarsky, G. (2002). Identifying "deterrable" offenders: Implications for research on deterrence. *Justice Quarterly, 19*(3), 343–369.

Porter, N. (2010). *The state of sentencing 2009: Developments in policy and practice.* Washington, DC: The Sentencing Project.

Porter, N. (2013). *The state of sentencing 2012: Developments in policy and practice.* Washington, DC: The Sentencing Project.

Proctor, J. (1999). The "new parole": An analysis of parole board decision making as a function of eligibility. *Journal of Crime and Justice, 22*(2), 193–217.

Rosenmerkel, S., Durose, M., & Farole, D. (2009). *Felony sentences in state courts, 2006: Statistical tables.* Washington, DC: Bureau of Justice Statistics.

Rottman, D., Flango, C., Cantrell, M., Hansen, R., & LaFountain, N. (2000). *State court organization, 1998.* Washington, DC: Bureau of Justice Statistics.

Rottman, D., & Strickland, S. (2006). *State court organization, 2004.* Washington, DC: Bureau of Justice Statistics.

Saint-Germain, M., & Calamia, R. (1996). Three strikes and you're in: A streams and windows model of incremental policy change. *Journal of Criminal Justice, 24*(1), 57–70.

Sample, L., & Kadleck, C. (2008). Sex offender laws: Legislators' accounts of the need for policy. *Criminal Justice Policy Review, 19,* 40–62.

Schoepfer, A., Carmichael, S., & Piquero, N. (2007). Do perceptions of punishment vary between white-collar and street crimes? *Journal of Criminal Justice, 35*(2), 151–163.

Schwartz, M., & Travis, L. (1996). *Corrections: An issues approach* (4th ed.). Cincinnati, OH: Anderson.

Shover, N. (1996). *Great pretenders: Pursuits and careers of persistent thieves.* Boulder, CO: Westview.

Skove, A. (2004). *Blakely v. Washington: Implications for state courts.* Williamsburg, VA: National Center for State Courts.

Smith, W., & Smith, D. (1998). The consequences of error: Recidivism prediction and civil-libertarian ratios. *Journal of Criminal Justice, 26*(6), 481–502.

Snell, T. (2013). *Capital punishment, 2011—Statistical tables.* Washington, DC: Bureau of Justice Statistics.

Spohn, C. (1994). Crime and the social control of Blacks: Offender/victim race and the sentencing of violent offenders. In G. Bridges & M. Myers (Eds.), *Inequality, crime, and social policy.* Boulder, CO: Westview.

Spohn, C., DeLone, M., & Spears, J. (1998). Race/ethnicity, gender and sentence severity in Dade County, Florida: An examination of the decision to withhold adjudication. *Journal of Crime and Justice, 21*(2), 111–138.

Steffensmeier, D., & Demuth, S. (2006). Does gender modify the effects of race-ethnicity on criminal sanctioning: Sentences for male and female White, Black, and Hispanic defendants. *Journal of Quantitative Criminology, 22*(1), 241–261.

Steffensmeier, D., Ulmer, J., & Kramer, J. (1998). The interaction of race, gender, and age in criminal sentencing: The punishment cost of being young, black, and male. *Criminology, 36*(4), 763–797.

Tonry, M. (1996). *Sentencing matters.* New York: Oxford University Press.

Tonry, M. (1999). The fragmentation of sentencing and corrections in America. In *Sentencing and corrections issues for the 21st century,* September. Washington, DC: National Institute of Justice.

Travis, L. F., III (2012). Criminal sentencing: Goals, practices, and ethics. In M. Braswell, B. McCarthy, & B. McCarthy (Eds.), *Justice, crime, and ethics* (7th ed.) (p. 165). Boston: Elsevier Anderson Publishing, 10.

Turner, S., Greenwood, P., Fain, T., & Chiesa, J. (2006). An evaluation of the federal government's violent offender incarceration and truth-in-sentencing incentive grants. *The Prison Journal, 86*(3), 364–385.

Turner, M., Sundt, J., Applegate, B., & Cullen, F. (1995). "Three strikes and you're out" legislation: A national assessment. *Federal Probation, 59*(3), 16–35.

Turpin-Petrosino, C. (1999). Are limiting enactments effective? An experimental test of decision making in a presumptive parole state. *Journal of Criminal Justice, 27*(4), 321–332.

U.S. Division of Probation (1974). The selective presentence investigation report. *Federal Probation, 38*(4), 52–53.

Ulmer, J. (1997). *Social worlds of sentencing: Court communities under sentencing guidelines.* Albany, NY: SUNY Press.

Umbreit, M. S. (1981). Community service sentencing: Jail alternative or added sanction? *Federal Probation, 45*(3), 3–14.

Van Dine, S., Conrad, J. P., & Dinitz, S. (1979). The incapacitation of the chronic thug. *Journal of Criminal Law and Criminology, 65,* 535.

Vining, A. R. (1983). Developing aggregate measures of disparity. *Criminology, 21*(2), 233–252.

Visher, C. (1987). Incapacitation and crime control: Does a "lock 'em up" strategy reduce crime? *Justice Quarterly, 4*(4), 513–543.

Vito, G. F., & Wilson, D. G. (1988). Back from the dead: Tracking the progress of Kentucky's *Furman* commuted death row population. *Justice Quarterly, 5*(1), 101–111.

von Hirsch, A. (1976). *Doing justice.* New York: Hill & Wang.

von Hirsch, A., & Hanrahan, K. J. (1979). *The question of parole.* Cambridge, MA: Ballinger.

Weinrath, M. (1999). Are new directions warranted for the presentence report? An empirical assessment of its predictive utility in the adult court system. *Journal of Crime and Justice, 22*(1), 113–129.

Wellford, C. (2007). Editorial introduction: Sentencing reform. *Criminology and Public Policy, 6*(3), 399–402.

Wenk, E. A., Robison, J. O., & Smith, G. W. (1972). Can violence be predicted? *Crime & Delinquency, 18*(3), 393–402.

Whitehead, J., Dodson, K., & Edwards, B. (2013). *Corrections: Exploring crime, punishment, and justice in America* (3rd ed.). Boston: Elsevier (Anderson Publishing).

Wilkins, L. T., Kress, J. M., Gottfredson, D., Calpin, J. C., & Gelman, A. (1976). *Sentencing guidelines: Structuring judicial discretion.* Albany, NY: Criminal Justice Research Center.

Wonders, N. (1996). Determinate sentencing: A feminist and postmodern story. *Justice Quarterly, 13*(4), 611–648.

Wood, P. (2007). Exploring the positive punishment effect among incarcerated adult offenders. *American Journal of Criminal Justice, 31,* 8–22.

Wooldredge, J. (2009). Short- versus long-term effects of Ohio's switch to more structured sentencing on extralegal disparities in prison sentences in an urban court. *Criminology and Public Policy, 8*(2), 285–312.

Wright, R., & Decker, S. (1994). *Burglars on the job: Streetlife and residential break-ins.* Boston: Northeastern University Press.

Zalman, M. (1987). Sentencing in a free society: The failure of the President's Crime Commission to influence sentencing policy. *Justice Quarterly, 4*(4), 545–569.

Zatz, M. (2000). The convergence of race, ethnicity, gender, and class on court decision making: Looking toward the 21st century. In J. Horney (Ed.), *Criminal justice 2000: Policies, processes, and decisions of the criminal justice system,* Vol. 3. (pp. 503–552). Washington, DC: National Institute of Justice.

Important Cases

Blakely v. Washington, 542 U.S.296 (2004).

Furman v. Georgia, 408 U.S. 238 (1972).

Gardner v. Florida, 430 U.S. 349 (1977).

Gregg v. Georgia, 428 U.S. 153 (1976).

Mempa v. Rhay, 389 U.S. 128 (1967).

United States v. Booker, 543 U.S. 220 (2005).

Williams v. New York, 377 U.S. 241 (1949).

CHAPTER 10

Incarceration

On any given day more than 2.2 million people are incarcerated in thousands of jails and hundreds of prisons across the United States (Glaze & Herberman, 2013). By midyear 2011, one in every 108 adult residents of the United States was either in prison or jail. The overwhelming majority of those incarcerated is male, and racial minorities make up a disproportionate number of those behind bars (Carson & Sabol, 2012). In 2010, expenditures for state prisons were more than $38 billion (Kyckelhahn, 2012). About 80% of state expenditures for correctional services are devoted to prisons. For a variety of reasons, the prison traditionally is our response to crime.

The public often views nonprison sentences as leniency (Newman, 1983; Rhine, 1992). The use of prisons as punishment for serious criminal behavior is an American invention. Most of us view incarceration as the most appropriate penalty to impose on those who violate the criminal laws (Durham, 1989; Tewksbury & DeMichele, 2003). Although most offenders do not receive sentences to terms of imprisonment, it seems to be our belief that prisons are the core of corrections in the United States.

There is good reason to believe that prisons are central to American corrections. By virtue of their size, history, and cost, prisons receive the lion's share of attention from correctional administrators (and, until recently, from persons studying corrections as well). Furthermore, the threat of imprisonment is considered necessary to make less severe sanctions workable (Connolly, 1975). The argument is that without the threat of imprisonment, offenders would not take seriously such sanctions as fines or probation.

Incarceration of criminals (and those accused of criminal behavior) takes place in prisons and jails. These are two distinct types of institutions (see comparison in Table 10.1). **Prisons** generally are state or federal facilities, segregated according to the sex of inmates, that house persons convicted of felonies who are serving sentences of 1 year or more. **Jails** are usually local municipal institutions and house a variety of people convicted of misdemeanors or at various stages of criminal case processing. As might be expected, there are far more jails in the country than prisons, but most of the jails are small and experience a greater turnover in population than prisons (Sabol, Minton, & Harrison, 2007).

Important Terms

clear and present danger
compelling state interest
congregate system
"hands-off" doctrine
institutionalization
jailhouse lawyers
jails
least restrictive alternative
multijurisdictional jails
pains of imprisonment
penitentiary
Prison Litigation Reform Act
prisonization
prisons
reformatory
role stress
segregate system
smug hack
total institution

Table 10.1	Characteristics of Prisons and Jails		
What Are the Characteristics of Confinement Facilities?			
Prisons		**Jails**	
Number of prisons	1,821	Number of jails	3,283
Maximum security	372	Population	
Medium security	480	<50	1,129
Minimum security	969	50–99	552
Average population		100–249	584
<500	946	250–499	272
500–999	304	500–999	173
1,000–2,499	495	1,000 or more	149
2,500+	76		
2,500+	64		
2,000+	156		

Sources: Stephan (2008); Stephan and Walsh (2011)

This chapter examines incarceration in the American criminal justice system. It describes the history, organization, and practice of incarceration in both prisons and jails. In the following chapter, we address several contemporary issues in the operation of prisons and jails.

THE ORIGINS OF AMERICAN INCARCERATION

The jail was established in England during the reign of Alfred the Great. Its purpose was to serve as a detention facility for those accused of seriously breaching the peace. In addition to tax collecting and other duties, the shire reeve (sheriff) was responsible for maintaining the jail. Then, as now, the jail operated on a local level in holding prisoners for a centralized authority.

The American colonists brought the jail with them to the New World but generally did not need to use it within their small, close-knit communities. As had happened earlier in England, however, towns in the colonies grew larger and jails began to receive more use. Those incarcerated in jails were arrested persons not yet convicted, or were debtors or people who failed to pay fines. We did not yet use incarceration as a punishment for crime (Moynahan & Steward, 1980).

Incarceration as a response to criminal behavior developed as part of a larger "discovery" of the asylum in American society in the early 1800s (Rothman, 1971). The American Revolution changed the nature of American society. No longer was it common for people to know all of their neighbors and to maintain a sense of small community in their dealings with others. Mobility (caused by the war), the beginnings of industrialism and immigration, and the growth of commerce and cities led to a more impersonal, less intimate social climate. Problems of poverty, dependency, and crime became increasingly common and seemed to require a more centralized solution than had been characteristic of the colonial response. Americans found the solution to social problems of poverty, insanity, and crime in the asylum or institution. Poorhouses, insane asylums, and jails became more common around the nation in the latter part of the 1700s. The first prison in the United States opened in Newgate, Connecticut, before the Revolution in 1773. The general use of imprisonment did not spread until afterward (Durham, 1990).

The **penitentiary**, a place of punishment and repentance, as a response to crime was particularly attractive. The harsh criminal code of England had been transported to the colonies with the result that most offenses were punished with what Langbein (1976) termed "blood punishments." It was common practice to torture, mutilate, or execute offenders. These barbaric penalties violated the assumptions of the Enlightenment, which underlay the New Republic. When Patrick Henry addressed the Virginia House of Burgesses and declared, "Give me liberty or give me death!" he unwittingly identified the perfect penalty. Incarceration gives the convicted offender neither liberty nor death.

Pragmatically, incarceration solved a pressing problem of administration for penal codes that provided for severe punishments. When the penalties for crimes were perceived as being too harsh (e.g., lashes or branding for petty theft, death for repeat offenses), juries dealt with the dilemma by failing to convict the offenders. Some observers saw this as a major obstacle to meeting the deterrent functions of the law. Furthermore, in a rational penalty system, it was difficult to grade penalties to crimes when physical pain was the standard. Incarceration seemed more humane and likely to result in higher conviction rates. It also made an easier task of matching lengths of term to seriousness of offense.

The problem of harsh penalties was very troublesome. If the penalty for stealing a pig was death, what should be the penalty for stealing a cow? What would deter a burglar who faced hanging from killing the homeowner? Jurors faced tough decisions as well. Voting to convict a hungry offender who stole a loaf of bread could ensure that the offender suffered branding, mutilation, or death. By establishing time as a punishment, and describing the prison as a harsh but humane environment, it was possible to better match penalties to offenses, such as 1 year for stealing a pig or 3 years for stealing a cow. The availability of incarceration as a sentencing option also led to a higher rate of conviction, as juries were more willing to see a hungry thief spend a few months in prison (where food and clothing would be available).

Jeremy Bentham established the centrality of the prison as an appropriate sanction for deterrent purposes, although later historians have overlooked Bentham's focus on deterrence. Sullivan (1996) reviewed Bentham's original work, concluding that, to Bentham, the prison provided a technology that allowed precise alteration of the intensity and duration of punishment. According to Bentham, this precision would allow punishers to achieve, via scientific application, optimal deterrent value from criminal punishment.

Ideologically, incarceration appeared well suited to the needs of offender reform. Without the opportunity to transport prisoners to penal colonies, penitentiaries provided internal penal colonies to which offenders could be sentenced. The penitentiary removed the offender from the evil environment of the city, allowed the person to reflect on the error of his or her ways, and taught good work habits. Indeed, in the early days of incarceration, some viewed the penitentiary as a utopia. Most proponents of the penitentiary believed crime was the result of an evil environment, and believed the penitentiary would insulate the offender from further criminal influences. The French philosopher Foucault (1979) is perhaps the best known proponent of the view that the prison emerged as a means of disciplining or controlling people. The prison emerged as a primary means of criminal punishment for a variety of reasons (Garland, 1990).

The Congregate/Segregate System Debate

During the 1820s, two systems of penitentiary discipline developed. They are compared in Box 10.1. The first emerged in Pennsylvania, known as the **segregate system** or the Pennsylvania system. Here, inmates were housed separately in individual cells, took their meals in their cells, exercised in separate yards, and never interacted with other offenders. Any industry conducted was cottage industry, in which inmates completed the entire product in their cell.

This system had the advantage of ensuring that offenders were protected from the corrupting influence of other offenders. The major disadvantages were that offenders suffered psychologically from isolation, and the prison was expensive to operate and was not always able to produce a profit from its industry. Nonetheless, the Pennsylvania system had its supporters because it was true to an ideal of penance and isolation.

In contrast, the second penitentiary in the United States developed in Auburn, New York, and was known as the **congregate system** or the Auburn system of prison discipline. Here, although housed in separate cells, inmates ate, worked, and exercised in groups. The prison maintained isolation by a strict rule of silence that prohibited inmates from conversing with each other. This organization reduced costs because of mass movement and feeding of prisoners. Further, the ability of offenders to work in groups allowed assembly-line methods of production and a wider variety of prison-made products.

The strengths of this system were the more humane mingling of prisoners (even if they had to remain silent, inmates at least were able to see each other) and the cost-effectiveness of the system. The disadvantages were that the congregate system required closer surveillance of inmates to enforce silence, and that prison administrators were unable to keep inmates isolated. In addition, in the congregate system, there was greater potential for riots and fights among inmates.

For several decades, a debate raged about which of these systems was the better method for handling inmates. In the end, the cost-effectiveness of the congregate system emerged the victor of the debate, at least in the United States. Later generations of American penitentiaries most often operated under the Auburn system of congregate feeding, work, and exercise.

The experience of the Virginia Penitentiary illustrates this point. In an attempt to benefit from both the congregate and segregate systems, Virginia law required that inmates, housed in larger dormitories under a "silent system" at first, spend

BOX 10.1 SEGREGATE VERSUS CONGREGATE SYSTEMS

The Eastern State Penitentiary, designed by John Haviland and completed in 1829, became the model and primary exponent of the Pennsylvania "separate" system. The prison had seven original cell blocks radiating from the hublike center, a rotunda with an observatory tower, and an alarm bell.

A corridor ran down the center of each block, with the cells at right angles to the corridor. Each cell had a back door to a small, uncovered exercise yard and double front doors, the outer one made of wood, and the other of grated iron with a trap so that meals could be passed to prisoners.

In 1816, New York began the construction of a new prison at Auburn. It was patterned after other early American prisons with a few solitary cells to conform to the law of solitary confinement to be used for punishment, and with sizable night rooms to accommodate most prisoners.

To test the efficiency of the Pennsylvania system, an experiment was tried in 1821 with a group of inmates who were confined to their cells without labor. Many of these inmates became insane and sick. The experiment was abandoned as a failure in 1823, and most of the inmates studied were pardoned.

A new plan was adopted whereby all inmates were locked in separate cells at night, but worked and ate together in congregate settings in silence under penalty of punishment.

Source: American Correctional Association (1983)

their last 3 months in solitary confinement. Keve (1986:41) cited the 1832 report of a legislative study committee, which found the solitary confinement requirement of Virginia prison terms counterproductive:

> Upon the subject of the three month's solitary confinement required by law to be inflicted upon convicts immediately preceding their discharge, the committee have had much reflection; and they have come to the conclusion that this portion of the close confinement ought to be abolished. They believe that it is productive of no substantial benefit, but is on the contrary, decidedly injurious. It obliterates the habits of industry previously acquired. Upon the score of more interest to the state it is inexpedient because it abstracts from the institution the most valuable portion of the time and labor of the convicts. It exceeds the requisitions of stern justice.... But above all it ruins the health of the victim and indirectly takes away human life.... In any aspect which it may be viewed experience proves its inexpediency, if not its absolute inhumanity and injustice.

The Changing Purposes of Prisons

Initially, people believed that the experience of incarceration alone would lead to improved behavior on the part of offenders. The learning of good work habits, the removal from contaminating influences, and other benefits of incarceration were supposed to result in better citizens. However, over time, it became clear that the reform (prison) was itself in need of reform. By the middle of the nineteenth century, penitentiaries were replaced with reformatories in which offenders were trained to be law-abiding citizens and released from incarceration as soon as it was clear that they had been reformed.

Created as a humanitarian and practical alternative to the corporal and capital punishments of the eighteenth century and earlier, the penitentiary soon came to be recognized as flawed. The early developers of the penitentiary supported isolation of prisoners because they sincerely believed that criminality was caused when the environment tempted people. The term "penitentiary" was applied because it was designed to be a place where the offender could do penance. Designers thought lack of adequate discipline and training from the family, combined with the lure of taverns and bawdy houses, led otherwise law-abiding citizens into a life of crime. Isolation, solitary contemplation on right and wrong, and the discipline of hard work in a sanitized environment free from criminal temptations would work to improve offenders and prepare them for lawful living.

By the Civil War period, however, observers had come to believe that simple incarceration was not enough. The penitentiary lacked an incentive to offenders to make them want to change. Furthermore, the imposition of a definite term of confinement seemed counterproductive. If a prisoner with a 5-year term had reformed in 1 year, these observers saw no reason to continue his or her confinement for an additional 4 years. It was important that prisons take active steps to reform criminals. These steps would include instilling discipline and industry as habits in the inmates, and offering the possibility of early release from incarceration as an incentive to reform.

In the **reformatory**, inmates were raw materials to be shaped into law-abiding citizens (that is, reformed). Upon entering the reformatory, the prisoner lost his or her civilian identity, contact with the outside world, and nearly all rights. The reformatory was a factory producing useful citizens. The process through which this production was to be accomplished was training. Prisoners were conditioned to industry and discipline in the belief that once the habits were established in the prison, they would not be broken after release. As an ex-convict, author Braly (1976:202) noted that the habits acquired in the penitentiary did endure, at least for a while. Describing his first few days of freedom after release from San Quentin, Braly wrote, "That first morning and every morning for several weeks I woke exactly at six-thirty when the big bell had begun to pound in the blocks. Rise and shine. It's daylight in the swamps."

Within 50 years of the creation of reformatories, a new correctional ideology developed (O'Leary & Duffee, 1971). The mere training of offenders was not sufficient. Rather, offenders were regarded as ill and in need of treatment to cure them of their proclivities toward crime. The rehabilitative correctional institution had arrived, with a treatment staff in addition to the custody and industry staffs.

Several problems had plagued the reformatory ideal. First, the habits established in prison did not last long for many prisoners after they were released. Second, over time, prison administrators increasingly used early release as a prison management tool rather than recognition of inmate reformation. If the prison became crowded, they released inmates. If a particular inmate was needed (e.g., if he or she was the only barber in the institution), he or she might not be released, no matter how reformed he or she became. Finally, the view of the cause of criminality also changed.

The growth of the social and behavioral sciences, and the development of service professions related to these disciplines, fostered a reexamination of institutional corrections. Spalding (1897), secretary of the Massachusetts Prison Association, remarked (1897:47), "The State is not an avenger, with a mission to right the wrong which the criminal has done, but is to try to right the criminal, that he may cease to do wrong." The emphasis on the individual offender, and on the motives and causes of the individual's criminality, grew in the early twentieth century (Fogel, 1979:50–61). This was the Progressive Era, when there was a general trust in the ability of the state to do good for individuals, and when reformers wanted prisons that met the needs of individual criminals rather than the general needs of society (Rothman, 1980).

In the middle 1960s, yet another shift occurred in correctional ideology. Observers now viewed prisons themselves as part of the problem of crime. The best solution to reforming criminal offenders was thought to rest in keeping the criminal in the community where he or she could learn how to live a law-abiding life. Prison populations fell, and those kept in prison increasingly were able to take advantage of furlough programs and to enjoy increased contact with the outside world. Observers of the nation's prisons came to believe that attempts at individualizing treatment, and the focus on the cause of crime as being inside the offender, were ineffective. Rather, to succeed in changing offenders into law-abiding citizens, it would be necessary to deal with the criminal in society. A survey of prison inmates in Norway revealed that the inmates themselves believed that imprisonment alone would neither deter nor rehabilitate inmates (Kolstad, 1996).

Another prison writer, Torok (1974:91), succinctly summarized the arguments in favor of the reintegration philosophy of corrections, which flourished for a decade from the mid-1960s:

> It costs the taxpayer up to six thousand dollars each year to keep one convict locked up uselessly in prison. On the other hand, it would only cost about three hundred dollars a year to keep the same man in the community, under close supervision, on parole or probation, where he will pay his own way, earn a salary, keep his family off welfare and live a law-abiding life. Both society and the offender would benefit from this approach but so many people are unwilling to examine the facts and figures objectively. They continue to pour millions of dollars of tax money into an archaic prison system which does not correct, does not reform, simply does not, in any sense work.

In the mid-1970s, correctional ideology again shifted. The purpose of imprisonment came to be defined principally as punishment. Inmates served time as punishment for criminal offenses. Whatever programs and industries were available to inmates were there for voluntary use. Release from incarceration was based on service of sentence, not on evidence of reform or rehabilitation. Further, more offenders were expected to serve prison sentences as punishment, although the lengths of terms were reduced for most offenders (Twentieth Century Fund, 1976).

One argument in favor of this newest purpose of prisons was that, in the end, punishment had been the only purpose that the tradition of the prison had shown incarceration could serve. Torok (1974:88) wrote, "In actual practice, prisons do little more than punish." Similarly, Braly (1976:362) wrote of the new prisons, "The old timers scorned these new prisons and dismissed them as Holiday Motels. We couldn't be conned by departmental [Department of Corrections] window dressing. We were still under the Man, and the Man still had a gun locked away somewhere nearby.... Essentially, it was only Folsom with Muzak." A number of commentators support the notion of the prison as a place of punishment. Logan and Gaes (1993) suggested that prisons follow a confinement model in which the purpose is the secure, safe, humane custody of inmates. This notion of the purpose of the prison fits well with a resurgence of retributive punishment. If the purpose of punishment is to return harm for harm, then the prison should impose pain safely and humanely (Clear, 1994; Cullen, 1995). When combined with tremendous crowding in prisons, the retributive ideal led to what some called a "new penology" (Feeley & Simon, 1992). In this new penology, the primary purpose of the prison was the efficient management of a large population (Holcomb & Williams, 2003; Rutherford, 1993).

At the turn of the century, the purpose of prisons was again the subject of intense debate (Clear, 1997). Several observers noted that the move to more punitive policies concerning the use of prisons and jails is at least partly responsible for the tremendous growth in America's inmate population during the past 40 years (Cook, 2009). Critics blamed punitive conditions in prisons and jails for failing to prepare inmates for life after incarceration, and for making the management of correctional institutions more difficult (Rhine, 1992; Seiter, 1997; Wright, 2000). In response, a growing number of commentators called for the reinstitution of rehabilitative programming in correctional institutions (Listwan, Jonson, Cullen, & Latessa, 2008; Schriro, 2000). Most Americans believe rehabilitation should be a primary objective of prison programming (Applegate, Cullen, & Fisher, 2002).

The American prison developed as a humane alternative to the harsh punishments of colonial justice. In a history of slightly less than 200 years, the purpose of prisons changed several times in accord with changing public and social attitudes regarding crime and human behavior. Through it all, the prison has survived. It is instructive to recognize that one of the first prisons ever erected, Auburn Penitentiary, is still in operation today. It has undergone several renovations and name changes, yet it still houses inmates. Pennsylvania opened the Eastern State Penitentiary in Philadelphia in 1829 (see Figure 10.1). In 1970, the state closed the penitentiary, but the city of Philadelphia used it to house

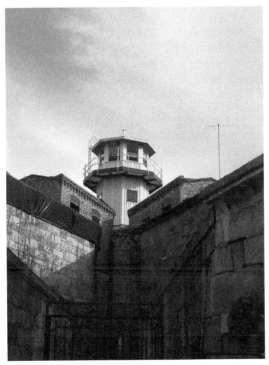

FIGURE 10.1
Eastern State Penitentiary in Philadelphia became the model and primary exponent of the Pennsylvania "separate" system. It is now a museum open to visitors.
Ellen S. Boyne

inmates from the county prison after a riot there. In 1971, the city finally closed the penitentiary as a prison. It is now a museum open to visitors (Eastern State Penitentiary, 2010).

The history of prisons in the United States reveals that these institutions are enduring (Schwartz & Travis, 1996). The prison represents the core of our views on how to respond to criminal behavior. It is likely to do so at least into the foreseeable future.

THE ORGANIZATION OF AMERICAN INCARCERATION

Given the distinct (although related) natures and functions of jails and prisons, it is necessary to give separate treatment to the organizations of the two types of institutions. Although both types of institutions hold convicted offenders, their widely divergent structures cannot be combined easily.

JAIL ORGANIZATION

Local control, multiple functions, and a transient, heterogeneous population have shaped the major organizational characteristics of jails. Box 10.2 provides a partial answer to the question, "Who is in jail?" Typically, jails are under the jurisdiction of county government. In most instances, the local area has neither the necessary tax base from which to finance a jail adequately nor sufficient size to justify even the most rudimentary correctional programs. In addition, local control has inevitably meant involvement with local politics. Jails are in a paradoxical situation: Although clung to tenaciously by localities, they often have been unwilling or unable to meet even minimal standards (National Advisory Commission, 1973:274).

County sheriffs operate most jails in the United States. Of 3,283 jails in the nation, over 99% operate at the county or city level. In recent years, the use of **multijurisdictional jails** has increased. These facilities serve more than one

---

BOX 10.2 WHO'S IN JAIL?

- Persons pending court proceedings such as arraignment, trial, or sentencing, including both those unable to secure pretrial release and those denied release
- Probation, parole, and bail violators and absconders
- Juveniles pending transfer to juvenile authorities
- Persons with mental illnesses pending movement to mental health facilities
- Military personnel for protective custody, contempt, or as witnesses
- Persons awaiting transfer to state or federal correctional facilities
- Federal and state prisoners held because of prison crowding
- Convicted offenders sentenced to short terms (generally under 1 year)
- Material witnesses
- Prison inmates on furlough or other temporary release status

Source: James (2004)

municipality or jurisdiction and provide the economic benefits of scale. There are at least 68 regional jails operating in the United States. As a result, the number of jail facilities decreased by 3% between 1999 and 2006 even as the jail inmate population increased 23% during that time (Stephan & Walsh, 2011).

As local institutions, jails must often compete for resources within a larger sheriff's or police department and with other municipal services such as public works, sanitation, health, and education departments. Moreover, nearly 40% of American jails are designed to house fewer than 50 inmates. About 20% of jails are capable of housing more than 250 inmates. Yet, the largest 5% of jails housed one-half of all jail inmates (Stephan & Walsh, 2011). The presence of large jails varies widely by jurisdiction. In the most recent census of jails, 14 states reported no jails capable of housing 1,000 inmates or more, whereas two states had no inmates in jails holding fewer than 50 inmates.

On any given day, our nation's jails hold more than 735,000 prisoners (Minton, 2013). Annually, jails process more than 11 million inmates with a weekly turnover rate of approximately 60%. Over half of those incarcerated in jails are awaiting trial and not yet convicted of a criminal offense. Including those who will receive pretrial release or a sentence to a penalty other than incarceration, the Bureau of Justice Statistics estimated the average length of stay for persons entering jails at 3 days (Snell, 1993). Figure 10.2 shows the average daily jail population over the past decade.

Most jail inmates are male, under the age of 35, unmarried, and minority-group members, with just under 40% having completed high school (James, 2004). Only about 12% of jail inmates are female, and 92% were U.S. citizens (James, 2004:2). Nearly half of all jail inmates have not graduated high school (Harlow, 2003). Because of short terms and small total population sizes, programs for jail inmates generally either do not exist or are inadequate. Most jails have programs for

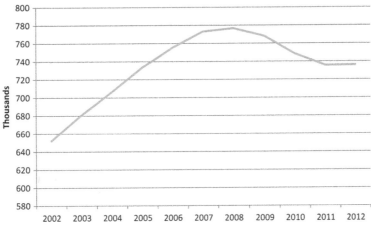

FIGURE 10.2
Average daily jail population, 2002–2012.
Source: Minton (2013)

education and health care. Table 10.2 describes programs available to jail inmates. Jail inmates spend much of their incarceration time in idleness, viewing television, or otherwise attempting to pass the hours. Jail inmates have high levels of medical needs and substance dependence and abuse, posing problems for jail treatment programs (Karberg & James, 2005; Maruschak, 2006). It is an understatement to say that the jail population comprises offenders with high service needs.

The majority of jail staff consists of custodial officers, and because of the administration of jails by sheriffs and police, many custodial officers are sworn

Table 10.2	Jail Jurisdictions Reporting Programs Available to Jail Inmates	
	Jail Jurisdictions with a Program	
Program or Policy	**Number**	**Percent**
Education		
Secondary	1,545	55
Basic adult	696	25
Special	303	11
Study release	260	9
Vocational	182	6
College	94	3
Counseling		
Religious/spiritual	1,960	70
Alcohol	1,724	61
Drug	1,528	54
Psychological	1,306	47
Life skills	601	21
Domestic violence	488	17
Pretrial services	468	17
Job seeking	411	15
Health care delivery system		
Fee-for-service	1,101	39
On-site staff	882	31
Managed care	500	18
Local government physicians	338	12
Mental health services		
Screening at intake	2,152	78
Psychotropic medication	1,832	66
24-hour care	1,309	47
Routine therapy/counseling	1,283	46
Psychiatric evaluation	1,044	38

Note: The following numbers of jail jurisdictions reported data on policies and programs: education, 2,821 jurisdictions; counseling, 2,804; health care delivery systems, 2,802; and mental health services, 2,769.

Source: Stephan (2001)

police officers who would rather not be serving in jails. Fewer than 10% of jail personnel are service staff members, such as doctors, social workers, and teachers (Stephan, 2001). Most jail personnel are Caucasian, non-Hispanic (66%), and male (66%). In 1999, the ratio of inmates to correctional officers in jails was 4.3 to 1. Twenty-six percent of correctional officers were African-American, most were non-Hispanic, and 28% were female.

The organization and administration of jails have remained relatively unchanged over the years, and there is little chance that speedy change in jail organization will occur (Skoler, 1978:11). Historically jail critics complained of the lack of programs for inmates, poor physical condition, and inadequate staffing (Fishman, 1923; Goldfarb, 1975; McGee, 1971). Ruddell and Mays (2007:258) studied rural jails and concluded, "Perhaps the most significant finding of this study was that the problems identified in Cronk's (1982) study of rural crime and justice were still major challenges over two decades later."

Although there has been improvement in jails over the years, much remains to be done (Katsampes & Neil, 1981). Newer jails often incorporate a redesign of jail facilities. An increasing number of new jails have been built using alternatives to the traditional row of cells. Often called podular designs, these jails contain housing units with cells arranged along the exterior walls with a common living/dining area in the center. This design is coupled with the delivery of most services to inmates within the housing unit. Researchers have reported that this design seems to reduce tension and inmate misbehavior (Zupan, 1991; Zupan & Menke, 1988). Senese (1997) evaluated the effect of jail design on inmate behavior and concluded that the new design is associated with lower rates of inmate misbehavior of some types (violence, escape, destruction), but that general disorder infractions are higher. Unfortunately, in many places the construction of these new facilities has not meant the closing of older, traditional jails (Bikle, 2000). Instead, because of growing populations, many jurisdictions now operate both types of jails. In addition, nearly 8% of persons under jail supervision nationally are supervised outside the jail facility, as shown in Table 10.3.

Prison Organization

Prisons exist on either the state or federal level. Unlike jails, prisons suffer from problems associated with their large size. The National Advisory Commission on Criminal Justice Standards and Goals observed the detrimental consequences of overly large institutions (1973:355):

> The usual response to bigness has been regimentation and uniformity. Individuals become subjugated to the needs generated by the institution. Uniformity is translated into depersonalization. A human being ceases to be identified by the usual points of reference, such as his name, his job, or family role. He becomes a number, identified by the cellblock where he sleeps. Such practices reflect maladaptation resulting from size.

Table 10.3	Persons under Jail Supervision by Confinement Status
Percent of jail inmates confined	
Inside jails	92.1
Outside jails	7.9
Status of jail inmates not confined in jail (%)	
Weekender program	16.1
Electronic monitoring	21.5
Home detention	3.3
Day reporting	6.1
Community service	23.0
Other pretrial supervision	12.1
Other work programs	11.1
Treatment programs	3.4
Other	3.4

Source: Minton (2013:9)

State governments operate the majority of prisons in the United States. Of the nearly 1,300 prisons in America, 102 are federal prisons (Stephan, 2008). Every state has a prison, or state confinement facility, and about one-third of states operate more than 20 (see Figure 10.3). About one-half of state and federal facilities house fewer than 750 inmates, but, as with the jail population, large prisons house most prison inmates. The Bureau of Justice Statistics reported that three jurisdictions, California, Texas, and the federal prison system, housed one-third of all inmates in 2012 (Carson & Golinelli, 2013a).

FIGURE 10.3
The Maryland Correctional Institution in Hagerstown is an adult male correctional institution located just south of Hagerstown. The construction of the facility was initiated in the early 1930s with the use of inmate labor.
Ellen S. Boyne

At the end of 1984, the Bureau of Justice Statistics (1985) reported more than 480,000 offenders held in American prisons. That population increased more than 17% by the end of 1986, when there were 546,659 prison inmates in the United States (Bureau of Justice Statistics, 1987:1). At the end of 1996, there were nearly 1,182,169 inmates in state and federal prisons, an increase of almost 250% (Mumola & Beck, 1997). By the end of 2008, there were more than 1.6 million people in prison. However, in 2009, prison releases exceeded admissions for the first time in 31 years. The prison population at year-end 2012 had fallen to approximately 1.57 million prisoners (Carson & Golinelli, 2013b). Most of these prisons are single-sex facilities. Fewer than 8% of prisons were coeducational in 2000 (Stephan & Karberg, 2003:6). Because prisons have a much lower turn-over rate than jails, fewer than 1.3 million inmates were admitted and released in prisons each year. In 2011, 13.7% of all offenders were sentenced to between 1 and 2 years in prison. The most common prison sentence is between 2 and 4 years, accounting for more than 43% of all new sentences. The vast majority of prisoners (94%) are sentenced to fewer than 20 years of imprisonment (Carson & Golinelli, 2013b). Figure 10.4 displays the growth in prison populations in the United States.

Most prison inmates, like their counterparts in jails, are male, minority-group members, and young (West, 2010). Recent data reveal that nearly one-third are age 40 or older and most have graduated from high school and have a history of some drug use. The Bureau of Justice Statistics reports only about 7% of inmates are female, 35% are Caucasian, 40% are African American, and nearly 20% are of Hispanic origin (West, 2010). Greenfeld (1992:16) reported that 93% of prisoners in 1991 were convicted of a violent crime or were recidivists. This is a tricky statistic, however, because it combines violence and recidivism. In 2011, only 30% of new admissions to prison were convicted of a violent offense (Carson & Golinelli, 2013b). Most persons sentenced to prison have a prior record of

FIGURE 10.4
Prison population in the United States, 2002–2012.
Source: Carson and Golinelli (2013a)

Prison employee job categories

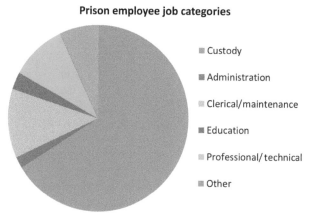

- Custody
- Administration
- Clerical/maintenance
- Education
- Professional/technical
- Other

FIGURE 10.5
Distribution of prison employees by job category, 2005.
Source: Stephan (2008)

criminal behavior and, at any time, about half of state prisoners have a current conviction for a violent crime.

Because of the longer terms of confinement and generally larger populations, prisons are able to provide a wide range of programs to inmates, including educational, vocational, recreational, social, and psychological counseling programs. Stephan (2008:5–6) reported that 85% of confinement facilities offered educational programs, 92% offered counseling programs, and most facilities provided work assignments to inmates. In fact, some states require inmates to either obtain education or work while incarcerated. Despite this, many inmates find themselves idle, having neither an academic nor a work assignment (Batchelder & Pippert, 2002).

Similar to jails, the majority of prison staff holds custodial positions (66%). There are, however, higher percentages of prison staff holding administrative (2%), education (3%), professional/technical (10%), maintenance/clerical (12%), and other (7%) job titles (Stephan, 2008:4). Figure 10.5 describes the distribution of prison personnel across job titles. Unlike those working in jails, prisons hire personnel solely as correctional personnel. The organization and administration of prisons have changed little over the years and do not seem likely to change much in the future.

DOING TIME

Incarceration is the foundation of American corrections. With the exception of capital punishment, it is the most severe sanction available to the state. Incarceration is the "stick" that supports community corrections programs, such as halfway houses, probation, and parole (Reasons & Kaplan, 1975). Prisons are an American invention, and Americans rely on the use of incarceration as a response to criminal behavior.

The experience of incarceration differs depending on where an inmate serves the sentence; yet, in large measure, it is the same wherever and whenever it occurs. The inmate in either prison or jail is typically under control and is not a contributing member of any policymaking body. This fact leads to a similarity of experience for all inmates. The experience of "doing time" is painful. Gresham Sykes (1969) identified the **pains of imprisonment** as (1) deprivation of liberty, (2) deprivation of goods and services, (3) deprivation of heterosexual relations, (4) deprivation of autonomy, and (5) deprivation of security. Hassine (1996:18), an inmate in the Pennsylvania prison system, described these pains as follows: "At first, I missed the obvious, sex, love, family, and friends. But it wasn't long before I stopped missing these things and started focusing on the next wave of things I no longer have: privacy, quiet, and peace of mind, intangibles that I have never stopped missing to this day."

Many observers have identified what has been called **prisonization**. This refers to the apparent fact that prison inmates become socialized into a specific prison subculture. Some contend that the experience of deprivation creates a prison subculture that provides inmates with norms and rules for living in prison. In contrast, others suggest that offenders import the prison subculture from outside. That is, the type of people sent to prison already have a set of values, norms, and beliefs that is different from and counter to conventional society (Zaitzow, 1999). The research evidence on whether the prison subculture is a product of the characteristics of inmates coming to prison (importation model) or emerges from the experience of imprisonment (deprivation model) is unclear. Paterline and Petersen (1999:438) surveyed more than 400 federal prisoners and concluded, "The findings of this investigation coincide with some previous research, which concludes that the merger of the importation and deprivation models explains more of the variation in prisonization than either analyzed separately." McDonald (1999) studied drug use and violence while incarcerated among youths released from California facilities. He also suggested that his research supports a merger of the importation and deprivation models. Hochstetler and DeLisi (2005) expanded on this by observing that different types of inmates are more likely to place themselves in circumstances in which they are exposed to opportunities for good or bad behavior in prison. They suggested that the reality of living in prison is quite complex and that it is a combination of inmate and institution characteristics that explains inmate behavior in prison. Whatever the source, the subculture provides inmates with a means of making sense of the prison and enduring the hardships of incarceration.

Deprivation of Liberty

By definition, those confined in correctional institutions do not have any liberty of movement. Even within the institution, the inmate is not at liberty to move around. As Sykes (1969:65) observed, "In short, the prisoner's loss of liberty is a double one: first, by confinement to the institution and second, by confinement within the institution." Figure 10.6 shows the Federal Correctional Complex, Terre Haute.

FIGURE 10.6
The Federal Correctional Complex, Terre Haute (FCC Terre Haute) is a U.S. federal prison complex for male inmates in Terre Haute, Indiana. It consists of two facilities: the Federal Correctional Institution, Terre Haute (FCI Terre Haute), a medium-security facility with a Communication Management Unit, and the U.S. Penitentiary, Terre Haute (USP Terre Haute), a high-security facility that holds federal death row for men.

Prisoners move en masse from cellblock to activity, to dining facility, to activity, and back to cellblock. Few inmates get the privilege of moving about the institution without an escort. Inmates also are not free to choose to whom they may write or with whom they may otherwise interact. The net effect of this deprivation is isolation from the outside community. This loss of liberty is symbolic of a loss of status as a trusted member of society. As one inmate put it:

> Freedom is the only meaningful thing to a human. Without freedom things lose meaning. The whole system in prison is designed to degenerate a human being, to break him as a man. They take away all of his freedom, his freedom to express himself and his feelings. How can you be human if you can't express yourself? (Wright, 1973:146).

Deprivation of Goods and Services

Although inmates have more options now than when Sykes made his observations, prisons still deprive inmates of access to, and ownership of, a wide variety of goods and services. Most prisons do not allow inmates to possess money, and most require standardization of clothing and other possessions.

Upon admission to a prison or jail, the "civilian" possessions of inmates (e.g., jewelry, money, and clothing) are confiscated and either stored until release or shipped to a destination chosen by the inmate (usually home). On admission to the prison, the inmate loses all of the amenities of free society by which we make a statement about who we are, such as the clothes we wear, the way we wear our hair, the car we drive, and the like. Instead, the inmate receives a uniform, a prison haircut, and generally cannot exercise personal taste in the selection and purchase of goods and services. Hassine (1996:19–21) described his first disciplinary infraction as the result of a desire to have a hamburger "his way." He wrote, "My first misconduct at Graterford resulted from missing one of life's simplest pleasures: a fresh-cooked burger." He bought contraband hamburger, buns, butter, onions, and a heating element. While preparing his hamburger, he was discovered and written up. He concluded this tale, writing, "For many years afterward, my prison handle became 'Burger King,' even though I had never gotten a chance to taste the object of my crime."

Most penal facilities now have commissaries, where inmates can purchase toiletries, candy bars, and other small items. Some prisons allow inmates to wear certain articles of civilian clothing, such as hats or T-shirts, but the range of options available to the inmate is very restricted. The effect of this deprivation is that the inmate feels impoverished. His or her self-worth is lessened by virtue of the reduced net worth.

> In prison the slightest distinction is cherished and enlarged.... Bob, since he had bad feet, had been allowed to keep his own shoes rather than wear the Santa Rosa hightops which were standard issue. He had polished these shoes until they glittered, and, as we spoke, he continued to rub one shoe and then the other against his pants leg. He also wore the watch Big John had given him, and he glanced at it frequently as if he had an important appointment and wasn't just standing around, as I was, killing time until lunch (Braly, 1976:156).

Deprivation of Heterosexual Relations

As noted earlier, most penal facilities in the United States are segregated by sex. The inmate is not only denied liberty and impoverished by incarceration but is also forced to endure involuntary celibacy. The lack of members of the opposite sex in the prison society leads to anxieties about sexual identity among inmates. Some observers have characterized the prison culture as being "ultramasculine" (Lutze & Murphy, 1999).

The effect of sex segregation is not only physical but also psychological in that the inmate has lost one-half of the audience and comparison group from whom he or she receives a validation of sexual identity. That is, it is more difficult to be masculine or feminine in an all-male or all-female society (respectively) than in mixed company. One of the principal ways in which we know who we are sexually is by comparison with members of the opposite sex. In prison, these comparisons are largely absent (Nacci & Kane, 1984).

> Some men look feminine and looks are enough alone for a man behind these walls to try and get him. It is a hell of a thing to say, but here you are another man and you are behind these walls and before long another man begins to look like a woman to you. (Lockwood, 1982:54)

Deprivation of Autonomy

The prison is a "total institution," as described by Goffman (1961). The **total institution** provides all of the necessities for the individual and makes all of the decisions for its residents. This fact leads to what has been called "**institutionalization**," which is the formation of individuals who are almost wholly dependent on the institution and incapable of caring for themselves in the free society.

The prison inmate is not allowed to decide when to eat, what to eat, when or how often to take a shower, when to go to sleep, when to awaken, what job to do, and how to make other seemingly trivial decisions. Rather, the inmate is subjected to a life in which all major, and most minor, decisions are made by others. The refusal of inmate requests is generally not accompanied by any explanation, thereby adding insult to injury.

The net effect of the loss of autonomy is a reduction in feelings of self-worth, as inmates come to recognize that they are no longer in control of their own destinies. The inmate is reduced to a state of childlike dependency on the parent (the state). As Sykes (1969:76) explained, "But for the adult who has escaped such helplessness with the passage of years, to be thrust back into childhood's helplessness is even more painful." In the words of an inmate at San Quentin:

> The worst thing here is the way your life is regulated, always regulated, day in and day out. They tell you what to do almost every moment of the day. You become a robot just following instructions. They do this, they say, so that you can learn to be free on the outside (Wright, 1973:146).

Deprivation of Security

The final pain of imprisonment mentioned by Sykes is paradoxical: the loss of security. In a prison, even one classified as maximum security, the prisoner experiences a real loss of personal security. Prisons are not safe places in which to reside. Consider living in a neighborhood where all of those around you are accused criminals, convicted felons, and other criminal offenders. How many people would voluntarily move into such a neighborhood?

At any time, the prisoner must be prepared to fight to protect his or her belongings and personal safety. Living with the constant threat of victimization is stressful, and this constant stress adds to the pain of imprisonment. Cell doors may serve not only to lock in the inmate but also to lock out others who may harm the prisoner. Many prison inmates request placement in segregation (solitary confinement) for reasons of personal safety. Existing in the general prison population is generally a frightening experience.

> It used to be a pastime of mine to watch the change in men, to observe the blackening of their hearts. It takes place before your eyes. They

enter prison more bewildered than afraid. Every step after that, the fear creeps into them.... No one is prepared for it.

Everyone is afraid. It is not an emotional, psychological fear. It is a practical matter. If you do not threaten someone, at the very least, someone will threaten you (Abbott, 1981:144).

CORRECTIONAL OFFICERS: THE OTHER INMATES

If imprisonment is frustrating and painful to inmates, it is not much less so for those whose job it is to work within the walls of penal facilities each day. The correctional officer serves a dual role: (1) manager of inmates and (2) line-level worker within the prison. As a line worker, the officer is subjected to frequent "shake-downs" (to control the possibility of officers smuggling contraband into the prison), supervision, and disciplinary action by superior officers, and other controls, which make the occupation of correctional officer similar to the role of prison inmate (Clear & Cole, 1986:306).

In recent years, increasing attention has been paid to the stressful role of custodial officers in prisons and jails (Dowden & Tellier, 2004; Griffin, 2006; Lambert, 2003; Lambert, Hogan, & Tucker, 2009). Research links this stress to physical illness, job dissatisfaction, and job turnover among correctional officers. What happens on the job, stress, and level of job satisfaction also spill over to influence general satisfaction with life. Research indicates that correctional officers who report being less satisfied at work are also likely to report lower levels of satisfaction with their lives in general (Lambert et al., 2010). Although they may be able to leave the institution at the end of their shifts, most correctional officers, over the span of their careers, will spend more time in prison or jail than will the inmates. They too suffer several pains of imprisonment.

Research shows that concerns about safety and career development are important sources of stress for correctional officers (Triplett, Mullings, & Scarborough, 1996). Much of the current research focuses on what many commentators have termed **role stress**. For example, an early survey of correctional officers in New Jersey (Cheek & Miller, 1983) identified 21 items that the officers thought were the most stressful aspects of the job. The most important of these fell into the categories of organizational or administrative problems. The officers reported being most troubled by a lack of clear job description, absence of support from superiors, and not being able to exercise personal judgment. Cheek and Miller (1983:19) concluded:

The officer gets no respect from anyone. Not from the outside community, which sees him as the brute portrayed in the old James Cagney movies, not from the inmates who use him as a dumping ground for their hostility, not from prison administrators who expect him to play the tin soldier.... A stressful job indeed!

Recent research has confirmed the existence of role stress. It appears that role stress can be alleviated by creating a work environment that clarifies the roles and responsibilities of the officers, provides the officers an input into decision making, and gives officers greater control over their jobs (Dowden & Tellier, 2004; Garland, Hogan, & Lambert, 2013; Lambert et al., 2009). Finally, research shows that officers who believe the prison administration treats them fairly are less likely to experience stress or leave the job (Lambert, Hogan, & Griffin, 2007; Taxman & Gordon, 2009).

Starting pay for correctional officers is generally low, and there is little hope for advancement to managerial positions (Fogel, 1979:95–96). Requirements for officers are also minimal and turnover in the custodial ranks is high. By virtue of the low entrance criteria, relatively low pay, and low status associated with their job, custodial officers suffer many of the same kinds of deprivations as do inmates (Pollock, 2004).

Although more than 60% of the prison staff hold correctional officer positions, the role of correctional officer had often been ignored. Investigations of the correctional officer's role have identified the importance of the officer to the operation of the prison (Jacobs & Crotty, 1978; Lombardo, 1989). Guards have the greatest contact with prison inmates and are most directly responsible for the smooth operation of the prison (Johnson, 2001; Pollock, 2004). Correctional officers have been shown to engage in many types of misconduct, which can serve to undermine the safety and operation of the prison (see Box 10.3).

As with any occupational group, it is difficult to generalize about guards, because they differ widely among themselves in terms of how they perceive and perform their jobs. However, some research has examined the effect of diversity among correctional officers. Traditionally, women have faced obstacles when working in a correctional facility. Among these obstacles was the idea that women could not respond reliably to violent situations or that they were not able to handle the mental stress of working in a prison (Jurik, 1985). To an extent, these perceptions still exist today. Although women make up approximately one-third of correctional personnel, only 25% of correctional officers with direct contact with inmates were women (Stephan, 2008). The research on the effects of diversity in the correctional officer field undermines these perceptions. For example, Jackson and Ammen (1996) investigated changes in the composition of the correctional officer force resulting from affirmative action regulations in Texas. They concluded that the recruitment of females and individuals from minority groups resulted in a wider range of officer perceptions of inmates and prison treatment. Camp, Saylor, and Wright (2001) found that diversity in the prison workforce was associated with lower job commitment among white, male officers, but did not seem to affect teamwork and job performance. Further, Tewksbury and Collins (2006) found that women respond similarly to instances of inmate challenges and misbehavior. Finally, Griffin (2006) reported no significant difference in the levels of stress experienced between male and female

---

BOX 10.3 TYPES OF CORRECTIONAL OFFICER DEVIANCE

Deviance against the Institution
Improper use of agency equipment
Purposely failing to perform one's duties
Theft of correctional facility property
Abuse of sick time
Accepting gifts from inmates and contractors

Deviance against Inmates
Abuse of authority
Mishandling/theft of inmate property
Discrimination toward inmates
Violence/excessive force
Sexual relations with or assault of inmates

Deviance against Other Correctional Officers
Drinking on the job
General boundary violations (minimize professional distance between correctional staff and prisoners)
Discrimination
Sexual harassment of fellow correctional officer
Smuggling contraband

Source: Ross (2013)

---

correctional officers. However, she also found that female officers report greater concerns regarding safety and perceptions of organizational support for equitable treatment of employees.

Toch and Klofas (1982) reported that perhaps one-fourth of all custodial officers fit the Hollywood image of the brutal, uncaring guard. They called this type of officer the "**smug hack**." However, this estimate means that 75% of the custodial force does not fit the stereotype. Johnson (2001) suggested that most guards are not "hacks," but play an important role in providing services to inmates. The guards do this, Johnson argued, at least partly in response to their need to make the job more challenging and important than either the public or the prison administration believes it to be.

Many officers, however, try to solve the problem of alienation by expanding their roles and making them more substantial and rewarding. These officers discover that in the process of helping inmates, and thereby giving them more autonomy, security, and emotional support, the officers gain the same benefits: more control over their environment, more security in their daily interactions with prisoners, and a sense of community—however, inchoate or ill defined—with at least some of the people under their care. In other words, in solving inmate adjustment problems, staff solve their own problems as well. Hassine (1996:117–118) commented on the symbiotic relationship between guards and inmates:

> [A]n unwritten agreement has been established between inmates and guards: inmates get what they want by being friendly and nonaggressive, while guards ensure their own safety by not strictly enforcing the rules. For the most part, inmates manipulate the guards' desire for safety, and guards exploit the inmates' need for autonomy.

Prison custodial officers then, like inmates and like police in the community, reflect the nature of their positions within the justice system. Traditionally, correctional officers are less supportive of treatment efforts than any other group in the prison (Young, Antonio, & Wingeard, 2009). In a classic experiment on the effects of incarceration, Zimbardo (1972) concluded that incarceration profoundly affected both the inmates and the guards. He concluded that the social situation (role definitions of guard or prisoner, presence or absence of power, etc.) determines how people will act. Riley (2000) explored the influence of social setting on guard behavior. He found that correctional officers developed "sense-making" tactics whereby they could define inmates as different, and less than human, thus justifying their exercise of control. Hemmens and Marquart (2000) reported a study of prisoners that indicated that inmates tended to report lower levels of satisfaction with correctional officers. Marquart (2005) suggested that relationships between inmates and officers are generally cooperative as both groups attempted to maintain order in the institution. Whether because of administrative rules, a lack of training, or some other reason, prison officers have a limited range of actions open to them. As part-time prison inmates, correctional officers also face deprivations of liberty, autonomy, and security. What these officers seem to want is not just more respect or support from the public and superiors, but more options. That is, officers seem to believe they will achieve greater security in the prison if they are granted the liberty to perform their jobs in a more autonomous fashion (Hepburn, 1987).

INCARCERATION IN THE CRIMINAL JUSTICE SYSTEM

For years, the operations of penal facilities were not open to public or court scrutiny. Rather, the prisons and jails were assumed to require no supervision by outsiders, and indeed, it was believed that outside interference would be more harmful than beneficial. In the 1970s, however, this condition changed with the emergence of prisoners' rights.

Fogel (1979) suggested that our perceptions of prison inmates have traveled along a continuum, from the earliest days when the offender was seen as a pariah, through periods of viewing the offender as penitent, prisoner, and patient, to the current view of the prisoner as a peer. This shift to seeing prisoners as peers has been costly to the status of correctional authorities, because they must now deal with inmates as individuals who retain certain rights. The unreviewed, nearly total power over inmates that traditionally rested with correctional authorities is now subject to judicial review upon the filing of lawsuits by the inmates themselves. In the 1941 case of *Ex parte Hull*, the U.S. Supreme Court ruled that inmates had the right to access the courts. Initially, this right of access was more theoretical than practical. For years, appellate courts adopted a **"hands-off" doctrine**, refusing to consider prisoner petitions and keeping the court's hands off correctional institutions when deciding cases concerning the rights of inmates (Vito & Kaci, 1982). In a series of appellate court decisions, though, courts identified the rights of inmates and placed due process controls on the exercise of discretion by prison authorities.

In 1964, the U.S. Supreme Court decided the case of *Cooper v. Pate*, ruling that prisoners in state and federal institutions were protected from arbitrary and capricious violations of their civil rights. Prison inmates were entitled to the protections of the Civil Rights Act of 1871. In deciding the case, the Court provided a vehicle by which inmates could challenge conditions of confinement in the nation's courts. A later decision, *Johnson v. Avery* (1969), further strengthened the position of inmates. In this case, the Court ruled that prison authorities must either allow inmates the use of **jailhouse lawyers** (inmates who assist others in the preparation of court documents) or provide an adequate alternative. In combination, these two rulings meant that inmates were not only entitled to certain rights but also that the state must provide them with the necessary resources to secure those rights in court. As Cohen (1972:862) noted, "To hold, for example, that a prisoner must be guaranteed reasonable access to the courts, that he must suffer no reprisals for his efforts, and that there is a right to some form of assistance, recognizes the prisoner as a jural entity."

Wallace (1992) observed that commentators often rely on the decision of the Virginia Supreme Court in *Ruffin v. Virginia* (1871) as support for the hands-off approach of the courts to prisoners' rights. In this decision, the court wrote that the prisoner was a "slave of the state," and thus had no protected rights. Wallace observed that indeed there has been a tradition of judicial oversight of prisons and concern with prisoners' issues. The problem for prisoners, however, was that courts were reluctant to intervene directly, except in the most extreme cases, and inmates were often unable to get the attention of either the courts or the public. Abandonment of a general hands-off attitude made court oversight of prisons more likely.

With access to the courts thereby ensured, the next stage in the development of prisoners' rights began. It was now time for prisoners to seek protections from the more onerous conditions of confinement. In a flurry of litigation, this is precisely what happened. The more important developments in prisoners' rights occurred in three areas, relating to the protections of the First, Eighth, and Fourteenth Amendments.

In deciding questions of prisoners' rights, the courts generally have applied three tests to the reasonableness of prison conditions and regulations: (1) compelling state interest, (2) least restrictive alternative, and (3) clear and present danger. A **compelling state interest** is any concern of the state (prison administration) that is so important that it overrides the protections afforded in the Constitution. Such an interest, for example, would be evident if an inmate were to request the right to go on a pilgrimage for religious reasons; the state interest in custody is compelling and justifies the denial of the right to go on a pilgrimage. The **least restrictive alternative** refers to the desire to be no more oppressive than is necessary to meet the needs of the state. For example, a rule punishing an inmate for possession of lewd photographs would probably be too restrictive, given that a rule prohibiting display of the material would meet the state's interests in not arousing other inmates. Finally, **clear and present danger** refers to conditions or behaviors that pose an immediate threat to safety or order and relates to controls on the activities of inmates that pose a direct threat to the smooth operation of the facility. For example, courts will uphold rules prohibiting inmates from assembling and making inflammatory speeches, because such activities pose a clear and present danger of instigating riots.

PRISONERS' RIGHTS
First Amendment Protections

The First Amendment to the U.S. Constitution provides for the freedoms of religion, speech, the press, and assembly, as well as the right to petition the government for redress of grievances. Some of the more noteworthy prisoners' cases focused on the question of freedom of religion, although other First Amendment issues also emerged. The examples above illustrate some of the kinds of issues that have been decided in the courts. The U.S. Supreme Court upheld restrictions on the right of inmates to correspond or communicate with other prisoners, but struck down rules that prevented prisoners from marriage [*Turner v. Safley*, 482 U.S. 78 (1987)]. These issues relate to the First Amendment right to freedom of assembly.

The major decisions regarding freedom of religion dealt with the emergence and spread of Islam in the prisons. Black Muslims in prisons were initially (and perhaps are to this day) viewed with suspicion by prison administrators. The Muslims were seen more as a political group than as a religious sect. Correctional personnel saw requests for special diets, spiritual mentors (chaplains), access to the Koran, and the like as challenges to prison authority rather than as attempts to practice a religion. The Muslims were required to litigate almost every issue involved in the practice of their religion in prison.

Similar litigation was required to clarify other First Amendment issues, such as access to the media, censorship of mail, visitation rights, formation of prisoners' unions, and other activities. Employing the three reasonableness tests described above, the courts have decided hundreds of cases dealing with First Amendment rights of prisoners.

Eighth Amendment Protections

The Eighth Amendment to the U.S. Constitution prohibits cruel and unusual punishments. Prisoners sued under this amendment to protest perceived deficiencies in nearly every aspect of prison life, from food to medical treatment. With the recent surge in prison populations, these suits have become more controversial as inmates seek relief from overcrowded prisons and overburdened prison resources. In *Rhodes v. Chapman* (1981), the U.S. Supreme Court ruled that crowding (housing two inmates in cells designed for one) by itself does not constitute cruel and unusual punishment. However, in *Brown v. Plata* (2011), the Court required the California Department of Corrections to reduce its prison population by 137.5% to alleviate serious overcrowding issues. The Court determined that California could not provide adequate medical care to inmates owing to the excessive overcrowding problem within its prison system.

Eighth Amendment suits have been responsible for the cessation of corporal punishment and a general improvement in prison conditions. There is evidence, however, that the courts are reluctant to interfere in the operation of prisons. An important case in prison conditions was *Holt v. Sarver* (1970), the basis for the movie *Brubaker*. In this case, inmates in Arkansas protested a wide range of prison conditions, from poor sanitary facilities to the use of inmate trustees (including allegations of inadequate medical care, food, sleeping quarters, and almost everything else). The Court found that many of the specific allegations did not constitute cruel and unusual punishment, but when it considered the claims together (the totality of the circumstances), the Court decided that conditions at the prison combined to make life there cruel and unusual. Later cases similar to this have led to the appointment of "masters," who are charged by the Court with the responsibility of bringing a prison, or even an entire prison system, into compliance with the Constitution.

Fourteenth Amendment Protections

The third major area of development in prisoners' rights lies within the purview of the Fourteenth Amendment, which provides that no state may deprive any citizen of life, liberty, or property without due process of law. This amendment also ensures that the federal courts can apply the requirements of the U.S. Constitution to the states.

The U.S. Supreme Court decided what might be the most important due process case in the area of prisoners' rights in 1974. In *Wolff v. McDonnell*, the Court determined what due process rights applied to prison disciplinary hearings. Prior to this decision, prisoners often faced a presumption of guilt and were granted no constitutional protections in disciplinary hearings. The *Wolff* decision required that correctional authorities provide the following to any prisoner charged with a rules violation: (1) written notice of the charges, (2) a hearing within 72 hours of notice, (3) warnings of possible criminal proceedings that could result from the hearing, (4) a written statement of the findings and evidence, and (5) the right to appeal within 5 days.

The impact of these rights on the daily lives of prisoners is unclear. Although prisons are still not country clubs by any stretch of the imagination, one effect of the prisoners' rights movement has been to make prisons less oppressive than they had been. Even though the pains of imprisonment still do exist, inmates today have somewhat more freedom and autonomy within the institution than did inmates at the time Sykes identified the five deprivations associated with prison life. Yet, correctional officials have ways to circumvent the requirements of court rulings such as the procedural protections afforded in *Wolff* (Thomas, Mika, Blakemore, & Aylward, 1991). Further, a number of court decisions have limited the ability of inmates to bring suits alleging violations of their rights. Alexander (1993:115) contended that the courts have "slammed the door" on inmates: "Whether in personal liability, habeas corpus, or rights emanating from the amendments to the U.S. Constitution, the Supreme Court of the 1980s and early 1990s has made it much more difficult for inmates to prevail."

Legal Issues in Incarceration

Courts have decided most of the major issues in prisoners' rights. A number of issues remain, however, that continue to bring prisoners' rights cases to the courts. Stephan and Walsh (2011) reported that approximately 7% of jails in the United States were under court order to reduce the inmate population, and about 6% were under court order for specific conditions. These specific conditions include issues regarding medical facilities, exercise, food service, religious practices, and other issues. Recent efforts to make imprisonment more painful have focused on restricting recreational opportunities for inmates. These efforts include calls for the removal of weight-lifting equipment, television, and similar "frills." The right of inmates to recreational time and pursuits has been established, but the definition of what kinds of activities are protected has not been resolved (Lee, 1996). Increasingly, issues associated with the concept of prisoners' rights are being litigated as civil liability cases. Perhaps the prisoners' rights movement has overcome restrictions on the use of criminal law appeals by entering the civil courts (Vaughn, 1996).

Table 10.4 provides a table of selected court cases on prisoners' rights.

DUE PROCESS, CRIME CONTROL, AND INCARCERATION

The issue of prisoners' rights demonstrates the conflict between due process and crime control in the incarceration process. Even after conviction of a felony offense and a sentence to prison, individuals retain rights and interests protected by our laws. Before the government can restrict the liberty of individuals (even incarcerated individuals), it must justify its decisions. Requirements for tests of state interest and the least drastic alternative represent limits on the authority of prison and jail staff. Viewing these concerns within a framework of the totality of circumstances, however, allows courts to consider the operational and crime control effects.

Table 10.4 Selected Court Cases on Prisoners' Rights	
Ruffin v. Virginia, 62 VA 790 (1871)	Declared prison inmates to be "slaves of the state" while imprisoned
Cooper v. Pate, 378 U.S. 546 (1964)	Granted inmates protection from arbitrary and capricious violations of civil rights
Ex parte Hull, 312 U.S. 546 (1941)	Granted prison inmates the right of access to the courts
Johnson v. Avery, 393 U.S. 483 (1969)	Required prison administrators to provide legal assistance to inmates
Holt v. Sarver, 309 F. Supp. 362 (1970)	Used "totality of circumstances" test to determine that conditions which shocked the conscience of the court violated the Eighth Amendment
Wolff v. McDonnell, 418 U.S. 539 (1974)	Specified due process protections for inmates facing disciplinary charges
Rhodes v. Chapman, 452 U.S. 337 (1981)	Declared that prison crowding, by itself, does not violate the ban on cruel and unusual punishment
Porter v. Nussle, 534 U.S. 516 (2002)	Held that the exhaustion requirement of the Prison Litigation Reform Act (PLRA) of 1995 applies to all inmate suits about prison life, regardless of whether they involve systemic conditions or isolated acts of wrongdoing

After conviction, and certainly after incarceration, the balance between due process and crime control concerns shifts to some degree. Alexander's (1993) observation that the federal courts are slamming the door on inmates is partly a reaction to this shift in balance. The courts are attempting to limit the disruption of crime control and operational efforts of correctional administrators by defining causes of action more narrowly. The U.S. Congress passed the **Prison Litigation Reform Act** of 1995 (PLRA), a law requiring inmates to exhaust all administrative remedies (appeals through the prison administration and department of corrections) before they could file a suit in federal court. In 2002, the U.S. Supreme Court decided *Porter v. Nussle*, ruling that the requirement of exhausting all administrative remedies was mandatory, no matter what the basis of the inmate's appeal, including allegations of excessive force.

This narrowing of definition, compared to the heyday of prisoners' rights, seems to be a victory for crime control supporters over those concerned with due process. In all likelihood, it is a natural attempt by the justice system to achieve equilibrium between these conflicting concerns. One thing that has not changed is the right of inmates to protection from unreasonable or malicious interventions by correctional staff. The creation of a prisoners' rights movement settled the question of the existence of due process protections for inmates. What remains is to determine how we can balance those protections against the crime control concerns of society.

REVIEW QUESTIONS

1. Why can we consider incarceration to be the cornerstone of American corrections?
2. Briefly relate the history of American prisons and jails. Distinguish between the Auburn and Pennsylvania systems of incarceration.
3. With reference to organizational and legal differences, distinguish between prisons and jails.
4. Identify the pains of imprisonment.
5. Who are the other inmates?
6. What is the hands-off doctrine.
7. What are the basic tests the courts use to assess prisoners' rights claims?
8. Identify three areas in which courts recognized prisoners' rights.

References

Abbott, J. H. (1981). *In the belly of the beast: Letters from prison*. New York: Vintage.

Alexander, R. (1993). Slamming the federal courthouse door on inmates. *Journal of Criminal Justice, 21*(2), 103–116.

American Correctional Association (1983). *The American prison: From the beginning ... A pictorial history*. College Park, MD: Author (pp. 39, 48).

Applegate, B., Cullen, F., & Fisher, B. (2002). Public views toward crime and correctional policies: Is there a gender gap? *Journal of Criminal Justice, 30*(2), 89–100.

Batchelder, J. S., & Pippert, J. M. (2002). Hard time or idle time: Factors affecting inmate choices between participation in prison work and education programs. *The Prison Journal, 82*(2), 269–280.

Bikle, B. (2000). *Direct supervision jails: What have we learned?* Paper presented at the annual meeting of Midwestern Criminal Justice Association, October 2000.

Braly, M. (1976). *False starts: A memoir of San Quentin and other prisons*. New York: Penguin Books.

Bureau of Justice Statistics (1985). *Jail inmates, 1983*. Washington, DC: U.S. Department of Justice.

Bureau of Justice Statistics (1987). *Prisoners in 1986*. Washington, DC: U.S. Department of Justice.

Camp, S., Saylor, W., & Wright, K. (2001). Racial diversity of correctional workers and inmates: Organizational commitment, teamwork, and worker's efficacy in prisons. *Justice Quarterly, 18*(2), 411–427.

Carson, E. A., & Golinelli, D. (2013a). *Prisoners in 2012—Advance counts*. Washington, DC: Bureau of Justice Statistics.

Carson, E. A., & Golinelli, D. (2013b). *Prisoners in 2012—Trends in admissions and releases, 1991–2012*. Washington, DC: Bureau of Justice Statistics.

Carson, E. A., & Sabol, W. (2012). *Prisoners in 2011*. Washington, DC: Bureau of Justice Statistics.

Cheek, F. E., & Miller, M. D. (1983). The experience of stress for correction officers: A double-bind theory of correctional stress. *Journal of Criminal Justice, 11*(2), 105–120.

Clear, T. R. (1994). *Harm in American penology: Offenders, victims, and their communities*. Albany, NY: SUNY Press.

Clear, T. R. (1997). Ten unintended consequences of the growth in imprisonment. *Corrections Management Quarterly, 1*(2), 25–31.

Clear, T. R., & Cole, G. F. (1986). *American corrections*. Monterey, CA: Brooks/Cole.

Cohen, F. (1972). The discovery of prison reform. *Buffalo Law Review, 21*(3), 855–887.

Connolly, P. K. (1975). The possibility of a prison sentence is a necessity. *Crime & Delinquency, 21*(4), 356–359.

Cook, P. (2009). Explaining the imprisonment epidemic. *Criminology & Public Policy, 8*(1), 25–28.

Cullen, F. (1995). Assessing the penal harm movement. *Journal of Research in Crime and Delinquency, 32*(2), 338–358.

Dowden, C., & Tellier, C. (2004). Predicting work-related stress in correctional officers: A meta-analysis. *Journal of Criminal Justice, 32*(1), 49–62.

Durham, A. (1989). Judgments of appropriate punishment: The effects of question type. *Journal of Criminal Justice, 17*(2), 75–86.

Durham, A. (1990). Social control and imprisonment during the American revolution: Newgate of Connecticut. *Justice Quarterly, 7*(2), 293–323.

Eastern State Penitentiary (2010). *Timeline.* Retrieved July 26, 2010, from http://easternstate.org/history.

Feeley, M., & Simon, J. (1992). The new penology: Notes on the emerging strategy of corrections and its implications. *Criminology, 30*(3), 449–474.

Fishman, J. F. (1923). *Crucibles of crime: The shocking story of the American jail.* Montclair, NJ: Patterson Smith, 1969.

Fogel, D. F. (1979). *We are the living proof … The justice model for corrections.* Cincinnati, OH: Anderson.

Foucault, M. (1979). *Discipline and punish: The birth of the prison.* New York: Vintage Books.

Garland, B., Hogan, N., & Lambert, E. (2013). Antecedents of role stress among correctional staff: A replication and expansion. *Criminal Justice Policy Review, 24*(5), 527–550.

Garland, D. (1990). *Punishment and modern society.* Chicago: University of Chicago Press.

Glaze, L., & Herberman, E. (2013). *Correctional populations in the United States, 2012.* Washington, DC: Bureau of Justice Statistics.

Goffman, E. (1961). *Asylums: Essays on the social situations of mental patients and other inmates.* Chicago: Aldine.

Goldfarb, R. (1975). *Jails: The ultimate ghetto.* New York: Anchor-Doubleday.

Greenfeld, L. (1992). *Prisons and prisoners in the United States.* Washington, DC: U.S. Department of Justice.

Griffin, M. (2006). Gender and stress: A comparative assessment of sources of stress among correctional officers. *Journal of Contemporary Criminal Justice, 22,* 4–25.

Harlow, C. (2003). *Education and correctional populations.* Washington, DC: Bureau of Justice Statistics.

Hassine, V. (1996). *Life without parole: Living in prison today.* Los Angeles: Roxbury.

Hemmens, C., & Marquart, J. (2000). Friend or foe? Race, age, and inmate perceptions of inmate-staff relations. *Journal of Criminal Justice, 28*(4), 297–312.

Hepburn, J. (1987). The prison control structure and its effects on work attitudes: The perceptions and attitudes of prison guards. *Journal of Criminal Justice, 15*(1), 49–64.

Hochstetler, A., & DeLisi, M. (2005). Importation, deprivation, and varieties of serving time: An integrated-lifestyle-exposure model of prison offending. *Journal of Criminal Justice, 33*(3), 257–266.

Holcomb, J., & Williams, M. (2003). From the field: "Bad Time": The rise and fall of penal policy in Ohio. *Journal of Crime and Justice, 26*(2), 153–175.

Jackson, J., & Ammen, S. (1996). Race and correctional officers' punitive attitudes toward treatment programs for inmates. *Journal of Criminal Justice, 24*(2), 153–166.

Jacobs, J., & Crotty, N. (1978). *Guard unions and the future of prisons.* Ithaca, NY: New York State School of Industrial and Labor Relations.

James, D. (2004). *Profile of jail inmates 2002.* Washington, DC: Bureau of Justice Statistics.

Johnson, R. (2001). *Hard time: Understanding and reforming the prison (3rd ed.)*. Monterey, CA: Brooks/Cole.

Jurik, N. (1985). An officer and a lady: Organizational barriers to women working as correctional officers in men's prisons. *Social Problems, 32*(4), 375–388.

Karberg, J., & James, D. (2005). *Substance dependence, abuse, and treatment of jail inmates, 2002*. Washington, DC: Bureau of Justice Statistics.

Katsampes, P., & Neil, T. C. (1981). A decade of improvement for our sick jails. *Federal Probation, 45*(3), 45–48.

Keve, P. W. (1986). *The history of corrections in Virginia*. Charlottesville: University Press of Virginia.

Kolstad, A. (1996). Imprisonment as rehabilitation: Offenders' assessment of why it doesn't work. *Journal of Criminal Justice, 24*(4), 323–335.

Kyckelhahn, T. (2012). *State corrections expenditures, fy: 1982–2010*. Washington, DC: Bureau of Justice Statistics.

Lambert, E. (2003). The impact of organizational justice on correctional staff. *Journal of Criminal Justice, 31*(2), 155–168.

Lambert, E., Hogan, N., & Griffin, M. (2007). The impact of distributive and procedural justice on correctional staff job stress, job satisfaction, and organizational commitment. *Journal of Criminal Justice, 35*(6), 644–656.

Lambert, E., Hogan, N., Jiang, S., Elechi, O., Benjamin, B., Morris, A., et al. (2010). The relationship among distributive and procedural justice and correctional life satisfaction, burnout, and turnover intent: An exploratory study. *Journal of Criminal Justice, 38*(1), 7–16.

Lambert, E., Hogan, N., & Tucker, K. (2009). Problems at work: Exploring the correlates of role stress among correctional staff. *The Prison Journal, 89*(4), 460–481.

Langbein, J. H. (1976). The historical origins of the sanction of imprisonment for serious crime. *Journal of Legal Studies, 5*(1), 35–60.

Lee, R. (1996). Prisoners' rights to recreation: Quantity, quality, and other aspects. *Journal of Criminal Justice, 24*(2), 167–178.

Listwan, S., Jonson, C., Cullen, F., & Latessa, E. (2008). Cracks in the penal harm movement: Evidence from the field. *Criminology & Public Policy, 7*(3), 423–466.

Lockwood, D. (1982). The contribution of sexual harassment to stress and coping in confinement. In N. Parisi (Ed.), *Coping with imprisonment* (pp. 45–64). Beverly Hills, CA: Sage.

Logan, C., & Gaes, G. (1993). Meta-analysis and the rehabilitation of punishment. *Justice Quarterly, 10*(2), 245–262.

Lombardo, L. X. (1989). *Guards imprisoned (2nd ed.)*. Cincinnati, OH: Anderson.

Lutze, F., & Murphy, D. (1999). Ultramasculine prison environments and inmates' adjustment: It's time to move beyond the "boys will be boys" paradigm. *Justice Quarterly, 16*(4), 709–733.

Marquart, J. (2005). Understanding the power of social contexts on criminal justice institutions. *Journal of Criminal Justice Education, 16*(2), 213–225.

Maruschak, L. (2006). *Medical problems of jail inmates*. Washington, DC: Bureau of Justice Statistics.

McDonald, J. (1999). Violence and drug use in juvenile institutions. *Journal of Criminal Justice, 27*(1), 33–44.

McGee, R. (1971). Our sick jails. *Federal Probation, 35*(1), 3–8.

Minton, T. (2013). *Jail inmates at midyear 2012—Statistical tables*. Washington, DC: Bureau of Justice Statistics.

Moynahan, J. M., & Steward, E. (1980). *The American jail*. Chicago: Nelson-Hall.

Mumola, C., & Beck, A. (1997). *Prisoners in 1996*. Washington, DC: Bureau of Justice Statistics.

Nacci, P. L., & Kane, T. R. (1984). Sex and sexual aggression in federal prisons: Inmate involvement and employee impact. *Federal Probation, 48*(1), 46–53.

National Advisory Commission on Criminal Justice Standards and Goals (1973). *Corrections.* Washington, DC: U.S. Government Printing Office.

Newman, G. R. (1983). *Just and painful.* New York: Macmillan.

O'Leary, V., & Duffee, D. (1971). Correctional policy: A classification of goals designed for change. *Crime & Delinquency, 17*(4), 373–386.

Pastore, A., & Maguire, K. (Eds.) (2010). *Sourcebook of criminal justice statistics.* (Table 6.28) [online]. Retrieved July 25, 2010, from http://www.albany.edu/sourcebook.

Paterline, B., & Petersen, D. (1999). Structural and social psychological determinants of prisonization. *Journal of Criminal Justice, 27*(5), 427–441.

Pollock, J. (2004). *Prisons and prison life.* Los Angeles, CA: Roxbury.

Reasons, C. E., & Kaplan, R. L. (1975). Tear down the walls? Some functions of prisons. *Crime & Delinquency, 21*(4), 360–372.

Reisig, M., & Lovrich, N. (1998). Job attitudes among higher-custody state prison management personnel: A cross-sectional comparative assessment. *Journal of Criminal Justice, 26*(3), 213–226.

Rhine, E. (1992). Sentencing reform and correctional policy: Some unanswered questions. In C. Hartjen & E. Rhine (Eds.), *Correctional theory and practice* (pp. 271–287). Chicago: Nelson-Hall.

Riley, J. (2000). Sensemaking in prison: Inmate identity as a working understanding. *Justice Quarterly, 17*(2), 359–376.

Ross, J. (2013). Deconstructing correctional officer deviance: Toward typologies of actions and controls. *Criminal Justice Review, 38,* 110–126.

Rothman, D. (1971). *The discovery of the asylum.* Boston: Little, Brown & Company.

Rothman, D. (1980). *Conscience and convenience: The asylum and its alternatives in progressive America.* Boston: Little, Brown.

Ruddell, R., & Mays, G. (2007). Rural jails: Problematic inmates, overcrowded cells, and cash-strapped counties. *Journal of Criminal Justice, 35*(3), 251–260.

Rutherford, A. (1993). *Criminal justice and the pursuit of decency.* Oxford, UK: Oxford University Press.

Sabol, W., Minton, T., & Harrison, P. (2007). *Prison and jail inmates at midyear 2006.* Washington, DC: Bureau of Justice Statistics.

Schriro, D. (2000). *Correcting corrections: Missouri's parallel universe.* Washington, DC: National Institute of Justice.

Schwartz, M., & Travis, L. (1996). *Corrections: An issues approach* (4th ed.). Cincinnati, OH: Anderson.

Seiter, R. (1997). A view from the inside: Setting correctional policies. *Corrections Management Quarterly, 1*(2), 81–83.

Senese, J. (1997). Evaluating jail reform: A comparative analysis of podular/direct and linear jail inmate infractions. *Journal of Criminal Justice, 25*(1), 61–73.

Skoler, D. L. (1978). *Governmental structuring of criminal justice services: Organizing the non-system.* Washington, DC: U.S. Government Printing Office.

Snell, T. (1993). *Correctional populations in the United States, 1991.* Washington, DC: Bureau of Justice Statistics.

Spalding, W. F. (1897). Indeterminate sentences. In *Proceedings of the National Conference of Charities and Correction at the 24th annual session.* Toronto, Canada: July (pp. 7–14, 46–51).

Stephan, J. (2001). *Census of jails, 1999.* Washington, DC: Bureau of Justice Statistics.

Stephan, J. (2008). *Census of state and federal correctional facilities, 2005.* Washington, DC: Bureau of Justice Statistics.

Stephan, J., & Karberg, J. (2003). *Census of state and federal correctional facilities, 2000*. Washington, DC: Bureau of Justice Statistics.

Stephan, J., & Walsh, G. (2011). *Census of jail facilities, 2006*. Washington, DC: Bureau of Justice Statistics.

Sullivan, R. (1996). The birth of the prison: Discipline or punish? *Journal of Criminal Justice, 24*(5), 449–458.

Sykes, G. M. (1969). *The society of captives*. Princeton, NJ: Princeton University Press.

Taxman, F., & Gordon, J. (2009). Do fairness and equity matter?: An examination of organizational justice among correctional officers in adult prisons. *Criminal Justice and Behavior, 36*(7), 695–711.

Tewksbury, R., & Collins, S. C. (2006). Aggression levels among correctional officers: Reassessing sex differences. *The Prison Journal, 86*(3), 327–343.

Tewksbury, R., & DeMichele, M. (2003). The good, the bad, and the (sometimes) ugly truths: American penal goals and perspectives. *American Journal of Criminal Justice, 28*(1), 1–14.

Thomas, J., Mika, H., Blakemore, J., & Aylward, A. (1991). Exacting control through disciplinary hearings: "Making do" with prison rules. *Justice Quarterly, 8*(1), 37–57.

Toch, H., & Klofas, J. (1982). Alienation and desire for job enrichment among correctional officers. *Federal Probation, 36*, 35–47.

Torok, L. (1974). *Straight talk from prison: A convict reflects on youth, crime and society*. New York: Human Sciences Press.

Triplett, R., Mullings, J., & Scarborough, K. (1996). Work-related stress and coping among correctional officers: Implications from organizational literature. *Journal of Criminal Justice, 24*(4), 291–308.

Twentieth Century Fund (1976). *Fair and certain punishment*. New York: McGraw-Hill.

Vaughn, M. (1996). Prison civil liability for inmate-against-inmate assault and breakdown/disorganization theory. *Journal of Criminal Justice, 24*(2), 139–152.

Vito, G. F., & Kaci, J. H. (1982). Hands on or hands off? The use of judicial intervention to establish prisoners' rights. In N. Parisi (Ed.), *Coping with imprisonment* (pp. 79–100). Beverly Hills, CA: Sage.

Wallace, D. (1992). *Ruffin v. Virginia* and slaves of the state: A nonexistent baseline of prisoner's rights jurisprudence. *Journal of Criminal Justice, 20*(4), 333–342.

West, H. (2010). *Prison inmates at midyear 2009—Statistical tables*. Washington, DC: Bureau of Justice Statistics.

Wright, E. O. (Ed.) (1973). *The politics of punishment: A critical analysis of prisons in America*. New York: Harper Torchbooks.

Wright, K. (2000). The evolution of decision making among prison executives, 1975–2000. In J. Horney (Ed.), *Policies, processes, and decisions of the criminal justice system* (pp. 177–224). Washington, DC: National Institute of Justice.

Young, K., Antonio, M., & Wingeard, L. (2009). How staff attitude and support for inmate and rehabilitation differs by job category: An evaluation of findings from Pennsylvania's Department of Corrections' employee training curriculum "Reinforcing Positive Behavior." *Journal of Criminal Justice, 37*(5), 435–441.

Zaitzow, B. (1999). Doing time: A case study of a North Carolina youth institution. *Journal of Crime and Justice, 22*(2), 91–124.

Zimbardo, P. G. (1972). The pathology of imprisonment. *Society, 9*(6), 4–8.

Zupan, L. (1991). *Jails: Reform and the new generation philosophy*. Cincinnati, OH: Anderson.

Zupan, L., & Menke, B. (1988). Implementing organizational change: From traditional to new generational jail operations. *Policy Studies Review, 7*, 614–625.

Important Cases

Brown v. Plata, 131 S. Ct. 1910 (2011).

Cooper v. Pate, 378 U.S. 546 (1964).

Ex parte Hull, 312 U.S. 546 (1941).

Holt v. Sarver, 309 F. Supp. 362 (1970).

Johnson v. Avery, 393 U.S. 483 (1969).

Porter v. Nussle, 534 U.S. 512 (2002).

Rhodes v. Chapman, 452 U.S. 337 (1981).

Ruffin v. Virginia, 62 Va. 790 (1871).

Turner v. Safley, 482 U.S. 78 (1987).

Wolff v. McDonnell, 418 U.S. 539 (1974).

CHAPTER 11

Problems and Issues in Incarceration

351

The development of prisoners' rights is a core issue in the use of incarceration as a sanction for criminal offenders. Like other areas of the justice system, the incarceration of offenders is a practice surrounded by controversy. Indeed, the concept of incarceration—especially as practiced in the United States—is itself controversial (Webster & Doob, 2008). Critics often note that, among all the nations in Western civilization, the United States has the highest rate of imprisonment and imposes the longest prison terms on offenders (Austin & Irwin, 2001; Doleschal, 1971). Although the recent economic struggles have prompted many states to rely less on incarceration as a criminal punishment, it is unclear whether these changes will have long-lasting impacts (Brown, 2013). Many have questioned the impact of incarceration on reducing crime and helping criminals and described the negative effects of imprisonment (Crutchfield, 2004; DeFina & Hannon, 2013). Still, others defend the use of incarceration. Wright (1994, 1997) provided a strong argument for prisons as both a deterrent and an incapacitative sanction, and Zedlewski (1997) noted that there is a value to prisons meeting society's desire to inflict some vengeance on criminal offenders.

It is clear that the United States incarcerates a large number of individuals, but we do not know enough about whom we incarcerate and how patterns of incarceration change over time. Those incarcerated most often come from the lower classes of society. Jail inmate populations tend to reflect the ethnic composition of our lower and working classes (Stojkovic, Pope, & Feyerherm, 1987). In addition, jail use varies by community (Klofas, 1987). Just as with the police and courts, some of the explanation for incarceration involves community attitudes and values. The early differences found in the treatment of crack cocaine users versus powder cocaine users illustrate this point. Viewing crack cocaine use as a more serious drug offense than powder cocaine use seems to have added to over-representation of minority-group members in the prison population (Barnes & Kingsnorth, 1996).

The war on drugs affected all areas of incarceration in the United States by increasing the numbers of offenders incarcerated, and resulted in disproportionate incarceration of minorities (Snyder, 1990). Lynch and Sabol (2000) argued that the long-term consequences of incarcerating large numbers of young, poor, minority males may be an increase in crime. They suggested that current

Important Terms

classification
consent decrees
contract system
deprivation model
design capacity
importation model
lease system
net-widening
operational
  capacity
piece price
  system
prison industrial
  complex
Prison Industry
  Enhancement
  Certification
  Program
  (PIECP)
Prison Rape
  Elimination Act
privatization
protective custody
public account
  system
public works
  system
rated capacity
state-use system

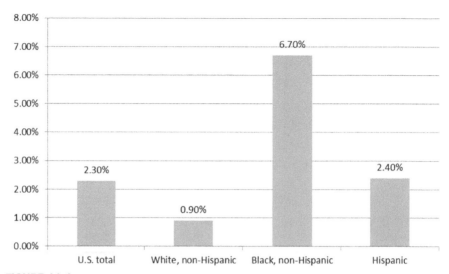

FIGURE 11.1
Percentage of children with a parent in state or federal prison, by race and Hispanic origin.
Source: Glaze and Maruschak (2008)

patterns of incarceration serve to disrupt family and social life in poor, minority neighborhoods, creating conditions that are ripe for crime. Approximately 1.7 million children in the United States have a parent in prison (see Figure 11.1). Liedka, Piehl, and Useem (2006) suggested that the effect of imprisonment on crime is curvilinear. They argued that increasing the rate of imprisonment from low levels probably reduces crime, but eventually the increase reaches a point of diminishing returns at which continuing to increase the rate of incarceration may actually lead to increases in crime. The trick is to discover the optimum level of imprisonment at which we can obtain the greatest reductions in crime.

Reacting to these observations, several commentators have joined long-standing critics of incarceration by suggesting that the most appropriate strategy for the control of criminal offenders is one that reduces reliance on incarceration (Meares, 2004; Nagel, 1973; Piehl, 2004; Rector, 1975). Morris (1974) took a middle-ground approach in suggesting that prisons are necessary and useful in the control of the small percentage of dangerous offenders, but that the United States currently overuses incarceration.

Logan and DiIulio (1992) challenged such assumptions about the rates of incarceration in the United States. They noted that the large number of persons incarcerated in the United States compared to other nations is a function of our higher crime rate. They also observed that whereas some "petty" criminals may go to prison, such offenders tend to get early release. Serious offenders serve longer terms, thus "stacking up" inside prisons. The net result is that most prisoners have committed serious crimes. They also observed that Americans make widespread use of alternatives to incarceration. They concluded that incarceration, if justly imposed, is a positive feature of our law.

Other observers believe that the problem with American prisons is that they are underused. Some suggest that the solution to the crime problem lies in the incarceration of offenders for incapacitative purposes (Greenwood, 1982; Wilson, 1975). The approach taken by these observers mirrors that of Morris in that they view prison as a scarce resource. They suggested that we reserve prison sentences for those criminals who commit the most serious offenses.

Some less discriminating scholars support incarceration for many more offenders. Zedlewski (1987) argued that incarceration of the average offender would save money. He calculated that, on average, it cost $25,000 to incarcerate a felon in prison for 1 year. Basing estimates on a survey of prison inmates, he concluded that the average inmate committed 187 crimes each year, at an average cost of $2,300 each. Thus, according to Zedlewski's model, investing $25,000 to incarcerate an offender would have saved $430,000 in crime costs. The reliability and accuracy of these estimates are questionable, but the model supports a broader use of incarceration.

Fox (1983:299) reported, "The viewpoint taken by the majority of correctional administrators is that prisons are overused and that many people in prison today do not need to be there." Yet, it is also true that abolition of the prison is not likely to occur in the near future. Whether because of its long tradition as a criminal sanction or, as Johnson (2001) suggested, because the urge to incarcerate may be "natural," the continued use of prisons seems assured. Assuming that we will continue to employ incarceration as a sanction for criminal offenses, the issues and controversies surrounding prison and jail operations today are significant. Although the processes are unclear, it seems apparent that the experience of imprisonment has effects on prisoners and staff.

It is difficult to choose the issues on which to focus because so many problems are found in our prisons and jails. The increasing use of imprisonment, along with the lengthening of prison terms imposed, has created a new class of geriatric prisoners. Increasing numbers of elderly offenders are serving time in American prisons, and these inmates pose management and medical problems for prison operation (Maruschak & Beck, 2001; McDonald, Hassol, & Carlson, 1999; Williams, Stern, Mellow, Safer, & Greifinger, 2012). In addition, higher rates of AIDS infection among intravenous drug users have produced a disproportionate number of AIDS-infected inmates, partly because of the war on drugs. The health problems posed by these inmates are another contemporary problem in prisons and jails (Maruschak, 2004).

A renewed focus on prison treatment of offenders to reduce the risk of future criminality has produced a variety of new programs and rekindled interest in traditional programming, such as education (Batiuk, Moke, & Rountree, 1997), work (Saylor & Gaes, 1997), and activities by religious groups (Johnson, Larson, & Pitts, 1997). Increases in the number of drug-involved persons in prisons and jails, and concern about the mental health problems of inmates, have spurred recent interest in drug and mental health treatment programs in correctional facilities (Mumola & Karberg, 2006). Personnel issues, ranging from changes in correctional officer recruitment and selection (Jackson & Ammen, 1996; Lommel, 2004) through staff training (Stohr, Lovrich, & Wood, 1996), as well as officer stress discussed in Chapter 10, have received much attention. Continuing issues, such as the influence of gangs in prisons, the prisoner subculture, the civil liability of prison administrators and systems, and facility design and size (Stohr, Lovrich, Menke, & Zupan, 1994) remain.

In this chapter, we discuss four continuing issues in American incarceration: (1) privatization, (2) crowding, (3) prison industries, and (4) prison violence. Because the history of incarceration has been fraught with problems, it may be safe to say that there are no new issues in American prisons and jails (Schwartz, Travis, & Clear, 1980:212). These problem areas represent continuing issues around incarceration that reveal the structural limitations on the ability of correctional institutions to change—and show the effects of broader social changes on criminal justice system operations.

PRIVATIZATION

For decades, correctional institutions have contracted for services with private corporations, ranging from facility design and construction to the provision of medical care or food service for the inmate population. There has been increasing **privatization**, that is, contracting with a private vendor for the entire operation of a prison or jail (Ericson, McMahon, & Evans, 1987). The private company will typically charge the government a daily rate per inmate that covers the operating costs of the prison in addition to the company's profit. Greenwood (1981) suggested that private enterprise could do a better job of running the nation's prisons, at less cost. In 1985, the delegate assembly of the American Correctional Association (ACA) passed a policy statement that was generally supportive of further privatization (*Criminal Justice Newsletter*, 1985:1–2).

Privatizing the operation of correctional facilities began with several detention facilities operated by private businesses (Krajick, 1984). Most of these institutions dealt with special offender populations, such as illegal aliens or juvenile offenders. What followed was the suggestion that private companies operate general-purpose prisons and jails (Logan, 1987). The effects of private operation are still controversial, but as Table 11.1 illustrates, private firms operate many penal facilities.

By the mid-1990s, contracts for the provision of medical care and food service were common (Camp & Camp, 1996:70). Twenty-eight states reported the private operation of halfway houses, prerelease centers, or related transitional residential programming. Only three states reported that they had contracted for the operations of institutions for adults under state jurisdiction (with 61 beds in total). Obviously, private operation of penal institutions was limited at that time.

By 1987, however, privatization had spread. Hackett et al. (1987) reported that, by the end of 1986, secure facilities operated by private organizations housed

Table 11.1	Correctional Facilities Run by Private Firms
Number of facilities under contract	415
Rated capacity of all facilities under contract	114,706
Total inmates in operating facilities	105,451
Percent occupancy of operating facilities	95
Security level of facilities	
Maximum	8
Medium	43
Minimum	364

Source: Stephan (2008)

about 1,200 adults. The state of Kentucky contracted for the operation of a 200-bed minimum-security facility that opened in January 1986. The authors concluded (1999:1), "State and local experience in contracting for the entire operation and management of a secure adult institution is still quite limited." The effect of private prisons is still not well understood (Thomas, 2005).

Nonetheless, privatization has emerged as an alternative for providing incarceration for all jurisdictions. Shover and Einstadter (1988) have suggested that privatization came to the fore in the 1980s because it was congruent with a national social view that the private sector and the marketplace are proper forums for the resolution of social problems. This is another example of how corrections reflects changes in social and political ideology.

The rapid growth of privately operated prisons and detention centers was part of what Dyer (2000) called the "prison industrial complex." The **prison industrial complex** refers to the relationships between governments, correctional authorities, and private corrections companies that combine to support increased use of prison. President Dwight Eisenhower identified a "military industrial complex" in his farewell speech in 1961. He warned that the combination of a large-scale weapons industry and the military produced pressure to maintain and increase military spending at the federal level. Pollock (2004) described the effects of this prison industrial complex on prison policy. Facing economic hardship, communities agree to the construction of private prisons. These prisons become so important to the local economy that voters and local officials exert pressure to ensure that the prisons remain open, even if prison populations were to decline. These economic incentives for keeping prisons, of course, also apply to public institutions.

At year-end 2012, prisons operated by private contractors housed more than 137,000 inmates, comprising more than 8% of the total prison population and representing a 57% increase since year-end 2000 (Carson & Golinelli, 2013; West, 2010). Six states (Alaska, Hawaii, Idaho, Montana, New Mexico, and Oklahoma) had at least a quarter of their prison population housed in private prisons at year-end 2012. More than 18% of federal inmates were in private facilities at that time.

Legal and Ethical Issues of Privatization

A primary concern regarding the privatization of prisons is the unresolved legal and ethical issues involving the privatization movement. Can a government authorize a private company and its agents to exercise force (including deadly force) to prevent escapes, quell riots, and otherwise control an inmate population? Perhaps more basic is the question of whether a private company can be empowered to deprive citizens of their liberty. Related legal issues surround the question of liability. If an inmate is injured through the negligence of a private company, would the committing state or local government also be liable for damages? These questions need answers before any large-scale movement to private prisons can take place. Logan (1987) suggested that the right of the state to imprison people derives ultimately from the citizens, and states can delegate it properly to a private company. Furthermore, he argued that we cannot assume the motives of state agencies are any better than the profit motive of a private firm. In contrast, Reisig and Pratt (2000) concluded that private prison management runs counter to our moral and philosophical tradition concerning liberal-democratic constitutional government.

Another set of concerns deals with accountability for the operation of the institution. If a prison or a jail is contracted, the contracting governmental authority is still accountable for the delivery of incarceration services (Gowdy, 1997:61). The task changes from that of managing the facility to that of overseeing and managing the contract. In addition, other problems of accountability arise because a new layer of administration has been created.

Do we allow the manager of a private prison to cap the population of the facility? Can a private facility refuse to accept inmates suspected of being troublemakers? It is most likely that the governmental agency contracting for the private prison remains accountable for its operation, but now must negotiate with the contractor over most aspects of institutional operation (Cooper, 1993). What happens if the contracting government cannot supply enough inmates to make the private facility profitable? Clear (1997) reported that when this happened in Connecticut, investors in the private jail lobbied to import offenders from other regions for local incarceration. Until these and other issues are resolved, privatization will pose as many problems as it does solutions (Bowditch & Everett, 1987; Ogle, 1999).

Bowditch and Everett (1987) voiced concern over the philosophical implications of the profit motive in the operation of prisons. Ethridge and Marquart (1993), after reviewing the development of privatization in Texas, suggested that private prisons might be limited to particular parts of the incarceration system, notably the operation of minimum-security and prerelease institutions. It would appear that in the twenty-first century, private prisons and jails have become a fixture in American corrections. Gowdy (1997:62) concluded, "As the industry grows and thereby establishes track records for its usage, the demand on corrections officials to consider using privatization as a means of quickly and economically addressing prison crowding problems is likely to become more prominent."

Even though private prisons house a substantial number of inmates, there has not been a rapid growth in their use. Private prisons and jails have emerged as a supplement to public facilities. One of the greatest users of private incarceration is the federal government. With many states facing severe economic times and large prison populations, there is increased interest in private prisons today.

Effectiveness of Private Prisons

Even as many of the legal and ethical issues surrounding privatization remain unsettled, the fact is that the privatization of prisons is increasing. Thus, it is important to examine the evidence regarding how effective private prisons are compared to their public counterparts. As mentioned, the primary motivation behind the privatization of prisons appears to be costs. With many services, contracting with private agencies appears to be more cost-efficient than governmental operation. Yet, the question of cost is less clear when discussing the possibility of an entire institution operated by a contractor. Any cost savings realized may come from lowering quality control. Might a private company hire custodial officers at minimum wage, thereby limiting the pool from which candidates might be drawn, and enhancing the likelihood of employee turnover? Assessments of private prison and jail operations must attend to both cost concerns and the impact of different types of facilities on future criminality by those incarcerated there (Pratt & Maahs, 1999). In a recent meta-analysis, Lundahl, Kunz, Brownell, Harris, and Van Vleet (2009) found mixed evidence regarding cost-effectiveness. Private prisons were more cost-effective in half of the studies included in the analysis. Of the remaining studies, private prisons were either as costly as or more costly than their publicly managed counterparts. Ultimately, it is very difficult to compare private and public prison costs. Comparisons of public and private prisons are sensitive to choices made by evaluators. Results will vary depending on what costs evaluators include and how they measure costs (Gaes, 2008). It is also difficult for researchers to compare prisons of different ages, design, and security levels, all of which will affect the cost of operating the prison.

Results are also mixed regarding future recidivism of inmates from private prisons. In one of the few published comparisons of private and public correctional facilities, Lanza-Kaduce, Parker, and Thomas (1999) concluded that privately operated juvenile facilities were more effective than their public counterparts. This study had some limitations, especially the fact that insufficient time had passed to be sure the youths housed in private facilities would continue to refrain from crime. Geis, Mobley, and Shichor (1999) criticized this evaluation because of links between its authors and private prison operations. They suggested that a potential conflict of interest might have influenced the results of the evaluation. A later comparison of public and private prisons in Florida revealed no difference in recidivism rates for inmates housed in those facilities (Bales, Bedard, Quinn, Ensley, & Holley, 2005). The two most recent evaluations of recidivism found that inmates serving their time in private prisons have a slightly increased rate of recidivism than those serving their time in public prisons (Duwe & Clark, 2013; Spivak & Shard, 2008).

McDonald and Patten (2003) reported on the management of privatization by government. They studied the operation of private prisons for convicted offenders in 1997, focusing on how government agencies established, monitored, and administered contracts for prisons. They identified two basic models. In the first, the government agency gets bids either for the operation of a state-owned prison or for the opening of a new prison in the state. In the second model, the state enters an agreement to house inmates in a contractor's facility that is located out of state. Of the two, McDonald and Patten found that contracts for in-state facilities were better monitored and less costly than those for housing inmates out of state. Whatever else happens, their research indicates that states exercise more control over private facilities when those prisons operate within the state jurisdiction.

CROWDING

Perhaps the most pressing concern of correctional administrators in many jurisdictions is crowding. At midyear 1990, jails in the United States were operating at 104% capacity (Stephan & Jankowski, 1991). Between 1990 and 2012, the jail inmate population nearly doubled from just over 400,000 inmates to more than 744,000 inmates (Minton, 2013). Clearly, this large increase to an already overcrowded jail system placed stress on many local jurisdictions to increase the amount of available jail space. Many of these local jurisdictions have responded over the last 3 decades by building new, larger facilities. From 1990 to 2012, jail capacity in the United States rose from approximately 295,000 to nearly 900,000. By 2012, jails were operating at an average of 84% capacity, reflecting the lowest level of jail crowding since 1984 (Minton, 2013). The reduction in crowding in jails is a positive development, but one that has come at a significant cost to local jurisdictions. Local governments currently spend more than $22 billion a year on jails (Kyckelhahn, 2013).

A similar situation exists with prisons. In the early 1980s, the majority of prison systems in the United States were crowded to the point that court intervention had occurred or inmates threatened lawsuits. In 1983, eight state prison systems (Alabama, Florida, Michigan, Mississippi, Oklahoma, Rhode Island, Tennessee, and Texas) were either operating under court order to change or courts had declared their operations unconstitutional. In addition, the District of Columbia and 21 states had one or more institutions operating under court order, while nine others had litigation pending and two states were operating under **consent decrees** (whereby the court and the state enter into a voluntary agreement about issues raised in court). Figure 11.2 describes the types of prison conditions leading to court orders through the end of the twentieth century.

The Bureau of Justice Statistics (1986) reported that 32 jurisdictions were housing more inmates than their highest capacity. Using a different estimate of capacity, it was reported that as many as 41 jurisdictions could be classified as crowded. At the end of 2012, the federal system and 18 states were operating at or above their highest capacity (Carson & Golinelli, 2013). One of the difficulties in assessing prison crowding is the determination of prison population capacity. The state,

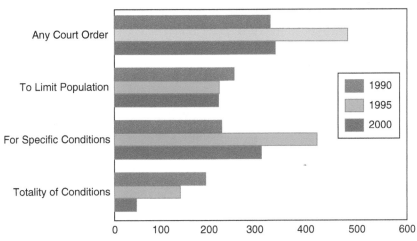

FIGURE 11.2
Changes in prison conditions leading to court orders, 1990–2000.
Sources: Stephan (1997:1) and Stephan and Karberg (2003:9)

federal, and District of Columbia jurisdictions apply a wide variety of capacity measures to reflect both the available space to house inmates and the ability to staff and operate an institution. Box 11.1 presents three definitions of prison capacity: (1) **rated capacity**, (2) **operational capacity**, and (3) **design capacity**. Nationally, the state prison inmate population equaled 99% of the highest capacity of prisons—usually the operational capacity and 109% of the lowest rating (Guerino, Harrison, & Sabol, 2011).

Crowding in correctional institutions poses several problems for inmates, correctional staff, and correctional administrators. For these reasons, it is simply not acceptable to jam more prisoners into existing space, at least not as a long-term response to crowding. Rather, we must develop alternatives that ensure adequate capacity to house the large numbers of offenders now populating the nation's prisons and jails.

For inmates, crowding places severe demands on available resources. Simple things that would generally be taken for granted (e.g., hot water for showers)

BOX 11.1 DEFINITIONS OF PRISON CAPACITY

Rated capacity: The number of beds or inmates assigned by a rating official (such as a fire marshal) to institutions within the jurisdiction.

Operational capacity: The number of inmates that can be accommodated based on a facility's staff, existing programs, and services.

Design capacity: The number of inmates that planners or architects intended for the facility.

Source: Harrison and Beck (2006:7)

become scarce resources. Privacy, always at a premium in penal facilities, becomes almost totally beyond the reach of most inmates. A crowded facility generally lacks the ability to provide activities or meaningful work experiences for inmates. They must share recreational, educational, vocational, and other resources with more inmates. It may even become difficult to find a seat from which to view television.

The Supreme Court has been reluctant to rule that prison overcrowding by itself is unconstitutional. However, overcrowding can lead to inhumane and dangerous conditions, which, at that point, violate the constitutional protections against cruel and unusual punishment. Approximately 7% of all jurisdictions are under a court order to limit their prisoner population (Stephan & Walsh, 2011). In a landmark decision (*Brown v. Plata*, 2011), the Supreme Court ruled that the California prison system had become so crowded that the state could not provide adequate supervision. In the majority opinion, Justice Kennedy illustrates an example of the conditions in California:

> A medical expert described living quarters in converted gymnasiums or dayrooms, where large numbers of prisoners may share just a few toilets and showers as "breeding grounds for disease." Cramped conditions promote unrest and violence, making it difficult for prison officials to monitor and control the prison population... After one prisoner was assaulted in a crowded gymnasium, prison staff did not even learn of the injury until the prisoner had been dead for several hours.

At the time of the *Plata* ruling, California's prison population was at roughly 200% capacity. The ruling required the state to reduce the prison population to 137.5% of capacity. In response to the ruling, the state implemented a policy designed to reduce the prison population by targeted releases of inmates and incarcerating new nonviolent, nonsexual offenders under county jurisdiction in local jails. Unconditional releases of California inmates increased by nearly 700% from 2010 to 2011 (Carson & Sabol, 2012).

Prison staff also feels the pressures of crowding. In addition to the increased tension in the institution and the perceived increase in the likelihood of attack by inmates, the workload of staff increases. Doubling the inmate population means doubling the caseloads of correctional counselors, increasing the class sizes of educational staff, doubling the demands on food service staff, and increasing activity for the custody staff. There are twice as many inmates to count, escort, search, counsel, and watch. The sheer numbers of inmates can overwhelm correctional officers. The crowded institution becomes more anonymous and impersonal, making it difficult for officers to recognize and know inmates or to provide adequate service and protection to them. As a result, correctional officers in crowded institutions are likely to be less attuned to the population and more distant from it.

Martin, Lichtstein, Jenkot, and Forde (2012) interviewed correctional officers to determine the effects of prison crowding. A prominent theme among the officers interviewed was the fear that being outnumbered would lead to increased levels of violence. As one correctional officer said, "[I]nmates allow us to be in this institution every day, and they allow us to leave. I think that anytime they want to take over, then they can" (Martin et al., 2012:97). Criminal justice system officials continue to identify prison and jail crowding as one of their most pressing problems (McEwen, 1995).

Correctional managers must provide for the needs of larger numbers of inmates with a constant level of resources (Vanyur, 1997). Managers become more concerned with tranquility and bed space than with the provision of services and opportunities. As Johnson (1987:182) noted, "When prisons become overcrowded, moreover, the temptation to warehouse inmates as a matter of policy, rather than as a failure of policy, is strong." That is, correctional managers facing crowded prisons seek to survive without disruption, rather than to improve either their institutions or the lives of inmates. As McEwen (1995:7) noted, "[W]ith the numbers increasing, the emphasis must shift from treatment and programming to containment, diverting resources from programs to security. Mental health programs and recreational programs were among those affected by crowding." For example, several jurisdictions are using what some euphemistically call "bus housing." It has been estimated that large jurisdictions, such as California, may have 1,000 or more inmates "in transit" between prisons at any time. Inmates on a bus do not require cells. Surely, routine transfers for the sake of bed space do not well serve the needs of prisoners (or of the prison system). Yet, correctional managers facing severe crowding can use this strategy to retain custody over inmates when there is insufficient space to house them.

The causes of prison crowding are not clear. Some suggest that the aging of the baby-boom generation produced a demographic bulge, a large number of persons in the age group most likely to be imprisoned. Yet, if demography were the cause, crowding should be on the decline. Marvell and Moody (1997) found that demography is related to prison population size, but that other factors must also be contributing to prison population growth. Among these other factors are increased punitiveness (more mandatory prison sentences and longer terms), improvements in detection and prosecution, and a widening of the definition of types of offenses requiring imprisonment. Beck and Mumola (1999) reported that increases in the number of parole violators returned to prison, declining rates of parole release, and increasing time served are key contributors to rising prison populations.

Solutions to the crowding problem are of two basic types (see Schwartz & Travis, 1997:77–80): (1) capacity expansion and (2) demand reduction. We must either increase the amount of prison space available or reduce our demand for prison space. These two solutions involve a variety of strategies. The capacity expansion strategy relies on construction of more prisons, the conversion of facilities built for other purposes (such as mental hospitals or military bases), and renovations of existing facilities to increase the number of prisoners they can accommodate. The demand reduction solution is a bit more complex. As Clear and Austin (2009) point out, the size of America's prison population is a result of two factors: (1) the number of people sentenced to prison and (2) how long they stay there. One strategy would be to reduce the number of offenders sent to prison by increasing diversion programs and the use of community-based alternative sentences. However, evaluations of diversion programs often show a **net-widening** effect. In other words, instead of reducing the prison population, diversion programs are often focused on offenders who would otherwise not have been arrested or prosecuted at all (Walker, 2011). Another strategy is to reduce the amount of time inmates are kept in prison and, thereby, reduce prison populations. If release dates were accelerated so that offenders served only one-half as much time as they currently do, the present supply of prison space could accommodate twice as many inmates. This strategy could also offer false hope for reducing the prison population, though. For example, if a substantial number of inmates who are released early on parole are quickly rearrested or violate the terms of parole, those offenders will return to prison. The recent economic pressures have resulted in many state-level efforts to reduce prison populations. Clear and Schrantz (2011) describe a variety of the strategies that have been considered to help relieve prison overcrowding (see Box 11.2).

PRISON INDUSTRIES

In the early days of prisons in America, government officials expected inmates to pay for the costs of incarceration by working in prison industries. Indeed, the early proponents of incarceration hoped that prisons would not only be self-sufficient, but that they might even become profit centers for the state. After decades of prison industry, including contracting prison labor with private companies and state-run industries, prison factories have not been profitable.

"Self-sufficiency was a goal pursued by all states where prisons were instituted. Legislators persistently demanded that their penitentiaries pay their way, even

---

BOX 11.2 STRATEGIES FOR REDUCING THE PRISON POPULATION

Reduce Prison Intake Rate

- Strengthening probation
- Creating fiscal incentives for community corrections
- Reducing or eliminating mandatory penalties

Reduce Length of Stay

- Effective parole release and supervision
- Special early release (e.g., increasing amount of good time an inmate can receive)
- Reform stringent truth in sentencing laws
- Offense-specific statutory changes
- Eliminate repeat offender sentencing enhancements

Source: Clear and Schrantz (2011)

though private industries lobbied against prison manufacturing," observed Keve (1986:28). Officials believed the prison industry had a number of beneficial effects. First, especially in the early years of the penitentiary, they hoped that convict labor could defray the expense of constructing and operating prisons and jails, that is, that inmates could pay for their own punishment (Durham, 1989). Second, they hoped the activity of work would occupy inmates and keep them from breaking prison rules. Finally, they expected that a regimen of work for inmates would serve to instill good habits in them. As Johnson (1987:26–27) summarized the approach:

> It was hoped that silent laboring days and solitary contemplative nights would encourage communion with God and effect a transformation of at least some of the wayward prisoners' souls. But simple conformity to the prison routine, a life of pure habits if not pure intentions, was enough to get a prisoner by in the congregate systems.

According to Fox (1983), prisons have organized their industry in many ways over time. Six of the more common of these are (1) piece price, (2) contract, (3) lease, (4) public account, (5) state use, and (6) public works. Each has its strengths and weaknesses. The **piece price system** was common in the early years of prisons. The manufacturer supplied the raw materials to the prison, and inmates constructed the finished product, which the manufacturer purchased at an established price. The **contract system** involved an entrepreneur contracting with the prison for labor and the use of prison shops for the production of goods. The highest bidder won the right to use prison labor and shops. The **lease system** was common in Southern prisons after the Civil War. The prison simply leased its convicts to a contractor who produced goods with convict labor. All of these methods involved having a private contractor.

The other common methods of organizing prison industry relied on prison-run operations. In a **public account system**, prisoners in correctional industries produce goods and sell them on the open market. There have traditionally been severe restrictions on what prisons may produce and to whom they may sell their products. In a **state-use system**, the prison produces almost any products, but the sale or distribution of the product is limited to governmental agencies. The state-use method of organization does not allow the prison industry to compete on the open market. The **public works system** uses inmate labor for public service projects, such as road maintenance, construction of parks, and other government services. Sing Sing Prison in the state of New York was an early public works prison project; it was constructed largely through the labors of inmates brought from the penitentiary at Auburn.

Opposition to the use of "slave" convict labor and the unfair advantage given to manufacturers employing convicts led to the passage of several laws limiting the sale of prison-made goods across state lines, and within states to nongovernmental units (Cullen & Travis, 1984). The resulting decline in markets, as well as the lack of capital investment in prison industries, rendered most prison factories noncompetitive with free-world enterprises. More recently, however, there has been a resurgence of prison industries competing in free-world markets (Vito, 1985).

The new prison industries tend to be operated by either federal or state governments. These industries produce products such as furniture, signage, and garments to be sold to governmental agencies, public organizations, tax-supported entities, or markets in other countries (Chang & Thompkins, 2002). An alternate model for prison industries is the **Prison Industry Enhancement Certification Program (PIECP)**. The PIECP was created by Congress in 1979 to encourage states to provide inmates with employment opportunities that are similar to private-sector work opportunities (Bureau of Justice Assistance, 2004). Under PIECP, governments create joint ventures with private industries. Though different models exist, inmates are often employed by, trained by, and even supervised by the private company (Sexton, 1995). Unlike the government-operated prison industry, PIECP programs pay inmates wages comparable to the private sector, and the products produced can be sold in the free market. Currently, at least 175 partnerships exist with private businesses and prisons across 37 states. Inmate participation in prison industries is generally voluntary. Inmates are required to pay taxes, child support, and other expenses. Prison officials consult local unions prior to the development of industries to ensure that the new prison jobs do not cause unemployment among law-abiding citizens (Auerbach, 1982).

The cycle of prison industry—progressing from the production of goods for the open market, through restricted public use, and back again to the free market—shows how difficult it is to resolve the issue of what to do with prison inmates. Some analyses have suggested that introducing free-market practices and pay scales into prison industry programs will benefit both the inmates (Schwarz, 1986) and the general economy of the state (Lonski, 1986:52). Still, there is opposition to the idea of prisoners manufacturing and selling goods. Finally, the old hopes for the prison industry have not changed. Those advocating the expansion of prison industry programs still suggest that the results of these efforts will achieve many goals. The Bureau of Justice Assistance (2004:3) identified the goals of the Prison Industry Enhancement Certification Program, to benefit:

- The corrections administrator, as a cost-effective way to occupy a portion of the ever-growing prison population
- The crime victim, by providing a means of partial repayment for harm sustained
- The inmate, through offering a chance to work, meet financial obligations, learn job skills, and increase chances of meaningful employment on release
- The private sector, by providing a stable and readily available workforce
- The public, through reducing costs with inmate worker contributions to room and board, family support, victim compensation, and taxes

As is apparent from these goals, when compared to the history of prison industries, the only change has been that the supporters of industries no longer expect

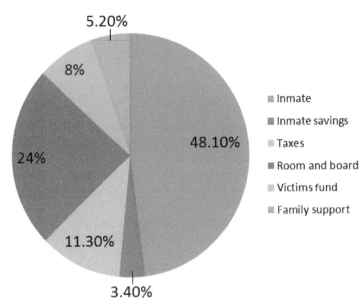

5.20%

8%

24%

11.30%

3.40%

48.10%

- Inmate
- Inmate savings
- Taxes
- Room and board
- Victims fund
- Family support

FIGURE 11.3
Distribution of wages paid inmates in PIECP.
Source: Moses and Smith (2007:35)

full self-sufficiency or complete rehabilitation to result from convict labor. Figure 11.3 presents the distribution of inmate wages under the PIECP. It shows that although inmates retained much of their earnings, almost one-half of gross wages went to inmate financial obligations (Moses & Smith, 2007). In addition, inmates used a portion of the net pay category (48% of total wages) for living expenses, including some health care costs, food, and toiletries. These payments by inmates further reduced state expenses.

Industry programs for inmates have expanded to include jail populations in recent years. Miller, Sexton, and Jacobsen (1991) reported on jail industry programs in 15 local and 1 federal jail/detention center operating inmate work programs. The purposes of jail work programs are similar to those in prison programs and include development of inmate work habits and skills, reduction of costs, reduction of inmate idleness, and the meeting of community needs. Most jail programs compensate inmates with "good time" reductions in sentence length, but some pay wages. Some counties allow inmates to continue to work at their own jobs, reporting to the jail after work each day. In cases in which inmates earn wages, it is typical for the jail to bill for room and board or other fees.

Still, relatively few inmates participate in prison industries. Almost all prisons operate some sort of work or employment programs, most commonly using inmates to perform tasks required for the operation of the prison. Not surprisingly, inmates rank prison jobs differently. Alarid (2003) found that although male and female inmates preferred somewhat different jobs, the best jobs according to inmates were those that provided some useful job skills, allowed a measure of independence, and were highest paid. No inmates indicated physical labor on prison maintenance under close supervision was attractive. Alarid also found no racial discrimination in inmate job assignments. The best jobs went to inmates having served the longest terms and those who were the lowest risks for escape or violence.

The resurgence of prison industries is a reflection of the current efforts to improve incarceration. Having learned from the past problems, correctional administrators are attempting to accentuate the positive aspects of past efforts while controlling the negative effects (Cullen & Travis, 1984). In a sense, the revitalization of prison industries represents a general return to incarceration as a preferred criminal sanction, which is an effect that has occurred since the early 1970s. The appeal of putting prisoners to work, both for their own good and for the good of the state, is strong. Figure 11.4 describes the distribution of work assignments in prisons. Inmate wage rates in most cases are substantially lower than wages in the free society. The question is whether it is possible to overcome objections to convict labor and to obtain the expected benefits of prison industries. Flanagan and Maguire (1993) have urged the adoption of a full-employment policy for prisons, believing that such an approach is both necessary and possible. Hopper (2013) reported that prisoners who participate in industry programs tend to have a lower recidivism rate upon release from prison.

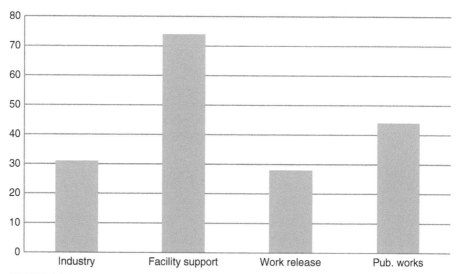

FIGURE 11.4
Percentage of prisons reporting types of work programs in prisons, 2005.
Source: Stephan (2008:5)

PRISON VIOLENCE

Violence has long been a part of the incarceration experience (Braswell, Montgomery, & Lombardo, 1994). The earliest prison riot in the United States occurred in 1774, when inmates at Newgate Prison of Connecticut revolted (Fox, 1983:114). Newgate was an abandoned copper mine where offenders served terms in the old underground mine shafts (see Figure 11.5). Riots and nonviolent strikes by inmates have occurred throughout the history of prisons and jails. In addition, violence on a smaller scale, between inmates and officers, and among inmates, has a long tradition. Prison violence occurs in many forms. We shall briefly examine interpersonal assaults, homicide, sexual assaults, and riots.

Interpersonal Assaults and Homicide

Conrad (1982) suggested that prison violence results from five factors: (1) violence-prone inmates; (2) the "lower-class value system," which emphasizes masculinity, toughness, and violence; (3) the use of violence by correctional administrators to control inmates; (4) the anonymity of large (especially crowded) prisons; and (5) the utility of violence in furthering inmate objectives. Given that prisons are places where aggressive, often violent, people live in proximity to each other, it is not surprising that so much violence occurs in prisons. Rather, it is surprising that so little violence occurs. Table 11.2 describes the types of offenses for which inmates were imprisoned in 2012. More than half had a current conviction for a violent crime. Added to this is the impact of truth in sentencing reforms (see Chapter 9), which seek to increase the amount of time inmates convicted of violent crimes serve in prison. It is likely that the overall

FIGURE 11.5
Postcard depicting Old Newgate Prison, a prison/mine in East Granby, Connecticut, where the first U.S. prison riot took place.
en.wikipedia.org

Table 11.2	State Prison Inmates by Type of Crime Conviction
Type of Crime	**Percentage of Inmates**
Violent	53.5
Property	18.9
Drug	16.6
Public order	10.6
Other	0.7
Total	100.0

Source: Carson and Golinelli (2013:5)

inmate population will comprise an even greater proportion of violent offenders as these inmates serve longer sentences and begin to stack up in prison.

Whether a high level of violence exists in any particular institution, the potential for violence is always there, and the threat of harm influences the behavior of inmates and staff alike (Bowker, 1980). Abbott (1981:150), a convict-writer who divulged his prison experiences in his book *In the Belly of the Beast*, wrote, "Everyone in prison has an ideal of violence, murder. Beneath all relationships between prisoners in prison is the ever-present fact of murder. It ultimately defines our relationship among ourselves." Abbott suggested that life in a modern prison is akin to life in the jungle. The rule is kill or be killed. Correctional officers are not immune to the constant threat of violence inside the institution, as evidenced by the growing interest in and market for body armor for correctional officers (Kaplan, 1987). Wolff, Shi, and Siegel (2009) reported that the climate of the prison relates to levels of violence. "Climate" refers to how the inmates perceive both staff and other inmates treat them. In prisons where inmates are satisfied with their treatment, there is less violence.

Most of what we know about violence and misbehavior in prisons comes from research focused on male offenders (Baskin, Sommers, & Steadman, 1991). There has been some research on the violence and misbehavior of female prisoners as well. Kruttschnitt and Krmpotich (1990) reported that about 25% of female inmates engaged in aggressive acts against other inmates. Tischler and Marquart (1989) reported no significant difference in disciplinary infractions between minimum-security male inmates and female inmates, but maximum-security female inmates posed the most disciplinary problems. In general, women were more likely to receive disciplinary reports for fighting than were men, but men were more likely to attack guards than were women. It may be that female prisoners are less violent because of the lower incidence of gang involvement in women's prisons. If women are less violent, it may also reflect differences in who goes to prison.

The majority of female violent offenders had attacked a victim known to them, whereas male violent criminals were more likely to have attacked strangers. Simon (1993) found that male inmates who had attacked strangers were significantly more likely to commit violent acts in prison than those who attacked people they knew. McCorkle (1995) compared male and female prisoners diagnosed with a mental health problem. He found that female inmates were both more likely than male inmates to receive medication for their illness while incarcerated and more likely to engage in disruptive behaviors in the institution. He suggested that different experiences with the stress of imprisonment for women as opposed to men aggravate these behavioral problems. It may be that women inmates convicted of violent crimes are qualitatively different from violent men in that their violent behavior was contextual and not a general pattern of adaptation to stress and conflict. We need more research before we can assess whether there are differences between men and women in terms of prison violence, and to be able understand any such differences. What is clear from these studies, however, is that violence and disciplinary infractions are not rare among female inmates.

In a study of women's perceptions and experiences in prison, Pogrebin and Dodge (2001) reported widespread violence and fear of violence among a sample of female prison inmates. This suggests that the experience of violence in prison by women is at least as common as that among men.

Fox (1983:107) wrote, "Homicides in prison appear to be grossly underreported." He further estimated that the official statistics should be doubled to approach a more accurate figure. Eichenthal and Jacobs (1991) noted the underreporting of criminal acts in prisons, and decried the lack of information concerning crimes of all types that occur in prisons. For example, the Bureau of Justice Statistics (Noonan & Ginder, 2013) reported 70 prison inmate homicides in 2011. Approximately 2% of inmate deaths were reported to be the result of homicide. Each year there are thousands of inmate assaults on other inmates. Wolff, Blitz, Shi, Siegel, and Bachman (2007) found that an estimated 20% of inmates reported being the victim of a physical assault either by staff or a fellow inmate during a 6-month period. In a self-report survey, 17% of inmates admitted to committing at least one inmate-on-inmate assault in the previous year (Lahm, 2008). Many factors contribute to the rates of reported physical violence in prisons, including the physical conditions of the prison in which the study is conducted and the way in which victimization is measured by researchers (Bierie, 2012; Wolff, Shi, & Bachman, 2008). Between midyear 1999 and 2000 (the most recent nationwide figures available), there were a reported 17,952 inmate assaults on staff, five of which resulted in the death of a prison staff member. Adjusting for the inmate population and number of prison staff for 2000, these yield rates of assault of 4,174 per 100,000 correctional staff and 2,622 per 100,000 inmates. These assault rates alone are 5–10 times higher than similar rates for members of the public. Figure 11.6 compares a violent crime rate of prisoners with the similar rate for aggravated assault. The figure shows that rates of violence in prisons greatly exceed those in the free society.

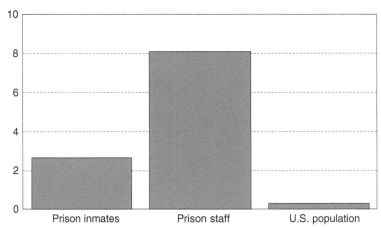

FIGURE 11.6
Comparison of U.S. and prison assault rates.
Source: Federal Bureau of Investigation (2001) and Stephan and Karberg (2003)

Sexual Assaults and Violence

Sexual assaults in prison are a special case of individual violence among inmates. Davis (1968) conducted the first reported study of sexual assaults among inmates. Davis studied this type of inmate violence in the Philadelphia prison system and in sheriff's vans transporting prisoners. He included verbal assaults with actual physical attacks in his definition of sexual assault. As a result, Davis concluded that nearly 5% of the prison population had been victims of sexual assaults. The problem of sexual violence in prisons has entered common knowledge so that the popular media depict and discuss sexual assaults in prisons.

In 2003, the U.S. Congress enacted the **Prison Rape Elimination Act**. This law provides for the development of better information about the nature and incidence of rape and sexual assault in prisons, and provides funding to correctional authorities to reduce and control sexual violence in prisons. In passing the law, Congress (45 USC 15601, Sec. 2) made several findings about sexual violence in prisons. They found that young, first offenders are at greater risk of sexual assault than older offenders are; prison rapes generally go unreported and victims are untreated; and the high incidence of prison rape "increases the levels of violence, directed at inmates and at staff, within prisons." See Figure 11.7.

The Bureau of Justice Statistics conducts annual surveys of prison and jail inmates, as well as youths confined in juvenile institutions (Beck & Harrison, 2007). Results of the 2012 survey of jail and prison inmates reveal that 4% of prison inmates and 3.2% of jail inmates reported being the victim of sexual misconduct. The rate of sexual victimization is highest among females, non-heterosexuals, and those with prior sexual victimization. Correctional staff was reported to be the offenders in approximately half of the victimizations, and roughly half of the staff sexual misconduct was reported by the inmate as

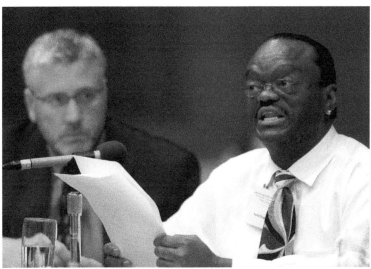

FIGURE 11.7
Kendell Spruce, right, testifies at a public hearing before the National Prison Rape Elimination Commission. Spruce, imprisoned on a forgery conviction, conveyed how he was assaulted by as many as 27 prisoners in an Arkansas prison. Listening at left is T. J. Parsell, who testified that as a 17-year-old he was gang-raped in an adult prison in Michigan. The National Prison Rape Elimination Commission was established by the 2003 Prison Rape Elimination Act to set new national policies to help prevent prison sexual assaults.
AP Photo/Eric Risberg

being consensual (Beck, Berzofsky, Caspar, & Krebs, 2013). Any sexual relations between staff and inmates, willing or not, is considered illegal and is reported as a sexual victimization.

True levels of sexual violence are very difficult to determine. Studies that rely on official records of sexual victimization are likely to underestimate the true prevalence of victimization in prisons (Jones & Pratt, 2008). For example, a survey of inmates at 10 prisons revealed that only 22% of the men and 34% of the women who had been victimized reported their incident to prison staff (Struckman-Johnson & Struckman-Johnson, 2006). Fowler, Blackburn, Marquart, and Mullings (2010) found that many of the same groups who are most at-risk for sexual victimization (e.g., homosexuals and those with prior victimizations) are the least likely to self-report the incident to prison officials.

The academic literature and popular media have portrayed sexual violence in correctional institutions as widespread (Lockwood, 1994). The image of such violence, however, has been that of the homosexual rape, which helps explain the relatively narrow title of the federal legislation. In fact, other studies (Lockwood, 1980; Nacci, 1988) have revealed that rape is a relatively rare event, with estimates of less than 1% of the inmate population being victims of physical sexual assaults. That the actual incidence of homosexual rape is low, however, tells only part of the story. One effect of sexual assault, or the threat of sexual assault, is a general increase in the level of violence in prisons. Fear of sexual assault leads otherwise peaceful inmates to commit acts of violence to deter attackers.

In terms of deterring inmate sexual assault, one useful result of fighting in prison is self-defense. Especially given the media portrayal of widespread rape and sexual victimization in prison, inmates may attempt to build a reputation in the institution to ensure they will not become targets of sexual aggressors. Thus, some inmates may assault others in nonsexual circumstances to avoid sexual attack. One inmate interviewed by Lockwood (1980:95–96) explained an assault on another in the dining hall as self-defense. The inmate Lockwood interviewed had been the victim of a sexual assault, and he attacked another inmate in the dining hall to prevent future sexual victimization. As the inmate explained his actions:

> They had a code in the prison on the chow line that said no man should cut ahead of you in the chow line. And this one man passed me a couple of times in the line, and he knew that I was aware of what he was doing. If I failed to do what I was supposed to do here, then I was lost again [would be a sexual victim again]. So the next day, when they come through the chow line, when this guy cut in front of me, I hit him in the head with a tray as hard as I could. And when he went to the ground, I hit him several more times before the guard could reach me. It is regrettable but it is the only way that you can handle it. And I didn't want to do it, but I did what I had to do to protect myself.

As Lockwood suggested, the importance of sexual violence in prisons may come more from the perception than the reality of sexual assaults. It appears that, in reality, there are relatively few cases of actual sexual assault in prisons. It also appears, however, that inmates believe the threat of sexual assault is both real and great. Many instances of individual violence in prisons, therefore, may result from the fear of sexual assault. In this way, it is possible that most prison violence is a form of sexual violence. We can infer a similar explanation for inmate violence from Hassine's (1996:23) observations on life in prison. He wrote, "In the life of an inmate, if you catch someone stealing from you, you're compelled to deal with it physically. This is not because you want to or you think it's the right thing to do, but because you absolutely must… If you choose to ignore the theft, the man will steal from you again and tell his friends, who in turn will also steal from you. Eventually, you will be challenged for more than just minor belongings."

From the perspective of the inmate, few choices are available for dealing with other inmates. Reliance on correctional authorities is a sign of weakness and is generally seen as ineffective. Not only are correctional officers often unable to protect victimized inmates, those inmates who report incidents to officers come to be labeled "snitches" and are then targets for increased violence. Often, inmates will find themselves being coerced into sexual behavior with a fellow inmate to gain protection from physical violence. Many inmates describe this behavior as consensual, although for others it is a form of sexual enslavement

(Trammell, 2011). Another alternative is to seek protective custody. **Protective custody** is usually a housing unit kept separate from the general inmate population so that inmates in the unit are separated from attackers. Most protective custody units, however, offer little programming, and inmates are kept locked in their cells for most of the day. The lack of alternatives to confrontation adds to the sense that the prison is a violent place.

Riots

To the relatively high level of violence among individuals, we must add the danger of riot. In the last third of the twentieth century, four large-scale prison riots captured media attention and illustrated the potential violence in prison riots. In 2001, there were more than 600 major incidents involving five or more inmates and resulting in serious injury or significant property damage in state prisons (Stephan & Karberg, 2003:10). There were an additional 639 other disruptions that same year. Riots or disturbances are common in prisons. What was unusual about the ones described here was the extent of damage and injury.

Although similar in some respects, each of the major riots between 1971 and 1993 had different outcomes. The riots at Attica (New York) and the New Mexico State Penitentiary in Santa Fe were among the bloodiest in history. The riots by Cuban detainees at federal institutions (in Atlanta, Georgia, and Oakdale, Louisiana) resulted in only one inmate death. The 1993 riot by inmates at the Southern Ohio Correctional Facility at Lucasville claimed 11 lives, including the life of one correctional officer.

On September 9, 1971, inmates rioted at the New York State Correctional Facility at Attica, where they took control of a large part of the prison. On September 13, state police and prison authorities stormed the prison and took command. When the smoke cleared, 43 people were dead; most of them (30) were inmates killed during the attack. It was the bloodiest prison riot in American history. Nine years later, on February 15 and 16, 1980, inmates rioted for 36 hours at the New Mexico State Penitentiary. When the incident was over, officials found that the rioting inmates had killed 33 prisoners, and many of these deaths occurred after the victims had been barbarically tortured (Rolland, 1997; Serrill & Katel, 1980). In late 1987, Cuban detainees rioted at the Federal Detention Center in Oakdale, Louisiana; 2 days later, Cuban inmates also rioted at the Federal Penitentiary in Atlanta (*Newsweek*, 1987). Two weeks after the beginning of the Oakdale disturbance, the Atlanta rioters finally surrendered.

The riots by the Cuban detainees did not involve anything near the level of personal violence that characterized the Attica and Santa Fe uprisings. Although only one inmate was killed, the extent of property damage caused by the rioting of Oakdale and Atlanta detainees was massive (Nacci, 1988). Rioters almost completely destroyed the two institutions. In this respect, the federal riots mirrored the Santa Fe experience, in which inmates caused extensive damage to the facility in addition to committing killings. (At Attica, damage to the institution was much less severe.) The Lucasville riot extended over several days and resulted in severe damage to the part of the prison that was under control of the rioting inmates. The death and damage toll at Lucasville was less than the damage at New Mexico, but the riot was the most serious in a decade.

Because of their intensity and the numbers of inmates and staff who are at risk, as well as the possibility of damage to the facility itself, riots are a major concern to correctional administrators. The problem is that we do not know enough about the causes of prison riots to allow adequate planning to avoid them (Rynne, Harding, & Wortley, 2008). The paradoxical nature of prison violence, including riots, is that the violence may be the result of efforts to reform the prison and improve the quality of life for prison inmates.

Camp, Gaes, Langan, and Saylor (2003) studied inmate misconduct, especially violence, in federal prisons. They concluded that characteristics of the prison itself account for much of the violence in prisons. In a similar fashion, Huebner (2003) reported that the style by which prison staff controls inmate behavior relates to levels of violence. As suggested by Conrad (1982), coercive control, or the use/threat of force may lead to higher levels of inmate violence than other controls. Marquart (2008) argued that correctional authorities must maintain control over the institution to prevent riots. The ability for the correctional institution to maintain control depends on factors such as the institution's security level, level of crowding, and characteristics of the inmate population (Griffin & Hepburn, 2013).

What makes prison violence a contemporary issue, although it has always been a part of the prison experience, is that there is evidence to suggest that violence in prisons today is qualitatively different from such violence in the past. As Johnson (1987:75) stated the issue, "Violence has always been a salient aspect of the convict world. In many of today's prisons, however, the convict culture of violence is unusually pronounced." The question remains: Why is the violence today more pronounced?

Observers point to many factors that they believe have changed the nature of American prisons and jails. Wright (2000) reported that the correctional administrators he interviewed mentioned the following as contributing to increased violence: the simple increase in the number of prisoners leading to increased chances of conflicts, the impact of crowding on prisoner classification and housing, the increase in gang membership among prisoners, and larger numbers of young predatory offenders. Two additional important contributors have been the emergence of professional prison administrators (Conrad, 1982; Fox, 1983; Johnson, 1987; Mahan, 1982) and the effect of court intervention on prison operations (Jacobs, 1977; Marquart & Crouch, 1984). In effect, the prisoners' rights movement and the prevalence of "professional" prison administrators served to lessen the authority of correctional staff by humanizing the prison.

Recognizing the prisoner as an individual deserving consideration and attention in making decisions about the running of the institution has the effect of lessening the power of correctional personnel. Fogel (1979) identified the prisoners' rights movement and the success of inmates in court as being "status costly" to correctional staff. It reduced the staff's position of social and physical superiority over inmates. Perhaps what this means is that a decrease in control over prisons and prisoners by correctional authorities has created a power vacuum in our institutions. The perceived increase in prison violence then represents a power struggle among inmates to fill that vacuum. As Johnson (1987:81) concluded, "Today's prisons are, as a result, more relaxed in their discipline but more dangerous in their daily operation. The iron hand of the custodian has given way to a 'rule of the cruel,' with the hard-core convicts now setting the tone of prison life."

There is some evidence to suggest that the violence of American prisons that seemed to follow the expansion of prisoners' rights was temporary. Crouch and Marquart (1990:120) stated the issue, writing, "If (court) intervention heightens violence and if prisoners thus are exposed not only to the danger of assault and death but also to the stresses created by greater risk, perhaps intervention is not worth the pain to prisoners." Reviewing events in Texas (discussed below), they noted that an immediate effect of court intervention was an increase in violence among inmates. However, they discovered that inmates did not view the prison as any less safe after court intervention.

In 1972, inmates sued the Texas prison system alleging that the crowding, health care practices, disciplinary policies, and security practices of the prisons were unconstitutional. In particular, Texas employed inmate trustees, called "building tenders," to maintain order in cellblocks. Correctional staff supported the tenders in their efforts, and the methods used by them included physical abuse and assault. In signing an agreement to settle the lawsuit, the Texas Department of Corrections agreed to abolish the position of building tender. With the building tenders (and correctional staff's use of force), the Texas prisons were orderly but oppressive. Removal of the building tenders meant reducing brutality against inmates, but it also reduced order in the prisons.

In 1985, the Texas Department of Corrections responded to escalating violence by placing all known gang members and inmates who had assaulted guards or other inmates into "administrative segregation." This meant that prisons locked the most dangerous inmates in single cells for an indefinite period. This segregated approximately 3,200 inmates from the general inmate population. As a result, rates of inmate violence decreased, and inmate perceptions of prison safety were improved. Even in the prison, we must make decisions that balance personal liberty against the need for order. The restriction of this 10% of inmates made life safer and more orderly for the remaining 90%.

The dilemma we face is to solve the problem, if possible, without resorting to the oppressive conditions characteristic of prison life prior to the 1970s. The question is whether it is possible to grant legal rights and protections to prison inmates, as well as giving inmates some level of self-determination, while maintaining control over the operation of the prison. If we can answer yes to that question, there is a chance that we can reduce the current level of prison violence and retain what progress we have made in conditions of confinement. The most promising developments are in the area of inmate classification.

Classification involves the testing and assessment of inmates to determine inmate treatment needs and prison custody and security needs. Accurate, effective inmate classification can lead to safer, less violent prisons (Berk, Ladd, Graziano, & Baek, 2003). Wooldredge (2003) observed that effective classification can produce benefits beyond reduced violence. He argued that controlling prison violence is a positive goal to protect inmates and staff, but also a requirement for effective correctional treatment.

CONTINUING PRESSURES ON INCARCERATION

It does not seem likely that we will soon solve the current problems of incarceration in the criminal justice system. Indeed, current events seem likely to increase the pressure on U.S. prisons and jails. As noted, efforts to achieve truth in sentencing for violent offenders promise to increase the population of and confine even more violent offenders to the prisons and jails. Improved police procedures, coupled with the war on drugs, will result in higher numbers of arrests, with corresponding pressures on jails, and higher numbers of convictions leading to increased prison populations.

As states try to deal with crowding, there is likely to be more emphasis on seeking solutions in the private sector and a greater reliance on private provision of incarceration. Thus far we have not been able to build our way out of the prison crowding crisis. Prison crowding influences privatization, violence, and limited inmate participation in industry programs. Current policy choices, whatever their other consequences, appear likely to aggravate crowding in both prisons and jails.

There are growing pressures to revise and improve prison treatment programs both as something that is owed to inmates and as a means of reducing crime and future prison populations (Listwan, Lero, Cullen, & Latessa, 2008). In the past 30 years, substantial progress has been made in the development of correctional programming. Research indicates that well-planned, carefully implemented treatment programs can substantially reduce recidivism among correctional populations. Although prisons will retain their punitive and security function, there are increasing calls for the development of more therapeutic efforts in correctional institutions.

INCARCERATION IN THE TOTAL SYSTEM

Prisons and jails are inextricably linked to the larger society in which they exist. As we saw, prison researchers identified what they called a prisoner subculture, a social system with its own set of values and language set apart from the broader society. The prison subculture placed a positive value on criminality, resistance to correctional officials, and inmate solidarity (Clemmer, 1940; Sykes, 1958). Two explanations for the existence of this subculture emerged: a deprivation model and an importation model (Schwartz & Travis, 1997:127–130). The **deprivation model** suggests that the inmate code or prison subculture develops as a reaction to the losses experienced by prisoners on arrival in the prison. The loss of freedom, autonomy, goods and services, and the like supports the development of a new social order based on the values of the prison inmates born in reaction to their plight as prisoners. The **importation model**, however, suggests that the prison subculture is actually a product of the selection of inmates. Those persons sent to prison, according to the importation model, already subscribe to an antiauthority code of conduct. Thus, the prison imports its problems from the free society. Cao, Zhao, and Van Dine (1997) argued that the importation model is a better explanation of prisoner behavior than the deprivation model, suggesting that much of the problem of inmate misbehavior in prisons is a reflection of subcultural conflict that exists in the free society.

All of the issues examined in this chapter display links between incarceration and the wider society. Privatization reflects a broader movement to reduce governmental bureaucracy that has trickled down to prisons and jails. Prisoners' rights represent, at some level, an expansion of the general due process revolution in American criminal justice that began under the Warren Supreme Court. Violence in institutions reflects the growing violence in American society, including gang- and drug-related violence. The problem of crowding in American prisons and jails, however, is perhaps the best illustration of how the criminal justice system and its subsystems interact with their environment. Crowding in correctional institutions is a product of changes in the justice system as well as broader social changes. All components of the justice system feel its effects.

One of the explanations for prison and jail crowding is demography. The maturing of the baby-boom generation means that the raw material for the justice system—the number of potential criminals—has increased dramatically. Thus, criminal justice agencies must respond to changes in the material environment. Similarly, the war on drugs, mandatory sentencing for drunk drivers, and a general rise in the desire for punitive solutions among Americans all help to explain both the increasing rate of imprisonment and the longer sentences imposed. Here, we can see criminal justice agencies reacting to changes in the philosophical environment.

Welsh (1993) reported on a study of police arrest practices in jurisdictions in which the courts had ordered jail populations reduced. He found no significant statistical support for the view that court intervention changed arrest practices. However, he concluded that part of the change in arrest practices might be attributable to court intervention with the jail. Recognizing the complexity of the justice system and its relationship with its environment, Welsh concluded that increasing the use of citations in lieu of arrest is probably the result of a number of forces. He (1993:112) wrote, "[T]he presence of court orders indeed may contribute to changes in police arrest policy in specific municipalities, but other factors (e.g., local politics, different organizational interests, exchange relationships with other justice agencies) also interact to shape citation policy at the local level." Klofas (1990) noted that jail crowding and policies aimed at reducing that crowding are intimately linked to the wider community. He suggested that jail crowding can be best understood as a product of changes in community structure and function in general. One response to jail crowding is to change arrest practices by the police, whereas one effect of jail crowding is to undermine the ability of the police to use arrest powers to enforce the law or maintain order. In this case, the link between the front end and the back end of the justice system is clear—as is their relationship to the society in which they exist.

Since the war on drugs and the development of sentencing guidelines for the federal courts, the composition of the inmate population has both increased and changed. The redefinition of drug offenses as more serious crimes and the attempt to ensure greater retribution in the allocation of criminal punishments increased the number of drug offenders sentenced to federal prisons. The proportion of the federal prison population comprised of violent offenders decreased as a result. Given the large increase in the total population, however, this change reflects the increased imprisonment of those convicted of drug crimes, not a reduction in the use of prison for violent offenders. At the state level, there has been an increase in the number of violent offenders partly because of increasing lengths of terms for those convicted of violent crimes, related to truth in sentencing. The greatly increased costs of incarceration, combined with little perceived reduction in crime, has caused some people to question the emphasis we place on prison as a response to crime. This questioning of imprisonment supports an expanded role for community alternatives to incarceration, raising issues in community corrections. Thus, changes in our views of crimes and improvements in our ability to detect and apprehend offenders have ripple effects throughout the justice system that are most keenly felt in the corrections component that is "at the end of the line."

THEORY AND INCARCERATION

Once again, we see multiple explanations for criminal justice issues. Some observers contend that crowding is the product of changes in the law that led to more people being sent to prison for longer periods. Others explain crowding as a function of changes in the criminal justice environment or the outcome of people and organizations pursuing economic advantages. Crowding, in turn, is an explanation for violence and privatization.

There are varying explanations of the effects of crowding on levels of violence, the influence of prison industry on offender recidivism, and the levels of violence found in different prisons have a number of explanations. Researchers report that the characteristics of individual inmates influence levels of violence in correctional institutions. They also report that much of the variation in violence is a product of the characteristics of the prison or jail as an organization.

A former governor of Alabama, Lester Maddox, once said that we never will improve prisons in America until we get a better class of prisoner. He presented an individual theory of prisons. By this logic, prison conditions are the product of the prisoners we confine. Other explanations suggest we can change prisons by changing correctional personnel. If we increase standards for hiring, or enhance training, prison conditions will improve. Alternatively, some suggest it is the organization itself. If prisons were smaller, or larger, or friendlier, or more caring of inmates, conditions would be better.

Remember the factors we have identified that might explain differences in prisons and prison issues. Each of these factors can represent a theory of prison, and by extension, can contribute to a theory of criminal justice. What explains prisons? Do those same things also explain police and courts?

REVIEW QUESTIONS

1. Explain what is meant by privatization in institutional corrections, and identify at least three unresolved issues regarding the privatization trend.
2. Explain how the crisis of crowding impacted jail capacity.
3. Identify three strategies a state may employ to deal with prison crowding, and name some factors that may help explain why a particular state selects a specific option.
4. Identify the effects of prison crowding on inmates, staff, and prison administrators.
5. Identify the ways in which prison industry has been organized throughout the years.
6. What positive benefits are expected for the state and inmates from successful prison industry programs?
7. Why should we be concerned about prison riots?
8. Describe two strategies for reducing the prison population.
9. Describe how many of the problems faced by prisons and jails are reflections of broader changes and issues in the larger society.

References

Abbott, J. H. (1981). *In the belly of the beast: Letters from prison.* New York: Vintage.

Alarid, L. (2003). A gender comparison of prisoner selection for job assignments while incarcerated. *Journal of Crime and Justice, 26*(1), 95–116.

Auerbach, B. (1982). New prison industries legislation: The private sector re-enters the field. *The Prison Journal, 62*(2), 25–36.

Austin, J., & Irwin, J. (2001). *It's about time: America's imprisonment binge.* Belmont, CA: Wadsworth.

Bales, W., Bedard, L., Quinn, S., Ensley, D., & Holley, G. (2005). Recidivism of public and private state prison inmates in Florida. *Criminology & Public Policy, 4*(1), 57–82.

Barnes, C., & Kingsnorth, R. (1996). Race, drugs, and criminal sentencing: Hidden effects of the criminal law. *Journal of Criminal Justice, 24*(1), 39–55.

Baskin, D., Sommers, I., & Steadman, H. (1991). Assessing the impact of psychiatric impairment on prison violence. *Journal of Criminal Justice, 19*(3), 271–280.

Batiuk, M., Moke, P., & Rountree, P. (1997). Research note: Crime and rehabilitation: Correctional education as an agent of change. *Justice Quarterly, 14*(1), 167–180.

Beck, A., Berzofsky, M., Caspar, R., & Krebs, C. (2013). *Sexual victimization in prisons and jails reported by inmates, 2011–2012*. Washington, DC: Bureau of Justice Statistics.

Beck, A., & Harrison, P. (2007). *Sexual victimization in state and federal prisons reported by inmates, 2007*. Washington, DC: Bureau of Justice Statistics.

Beck, A., & Mumola, C. (1999). *Prisoners in 1998*. Washington, DC: Bureau of Justice Statistics.

Berk, R., Ladd, H., Graziano, H., & Baek, J. (2003). A randomized experiment testing inmate classification systems. *Criminology & Public Policy, 2*(2), 215–242.

Bierie, D. (2012). Is tougher better? The impact of physical prison conditions on inmate violence. *International Journal of Offender Therapy and Comparative Criminology, 56*(3), 338–355.

Bowditch, C., & Everett, R. (1987). Private prisons: Problems within the solution. *Justice Quarterly, 4*(3), 441–453.

Bowker, L. H. (1980). *Prison victimization*. New York: Elsevier.

Braswell, M., Montgomery, R., & Lombardo, L. (Eds.) (1994). *Prison violence in America*. (2nd ed.) Cincinnati, OH: Anderson.

Brown, E. (2013). Foreclosing on incarceration? State correctional policy enactments and the great recession. *Criminal Justice Policy Review, 24*(3), 317–337.

Bureau of Justice Assistance (2004). *Prison industry enhancement certification program*. Washington, DC: Bureau of Justice Assistance.

Bureau of Justice Statistics (1986). *Population density in state prisons*. Washington, DC: U.S. Department of Justice.

Camp, C., & Camp, G. (1996). *The corrections yearbook 1996*. South Salem, NY: Criminal Justice Institute.

Camp, S., Gaes, G., Langan, N., & Saylor, W. (2003). The influence of prisons on inmate misconduct: A multilevel investigation. *Justice Quarterly, 20*(3), 501–533.

Cao, L., Zhao, J., & Van Dine, S. (1997). Prison disciplinary tickets: A test of the deprivation and importation models. *Journal of Criminal Justice, 25*(2), 103–113.

Carson, E. A., & Golinelli, D. (2013). *Prisoners in 2012: Trends in admissions and releases, 1991–2012*. Washington, DC: U.S. Department of Justice.

Carson, E. A., & Sabol, W. (2012). *Prisoners in 2011*. Washington, DC: Bureau of Justice Statistics.

Chang, T. F. H., & Thompkins, D. (2002). Corporations go to prisons: The expansion of corporate power in the correctional industry. *Labor Studies Journal, 27*, 45–69.

Clear, T. (1997). Ten unintended consequences of the growth in imprisonment. *Corrections Management Quarterly, 1*(2), 25–31.

Clear, T., & Austin, J. (2009). Reducing mass incarceration: Implications of the iron law of prison populations. *Harvard Law & Policy Review, 3*, 307–324.

Clear, T., & Schrantz, D. (2011). Strategies for reducing prison populations. *The Prison Journal, 91*, 38S–59S.

Clemmer, D. (1940). *The prison community*. Boston: Christopher.

Conrad, J. (1982). What do the undeserving deserve? In R. Johnson & H. Toch (Eds.), *The pains of imprisonment* (pp. 313–330). Beverly Hills, CA: Sage.

Cooper, L. (1993). Minimizing liability with private management of correctional facilities. In G. Bowman, S. Hakim, & P. Seidenstat (Eds.), *Privatizing correctional institutions* (pp. 131–137). New Brunswick, NJ: Transaction.

Criminal Justice Newsletter (1985). Controversial A.C.A. policy calls for "privatization." *Criminal Justice Newsletter, 16*(3), 1–3.

Crouch, B., & Marquart, J. (1990). Resolving the paradox of reform: Litigation, prisoner violence, and perceptions of risk. *Justice Quarterly, 7*(1), 103–123.

Crutchfield, R. (2004). Editorial introduction—Commentary: Mass incarceration. *Criminology & Public Policy, 3*(2), 265–266.

Cullen, F. T., & Travis, L. F., III. (1984). Work as an avenue of prison reform. *New England Journal on Criminal and Civil Confinement, 10*(1), 45–64.

Davis, A. (1968). Sexual assaults in the Philadelphia prison system and sheriff's vans. *Trans-Action, 6*, 13.

DeFina, R., & Hannon, L. (2013). The impact of mass incarceration on poverty. *Crime & Delinquency, 59*, 562–586.

Doleschal, E. (1971). Rate and length of imprisonment. *Crime & Delinquency, 23*, 51.

Durham, A. (1989). Managing the costs of modern corrections: Implications of nineteenth-century privatized prison-labor programs. *Journal of Criminal Justice, 17*(2), 441–455.

Duwe, G., & Clark, V. (2013). The effects of private prison confinement on offender recidivism: Evidence from Minnesota. *Criminal Justice Review, 38*(3), 375–394.

Dyer, J. (2000). *The perpetual prison machine.* Boulder, CO: Westview.

Eichenthal, D., & Jacobs, J. (1991). Enforcing the criminal law in state prisons. *Justice Quarterly, 8*(3), 283–303.

Ericson, R., McMahon, M., & Evans, D. (1987). Punishment for profit: Reflections on the revival of privatization in corrections. *Canadian Journal of Criminology, 29*(4), 355–388.

Ethridge, P., & Marquart, J. (1993). Private prisons in Texas: The new penology for profit. *Justice Quarterly, 10*(1), 29–48.

Federal Bureau of Investigation (2001). *Crime in the United States, 2000.* Washington, DC: Bureau of Justice Statistics.

Flanagan, T., & Maguire, K. (1993). A full employment policy for prisons in the United States: Some arguments, estimates, and implications. *Journal of Criminal Justice, 21*(2), 117–130.

Fogel, D. F. (1979). *"We are the living proof ..." The justice model for corrections* (2nd ed.). Cincinnati, OH: Anderson.

Fowler, S., Blackburn, A., Marquart, J., & Mullings, J. (2010). Would they officially report an in-prison sexual assault? An examination of inmate perceptions. *The Prison Journal, 90*, 220–243.

Fox, V. (1983). *Correctional institutions.* Englewood Cliffs, NJ: Prentice Hall.

Gaes, G. (2008). Cost, performance studies look at prison privatization. *National Institute of Justice Journal, 259*, 32–36.

Geis, G., Mobley, A., & Shichor, D. (1999). Private prisons, criminological research, and conflict of interest: A case study. *Crime & Delinquency, 45*(3), 372–388.

Glaze, L., & Maruschak, L. (2008). *Parents in prison and their minor children.* Washington, DC: Bureau of Justice Statistics.

Gowdy, V. (1997). Should we privatize our prisons? The pros and cons. *Corrections Management Quarterly, 1*(2), 56–63.

Greenwood, P. (1981). *Private enterprise prisons? Why not? The job would be done better and at less cost.* Santa Monica, CA: RAND.

Greenwood, P. (1982). *Selective incapacitation.* Santa Monica, CA: RAND.

Griffin, M., & Hepburn, J. (2013). Inmate misconduct and the institutional capacity for control. *Criminal Justice and Behavior, 40*, 270–288.

Guerino, P., Harrison, P., & Sabol, W. (2011). *Prisoners in 2010.* Washington, DC: Bureau of Justice Statistics.

Hackett, J. C., Hatry, H. P., Levinson, R. B., Allen, J., Chi, K., & Feigenbaum, E. D. (1987). *Contracting for the operation of prisons and jails.* Washington, DC: U.S. Department of Justice.

Harrison, P., & Beck, A. (2006). *Prisoners in 2005.* Washington, DC: Bureau of Justice Statistics.

Hassine, V. (1996). *Life without parole: Living in prison today*. Los Angeles: Roxbury.

Hopper, J. (2013). Benefits of inmate employment programs: Evidence from the prison industry enhancement certification program. *Journal of Business & Economics Research, 11*(5), 213–222.

Huebner, B. (2003). Administrative determinants of inmate violence: A multilevel analysis. *Journal of Criminal Justice, 31*(2), 107–117.

Jackson, J., & Ammen, S. (1996). Race and correctional officers' punitive attitudes toward treatment programs for inmates. *Journal of Criminal Justice, 24*(2), 153–166.

Jacobs, J. (1977). *Stateville: The penitentiary in mass society*. Chicago: University of Chicago Press.

Johnson, R. (1987). *Hard time: Understanding and reforming the prison*. Monterey, CA: Brooks/Cole.

Johnson, R. (2001). *Hard time: Understanding and reforming the prison* (3rd ed.). Monterey, CA: Brooks/Cole.

Johnson, B., Larson, D., & Pitts, T. (1997). Religious programs, institutional adjustment, and recidivism among former inmates in prison fellowship programs. *Justice Quarterly, 14*(1), 145–166.

Jones, T., & Pratt, T. (2008). The prevalence of sexual violence in prison: The state of the knowledge base and implications for evidence-based correctional policy making. *International Journal of Offender Therapy and Comparative Criminology, 52*(3), 280–295.

Kaplan, S. (1987). Solid protection—New advances in body armor. *Corrections Today, 49*(4), 80–82.

Keve, P. (1986). *The history of corrections in Virginia*. Charlottesville: University of Virginia Press.

Klofas, J. (1987). Patterns of jail use. *Journal of Criminal Justice, 15*(5), 403–412.

Klofas, J. (1990). The jail and the community. *Justice Quarterly, 7*(1), 69–102.

Krajick, K. (1984). Punishment for profit. *Across the Board, 21*(3), 20–27 (March).

Kruttschnitt, C., & Krmpotich, S. (1990). Aggressive behavior among female inmates: An exploratory study. *Justice Quarterly, 7*(2), 371–389.

Kyckelhahn, T. (2013). *Local government corrections expenditures, FY 2005–2011*. Washington, DC: Bureau of Justice Statistics.

Lahm, K. (2008). Inmate-on-inmate assault: A multilevel examination of prison violence. *Criminal Justice and Behavior, 35*, 120–137.

Lanza-Kaduce, L., Parker, K., & Thomas, C. (1999). A comparative recidivism analysis of releases from private and public prisons. *Crime & Delinquency, 45*(1), 28–47.

Liedka, R., Piehl, A., & Useem, B. (2006). The crime-control effect of incarceration: Does scale matter? *Criminology & Public Policy, 5*(2), 245–276.

Listwan, S., Lero, C., Cullen, F., & Latessa, E. (2008). Cracks in the penal harm movement: Evidence from the field. *Criminology & Public Policy, 7*(3), 423–466.

Lockwood, D. (1980). *Prison sexual violence*. New York: Elsevier.

Lockwood, D. (1994). Issues in prison sexual violence. In M. Braswell, R. Montgomery, & L. Lombardo (Eds.), *Prison violence in America* (pp. 89–97) (2nd ed.). Cincinnati, OH: Anderson.

Logan, C. H. (1987). The propriety of proprietary prisons. *Federal Probation, 51*(3), 35–40.

Logan, C. H., & DiIulio, J. (1992). Ten deadly myths about crime and punishment in the U.S. *Wisconsin Interest, 1*, 21–35 (Winter/Spring).

Lommel, J. (2004). Turning around turnover. *Corrections Today, 66*(5), 54–63 (August).

Lonski, P. D. (1986). Illinois shatters myth—Industries boost local economy. *Corrections Today, 48*(7), 52–56.

Lundahl, B., Kunz, C., Brownell, C., Harris, N., & Van Vleet, R. (2009). Prison privatization: A meta-analysis of cost and quality of confinement indicators. *Research on Social Work Practice, 19*(4), 383–394.

Lynch, J., & Sabol, W. (2000). Prison use and social control. In J. Horney (Ed.), *Policies, processes, and decisions of the criminal justice system* (pp. 7–44). Washington, DC: National Institute of Justice.

Mahan, S. (1982). An orgy of brutality at Attica and the "killing ground" at Santa Fe: A comparison of prison riots. In N. Parisi (Ed.), *Coping with imprisonment* (pp. 65–78). Beverly Hills, CA: Sage.

Marquart, J. (2008). Addicted to prisons and asking "why don't they riot?" *Criminology & Public Policy, 7*(1), 153–158.

Marquart, J. W., & Crouch, B. M. (1984). Co-opting the kept: Using inmates for social control in a southern prison. *Justice Quarterly, 1*(4), 491–509.

Martin, J., Lichtstein, B., Jenkot, R., & Forde, D. (2012). "They can take us over any time they want": Correctional officers' responses to prison crowding. *The Prison Journal, 92,* 88–105.

Maruschak, L. (2004). *HIV in prisons, 2001.* Washington, DC: Bureau of Justice Statistics.

Maruschak, L., & Beck, A. (2001). *Medical problems of inmates, 1997.* Washington, DC: Bureau of Justice Statistics.

Marvell, T., & Moody, C. (1997). Age-structure trends and prison populations. *Journal of Criminal Justice, 25*(2), 115–124.

McCorkle, R. (1995). Gender, psychopathology, and institutional behavior: A comparison of male and female mentally ill prison inmates. *Journal of Criminal Justice, 23*(1), 53–61.

McDonald, D., Hassol, A., & Carlson, K. (1999). Can telemedicine reduce spending and improve prisoners health care? *National Institute of Justice Journal, 239,* 20–25 (April).

McDonald, D., & Patten, C. (2003). *Government's management of private prisons.* Washington, DC: National Institute of Justice.

McEwen, T. (1995). *National assessment program: 1994 survey results.* Washington, DC: National Institute of Justice.

Meares, T. (2004). Mass incarceration: Who pays the price for criminal offending? *Criminology and Public Policy, 3*(2), 295–302.

Miller, R., Sexton, G.E. & Jacobsen, V.J. (1991). *Making jails productive.* Washington, DC: National Institute of Justice.

Minton, T. (2013). *Jail inmates at midyear 2012—Statistical tables.* Washington, DC: Bureau of Justice Statistics.

Morris, N. (1974). *The future of imprisonment.* Chicago: University of Chicago Press.

Moses, M., & Smith, C. (2007). Factories behind fences: Do prison "real work" programs work? *National Institute of Justice Journal, 257,* 32–35 (June).

Mumola, C., & Karberg, J. (2006). *Drug use and dependence, state and federal prisoners, 2004.* Washington, DC: Bureau of Justice Statistics.

Nacci, P. L. (1988). The Oakdale–Atlanta prison disturbances: The events, the results. *Federal Probation, 52*(4), 3–12.

Nagel, W. G. (1973). *The new red barn: A critical look at the modern American prison.* New York: Walker & Co.

Newsweek, (1987, December 7). *A Cuban explosion.* 38–40.

Noonan, M., & Ginder, S. (2013). *Mortality in local jails and state prisons, 2000–2011—Statistical tables.* Washington, DC: Bureau of Justice Statistics.

Ogle, R. (1999). Prison privatization: An environmental catch-22. *Justice Quarterly, 16*(3), 579–600.

Piehl, A. (2004). The challenge of mass incarceration. *Criminology and Public Policy, 3*(2), 303–308.

Pogrebin, M., & Dodge, M. (2001). Women's accounts of their prison experiences: A retrospective view of their subjective realities. *Journal of Criminal Justice, 29*(6), 531–541.

Pollock, J. (2004). *Prisons and prison life.* Los Angeles, CA: Roxbury.

Pratt, T., & Maahs, J. (1999). Are private prisons more cost-effective than public prisons? A meta-analysis of evaluation research studies. *Crime & Delinquency, 45*(3), 358–371.

Rector, M. (1975). The extravagance of imprisonment. *Crime & Delinquency, 21*(3), 323–330.

Reisig, M., & Pratt, T. (2000). The ethics of correctional privatization: A critical examination of the delegation of coercive authority. *The Prison Journal, 80*(2), 210–222.

Rolland, M. (1997). *Descent into madness: An inmate's experience of the New Mexico State Prison riot.* Cincinnati, OH: Anderson.

Rynne, J., Harding, R., & Wortley, R. (2008). Market testing and prison riots: How public-sector commercialization contributed to a prison riot. *Criminology & Public Policy, 7*(1), 117–142.

Saylor, W., & Gaes, G. (1997). Training inmates through industrial work participation and vocational and apprenticeship instruction. *Corrections Management Quarterly, 1*(2), 32–43.

Schwartz, M. D., & Travis, L. F., III (Eds.) (1997). *Corrections: An issues approach* (4th ed.). Cincinnati, OH: Anderson.

Schwartz, M., Travis, L., & Clear, T. (Eds.) (1980). *Corrections: An issues approach* Cincinnati, OH: Anderson.

Schwarz, R. J. (1986). New Mexico: The anatomy of a riot. *Corrections Magazine, 6*(2), 6–24.

Serrill, M., & Katel, P. (1980). New Mexico: The anatomy of a riot. *Corrections Magazine, 6*(2), 6–24.

Sexton, G. (1995). *Work in American prisons: Joint ventures with the private sector.* Washington, DC: National Institute of Justice.

Shover, N., & Einstadter, W. (1988). *Analyzing American corrections.* Belmont, CA: Wadsworth.

Simon, L. (1993). Prison behavior and the victim–offender relationship among violent offenders. *Justice Quarterly, 10*(3), 490–506.

Snyder, H. (1990). *Growth in minority detentions attributed to drug law violators.* Washington, DC: Office of Juvenile Justice and Delinquency Prevention.

Spivak, A., & Shard, S. (2008). Inmate recidivism as a measure of private prison performance. *Crime and Delinquency, 54*, 482–508.

Stephan, J. (1997). *Census of state and federal correctional facilities, 1995—Executive summary.* Washington, DC: Bureau of Justice Statistics.

Stephan, J. (2008). *Census of state and federal correctional facilities, 2005.* Washington, DC: Bureau of Justice Statistics.

Stephan, J., & Jankowski, L. (1991). *Jail inmates, 1990.* Washington, DC: Bureau of Justice Statistics.

Stephan, J., & Karberg, J. (2003). *Census of state and federal correctional facilities, 2000.* Washington, DC: Bureau of Justice Statistics.

Stephan, J., & Walsh, G. (2011). *Census of jail facilities, 2006.* Washington, DC: Bureau of Justice Statistics.

Stohr, M., Lovrich, N., Menke, B., & Zupan, L. (1994). Staff management in correctional institutions: Comparing Diiulio's "Control Model" and "Employee Investment Model": Outcomes in five jails. *Justice Quarterly, 11*(3), 471–497.

Stohr, M., Lovrich, N., & Wood, M. (1996). Service versus security concerns in contemporary jails: Testing general differences in training topic assessments. *Journal of Criminal Justice, 24*(5), 437–448.

Stojkovic, S., Pope, C., & Feyerherm, W. (1987). Confinement patterns in the Milwaukee County House of Correction: 1907–1965. *Journal of Criminal Justice, 15*(4), 301–316.

Struckman-Johnson, C., & Struckman-Johnson, D. (2006). A comparison of sexual coercion experiences reported by men and women in prison. *Journal of Interpersonal Violence, 21*(12), 1591–1615.

Sykes, G. (1958). *The society of captives.* Princeton, NJ: Princeton University Press.

Thomas, C. (2005). Recidivism of public and private state prison inmates in Florida: Issues and unanswered questions. *Criminology and Public Policy, 4*(1), 89–100.

Tischler, C., & Marquart, J. (1989). Analysis of disciplinary infraction rates among male and female inmates. *Journal of Criminal Justice, 17*(6), 507–513.

Trammell, R. (2011). Symbolic violence and prison wives: Gender roles and protective pairing in men's prisons. *The Prison Journal, 91,* 305–324.

Vanyur, J. (1997). What it takes to be a warden in the 1990s. *Corrections Management Quarterly, 1*(2), 65–70.

Vito, G. (1985). Putting prisoners to work: Policies and problems. *Journal of Offender Counseling, Services, and Rehabilitation, 9*(3), 21–34.

Walker, S. (2011). *Sense and non-sense about crime, drugs, and communities* (7th ed.). Belmont, CA: West/Wadsworth.

Webster, C., & Doob, A. (2008). America in a larger world: The future of the penal harm movement. *Criminology and Public Policy, 7*(3), 473–487.

Welsh, W. (1993). Changes in arrest policies as a result of court orders against county jails. *Justice Quarterly, 10*(1), 89–120.

West, H. (2010). *Prisoners at midyear 2009.* Washington, DC: Bureau of Justice Statistics.

Williams, B., Stern, M., Mellow, J., Safer, M., & Greifinger, R. (2012). Aging in correctional custody: Setting a policy agenda for older prisoner health care. *American Journal of Public Health, 102*(8), 1475–1481.

Wilson, J. Q. (1975). *Thinking about crime.* New York: Basic Books.

Wolff, N., Blitz, C., Shi, J., Siegel, J., & Bachman, R. (2007). Physical violence inside prisons: Rates of victimization. *Criminal Justice and Behavior, 34,* 588–599.

Wolff, N., Shi, J., & Bachman, R. (2008). Measuring victimization inside prisons: Questioning the questions. *Journal of Interpersonal Violence, 23*(10), 1343–1362.

Wolff, N., Shi, J., & Siegel, J. (2009). Understanding physical victimization inside prisons: Factors that predict risk. *Justice Quarterly, 26*(3), 445–475.

Wooldredge, J. (2003). Keeping pace with evolving prison populations for effective management. *Criminology & Public Policy, 2*(2), 253–258.

Wright, R. (1994). *In defense of prisons.* Westport, CT: Greenwood Press.

Wright, R. (1997). The evidence in favor of prisons. In M. Schwartz, & L. Travis (Eds.), *Corrections: An issues approach* (4th ed.) (pp. 95–108). Cincinnati, OH: Anderson.

Wright, K. (2000). The evolution of decision making among prison executives, 1975–2000. In J. Horney (Ed.), *Policies, processes, and decisions of the criminal justice system* (pp. 177–224). Washington, DC: National Institute of Justice.

Zedlewski, E. (1987). *Making confinement decisions.* Washington, DC: U.S. Department of Justice.

Zedlewski, E. (1997). Why prisons matter: A utilitarian review. *Corrections Management Quarterly, 1*(2), 15–24.

Important Case

Brown v. Plata, 131 S. Ct. 1910 (2011).

CHAPTER 12

Probation, Parole, and Community Corrections

At any given time, there are roughly two times as many people under probation and parole supervision as there are people incarcerated in the United States. As of December 31, 2012, approximately 2% of the adult population of the United States were under either probation or parole supervision (Glaze & Herberman, 2013). Although incarceration may be the cornerstone of American corrections, the majority of criminal offenders receive sentences to probation.

By the end of 1985, the Bureau of Justice Statistics (1987:1) reported that more than 2.9 million persons were under correctional authority, and 74% of all those were under community supervision (probation or parole). By the end of 2012, more than 6.9 million adults were under correctional authority, with more than 4.7 million under probation or parole supervision (Glaze & Herberman, 2013). The majority of persons under community supervision (almost 4 million) were on probation. The combined probation and parole populations account for almost 70% of all those under the custody of correctional agencies. Although the percentage of the correctional population comprised of inmates (in jails and prisons) has increased during the past 25 years, community supervision is still the most common correctional setting.

Probation and parole supervision as currently operated, like the prison, are American inventions. Both involve the conditional release of convicted offenders into the community under supervision. Probationers and parolees experience similar treatment but, as we shall see, there are important differences between the two.

Probation and parole can be considered the "bookends" of imprisonment (see Box 12.1). **Probation** is a sanction generally imposed in lieu of incarceration and, thus, it occurs before imprisonment. **Parole** involves offenders released early from incarceration sentences, so it occurs after a period of imprisonment. Therefore, probation and parole flank imprisonment on either side as criminal sanctions.

This chapter examines community supervision in the criminal justice system of the United States. We will describe probation and parole supervision as

Important Terms

absconders
benefit of clergy
community
    service orders
discretionary
    release
diversion
furlough
halfway houses
home
    incarceration
judicial reprieve
mandatory
    release
mark system
"on paper"
parole
probation
reentry
reentry courts
release on
    recognizance
    (ROR)
restorative justice
special conditions
standard
    conditions
supervised
    release
suretyship
ticket of leave
work release

BOX 12.1 PROBATION AND PAROLE (2012): THE BOOKENDS OF IMPRISONMENT

Probation	Jail	Prison	Parole
3,942,800	744,500	1,483,900	851,200
56.8%	10.7%	21.4%	12.3%

- *Probation* is the sentencing of an offender to community supervision by a probation agency, often as a result of suspending a sentence to confinement. Such supervision normally entails specific rules of conduct while in the community. If the rules are violated, a sentence to confinement may be imposed. Probation is the most widely used correctional disposition in the United States.

- *Incarceration* is the confinement of a convicted criminal in a federal or state prison or a local jail to serve a court-imposed sentence. Confinement is usually in a jail, administered locally, or a prison, operated by the state or federal government. In many states offenders sentenced to 1 year or less are held in a jail; those sentenced to longer terms are committed to a state prison.

Release from prison generally occurs as the result of a decision of a paroling authority, mandatory release, or expiration of sentence.

- *Parole* is the release of a prisoner by the decision of a paroling authority. The offender is placed under the supervision of a parole officer who monitors the offender's compliance with rules of conduct imposed by the paroling authority. Violations of these rules may result in reimprisonment for the balance of the unexpired sentence.

- *Mandatory release* is based on earned "good time" (days earned for good behavior) or other statutory sentence-reduction measures and, though supervision is required after release, does not usually depend on the discretionary decision of a parole board. Supervision rules of conduct, if violated, may result in a return to prison for the time remaining on the sentence.

Source: Maruschak and Bonczar (2013)

well as some other forms of community control of offenders. We will explore the history and practice of probation and parole, and we will examine other community-based sanctions and the various populations involved in these sanctions.

THE ORIGINS OF COMMUNITY SUPERVISION

Probation and parole developed in the nineteenth century in the United States, although each had precursors in Western civilization. An examination of the history of community supervision shows how the justice system has changed with the social and intellectual currents in the larger society. Shortly after the creation of the penitentiary, many people came to view incarceration as a less-than-adequate response to all offenders. Probation and parole developed as alternatives to incarceration for select groups of offenders.

Probation evolved from several prior practices in the English courts that allowed judges to grant leniency to offenders and avoid the harsh corporal and capital punishments provided in the common law. Among these were the benefit of clergy, judicial reprieve, and release on recognizance (ROR) (Allen, Eskridge, Latessa, & Vito, 1985:37–40). Each of these practices allowed the sentencing judge to postpone or avoid the execution of sentence.

The **benefit of clergy** was a practice that developed during the medieval period so that members of the clergy were accountable to ecclesiastic (church) courts rather than civil courts. The accused could claim the benefit of clergy to have his or her case moved from the civil courts to the church courts. The test for benefit of clergy came to be one of literacy, in which the court required the accused to read the text of the fifty-first Psalm (see Box 12.2). In due time, illiterate common criminals committed the psalm to memory so that they could pretend to read it and thus avoid the punishments of the king's courts (Clear & Cole, 1986:232).

The fifty-first Psalm, because it allowed many offenders to avoid hanging as the penalty for their crimes, came to be known as the "neck verse." After a period of expansion of the benefit of clergy (from the fourteenth through the eighteenth centuries), the practice was disallowed by statute in 1827. No longer was it possible to escape in this way to the less severe sanctions of the church courts.

BOX 12.2 FIFTY-FIRST PSALM: THE NECK VERSE

Have mercy upon me, O God,
according to thy loving kindness,
According to the multitude of thy tender mercies
blot out my transgressions.

Judicial reprieve was a common practice in England in the nineteenth century. Under this practice, the offender could apply to the judge for a reprieve, which required that sentencing of an offender be delayed on the condition of good behavior for a specific period. After the allotted time, the offender could ask the king for a pardon. Here, we see the addition of two components of contemporary probation: (1) a set period and (2) the requirement that the offender abide by conditions of good behavior.

ROR was a practice (combined with peace bonds) that was a forerunner to bail. While awaiting the arrival of the circuit magistrate, an accused offender obtained release by posting a surety or by having someone vouch for him or her. This practice most directly led to the development of contemporary probation.

We generally credit John Augustus, a Boston boot maker, with being the father of probation. It was common practice in Massachusetts courts to release offenders on the recognizance of a third party. Augustus began a nearly 20-year career as a voluntary probation officer by posting bail in the Boston Police Court in 1841 for a man accused of drunkenness. Between 1841 and 1858, he supervised nearly 2,000 people. He was so successful that the state of Massachusetts passed legislation authorizing probation as a disposition and provided for the first paid probation officer. Over time, other states emulated the Massachusetts practice. Today, probation is the most common disposition of criminal cases.

Parole also developed in the mid-1800s. By the 1850s, observers of the penitentiary system grew dissatisfied with the effectiveness of incarceration in preventing further criminal behavior by offenders. These critics began to call for changes in incarceration practices that would serve to reform inmates and produce law-abiding citizens. The outcome of this reform movement was parole release and supervision. Parole has two components. The first is discretionary early release from prison. The second component is the period of supervision in the community that follows such a release.

In England and other European countries, several practices were already in place that laid the groundwork for the creation of parole. The term "parole" comes from the French phrase *parole de honeur*, meaning word of honor. Prisoners of war gained release on their "parole" that they would not again take up arms against their captors. This term was later applied to the procedure for allowing prison inmates to return to society prior to the expiration of their prison terms. Essentially, officials expected the prisoners to vow that they would not violate the law, in return for which they were granted release.

Banishment and transportation also have been considered to be precursors to parole, in that these procedures essentially allowed an offender to avoid a more harsh penalty on the condition that the offender not return to the land of the original crime (Barnes & Teeters, 1959). Closer to modern parole practice, however, were release procedures developed by Walter Crofton and Captain Alexander Maconochie. As superintendents of penal facilities, each of these men created a system of inmate discipline that allowed the prisoners to earn early release.

Crofton devised a "ticket of leave" for inmates in the Irish prison system. Prisoners were classified into three stages of treatment, ranging from segregated confinement, through work on public projects (which was increasingly free of supervision), until final release "on license." Successful inmates earned their ticket of leave through hard work and good behavior. When Crofton believed an inmate to be ready for release, he would issue a **ticket of leave**, which authorized the inmate to leave the prison, return home, and report to the local police. There was no supervision of the released inmate.

Alexander Maconochie is often called the father of parole. His system was very similar to that of Crofton. Maconochie operated the British penal colony on Norfolk Island, in the South Pacific. There he classified offenders into three groups and instituted a **mark system**. All inmates began at the penal stage, which involved close supervision while engaging in hard labor with a large group of fellow prisoners. Good behavior and industry earned "marks" for an inmate, and upon acquiring enough marks, the prisoner moved to the next stage. The social stage involved working and living in groups of about seven prisoners, with less supervision than the penal stage. Again, prisoners earned marks leading to promotion to the individual stage, during which the prisoner was allowed a cottage and was given individual work. Prisoners were subject to being moved back to earlier stages for misconduct or laziness. Those in the individual stage who continued to demonstrate good behavior and industry eventually earned a ticket of leave or conditional pardon. Often they were apprenticed to citizens on mainland Australia (Travis, 1985).

The apparent success of these programs was noticed in the United States. In 1870, the American Prison Association in Cincinnati provided the forum for reformers to push for the creation of parole and a system of reformatory discipline in the United States (Lindsey, 1925). With growing support for the early release and reformatory discipline, New York enacted legislation creating a reformatory at Elmira, where first offenders received sentences to terms that would last "until reformation, not to exceed five years." Parole release had been born in the United States.

Simon (1993) has reviewed and assessed the development of parole. He suggested that the practice of third-party recognizance, what he calls "suretyship," was a forerunner to modern parole. **Suretyship** was the practice of a person of good standing in the community taking responsibility for guaranteeing the lawful behavior of another person. When the prison became the dominant form of punishment, Simon suggested, people recognized that not all offenders needed to remain in prison, or at least not for full terms. Parole release and supervision allowed authorities to select worthy offenders and release them from prison. Officials used parole to support discipline, in that well-behaved, industrious inmates who could secure employment (and thus keep busy at socially acceptable activities) received parole. When employment opportunities decreased during the Great Depression, "clinical" parole replaced disciplinary parole. In this revised model, the purpose of parole was to support the treatment and rehabilitation of inmates. In both cases, parole enabled authorities to differentiate between those convicted criminals who could be reformed and those who could not.

We can apply a similar argument to the development of probation supervision, as the functions and definitions of probation have mirrored those of parole. The task of probation evolved from diverting selected offenders from prison through control and discipline in the community, to the provision of treatment and rehabilitative services to offenders who did not need the more intensive treatment of prison.

During the first 6 or 7 decades of its existence, parole faced a number of legal challenges. The practice of discretionary early release from incarceration gained acceptance by the 1940s. In addition, during this era (called the Progressive Era), increasing attention was focused on the role of postrelease supervision of offenders (as well as probation supervision). This led eventually to the current system of parole involving both early release and supervision in the community (Rothman, 1980).

Since the mid-1990s, there has been increased concern about **reentry**, the return of former inmates to life in the community. Throughout the 1990s, as prison populations continued to increase, it became apparent that relatively large numbers of parole violators accounted for a substantial portion of the inmate population (Burke, 2004). In 2012, more than one-quarter of all inmates admitted to state prisons were parole violators (see Figure 12.1).

The twin concerns of assisting released inmates to adjust to law-abiding life in the community and reducing the risk of new crime posed by released offenders led to the development of **reentry courts**, where services for and supervision of parolees are coordinated and monitored in a court environment. These operate much like drug courts in which a judge meets frequently with the offender

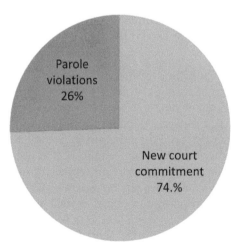

FIGURE 12.1
Source of new prison admissions.
Source: Carson and Golinelli (2013)

to monitor progress and, if needed, to change conditions of supervision and release (Lindquist, Hardison, & Lattimore, 2003; Travis, Solomon, & Waul, 2001). In many ways, the contemporary focus on prisoner reentry is similar to the original interest in developing parole (Burke & Tonry, 2006). We might say that we have rediscovered parole in the past decade.

An evaluation of one such program compared offenders enrolled in a specific reentry program with others who either received traditional prerelease services or no reentry programming at all (Wilson, 2007). Of the three groups, those who received no programming had fewer arrests and lower rates of revocation than either the reentry or traditional programming groups. The evaluators and others (Rhine, Mawhorr, & Parks, 2006) suggested that the reentry program was not properly designed and implemented. Correctional personnel seek to learn from their mistakes and improve programs for the future. A more recent evaluation of a different reentry court reported lower rates of rearrests and reconviction for parolees participating in the program (Hamilton, 2010). However, the closer supervision of the program did result in an increased rate of technical violations. It remains unclear how well reentry programs will do in improving parole supervision and outcomes.

THE ORGANIZATION OF COMMUNITY SUPERVISION: PROBATION AND PAROLE

Probation and parole, although very similar, differ in how they are organized. Whereas many states charge supervising officers with the responsibility of serving both parolees and probationers, there are other states where the two tasks are administratively separate (Bonczar, 2008). Probation tends to be a county and municipal function. Parole, on the other hand, usually is a state function, even in states where probation officers supervise parolees (U.S. Department of Justice, 1978).

According to the U.S. Department of Justice (1978), parole supervision was exclusively a state function in 44 states. Seven states (the total included the District of Columbia) supplement state-level authority with local systems. Probation supervision is a function of the criminal court, but in most cases, probation officers are employees of the executive branch of the state government. About a quarter of the agencies responsible for the supervision of adult and juvenile probationers are state level, whereas nearly 70% are organized at the county level. The remaining probation agencies are city and municipal organizations. For parole supervision, the numbers are reversed, with more than 90% of agencies charged solely with the supervision of parolees organized at the state level. In places where the same agency supervises both probationers and parolees, more than 90% of the organizations exist at the state level (U.S. Department of Justice, 1978). Thus, for the most part, probation is a local function and parole is a state function.

A survey of parole supervising agencies in 2006 (Bonczar, 2008) revealed that 35 (over two-thirds) of the systems reported combined probation and parole officers, while 17 maintained separate parole supervision staff. Even in states reporting dual roles for officers (probation and parole supervision), often there is a separate local system of probation. In many states, counties can choose to provide probation supervision themselves, or may turn responsibility for the supervision of probationers over to the state.

Probationers are under the jurisdiction of the sentencing court, and held to a set of conditions imposed by the sentencing judge. Probation officers are responsible for carrying out the wishes of the sentencing judge. Parolees, on the other hand, are under the jurisdiction of the state paroling authority, and held to a set of conditions imposed by that authority. Parole officers are responsible for carrying out the wishes of the parole authority, although in most cases parole supervision is independent of the parole release authority (Bonczar, 2008; Rhine, Smith, & Jackson, 1991). In jurisdictions in which the same officers supervise both parole and probation, the officers wear two hats, and their behavior is contingent on the legal status (probationer or parolee) of the client.

Inmates can be released from prison under a variety of terms. Several states allow prisoners to be released from a prison sentence with no parole supervision. These offenders are often said to have "maxed out" their sentence. Those inmates who enter parole supervision most often either receive a discretionary parole or achieve mandatory release. **Mandatory release** occurs at the expiration of a prison term reduced by good behavior, or when a sentencing law requires that inmates completing their prison terms receive supervision in the community for some period of time (Glaze & Bonczar, 2006:8). For the period of their supervision, they are on a conditional release and must obey the rules and conditions of parole or face a return to prison.

Discretionary release is granted by a parole board who will typically assess the inmate's perceived likelihood of successfully following the conditions of parole. The use of discretionary parole declined significantly from the 1970s until 2008. In 1977, 69% of inmates released from prison received discretionary parole release (Hughes, Wilson, & Beck, 2001). By 2008, discretionary parole represented fewer than 27% of parolees (Glaze & Bonczar, 2009). In 2012, discretionary release again became the most common type of entry to parole (Maruschak & Bonczar, 2013). Table 12.1 describes the number of offenders entering each type of parole supervision.

Table 12.1	Number of Adults Entering Parole, by Type of Entry, 2012
Discretionary	187,003
Mandatory	128,098
Supervised release	82,823
Reinstatement[a]	57,916

[a]*Reinstatement includes offenders returned to parole after serving time in prison due to a parole violation.*
Source: Maruschak and Bonczar (2013)

In 1984, Congress eliminated parole at the federal level and established a post-confinement monitoring system called **supervised release**. A term of supervised release is imposed at the initial sentencing hearing, requiring the offender to be monitored by a federal probation officer and to abide by certain conditions upon release from prison. Unlike parole, supervised release does not serve as a substitute for imprisonment. If the offender violates the terms of supervised release, he or she can be required to serve the term of supervised release in prison (United States Sentencing Commission, 2010).

Few systematic data exist on the characteristics of probationers and parolees. It is generally safe to say that probationers, for the most part, are offenders who have less extensive criminal records than prisoners. Auerhahn (2007), however, has estimated that the probation population in California is increasingly composed of offenders with prior felony records convicted of violent crimes. If this is true, then the traditional differences between probationers and parolees may be disappearing. Parolees, on the other hand, having been prisoners themselves, tend to mirror the prison population. In those states where release is discretionary, we might expect parolees to be slightly less dangerous than the general prison population, but this is speculation.

In 2012, more than 2 million adults were sentenced to probation, with an average supervision term of just under 2 years. At the same time, 496,100 persons entered parole supervision from state prisons (Maruschak & Bonczar, 2013). Table 12.2 presents a description of the characteristics of the probation and parole populations in 2012. The probation population contains more females,

Table 12.2	Characteristics of the Probation and Parole Population, 2012	
Characteristic	**Probation (%)**	**Parole (%)**
Sex		
Male	76	89
Female	23	11
Race		
White	54	41
African American	30	40
Hispanic	13	17
Other	**2**	**2**
Supervision status		
Active	72	82
Inactive	7	5
Absconded	10	6
Out-of-state	3	4
Other	8	3

Source: Maruschak and Bonczar (2013:18, 21)

fewer persons convicted of a violent offense, and fewer ethnic minorities than does the parole population. Given that ethnic minorities and males are more likely to receive prison sentences, it follows that the parole population (comprised of those who had been in prison) would have disproportionately fewer women and whites.

Not only do parole populations generally tend to be composed of offenders with more serious criminal records, but also, largely because of incarceration, parolees tend to have greater needs in the areas of housing, employment, and personal relations than do probationers. One major difference is that parole caseloads tend to be significantly smaller than probation caseloads. Camp and Camp (1996) reported that the average caseload for regular probation in the United States in 1995 was 142 offenders; for parole, the average caseload was 90 offenders. In 2006, the ratio of full-time equivalent officers supervising cases to active parolees was 1:38. However, even though parole caseloads are smaller, the greater needs of the parole population often make them more difficult to supervise than the probation population. Figure 12.2 compares supervision outcomes of probationers and parolees. Of those removed from supervision, nearly 70% of probationers successfully completed their terms, while 58% of parolees did so. Success rates for both probation and parole have increased since 2008 (Maruschak & Bonczar, 2013).

OTHER FORMS OF COMMUNITY SUPERVISION

Although probation and parole are the major components of community supervision of criminal offenders, other programs play a role in the nonincarceration treatment of convicted offenders. These programs include halfway houses, community service, furlough, work and education, home incarceration, and various diversion programs. Very frequently, courts or parole authorities require

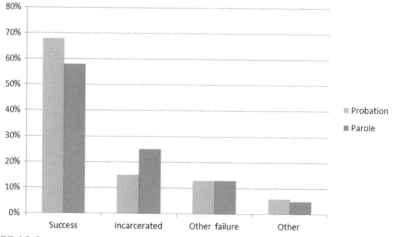

FIGURE 12.2
Supervision outcomes for adults leaving probation and parole, 2012.
Source: Maruschak and Bonczar (2013: 6, 9)

participation in these programs as conditions of release under probation or parole. Nonetheless, we will briefly discuss each of these separately.

Halfway Houses

Halfway houses are generally small residential programs based in the community that serve populations of fewer than 30 people (Wilson, 1985). Changes in thinking about the role of the community in the development of socially acceptable behavior spurred the development of halfway houses for both criminal offenders and the mentally ill (Beha, 1975). Although these houses have a long tradition, their application to criminal corrections has experienced tremendous growth in the past three decades (Allen, Carlson, Parks, & Seiter, 1978; Latessa & Travis, 1992).

Halfway houses are so-named because they represent an intermediate step that is halfway between incarceration and community supervision. They are either "halfway-out" houses that deal with parolees and other ex-inmates, or "halfway-in" houses for probationers and others not imprisoned (Keller & Alper, 1970). In either case, treatment is a part of the halfway-house routine.

In addition to providing room and board, halfway houses generally offer counseling services that include group and individual counseling sessions. Some halfway houses restrict their client population to special needs offenders, such as abusers of alcohol and other drugs. Other houses accept a wider range of persons and provide or contract for a wider range of services. Inasmuch as the popularity of halfway houses has increased, relatively little attention has been devoted to their effectiveness. Recent evidence is mixed regarding whether halfway houses reduce recidivism or provide a cost savings to states (Bell et al., 2013; White, Mellow, Englander, & Ruffinengo, 2011). In the past several years, the traditional halfway house name has been changing to "residential reentry center," though the function remains the same.

Community Service Programs

Community service orders are programs in which courts sentence convicted offenders to a number of hours of service to community organizations or governmental agencies (Perrier & Pink, 1985). The work takes place in the community, and the offender is generally at liberty except for the scheduled work hours. The work of the convicted offender is supervised (Umbreit, 1981). See Figure 12.3.

These programs have not been widely used with felons. Langan and Dawson (1993) reported that 4% of felons sentenced in state courts in 1990 were ordered to complete some form of community service. By 2006, that number had changed, with 11% of felons ordered to complete community service as part of their sentence (Rosenmerkel, Durose, & Farole, 2009).

Often community service is symbolically retributive in that the court requires the offender to render some service related to the offense. For example, drunk drivers might be ordered to assist in a hospital emergency room, vandals ordered

FIGURE 12.3
The Talbert House in Cincinnati, Ohio, was one of the first community-based agencies to receive accreditation from the American Correctional Association's Commission on Accreditation for Corrections.
Ellen S. Boyne

to clean and repair damaged buildings, and similar reflective penalties may be imposed on other offenders. A variant on community service is the chain gang, in which inmates work on public projects such as cleaning litter from roadsides while chained together in groups. Once discredited as too demeaning, chain gangs have recently resurfaced in some places. Probation officers typically supervise those completing community service sentences. Frequently, community service is a condition of probation (Tonry, 1998).

The Vera Institute of Justice in New York City operated one of the most ambitious community service sentencing programs reported to date (McDonald, 1986). In this program, courts sentenced minor offenders to perform 70 hours of community service work, such as cleaning and maintaining parks and senior citizen centers or restoring buildings for low-income housing. The community service sanction applied to those offenders likely to receive jail terms of 90 days or less and on those likely to receive no sanction because of the pettiness of their offenses. In a 5-year span, nearly 3,500 offenders served community service sentences in three boroughs of New York.

Community service is often a core component of restorative justice programs. The term **restorative justice** refers to efforts to repair the harm to victims and/ or communities caused by crime through interventions with the offender. Karp and Drakulich (2004) reported on a statewide program of restorative justice in Vermont that involved those convicted of less serious offenses receiving probation with a condition that they participate in the restorative justice program. Nearly two-thirds of restorative justice cases included community service orders. If restorative justice efforts increase, we can expect an increased reliance on community service in the future.

Furlough Programs

Furlough programs also are relatively recent alternatives to the traditional sanction of incarceration. At base, a furlough program allows an inmate to leave the penal facility for a specified period to perform an identified function. Several prisons and jails operate work and educational furlough programs. Inmates are released, without escort, to participate in educational programs or to report to work. After work or school, they return to the institution.

These programs seek to eliminate some of the more debilitating effects of incarceration, such as the loss of a job or the severance of community ties. Furloughs also help inmates prepare for reentry to the community by gradual exposure to release (Doleschal, 1971). Inmates on these types of furloughs seek work and housing, which they will need on release from the institution.

Furloughs have a relatively long history in American corrections, but their use has changed and grown in recent years. Traditionally, furloughs were available to prison inmates in cases of family emergencies (e.g., to visit seriously ill relatives or to attend funerals). In these traditional furloughs, the inmate and the inmate's family were required to pay all expenses, including the cost of an escorting officer (Fox, 1983:147). In the 1960s, several states began granting furloughs to qualifying inmates for social visits by issuing weekend passes to certain inmates. Today, many states use furlough programs to allow inmates that are near the time of their release on parole to seek employment or arrange for residences. Each year thousands of prison inmates receive furloughs from prison in more than 40 jurisdictions. The federal bureau of prisons grants three types of furloughs. Sixteen-hour furloughs require inmates to return to the institution in the evening, whereas overnight furloughs allow inmates to leave the facility for either 5 or 7 days.

LeClair and Guarino-Ghezzi (1991) studied furlough programs in Massachusetts. They found that prisoners who received furloughs were significantly less likely to commit new offenses after release than those who did not receive furloughs. They suggested that furlough programs serve as a positive reward for good behavior by inmates, and that by going on furlough, inmates may become more committed to adopting a lawful lifestyle. This is, indeed, the theory behind furlough programs. As LeClair and Guarino-Ghezzi suggested, we need to learn more about how furlough programs may work to reduce recidivism.

Work and Educational Release Programs

In a move related to furloughs, which tend to be brief releases for a specified period, correctional agencies are making use of work or study/educational release. Work or study release refers to the practice of allowing inmates of correctional facilities to leave the institution during the day to attend classes or work at a job. More than 9,000 jail inmates in 1995 were involved in work release programs (Gillard & Beck, 1996), and more than 55,000 prison inmates participated in work or study release programs in that year (Camp & Camp, 1996).

In 2005, 28% of confinement facilities operated work release programs for inmates (Stephan, 2008). More than 5,000 jail inmates were participating in work release programs in 2006 (Minton, 2010).

Work release programs allow inmates to secure or maintain employment while serving terms of incarceration. The opportunity for inmates released for work to maintain ties to conventional lifestyles and to their communities is a benefit of work release programs. Such inmates also can help support their families and often must contribute to the cost of their incarceration. This reduces overall correctional costs to the community. Although relatively few inmates participate in such release programs, those who do participate benefit from leaving the correctional facility and by being able to keep jobs or secure an education (Wright & Travis, 1996). See Figure 12.4.

Turner and Petersilia (1996) reported an evaluation of work release programming in the state of Washington. They found that almost 40% of inmates participated in work release programs at some point during their term. Most work release participants successfully completed the program, with only 5% committing new crimes. However, they did not find the work release program to reduce later recidivism or correctional costs when compared to what happened with inmates who did not receive a work release placement as is shown in Figure 12.5. In recent years, the use of work release programs has decreased compared to the early 1970s. Turner and Petersilia suggested that the decreased use of work release is a product of increased concerns about public safety and reduced program funding available from the federal government.

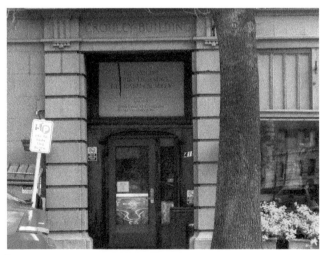

FIGURE 12.4
Located in Seattle, the Reynolds Work Training Release Facility is Washington State's largest work release facility for males.

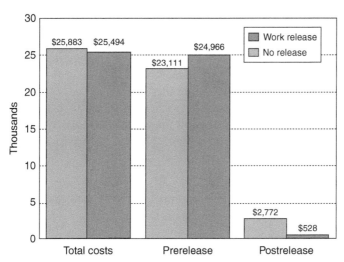

FIGURE 12.5
Work release costs: Comparison of released and nonreleased offenders.
Source: Turner and Petersilia (1996)

Home Incarceration

As a response to crowded prisons and jails, there has been a resurgence of interest in the practice of house arrest or **home incarceration** (Petersilia, 1986). Offenders sentenced to home incarceration are essentially grounded. They must remain at home except for approved absences, such as attending school, going to work, or keeping medical appointments. While thus incarcerated, the offender is out of society, yet not confined in a jail. The offender retains ties to family and the community, the state faces reduced costs, and the offender generally experiences better conditions of confinement than would exist in a penal facility.

Proponents of home incarceration argue that this practice is more humane and less costly than incarceration (Corbett & Fersch, 1985). These proponents suggest that, for many offenders, home incarceration represents a more satisfactory alternative to incarceration than do the traditional practices of fines or probation. With home incarceration, someone (usually a probation officer) must be responsible for monitoring the offender to ensure that he or she stays home. At midyear 2006, more than 800 jail inmates were on home detention with no other monitoring, and an unknown portion of the nearly 11,000 inmates under electronic monitoring were also on home detention (Sabol, Minton, & Harrison, 2007).

Diversion

The general rubric of **diversion** incorporates a wide variety of programs that occur at all stages of the justice system. Diversion is included in the discussion of community supervision because its most common formal application is at some point in the court process prior to conviction or sentencing. In most places, the same office provides supervision of both diverted and sentenced offenders: the probation department (McSparron, 1980).

Diversion programs prevent some offenders from passing through the justice system, or minimize the extent of their processing. Supporters hope diverting offenders from the system will enable them to avoid the stigma of a criminal label and other negative effects of justice system processing. Although used for adults in many jurisdictions, diversion programs are more common with juvenile offenders (Latessa, Travis, & Wilson, 1984).

BEING ON PAPER

We discuss additional types of community sanctions or forms of probation and parole supervision in Chapter 13. These include shock probation and parole, electronic monitoring, and day reporting programs. Just as the alternatives discussed above, each of these innovations either represents a form of community supervision or is imposed as a condition of probation or parole. Remember that probation and parole are the core components of community corrections, and that each of these is a form of conditional release from prison. The underlying assumption is that the offender would be in prison or jail if not for his or her participation in community programming.

Community supervision is the punishment of choice for most offenders. The pressures from prison crowding have enhanced the already important role community supervision plays in the justice system. Community supervision is an alternative to imprisonment. We generally hold offenders under community supervision to a higher moral standard than members of the free society, by virtue of the conditions of release. A term probationers and parolees often use to describe their status is to say they are **"on paper."** This refers to the written probation or parole agreements that set out the conditions of release.

Supervision Conditions

In the final analysis, probation and parole represent an agreement between the offender and the state. In return for the decision not to incarcerate (or for the decision to release from incarceration), the offender agrees to abide by several conditions while at liberty in the community. Violation of any of these conditions can be the basis for revocation of liberty and subsequent incarceration of the offender.

Probation and parole conditions cover a wide variety of behavior and serve a number of purposes (Travis & Latessa, 1984:599). The primary goal of supervision conditions is to prevent future criminality on the part of probationers and parolees. There are two general types of conditions: **standard conditions** that are imposed on everyone under supervision in a jurisdiction, and **special conditions** imposed on individual offenders that relate directly to the offender's status and characteristics (Travis & Stacey, 2010).

Standard conditions of parole and probation vary across jurisdictions. They usually include restrictions on travel and on the freedom to change addresses or jobs, and involve instructions on reporting to the supervising officer. These conditions ensure that the probation or parole officer will be able to monitor the offender. Table 12.3 presents standard conditions of parole in the United States during the past quarter century. Special conditions vary greatly (Jaffe, 1979). They include such things as restrictions on association with particular people, requirements of attending treatment programs, restrictions on the consumption of alcoholic beverages, and restitution orders.

The conditions of probation and parole serve a number of purposes. Some conditions are necessary to ensure that supervision can occur. Thus, offenders may not be allowed to change their jobs or addresses without notifying the supervising officer. They may be required to report to a probation or parole officer on a regular schedule. Offenders who fail to submit to supervision (do not report as directed, change jobs or addresses without notifying their supervising officer, etc.) are called **absconders**, as they absconded (escaped) from supervision. A study of probation absconders (Mayzer, Gray, & Maxwell, 2004) found that these offenders often seem to abscond in the face of probable revocation and they do not appear to differ from probationers who ultimately have their conditional liberty revoked. It seems likely that those who abscond from supervision have violated the conditions of release in other ways as well.

Other supervision conditions impose punishment, such as a requirement that an offender pay restitution, write a punishment lesson, or do community service

Table 12.3	Percentage of American Parole Jurisdictions Imposing Routine Conditions, 1982–2008		
Standard Condition	1982	1995	2008
Comply with the law	96	90	100
Change residence	92	79	98
Possess firearm/dangerous weapon	92	90	96
Maintain employment/education program	73	81	94
Report regularly	94	33	87
Permit home/work visits and searches	42	61	87
Out-of-state travel	100	88	87
Use controlled substances	63	88	81
Change employment	87	81	79
Pay fees/restitution	NA	46	79
Report arrest/questioning by law enforcement	50	63	71
Make first arrival report	75	58	63
Submit to medical/drug test	NA	40	63
Undesirable associates/locations	50	NA	60
Alcohol use	44	42	54
Obey PO instructions	NA	23	54
Give written/oral information	NA	55	NA
Waive extradition	50	NA	NA

Source: Travis and Stacey (2010)

work. A judge in Painesville, Ohio, sentenced men convicted of soliciting a prostitute to wear a chicken suit and carry a sign that read, "No Chicken Ranch in Painesville." The sign is a reference to a famous Chicken Ranch prostitution house in Nevada (*Cincinnati Enquirer*, 2007). Still other conditions seek to ensure that offenders receive treatment for their problems by requiring participation in educational, psychological, or substance abuse programs.

We also use special conditions to reduce the risk of new criminality. For instance, jurisdictions across the country have placed specialized conditions on the supervision of sex offenders. These conditions often require the sex offender to register on a public database and to live outside of a specified distance of schools, day care centers, parks, and so on. Finally, some conditions do not impose restrictions on behavior, but give the offender notice. This may be the case, for example, when a condition of supervision is that the offender remains on probation or parole until discharged. What this condition does, of course, is tell the offender that supervision does not end until released by the supervising authority.

Client Perspectives

The experience of being on paper reflects the number and content of conditions as well as the characteristics of the probation or parole officer. A probationer facing conditions that include a curfew, requirements of restitution, restriction on associating with friends, and some period of incarceration will have a qualitatively different experience than will a probationer under less restrictive conditions. Similarly, a parolee whose supervising officer is rule oriented and unsympathetic will experience a different sanction than one whose officer is flexible and empathetic.

The ability to impose special conditions of probation has led to the use of probation to accomplish many correctional goals not necessarily authorized by statute. For example, in a jurisdiction in which there is no law authorizing split sentences, a judge wishing to impose such a sentence can place the offender on probation on condition that he or she serves some time in jail (Talarico & Myers, 1987). In a like fashion, absent a statutory authority to impose restitution, a judge can simply make restitution a condition of probation. Probation and (to a lesser extent) parole are the most flexible of sanctions. This may account, in part, for their popularity among justice system officials.

Criminal justice scholars have asked probationers and parolees for their views on community supervision (Allen, 1985; Gibbs, 1985; Martin, Hanrahan, & Bowers, 2009; Spelman, 1995; Wood & May, 2003). In large part, these offenders prefer probation or parole to any form of incarceration. Many feel fortunate to have an opportunity to prove themselves in the community, but most also identify problems associated with being under supervision.

In some cases, offenders see community supervision as a less desirable sanction than incarceration (Crouch, 1993; Petersilia, 1990; Wood & May, 2003). If the prison or jail term will be short and followed by unsupervised release, but probation or parole supervision will entail close supervision and restrictive conditions, many offenders would rather just "get it over with." They would prefer a short term of incarceration followed by freedom instead of what they expect will be a period of close supervision followed by prison if they are found in violation of conditions. This suggests that, at some level, it is possible to design a community supervision sanction that is as unpleasant as incarceration.

Probationers and parolees most often complain about what they perceive as the pettiness and unfairness of some conditions of release. They also dislike the requirement that they seek approval of their supervising officers for many minor decisions (Williams, May, & Wood, 2008). Wood and May (2003) suggested that African Americans or other minority group members may perceive greater discrimination and unfairness in community supervision than in prison, leading them to conclude that prison is often a less severe sanction than community alternatives. Finally, many are dissatisfied with their officers. Many probationers and parolees believe their officers do not act as advocates for them, and many believe their officers are too intrusive. Offenders also complain about the social distance between themselves and their supervising officer (Helfgott, 1997). In other words, the offenders perceive the officers as having too little in common with them, making it difficult for the officers to appreciate the daily struggles faced by those under community supervision.

As probation and parole have become more intrusive and controlling in recent years, the perceived difference between being on paper and doing time may have decreased. Chapter 13 describes these changes in supervision in more detail, but in general, the increase in punitiveness has made community supervision more troublesome to offenders. At the same time, because of crowding, many jurisdictions have shortened incarceration terms. As a result, when offered release on parole for a given period or incarceration for a short period, many offenders choose incarceration. In a sample of Texas prisoners, Crouch (1993:79) found that almost half would choose 1 year in prison instead of 5 years of probation. A study compared probationer and probation officer perceptions of the burden of certain community sanctions relative to imprisonment and found that officers routinely overestimated the severity of sanctions. In general, probationers were much less likely to agree to additional sanctions, such as fines, restitution, and the like to avoid incarceration. Similarly, offenders reported that community service was much less onerous than probation officers thought it to be. The implications of this research are that probation and parole officers may be very limited in their ability to control offender behavior through the threat of sanctions (Flory, May, Minor, & Wood, 2006). If offenders would prefer jail time to intensive supervision, the threat of jail is unlikely to convince them to abide by the conditions of supervision.

Officer Perspectives

Probation and parole officers lead a "schizophrenic" existence in relation to their jobs. For years, research into the role of the community supervision officer has identified conflicting dimensions of the responsibilities to help but also to control (Clear & Cole, 1986). The officer is expected to befriend and assist his or her clients, as well as to monitor and control them. Most officers think that offender success is primarily a function of rational choice and generally view the offender's complaint of social distance as an excuse (Gunnison & Helfgott, 2011). With reference to parole officers, Studt (1973) identified officer "style" as critical to an understanding of the supervision process. She observed two basic styles: service (emphasis on helping the offender) and surveillance (emphasis on controlling criminal conduct).

Crean (1985:118) reported, "Within a typical work week, a line officer is usually called upon to be an investigator, a biographer, a watchdog, counselor, friend, confidant, reporter, expert witness, and broker of outside services." The line officer is a public employee and responsible to the authority that placed the offender under the officer's supervision. Further, the officer must interact on a regular basis with the offender, the offender's family, law enforcement officials, and representatives of community agencies (Sigler, 1988).

As with most criminal justice jobs, community supervision involves a rather large degree of discretion and responsibility. It also entails a tremendous amount of paperwork. Even though there are psychological, monetary, and social rewards in being a probation or parole officer, there are the concomitant costs of dealing with offenders, danger, and bureaucracy. Nevertheless, probation and parole officers exhibit the characteristics of professionals, and they frequently do not work steady hours. Those who remain at their positions learn to separate work from the other aspects of their lives.

In a study of role conflict among probation officers working in intensive supervision programs, Clear and Latessa (1993) failed to find evidence of effects of different role definitions on individual officers. They compared officers working in one program that was clearly control oriented with those working in another that was clearly treatment oriented. They found that individual officers displayed differences in role definition (seeing themselves as more control or treatment/support oriented), but not in how they approached the jobs. The organizational philosophy of the probation agency appeared to be more important in explaining differences in case treatment than did individual attitudes. Regardless of whether the officer personally prefers control or support as an orientation to the job, the officer is able to perform only in compliance with organizational expectations. As Clear and Latessa noted, a key question that remains is to discover how agencies select officers whose role definitions meet agency philosophy, or how agency philosophy is transmitted to officers and how it influences officer behavior. Fulton, Stichman, Travis, and Latessa (1997) reported that officer role orientation can be changed through training, again suggesting that it is the organizational policy more than the individual officer attitudes that affects a probation or parole officer's style of work.

Probation and (to a lesser extent) parole are correctional interventions that often employ citizen volunteers. Inasmuch as a volunteer started probation, this volunteer involvement is not surprising. Because the primary task of community supervision is to see that offenders can reside safely in the community, there are good reasons for using volunteers. Volunteers can perform many functions for probation and parole officers. The use of volunteers also helps clients by connecting them with law-abiding citizens (Lucas, 1987).

The dual roles of service and surveillance, coupled with heavy caseloads and frequently inadequate community services, often frustrate probation and parole officers and managers. Some areas of inquiry have included burnout and job satisfaction among the ranks of probation and parole officers (Whitehead, 1986). Although the job of community supervision agent has many demoralizing facets, most officers report that the benefits outweigh the drawbacks of the job.

OFFENDER RIGHTS IN COMMUNITY SUPERVISION

Probation and parole normally are considered privileges and not rights (del Carmen, 1985). Once placed on probation or parole, however, the offender does have a constitutionally protected interest in retaining that status. To date, there have been relatively few U.S. Supreme Court decisions dealing with the acceptability of various conditions of release and supervision practices. State or federal appellate courts have decided most of the existing cases in this area. In 2006, the U.S. Supreme Court decided the case of *Samson v. California*. Samson's parole conditions required him to submit to warrantless searches by police or his parole officer. One such search uncovered criminal evidence resulting in his return to prison. The Court ruled that the search was acceptable because of the parole condition that authorized it.

Essentially, courts have supported all types of probation and parole conditions, as long as those conditions were constitutional, reasonably related to criminality, clearly written, and/or contributed to the rehabilitation of the offender. The decisions of courts vary across jurisdictions, and are indeed case specific. For example, the courts are likely to uphold a prohibition against the consumption of alcoholic beverages in a case in which the offender's criminality stemmed from drunkenness, but void it in a case in which the offender has no history of alcohol abuse.

Probation and parole conditions often serve as an arsenal of leverage for correctional authorities. Because violation of any of the conditions of parole or probation constitutes grounds for revocation and incarceration, the conditions provide the officer with tools for controlling the offender. With regard to revocation, however, the U.S. Supreme Court has set forth due process protections for probationers and parolees.

In 1972, the Court decided the case of *Morrissey v. Brewer*, in which a parolee sought relief after his parole had been revoked. The Court ruled that parolees facing revocation must be granted the following protections: (1) written notice of the claimed violations, (2) disclosure of evidence against the parolee, (3) the opportunity to be heard and to present evidence, (4) a limited right to confront and cross-examine witnesses, (5) a hearing before a neutral body, and (6) a written statement of the decision and evidence on which it was based.

The following year, the Court decided the case of *Gagnon v. Scarpelli* (1973), which dealt with probation revocation. In this case, the Court stated that, at least regarding revocation procedures, there was no substantial difference between probationers and parolees. They granted probationers the same protections as those given to parolees.

Persons under community supervision generally are less restricted and suffer fewer pains than those who are incarcerated. Nonetheless, community supervision is still a punishment for crime, and the status of conviction and being under sentence sets probationers and parolees apart from free citizens. Even with the protections afforded by the *Morrissey* and *Gagnon* decisions, probationers and parolees may have their liberty revoked and may be incarcerated for offenses that would not carry similar penalties for free citizens. In addition, incarceration may follow hearings for which the burden of proof is not as high as the trial standard of proof beyond a reasonable doubt.

Hoffman and Beck (2005) described a pilot program of the U.S. Parole Commission that involved expedited revocation hearings. In many cases, the alleged misbehavior involves violations of the technical conditions of parole and the parolee admits the violation. In these cases, the function of the revocation hearing is to determine the sanction. If the parolee consents, they waive the probable cause hearing and return the parolee to the institution for a dispositional hearing. The researchers concluded that the expedited process was cost-effective and supported by all parties, including defense counsel.

Community supervision serves crime control functions by allowing the state to limit the risk of new crimes being committed through relaxed requirements for revocation (as compared to conviction). Yet, probationers and parolees have protected interests in conditional liberty, and the actions and decisions of probation and parole authorities are constrained by some due process requirements. It is instructive to observe that although a number of states and the federal government have taken steps to eliminate discretionary parole release, most have retained a period of postrelease supervision. Community supervision itself represents a balance between individual interests in avoiding incarceration and community interests in controlling potential criminality.

See Box 12.3 for a table of selected court cases on probation and parole.

Supervision conditions also represent part of the arsenal of the prosecutor. As we discussed earlier, it is common for prosecutors to dismiss new criminal charges when they can proceed to a probation or parole revocation. Kingsnorth, MacIntosh, and Sutherland (2002) studied probation violation processing in eight California counties. They reported that prosecutors frequently seek probation violations rather than file new criminal charges. This is especially true when the new offense is less serious than the one for which the offender was placed on probation.

BOX 12.3 SELECTED CASES ON COMMUNITY SUPERVISION

Morrissey v. Brewer 408 U.S. 471 (1972)	Parolees facing revocation must be granted: written notice of the claimed violations; disclosure of evidence against the parolee; the opportunity to be heard and to present evidence; a limited right to confront and cross-examine witnesses; a hearing before a neutral body; and a written statement of the decision and the evidence on which it was based
Gagnon v. Scarpelli 411 U.S. 778 (1973)	At least in regard to revocation procedures, there is no substantial difference between probationers and parolees; therefore, probationers are granted the same protections as parolees (for specific protections granted, see *Morrissey v. Brewer*)
Samson v. California 547 U.S. 843 (2006)	Supreme Court affirmed the decision holding that suspicionless searches of parolees are lawful under California law and reasonable under the Fourth Amendment

COMMUNITY SUPERVISION IN THE WHOLE SYSTEM

In previous chapters, we have discussed several areas of overlap between community supervision and other components of the justice system. Pretrial release, diversion from court, prosecutorial charging, incarceration, and the size of the prison population all involve decisions that depend (more or less) directly on the operation of community supervision. For example, if probation and parole were not available as alternatives to incarceration, absent the development of other practices, the prison and jail population would increase threefold. The growth of intermediate sanctions and other changes in community supervision practices show how the criminal justice process is an open system.

The development of intermediate sanctions and their effects on community supervision agencies and practices illustrate the open nature of the criminal justice system. The primary motivation for these new alternatives has been the need to control correctional costs, and the prison population specifically. As the prison population grew, so did community supervision populations. The same forces that produced the increase in prisoners have worked to swell community supervision populations. The war on drugs, for example, brought a large number of offenders into the justice system. Low-level drug offenders are now prime candidates for intermediate sanctions while under community supervision. A common adjustment to truth in sentencing, which requires longer prison terms for violent offenders, has been to divert property and public order offenders from prison to probation or parole.

The prison population crisis has changed the nature of the community supervision population so that there are increased numbers of felons and more serious offenders under probation and parole supervision than historically was the case. The increase in the numbers of offenders provides the impetus for changes in community supervision management, financing, and programs. Because they involve closer supervision and impose more restrictive conditions of release, some of these programs have relatively high rates of supervision failure. Those revoked from intermediate sanction programs often are imprisoned, but now come to prison as community supervision failures.

In these ways, we can see the links between the components of the justice system, and between the justice system and the larger society. A redefinition of the seriousness of drug offenses led to enhanced drug crime enforcement. Increased enforcement changed the size and composition of the correctional population, both those incarcerated and those under community supervision. Seeking ways of managing the larger populations, we have developed intermediate sanctions that have altered traditional community supervision programs. Changes in community supervision, in turn, seem to have put increased pressure on prison populations through increased numbers of supervision failures. The next chapter explores changes in community supervision in more detail.

REVIEW QUESTIONS

1. Distinguish between probation and parole.
2. Briefly trace the origins of community supervision in corrections.
3. Describe the organization of community supervision.
4. Tell what is meant by the term "reentry."
5. Identify five forms of community supervision, excluding traditional probation and parole.
6. Distinguish between standard and special conditions of probation or parole.
7. Describe the role and importance of community supervision in the criminal justice system.
8. Identify the due process rights of probationers and parolees at revocation.

References

Allen, G. F. (1985). The probationers speak: Analysis of probationer's experiences and attitudes. *Federal Probation, 49*(3), 67–75.

Allen, H. E., Carlson, E. W., Parks, E. C., & Seiter, R. P. (1978). *Halfway houses.* Washington, DC: U.S. Government Printing Office.

Allen, H. E., Eskridge, C. W., Latessa, E. J., & Vito, G. F. (1985). *Probation and parole in America.* Monterey, CA: Brooks/Cole.

Auerhahn, K. (2007). Do you know who your probationers are? Using simulation to estimate the composition of California's felony probation population, 1980–2000. *Justice Quarterly, 24*(1), 28–47.

Barnes, H. E., & Teeters, N. D. (1959). *New horizons in criminology.* Englewood Cliffs, NJ: Prentice Hall.

Beha, J. A. (1975). Halfway houses in adult corrections: The law, practice, and results. *Criminal Law Bulletin, 11*(4), 437–477.

Bell, N., Bucklen, K. B., Nakamura, K., Tomkiel, J., Santore, A., Russell, L., et al. (2013). *Recidivism report, 2013*. Mechanicsburg, PA: Pennsylvania Department of Corrections.

Bonczar, T. (2008). *Characteristics of state parole supervising agencies, 2006*. Washington, DC: Bureau of Justice Statistics.

Bureau of Justice Statistics (1987). *Probation and parole 1985*. Washington, DC: U.S. Department of Justice.

Burke, P. (2004). Parole violations: An important window on offender reentry. *Perspectives, 28*(1), 24–31.

Burke, P., & Tonry, M. (2006). *Successful transition and reentry for safer communities: A call to action for parole*. Silver Spring, MD: Center for Effective Public Policy.

Camp, C., & Camp, G. (1996). *The corrections yearbook 1996*. South Salem, NY: Criminal Justice Institute.

Carson, E. A., & Golinelli, D. (2013). *Prisoners in 2012: Trends in admissions and releases, 1991–2012*. Washington, DC: U.S. Department of Justice.

Clear, T. R., & Cole, G. F. (1986). *American corrections*. Monterey, CA: Brooks/Cole.

Clear, T. R., & Latessa, E. J. (1993). Probation officers' roles in intensive supervision: Surveillance versus treatment. *Justice Quarterly, 10*(3), 441–459.

Corbett, R. P., & Fersch, E. A. I. (1985). Home as prison: The use of house arrest. *Federal Probation, 49*(1), 13–17.

Crean, D. M. (1985). Community corrections: On the line. In L. F. Travis (Ed.), *Probation, parole and community corrections* (pp. 109–124). Prospect Heights, IL: Waveland.

Crouch, B. (1993). *Is incarceration really worse? Analysis of offenders' preferences for prison over probation.* In *Parole and community corrections* (pp. 47–70). Prospect Heights, IL: Waveland.

del Carmen, R. V. (1985). Legal issues and liabilities in community corrections. In L. F. Travis, III (Ed.), *Probation, parole, and community corrections* (pp. 47–70). Prospect Heights, IL: Waveland.

Doleschal, E. (1971). *Graduated release*. Rockville, MD: National Institute of Mental Health.

Cincinnati Enquirer (2007). *Sex offenders must wear chicken suit*. Retrieved July 27, 2007, from http://news.enquirer.com.

Flory, C., May, D., Minor, K., & Wood, P. (2006). A comparison of punishment exchange rates between offenders under supervision and their supervising officers. *Journal of Criminal Justice, 34*(1), 39–50.

Fox, V. (1983). *Correctional institutions*. Englewood Cliffs, NJ: Prentice Hall.

Fulton, B., Stichman, A., Travis, L., & Latessa, E. (1997). Moderating probation and parole officer attitudes to achieve desired outcomes. *The Prison Journal, 77*(3), 295–312.

Gibbs, J. J. (1985). Client's views of community corrections. In L. F. Travis (Ed.), *Probation, parole and community corrections* (pp. 97–108). Prospect Heights, IL: Waveland.

Gillard, D., & Beck, A. (1996). *Prison and jail inmates, 1995*. Washington, DC: Bureau of Justice Statistics.

Glaze, L., & Bonczar, T. (2006). *Probation and parole in the United States, 2005*. Washington, DC: Bureau of Justice Statistics.

Glaze, L., & Bonczar, T. (2009). *Probation and parole in the United States, 2008*. Washington, DC: Bureau of Justice Statistics.

Glaze, L., & Herberman, E. (2013). *Correctional populations in the United States, 2012*. Washington, DC: Bureau of Justice Statistics.

Gunnison, E., & Helfgott, J. (2011). Factors that hinder offender reentry success: A view from community corrections officers. *International Journal of Offender Therapy and Comparative Criminology, 55*(2), 287–304.

Hamilton, Z. (2010). *Do reentry courts reduce recidivism? Results from the Harlem parole reentry court*. New York, NY: Center for Court Innovation.

Helfgott, J. (1997). Ex-offender needs versus community opportunity in Seattle, Washington. *Federal Probation, 61*, 12–24.

Hoffman, P., & Beck, A. (2005). Revocation by consent: The United States Parole Commission's expedited revocation procedure. *Journal of Criminal Justice, 33*(5), 451–462.

Hughes, T., Wilson, D., & Beck, A. (2001). *Trends in state parole, 1991–2000*. Washington, DC: Bureau of Justice Statistics.

Jaffe, H. J. (1979). Probation with a flair: A look at some out-of-the-ordinary conditions. *Federal Probation, 43*(1), 25–36.

Karp, D., & Drakulich, K. (2004). Minor crime in a quaint setting: Practices, outcomes, and limits of Vermont reparative probation boards. *Criminology & Public Policy, 3*(4), 655–686.

Keller, O., & Alper, B. (1970). *Halfway houses: Community centered corrections and treatment*. Lexington, MA: D.C. Heath.

Kingsnorth, R., MacIntosh, R., & Sutherland, S. (2002). Criminal charge of probation violation? Prosecutorial discretion and implications for research in criminal court processing. *Criminology, 40*(3), 553–578.

Langan, P., & Dawson, J. (1993). *Felony sentences in state courts, 1990*. Washington, DC: Bureau of Justice Statistics.

Latessa, E. J., & Travis, L. F., III. (1992). Residential community correctional programs. In J. Byrne, A. Lurigio, & J. Petersilia (Eds.), *Smart sentencing: The emergence of intermediate sanctions* (pp. 166–181). Beverly Hills, CA: Sage.

Latessa, E. J., Travis, L. F., III, & Wilson, G. P. (1984). Juvenile diversion: Factors related to decision making and outcome. In S. H. Decker (Ed.), *Juvenile justice policy* (pp. 145–165). Beverly Hills, CA: Sage.

LeClair, D., & Guarino-Ghezzi, S. (1991). Does incapacitation guarantee public safety? Lessons from the Massachusetts furlough and prerelease programs. *Justice Quarterly, 8*(1), 9–36.

Lindquist, C., Hardison, J., & Lattimore, P. (2003). *Reentry courts process evaluation (Phase 1)*. Washington, DC: National Institute of Justice.

Lindsey, E. (1925). Historical sketch of the indeterminate sentence and parole system. *Journal of Criminal Law & Criminology, 16*(1925), 9–126.

Lucas, W. (1987). Perceptions of the volunteer role. *Journal of Offender Counseling, Services & Rehabilitation, 12*(1), 141–146.

Martin, J., Hanrahan, K., Bowers, J., Jr. (2009). Offenders' perceptions of house arrest and electronic monitoring. *Journal of Offender Rehabilitation, 48*, 547–570.

Maruschak, L., & Bonczar, T. (2013). *Probation and parole in the United States, 2012*. Washington, DC: Bureau of Justice Statistics.

Mayzer, R., Gray, M., & Maxwell, S. (2004). Probation absconders: A unique risk group? *Journal of Criminal Justice, 32*(2), 137–150.

McDonald, D. (1986). *Punishment without walls: Community service sentences in New York City*. New Brunswick, NJ: Rutgers University Press.

McSparron, J. (1980). Community corrections and diversion: Cost and benefit, subsidy models, and start-up recommendations. *Crime & Delinquency, 26*(2), 226–247.

Minton, T. (2010). *Jail inmates 2009—Statistical tables*. Washington, DC: Bureau of Justice Statistics.

Perrier, D. C., & Pink, F. S. (1985). Community service: All things to all people. *Federal Probation, 49*(2), 32–38.

Petersilia, J. (1986). Exploring the option of house arrest. *Federal Probation, 50*(2), 52–55.

Petersilia, J. (1990). When probation becomes more dreaded than prison. *Federal Probation, 54*(1), 23–27.

Rhine, E., Mawhorr, T., & Parks, E. (2006). Implementation: The bane of effective correctional programs. *Criminology and Public Policy, 5*(2), 347–358.

Rhine, E., Smith, W., & Jackson, R. (1991). *Paroling authorities: Recent history and current practice.* Gaithersburg, MD: American Correctional Association.

Rosenmerkel, S., Durose, M., & Farole, D. (2009). *Felony sentences in state courts, 2006—Statistical tables.* Washington, DC: Bureau of Justice Statistics.

Rothman, D. J. (1980). *Conscience and convenience.* Boston: Little, Brown.

Sabol, W., Minton, T., & Harrison, P. (2007). *Prison and jail inmates at midyear 2006.* Washington, DC: Bureau of Justice Statistics.

Sigler, R. (1988). Role conflict for adult probation and parole officers: Fact or myth? *Journal of Criminal Justice, 16*(2), 121–130.

Simon, J. (1993). *Poor discipline.* Chicago: University of Chicago Press.

Spelman, W. (1995). The severity of intermediate sanctions. *Journal of Research in Crime and Delinquency, 32*(1), 107135.

Stephan, J. (2008). *Census of state and federal correctional facilities, 2005.* Washington, DC: Bureau of Justice Statistics.

Studt, E. (1973). *Surveillance and service in parole.* Washington, DC: U.S. Government Printing Office.

Talarico, S., & Myers, M. (1987). Split sentencing in Georgia: A test of two empirical assumptions. *Justice Quarterly, 4*(4), 611–629.

Tonry, M. (1998). *Sentencing matters.* New York, NY: Oxford University Press.

Travis, L. F., III. (1985). The development of American parole. In H. E. Allen, C. Eskridge, E. J. Latessa, & G. F. Vito (Eds.), *Probation and parole in America* (pp. 19–35). New York: Free Press.

Travis, L. F., III, & Latessa, E. J. (1984). "A summary of parole rules—Thirteen years later": Revisited thirteen years later. *Journal of Criminal Justice, 12*(6), 591–600.

Travis, J., Solomon, A., & Waul, M. (2001). *The dimensions and consequences of prisoner reentry.* Washington, DC: Urban Institute.

Travis, L., & Stacey, J. (2010). A half century of parole rules: Conditions of parole in the United States, 2008. *Journal of Criminal Justice, 38*(4), 606.

Turner, S., & Petersilia, J. (1996). *Work release: Recidivism and corrections costs in Washington State.* Washington, DC: National Institute of Justice.

U.S. Department of Justice (1978). *State and local probation and parole systems.* Washington, DC: U.S. Government Printing Office.

Umbreit, M. S. (1981). Community service sentencing: Jail alternative or added sanction? *Federal Probation, 45*(3), 3–14.

United States Sentencing Commission (2010). *Federal offenders sentenced to supervised release.* Washington, DC. Retrieved from http://www.ussc.gov/Education_and_Training/Annual_National_Training_Seminar/2012/2_Federal_Offenders_Sentenced_to_Supervised_Release.pdf.

White, M., Mellow, J., Englander, K., & Ruffinengo, M. (2011). Halfway back: An alternate to revocation for technical parole violators. *Criminal Justice Policy Review, 22*, 40–66.

Whitehead, J. (1986). Job burnout and job satisfaction among probation managers. *Journal of Criminal Justice, 14*(1), 25–36.

Williams, A., May, D., & Wood, P. (2008). The lesser of two evils? A qualitative study of offenders' preferences for prison compared to alternatives. *Journal of Offender Rehabilitation, 46*(3,4), 71–90.

Wilson, G. P. (1985). Halfway house programs for offenders. In L. F. Travis III, (Ed.), *Probation, parole and community corrections* (pp. 151–164). Prospect Heights, IL: Waveland.

Wilson, J. (2007). Habitation or harm: Project Greenlight and the potential consequences of correctional programming. *National Institute of Justice Journal, 257*, 2–7 (June).

Wood, P., & May, D. (2003). Racial differences in perceptions of the severity of sanctions: A comparison of prison with alternatives. *Justice Quarterly, 20*(3), 605–631.

Wright, J., & Travis, L. (1996). Work release. In M. McShane & F. Williams (Eds.), *The encyclopedia of American prisons* (pp. 510–512). New York: Garland.

Important Cases

Gagnon v. Scarpelli, 411 U.S. 778. (1973).

Morrissey v. Brewer, 408 U.S. 471. (1972).

Samson v. California, 547 U.S. 843. (2006).

CHAPTER 13

Issues in Community Supervision

Many important issues in community supervision center on developments in the financing, management, and technology involved in probation and parole. Largely in response to crowded institutions, there is continuing interest in community supervision as an alternative to incarceration. Burrell (2005) identified emerging trends in probation and parole. He recognized several emerging issues, concluding that community supervision will continue to play a central role in the American system of criminal justice.

Many recent developments are attempts to improve and enhance the effectiveness and economy of probation and parole. In the past 30 years, however, the central practices of community supervision (probation and parole supervision) have themselves come under attack. This chapter examines the current controversy over community supervision, and discusses specific attempts to improve the efficiency of community corrections.

DOES COMMUNITY SUPERVISION WORK?

Von Hirsch and Hanrahan (1978) published a report for the U.S. Department of Justice titled "Abolish Parole?" In this brief document, they suggested that parole supervision might be useless. On both rational (practical) and philosophical grounds, the authors concluded that there was little reason to continue the practice of parole supervision. They held that a period of supervision under conditions constituted an added penalty. That is, assuming the offender served a prison sentence as punishment, there was no reason to impose conditional release in addition to incarceration. From a practical standpoint, they argued that the research to date did not support parole supervision as a crime control strategy. The authors also argued that parole officers were not very effective in providing needed services to parolees. Figure 13.1 illustrates many of the serious problems faced by ex-offenders after prison.

Von Hirsch and Hanrahan were not the first to question parole supervision, but they may have been the most eloquent critics. Later reports (e.g., Gottfredson, Mitchell-Herzfeld, & Flanagan, 1982) showed that success of supervision in preventing crimes by parolees often depends on how "new crimes" are defined. If a parolee returned to prison for violating the conditions of release without

Important Terms

boot camp
casework model
community
  corrections
  legislation
day reporting
drug testing
electronic
  monitoring
global positioning
  system (GPS)
intensive
  supervision
model case
  management
  system
net-widening
nonrevocable
  parole
Probation Subsidy
  Act
radio frequency
restitution
shock
  incarceration
shock parole
shock probation
split sentence
supervision fees
team supervision
technical
  violations
Transition from
  Prison to the
  Community
  (TPC)

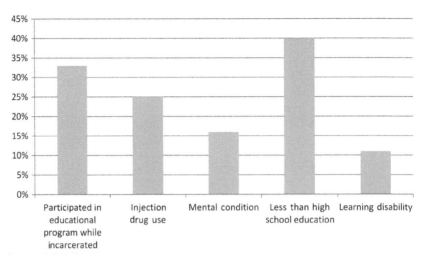

FIGURE 13.1
Characteristics of former offenders returning to the community.
Source: Petersilia (2005)

committing a new crime counts as a failure, parole supervision may be less effective in preventing recidivism than no supervision at all. Because parolees must obey the conditions of release, they may be returned to prison for technical violations. **Technical violations** are infractions of the rules of supervision that do not involve any new criminality. Examples include violating curfew, failing to report to a parole officer, and other noncriminal behavior. If returns to prison based on technical violations count as failures, parolees have more chances to fail than do nonparolees, who must be convicted of new crimes to be incarcerated. The research shows mixed findings. It is difficult, if not impossible, to decide whether parole supervision is an effective crime prevention method (Flanagan, 1985).

With the increased use of both probation and parole in response to prison crowding, these concerns have grown. Observers believe that not only are more offenders being placed under community supervision but also that probation and parole now include more dangerous offenders (Auerhahn, 2007; Guynes, 1988). Critics are beginning to reexamine the degree to which community supervision protects public safety.

Petersilia (1985) studied probationers convicted of felonies in two large California counties. Her conclusions raised serious questions about the ability of community supervision to control crime. Petersilia, Turner, and Peterson (1986:2) concluded that a 65% rate of new criminality among their sample showed that granting probation to those convicted of felonies was not in the best interest of public safety. She later summarized the results of this study:

> These results would seem to support the contention that routine probation is not an appropriate or effective sanction for convicted felons. It evidently could not provide the kind of supervision that might have prevented the majority of our sample of felony offenders from returning to crime.

The news media exaggerated the importance of Petersilia's study (Goldstein, Burrell, & Talty, 1985). In the weeks following the release of her report by the RAND Corporation, newspapers across the country reported the story. They summarized the research, often with forbidding headlines telling of the dangers posed by felony probation. Reactions to the report were quick but failed to achieve the same level of media coverage.

Vito (1986) replicated the RAND study on a sample of Kentucky probationers. He reported that felons on probation in Kentucky were much less likely to commit new crimes than were those studied by Petersilia. Similarly, McGaha, Fichter, and Hirschburg (1987) replicated the study with probationers in Missouri, finding results similar to those found by Vito. In addition, Goldstein et al. (1985) concluded that probationers in New Jersey did not pose as great a threat to public safety as those examined in Petersilia's study in California. It is possible that the results of Petersilia's study were unique to California, as they are different from findings in other states. In support of this conclusion, the Bureau of Justice Statistics (Hughes, Wilson, & Beck, 2001) noted that national averages of successful completion of parole supervision increase when California's cases are removed from the sample.

In attempting to answer the question of whether community supervision works, we must first determine what we mean by the word "work." In the evaluations of felony probation reported by Petersilia, Vito, and Goldstein, the criterion was new crime by probationers. That is, probation "works" if people under supervision did not commit too many new crimes. In general, we can apply three criteria to community supervision to determine "what works." Harland (1996:2–3) noted that the definition of what works depends on the perspective of the individual asking the question. Elected officials and the public often define "working" as reducing rates of recidivism. Policymakers may define "working" as reducing rates of commitment or lengths of stay for prison and jail inmates. Budget officials may define what works as managing offenders at a lower cost. For retributivists, what works is a system of sanctions that matches the pain of punishment with the harm of the crime and blameworthiness of the offender. In short, probation, parole, and other community supervision practices work to the degree that they can (1) control risk of new crime, (2) reduce incarceration and correctional costs, and/or (3) match punishments with offenders.

Wodahl, Ogle, and Heck (2011) observed that community-based corrections is facing a crisis of legitimacy resulting from high rates of probation and parole revocation. With large numbers of revocations, the potential cost savings and impact on prison crowding is not realized. Byrne (2008) observed that community corrections systems have tried to become more like the police. Probation and parole officers seem more interested in arresting violators than in helping offenders. In this environment, high rates of supervision failure are not surprising. Many jurisdictions have responded to this issue by implementing various strategies including increased funding for reentry programs, stronger departmental policies to guide officers' discretion in the event of noncompliance, graduated sanctions that provide incremental responses to noncompliant behavior, and limiting the consequences offenders receive when they do not comply with supervision conditions (Wodahl et al., 2011).

Controlling Risk

Jones (1991) discussed the development of community corrections in Kansas. One of the primary goals of the movement toward community correctional alternatives to imprisonment in that state was to protect public safety. As Jones (1991:51) observed, however, "while a public-safety interest was frequently cited, it was usually in the sense of representing an obvious and necessary constraint on how the other goals (reducing prison crowding and developing more appropriate responses for offenders) would be pursued." Thus, protecting public safety was a baseline concern. In the extreme, we could reduce crowding by not sending anyone to prison. If doing so led to a significant increase in crime, however, this policy would be unacceptable.

Much attention has been paid to the ability or inability of community correctional programs to control risk. As Bennett (1991:95) noted, "The public is upset, and perhaps rightly so, that people placed on regular probation often do not receive either help or supervision because of large caseloads and inadequate supervision." The critical question is how safe is safe enough? As Jones (1991) described it, risk control can range from a definition of no new criminality through acceptance of levels of crime no greater than those among persons incarcerated. Harland and Rosen (1987) suggested that minimizing public risk is the primary goal of most intermediate sanctions. Thus, although no new crime would be preferred, achieving similar levels of new crime among a population diverted from prison that is less than (or no more than) the level among incarcerated offenders may be "safe enough." There is also the question of what kind of "crime" is being committed.

In an assessment of recidivism among parolees in Tennessee, Wilson (2005) observed that wide fluctuations in the rate of discretionary parole release did not correlate with changes in revocation rates. This indicates that we could place more offenders on parole with little or no change in the rate of parole failures. In addition, a major explanation for the levels of failure had to do with increasingly harsh responses (revocation) for technical violations of parole. Those parolees did not endanger public safety in terms of the threat of new crime. In contrast, Hipp and Yates (2009) reported that in one city, the return of parolees led to increases in neighborhood crime rates. Their data indicate that parolees resume their criminal ways, or otherwise produce increased rates of crimes in neighborhoods in which they reside.

Evaluations of the effectiveness of community supervision use different measures of outcome. The inclusion of violations of technical conditions of supervision, including absconding, with new criminality produces relatively high rates of failure but may not represent high rates of crime. Worrall, Schram, Hays, and Newman (2004) studied the link between the size of the probation caseload and the crime rate in California counties. They concluded that the size of the probation caseload is positively associated with the rate of property crime. It is not possible to tell if the crime rate causes probation or the number of probationers causes the crime rate, but there is no evidence that large probation caseloads are associated with any reduction in crime rates. Worrall and colleagues observed that large caseloads are also associated with reduced levels of treatment and reintegration services for probationers. The administration of supervision (large numbers of offenders assigned to too few officers) may explain failure. In contrast, some observers contend that smaller caseloads provide close supervision, which translates into higher rates of technical violations and higher rates of failure. In a study of "community probation" in Maryland, Piquero (2003) suggested that probationers receiving the closest supervision were more likely to fail early.

During the past 2 decades, substantial progress has been made in the development and use of risk-assessment devices in both probation and parole. Many classification and prediction instruments exist, and several appear to offer valid predictions of the risk of recidivism among correctional populations (Holsinger, Lowenkamp, & Latessa, 2006). One problem with these instruments is the incredible diversity of correctional populations. Most risk-assessment devices do not account for specific subpopulations such as females or racial and ethnic minorities. As a result, the accuracy of risk predictions can vary across different groups (Taylor & Blanchette, 2009). As important is that these general risk-screening instruments are not especially well suited to the prediction of specific risks, such as the risk that a particular offender will commit a violent offense (Davies & Dedel, 2006).

Surely, the safest course of action in terms of protecting the community from convicted offenders is to incarcerate the offenders. To do so, however, does not really manage risk but rather seeks to avoid it. At some point, most of these offenders will return to the community, regardless of their level of risk. Attempts to identify and manage risk through probation and parole supervision are necessary, if difficult. Baird (2009) criticized current risk-classification efforts as being too complicated and lacking accuracy in their conclusions. Baird warned that classification may be more accurate in assessing risk than in identifying ways to reduce risk.

Reducing Incarceration and Costs

As Jones (1991) observed in Kansas, a primary factor motivating the development and spread of community supervision sanctions is a desire to reduce prison crowding and correctional costs. Clear and Byrne (1992:321) flatly said, "The frank bottom line for the intermediate sanction movement must be whether it is able to reduce overcrowding in corrections." The impetus behind the movement to expand community supervision sanctions is our inability to deal with the large numbers of persons whom we believe need or deserve more severe sentences than traditional probation. Our inability emerges, in large part, from the cost of incarceration. Thus, if we had excess prison space, we would simply incarcerate offenders who required tougher punishment than probation. We do not have that excess, and we cannot afford to build enough prisons to house all of these offenders.

The creation of alternative sanctions in the community can have the effect of reducing demand for prison space (Gowdy, 1993). Conversely, the development of more severe community-based sanctions may simply result in **net-widening**. Morris and Tonry (1990) argued that in many cases, the result of alternative sanctions has been to make sentences more severe for those who would not have gone to prison anyway. In this way, we cast the "net" of punishment wider to catch more people. If they are correct, alternative sanctions as presently developed will not meet the goal of reducing correctional costs and prison crowding. To the extent that community supervision agencies strive to identify and punish violators, the "failure" rates for probation and parole increase, and more community supervision violators go to prison.

Community supervision can work as an alternative to incarceration and many intermediate punishments developed in the past few decades seek to accomplish just that purpose. The problem arises when, because of these more restrictive community punishments, failure rates increase, leading to increased levels of imprisonment. Concerns over prison crowding recently led California to experiment with **nonrevocable parole**. Under the program, which was implemented in 2011, low-risk inmates who were eligible for parole were released into the community without being subject to traditional parole conditions. Parolees under nonrevocable parole were still subject to warrantless searches but could not be returned to prison unless they were convicted of a felony. In essence, California sought to reduce parole revocations by limiting the state's ability to detect noncompliance. If implemented correctly, this policy would have reduced incarceration costs, the prison population, and the cost of community supervision. However, an evaluation of the program determined that more than 15% of those given nonrevocable parole in the first year of the program were inappropriately classified as low risk (Monfross, 2011). More recently, California passed legislation replacing nonrevocable parole with a policy to shift supervision of these low-risk parolees from the state parole authorities to county-level probation officers.

Matching Punishments with Offenders

A third goal of the development of intermediate sanctions in the community is to create a range of penalties appropriate to the range of offenses and offenders who come before the courts. Many see the traditional choice between probation and incarceration as inadequate for responding to the wide array of crimes and criminals that exist. Morris and Tonry (1990:38) argued that a "variety of intermediate punishments, along with appropriate treatment conditions, should be part of a comprehensive, integrated system of sentencing and punishment."

Community supervision programs and practices have undergone tremendous change in recent times as we struggle to develop this range of punishments.

The matching of punishments to offenders includes two dimensions as anticipated by Morris and Tonry (1990). First, the severity of the penalty should reflect more closely the seriousness of the crime. In this way, there needs to be a range of punishments. Second, punishments should be sensitive to the needs of specific offenders. This necessitates a range of appropriate treatment conditions.

Even if Petersilia's findings of risk among probationers are not accurate for the nation, the ability of probation supervision to provide for community safety remains critical. At a minimum, the perception exists that probation populations are more dangerous today than ever before. There is growing concern about the risk posed by offenders placed under community supervision. Probation and parole officers are changing the way they do their jobs. There is greater emphasis on enforcement and surveillance than in the past. Matejkowski, Festinger, Benishek, and Dugosh (2011) advocated for policies that would encourage probation and parole officers to distinguish between offender behavior that is willfully criminal (noncompliant) and behavior that is a result of a psychiatric disorder (nonresponsive). This distinction would allow probation and parole officers to respond appropriately based on the needs of the offender. Other changes involve making both probation and parole more punitive, such as the increasing use of shock incarceration and intensive supervision, electronic monitoring, day reporting, and other sanctions that are more severe than traditional probation or parole supervision. Table 13.1 shows the imposition of selected supervision conditions on adult probationers.

Harris, Petersen, and Rapoza (2001) investigated the use of intermediate sanctions in one county to assess the use of a range of intermediate sanctions. The focus of the research was to determine whether a true continuum of sanctions was in place so that the severity of the punishment reflected the seriousness of the crime. They found that there was a significant relationship between severity of sanction and seriousness of offense, but that the link was relatively weak. They interpreted this to mean that the availability of a range of intermediate sanctions supports efforts to match penalties to crimes. However, other factors still influence the application of penalties in specific cases. They concluded that without the range of intermediate penalties, it would be much more difficult, if even possible, to link crimes and punishments in any meaningful fashion.

Table 13.1 Felons Having Additional Penalties, 2006	
Additional Penalty	**Percent of Felons Receiving**
Fine	38
Restitution	18
Community service	11
Treatment	11
Other	2

Source: Rosenmerkel, Durose, and Farole (2009)

SHOCK INCARCERATION

Programs of shock incarceration and intensive supervision have affected the operation of traditional probation and parole. They illustrate clearly how community supervision serves as an alternative to incarceration. In both programs, the attempt is to use community supervision to meet sentencing goals normally associated with incarceration. Specifically, the desired result is the enhancement of both the deterrent and incapacitation effects of community supervision.

Shock probation and shock parole attempt to deter offenders from continued criminality by imposing a prison sentence that is later commuted to a period of supervision. The initial incarceration "shocks" the offender by the severity of the punishment. It also informs offenders what to expect if they continue to break the law (Vito, 1985). Thus, with **shock probation**, the judge might sentence the offender to a long prison term but, within 6 months, alter the sentence to a probation period. In some states, such as Ohio, the inmate could petition the court for shock probation. In other states, such as Texas, shock probation is administered solely at the discretion of the judge.

Shock parole is similar to shock probation in that it involves an early release from a relatively long prison term. The difference here is that it is the parole authority rather than the judge who grants an early release from incarceration to parole supervision. For example, a convicted forger who receives a 10-year prison sentence could receive shock probation from the judge after 4 or 5 months. If there is no shock probation, in several states the parole authority is empowered to grant early or shock parole to the offender at his or her first hearing before the board. Like shock probation, states differ as to whether inmates must petition the parole board for shock parole.

In practice, the effectiveness of shock programs is unclear. Many of the programs provide no shock value because offenders expect release. Ideally, the incarcerated offender is shocked when released. In practice, however, the only shock may come if the court does not grant early release. Through a combination of a short prison term followed by community supervision, shock programs attempt to gain the benefits of both incarceration and supervision as sanctions. We hope the sentence will deter the offender. In theory, shock probation and parole provide a stern warning to the inmate. Without the kindness of the judge or parole authority, the offender would be serving a long prison term. In effect, the released inmate realizes that he or she is living "on borrowed time" and will face a long term of incarceration if supervision is unsuccessful.

An innovation to the practice of shock probation and parole has been the development of the prison **boot camp** (Anderson, Dyson, & Burns, 1999). These programs, sometimes called **shock incarceration** because the conditions of incarceration are very severe but limited in duration, also seek to increase punitiveness. Boot camp programs in prisons subject inmates to austere conditions, including physical conditioning and strict discipline combined with hard labor, akin to the boot camp experience of new recruits in the military. We discussed boot camps in Chapter 9 as evidence of attempts to make punishment more physically painful for offenders (Kurlychek, 2010). These camps relate to community supervision because they serve to reduce the length of term served by participants. The boot camp provides a harsher penalty for a shorter time than traditional imprisonment. Inmates participate in boot camp programs operating in scores of correctional facilities across the nation. Many of these programs release their graduates to community supervision as probationers or parolees.

Mackenzie and Parent (1991) studied the impact of boot camps on prison crowding in Louisiana. They observed that if careful selection criteria are developed, camps could reduce the number of inmates admitted to regular prison terms. Further, Mackenzie and Shaw (1990) reported that graduates of boot camps appear to have more socially positive attitudes. They suggested that boot camps may meet offender needs in ways that will improve their chances of avoiding crime in the future. Lutze (1998) surveyed prisoners and found that although boot camp programs provide stricter controls on inmate behavior in prison, they are no more likely to support personal growth and development among inmates than traditional minimum-security incarceration. That is, boot camp participants do not differ from regular prisoners in terms of their learning ways to avoid future problems with the law. In a later study, Lutze (2001) reported that the increased severity of boot camp was associated with negative attitudes and adaptations to prison, when not linked to supporting future improvement for inmates. Inmates may see being "tough" for the sake of being tough as unnecessary and unfair. As Mackenzie and Parent noted, legislators may support boot camp programs because the conditions in these programs are more punitive than in the typical prison, and thus shorter terms can be equally tough on crime. However, the available evidence suggests that boot camps do not reduce rates of new crime (recidivism) by program graduates and may actually hinder inmates in making a positive adjustment (Bottcher & Ezell, 2005; Mackenzie, 1997). Benda, Toombs, and Peacock (2006) found that boot camp programs appear to have different effects for different kinds of offenders. Similar to the problem of applying general risk assessments to diverse populations, boot camp programs seem to help some offenders but are harmful to others. Improvement in boot camps (and other correctional efforts) may depend on our ability to match the right program to the right type of offender.

Another practice that is somewhat akin to shock probation is the imposition of split sentences. A **split sentence** is a penalty that is divided (split) between a period of incarceration and a period of probationary supervision. Because of the great flexibility that judges are allowed in determining the conditions of probation, split sentences are relatively widely used. This is true even in jurisdictions where there is no law that specifically allows the judge to use split sentencing.

Status of probation

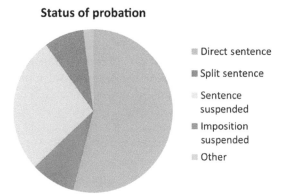

- Direct sentence
- Split sentence
- Sentence suspended
- Imposition suspended
- Other

FIGURE 13.2
Types of sentences to probation, 2007.
Source: Glaze, L., & Bonczar, T. (2009). Probation and Parole in the United States, 2007 Statistical Tables. Washington, DC: Bureau of Justice Statistics: 6

Parisi (1980) described four historical methods of imposing split sentences, including shock probation as practiced in several states:

1. With a defendant convicted of several offenses or counts, the judge may order incarceration for some offenses and probation for others. Thus, a defendant convicted of two counts of theft receives sentences to 90 days on the first count and 2 years of probation on the second.
2. In shock probation, the same offender may receive an initial 5-year prison term, and be "shocked" to probation in 90 days.
3. Legislation that allows the judge to combine incarceration and probation in one sentence, such as a sentence of 90 days of incarceration followed by 2 years of probation, is another way to impose split sentences.
4. Finally, most states have legislation allowing the judge to use incarceration as a condition of probation. In this case, the offender might receive 2 years of probation with the condition that the offender serves the first 90 days in jail.

Regardless of the method used to impose split sentences, the outcomes are the same. Judges, offenders, and the public often see probation as a lenient sanction. The use of split or combination sentences allows judges to increase the harshness of the penalty. A judge may not wish to send a minor offender to prison for a long period but may want the offender to spend some time in jail. Split sentences allow judges to adjust the severity of sanctions. Figure 13.2 shows that in 2007, 9% of offenders sentenced to probation received a split sentence and more than half were sentenced directly to probation.

INTENSIVE SUPERVISION

Intensive supervision programs (ISPs) seek to provide more control and service to offenders who otherwise would be incarcerated (Travis, 1984). In practice, these programs rely on lower client-to-officer ratios and, thus, they assume a higher level of supervision and service delivery (Cullen, Wright, & Applegate, 1996; Latessa, 1980). Evaluations of ISPs show some promise of their effectiveness. However, they do not show that intensive supervision yields better results for the intensive populations than does regular supervision for the regular caseload (Fulton, Latessa, Stichman, & Travis, 1997; Mackenzie, 1997).

ISPs in which the level of service delivery actually increases appear to be modestly effective. Intensive supervision appears to affect the release of many offenders otherwise destined for prison. What is perhaps more important is that the mental picture caused by the label "intensive supervision" may make it politically possible to retain a number of relatively serious or persistent offenders under community supervision, as opposed to incarcerating them (Clear & Shapiro, 1986). This is consistent with the traditional role of community supervision as the "overflow valve" for incarceration.

Several states have implemented ISPs. Typically, an ISP requires the probationer to have more contacts with his or her probation officer. By reducing the size of caseloads, we expect officers to be more vigilant in ISPs (Byrne, 1986). The net effect of these differences is to make the penalty more painful. The probationer experiences more intrusions by the officer. The penalty is also more incapacitative. The officers supervise the offender more closely and this prevents the offender from relapsing into crime.

Reviews of intensive supervision have been mixed. In an assessment of one state's intensive parole supervision, Georgiou (2014) found that intensive supervision did not result in a lower recidivism rate. Drake, Aos, and Miller (2009) reviewed several evaluations of ISPs while distinguishing programs that were treatment-oriented from those that were surveillance-oriented. They reported that intensive supervision alone is not effective at reducing recidivism. However, intensive supervision was effective when coupled with treatment. Finally, Lowenkamp, Flores, Holsinger, Makarios, and Latessa (2010) found that not only should ISPs have a treatment philosophy, but that the staff's commitment to this philosophy was equally important. The importance of treatment within ISPs is not a new finding. Fulton et al. (1997:74) concluded a review of ISPs, writing,

> ISP has held its ground as a key element of community corrections programming since its reemergence in 1982. Although the research suggests that ISP has not fulfilled its promise of alleviating prison crowding, it does appear to be serving the important function of providing an intermediate sanction… More importantly, it appears that ISPs that emphasize treatment and services are producing better results than strict surveillance-based ISPs in terms of addressing offender needs and reducing recidivism.

ELECTRONIC MONITORING

In **electronic monitoring** programs, offenders are fitted with transmitting devices that allow correctional staff to monitor their whereabouts. In recent years, electronic monitoring has gained popularity as a practical tool used to supervise pretrial offenders released on bail, or used by probation and parole officers to increase supervision of certain offenders. As of 2009, 19 states had passed legislation requiring the use of electronic monitoring in the supervision of sex offenders (Button, Demichele, & Payne, 2009).

Although the use of surveillance technology to monitor criminal offenders is relatively new, we have long recognized the potential of such technology for crime control. As early as 1966, Schwitzgebel described a potential telemetric monitoring system for probationers and parolees. In 1968, a prototype of the system was developed and tested. An assessment of the legal ramifications of electronic monitoring appeared in the *Harvard Law Review* in 1966. Later, Schwitzgebel, Ralph's brother, experimented with telemetric monitoring with volunteers in California (Schwitzgebel, 1969). For years, a debate about the acceptability of electronic monitoring continued (Corbett & Marx, 1991; del Carmen & Vaughn, 1986; Ingraham & Smith, 1972; Szasz, 1975), but the sheer practicality of the technology has meant that, although many important issues remain to be solved, electronic monitoring of criminal offenders is an ongoing practice. There are two types of technology available for electronic monitoring: **radio frequency** and **global positioning system (GPS)**.

Currently, two basic types of radio frequency electronic surveillance systems are in use (Ford & Schmidt, 1985; Huskey, 1987; National Institute of Justice, 1999; Schmidt, 1987). These systems are either active or passive surveillance. In an active system, the supervising agency takes positive steps to monitor the offender. Generally, this system involves fitting the offender with a transmitting device, and the transmitter sends a tone over the telephone. A computer program randomly calls offenders at times when they are supposed to be at home. The offender must answer the phone and place the transmitter in a special telephone connection, so that the transmitter sends a message to the computer. In the passive system, a transmitter attached to the offender emits a continuous signal. The offender must keep the transmitter within range of an amplifier/transmitter or the signal will not reach a monitoring computer. This continuously signaling system requires the offender to remain within 150–200 feet of the fixed amplifier, usually installed in the offender's home (Huskey, 1987:19–20).

The random calling system allows for both voice identification and the transmission of a monitoring signal. Because it operates over telephone lines, this system is unaffected by interruptions in transmission caused by walls, structural steel, or other radio transmissions. The active surveillance random calling system appears to have a lower false-alarm rate than the passive surveillance system. The passive-surveillance continuous-transmission system, although more prone to false alarms, provides a continuous monitoring of the offender's whereabouts.

A more recent innovation is the use of a GPS unit to maintain constant surveillance of the whereabouts of a person being electronically monitored (Padgett, Bales, & Blomberg, 2006). GPS units are also available in active and passive formats. Similar to radio frequency systems, active GPS monitoring works through an ankle bracelet attached to the offender. The GPS connects to a satellite system, providing real-time monitoring without requiring the offender to have a landline telephone. Passive GPS systems collect and store tracking information throughout the day and then send a day's worth of data to the probation and parole officer (National Institute of Justice, 2011). Although GPS is typically considered to be a more advanced technology than radio frequency systems, there are important limitations. One of the greatest challenges of using GPS to track offenders involves the technological limitations of the GPS signal inside large buildings (Drake, 2008). Table 13.2 provides advantages and disadvantages to using a GPS monitoring system.

Most jurisdictions have adopted one or the other form of monitoring technology, and a few have used both. The random calling system allows somewhat greater freedom. For example, the offender could be next door at a neighbor's house and still be called to the telephone. The use of both systems could provide a gradation in the severity of monitoring. A probationer ordered to the random calling monitor who then misses a call could be "punished" by being issued a continuous transmission monitor. The possibility of varying the level of restriction within a category of penalty called "monitoring" adds to the attractiveness of this sanction.

Renzema and Mayo-Wilson (2005) reviewed scores of studies on electronic monitoring and concluded that the best evidence available suggests that the effect of electronic monitoring on reducing recidivism is limited. However, Padgett and colleagues (2006) found that electronic monitoring was effective at reducing the likelihood of reoffending and absconding from supervision. More recently, Bales and his colleagues (2010) conducted a comprehensive assessment of electronic monitoring outcomes in Florida. Results showed that offenders placed on electronic monitoring were 31% less likely to fail, compared to offenders participating in other forms of community supervision. Electronic monitoring

Table 13.2	Advantages and Disadvantages of GPS Monitoring
Advantages	**Disadvantages**
• Provides real-time tracking of an offender's location	• Cannot track signal inside large buildings, subways, etc
• Triggers an instant alarm if it is tampered with or removed	• Limited to areas with good-quality cellular telephone coverage
• Permits creation of customized inclusion zones and exclusion zones	• Initial and replacement costs are high
• Does not require the offender to have a landline telephone in his or her residence	• Requires timely responses to notice of violation
• Allows the offender to return to the work force while still being monitored	• Requires comprehensive training
• Has been shown to positively alter the behavior of those who comply with the programs	• Active system operating costs can be relatively high
	• Notice will be sent any time the offender enters an exclusion zone, even if accidentally

Source: Downing (2006:44)

was effective regardless of offense type and offender age, but GPS was shown to be more effective than radio frequency supervision. Despite the positive findings, interviews with offenders showed that electronic monitoring often had a negative impact on personal relationships and the ability to obtain employment (Bales et al., 2010).

George Orwell published his book *1984* in 1949. In the book, Orwell assessed the future of the human race under the conditions of the arms race. He suggested that society would become bureaucratic, and governments would be totalitarian. The leader of one government, "Big Brother," would retain power through torture and brainwashing. The dominant aspect of life in this society would be that everyone was under surveillance by the government. It was in *1984* that Orwell coined the slogan, "Big Brother is watching." Because of the time in which he wrote the book, much of what he described appeared to be science fiction. Given current capabilities, Orwell only missed by a few years when he titled his book *1984*.

The issues involved in electronic surveillance recall the questions raised about the development of probation and parole supervision. On the one hand are critics who suggest that monitoring is an insufficient penalty for many offenders. They contend that this leniency reduces the deterrent effect of the law. Other critics argue that the use of monitoring technology to allow the release from incarceration of "dangerous" offenders poses too great a risk to the community. In contrast are those who criticize this technology as too oppressive because it violates current standards of privacy and infringes on constitutional rights to protection against unreasonable searches and seizures. Finally, some critics fear that electronic monitoring, in practice, will increase the severity of community supervision for offenders who otherwise would receive traditional probation or parole.

Proponents of surveillance argue that the technology enhances public safety by ensuring supervision of offenders in the community. Further, surveillance itself deters offenders from committing crimes. Similarly, the proponents suggest that the ability to monitor offenders results in a lessening of penalty severity. They argue that some offenders are in prison who do not actually need to be incarcerated. Continual supervision will allow judges and parole boards to leave these offenders in the community. Whereas the current focus may be on the electronics of contemporary surveillance, at base, the questions and criticisms are the same ones that have always surrounded community supervision.

Despite the ongoing debate, electronic monitoring as a sanction, either alone or in combination with other forms of community supervision, appears to be here to stay. Most observers believe that electronic monitoring is a cost-effective alternative to incarceration for many offenders (Evans, 1996; Yeh, 2010). Learning how well electronic monitoring can meet the other goals of community supervision (fairness, a reduction in future crime, etc.) must await further study. Payne and DeMichele (2010) observed that the use of electronic monitoring with sex offenders provides a false sense of security and affects officer workloads. Monitoring is more compatible with some approaches to community supervision than others.

DAY REPORTING AND OTHER SANCTIONS

Unlike many other intermediate sanction alternatives, **day reporting** is of relatively recent origin. Although England has used day reporting in the past, the first day reporting program in the United States was started in Massachusetts in 1986 (McDevitt, 1988). This program worked as an early release alternative for prison and jail inmates near the date of their parole. Participants in the program were required to report to the center each day, prepare an itinerary for their next day's activities, and report by telephone to the center throughout the day (Larivee, 1990).

At midyear 2012, jails reported supervising almost 3,900 offenders in day reporting programs (Minton, 2013). Parent (1990) reported that day reporting programs were operational in six states by the late 1980s, and many more states were considering the option. A Google search of day reporting yields scores of day reporting programs in courts and local correctional systems across the United States. These programs (and the clients they served) varied. McDevitt and Miliano (1992:153) observed that programs tend to have similar components, including frequent contact, formalized scheduling, and drug testing. Day reporting represents a significant increase in surveillance and contact over even ISPs. By 1992, there were six reporting centers in operation in Massachusetts, with a total average daily population of several hundred offenders. By 1994, there were 114 reporting centers operating in the United States (Parent et al., 1995). Table 13.3 offers a description of these early day reporting centers.

Day reporting clients typically make at least one in-person and several telephone contacts with center staff daily, yet they are allowed to remain in the community throughout much of the day. Most programs are limited to between 2 and 4 months in duration, followed by a period of probation or parole supervision. Often, day reporting clients work with program staff to develop and obtain substance abuse,

Table 13.3	Services Provided by Day Reporting Centers			
Total Number of Centers: 114				
Services	**At center (%)**	**Elsewhere (%)**	**Both (%)**	**Centers Providing (%)**
Job-seeking skills	79	13	8	98
Drug abuse education	69	17	14	96
Group counseling	80	12	18	96
Job placement	62	34	14	93
Education	55	31	14	93
Drug treatment	31	54	15	92
Life skills training	92	16	12	91
Individual counseling	72	17	11	89
Transitional housing	13	81	16	63
Recreation and leisure	74	16	10	60

Source: Parent, Byrne, Tsarfaty, Valade, and Esselman (1995:13)

psychological, and employment treatment and services. These programs promise to reduce prison crowding and costs, protect community safety, and provide needed services to offenders.

In Chapter 12 we discussed furlough programs. Work and study furloughs, as well as prerelease programs, help inmates make the adjustment from incarceration to living in the community. Placements in residential community corrections facilities also provide custodial supervision of offenders not needing or deserving jail or prison incarceration (Holsinger, Latessa, Turner, & Travis, 1997). Other changes in probation and parole have similarly bridged the gap between traditional supervision and incarceration. There has been an increasing use of community service sentencing and the imposition of monetary penalties (such as fines and restitution to crime victims). All these changes in traditional community supervision have worked to make probation and parole more severe as penalties, and to provide greater restrictions and controls over offenders in the community.

Shock probation and parole, split sentencing, and ISPs blur the distinction between incarceration and community supervision. The experience of being "on paper" becomes much more like that of incarceration. In these programs, the probationer or parolee faces additional deprivations of autonomy, liberty, and the like. It is difficult to determine whether the development of these programs has led to the increasing use of community supervision for felons and dangerous offenders. It is possible that these developments are in response to a changing population. Alternatively, these changes may have been successful in creating community-based sanctions that are seen as appropriate for prison and jail-bound offenders. In that case, the changing population of community corrections programs may be a response to changes in programs available.

ISSUES IN COMMUNITY SUPERVISION

Identifying trends in probation and parole, Burrell (2005) noted developments in management and organization. Broad trends, including results-driven management and the reemergence of a correctional rehabilitation, have had an influence on community supervision. As with the police and courts, an increased emphasis on collaboration across agencies in communities is common to probation and parole. Specialization, in the form of focused caseloads and services, is common. Drug courts and other problem-solving courts typically work through probation departments. It is once again difficult to select issues for specific attention given the range of available topics. Perhaps the greatest demand on community supervision is that it respond to the burgeoning growth in correctional populations.

As prison populations have increased since the 1970s, so have the numbers of people under community supervision. The change in types of offenders on probation and parole supervision is an important factor in understanding changes in community supervision. The simple growth in the size of the population, regardless of its characteristics, also has led to changes. Three areas in which we observe changes are the financing, management, and technology of probation and parole. These changes merit attention, regardless of whether they involve special programs such as shock or intensive supervision.

Financing

Several states have implemented **community corrections legislation** that includes various funding formulas to support community supervision activities. These laws provide financial incentives to counties to reduce their prison commitments and to retain offenders in the community. The typical law either authorizes a subsidy for counties that reduce their commitment rates or provides financial support for improved and increased community corrections programs (Austin, 2010; Clear & Schrantz, 2011).

California was the first state to employ an incentive program to encourage communities to keep offenders out of the prison system. In 1965, the California legislature passed the **Probation Subsidy Act**, which paid counties for each offender not sentenced to prison in each county. The state developed a formula that estimated the number of offenders expected to be sentenced to prison, and then paid $4,000 to the county for each offender, less than that number that was not sentenced to prison. If a county was expected to commit 1,000 offenders to prison but actually committed only 900, the county received a subsidy of $400,000 ($4,000 × 100). Subsidy funds were earmarked for the improvement of local correctional services. Other states subsequently developed similar models.

The California subsidy program faced several obstacles (Clear & Cole, 1986). There was no subsidy assistance to law enforcement, although the effect of the program was to keep offenders in the community. No inflation factor was included, so that within 10 years, the purchasing power of the subsidy declined by more than one-third. The formula did not consider counties that historically had kept offenders in local correctional custody. For example, a county traditionally may have kept nonviolent offenders in the community on probation. Under the subsidy formula, that county had a lower estimate of commitments. Another county may have traditionally incarcerated nearly every felony offender. Under the subsidy program, the first county could only receive aid by keeping violent or more serious offenders in the community. The second county could begin to use probation for minor, nonviolent offenders, and could reap a large subsidy.

Later funding formulas for community corrections attempted to overcome some of the original difficulties in the California subsidy program. Minnesota, Oregon, and Colorado passed community corrections legislation that included more options for counties. These states also tried to adjust for crime and incarceration rates and included inflation factors. Other states, such as Ohio, began subsidy programs for specific practices that counties could adopt to reduce prison commitments. In each of these cases, funding relates to the development and expansion of community programs. The effects are to support probation and other community services and to assist the counties in handling their increasing caseloads.

Clear (2011) proposed a model to provide incentives for states to reduce incarceration costs and to reinvest much of the savings into the local communities plagued by high incarceration rates. His model consists of four elements:

1. The state creates a voucher system to translate savings from diversion from prison into dollars to be used for other purposes.
2. Community-based organizations use the vouchers as funding sources for their work (both profit and nonprofit).
3. An oversight function is included to audit all activities using the funds.
4. A risk-management and victim-restoration plan is developed for each offender. The plan would detail a strategy to keep the offender in the community at a reduced level of risk and restore the damage suffered by the victim.

Another recent development is in the charging of **supervision fees**. Many state parole authorities and probation offices now require that the client make a monthly payment to the agency to offset the costs of supervision (Teague, 2011). This requirement further increases the cost advantage of probation and parole over incarceration. Similarly, it is common for a condition of supervision to be the payment of court costs. This requires that probation and parole officers serve (at least part time) as bill collectors for the courts.

A related financial alteration in the operation of probation and parole is the growing use of **restitution**. Offenders on probation and parole increasingly must make restitution to the victims of their crimes. Thirty-eight percent of felony convicts in 2006 were assessed fines, and 18% were ordered to pay restitution (Rosenmerkel et al., 2009). Probation and parole officers are then required to manage the payment process for restitution and fines (Weisburd, Einat, & Kowalski, 2008).

On the one hand, these developments assist community supervision by providing enhanced resources and by reducing costs of operation. On the other hand, these programs also add to the burden of probation and parole officers, who generally dislike working in the role of bill collector. These practices reflect the tradition of experimentation with correctional practices in probation and parole. Figure 13.3 shows financial conditions imposed on probationers in 1995, the most recent year for which data are available.

Management

The traditional approach to probation and parole supervision consisted of the casework model. In casework, each officer was responsible for a caseload of offenders. The officer was a generalist expected to supervise a variety of persons having a variety of needs. The **casework model** expected the single officer to be capable of providing needed services to all of the offenders. A recent survey of members

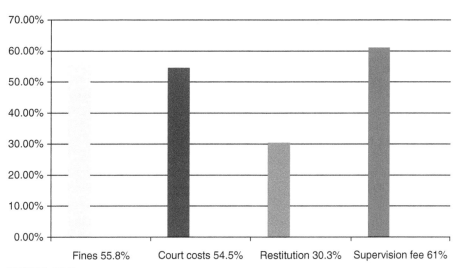

FIGURE 13.3
Percent of probationers with selected financial conditions imposed, 1995.
Source: Bonczar, T. (1997). Characteristics of Adults on Probation, 1995. *Washington, DC: Bureau of Justice Statistics: 7*

of the American Probation and Parole Association revealed that the majority of respondents still used a caseload organization structure (DeMichele, 2007).

Several other models of organization and caseload management have been proposed and adopted. Several jurisdictions use teams of officers responsible for large groups of offenders. In **team supervision**, officers can take advantage of their varied strengths and skills. Thus, an officer who is particularly effective with offenders that require employment services can concentrate on that type of case for the entire team (Dell'Apa, Adams, Jorgensen, & Sigurdson, 1976).

Another development involves the classification of offenders by objectives of supervision, rather than the general assignment of offenders to officers. This process clarifies the goals of supervision for the officer, and it allows officers to set priorities in responding to the needs of offenders (Clear & O'Leary, 1983). A related adaptation involves identifying the offenders who are least in need of supervision and service and assigning them to a very low level of monitoring. This practice reduces the caseloads of officers who are providing service, and it maximizes (at least in theory) utilization of supervision resources (Vito & Marshall, 1983). As with objectives-based supervision classification, recent practice involves the identification of supervision levels based on assessments of both the needs and risk of offenders.

The National Institute of Corrections (1981) developed a **model case management system**. The system relies on two case assessment instruments: a risk assessment and a needs assessment. Each supervising officer completes these two questionnaires and then reviews them with the offender. Through discussion of the instruments, the officer and the offender develop a plan for dealing with needs. They develop case objectives from that plan. This system helps identify concrete actions that the officer should take, and it provides an ability to assess case progress.

As a management system, the model system involves three components: (1) classification, (2) case planning, and (3) the assignment of workload units. Classification reflects the assessments mentioned above. Depending on the levels of need or risk, or on combinations of the two, the offender is placed in a supervision category that is somewhere between high (frequent officer attention) and low (little or no direct contact by officer). The second component, case planning, creates case objectives based on a structured interview with the client. The officers' supervisors review the objectives and approve or modify them. Finally, cases are assigned varying degrees of difficulty or workload units. These units describe how much of an officer's time will be consumed by the case. In this manner, the officer and his or her supervisor know how much effort to expend on that case, and how much effort to spend on the total caseload.

From the information derived through individual case planning, it is possible for the agency or office to assess its needs, objectives, and progress. If 35% of the agency's caseload has high employment needs, administrators can see the utility in providing officers with employment development training. The agency might assign some officers as employment specialists. If a large enough percentage of the caseload has high-risk scores, administrators may want to create special surveillance units that would serve risk-control goals distinct from service delivery (Clear & O'Leary, 1983).

In 2001, the National Institute of Corrections developed the **Transition from Prison to the Community (TPC)** case management model. The TPC model reflects a renewed interest in managing an offender's successful reentry to the community. Unlike traditional case management, the TPC model approaches offender reentry as a process that begins at sentencing and continues until discharge from community supervision. Thus, case management is a continuous process consisting of three phases:

1. *The institutional phase*: the period of incarceration
2. *The release phase*: the months just before and just after release
3. *The community phase*: the period after an offender reenters and stabilizes in the community through supervision, discharge from supervision, and beyond (Thigpen et al., 2010:7)

The National Institute of Corrections (NIC) devoted considerable resources to the development and dissemination of this case management program. From 2001 to 2009, eight states received technical assistance and guidance from the NIC. In 2009, six states were selected for additional technical assistance, with the technical assistance period ending in 2012. To implement the TPC model effectively, participating states increased collaboration between institutional corrections, field supervision, and the parole boards (Jannetta, Neusteter, Davies, & Horvath, 2012). Box 13.1 describes a sample postrelease supervision model.

BOX 13.1 SAMPLE POSTRELEASE SUPERVISION MODEL

Extremely high-risk offenders: surveillance and monitoring for risk management.

Medium- to high-risk offenders: supervision and case management specifically directed toward risk reduction, along with addressing factors that can contribute to community stability-obtaining forms of identification, housing, employment, and so forth.

Low-risk offenders: minimum supervision and correctional case management with attention to stability factors, including referral to noncorrectional resources to address other needs.

Administrative cases: the major issue for an offender is completion of financial and administrative compliance.

Source: Thigpen, Beauclair, Moore, and Humphries (2010:48)

Management innovations in community supervision include the development and adoption of automated information systems to improve case supervision and monitoring. Existing software programs designed for salespeople are also well suited to probation and parole use. This software manages scheduling, keeps tracks of contacts, and otherwise performs the information storage and retrieval functions most useful to probation and parole officers. In recent years there has been increased emphasis in two important management areas. First, community supervision agencies are moving toward "evidence-based practice" (Carter, Gibel, Giguere, & Stroker, 2007; DeMichele, 2007). Coupled with automated information systems, administrators seek to assess the effects of different practices on specific types of offenders or specific problems. Boone and Fulton (1996) reported the development of performance-based measures of community supervision effects. Increasingly, community supervision managers seek information about how to affect the behaviors of offenders. In 2001, the American Probation and Parole Association began revising accreditation standards for probation and parole agencies to include performance-based standards. As described by Taylor (2004:21), the new standards not only include compliance with policies and procedures but also include "measurement not only of what an agency does, but how well it does it."

Technology

A final area of recent innovations in community supervision involves the application of communications and other technologies to supervision. These applications have taken a number of forms, such as the information technologies mentioned above. Developments in areas including word processing, telecommunications, and video recording have had some effects and will play a larger role in the future. We have already addressed some of the effects of improved information systems and classification and assessment procedures as a form of information technology.

Drug testing is currently common throughout all of our society. Repeated or continuing wars on drugs, increasingly tough drunk-driving laws, deaths of celebrities from drug-related causes, and notorious transportation accidents attributed to drug use all have focused attention on substance abuse. Today, a number of relatively simple technologies are available for the detection of alcohol and other drug consumption. They range from the Breathalyzer test to determine if a person has been driving under the influence of alcohol, to blood tests to determine alcohol or other drug content. Urine testing is becoming an increasingly common component of community supervision conditions. Every parole supervision agency in the country reports using drug testing with parolees (Bonczar, 2008).

Judges and parole boards seek to reduce the incidence of substance abuse among convicted offenders in the hopes of reducing future criminality. They traditionally have prohibited probationers and parolees from the consumption of excessive amounts of alcohol or the use of other recreational drugs. When this author worked for the Oregon Board of Parole, a standard condition of parole limited drinking for all parolees. Parolees were either not allowed to drink alcohol to excess, not allowed to drink alcohol at all, or required to take Antabuse. Antabuse is a drug that reacts with alcohol to produce very unpleasant symptoms in the drinker. These symptoms include nausea, shortness of breath, dizziness, and other sensations that are generally unpleasant enough to deter the drinker.

Regardless of the attempts to control substance abuse, probationers and parolees continue to acquire and use alcohol and other drugs. The development of easily administered detection tests has strengthened the ability of probation and parole officers to identify and control substance abuse among their clients. Many believe that merely testing for use will deter offenders. As Atmore and Bauchiero (1987) reported:

> We have noted significant behavioral improvements when we test regularly, because it serves as a deterrent. Therefore, we are returning less people to higher security for positive urines because they know they are taking a huge risk by substance use. In other words, test regularly! You need to have a consistent policy for testing and sanctions for positive results, or else word will get around quickly that one should not take this seriously.

In addition to urine tests, probation and parole officers have a wide array of other testing technologies available to them. These include the Breathalyzer and blood tests, as well as some newer developments, such as a saliva test for alcohol use. With the saliva test, the subject's saliva is placed on a "blotter" that is actually a form of litmus paper. If the subject has recently used alcohol, the paper will change colors. Efforts are currently under way to develop similar saliva tests for other drug use. Finally, alcohol use can now be detected by a device that is fitted on one's wrist or ankle (Leffingwell et al., 2013) (see Figure 13.4).

Camp and Camp (1996:158–159) reported that all community supervision agencies responding to their survey used drug testing in 1995. These agencies

FIGURE 13.4
An official attaches a SCRAM (Secure Continuous Remote Alcohol Monitor) anklet at the Municipal
Courthouse in North Las Vegas, Nevada. The court-ordered device tests vapor in the skin for alcohol and
sends the results wirelessly to a phone modem.
AP Photo/Las Vegas Sun/Steve Marcus

reported nearly 3.7 million drug tests. Most of these tests (98.7%) did not result
in revocation of supervision for offenders. Often, even positive drug tests do not
result in revocation. The development of drug courts, with their emphasis on
drug treatment, for example, use tests as measures of case progress. A positive
test result (showing the use of drugs) is likely to result in some change in status
(assignment to a new treatment, increased contact, etc.), but is unlikely to result
in revocation. Nonetheless, offenders seek ways to avoid detection, and officers
must continually guard against altered urine samples (Elbert, 1997).

Substance-abuse testing technologies enhance the ability of officers to control
the risks of crime posed by their clients. These procedures also may change the
nature of the job. The officers must now test their clients, serve as medical techni-
cians, and otherwise assume the role of "cop" instead of "helper." Some believe
that testing alters the nature of the officer's job and his or her relationship with
offenders. The Georgia Intensive Supervision program used special officers, designated as "surveillance officers," and charged them with conducting urine tests
and investigations. Using special officers protected the helping relationship
between the probation or parole officer and the offender (Erwin & Clear, 1987).

Developments in geographic information systems have been applied to community supervision. Harries (2003) described a program in which the Maryland
Division of Probation and Parole used geographic information to improve supervision. As described by Piquero (2003), Maryland used geographic analysis of
crime to develop programs involving police, probation, community members,
and other agencies to develop coordinated efforts to reduce and prevent crime.
Geographic analysis can improve community supervision in a variety of ways
ranging from describing "good" and "bad" environments in which to place

offenders through minimizing officer travel time by assigning caseloads based on geography. As mentioned, it is now possible to use GPS units to track offenders. With GPS monitors, officers can monitor the location of probationers and parolees at all times. Mellowa, Schlager, and Caplan (2008) reported on the process of using geographic analysis to evaluate parole services. By mapping the residential locations of parolees and the locations of required services, the evaluators were able to assess the adequacy of services easily available to parolees.

THEORY AND COMMUNITY SUPERVISION

We explored community supervision in this and the preceding chapter. This assessment identified several issues in contemporary community corrections and described a range of changes during the recent past. A number of explanations for the emergence of issues or the implementation of changes exist. Each of these explanations may represent a theory of community supervision.

The impact of supervision on recidivism depends on organizational goals and structures. Recidivism also seems to reflect the characteristics of the offenders under supervision as well as the qualifications and efforts of supervising officers. Changes in the law, or in public perceptions of offense seriousness, are related to changes to community supervision populations and practices. Finally, the growth of community supervision is directly related to the fiscal burden created by overcrowded prisons (Wodahl & Garland, 2009).

Once again, we can identify individual, organizational, and social theories of community supervision. It appears the same types of explanations offered for policing, courts, and incarceration apply to community supervision. We will return to this topic in the final chapter, but it seems possible to identify theories of criminal justice.

DUE PROCESS, CRIME CONTROL, AND COMMUNITY SUPERVISION

Many changes in community supervision were grafted onto existing practices of probation and parole supervision. Thus, we added restitution orders and supervision fees as conditions of probation. Periods of confinement have been added to supervision conditions to enable courts to achieve split sentences or to create programs such as shock incarceration. Supervision has changed to create intensive monitoring programs for the more serious offenders now placed in probation and parole caseloads.

Some of the changes in community supervision represent the development of new programs that complement traditional probation and parole supervision. Day reporting centers, for example, often operated as adjuncts of the jail or as institutional components of local community corrections agencies. The growth of residential community correctional facilities similarly has been outside of probation and parole agencies. Such facilities serve as a resource to those agencies.

Indeed, one of the problems inherent in estimating the numbers of persons participating in these various programs is that jurisdictions report the participants as members of the probation and parole population. Thus, probation and parole supervision now includes thousands of cases in which offenders are under electronic monitoring, residing in halfway houses, attending day reporting centers, or receiving other forms of intermediate sanctions. As perceptions about the adequacy of sentences have changed, and as the number of offenders eligible for correctional supervision has increased, a large proportion of the burden of adapting to these changes has fallen on the community supervision agencies of the criminal justice system.

Traditionally, community supervision has taken the role of assistance to convicted offenders through the provision of services and a reduction in the severity of criminal sanctions. In this regard, throughout most of the twentieth century, probation and parole supported the interests and needs of the individual, having a due process orientation. In recent years, however, the role of community supervision in crime control has come to dominate. Lutze, Johnson, Clear, Latessa, and Slate (2012) presented the argument that criminal justice policymakers must invest in community corrections if they hope to reduce crime in the future. They contend that community supervision and alternative sanctions can support crime control efforts efficiently if we utilize evidence-based practices and view community corrections as a human service profession. Probation and parole officers should be supported through reduced caseloads, better resources, and rewards for reaching positive outcomes. At the same time, they should be held professionally accountable for what they have control over.

Although crime control advocates might argue that sanctions short of incarceration inadequately protect the public and fail to deter offenders, due process advocates fear increasing the numbers of offenders subjected to criminal justice processing (i.e., net-widening) or increasing the restrictiveness of interventions on the lives of offenders. In addition, due process proponents fear that the proliferation of intermediate sanctions has simply meant that offenders who would otherwise have received regular probation now experience programs such as electronic monitoring, intensive supervision, and day reporting (Harland, 1996). They believe that instead of providing true alternatives to incarceration, intermediate sanctions have brought more offenders under tighter control by the correctional system.

The growth of the community corrections population, especially if coupled with that of the prison and jail populations, suggests the due process proponents may be correct. At the end of 2012, nearly 3% of the adult population of the United States was under correctional control (Glaze & Herberman, 2013). What remains unsettled is whether the offenders or society as a whole benefits from increased correctional intervention. Whereas more offenders than ever before are in the custody of corrections officials, intermediate sanctions may have saved tens of thousands of offenders from serving prison and jail terms, and may result in improved conditions for them in the future.

Community supervision represents a compromise between due process and crime control proponents. Offenders under community supervision face restrictions and control. Still, these offenders are under less onerous control than those incarcerated. Community supervision often seeks to provide the "right" level of state control over the lives and behavior of convicted offenders. We will return to this issue in the final chapter, but growing interest in restorative justice seeks to balance the interests of the community, victim, and offender. In most restorative justice programs, community supervision plays a key role precisely because it is well suited to serve both due process and crime control ends.

REVIEW QUESTIONS

1. How have probation and parole populations changed in recent years?
2. Name and describe two innovations in probation and parole that allow community supervision to approximate the severity of incarceration more closely.
3. What are split sentences, and how may they be imposed by a judge?
4. Take a position on the question of whether community supervision is effective. Include public risk, cost, and other relevant factors in arguments for your position.
5. Describe funding approaches that serve to encourage communities to keep offenders out of state prisons, and argue either in favor of or in opposition to them.
6. How can classification of probationers and parolees aid in the use of community supervision resources?
7. Describe two ways in which emerging technologies have affected the ability of probation and parole agencies to supervise offenders in the community.
8. Are current changes in community supervision evidence of a growing dominance of the crime control perspective in American criminal justice? Explain.

References

Anderson, J., Dyson, L., & Burns, J. (1999). *Boot camp: An intermediate sanction*. Lanham, MD: University Press of America.

Atmore, T., & Bauchiero, E. (1987). Substance abusers: Identification and treatment. *Corrections Today, 49*(7), 22–24, et seq.

Auerhahn, K. (2007). Do you know who your probationers are?: Using simulation modeling to estimate the composition of California's felony probation population, 1980–2000. *Justice Quarterly, 24*(1), 28–47.

Austin, A. (2010). *Criminal justice trends: Key legislative changes in sentencing policy, 2001–2010*. New York, NY: Vera Institute of Justice.

Baird, C. (2009). *A question of evidence: A critique of risk assessment models used in the justice system*. Madison, WI: National Council on Crime and Delinquency.

Bales, W., Mann, K., Blomberg, T., Gaes, G., Barrick, K., Dhungana, K., et al. (2010). *A quantitative and qualitative assessment of electronic monitoring*. Tallahassee, FL: Center for Criminology and Public Policy Research.

Benda, B., Toombs, N., & Peacock, M. (2006). Distinguishing graduates from dropouts and dismissals: Who fails boot camp? *Journal of Criminal Justice, 34*(1), 27–38.

Bennett, L. (1991). The public wants accountability. *Corrections Today, 53*(4), 92–95.

Bonczar, T. (2008). *Characteristics of state parole supervising agencies, 2006.* Washington, DC: Bureau of Justice Statistics.

Boone, H., & Fulton, B. (1996). *Implementing performance-based measures in community corrections.* Washington, DC: National Institute of Corrections.

Bottcher, J., & Ezell, M. (2005). Examining the effectiveness of boot camps: A randomized experiment with a long-term follow up. *Journal of Research in Crime and Delinquency, 42,* 309–332.

Burrell, W. (2005). *Trends in probation and parole in the states.* Lexington, KY: American Probation and Parole Association. Retrieved July 24, 2010, from http://www.appa-net.org.

Button, D. M., Demichele, M., & Payne, B. K. (2009). Using electronic monitoring to supervise sex offenders: Legislative patterns and implications for community corrections officers. *Criminal Justice Policy Review, 20*(4), 414–436.

Byrne, J. (1986). The control controversy: A preliminary examination of intensive probation supervision programs in the United States. *Federal Probation, 50*(2), 4–16.

Byrne, J. (2008). The social ecology of community corrections—Understanding the link between individual and community change. *Criminology & Public Policy, 7*(2), 263–274.

Camp, C., & Camp, G. (1996). *The corrections yearbook 1996.* South Salem, NY: Criminal Justice Institute.

Carter, M. M., Gibel, S., Giguere, R., & Stroker, R. (2007). *Increasing public safety through successful offender reentry: Evidence-based and emerging practices in corrections.* Silver Spring, MD: Center for Effective Public Policy.

Clear, T. R. (2011). A Private-sector, incentives-based model for justice reinvestment. *Criminology & Public Policy, 10*(3), 585–608.

Clear, T. R., & Byrne, J. (1992). The future of intermediate sanctions: Questions to consider. In J. Byrne, A. Lurigio, & J. Petersilia (Eds.), *Smart sentencing: The emergence of intermediate sanctions* (pp. 319–331). Beverly Hills, CA: Sage.

Clear, T. R., & Cole, G. F. (1986). *American corrections.* Monterey, CA: Brooks/Cole.

Clear, T. R., & O'Leary, V. (1983). *Controlling the offender in the community.* Lexington, MA: Lexington Books.

Clear, T. R., & Schrantz, D. (2011). Strategies for reducing prison populations. *The Prison Journal, 91,* 138S–159S.

Clear, T. R., & Shapiro, C. (1986). Identifying high-risk probationers for supervision in the community: The Oregon model. *Federal Probation, 50*(2), 42–49.

Corbett, R., & Marx, G. (1991). Critique: no soul in the new machine: Technofallacies in the electronic monitoring movement. *Justice Quarterly, 8*(3), 399–414.

Cullen, F., Wright, J., & Applegate, B. (1996). Control in the community: The limits of reform. In A. Harland (Ed.), *Choosing correctional options that work* (pp. 69–116). Thousand Oaks, CA: Sage.

Davies, G., & Dedel, K. (2006). Violence risk screening in community corrections. *Criminology & Public Policy, 5*(4), 743–770.

del Carmen, R., & Vaughn, J. (1986). Legal issues in the use of electronic surveillance in probation. *Federal Probation, 50*(2), 60–69.

Dell'Apa, F., Adams, W. T., Jorgensen, J. D., & Sigurdson, H. R. (1976). Advocacy, brokerage, community: The ABC's of probation and parole. *Federal Probation, 40*(4), 3–8.

DeMichele, M. (2007). *Probation and parole's growing caseloads and workload allocation: Strategies for managerial decision making.* Lexington, KY: American Probation and Parole Association.

Downing, H. (2006, October). The emergence of global positioning satellite (GPS) systems in correctional applications. *Corrections Today, 68*(6), 42–45.

Drake, E. (2008). *Offender tracking technologies: Where are we now?* Retrieved January 26, 2014, from http://www.cepprobation.org/uploaded_files/Pres%20EM09%20Dra.pdf.

Drake, E. K., Aos, S., & Miller, M. G. (2009). Evidence-based public policy options to reduce crime and criminal justice costs: Implications in Washington state. *Victims and Offenders, 4,* 170–196.

Elbert, M. (1997). The use of creatinine and specific gravity measurement to combat drug test dilution. *Federal Probation, 61*(4), 10.

Erwin, B., & Clear, T. R. (1987). Rethinking role conflict in community supervision. *Perspectives, 11*(2), 21–24.

Evans, D. (1996). Electronic monitoring: Testimony to Ontario's Standing Committee on Administration of Justice. *APPA Perspectives,* 8–10, Fall.

Flanagan, T. (1985). Questioning the other parole: The effectiveness of community supervision of offenders. In Travis, L. F., III (Ed.), *Probation, parole, and community corrections: A reader* (pp. 167–183). Prospect Heights, IL: Waveland.

Ford, D. & Schmidt, A. (1985). *Electronically monitored home confinement.* Washington, DC: National Institute of Justice.

Fulton, B., Latessa, E., Stichman, A., & Travis, L. (1997). Up to speed: The state of ISP: Research and policy implications. *Federal Probation, 61*(4), 65–75.

Georgiou, G. (2014). Does increased post-release supervision of criminal offenders reduce recidivism? Evidence from a statewide quasi-experiment. *International Review of Law and Economics, 37,* 221–243.

Glaze, L., & Herberman, E. (2013). *Correctional populations in the United States, 2012.* Washington, DC: Bureau of Justice Statistics.

Goldstein, H., Burrell, W., & Talty, R. (1985). Probation: The RAND report and beyond. *Perspectives, 9*(2), 11–12, et seq.

Gottfredson, M., Mitchell-Herzfeld, S., & Flanagan, T. (1982). Another look at the effectiveness of parole supervision. *Journal of Research in Crime & Delinquency, 18*(2), 277–298.

Gowdy, V. (1993). *Intermediate sanctions.* Washington, DC: National Institute of Justice.

Guynes, R. (1988). *Difficult clients, large caseloads plague probation, parole agencies.* Washington, DC: U.S. Department of Justice.

Harland, A. (Ed.), (1996). *Choosing correctional options that work.* Thousand Oaks, CA: Sage.

Harland, A., & Rosen, C. (1987). Sentencing theory and intensive supervision probation. *Federal Probation, 51*(4), 33–42.

Harries, K. (2003). Using geographic analysis in probation and parole. *National Institute of Justice, 249,* 32–33 (July).

Harris, P., Petersen, R., & Rapoza, S. (2001). Between probation and revocation: A study of intermediate sanctions decision-making. *Journal of Criminal Justice, 29*(4), 307–318.

Harvard Law Review Note (1966). Anthropotelemetry: Dr. Schwitzgebel's machine. *Harvard Law Review, 80,* 403.

Hipp, J., & Yates, D. (2009). Do returning parolees affect neighborhood crime? A case study of Sacramento. *Criminology, 47*(3), 619–656.

Holsinger, A., Latessa, E., Turner, M., & Travis, L. (1997). *High level alternatives to incarceration: Examining community based correctional facilities.* Paper presented at the annual meeting of the Academy of Criminal Justice Science, Louisville, KY, March 1997.

Holsinger, A., Lowenkamp, C., & Latessa, E. (2006). Exploring the validity of the level of service inventory—Revised with Native American Offenders. *Journal of Criminal Justice, 334*(3), 331–337.

Hughes, T., Wilson, D., & Beck, A. (2001). *Trends in state parole, 1990–2000.* Washington, DC: Bureau of Justice Statistics.

Huskey, B. (1987). Electronic monitoring: An evolving alternative. *Perspectives, 11*(3), 19–23.

Ingraham, B., & Smith, G. (1972). *Electronic surveillance and control of behavior and its possible use in rehabilitation and parole.* In *Issues in criminology Vol. 7.* (pp. 35–52) Beverly Hills, CA: Sage.

Jannetta, J., Neusteter, S. R., Davies, E., & Horvath, A. (2012). *Transition from prison to community initiative: Process evaluation final report.* Washington, DC: Urban Institute.

Jones, P. (1991). The risk of recidivism: Evaluating the public-safety implications of a community corrections program. *Journal of Criminal Justice, 19*(1), 49–66.

Kurlychek, M. (2010). Transforming attitudinal change into behavioral change: The missing link. *Criminology & Public Policy, 9*(1), 119–126.

Larivee, J. (1990). Day reporting centers: Making their way from the U.K. to the U.S. *Corrections Today, 52*(6), 84.

Latessa, E. J. (1980). Intensive diversion unit: An evaluation. In B. Price & P. J. Baunach (Eds.), *Criminal Justice Research* (pp. 101–124). Beverly Hills, CA: Sage.

Leffingwell, T. R., Cooney, N. J., Murphy, J. G., Luczak, S., Rosen, G., Dougherty, D., et al. (2013). Continuous objective monitoring of alcohol use: Twenty-first century measurement using transdermal sensors. *Alcoholism: Clinical and Experimental Research, 37*, 16–22.

Lowenkamp, C., Flores, A., Holsinger, A., Makarios, M., & Latessa, E. (2010). Intensive supervision programs: Does program philosophy and the principles of effective intervention matter? *Journal of Criminal Justice, 38*, 368–375.

Lutze, F. (1998). Are shock incarceration programs more rehabilitative than traditional prisons? A survey of inmates. *Justice Quarterly, 15*(3), 547–563.

Lutze, F. (2001). The influence of a shock incarceration program on inmate adjustment and attitudinal change. *Justice Quarterly, 29*(3), 255–267.

Lutze, F., Johnson, W. W., Clear, T., Latessa, E., & Slate, R. (2012). The future of community corrections is now: Stop dreaming and take action. *Journal of Contemporary Criminal Justice, 28*, 42–59.

Mackenzie, D. (1997). Criminal justice and crime control. In L. Sherman, D. Gottfredson, D. MacKenzie, J. Eck, P. Reuter, & S. Bushway (Eds.), *Preventing crime: What works, what doesn't, what's promising?* (pp. 9.1–9.76). Washington, DC: National Institute of Justice.

Mackenzie, D., & Parent, D. (1991). Shock incarceration and prison crowding in Louisiana. *Journal of Criminal Justice, 19*(3), 225–237.

Mackenzie, D., & Shaw, J. (1990). Inmate adjustment and change during shock incarceration: The impact of correctional boot camp programs. *Justice Quarterly, 7*(1), 125–150.

Matejkowski, J., Festinger, D., Benishek, L., & Dugosh, K. (2011). Matching consequences to behavior: Implications of failing to distinguish between noncompliance and nonresponsivity. *International Journal of Law and Psychiatry, 34*, 269–274.

McDevitt, J. (1988). *Evaluation of the Hampton County Day Reporting Center.* Boston: Crime and Justice Foundation.

McDevitt, J., & Miliano, R. (1992). Day reporting centers: An innovative concept in intermediate sanctions. In J. Byrne, A. Lurigio, & J. Petersilia (Eds.), *Smart sentencing: The emergence of intermediate sanctions* (pp. 152–165). Beverly Hills, CA: Sage.

McGaha, J., Fichter, M., & Hirschburg, P. (1987). Felony probation: A re-examination of public risk. *American Journal of Criminal Justice, 12*(1), 1–9.

Mellowa, J., Schlager, M., & Caplan, J. (2008). Using GIS to evaluate post-release prisoner services in Newark, New Jersey. *Journal of Criminal Justice, 36*(5), 416–425.

Minton, T. (2013). *Jail inmates at midyear 2012—Statistical tables.* Washington, DC: Bureau of Justice Statistics.

Monfross, B. (2011). *Special report: California Department of Corrections and Rehabilitation's implementation of the non-revocable parole program.* Sacramento, CA: Office of the Inspector General.

Morris, N., & Tonry, M. (1990). *Between prison and probation: Intermediate punishments in a rational sentencing system*. Oxford: Oxford University Press.

National Institute of Corrections (1981). *Model probation and parole management project*. Washington, DC: National Institute of Corrections.

National Institute of Justice (1999). *Keeping track of electronic monitoring*. Washington, DC: National Law Enforcement and Corrections Technology Center.

National Institute of Justice (2011). *Electronic monitoring reduces recidivism*. Washington, DC: Office of Justice Programs.

Padgett, K., Bales, W., & Blomberg, T. (2006). Under surveillance: An empirical test of the effectiveness and consequences of electronic monitoring. *Criminology & Public Policy, 5*(1), 61–92.

Parent, D. (1990). *Day reporting centers for criminal offenders: A descriptive analysis of existing programs*. Washington, DC: U.S. Department of Justice.

Parent, D., Byrne, J., Tsarfaty, V., Valade, L., & Esselman, J. (1995). *Day reporting centers, Volume 1: Issues and practices*. Washington, DC: National Institute of Justice.

Parisi, N. (1980). Combining incarceration and probation. *Federal Probation, 44*(2), 3–11.

Payne, B., & DeMichele, M. (2010). Electronic supervision for sex offenders: Implications for work load, supervision goals, versatility, and policymaking. *Journal of Criminal Justice, 38*(3), 276–281.

Petersilia, J. (1985). *Probation and felony offenders*. Washington, DC: U.S. Department of Justice.

Petersilia, J. (2005). Hard time: Ex-offenders returning home after prison. *Corrections Today, 67*(2), 66–71, to 155.

Petersilia, J., Turner, S., & Peterson, J. (1986). *Prison versus probation in California: Implications for crime and offender recidivism*. Santa Monica, CA: RAND.

Piquero, N. (2003). A recidivism analysis of Maryland's community probation program. *Journal of Criminal Justice, 31*(4), 295–307.

Renzema, M., & Mayo-Wilson, E. (2005). Can electronic monitoring reduce crime for moderate to high-risk offenders? *Journal of Experimental Criminology, 1*(2), 215–237.

Rosenmerkel, S., Durose, M., & Farole, D. (2009). *Felony sentences in state courts, 2006—Statistical tables*. Washington, DC: Bureau of Justice Statistics, 8.

Schmidt, A. (1987). Electronic monitoring: Who uses it? How much does it cost? Does it work? *Corrections Today, 49*(7), 28–34.

Schwitzgebel, R. (1969). A belt from big brother. *Psychology Today, 2*(11), 45–47, 65.

Szasz, T. (1975). The control of conduct: Authority vs. autonomy? *Criminal Law Bulletin, 11*, 617–622.

Taylor, D. (2004). Agency accreditation: The performance-based standards experience. *Perspectives, 28*(2), 21–23.

Taylor, K., & Blanchette, K. (2009). The women are not wrong: It is the approach that is debatable. *Criminology and Public Policy, 8*(1), 221–229.

Teague, M. (2011). Probation in America: Armed, private and unaffordable? *Probation Journal, 58*, 317–332.

Thigpen, M., Beauclair, T., Moore, J., & Humphries, K. (2010). *TPC case management handbook: An integrated case management approach*. Washington, DC: National Institute of Corrections.

Travis, L. F., III (1984). Intensive supervision in probation and parole. *Corrections Today, 46*(4), 34.

Vito, G. F. (1985). Probation as punishment: New directions. In Travis, L. F., III, (Ed.), *Probation, parole and community corrections* (pp. 73–80). Prospect Heights, IL: Waveland.

Vito, G. F. (1986). Felony probation and recidivism: Replication and response. *Federal Probation, 50*(4), 17–25.

Vito, G. F., & Marshall, F. H. (1983). The administrative caseload project. *Federal Probation, 46*(3), 33–41.

von Hirsch, A., & Hanrahan, K. (1978). *Abolish parole?* Washington, DC: U.S. Department of Justice.

Weisburd, D., Einat, T., & Kowalski, M. (2008). The miracle of the cells: An experimental study of interventions to increase payment of court-ordered financial obligations. *Criminology & Public Policy, 7*(1), 9–36.

Wilson, J. (2005). Bad behavior or bad policy? An examination of Tennessee release cohorts, 1993–2001. *Criminology & Public Policy, 4*(3), 485–518.

Wodahl, E. J., & Garland, B. (2009). The evolution of community corrections: The enduring influence of the prison. *The Prison Journal, 89*, 81S–104S.

Wodahl, E. J., Ogle, R., & Heck, C. (2011). Revocation trends: A threat to the legitimacy of community-based corrections. *The Prison Journal, 91*(2), 207–266.

Worrall, J., Schram, P., Hays, E., & Newman, M. (2004). An analysis of the relationship between probation caseloads and property crime rates in California counties. *Journal of Criminal Justice, 32*(3), 231–241.

Yeh, S. (2010). Cost-benefit analysis of reducing crime through electronic monitoring of parolees and probationers. *Journal of Criminal Justice, 38*, 1090–1096.

CHAPTER 14

The Juvenile Justice System

Misbehavior by juveniles poses special problems for agents of social control. Foremost among the concerns is the general societal belief that we should treat juveniles differently from adults. Indeed, an entire system of social control exists for dealing with problem youths. The juvenile justice system operates under a different set of assumptions about deviant behavior than does the adult criminal justice system, and it works somewhat independently of the adult system. This does not mean that there is no overlap between the adult and juvenile systems. In actuality, there is a great deal of similarity in the operations of the two systems. Some individuals claim that the differences are little more than semantic exercises. The aim of this chapter is to give the reader a brief overview of the problem of juvenile delinquency, the operations of the juvenile justice system, and the major issues currently facing that system.

DEFINING DELINQUENCY

Perhaps the first point of departure between the adult and juvenile systems appears in the behavior each handles. There are a number of definitions of delinquency. Many definitions reflect the same behavior outlined as criminal in the adult system. Such criminal law definitions often define a delinquent as a juvenile who violates the criminal laws of the jurisdiction. The Ohio Revised Code (see Box 14.1) is one such statute. The emphasis is on the same behavior prohibited for adults.

Besides adult criminal acts, the juvenile justice system intervenes in a variety of specific juvenile offenses usually referred to as status offenses because they are applicable only to persons of a certain "status." Acts typically considered status offenses include smoking, drinking, fighting, swearing, running away, being disrespectful to parents, truancy, and various others that are allowable for adults. Although "status offense" is the most common term for these actions, some jurisdictions refer to "unruliness," "incorrigibility," "dependency," and other similar terms. Regardless of the term used, such statutes are generally very vague, leaving the interpretation of what is not acceptable behavior to the reader's discretion, making it possible to intervene with almost all youths. An example of one such statute appears in Box 14.2.

Important Terms

abandonment
adjudication
    decision
apprenticeship
blended
    sentencing
cottage
    reformatories
deinstitutionaliza-
    tion
delinquent
detached workers
detention
    decision
disposition
    decision
divestiture
forays
GREAT
houses of refuge
infanticide
intake decision
involuntary
    servitude
juvenile
nonsecure
    detention
parens patriae
rumble
status offenses
waiver decision

BOX 14.1 A CRIMINAL LAW DEFINITION OF DELINQUENCY

(F) "Delinquent child" includes any of the following:

1. Any child, except a juvenile traffic offender, who violates any law of this state or the United States, or any ordinance of a political subdivision of the state, that would be an offense if committed by an adult;
2. Any child who violates any lawful order of the court ...;
3. Any child who violates [prohibitions against purchasing or owning a firearm or handgun (Section 2321.211)];
4. Any child who is a habitual truant and who previously has been adjudicated an unruly child for being a habitual truant;
5. Any child who is a chronic truant.

Source: Ohio Revised Code (2010)

BOX 14.2 A STATUS OFFENSE DEFINITION OF DELINQUENCY

Ohio Chapter 2151.022 defines an "unruly child" as:

A. Any child who does not submit to the reasonable control of the child's parents, teachers, guardian, or custodian, by reason of being wayward or habitually disobedient;
B. Any child who is an habitual truant from school and who previously has not been adjudicated an unruly child for being an habitual truant;
C. Any child who behaves in a manner as to injure or endanger the child's own health or morals or the health or morals of others;
D. Any child who violates a law ... that is applicable only to a child.

Source: Ohio Revised Code (2006)

Implicit in the various definitions of delinquency is a definition of "juvenile." Whereas some delinquency statutes provide a specific age, others simply refer to the age of majority defined in another statute. Clearly, juveniles are young persons who are not yet adults. The legal definition, however, varies from place to place (see Box 14.3). For example, 37 states and the District of Columbia set 18 years as the age at which youths move to adult court. Ten states move those aged 17 or older to adult court jurisdiction, and three states do so with those aged 16 and over (King & Szymanski, 2006). At the same time that an upper age limit is set, some states also set a lower age limit for system intervention (see Box 14.4). These lower ages typically range from age 6 to age 10. A further age consideration deals with the "waiver or transfer" of youths to adult jurisdiction. Although this issue will be dealt with later in the chapter, it is important to note that in 22 states and the District of Columbia there is no minimum age at which juveniles can be considered as adults and handled by the adult criminal justice system (see Box 14.5). Varying maximum age, minimum age, and waiver provisions mean that youths subject to the juvenile statutes in one location are adults in another jurisdiction.

BOX 14.3 AGES AT WHICH CRIMINAL COURTS GAIN JURISDICTION OVER YOUNG OFFENDERS

Age 16 (3 states)	Age 18 (38 states)	
Connecticut	Alabama	Montana
New York	Alaska	Nebraska
North Carolina	Arizona	Nevada
	Arkansas	New Jersey

Age 17 (10 states)		
Georgia	California	New Mexico
Illinois	Colorado	North Dakota
Louisiana	Delaware	Ohio
Massachusetts	District of Columbia	Oklahoma
Michigan	Florida	Oregon
Missouri	Hawaii	Pennsylvania
New Hampshire	Idaho	Rhode Island
South Carolina	Indiana	South Dakota
Texas	Iowa	Tennessee
Wisconsin	Kansas	Utah
	Kentucky	Vermont
	Maine	Virginia
	Maryland	Washington
	Minnesota	West Virginia
	Mississippi	Wyoming

Source: King and Szymanski (2006)

BOX 14.4 LOWER AGE LIMITS FOR JUVENILE COURT JURISDICTION

Age 6	Age 7	Age 8	Age 10	
North Carolina	Maryland	Arizona	Arkansas	Pennsylvania
	Massachusetts		Colorado	South Dakota
	New York		Kansas	Texas
			Louisiana	Vermont
			Minnesota	Wisconsin
			Mississippi	

No Specified Lowest Age in Statute or Court Rule

Alabama	Hawaii	Michigan	New Mexico	Tennessee
Alaska	Idaho	Missouri	North Dakota	Utah
California	Illinois	Montana	Ohio	Virginia
Connecticut	Indiana	Nebraska	Oklahoma	Washington, DC
Delaware	Iowa	Nevada	Oregon	West Virginia
Florida	Kentucky	New Hampshire	Rhode Island	Wyoming
Georgia	Maine	New Jersey	South Carolina	

Source: King and Szymanski (2006)

BOX 14.5 MINIMUM AGES FOR TRANSFER TO CRIMINAL COURT

Age 10	Age 12	Age 13	Age 14		Age 15
Kansas	Colorado	Illinois	Alabama	Michigan	New Mexico
Vermont	Missouri	Mississippi	Arkansas	Minnesota	
	Montana	New Hampshire	California	New Jersey	
		New York	Connecticut	North Dakota	
		North Carolina	Iowa	Ohio	
		Wyoming	Kentucky	Texas	
			Louisiana	Utah	
			Massachusetts	Virginia	

No Minimum Age

Alaska	Georgia	Nebraska	South Carolina
Arizona	Hawaii	Nevada	South Dakota
Delaware	Idaho	Oklahoma	Tennessee
District of	Indiana	Oregon	Washington
Columbia	Maine	Pennsylvania	West Virginia
Florida	Maryland	Rhode Island	Wisconsin

Source: Griffin (2006)

MEASURING THE SCOPE OF THE PROBLEM

How large is the delinquency problem? What characterizes the typical delinquent? Answers to both of these questions can present different images. The varied responses are attributable to the range of possible considerations in defining delinquents and the various methods used for measuring delinquency. Despite the potential variability, some common features about delinquency emerge.

Official Records

The most common source of information on delinquency is the official records of the criminal and juvenile justice system. The *Uniform Crime Reports* (UCR), court records, and correctional figures are among the official crime measures that present information about the level of juvenile misbehavior. Figure 14.1 presents data from the 2012 UCR. Youths under the age of 18 accounted for just under 11% of all arrests (approximately 1 million), 11.7% of the violent Index crimes (47,237), and 18% of the property Index crimes (230,803) (Federal Bureau of Investigation [FBI], 2012). The size of the juvenile problem appears even larger when you consider that youths between the ages of 10 and 17 (inclusive) make up roughly 10% of the total U.S. population (U.S. Census Bureau, 2010). Juveniles, therefore, are contributing their share to the arrest statistics.

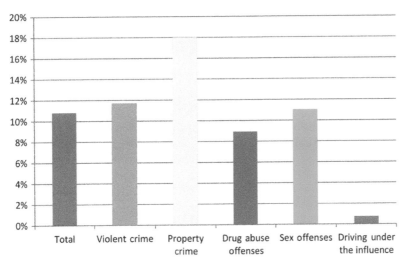

FIGURE 14.1
Percent of arrests by juveniles, by offense type.
Source: Constructed by author from the 2012 UCR

Official figures also serve to provide a profile of delinquents. In terms of type of offense, youths confine most of their deviance to property offenses. The sex distribution of juvenile offenders is heavily skewed; males represent 70% of all arrestees. Both males and females, however, commit more than one-quarter of their offenses in the Part I Index categories. The racial breakdown in official figures shows an overrepresentation of minorities. For example, black youths were arrested for robbery at 10 times the rate of white youths (Puzzanchera, 2013). The trend in youthful crime reveals declines over recent years. UCR data show significant decreases since 1989 for every Index category. Unfortunately, juveniles still account for more than 278,000 Index offense arrests and more than 1 million arrests for all offenses.

In summary, official statistics show that the delinquency problem mainly involves property offenses, is dominated by males, and is overrepresented by minority youths. The data, however, show signs of decreasing arrests in recent years. Although the official measures uncover a large amount of delinquency, these numbers probably underrepresent the actual level of juvenile misbehavior in society. First, not everyone reports all of the crimes they know about to the police; thus, any unreported deviant act is not included. Second, official records do not adequately reflect status offenses. The police may ignore or simply not record youthful misbehavior that is not also an adult criminal act. The possibility that official records underreport delinquency has led to the use of other measures of deviance. The greatest advantage of the official records lies in the fact that they are collected on an ongoing basis and in a reasonably consistent fashion.

Self-Reports of Delinquency

Researchers also measure delinquency through self-report surveys that ask the respondent what crimes he or she has committed. These measures have the potential of uncovering deviant acts not reported to the police. Indeed, self-report surveys emerged in part as a means of finding out about deviance about which the police were unaware.

Self-report surveys have a long history in juvenile justice. In fact, the earliest such surveys applied specifically to the study of juvenile misbehavior. One of the best-known self-report scales is the Short-Nye Self-Report Delinquency Scale (see Box 14.6). It is apparent that status and minor offenses dominate the items in the scale. Most surveys use a set of seven of the items (see the asterisks in Box 14.6) in place of the entire scale. These self-report scales typically uncover a great deal of delinquency. Studies using these types of scales show that virtually every person is a delinquent. This probably results from the minor nature of the acts probed in the questions.

BOX 14.6 SHORT-NYE SELF-REPORT DELINQUENCY ITEMS

Drove a car without a driver's license or permit[a]
Skipped school[a]
Had a fist fight with one person
Ran away from home
Was expelled from school or put on probation
Defied parents' authority[a]
Drove too fast or recklessly
Took little things (worth less than $2)[a]
Took things of medium value ($2–$50)
Took things of large value (over $50)
Used force (strong-arm methods) to get money from another person
Took part in "gang fights"
Took a car for a ride without the owner's knowledge
Bought or drank beer, wine, or liquor (including drinking at home)[a]
Bought or drank beer, wine, or liquor (outside the home)
Drank beer, wine, or liquor at home
Deliberately damaged property[a]
Used or sold narcotic drugs
Had sexual relations with another person of the same sex (not masturbation)[a]
Had sexual relations with a person of the opposite sex
Hunted or fished without a license (or violated other game laws)
Took things you didn't want
Beat up on kids who hadn't done anything to you
Hurt someone to see them squirm

---

[a]Commonly used items in subsequent self-report studies.
Source: Short and Nye (1958)

Criticisms that trivial acts dominate the scales prompted some researchers to construct scales that include more serious property and personal offenses. The National Youth Survey (NYS) included acts that qualify as felony assault, grand theft, sale of stolen items, and robbery. Unfortunately, the NYS is no longer collected. An ongoing self-report survey, the Monitoring the Future (MTF) project, questions high school students and young adults every year. As with the NYS, the MTF includes serious offenses, such as hitting a teacher, using a weapon to steal something from someone, stealing a car, and fighting in a group. The result of including these more serious items is a reduction in the number of persons claiming to have participated in deviance. In fact, the level of offending for the serious crimes is often close to that uncovered in official records. The level of minor offending, however, remains high.

The demographic profile of offenders presented by self-report studies is somewhat different from the picture evident in official records. First, the peak age of offending appears around ages 13–15. This earlier peak may be partly due to the use of minor and status offenses in the surveys. Second, differences in the racial and social class distribution are minimal in self-report surveys. Where racial and social class differences appear, they are generally small (Elliott, Ageton, Huizinga, Knowles, & Canter, 1983; Hindelang, Hirschi, & Weis, 1981). The greatest similarity to official records appears in the sex distribution of offenses. Males again exceed females in the level of offending. An interesting point to note is that, despite the numerical differences, males and females tend to commit similar types of behaviors. That is, there do not appear to be any acts that are primarily restricted to one or the other sex (Elliott et al., 1983).

Comparing the Delinquency Measures

The different sources of delinquency data show both similarities and differences. In general, both show that delinquency is a widespread problem. It is not restricted to any one group or type of offense. The level of offending increased throughout the 1960s and early 1970s, leveled off and showed some decreases in the late 1970s and 1980s, increased in the late 1980s and early 1990s (particularly in serious personal offenses), and has been decreasing in recent years. There is a clear diversity in offending. Youths are involved in all types of behavior—from status offenses to serious personal crimes. Property crimes dominate in all measures, and personal offenses are the least common. Males dominate in all but a couple of delinquency categories, such as prostitution and running away.

Most differences in the measures appear in the relative magnitude of offending and by offending subgroups in the population. Self-report measures uncover more offending than do official measures. In terms of demographics, official figures show a much larger number of African American offenders than self-report measures. Self-report statistics find little racial difference in offending. Social class differences also tend to disappear when most self-report data are considered. Similar discrepancies emerge when considering the sex of the offenders. Even though males dominate in magnitude of offending, official figures show the sexes committing different types of offenses. Self-report data, however, tend to portray the sexes as participating in the same types of behavior.

The differences between the measures are a result of the measurement techniques. Official records provide an ongoing look at the level and change in delinquency from year to year according to the formal justice system. These records reflect offenses brought to the attention of the authorities. Actions not reported are withheld from public officials and are lost to these records. Self-reports typically portray a larger delinquency problem than official figures. The cause of this is the type of activities probed in the survey. Surveys that inquire about minor status offenses will always find high delinquency levels. When serious offenses form the core of the questionnaire, however, the number of delinquents falls to lower levels.

No single method of measuring delinquency is better than the others. The usefulness of the measures depends entirely on the question being answered. Each method provides a different set of information about delinquency. Official records are useful for noting change in official processing and handling of youths over time. They also provide a long-term set of data that allows the inspection of changes over time. Official data are also rich in information about various demographic and offense factors not found in other measures. Self-reports provide a measure of delinquency based on the offender's viewpoint. They are capable of addressing behaviors that may not result in arrests and lead to official records. Self-reports yield information on minor crimes, the number of offenses an individual commits, offender demographics, and why an individual acts in a certain way.

GANG DELINQUENCY

The study of juvenile misbehavior consistently portrays delinquency as a group phenomenon (Erickson, 1971; Erickson & Jensen, 1977; Hindelang, 1971). Much of the interest in group delinquency revolves around the existence of juvenile gangs. One source of the public's concern about gangs may be the portrayal of gang behavior in the mass media. Movies and plays such as *The Blackboard Jungle* and *West Side Story* in the 1950s, and *Colors*, *Boyz N the Hood*, and *The Freedom Writers* in more recent years dramatize the lure of gangs for youths and the aggressive nature of these groups. Social and scholarly interest in gangs was particularly high in the early 1900s until the early 1960s. For a variety of reasons, including overall increases in social unrest and changes in theoretical approaches to deviance, gangs received little specific attention in the late 1960s, 1970s, and early 1980s. It is only within the past 30 years, as gang-related violence has increased, that academic and social interest in gangs reemerged.

Defining Gangs

Although there has been a great deal of interest and research in gang activity, no single, universally accepted definition of a gang has developed. Curry and Decker (1998) identify a number of factors that are common to most definitions (see Box 14.7). These elements are a group, symbols, communication,

BOX 14.7 TYPICAL ELEMENTS OF A "GANG" DEFINITION

Group	Usually a specified minimum number of members, certainly more than two
Symbols	Clothes, hand signs, colors, etc., which serve to indicate membership
Communication	Verbal and nonverbal forms, such as made-up words, graffiti, hand signals, etc.
Permanence	Gangs must persist over time, generally at least 1 year or more
Turf	Territory claimed and/or controlled by the gang (not as common in many definitions)
Crime	Involvement in criminal behavior

Source: Compiled from Curry and Decker (1998)

permanence, turf, and criminal behavior. Gangs also are more common in poor, disorganized areas of the community.

Rather than attempt to arrive at a single definition for gangs, some authors opt to identify different types of gangs. Knox (1991) offered a typology that presents gangs as developing through identifiable stages from a loose group of youths only marginally involved in criminal activity to a formal gang organized around criminal behavior for profit. Not all gangs will successfully move to the most formalized end of the development continuum. Taylor (1990) offered a typology of gangs based on the motivational factors underlying the gang behavior. Although some gangs center on protecting territory, others may exist to make money for its members. Using typologies of gangs negates the need for a single definition. By suggesting that there are different degrees or types of gangs, such typologies suggest that different types of gangs pose different problems and require different solutions.

The Extent of Gang Deviance

The extent of gang deviance is very difficult to gage, particularly given the varied definitions one can use to identify a gang. What was perhaps the earliest study of gangs identified 1,313 gangs with roughly 25,000 members in Chicago (Thrasher, 1936). These gangs comprised mostly adolescent males and usually ranged in size from 6 to 20 members, although some had as few as two to three members and others numbered more than 100. The great number of gangs in part reflected the fact that Thrasher considered almost any consistent grouping of youths (what he referred to as "play groups") to be a gang. Based on data from six U.S. cities in the 1970s, Miller (1975, 1980) estimated the number of gangs and the number of gang members (see Table 14.1). His top estimate for these cities was 2,700 gangs with roughly 81,500 members. Research since the 1970s, relying primarily on the National Youth Gang Survey (NYGS) of police and sheriff's departments, suggests that the gang problem is large and appears in every state and in cities of every size. Although we do not know the exact extent of gang

Table 14.1	Estimates of the Number of Gangs and Gang Members	
	Number of Gangs	**Number of Members**
Miller (1975)—6 cities		
Low estimates	700	28,450
High estimates	2,700	81,500
Spergel, Curry, Ross, and Chance (1990)—45 cities	1,400	121,000
Curry, Fox, Ball, and Stone (1993)—79 cities	4,881	~250,000
Office of Juvenile Justice and Delinquency Prevention (1999b)—3,440 jurisdictions	23,388	~665,000
Egley and Arjunan (2002)		
2,542 jurisdictions	24,500	>772,000
Egley and Major (2004)		
2,182 jurisdictions	21,500	731,500
Egley and Howell (2013)		
3,300 jurisdictions	29,900	782,500

participation, we do know that gangs are common, and they exist in all 50 U.S. states (Office of Juvenile Justice and Delinquency Prevention, 1999a, 1999b). The most recent estimate indicates that there are nearly 30,000 gangs with about 782,000 members. Slightly less than one-third (31.6%) of local law enforcement agencies report youth gang activity in their jurisdictions (Egley & Howell, 2013).

Why Do Youths Join Gangs?

Gang members come together and associate with one another for a wide array of reasons. Among these are the following:

- The economic benefits offered by the gang, which can be more lucrative than a minimum-wage job
- Close relationships with friends and family who may already be involved in gang activity
- A feeling of protection where gang members may believe they are less likely to be victimized by members of the community
- To fill a need for support when the youth has experienced rejection in other areas of life, such as family or school
- An enhanced social status among peers, often symbolized by materialistic items such as clothing or jewelry
- Rebellion against traditional middle-class values and ethics (Taylor & Smith, 2013)

Clearly, juveniles who find themselves faced with poverty, poor opportunities for advancement, poor school performance, lack of familial support, or other factors may find support and acceptance in a gang.

Gang Activity

The typical view of gang activity, especially as portrayed in the media, has not changed much over the years. The media portray gangs in constant violent confrontation with one another and with the public. Contrary to this media portrayal, gangs participate in a variety of different behaviors. This does not mean that the gang fights and drive-by shootings are fictional. Such confrontations have taken place in the past and continue to occur today. The media portrayal, however, distorts reality. Research reveals such violent confrontations are rare relative to other gang behavior. Jankowski (1991) pointed out that gangs provide a forum for recreation, partying, and companionship. Although evidence shows that involvement in a gang increases one's risk of arrest, Tapia (2011) noted that part of this increased risk is likely due to newly enacted "arrest on sight" injunctions which make gang membership in itself a risk factor for being arrested.

Even though gang violence is not as common as many believe, gang violence does occur and has changed greatly over the years. The gang fight, or rumble, was the traditional image associated with gang confrontations. The common scenario was two groups of youths in leather jackets and wielding chains, knives, or broken bottles in a prearranged fight. Such rumbles were relatively rare and resulted in few deaths. Violence in recent years does not conform to the image of a rumble. Instead, rumbles have given way to forays, in which one or two gang members attack a single rival gang member. The attack usually involves a firearm fired from a moving vehicle. The victim's gang then reciprocates against the transgressor's gang in a like fashion. From this emerges an ongoing series of small, isolated attacks between gangs. Counter to public perception, the forays target rival gang members and not the public in general. Violence against the public mainly appears in accidental injuries to bystanders. Two factors often pointed to as causes of modern gang violence are the heavy use of firearms and the role of violence in the drug trade.

The role of firearms in increased levels of violence, whether by gang members or individual youths, is very clear. Sheppard, Grant, Rowe, and Jacobs (2000) noted that the great increase in juvenile homicides in the mid- to late 1980s and early 1990s was due to the increased availability and use of firearms by youths. From 1984 to 1993, there was a 158% increase in the homicide rate involving handguns among 15–24-year-olds (Sheppard et al., 2000). According to UCR data, 80% of murdered juveniles aged 13 and older were killed with a firearm (Puzzanchera & Adams, 2011).

Firearms use by gang members is a major problem. According to the 1998 NYGS, more than half of law enforcement respondents claimed that gang members used firearms often (21%) or sometimes (32%) in assault crimes (National Youth Gang Center, 2000). Gang members are more likely than nongang members to possess, carry, and use guns (Watkins, Huebner, & Decker, 2008). Access to firearms has altered the confrontational approach of gangs from more face-to-face personal interaction to more impersonal drive-by shootings. The result of this use of lethal weapons by gangs is a much higher mortality rate among gang members when compared to the general population (Decker & Van Winkle, 1996; Morales, 1992). There is evidence that possession of firearms is a better explanation for criminal victimization than gang membership. Whether or not youths belong to gangs, those who carry firearms are more likely to be crime victims than those who do not (Spano, Freilich, & Bolland, 2008).

The involvement of drugs in gang activity has changed in recent years. There is no doubt that many gang members use and sell drugs, and that the sale of drugs is an integral part of some organized gangs. The degree to which gangs are involved in drugs, however, is highly variable. Drug sales in one gang may involve simple sale among its own members, really amounting to little more than a pattern of use, whereas another gang may be integrally involved in the drug trade throughout the community. Fagan (1990), in a survey of gang members in Los Angeles, San Diego, and Chicago, found that roughly 28% were rarely involved in drug use, but 35% were seriously involved in drug use and sales. In addition, he found little support for the claim that drug sales were integral to the formal organization of the gang. Similarly, Klein, Maxson, and Cunningham (1991) noted that gangs did not dominate drug sales in Los Angeles County. Whether drug involvement is a driving force behind gang violence is not clear. Klein and colleagues reported little evidence that drugs are more prevalent in gang homicides than nongang homicides, and that violence is rare in both gang and nongang drug arrests. Recent research is mixed regarding whether gang members who sell drugs engage in more violence than those who do not sell drugs (Bellair & McNulty, 2009; Bjerregaard, 2010). Despite these findings, there is no doubt that conflicts over drugs and sales territories do escalate to violence. It is the extent to which such instances occur that needs further exploration.

Responding to Gangs

Responding to gangs and gang problems is an area in which much work remains. Unfortunately, the first response by many cities to an emerging gang problem is one of denial (Hagedorn, 1988). Cities often do not want to admit that they have gangs. The outcome of such denial is the emergence of a full-blown problem before the authorities are prepared to deal with it.

The most common approach for dealing with gangs in the past involved the use of detached workers. This approach places gang workers into the environment of the gang. The workers spend considerable time in the neighborhoods, maintain contact with the gangs, and provide input geared toward acceptable activities. One key problem of these programs, however, was the inadvertent strengthening of gangs by the workers' presence and the provision of activities (Klein, 1971). Consequently, the impact of these programs on the level of deviance was negligible.

BOX 14.8 GANG INTERVENTION STRATEGIES

Suppression	Any form of social control in which the criminal justice system (police, courts, or corrections) or society attempt to impose formal or informal limits on behavior
Social Intervention	Basically a social work approach to working with gangs in the neighborhoods (such as detached worker programs)
Organizational Change and Development	An approach designed to alter the organization(s) that respond to gang problems, such as through the establishment of gang units or specialized training of personnel
Community Organization	Efforts aimed at mobilizing the community toward self-improvement and change, including both physical and social alterations
Opportunities Provision	An approach recognizing the lack of meaningful jobs and the training needed to succeed, and taking steps to change the problems; education, vocational training, and job placement are elements

Source: Adapted from Spergel and Curry (1990)

A wide variety of alternative responses has emerged over the years. Box 14.8 lists five general gang intervention strategies identified in a survey of personnel in 245 cities (Spergel & Curry, 1990). The strategies, listed in order of prevalence, show 44% of the cities reporting the use of suppression of gangs through arrest, incarceration, and supervision, closely followed by social interventions (31.5%). The least-used response is opportunities provision, although most survey respondents claimed that this is the most effective approach.

One of the interventions growing in popularity is the Gang Resistance Education and Training (GREAT) program. GREAT began in 1991 under a grant from the Bureau of Alcohol, Tobacco, and Firearms (known as the ATF, and now named the Bureau of Alcohol, Tobacco, Firearms, and Explosives) to the Phoenix, Arizona, Police Department. GREAT mimics the Drug Abuse Resistance Education (D.A.R.E.) program with police officers instructing middle-school youths. Lessons deal with individual rights, cultural sensitivity, conflict resolution, drugs, neighborhoods, personal responsibility, and goal setting. The program also targets self-esteem. An initial evaluation failed to find any significant impact on the level of self-reported gang participation (Esbensen & Osgood, 1997; Esbensen, Osgood, Taylor, Peterson, & Freng, 2001). However, program participants did display "more prosocial behaviors and attitudes" toward police, school, family, and peers. The promising results found in the evaluation led to the revised curriculum displayed in Box 14.9. A recent evaluation (Esbensen, Peterson, Taylor, & Osgood, 2012) found the revised curriculum to be effective at preventing gang membership.

BOX 14.9 GREAT MIDDLE-SCHOOL CURRICULUM

1. Welcome to GREAT
   - Program Introduction
   - Relationship Between Gangs, Violence, Drugs, and Crime
2. What's the Real Deal?
   - Message Analysis
   - Facts and Fiction About Gangs and Violence
3. It's About Us
   - Community
   - Roles and Responsibilities
   - What You Can Do About Gangs
4. Where Do We Go From Here?
   - Setting Realistic and Achievable Goals
5. Decisions, Decisions, Decisions
   - GREAT Decision-Making Model
   - Impact of Decisions on Goals
   - Decision-Making Practice
6. Do You Hear What I Am Saying?
   - Effective Communication
   - Verbal vs. Nonverbal
7. Walk in Someone Else's Shoes
   - Active Listening
   - Identification of Different Emotions
   - Empathy for Others
8. Say It Like You Mean It
   - Body Language
   - Tone of Voice
   - Refusal-Skills Practice
9. Getting Along Without Going Along
   - Influences and Peer Pressure
   - Refusal-Skills Practice
10. Keeping Your Cool
    - GREAT Anger Management Tips
    - Practice Cooling Off
11. Keeping It Together
    - Recognizing Anger in Others
    - Tips for Calming Others
12. Working It Out
    - Consequences for Fighting
    - GREAT Tips for Conflict Resolution
    - Conflict Resolution Practice
    - Where to Go for Help
13. Looking Back
    - Program Review
    - "Making My School a GREAT Place" Project Review

Source: Bureau of Justice Assistance (2005)

Miller (1990) offered four reasons for our failure to deal with gangs. First, we have no comprehensive national strategy to deal with the problem. Instead, most programs are local and implemented on a piecemeal basis. Second, the resources provided to deal with the problem are inadequate. Third, there is no central focus for the implementation and evaluation of gang programs. Finally, we have failed to identify the problems of the social context within which gang activity flourishes. Miller argued that until we seriously commit ourselves to dealing with gangs, we will not have any appreciable impact on gangs.

Some jurisdictions have focused on violence rather than on gangs. Where violence is linked to gangs and gang activities, interventions aimed at gangs are part of the violence control effort. These strategies fall under a general heading of "pulling levers," because officials apply any pressure they can to influence violence. Police and other justice officials use probation and parole conditions, enhanced sentencing, refusal to enter plea negotiations, and other tactics to deter or incapacitate gang members. Evaluations of these efforts indicate they are generally successful in reducing rates of gun violence and homicide (Braga, 2012).

THE HISTORY OF JUVENILE JUSTICE

The history of juvenile delinquency and juvenile justice is relatively short. Although deviance on the part of young persons has always been a fact, societal intervention and participation in the handling of juvenile transgressors has gained most of its momentum in the last 100–150 years. The reasons for this are easy to see. Throughout most of history, youthful members of society did not enjoy a distinct status as "child." The young were either property or people. The very young, from birth to age 5 or 6, had much the same status as any other piece of property. The owner (parents) could buy, sell, or otherwise dispose of children as they wished. Once the individual reached the age of 5 or 6, he or she became a full-fledged adult member of society, subject to the same rules of conduct governing all "adults."

This state of indifference toward youths resulted from the health and economic conditions in society. The infant mortality rate typically exceeded 50%. The failure to develop a personal, caring attitude toward infants, therefore, was an emotional defense mechanism for reducing or eliminating any pain or sorrow attached to the death of a child. The economic conditions also meant that the birth of an infant was a financial burden on the family. Families lived from day to day on what they could produce. The very young were dependent and did not contribute to the family. A child represented a drain on the family's resources.

Over the centuries practices developed for dealing with unwanted or burdensome children. One practice was infanticide, or the deliberate killing of an infant, usually by the mother. Infanticide was a common practice prior to the fourth century and appeared as late as the fourteenth century. A similar practice, which gained prominence after the fourth century, was abandonment. Abandoning children was less offensive than outright infanticide despite the fact that the result was the same. Parents subjected children who survived the first few years to actions such as apprenticeship and involuntary servitude. These actions were similar to the sale of youths by families. This again alleviated the need to care for the youth and brought an economic return to the family. In addition, these youths provided labor during the rise of industrialization.

Once children entered the labor force, they were viewed as adults and subject to the same rules and regulations as adults. A separate system for dealing with youthful offenders did not exist. At best, the father was responsible for controlling the child and his choices for punishment had no bounds. At the societal level, youths could be (and were) sentenced to the same penalties (including death) as were adults. Where due process protections existed, there is little evidence that the youths received them (Faust & Brantingham, 1979; Platt, 1977).

Changes in the societal view of children did not occur until the seventeenth and eighteenth centuries (the Progressive Era). During this time, medical advances were beginning to have a major impact on infant mortality and life expectancy. Additionally, scholars and religious leaders began to pay attention to the young as a means of attacking the ills of society. They saw education and protection of the young as a means of creating a moral society. Accompanying these views were alterations in beliefs about disciplining youthful offenders.

Methods for dealing with problem youths grew out of the establishment of ways to handle the poor. A key method of dealing with the poor was the removal of children from the bad influences and substandard training of poor parents. The establishment of houses of refuge in the early 1800s conformed to this idea. The first such institution opened in New York in 1825. Key features of these institutions were the use of education, skills training, hard work, and apprenticeships—all geared toward producing productive members of society. Despite the goals of the houses of refuge, various problems emerged. Among the concerns were the mixing of adults and juveniles, the mixing of criminals and noncriminals, overcrowding, the failure to supply intended education and training, the use of harsh physical punishment, and the exploitive use of the clients for monetary gain.

The failure of the early houses of refuge gave rise to the establishment of cottage reformatories in the second half of the 1800s. These new institutions closely paralleled a family; surrogate parents provided the education and moral training for a small number of youths. Probation and the use of foster homes also emerged at the same time as the reformatories. Unfortunately, like the earlier houses of refuge, these new alternatives suffered from many of the same problems.

In response to the failures of institutions to deal with problem youths and the call for new interventions, Chicago created a juvenile court in 1899. The late 1800s continued to experience great levels of immigration by lower-class Europeans, delinquency was on the rise, and there was an emergent body of sociological and psychological study attempting to explain the reasons for social ills. The new juvenile court reflected the general belief in the ability to alter youthful

> ### BOX 14.10 MILESTONES IN THE HISTORY OF JUVENILE JUSTICE
>
> | | |
> |---|---|
> | Pre-1800s | Children viewed as property or little adults
Deviant youths handled in adult criminal system |
> | 1825 | Establishment of Houses of Refuge—view that youths can be saved through education, moral training, hard work |
> | 1838 | *Ex parte Crouse*—establishment of *parens patriae* as basis of intervention with youths |
> | 1869 | Juvenile probation established in Massachusetts |
> | Late 1880s | Move to cottage reformatories—same rationale as Houses of Refuge provided in surrogate family setup |
> | 1899 | Juvenile court established in Chicago—totally separate from adult court, heavy reliance on *parens patriae* doctrine |
> | 1905 | *Commonwealth v. Fisher*—court rules that *parens patriae* and good intentions are sufficient for intervention without concern for due process |
> | 1920–1960s | Various new approaches to treatment |
> | 1966 | *Kent v. United States*—Justice Abe Fortas questions whether the juvenile system is providing the benevolent treatment promised by *parens patriae*, beginning of move toward due process in juvenile court |

behavior through application of informal intervention and a desire to educate and train the child. Benevolent assistance, caring, training, and guidance were the watchwords of the new juvenile court. The mandate to help youths did not restrict the court to dealing with youths who committed criminal acts. Rather, the court could intervene in any situation in which a youth was in need of assistance. It was during this time that status offenses were included under the purview of the court. The growth of the court was phenomenal, and almost every state had at least one juvenile court by 1920 (see Box 14.10).

THE PHILOSOPHY OF THE JUVENILE JUSTICE SYSTEM

The underlying philosophy of the new juvenile court was the doctrine of *parens patriae*. Parens patriae, or the "state as parent," was based on the actions of the English Chancery Court, which dealt with overseeing the financial affairs of orphaned juveniles. The court was to act as guardian until the child was mature enough to assume responsibility. Early interventions with juveniles also relied on the doctrine of *parens patriae*. In the case *Ex parte Crouse* (1838), the Pennsylvania Supreme Court ruled that the state had a right to intervene into a juvenile's life, against the wishes of the juvenile or the juvenile's parents, if the state thought that the parents were not capable of properly caring for the youth.

The new juvenile court borrowed this idea of guardianship for the cornerstone of its operations. Debate over the *parens patriae* doctrine was largely settled in 1905 when the Pennsylvania Supreme Court ruled in *Commonwealth v. Fisher* that intervention based on protecting, caring for, and training a youth was a duty of the state and did not violate the constitution, regardless of the youth's actions. The *parens patriae* philosophy stood largely unchallenged until the 1966 case of *Kent v. United States*. In this case, Justice Abe Fortas questioned the denial of due process for juveniles when he noted:

> There is evidence … that there may be grounds for concern that the child receives the worst of both worlds: that he gets neither the protections accorded to adults nor the solicitous care and regenerative treatment postulated for children.
>
> **Kent v. United States (1966)**

Parens patriae remained the dominant force behind interventions with juveniles through the 1970s. Several critics, however, have proposed radical changes in juvenile justice that threaten the traditional *parens patriae* philosophy.

THE JUVENILE COURT PROCESS

Once a police officer takes a youth into custody, it is likely that the police will refer that youngster to juvenile court. In 2012, police referred 68% of youths taken into custody to juvenile court. They either referred the remaining cases to other authorities or the police handled them (FBI, 2012). When police refer a youth to juvenile court, the court personnel must then make one or more critical decisions: whether or not to detain (jail) the youth, whether or not to actually file a petition (charges) against the youth, whether to find (adjudicate) the youth a delinquent, and how to dispose of the petition. These decisions correspond to the adult court decisions of bail or jail, the filing of a formal charge versus dismissal, determination of guilt by plea or by trial, and sentencing. Several juvenile court actors—probation officers, defense attorneys, prosecutors, and judges—are involved in these important decisions. Whereas the judge is the primary decision maker, other court personnel play important roles in deciding the fate of juvenile suspects.

This section examines the critical decision points in the juvenile court process: detention, intake, waiver (transfer), adjudication, and disposition. We look at the roles the various court personnel play (and should play) in the court process. We describe what happens when a juvenile suspect goes through the juvenile court process, and compare the ideal with the reality. Finally, we examine some of the controversial issues facing juvenile court today, such as the question of how adversarial the attorneys in juvenile court should be and whether juveniles should have the right to a jury trial. Note that we do not focus on the critical question of the police and juveniles. However, many of the law enforcement issues raised earlier in the book apply to juveniles as well as to adults.

The Detention Decision

The first decision that juvenile court personnel must make is the detention decision. They must decide whether to keep a juvenile in custody or allow the youth to go home with his or her parents to await further court action. The detention decision is the juvenile court counterpart of the bail decision in adult court. It is very important because it concerns the freedom of the child and, therefore, resembles the disposition (sentencing) decision. In fact, children sent to detention may stay there for an extensive period, perhaps even longer than those sent to state training schools (youth prisons for juveniles determined to be delinquent). Sickmund and Baunach (1986) reported that youths sentenced to detention spent an average of 12 days in detention even though they had not yet been adjudicated delinquent. As with adult bail, youths who are detained face a higher likelihood of being committed to a juvenile correctional institution (Lin, Miller, & Fukushima, 2008).

Detention workers or probation officers usually make the initial detention decision and have several options. Releasing a child to his or her parents is the most frequently used option and the preferred decision in most states. Secure detention—placing a child in the juvenile equivalent of a local jail—is another alternative. It involves placement in a locked facility that houses 10, 20, or more youths who are awaiting further court action or are awaiting transfer to a state correctional facility. Nonsecure detention is another option in some places—for youths involved in less serious crimes, youths who do not pose much threat to the community, and youths who are not a threat to themselves. Such youngsters may be placed in small group homes that are either not locked at all or at least not locked as comprehensively as a secure detention facility (hence the term "nonsecure"). Youngsters in nonsecure detention centers may even go to regular public school classes during the day. Alternatives to detention, such as home detention, have developed in recent years. These alternatives are important in light of extensive overuse of detention in the past (McCarthy, 1987).

The Intake Decision

The second major decision point in juvenile court is the intake decision, analogous to the filing or charging decision in adult court. At intake, a court official (probation officer, prosecutor, or both) decides whether to file a court petition of delinquency, status offense, neglect, abuse, or dependency in a particular case. Traditionally, a probation officer makes the intake decision. The *parens patriae* philosophy of the court dictated this approach because its treatment orientation indicated that the probation officer, ideally a trained social worker, should consider the best interests of the child as well as the legal aspects of the case (as an adult court prosecutor might). That is, an intake probation officer is supposed to consider the welfare of the child and the legal demands of the police and victim, and then attempt to resolve every case in light of those considerations.

A frequent decision of the intake officer is to refrain from filing a petition alleging delinquency or a status offense. Called "adjustment at intake" or "informal adjustment," the officer resolves the matter without resorting to a formal petition against the child. Informal adjustment practices occur as frequently as 25% of the time (Knoll & Sickmund, 2011) and have been part of juvenile court since its inception.

The Prosecutor's Role

If an intake probation officer decides to file a petition against a child, often that decision requires the approval of an attorney, normally the prosecutor. The prosecutor's approval of the probation officer's decision to file a petition ensures that a legally trained official has reviewed the legal criteria for a properly authorized petition. The prosecutor checks the legal wording of the petition, determines that enough evidence is available for establishing the petition (finding the delinquent or status offender "guilty"), and ensures that the offense occurred in the court's jurisdiction and that the child was of proper age at the time of the offense.

Because of the importance of such legal criteria, and because of the growing emphasis on more punitive juvenile models, some jurisdictions have turned away from the traditional probation officer model of intake to models in which the prosecutor is either the first or the only intake decision maker. Such models are more consistent with legalistic views of juvenile court in which the state has abandoned the traditional *parens patriae* philosophy. For example, the state of Washington has switched responsibility for the intake decision to the prosecutor for all felony charges and most misdemeanors. This action represents a radical break with traditional juvenile court thinking and practice. It constitutes a close approximation of adult processing with its retributive emphasis.

The Waiver Decision

For some youths petitioned to juvenile court, the most critical decision point is the waiver decision (also called the "transfer decision"). Many states allow the court to waive or transfer certain offenders (generally older offenders who commit serious crimes) to adult court. This is a crucial decision because transfer to adult court makes the youth subject to adult penalties (such as lengthy incarceration in an adult prison or even the death penalty) as opposed to a relatively short period of incarceration in a juvenile training school. Such a decision also results in the creation of an adult criminal record, which is public and may hinder future opportunities for employment in certain occupations. In contrast, a juvenile court record is confidential.

Waivers occur through a variety of methods (see Box 14.11). The most common is in a hearing that is analogous to the preliminary hearing in adult court. At a waiver hearing, the prosecutor only must show probable cause that an offense occurred and that the juvenile committed the offense. The prosecutor does not have to prove guilt beyond a reasonable doubt. Proof of guilt is reserved for the trial in adult court if the court waives the juvenile or for the adjudication stage in juvenile court if the waiver motion fails. The juvenile transfer hearing differs from an adult court preliminary hearing in that the prosecutor must establish

---

BOX 14.11 FORMS OF WAIVER

Discretionary—Judge makes decision to waive youths after hearing

Mandatory—State mandates the juvenile court judge to waive jurisdiction under certain circumstances; requires a hearing

Presumptive—Statute sets presumption that certain cases are to be waived; not mandatory

Direct File—Prosecutor has right to choose whether to file in adult or juvenile court

Statutory Exclusion—State excludes certain categories of cases from juvenile court jurisdiction

Reverse Waiver—Permits waiving a juvenile being prosecuted in adult court to be transferred back to juvenile court

Once an Adult/Always an Adult—Juvenile court jurisdiction is permanently terminated once prosecuted as an adult

Blended Sentencing—Either the juvenile court or the adult court imposes a sentence that involves either the juvenile or adult correctional systems, or both

---

Source: Based on Griffin, Torbet, and Syzmanski (1998) and Office of Juvenile Justice and Prevention (2002)

---

that the juvenile is not amenable to juvenile court intervention or that the juvenile is a threat to public safety.

An example of nonamenability would be the case of a youth who is already on parole from a state training school for an earlier delinquent act who then commits another serious offense (e.g., armed robbery). If probable cause were established that the youth committed the robbery, then the judge would have to find that the juvenile court had a history of contacts with the youth dating back several years and that more juvenile court effort to deal with the youth's problems, either through probation or a training school placement, would be futile. An example of a case involving a threat to public safety would be a murder case or an offender with a history of violent offenses.

A number of other forms of waiver have emerged in recent years, including direct file, presumptive waiver, and statutory exclusion. Many of these are due to the more punitive attitudes toward juvenile delinquents. Table 14.2 shows the use of the varying forms of waiver found throughout the United States. Because these measures are relatively new, there are no national data available on the exact number of youths waived to adult criminal court in such ways.

In 2008, approximately 8,900 juveniles were waived to adult court (Adams & Addie, 2011). This was considerably below the peak of 13,700 cases waived in 1994, but 13% more than in 2001. Overall, approximately 1% of the juvenile cases handled formally were waived to adult court. Fifty percent of waived cases in 2008 involved personal crimes, and 29% involved property offenses (Adams & Addie, 2011). One reason that the number of waiver cases is lower than in 1994 is that states use other methods (such as direct file or statutory exclusion)

| Table 14.2 | States' Use of Waiver and Blended Sentencing |

	Judicial Waiver			Direct File	Statutory Exclusion	Reverse Waiver	Once/ Always	Juvenile Blended	Criminal Blended
	Discretionary	Presumptive	Mandatory						
Total States	45	15	15	15	29	25	34	15	17
Alabama	X				X		X		
Alaska	X	X			X			X	
Arizona	X			X	X	X	X		
Arkansas	X				X	X		X	X
California	X	X		X	X	X	X		X
Colorado	X	X		X		X		X	X
Connecticut			X			X		X	
Delaware	X		X		X		X		
DC	X	X		X			X		
Florida	X			X	X		X		X
Georgia	X		X	X	X	X			
Hawaii	X						X		
Idaho	X				X		X		X
Illinois	X	X	X		X	X	X	X	X
Indiana	X		X		X		X		
Iowa	X				X	X	X		X
Kansas	X	X					X	X	
Kentucky	X		X			X			X
Louisiana	X		X	X	X				
Maine	X	X					X		
Maryland	X				X	X	X		
Massachusetts					X			X	X
Michigan	X			X			X	X	X
Minnesota	X	X			X		X	X	
Mississippi	X				X	X	X		
Missouri	X						X		X
Montana				X	X	X		X	
Nebraska				X		X			X
Nevada	X	X			X	X	X		
New Hampshire	X	X					X		
New Jersey	X	X	X						
New Mexico					X			X	X
New York					X	X			
North Carolina	X		X				X		
North Dakota	X	X	X				X		
Ohio	X		X				X	X	
Oklahoma	X			X	X	X	X		X
Oregon	X				X	X	X		
Pennsylvania	X	X			X	X	X		
Rhode Island	X	X	X				X	X	
South Carolina	X		X		X				
South Dakota	X				X	X	X		
Tennessee	X					X	X		
Texas	X						X	X	
Utah	X	X			X		X		
Vermont	X			X	X	X		X	
Virginia	X		X	X		X	X		X
Washington	X				X		X		
West Virginia	X		X						X
Wisconsin	X				X	X	X		X
Wyoming	X			X		X			

Source: Griffin (2006)

to prosecute juveniles in adult criminal courts. For example, a survey of 40 of the nation's largest urban counties showed that of 7,100 juveniles charged with felonies in adult criminal court in 1998, three-quarters reached criminal court by direct file or statutory exclusion (Rainville & Smith, 2003). If these proportions apply to the entire nation, then the 2008 juvenile court number of 8,900 juveniles waived would suggest a significantly higher total number of youths overall being tried in adult court.

Research on transfer and other methods of placing youths into adult court has produced mixed results. In general, youths charged with serious offenses tend to receive harsher sentences in adult courts whereas those charged with less serious crimes receive harsher sentences in juvenile courts. Steiner (2009) reported that youths transferred to adult courts were more likely to receive prison sentences than a comparison group of young adults in the same courts. Donna Bishop and her colleagues (Winner, Lanza-Kaduce, Bishop, & Frazier, 1997) have done extensive research on transfer in the state of Florida. Comparing a sample of 2,738 youths transferred in 1987 to youths retained in the juvenile court, they reported that the transferred youths were more likely to receive longer sentences in the adult system than youths in the juvenile system. They were also more likely actually to be incarcerated for longer periods (they actually served longer sentences) than other youths. The two groups had similar recidivism rates, but the transferred youth had more arrests more quickly than nontransferred youths (Winner et al., 1997).

Examining juvenile cases in Pennsylvania, Myers (2003) tested the idea that a higher recidivism rate among juveniles transferred to adult court might be a result of selection bias. In other words, it is possible that the juveniles transferred to adult court are those at the greatest risk of engaging in subsequent criminal activity. However, Myers (2003) found that even after controlling for selection bias, juveniles transferred to adult court have greater rates of recidivism than those processed by the juvenile court.

A study of 1,042 juveniles prosecuted and sentenced in Pennsylvania adult criminal court between 1997 and 1999 showed that juveniles received harsher sentences in adult court than did young adults, even controlling for legal factors such as offense seriousness and prior record. Specifically, the juveniles were 10% more likely to be incarcerated and received a 29-percent increase in sentence length (average sentence length of 2.18 months per juvenile, compared to 1.69 months per adult). These findings "suggest that judges may assign greater levels of culpability and dangerousness to transferred juveniles than to young adult offenders" (Kurlychek & Johnson, 2004:505).

In general, the research suggests that transfer and other means of putting juveniles into adult court are not magic solutions to some of the perceived problems in the juvenile court. There is conflicting evidence regarding whether youths placed into adult court are more likely to receive prison sentences or to serve longer time in incarceration. Recidivism statistics do not indicate any advantage for transferred youths. In several studies, the transferred youths do worse than nontransferred youths. Nevertheless, the current climate favoring punishment suggests that transfer and other mechanisms to get juveniles into adult court will continue. This probably will occur even despite the fact that some research evidence questions whether this trend is actually protecting the public more than juvenile court processing could.

Adjudication and Disposition

For children not waived to adult criminal court, the next steps after the filing of a petition are adjudication and disposition. In the adjudication and disposition decisions, a judge determines whether there is enough evidence to establish the petition and then decides what to do if there is enough evidence. The adjudication decision is comparable to the conviction (plea or trial), and the disposition decision is like the sentencing decision in adult court.

The U.S. Supreme Court ruled certain procedural rights apply to juveniles as well as to adults (see Table 14.3 for a summary of key court decisions). In the ideal, the determination of the truth of the petition occurs in a rational fashion, with the prosecutor, defense attorney, and judge using their abilities and training to seek justice. Realistically, juvenile court sessions often are hectic and hurried, and they may reflect the self-interests of the parties involved rather than justice or the best interests of the child (Baker, 1991; Prescott, 1981).

Attorneys in the Juvenile Courtroom

There are several problems concerning attorneys in juvenile court. First, many juveniles do not have attorneys (Feld & Schaefer, 2010). Many juveniles waive their right to an attorney, often because they do not fully understand their rights, especially the importance of the right to an attorney (see e.g., Schwartz & Levick, 2010). A second critical problem is the burden of high caseloads for public defenders in juvenile court. Depending on the state, the caseload for the average public defender can range from 360 to 1,000 cases per defender (Jones, 2004). With attorneys overworked, many juvenile defendants have gotten the clear impression that "their attorneys do not care about them" (Puritz, Burrell, Schwartz, Soler, & Warboys, 1995:47).

Many attorneys in juvenile court, both public defenders and private attorneys, are reluctant to utilize the zealous advocate approach that is, at least theoretically, the norm in adult criminal court (Kempf-Leonard, 2010). Attorneys in adult criminal courts justify such zealous advocacy (in which the attorney fights as hard as possible for all defendants, even defendants who have admitted that they are factually guilty) on the grounds that the system is adversarial and that the adversarial process is best for bringing out the truth. In juvenile court, some attorneys, parents, and judges believe that the adult criminal court norm of zealous advocacy is inappropriate. They may worry that strong advocacy can result in an outcome in which a child who "needs help" will not get it because failure to establish the petition leaves the court with no jurisdiction over the child. As

Table 14.3	Selected Court Decisions on Juveniles
Kent v. United States, 383 U.S. 541 (1966)	Certain minimum safeguards apply to transfer (waiver) cases. The juvenile being considered for transfer to adult criminal court has the right to the assistance of counsel (an attorney), the right to a hearing, and a statement of the reasons for transfer if the judge decides to transfer the case to adult court
In re Gault, 387 U.S. 1 (1967)	The Fifth Amendment privilege against self-incrimination (the right to remain silent) and Sixth Amendment rights to adequate notice of charges against oneself, the right to confront and cross-examine accusers, and the right to the assistance of counsel do apply in delinquency proceedings with the possibility of confinement
In re Winship, 397 U.S. 358 (1970)	The standard proof of guilt beyond a reasonable doubt applies to juvenile delinquency proceedings as well as to adult criminal trials
McKeiver v. Pennsylvania, 493 U.S. 528 (1971)	Juveniles do *not* have a constitutional right to a jury trial
Breed v. Jones, 421 U.S. 519 (1975)	Juveniles cannot be adjudicated delinquent in juvenile court and then waived to adult court for trial without violating double jeopardy
Fare v. Michael C., 442 U.S. 707 (1979)	Trial court judges must evaluate the voluntariness of any confession obtained from a juvenile based on all circumstances of the confession. There is no rule that mandates the police consult the child's parent or an attorney before they can question a juvenile suspect. The child can waive his or her privilege against self-incrimination and the right to consult an attorney prior to interrogation
Eddings v. Oklahoma, 455 U.S. 104 (1982)	The age of the defendant should be considered as a mitigating factor in death penalty deliberations
Schall v. Martin, 467 U.S. 361 (1984)	A juvenile who is awaiting court proceedings can be held in preventive detention if there is adequate concern that the juvenile would commit additional crimes while the primary case is pending further court action
Stanford v. Kentucky, 492 U.S. 361 (1989)	The constitutionality of the death penalty was upheld for youths who were either age 16 or 17 at the time they committed a murder
Roper v. Simmons, 543 U.S. 551 (2005)	The death penalty for juveniles was ruled unconstitutional
Graham v. Florida, 560 U.S. 48 (2010)	Life without parole sentences are unconstitutional for youths in nonhomicide cases
Miller v. Alabama, 132 S. Ct. 2455 (2012)	Mandatory life without parole sentences are unconstitutional for juveniles

a result, at least some attorneys act more like a concerned adult, encouraging youths to admit to petitions in cases in which an adversarial approach may have resulted in a dismissal of the petition.

The situation in America's juvenile courts appears to be that some attorneys are adversarial, some are still traditional and act as concerned adults, and some are in between the two extremes. The chief advantage of the zealous advocate model is that it is probably the best insurance that only truly guilty youths will come under court jurisdiction. Because the attorney does not pressure the child to admit to the petition (plead guilty), there is less danger that the court will attempt some type of intervention program with youths who are not guilty. An added advantage is that this approach may well generate the most respect from juveniles for the court system. Fewer youths will feel betrayed or will feel tricked into something that some adult thought was best for them, despite their own wishes.

The biggest danger of the zealous advocate approach is that it may contribute to what Fabricant (1983) called the contemporary version of benign neglect. Because many youths appearing in juvenile court come from families racked with problems, such as low income, public assistance, and/or broken homes, they indeed do need assistance. An adversarial approach may avoid forcing these children into juvenile prisons or other types of intervention owing to insufficient legal defense.

The advantage of the concerned adult model is that it seeks to address the problems of the child that presumably led the child into delinquency. The problem is that this helping philosophy has been the rationale of the juvenile court since 1899 and, as Rothman (1980) has so aptly phrased it, the rhetoric of individualized attention has always far outstripped the reality of ineffective if not abusive programs.

Although the assumption is that legal assistance will result in less severe punishments, recent evidence is mixed. For example, Armstrong and Kim (2011) found that juveniles who were represented by a lawyer were more likely to receive a placement outside the home than juveniles who waived their right to counsel. This effect was true regardless of whether the juvenile was represented by a public defender or private attorney.

Jury Trials for Juveniles

Because the U.S. Supreme Court has not mandated the right to a jury trial for all juveniles, only nine states specify that juveniles have a right to a jury trial, and another 11 allow juries in special circumstances (Szymanski, 2008). Some maintain that it is critical for juveniles to have the right to a jury trial. For example, Barry Feld (1987, 1993) has argued that judges require less proof than juries require and, therefore, it is easier to convict a youth in front of a judge than in front of a jury. The American Bar Association agrees that judges may be biased and thus it calls for jury trials in juvenile court (Institute of Judicial Administration–American Bar Association, 1980).

Having the right to a jury trial, however, may not make very much difference in juvenile court. In her study of a suburban juvenile court, Mahoney (1985) found that only seven cases out of the 650 she studied actually went to trial. For those seven youths, and for 87 other youths who initially requested a jury trial but later settled without a jury trial, there appeared to be no impact of setting (scheduling) a case for trial on outcomes. Recent research in Ohio showed that most attorneys reported that 10% or fewer cases went to trial, and trials were almost nonexistent in some counties (Brooks & Kamine, 2003).

ISSUES IN JUVENILE JUSTICE

Modern juvenile justice faces a variety of concerns and issues. Many of these topics are interrelated and reflect different approaches and concerns. Among the issues are the emphasis on punitiveness, constitutional limitations of punishment for youths, and jurisdiction over status offenders.

The Emphasis on Punitiveness

Traditionally, the disposition stage of juvenile court has been the epitome of the *parens patriae* philosophy. With the advice of probation officers, social workers, psychologists, and psychiatrists, we presumed that the judge would do his or her best to act in the best interests of the child. Beginning in the 1980s, however, disposition (sentencing) in juvenile justice began to take on an increasingly punitive character.

One indicator of this increasingly explicit focus on punishment is the revision of the purpose clauses of state juvenile codes. Forty-two states have more punitive purpose clauses, and virtually all have some mention of what amounts to a focus on the best interests of the child. However, a number of states have amended their juvenile code purpose clauses to include such goals as punishment, the protection of society, or accountability (Hemmens, Fritsch, & Caeti, 1997).

Parallel to the amendment of the purpose clauses, the states have taken concrete measures to emphasize punishment. Three states (Washington, New Jersey, and Texas) have adopted determinate sentencing statutes with an emphasis on proportionality. The law in such states limits the discretion of judges at disposition and attempts to set penalties that are proportionate to the seriousness of the offense. Some states have enacted mandatory minimum provisions. This means that if the judge commits a child to the state youth authority, the law dictates that the youth must serve a certain minimum amount of time. Some states have adopted dispositional guidelines or suggested sentences for most adjudicated delinquents. Unless a case has some unusual factors, judges following the guidelines impose a sentence that falls within the ranges identified in the guidelines. Finally, there is the concern that the conditions of confinement have become more negative. For example, in 1991 almost two-thirds of all juveniles in long-term public institutions were in a facility in which the population exceeded design capacity (Office of Juvenile Justice and Delinquency Prevention, 1995).

Blended sentencing represents another punitive development. Blended sentencing allows either the juvenile court or the adult court to impose a sentence that can involve either the juvenile or the adult correctional system or both. The court can suspend the adult sentence pending either a violation or the commission of a new crime. The rationale is to give the judge greater flexibility in sentencing. The judge has greater discretion to adjust the sentence to the offender and the offense. At the end of 1997, 20 states had laws authorizing some type of blended sentencing. It is still too early, however, to gage the impact of these reforms. Preliminary lessons are that resources have not kept up with legislative changes, the laws seem to encourage plea-bargaining, and minorities are over-represented in the affected populations (Torbet, Griffin, Hurst, & MacKenzie, 2000).

Constitutional Limitations of Punishment

In 2010, an estimated 1,000 juveniles (youths under 18 years of age) were arrested for murder. This continued a downward trend since the peak in 1993. Following an increase in the mid-1980s and the peak in 1993, the juvenile murder rate is currently at a historically low level (Puzzanchera, 2013). Despite this decrease, we will probably see continued media attention on juveniles who kill.

Considerable discussion has taken place about the appropriateness of sentences such as the death penalty and life without the possibility of parole for juveniles accused of the most heinous crimes. Although the 2010 statistics represent a continuing decline since 1993, involvement in murder by juveniles is still alarming and prevalent enough that states will likely continue to punish these juveniles harshly. However, several recent court rulings have somewhat limited the range of punishments available for juvenile offenders.

The Supreme Court ruled that the death penalty is unconstitutional for juveniles. In *Roper v. Simmons* (2005), writing for the majority, Justice Kennedy wrote, "The Eighth and Fourteenth Amendments forbid imposition of the death penalty on offenders who were under the age of 18 when their crimes were committed." The ruling came in a case in which Christopher Simmons, age 17, with two accomplices, broke into and entered a home at 2:00 A.M., took a woman captive, drove away, and threw the woman from a railroad trestle into a river. The majority opinion reasoned that the majority of states rejected the juvenile death penalty and it is used infrequently in states that authorize it. The majority went on to cite scientific evidence that juveniles under age 18 are less mature and responsible than adults, more susceptible to peer pressure, and have character less well-formed than that of an adult.

The Supreme Court has recently decided a series of cases involving juveniles sentenced to life without parole. In *Graham v. Florida* (2010), the Court ruled that sentencing a juvenile to life without parole in nonhomicide cases violates the Constitution's ban on cruel and unusual punishment. The Court noted that a consensus had developed in the United States and worldwide against sentencing juveniles to life sentences without the possibility of parole.

The most recent application of the Eight Amendment in juvenile sentencing is *Miller v. Alabama* (2012). In *Miller*, the Court struck down a criminal law that mandated a life without parole sentence for juveniles convicted of murder. It is important to note that the Court did not rule that a life without parole sentence was unconstitutional per se. As stated by the Court, "Although we do not foreclose a sentencer's ability to make that judgment in homicide cases, we require it to take into account how children are different, and how those differences counsel against irrevocably sentencing them to a lifetime in prison." It is difficult to predict whether the Supreme Court will eventually determine that life without parole is unconstitutional in itself.

Jurisdiction over Status Offenses

A controversial issue facing the juvenile justice system is the issue of divestiture, the elimination of juvenile court jurisdiction over status offenders. For example, family crisis centers, county attorneys, and social service agencies have assumed the responsibility of processing juvenile status offenses in many jurisdictions (Puzzanchera & Hockenberry, 2013). Most states have retained jurisdiction but have implemented policies of deinstitutionalization (i.e., they have stopped confining status offenders in state institutions). Additionally, they have established diversion programs to handle status offenders instead of relying on the juvenile justice system (Schneider, 1985).

Despite such efforts, status offenses and status offenders continue to take up a considerable portion of the juvenile court's time and effort. In 1997, juvenile courts handled 158,500 petitioned status offense cases, an increase of more than 90% over 1986. Runaway, truancy, and liquor law violations increased more than 50%, whereas ungovernable cases increased only 14%. Despite more than a decade of discussion about ending juvenile court jurisdiction over status offenses, approximately 6,100 youths were adjudicated status offenders and placed in out-of-home placements in 2010 (Puzzanchera & Hockenberry, 2013). See Figure 14.2.

ARGUMENTS FOR ENDING JURISDICTION

There are several arguments in favor of complete divestiture. First, it allows the juvenile court more time and resources to deal with juvenile delinquents, especially violent and chronic delinquents. Second, the elimination of status offense jurisdiction would prevent violations of the due process rights of status offenders, such as prosecution for very vague charges. Status offense statutes typically are unclear or vague on when youthful disobedience or adolescent rebellion turns into a status offense. Third, elimination of this jurisdiction recognizes the reality that juvenile courts are not adequately staffed and equipped to deal with status offenders. Elimination of jurisdiction over status offenses would be an admission that private agencies with trained social workers and counselors are better equipped to handle the complex personal and interpersonal problems of status offenders, by means of individual, group, and family counseling as well as other professional techniques. Furthermore, elimination of juvenile court

FIGURE 14.2
The Hamilton County (Ohio) Juvenile Court Youth Center is a county detention facility that contains two court rooms, a psychological/psychiatric clinic, an intake complaint processing center, and a counseling center. The Youth Center is recognized as a model facility with special recognition for its Suicide Assessment/Management program.
Ellen S. Boyne

jurisdiction would force any intervention to be voluntary, which some writers argue is the proper way to deal with status offenders.

ARGUMENTS FOR CONTINUING JURISDICTION

Some still believe, however, that juvenile court jurisdiction over status offenses is both desirable and necessary. Proponents of continued jurisdiction contend that parents and schools need the influence or authority of juvenile court to impress adolescents with the need to obey their parents, attend school, and not run away from home. In addition, proponents of court jurisdiction argue that private agencies in the community will not handle (or will not be able to handle) all of the status offense cases if the juvenile court cannot intervene. Private agencies intervene only with willing clients, and many status offenders taken to such agencies will simply refuse assistance.

Proponents also contend that status offenders are properly under juvenile court jurisdiction because their behavior often escalates into delinquent activity. Hence, they think that early intervention can prevent much delinquency. This escalation hypothesis, however, is controversial. Some proportion of status offenders do indeed escalate or progress but most do not (Lab, 1984; Rojek & Erickson, 1982; Shannon, 1982). Therefore, it is questionable whether all status offenders should be subject to juvenile court jurisdiction. Proponents of court jurisdiction over status offenses believe that court jurisdiction might prevent some children from becoming involved in associated dangerous behaviors. Another argument in favor of continued jurisdiction is that it prevents status offenders from treatment as delinquents. Where states have ended system processing of status offenders, there is some evidence of treating status offenders as minor delinquents and thereby "relabeling" them (Schneider, 1985).

THE FUTURE OF JUVENILE JUSTICE

The juvenile justice system has a cyclical history (Lipsey, Howell, Kelly, Chapman, & Carver, 2010). As mentioned previously, many states have shifted from the traditional *parens patriae* philosophy to a more punitive model. Recent developments point to a new balance in juvenile justice policy (Bishop & Feld, 2012). We will examine several of these developments that, together, appear to be leading to a renewed focus on the rehabilitative mission of the juvenile justice system.

Developmental Approach

The past decade has seen many advances in the science of adolescent development. Specifically, empirical research shows that adolescents lack the ability to control their behavior when placed in emotional situations, are particularly sensitive to social influences such as peer pressure, and lack the ability to consider long-term consequences of their actions (Bonnie, Johnson, Chemers, & Schuck, 2013). Researchers have long studied the impact of a juvenile's social environment on delinquency. Adolescents are influenced by a variety of parental, peer group, and school factors. However, it is only recently that attention has also focused on a child's brain development. Evidence shows that the brain system influencing pleasure-seeking activity develops more rapidly than the system that supports self-control (Bonnie et al., 2013). The advances in knowledge provide support to juvenile justice policies designed to help the juvenile make a successful transition to adulthood. In addition, they challenge the wisdom of excessively punitive punishments such as life in prison without the opportunity for parole.

Evidence-Based Practices

An important trend in the area of juvenile justice involves the increased focus on evidence-based practices. There is considerable research on "what works" in juvenile corrections. Program evaluation research has increased in rigor over the past decade, and can determine whether a particular delinquency prevention program is effective. By reviewing this research, policymakers are able to identify the types of programs that are most successful. States are increasingly using these research-based solutions to help shape their juvenile corrections policies (Greenwood & Welsh, 2012).

Several sources of information regarding the effectiveness of delinquency programs exist. For example, the Blueprints for Violence Prevention initiative reviewed more than 600 programs to identify 11 model programs that have demonstrated the greatest level of empirical support (Mihalie, Fagan, Irwin, Ballard, & Elliot, 2004). The Blueprints website (see http://www.blueprintsprograms.com) serves as a tool that government agencies can use to identify a program that meets the needs of their community. Another approach is to identify common characteristics of successful programs. After reviewing 548 evaluation studies, Lipsey (2009) reported that successful delinquency programs were those that were implemented well, targeted high-risk juveniles, and were therapeutic (rather than punitive) in nature. Although this research does not endorse specific programs, the information can assist communities who are interested in developing their own programs based on evidence-based principles.

Reemphasizing Juvenile Court

During the punitive era of juvenile justice, most states revised their laws to diminish the jurisdiction of the juvenile court. For example, many states removed certain crimes from the juvenile court regardless of age. Other states simplified the process to transfer youths to adult court or lowered the upper age of which a youth could be processed in juvenile court (Feld, 1998). The recent decline in juvenile crime and enhanced focus on evidence-based practices has motivated many states to reverse course. Many states have begun to reform their juvenile transfer and direct file laws, reserving the adult court system to only the most serious youth offenders. Another major trend in the past decade has been to expand the upper age of jurisdiction, in some cases back to 18. From 2001 to 2011, 21 states enacted legislation that in some way restored the jurisdiction of juvenile court (Brown, 2012).

Restorative Justice

Many communities have invested substantial resources into the development of restorative justice programs. Restorative justice can come in many forms (Van Ness & Strong, 2015). Often, the victim and offender will meet with a trained mediator to talk about the crime, its consequences, and how to make things right. Restorative justice can also take place as a conference in which the victim, offender, their families, and possibly even the arresting police officer are present. Another model takes the form of a circle in which members of the community and other interested parties can meet with the victim and offender. After forming a circle, participants speak one at a time about the crime and a possible resolution (Van Ness & Strong, 2015). What all of these efforts have in common is a focus that emphasizes the victim and the community. The approach is "focused less on achieving public safety by incarcerating individual offenders and more on reducing fear, building youth–adult relationships, and increasing the capacity of community groups and institutions to prevent crime and safely monitor offenders in the community" (Bazemore, 1999:98).

This represents a radical rethinking of the role of juvenile court. Instead of sanctioning and supervising offenders, the role of the court would be to build community so that neighborhoods can better respond to, but also prevent, delinquency. Communities would be more involved in sentencing through community panels, conferences, or dispute resolution programs. Communities would return to their role of being responsible for youths. Bergseth and Bouffard

(2013) reported that restorative justice programs seem to be effective with a wide range of juvenile offenders.

As noted, numerous communities already are working at restorative justice. A major question, however, is how far restorative justice can go. How willing are citizens to assume the responsibilities that restorative justice would give them in deciding cases and monitoring sanctions such as community service? If people are not available to staff the restorative justice programs, they will not work.

DUE PROCESS, CRIME CONTROL, AND THE JUVENILE JUSTICE SYSTEM

In some sense, the juvenile justice process is a separate and parallel system to the adult criminal justice system. Yet, both of these formal social control systems are designed to respond to behaviors that have been defined as criminal. Further, each is composed of subsystems of policing, courts, and corrections. What separates the two is the distinction drawn between adult and juvenile offenders.

The juvenile justice process is a product of the open-system nature of criminal justice. As attitudes and perceptions about children and childhood changed in the late 1800s, a separate system for the control and provision of assistance to youthful offenders was created. Originally designed to be helpful rather than punitive, the juvenile justice system was not seen as adversarial (where the interests of the juvenile were in conflict with the desires of the state for order). As a result, due process protections were largely absent from the juvenile justice process.

A growing recognition of the punitive aspects of the juvenile justice process led to concern about the rights of juvenile offenders. To protect the rights and interests of those accused of delinquency, due process protections were introduced into the juvenile justice system. The system increasingly came to resemble the adult process. What did not change was the goal of juvenile justice as "saving children." Inasmuch as the spread of due process protections in juvenile justice was not complete, the power of the juvenile justice system was constrained. Although juvenile offenders do not have a right to trial by jury, neither can the juvenile court impose a death sentence or life imprisonment. The juvenile process balances limits on the liberties of juveniles with limits on the power of the state.

For those deemed unsavable or otherwise inappropriate subjects for the juvenile courts, procedures to transfer their cases to the adult justice system are available. The existence of the juvenile justice system allows us, as a society, to resolve the dilemma of what should be done about the "criminality" of children. It lets us achieve a measure of social protection while requiring, in theory at least, that our protective efforts also be corrective or helpful to the offender.

The existence of a separate juvenile justice process by itself illustrates our deep ambivalence about the balance between due process and crime control. We want and need to control the dangerous and disruptive acts of youths, we also want to avoid doing long-term harm to these offenders. Rather than use a justice system that decides what interests will prevail (individual liberty or social control), we have created a compromise system that attempts to balance these interests in each case. As is usually true of compromises, the arrangement is uneasy. The juvenile justice system demonstrates the difficulty of balancing our competing interests in liberty and order. Hopefully, whatever changes continue to be implemented for court processing and correctional intervention with juveniles will retain some of the hope that the founders of juvenile court had for troubled youths.

REVIEW QUESTIONS

1. What is "delinquency"?
2. Why do juveniles join gangs?
3. How did the juvenile court come to be?
4. What is meant by *parens patriae*?
5. Briefly describe the juvenile justice system.
6. How does the juvenile justice system differ from the adult criminal system?
7. Describe how restorative justice is different from traditional punishment.

References

Adams, B., & Addie, S. (2011). *Delinquency cases waived to criminal court, 2008*. Washington, DC: Office of Juvenile Justice and Delinquency Prevention.

Armstrong, G., & Kim, B. (2011). Juvenile penalties for "lawyering up": The role of counsel and extra-legal case characteristics. *Crime & Delinquency, 57,* 827–848.

Baker, F. (1991). *Saving our kids from delinquency, drugs, and despair*. New York: Harper Collins.

Bazemore, G. (1999). The fork in the road to juvenile court reform. *Annals of the American Academy of Political and Social Science, 564,* 81–108.

Bellair, P., & McNulty, T. (2009). Gang membership, drug selling, and violence in neighborhood context. *Justice Quarterly, 26*(4), 644–669.

Bergseth, K., & Bouffard, J. (2013). Examining the effectiveness of a restorative justice program for various types of juvenile offenders. *International Journal of Offender Therapy and Comparative Criminology, 57*(9), 1054–1075.

Bishop, D. M., & Feld, B. C. (2012). Trends in juvenile justice policy and practice. In B. C. Feld & D. M. Bishop (Eds.), *The Oxford Handbook of Juvenile Crime and Juvenile Justice* (pp. 898–926). New York: Oxford University Press.

Bjerregaard, B. (2010). Gang membership and drug involvement: Untangling the complex relationship. *Crime & Delinquency, 56,* 3–34.

Bonnie, R., Johnson, R., Chemers, B., & Schuck, J. (2013). *Reforming juvenile justice: A developmental approach*. Washington, DC: National Academies Press.

Braga, A. (2012). Getting deterrence right? Evaluation evidence and complementary crime control mechanisms. *Criminology & Public Policy, 11*(2), 201–210.

Brooks, K., & Kamine, D. (2003). *Justice cut short: An assessment of access to counsel and quality of representation in delinquency proceedings in Ohio*. Columbus: Ohio State Bar Association.

Brown, S. A. (2012). *Trends in juvenile justice state legislation: 2001–2011*. Denver, CO: National Conference of State Legislatures.

Bureau of Justice Assistance (2005). Gang Resistance Education and Training from http://greatonline.org.

Curry, G. D., & Decker, S. H. (1998). *Confronting gangs: Crime and community*. Los Angeles: Roxbury.

Curry, G. D., Fox, R. J., Ball, R. A., & Stone, D. (1993). *National assessment of law enforcement antigang information resources: Final report*. Washington, DC: National Institute of Justice.

Decker, S. H., & Van Winkle, B. (1996). *Life in the gang: Family, friends, and violence*. New York: Cambridge University Press.

Egley, A., & Arjunan, M. (2002). *Highlights of the 2000 National Youth Gang Survey. OJJDP Fact Sheet (February, #4)*. Washington, DC: Office of Juvenile Justice and Delinquency Prevention.

Egley, A., & Howell, J. (2013). *Highlights of the 2011 National Youth Gang Survey*. Washington, DC: Office of Juvenile Justice and Delinquency Prevention.

Egley, A., & Major, A. K. (2004). *Highlights of the 2002 National Youth Gang Survey. OJJDP Fact Sheet*. Washington, DC: Office of Juvenile Justice and Delinquency Prevention.

Elliott, D. S., Ageton, S. S., Huizinga, D., Knowles, B. A., & Canter, R. J. (1983). *The prevalence and incidence of delinquent behavior: 1976–1980*. Boulder, CO: Behavioral Research Institute.

Erickson, M. L. (1971). The group context of delinquent behavior. *Social Problems, 19*, 114–129.

Erickson, M. L., & Jensen, G. (1977). Delinquency is still group behavior: Toward revitalizing the group premise in the sociology of deviance. *Journal of Criminal Law and Criminology, 68*, 262–273.

Esbensen, F., & Osgood, D. W. (1997). *National evaluation of GREAT. NIJ research in brief*. Washington, DC: National Institute of Justice.

Esbensen, F., Osgood, D. W., Taylor, T. J., Peterson, D., & Freng, A. (2001). How great is G.R.E.A.T.? Results from a longitudinal quasi-experimental design. *Criminology & Public Policy, 1*, 87–118.

Esbensen, F., Peterson, D., Taylor, T., & Osgood, D. W. (2012). Results from a multi-site evaluation of the G.R.E.A.T. program. *Justice Quarterly, 29*, 125–151.

Fabricant, M. (1983). *Juveniles in the family courts*. Lexington, MA: Lexington Books.

Fagan, J. (1990). Social processes of delinquency and drug use among urban gangs. In C. R. Huff (Ed.), *Gangs in America*. Newbury Park, CA: Sage.

Faust, F. L., & Brantingham, P. J. (1979). *Juvenile justice philosophy: Readings, cases and comments*. St. Paul, MN: West.

Federal Bureau of Investigation (2012). *Crime in the United States 2012: Uniform crime reports*. Washington, DC: U.S. Department of Justice.

Feld, B. (1987). The juvenile court meets the principle of the offense: Legislative changes in juvenile waiver statutes. *Journal of Criminal Law and Criminology, 78*, 471–533.

Feld, B. (1993). Juvenile (in)justice and the criminal court alternative. *Crime & Delinquency, 39*, 403–424.

Feld, B. (1998). Juvenile and criminal justice systems' response to youth violence. *Crime and Justice, 24*, 189–261.

Feld, B., & Schaefer, S. (2010). The right to counsel in juvenile court: Law reform to deliver legal services and reduce justice by geography. *Criminology & Public Policy, 9*(2), 327–356.

Greenwood, P. W., & Welsh, B. C. (2012). Promoting evidence-based practice in delinquency prevention at the state level: Principles, progress, and policy directions. *Criminology & Public Policy, 11*(3), 493–513.

Griffin, P. (2006). *"National overviews," State juvenile justice profiles*. Pittsburgh, PA: National Center for Juvenile Justice.

Griffin, P., Torbet, P., & Syzmanski, L. (1998). *Trying juveniles as adults in criminal court: An analysis of state transfer provisions.* Washington, DC: U.S. Department of Justice.

Hagedorn, J. M. (1988). *People and folks: Gangs, crime, and the underclass in a rustbelt city.* Chicago: Lake View Press.

Hemmens, C., Fritsch, E., & Caeti, T. (1997). Juvenile justice code purpose clauses: The power of words. *Criminal Justice Policy Review, 8,* 221–246.

Hindelang, M. J. (1971). The social versus solitary nature of delinquent involvement. *British Journal of Criminology, 11,* 167–175.

Hindelang, M. J., Hirschi, T., & Weis, J. G. (1981). *Measuring delinquency.* Beverly Hills, CA: Sage.

Institute of Judicial Administration–American Bar Association (1980). *Juvenile justice standards: Standards relating to adjudication.* Cambridge, MA: Ballinger.

Jankowski, M. S. (1991). *Islands in the street: Gangs and American urban society.* Berkeley: University of California Press.

Jones, J. B. (2004). *Access to counsel.* Washington, DC: U.S. Department of Justice.

Kempf-Leonard, K. (2010). Does having an attorney provide a better outcome?: The right to counsel does not mean attorneys help youths. *Criminology & Public Policy, 9*(2), 357–364.

King, M., & Szymanski, L. (2006). National overviews. State juvenile justice profiles. Pittsburgh, PA: National Center for Juvenile Justice. Retrieved from http://www.ncjj.org/stateprofiles.

Klein, M. W. (1971). *Street gangs and street workers.* Englewood Cliffs, NJ: Prentice Hall.

Klein, M. W., Maxson, C. L., & Cunningham, L. C. (1991). "Crack," street gangs, and violence. *Criminology, 29,* 623–649.

Knoll, C., & Sickmund, M. (2011). *Delinquency cases in juvenile court, 2008.* Washington, DC: Office of Juvenile Justice and Delinquency Prevention.

Knox, G. W. (1991). *An introduction to gangs.* Berrien Springs, MI: Vande Vere.

Kurlychek, M. C., & Johnson, B. D. (2004). The juvenile penalty: A comparison and young adult sentencing outcomes in criminal court. *Criminology, 42,* 485–515.

Lab, S. P. (1984). Patterns in juvenile misbehavior. *Crime & Delinquency, 30,* 293–308.

Lin, J., Miller, J., & Fukushima, M. (2008). Juvenile probation officers' dispositional recommendations: Predictive factors and their alignment with predictors of recidivism. *Journal of Crime and Justice, 31*(1), 1–34.

Lipsey, M. W. (2009). The primary factors that characterize effective interventions with juvenile offenders: A meta-analytic overview. *Victims and Offenders, 4,* 124–147.

Lipsey, M. W., Howell, J. C., Kelly, M. R., Chapman, G., & Carver, D. (2010). *Improving the effectiveness of juvenile justice programs: A new perspective on evidence-based practice.* Washington, DC: Center for Juvenile Justice Reform.

Mahoney, A. R. (1985). Jury trial for juveniles: Right or ritual? *Justice Quarterly, 2,* 553–565.

McCarthy, B. R. (1987). Preventive detention and pretrial custody in the juvenile court. *Journal of Criminal Justice, 15,* 185–200.

Mihalie, S., Fagan, A., Irwin, K., Ballard, D., & Elliot, D. (2004). *Blueprints for violence prevention.* Washington, DC: Office of Juvenile Justice and Delinquency Prevention.

Miller, W. B. (1975). *Violence by youth gangs and youth groups as a crime problem in major American cities.* Washington, DC: National Institute for Juvenile Justice and Delinquency Prevention.

Miller, W. B. (1980). Gangs, groups and serious youth crime. In D. Shichor & D. H. Kelly (Eds.), *Critical issues in juvenile delinquency* (pp. 115–138). Lexington, MA: Lexington Books.

Miller, W. B. (1990). Why the United States has failed to solve its youth gang problem. In C. R. Huff (Ed.), *Gangs in America.* Newbury Park, CA: Sage.

Morales, A. (1992). A clinical model for the prevention of gang violence and homicide. In R. C. Cervantes (Ed.), *Substance abuse and gang violence* (pp. 105–118). Newbury Park, CA: Sage.

Myers, D. (2003). The recidivism of violent youths in juvenile and adult court: A consideration of selection bias. *Youth Violence and Juvenile Justice, 1,* 79–101.

National Youth Gang Center (2000). *1998 National Youth Gang Survey: Summary.* Washington, DC: Office of Juvenile Justice and Delinquency Prevention.

Office of Juvenile Justice and Delinquency Prevention (1995). *Juvenile offenders and victims: A national report.* Washington, DC: U.S. Department of Justice.

Office of Juvenile Justice and Delinquency Prevention (1999a). *Promising strategies to reduce gun violence.* Washington, DC: Office of Juvenile Justice and Delinquency Prevention.

Office of Juvenile Justice and Delinquency Prevention (1999b). *1997 National Youth Gang Survey.* Washington, DC: Office of Juvenile Justice and Delinquency Prevention.

Office of Juvenile Justice and Delinquency Prevention (2002). *OJJDP statistical briefing book,* retrieved from http://ojjdp.ncjrs.org/ojstatbb/html/qa088.html.

Ohio Revised Code (2006). Section 2151.022, retrieved from http://statutes.laws.com/ohio/title21/chapter2151/2151_022.

Ohio Revised Code (2010). Section 2152.02, retrieved from http://statutes.laws.com/ohio/title21/chapter2152/2152_02.

Platt, A. M. (1977). *The child savers: The invention of delinquency.* Chicago: University of Chicago Press.

Prescott, P. S. (1981). *The child savers: Juvenile justice observed.* New York: Alfred A. Knopf.

Puritz, P., Burrell, S., Schwartz, R., Soler, M., & Warboys, L. (1995). *A call for justice: An assessment of access to counsel and quality of representation in delinquency proceedings.* Washington, DC: American Bar Association Juvenile Justice Center.

Puzzanchera, C. (2013). *Juvenile arrests 2010.* Washington, DC: Office of Juvenile Justice and Delinquency Prevention.

Puzzanchera, C., & Adams, B. (2011). *Juvenile arrests 2009.* Washington, DC: Office of Juvenile Justice and Delinquency Prevention.

Puzzanchera, C., & Hockenberry, S. (2013). *Juvenile court statistics 2010.* Pittsburgh, PA: National Center for Juvenile Justice.

Rainville, G. A., & Smith, S. K. (2003). *Juvenile felony defendants in criminal courts: Survey of 40 counties, 1998.* Washington, DC: U.S. Department of Justice.

Rojek, D. G., & Erickson, M. L. (1982). Delinquent careers: A test of the career escalation model. *Criminology, 20,* 5–28.

Rothman, D. (1980). *Conscience and convenience.* Boston: Little, Brown.

Schneider, A. L. (1985). *The impact of deinstitutionalization on recidivism and secure confinement of status offenders.* Washington, DC: U.S. Department of Justice.

Schwartz, R., & Levick, M. (2010). When a "right" is not enough: Implementation of the right to counsel in an age of ambivalence. *Criminology and Public Policy, 9*(2), 365–374.

Shannon, L. W. (1982). *Assessing the relationship of adult criminal careers to juvenile careers.* Iowa City: Iowa Urban Community Research Center, University of Iowa.

Sheppard, D., Grant, H., Rowe, W., & Jacobs, N. (2000). *Fighting juvenile gun violence. OJJDP Juvenile Justice Bulletin.* Washington, DC: Office of Juvenile Justice and Delinquency Prevention.

Short, J. F., & Nye, I. (1958). Extent of unrecorded delinquency: Tentative conclusions. *Journal of Criminal Law, Criminology, and Police Science, 49,* 296–302.

Sickmund, M., & Baunach, P. J. (1986). *Children in custody: Public juvenile facilities, 1985. Bureau of Justice Statistics Bulletin.* Washington, DC: U.S. Department of Justice.

Spano, R., Freilich, J., & Bolland, J. (2008). Gang membership, gun carrying, and employment: Applying routine activities theory to explain violent victimization among inner city, minority youth living in extreme poverty. *Justice Quarterly, 25*(2), 381–410.

Spergel, I. A., & Curry, G. D. (1990). Strategies and perceived agency effectiveness in dealing with youth gang problems. In C. R. Huff (Ed.), *Gangs in America*. Newbury Park, CA: Sage.

Spergel, I., Curry, G., Ross, R., & Chance, R. (1990). *Survey of youth gang problems and programs in 45 cities and 6 sites*. Washington, DC: Office of Juvenile Justice and Delinquency Prevention.

Steiner, B. (2009). The effects of juvenile transfer to criminal court on incarceration decisions. *Justice Quarterly, 26*(1), 77–106.

Szymanski, L. A. (2008). *Juvenile delinquents' right to a jury trial (2007 update)*. NCJJ Snapshot 13(2) Pittsburgh, PA: National Center for Juvenile Justice.

Tapia, M. (2011). Gang membership and race as risk factors for juvenile arrest. *Journal of Research in Crime and Delinquency, 48*(3), 364–395.

Taylor, C. S. (1990). Gang imperialism. In C. R. Huff (Ed.), *Gangs in America*. Newbury Park, CA: Sage.

Taylor, C. S., & Smith, P. R. (2013). The attraction of gangs: How can we reduce it? In T. Simon, N. Ritter, & R. Mahendra (Eds.), *Changing course. Preventing gang membership*. Washington, DC: National Institute of Justice.

Thrasher, F. M. (1936). *The gang*. Chicago: University of Chicago Press.

Torbet, P., Griffin, P., Hurst, H., Jr., & MacKenzie, L. R. (2000). *Juveniles facing criminal sanctions: Three states that changed the rules*. Washington, DC: Office of Juvenile Justice and Delinquency Prevention.

U.S. Census Bureau (2010). *National population projects released 2008*. Washington, DC: U.S. Department of Commerce. Retrieved August 2, 2010, from, http://www.census.gov/population/projections/summarytables.html.

Van Ness, D. W., & Strong, K. H. (2015). *Restoring justice: An introduction to restorative justice* (5th ed.). Boston: Elsevier (Anderson Publishing).

Watkins, A. M., Huebner, B. M., & Decker, S. H. (2008). Patterns of gun acquisition, carrying, and use among juvenile and adult arrestees: Evidence from a high-crime city. *Justice Quarterly, 25*(4), 674–700.

Winner, L., Lanza-Kaduce, L., Bishop, D.M. & Frazier, C.E. (1997). The transfer of juveniles to criminal court: Reexamining recidivism over the long term. *Crime & Delinquency, 43*, 548–563.

Important Cases

Breed v. Jones, 421 U.S. 519 (1975).

Commonwealth v. Fisher, 213 Pa. 48 (1905).

Eddings v. Oklahoma, 455 U.S. 104 (1982).

Ex parte Crouse, 4 Wheaton (Pa.) 9 (1838).

Fare v. Michael C., 442 U.S. 707 (1979).

Graham v. Florida, 560 U.S. 48 (2010).

In re Gault, 387 U.S. 1 (1967).

In re Winship, 397 U.S. 358 (1970).

Kent v. United States, 383 U.S. 541 (1966).

McKeiver v. Pennsylvania, 403 U.S. 528 (1971).

Miller v. Alabama, 132 S. Ct. 2455 (2012).

Roper v. Simmons, 543 U.S. 551 (2005).

Schall v. Martin, 467 U.S. 253 (1984).

Stanford v. Kentucky, 492 U.S. 361 (1989).

CHAPTER 15

Discharge and Developments

In 2012, approximately 3.1 million persons obtained release from some form of prison, probation, or parole supervision (Carson & Golinelli, 2013; Maruschak & Bonczar, 2013). In 1987, Burton, Cullen, and Travis estimated that more than 14 million convicted felons lived in the population at large. In the quarter century since then, it is almost certain that the number of felons in the population has increased. Experts estimate that more than 5% of all Americans will serve a prison sentence some time in their lives, and only about one-half of all felons go to prison, so as much as 10% of the adult population may become ex-offenders.

This chapter examines what happens to those people who progress through the justice system to the point of discharge from custody, or to where the justice system stops. In doing so, we see that, for many, the effects of justice system processing do not stop, but start anew. We will also examine changes in the criminal justice system we can anticipate, or that seem to be beginning now.

DISCHARGE

The last major point in the criminal justice process is the **discharge** of offenders. In many cases, discharge is not actually a decision point but rather an event that occurs at a point in time. For example, if you received a sentence to 5 years in prison on January 1, 2014, the sentence would expire at midnight on December 31, 2018. The state must discharge you from custody at that point, because there would no longer be a legal justification for custody. In many states, however, discharge itself is a decision.

Traditionally, we considered a convicted offender to be under the custody of the justice system until his or her sentence had expired. With the imposition of relatively long sentences, this meant that a person sentenced to a life term could be in custody for his or her entire lifetime. Most states developed mechanisms for limiting the period of custody, and empowered the parole authority to grant a discharge from sentence after a period of successful parole supervision. As a pragmatic alternative, many parole authorities created a custody class of **unsupervised parole**, in which the offender was no longer required to report to a parole officer nor subjected to supervision. Unsupervised parole allowed an offender to

Important Terms

civil death
collateral
  consequences
community justice
CPTED
crime-stopper
  programs
discharge
dispute resolution
executive
  clemency
identity theft
intelligence
  gathering
Neighborhood
  Watch
recidivism
unsupervised
  parole
victim
  compensation
victim impact
  statement
victim/offender
  mediation
victims' rights

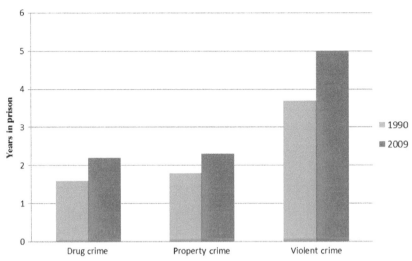

FIGURE 15.1
Average time served in prison, by release year.
Source: Pew Center on the States (2012)

"serve" a sentence until discharge without actually being restricted. Further, many states have specifically empowered correctional officials to grant final releases or discharges from sentence. Figure 15.1 shows the distribution of time served in prison offenders released in 2009. Time served in prison prior to release on parole has increased, and the rate of parole release from prison has decreased. It is likely that today's prisoners will spend more time in prison and less time under parole supervision before discharge.

Some states allow offenders to apply for **executive clemency**, or mercy. A convict could ask the governor for a commutation or pardon. If granted, the prisoner would receive a discharge from sentence. Someone serving a 20-year term, for example, might be imprisoned for 2 years, serve an additional 2 years under parole supervision, and still "owe" 16 years on the sentence. That offender could ask the governor to commute the sentence to 4 years and receive a discharge, or the governor could grant a pardon for the offense.

Regardless of the method, the fact remains that, at some point, most offenders receive a discharge from sentence. At the point of discharge, whether by the discretionary decision of a justice system official, or at the expiration of sentence, the offender is free from direct intervention by the criminal justice system. The effects of conviction, however, will linger.

COLLATERAL CONSEQUENCES OF CONVICTION

Once convicted of a criminal offense, an individual experiences several negative effects. The sentence imposed for crime is a direct consequence of conviction, and is intentionally painful. Other effects that result from conviction called

> **BOX 15.1 VOTING RESTRICTIONS**
>
> Almost every state currently has voting restrictions for convicted felons. Restrictions range from only current inmates to convicted felons who are released and are no longer under any type of correctional supervision. A breakdown of restrictions is as follows:
>
> **No restriction:** 2 states (Maine, Vermont)
> **Inmates only:** 14 states (District of Columbia, Hawaii, Illinois, Indiana, Massachusetts, Michigan, Montana, New Hampshire, North Dakota, Ohio, Oregon, Pennsylvania, Rhode Island, and Utah)
> **Inmates and parolees:** 4 states (California, Colorado, Connecticut, and New York)
> **Inmates, parolees, and probationers:** 20 states (Alaska, Arkansas, Georgia, Idaho, Iowa, Kansas, Louisiana, Maryland, Minnesota, Missouri, New Jersey, New Mexico, North Carolina, Oklahoma, South Carolina, South Dakota, Texas, Washington, West Virginia, and Wisconsin)
> **Inmates, parolees, probationers, and ex-felons:** 11 states (Alabama, Arizona, Delaware, Florida, Kentucky, Mississippi, Nebraska, Nevada, Tennessee, Virginia, and Wyoming)
>
> Source: Chung (2013)

collateral consequences are not part of the stated penalty for the crime. In many ways, these effects can be more disturbing and painful than the imposed sentence. Box 15.1 describes the voting restrictions placed on those convicted of a felony.

A stigma attaches to a person convicted of a crime. The label of "ex-con" is difficult to overcome. If you were hiring people to work for a company and had two equally qualified candidates, one of whom was an ex-con, which applicant would you hire? At a party, how would you react when meeting someone who was an ex-con? That we can discuss a set of people simply by using the label "ex-con" illustrates the point of stigma. The fact of a prior conviction is meaningful to us in our dealings with ex-cons (Blumstein & Nakamura, 2009).

In addition to the stigma of having a criminal record, other collateral consequences attend criminal conviction. Conviction closes some avenues of employment to offenders (Finn & Fontaine, 1985). Many jobs in our society require that the employee be bonded (insured), and ex-offenders normally are not considered good risks by bonding companies. Thus, an ex-offender may even have difficulty obtaining employment as a cashier in a convenience store. Other occupational groups, such as barbers, beauticians, teachers, physicians, nurses, and attorneys, require licensure. In many cases, a felony conviction is a bar to licensure (Davidenas, 1983).

Assuming the offender served a prison term, he or she may have a particularly difficult time in securing credit or employment because of the incarceration. How does an ex-inmate answer questions about where he or she worked for the past 2 years, or about where he or she resided? (One of the author's students, an ex-convict, routinely answered such questions by saying that he had "worked for the state" for the past 7 years). Kurlychek, Brame, and Bushway (2006) reported that employers are conducting criminal history checks of employees and applicants more frequently now. In some cases, state laws require employers to check the criminal history of workers. They found that in most cases, there was little difference between employees with and without prior arrest records, and that in some cases employers dismissed "good" employees when they found a previous arrest. The impact of a prior conviction on employment prospects continues to be negative.

Stoll and Bushway (2008) reported that firms conducting criminal background checks were less likely to hire ex-offenders. There is clear evidence that those released from prison do not fare well in the job market (Western, 2008). The exact contribution of the stigma of "ex-offender" to poor employment is less clear. Not only do ex-offenders have the stigma of conviction, they also tend to have less education and job experience, and more physical and mental health issues.

Many states require ex-offenders to register with the local police, or maintain registries of released offenders that are available to the public. All states require registration of some offenders, especially some sexual offenders, and most restrict locations where at least some sex offenders can reside. Research into the effect of residence restrictions and registration requirements does not support the practices. Zgoba and Levenson (2012) found that sex offenders who fail to register pose no greater risk of new sex offenses than those who do register. Recent research shows that residency restrictions for sex offenders are not effective at preventing sexual victimization by known sex offenders or at serving as a deterrent for sex crimes (Nobles, Levenson, & Youstin, 2012). Other research has reported that residency restrictions are not effective at keeping sex offenders away from protected locations (schools, parks, playgrounds, etc.). Further, the restrictions seem to result in the concentration of sex offenders in certain neighborhoods—typically poor, urban neighborhoods. The restrictions also place a heavy burden on ex-offenders in terms of their ability to find housing and employment (Hughes & Burchfield, 2008; Hughes & Kadleck, 2008; Socia & Stamatel, 2012).

As if the natural consequences of conviction were not severe enough, most states impose specific limitations on the rights of those convicted of felonies. These limitations are in addition to whatever sentences the courts order (Buckler & Travis, 2003; Burton, Cullen, & Travis, 1987; Vile, 1981). Two states, Idaho and New York, have provisions allowing certain offenders (generally, those receiving life sentences) to be declared civilly dead (Rottman & Strickland, 2006). **Civil death** means that as far as civil rights (contracting, marriage, voting, etc.) are concerned, the offender is "dead." Most states restrict some civil rights for at least as long as the offender is serving his or her sentence. In many jurisdictions, conviction of a felony carries the permanent loss of some civil rights. All states now require the registration of at least some sex offenders and more than half the states restrict parental rights for those convicted of specified crimes. Given the collateral consequences of conviction, for many offenders, criminal justice processing never ends.

Restoration of Rights

Most states today have provisions for the restoration of all, or most, of the civil rights that are lost on conviction of a felony. For example, Porter (2010) reported that since 1997, 23 states have expanded voter eligibility to convicted felons. In 2013, 48 states and the District of Columbia had some type of felony disenfranchisement restrictions. Only two states, Maine and Vermont, do not restrict a felon's voting rights in some way (Chung, 2013). However, states vary considerably in the level of restriction. In 14 states, felons are only restricted from voting as long as they are in prison. However, approximately 75% of disenfranchised felons live in the community, either under probation or parole supervision or having completed their sentence entirely (Chung, 2013). Uggen, Shannon, and Manza (2012) reported that nearly 7.7% of African American adults are disenfranchised, which is more than four times the rate of non-African Americans.

Many states automatically restore the felon's voting rights upon being eligible for restoration. Other states are much more restrictive, with some requiring the convicted felon to apply to the governor for a pardon. Eight states have recently eased the restoration process. For example, Florida has traditionally had one of the most restrictive disenfranchisement laws. Until recently, felons seeking voting restoration were required to appear personally at a hearing before the governor. A new policy allows for the automatic restoration of voting rights for nonviolent offenders. Felons convicted of serious offenses such as murder or sex crimes must either petition the clemency board for an in-person hearing or wait 15 years (crime-free) to apply without a hearing (Porter, 2010).

Those opposed to the imposition of collateral consequences of felony conviction argue restrictions may be counterproductive. Adding to penalties by limiting rights may cause ex-offenders to become bitter toward society in general and the justice system in particular. Restrictions regarding employment may be especially harmful. They limit an ex-offender's ability to lead a law-abiding life by closing opportunities for socially accepted means of earning a living. In addition, many restrictions on civil rights, such as restrictions on the voting rights of someone with a prior conviction for theft, are unrelated to the offender's crime. Finally, there are those who argue that the imposition of additional restrictions continuing after the sentence means that the offender can never pay his or her debt to society.

Those favoring the restriction of civil rights for people convicted of criminal offenses argue that such restrictions serve several purposes. First, rights are balanced by duties and, by failing to meet the duty of obeying the law, offenders have lost the privilege of exercising their rights (Vile, 1981). Others suggest that a "principle of least eligibility" applies, in that ex-offenders are least eligible of all citizens to be protected in their rights to vote, work, and so on

(Simon, 1993:265–266). Others suggest that the fact of conviction evidences unacceptable character flaws, so that restricting offenders from holding public office, serving on juries, and voting actually protects law-abiding citizens from possible election fraud and malfeasance in office by ex-offenders. Other restrictions on rights are justified by proponents as pragmatic concessions. In many states, incarceration is grounds for divorce; it is justified by the argument that it is not fair to require the spouse to stand by an absent mate. Loss of parental rights has been justified because a felony conviction represents proof of being an unfit parent. Finally, civil death has been justified to enable family members to dispose of the convicted offender's debts and property.

RECIDIVISM

Ex-convict Malcolm Braly (1977) wrote an autobiography, aptly titled *False Starts*, in which he recalled 20 years of criminal justice experience, during which he spent time in and out of reform school and prison. His first incarceration was in a reform school before he had turned 18. Describing his years as an offender, Braly remembered his "false starts" at living a conventional, law-abiding life. Through four releases from custody, three of which became failed paroles, Braly learned how to live in the free world, and finally successfully settled after his fifth release, at age 40.

As a "business," the criminal justice system is not supposed to encourage repeat "customers." If the system operated at peak effectiveness, no one who committed a crime would commit a second offense. Unfortunately, the data indicate that the justice system produces many customers who return repeatedly. We call these repeat offenders recidivists.

Defining Recidivism

Perhaps no other concept in criminal justice has been as fully studied and debated as has recidivism. **Recidivism** is hard to define, but generally means a return to crime or other trouble with the criminal justice system. The notion of recidivism is so controversial that contemporary writers tend to use other labels for it, such as "failure" or "return." At base, recidivism means repetition of crime. The term is confusing because it is not exactly clear what "repetition" should include. For example, if a convicted robber released from custody now commits a theft, has the offender repeated? If the offender is arrested, but not convicted, is it recidivism? If the offender's parole is revoked for failing to report to the supervising officer, is the offender a recidivist? These seem to be technical distinctions, but they can be very important.

Whatever definition one adopts the concept is crucial to evaluations of the effectiveness of criminal justice processing. Gottfredson, Mitchell-Herzfeld, and Flanagan (1982) suggested that the definition employed has an effect on the level of recidivism detected. For example, if recidivism includes technical violations of probation or parole rules, the rate of return to crime will be higher.

Counting arrests yields higher recidivism rates than counting only convictions. Counting only returns to prison as repeat offenses leads to still lower rates of recidivism, and counting only repeated convictions for the same crime yields the lowest rates of all.

Harris, Lockwood, and Mengers (2009) argued that time is yet another important component of the definition. The longer the period over which we track offenders, the higher will be the total level of recidivism. For example, Jung, Spjeldnes, and Yamatani (2010) tracked the recidivism rate of jail inmates in a Pennsylvania county over a 3-year time frame. Within a year, more than 36% of inmates had been rearrested. At the end of the 3-year tracking period, nearly 60% of inmates had been rearrested for a new crime. This finding illustrates the importance of a researcher's follow-up period. A study that examines a particular program's recidivism rate should be measured against research of competing programs using the same follow-up period. Likewise, any examination of recidivism trends should use a standard tracking period.

Recidivism and Criminal Justice Policy

One problem with recidivism is that it is very difficult to measure. Knowledge of the effectiveness of correctional programs and judicial sentencing decisions based on the rate of return to crime can help us to design crime control policies. The fact that recidivism depends so heavily on what we count, and for how long, means that we must be especially careful in interpreting and using recidivism statistics as the basis for policy decisions.

A study of boot camp effectiveness illustrates this point. Duwe and Kerschner (2008) followed participants of a Minnesota boot camp for an average of more than 7 years, and compared their recidivism rates to a control group. At the end of the follow-up period, 62% of the boot camp participants had been rearrested. However, only 32% were reconvicted, and 22% were sentenced to jail or prison terms. Offenders participating in boot camps returned to prison at virtually the same rate as the control group. However, the boot camp offenders were more likely to return to prison owing to a technical violation as opposed to a new crime (Duwe & Kerschner, 2008). As a policymaker, what does this information tell you about the use of boot camps as a correctional tool?

Unfortunately, it tells us little. Paradoxically, it also tells us much. Ultimately, the decision about using boot camps as a punishment will depend on this and other information, and on the attitudes of the policymakers themselves. If they count new prison terms as recidivism, 78% of boot camp participants will succeed, and boot camps are effective for eligible offenders. If the policymakers count arrests as failures, 62% of boot camp offenders will fail, and boot camps may be an inappropriate disposition for offenders in Minnesota. What is important is that to make an informed judgment, the decision makers need to know not only the statistics (62% or 22% "failures"), but also what the statistics mean. Duwe and Kerschner (2008) calculated that the boot camp program has resulted in significant cost savings to the state of Minnesota. Even though the boot camp offenders returned to prison at the same rate as the control group, the members of the control group received a longer average sentence because they were more likely to return for a new offense as opposed to a technical violation.

In a study of drug courts, Mitchell, Wilson, Eggers, and Mackenzie (2012) reported that drug court participants generally have lower recidivism rates than nonparticipants. However, results varied by type of drug court and the measure of effectiveness. They identified three distinct categories of recidivism: general recidivism, drug-related recidivism, and drug use. Results showed that participants in adult and juvenile drug courts have significantly lower rates of general recidivism. However, drug-related recidivism was only lower for the participants of the adult court. This suggests that the effectiveness of juvenile drug courts might vary depending on the different types of recidivism. Lumping all the ways in which offenders may fail into a single category of recidivism may actually make it more difficult to understand how to intervene successfully in the lives of offenders.

DEVELOPMENTS IN CRIMINAL JUSTICE

Bennett (1987) coined the phrase "crime-warps" to describe what she saw as changes in the future of criminal justice in the United States. Crime-warps referred to the alterations she expected to occur in our definitions of—and our responses to—crime. She anticipated that the form, if not the substance, of crime would take on new shapes in the future, and the justice system will need to adapt to these new developments. Bennett identified several crime-warps, ranging from new types of criminals to changes in the balance between the protection of individual liberties and the requirements of social defense. She predicted there would be increasing emphasis on white-collar and computer crimes. According to Bennett, many "victimless" crimes, such as prostitution, homosexuality, gambling, and drug use, would be legalized, whereas other offenses, such as manufacturing and distributing pornography, would be subjected to greater restrictions. She anticipated greater technological development in criminal justice, an enhanced role for private enterprise, and a reduction in privacy. In her view citizens would face increasing surveillance by both their neighbors and justice officials, threatening civil liberties.

It is always risky to predict the future. As we have seen, criminal justice practices and policies are the products of a complex set of forces. Ideological shifts, economic changes, demographic variations, organizational goals, and the attitudes of individual agents and offenders all affect criminal justice. Attempting to predict how these factors will change and develop, and how they will interact to produce different decisions and patterns of criminal justice practice, is hazardous and prone to error. Nonetheless, it is incumbent on us to attempt to foresee the future so that we can try to shape it.

Looking at the future of criminal justice in the United States, we examine three trends and project possible futures. In doing so, we must pay attention to the forces that gave rise to the trends, as well as to the powerful forces opposing any real change in the operation of the criminal justice system. Hedging our bets, we shall call these trends "possibilities." It should be remembered, of course, that it is likely that nothing much will change. The possibilities that we examine here are increased federalism, private justice, and technological justice. In the next two sections we examine two of the possibilities, federalism and private justice. We discuss the third, technological justice, in a later section.

Increased Federalism

We have described the American criminal justice system as fragmented, with multiple sets of crime control apparatus operating in thousands of counties and/or cities across the country. Traditionally, criminal justice and crime control policy have been local issues. America has not had a single national criminal justice system comprised of federal laws, police, courts, and corrections. Rather, each state has its own criminal code, and most municipalities have their own police and courts. During the past 60 years, however, the federal role in criminal justice has expanded greatly. In the late 1960s, the U.S. Congress passed the Omnibus Crime Control and Safe Streets Act, creating a federal bureaucracy that influenced local justice policy and practice through the provision of federal aid. As Friel (2000:2) put it, "Beginning with this Act and the Federal funds that then flowed to State and local criminal justice agencies, the Federal Government would become a major player in local crime control and justice policy...On top of the long litany of decisions by the Federal courts that have tempered almost every area of the justice system in the past 40 years, we now question whether there is too much federal involvement. Some argue for more, while others demand less."

During the last half century, the federal government has provided funding, training, and technical support to local criminal justice agencies on a variety of topics. The debate over the role of the federal government in local justice policy hinges on a disagreement about the motive for, and impact of, this assistance. Those who believe the federal government is exerting too much influence over local policy contend that this aid acts as an inducement, or bribe. Accepting federal support requires accepting any "strings" attached to the support. In essence, the federal government is paying local criminal justice agencies to change their policies and practices.

For example, in 1998, the Office of Juvenile Justice and Delinquency Prevention began funding what it called the Juvenile Accountability Incentive Block Grants (JAIBG) program. The program provides funding and other support to local juvenile justice systems that agree to implement "accountability" efforts. "Holding a juvenile offender 'accountable' in the juvenile justice system means that once the juvenile is determined to have committed law-violating behavior, by admission or adjudication, he or she is held responsible for the act through consequences of sanctions, imposed pursuant to law, that are proportionate to the offense. Consequences or sanctions that are applied swiftly, surely, and consistently, and are graduated to provide appropriate and effective responses to varying levels of offense seriousness and offender chronicity, work best in preventing, controlling, and reducing further law violations" (Hurst, 1999). To receive JAIBG funding, a state or local juvenile justice agency must demonstrate a plan to hold juveniles accountable in accordance with the JAIBG program's definitions and purposes.

Similarly, other federal assistance has been available for programs involving truth in sentencing, where federal support is available to states that propose to ensure that offenders convicted of violent crimes will serve at least 85% of their sentence in prison. Traditionally, these offenders would be incarcerated for one-half or less of their sentence. States received support for the construction of new prisons, or alternatives to prison for nonviolent offenders. They had to ensure, however, that violent offenders would serve 85% of their sentences in prison. There was also the federal initiative supporting community-oriented policing, in which the Office of Community Oriented Policing Services (COPS) disbursed funds to law enforcement agencies to support efforts to place an additional 100,000 police officers on the streets of the nation. Funding was available, over the life of the program, for hiring new officers, paying overtime to existing officers, and for other efforts (hiring civilians, implementing new technologies, etc.) aimed at making more time available for police officers to serve on the streets. Thousands of police agencies took advantage of these programs. Of course, it was not enough simply to increase the number of police officers on patrol. The increased personnel were required to be dedicated to "community policing." As of 2014, the COPS program is still operational and provides millions of dollars in funding to local police departments annually.

Critics view these funding and support programs as efforts by the federal government to standardize and direct local criminal justice practices. On the other side of the issue, however, are those who support and applaud this increased federal role. They argue that no one forces local officials to participate in the programs. Indeed, many jurisdictions did not apply to participate in each of these programs. Local justice officials are free to ignore offers of federal assistance that do not meet local needs, and to apply only for those that fit local priorities.

The impact of federal incentives on local operations is still unclear. Helms and Gutierrez (2007) reported that COPS funding is associated with important innovation and organizational change in large police agencies. Worrall and Kovandzic (2007), however, found that the influx of community policing dollars had little impact on rates of serious crime. It is also unclear how permanent any changes may be, with the expiration of federal funding for community policing. Some cynics suggest that local agencies "follow the money" and accept federal funding without planning any lasting reforms. For example, in 2003, fewer than half of local police departments had a written plan concerning terrorist attacks (Hickman & Reaves, 2006). With the advent of the Department of Homeland Security and the availability of some federal support for counterterrorism efforts, local justice agencies began to purchase additional equipment and increase terrorism response training. However, the grants often prevented local agencies from spending the funds according to their individual needs (Eisinger, 2006).

Beginning in 2005, the federal Bureau of Justice Assistance began offering federal grant money through the Justice Assistance Grant (JAG) program, awarding more than 2.78 million in fiscal year 2013.The distribution of JAG funds is illustrated in Figure 15.2. The Bureau of Justice Statistics calculates each state's fund allocation based on its share of violent crime and the population. Funds are shared between state and local governments, to be used for one of seven purposes: (1) law enforcement, (2) prosecution and courts, (3) prevention and education, (4) corrections and community corrections, (5) drug treatment, (6) planning, evaluation, and technology, and (7) crime victim and witness programs (Cooper, 2013).

With the passage of the Adam Walsh Act in 2006, the federal government created a set of national standards for the registration and community notification of sex offenders. States that did not comply with the national standards by July 2011 faced a 10% reduction in their JAG funds. These requirements created many challenges for states. As of November 2012, only 16 states have substantially implemented the new standards (GAO, 2013). Among the challenges facing states is the federal standard expanding sex offender registration to include many juvenile offenses. This requirement directly conflicts with many state's juvenile delinquency laws, and policymakers in these states have thus far been unwilling to implement a registration for juvenile sex offenders.

Beyond the provision of additional funds, the federal role in local justice policy and practice has also increased in two additional areas. First, the federal government

FIGURE 15.2
Allocation of Justice Assistance Grants, selected years.
Source: Cooper (2012a, 2012b, 2013); Cooper and Reaves (2011); Hickman (2005)

has taken the lead in publicizing successful criminal justice practices by supporting a range of conferences, training, and information dissemination activities. One result of this has been to make the same information available to criminal justice officials all over the nation, creating a common knowledge of criminal justice. Second, the past 2 decades have seen greatly increased collaboration between federal and local agencies. Einhorn (2003) has described the increasing collaboration between federal and local justice officials, especially police and prosecutors. He noted that federal criminal procedures are often less stringent than state rules, making investigation, prosecution, and conviction easier. Perhaps the most important criminal justice initiative of President George W. Bush's administration was "Project Safe Neighborhoods," which joins local and state police and prosecutors to crack down on gun crimes (Healy, 2002). And, of course, after the terrorist attacks of September 11, 2001, the provisions of the USA PATRIOT Act and the effort to prevent future acts of terrorism have combined to support increased centralization of terror prevention activities and broader information sharing between local, state, and federal law enforcement agencies (International Association of Chiefs of Police, 2004).

The past several decades have seen an increased role for the federal government in local criminal justice policy and practice. The provision of direct support for specific criminal justice policies has increased in recent years, and the federal courts have been involved in all aspects of the justice process. It remains to be seen what the ultimate impact of increased federal involvement may be, but at present, it seems certain that the federal role in local criminal justice is not likely to diminish in the near future.

Private Justice

In earlier chapters, we discussed developments that tend toward the privatization of criminal justice. These include, but are not limited to, contracted services for the operation of correctional programs and institutions, citizen crime prevention, private security, and alternative dispute resolution. Additionally, continuing developments in **victims' rights**, that is, efforts to protect the interests of crime victims, can be considered to be indicative of a trend toward a privatization of justice.

Historically, the criminal justice system evolved from a tradition of private retaliation for wrongdoing. In the past, if a member of one family should injure a member of another family, the families would settle the dispute. Either you or your kin would seek revenge, or my kin and I would pay reparations. With the emergence of stronger leaders and central governments, offenses became crimes against the state, rather than wrongs against individuals. With the growing division of labor within society, the duty to prevent and control crime came to be the province of a set of defined agents and organizations. This relieved the average citizen of the necessity to intercede in criminal matters. Over time, both the definition of crimes and the response to them became matters of public domain.

Today we can see a reversal of that trend. Increasingly, crime and crime control are becoming private concerns. This new definition goes beyond acceptance of private industry provision of criminal justice services, such as the contract prisons discussed earlier. There is recognition that crimes harm private individuals, and that private individuals must be involved in solving the problem of crime (Finn & Lee, 1988).

Rosenbaum, Lurigio, and Lavrakas (1986) reported that, between 1978 and 1986, the number of **crime-stopper programs** in the United States grew from just five to more than 600. Today, one function of community-oriented policing is to develop and support Neighborhood Watch and similar citizen crime-prevention programs. There is an increased awareness of the need for citizens to take steps on their own to prevent crime.

By granting anonymity and cash rewards for tips that lead to arrests and convictions in criminal cases, these programs encourage citizens to provide information to the police. Programs rely upon private citizens to provide leads and evidence to public law enforcement agencies. Further, the majority of funding for these programs comes from private (usually business and industry) donations.

Pfuhl (1992) characterized crime-stopper programs as legitimized snitching. He noted the long-held social disapproval of tattletales in the United States and assessed how it has happened that this form of snitching has become acceptable. He suggested that public fear of crime, media portrayals of the value of crime stoppers, and police support for crime-stopper programs combined to define this form of tattling as a positive public service. Nor did Pfuhl discount the effect of rewards paid to informers. He suggested that crime-stopper programs are congruent with general social attitudes that the citizenry must take an active role in the war on crime. In attempting to assess the implications of socially approved snitching, he is concerned about the promise of anonymity given to those who report to crime-stopper programs. Although unsure of the final effects of such programs on American society, Pfuhl (1992:525) noted that legitimizing anonymous informing might "pose an even greater threat than the criminality it was intended to combat."

Neighborhood Watch programs have experienced similar growth (Latessa & Travis, 1987). Beginning in 1967, criminal justice observers noted the importance of citizen involvement in assisting the police in controlling crime. Projects designed to increase citizen cooperation with the police began across the country. Variously named, the most common of these projects are Neighborhood Watch or crime-watch programs. They rely on citizen volunteers to act as "the eyes and ears" of the police. Again, the effect of these programs is that private citizens are taking responsibility for crime control. One interesting product of a crime-watch program studied by Latessa and Travis (1987:48) was that fewer citizens believed the police were successful in controlling crime. It may be that crime-watch programs led citizens to appreciate their role in crime control, and therefore, to devalue the role of the police. These programs may develop a "they-couldn't-do-it-without-us" attitude toward the police. Still, during the past

20 years, there has been a sustained national effort to increase citizen participation in crime prevention (Bureau of Justice Assistance, 1997).

Lab (1990) studied participation in crime prevention activities among a sample of American citizens. He found five distinct crime prevention activities: (1) personal access control (multiple locks, peepholes on doors), (2) target-hardening (installing alarms, marking property), (3) personal security (buying a gun or dog for self-defense), (4) surveillance (joining a crime-watch program), and (5) avoidance (changing behavior to reduce risk, e.g., staying at home at night). Moreover, different personal characteristics were associated with participation in different types of crime prevention. Thus, citizen participation in crime prevention actions is partly a product of the characteristics of the citizens themselves. For instance, Lab (1990:481) found that crime-watch participants were likely to be older, better educated females who did not own their homes and who had previously been victims of property crimes. Zhao, Gibson, Lovrich, and Gaffney (2002) found that citizens who volunteer to participate in crime prevention programs tend to report higher levels of fear of crime than those who do not. In that regard, participation in crime prevention programs may represent self-interest, as those most afraid of being crime victims are most likely to join programs.

Following the 2012 shooting of Trayvon Martin by a member of a Neighborhood Watch program, some scholars have argued for increased regulation of crime watch associations. Finegan (2013) proposed limitations on the ability of Neighborhood Watch members to confront suspects. As Finegan pointed out, members of a community crime prevention program are not held to the same legal and ethical standards as police officers. Private residents can act on their own biases, potentially targeting suspects on the basis of their race or ethnicity. Finegan (2013) further proposed increased training for members of community watch groups, as well as the expansion of the exclusionary rule to restrict evidence seized illegally by private citizens from being used in a trial of the suspect. The city where Trayvon Martin was killed announced changes in its community watch program, including increased training, background checks for all volunteers, and the recommendation that volunteers not be armed while on the streets (Karlamangla, 2013).

Another area receiving increased attention is known as "crime prevention through environmental design" or CPTED. **CPTED** (pronounced "sep-ted") programs change environmental conditions to reduce the likelihood of crime. Strategies such as the increased use of lighting, alarms, surveillance cameras, locks, bars, chains, and other security devices; the marking of property; and the changing of traffic flow patterns all seek to make crime less attractive to potential offenders (see Figure 15.3).

Zahm (2007) identified three basic objectives for CPTED (see Box 15.2). Wagner (1997) reported that blocking the through traffic in a neighborhood may reduce the amount of crime that occurs there. Hakim, Rengert, and Shachmurove (1996) calculated the costs and benefits of increased use of alarm systems by citizens. They concluded that such systems do save money by reducing the likelihood of

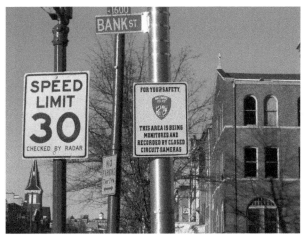

FIGURE 15.3
Increasingly our streets are being monitored by surveillance cameras, as evidenced by this sign in Baltimore, Maryland.

BOX 15.2 REDUCING CRIME OPPORTUNITIES WITH CRIME PREVENTION THROUGH ENVIRONMENTAL DESIGN (CPTED)

Control access by creating real and perceptual barriers to entry and movement: The environment should offer cues about who belongs in a place, when they are supposed to be there, and what they should be doing. For example, boundaries can be defined by the use of fences and hedges. Movement through space can be directed by the use of sidewalks and paths. A space might also be supported with the use of locks, alarm systems, or guards.

Provide opportunities to see and be seen: Providing opportunities to see a space from adjacent properties, from the site's perimeter, and from one part of the site to another. Strategies include improved lighting and windows. Proper building orientation and minimal landscaping can also serve to enhance the view of a space.

Define ownership and encourage maintenance of territory: Encouraging the use of territorial markings or fostering conditions that show signs of guardianship, such as Neighborhood Watch signs. Buildings, yards, gardens, and other features should be well maintained and in working order. Neighborhood cleanup and beautification efforts indicate that residents are observant and concerned about neighborhood conditions.

Source: Zahm (2007)

---

crimes at protected places, but that the costs of police investigating false alarms are higher than generally thought and usually not charged directly to the alarm owner. Ward (1997) found that even if such programs do not affect actual levels of crime, they appear to reduce the level of fear of crime among neighborhood residents. Giblin, Burruss, Corsaro, and Schafer (2011) reported that individuals often make assessments about their likelihood of victimization, and take protective measures such as locking their homes and increase lighting around their homes accordingly.

Dispute resolution is yet another area where there is a movement away from the criminal justice system as the solution to crime. Dispute resolution programs generally attempt to take less serious offenses and citizen disputes out of the criminal justice arena and put them into a private negotiation format. Rather than neighbors pressing criminal charges or property owners bringing charges against tenants, these programs provide a forum in which the conflicting parties can resolve their differences without recourse to the criminal law. Dispute resolution centers appear to provide alternatives to criminal justice processing, and participants generally seem satisfied with the programs.

Hanna (2008) described a successful dispute resolution program operating in Maricopa County, Arizona. Originally developed to alleviate increasing court dockets, this program allows judges to directly participate in plea negotiations between the prosecutor and defense attorney. These meetings are informal and often include the defendant and victim. Although the participating judges rarely participate in dispute resolutions in cases over which they will be presiding, the presence of a judge often helps the defendant understand and evaluate a plea offer.

A related development involves **victim/offender mediation** programs in which criminal offenders meet with their victims to negotiate a resolution to the criminal event (Umbreit & Greenwood, 2000). In a survey of programs, Umbreit and Greenwood identified nearly 300 operating mediation projects, the first of which started in the late 1970s. The majority of these programs were developed by private-sector organizations. The major goals of such projects are to provide sentencing alternatives, to allow the victim a voice in the justice process, to reduce the harm done to the victim (generally through restitution), and to increase the offender's accountability to the victim.

In a survey of mediation participants, McGarrell (2001) examined the satisfaction of victims who participate in these programs for young offenders. His conclusion was that victims obtain a greater sense of satisfaction through mediation programs than they do in traditional criminal justice processing. More than 90% of the victims were satisfied with the program, and 98% said that they would recommend the approach to a friend involved in a similar situation. Malsch and Carriere (1999) reported that mediation programs met the needs of victims for involvement in the process and being kept informed about case status and progress better than traditional justice system procedures. Umbreit (1989) suggested that most victims seek a resolution to the crime that they feel is fair in terms of both the offender and themselves. Table 15.1 presents Umbreit's typology of crime victims' perspectives.

Current interest in community courts, community prosecution (Brienza, 1998; Cunningham, Renauer, & Khalifa, 2006), and **community justice** (Clear, Hamilton, & Cadora, 2011) indicates that there has been an expansion of these earlier programs into a more comprehensive approach to the problem of crime

Table 15.1	Typology of Victim Perspectives of Fairness		
	Type A "The Healer" $N=24$	Type B "The Fixer" $N=14$	Type C "The Avenger" $N=12$
Focus	**Offender**	**Victim**	**Society**
Primary Concerns	(1) Kids need help, counseling, and guidance (2) Rehabilitation can reduce future criminal behavior (3) Punishment is important but not as important as taking responsibility for their lives	(1) Need to face consequences by repairing damages (2) Full compensation to victim is required (3) Direct accountability to victim is important	(1) [Criminal justice system] too lenient, most often just a slap on the hand (2) Firm punishment is needed, jail or institution (3) Rehabilitation: restitution often important, but secondary concern
Examples	(1) "I'm not so worried about the money as the kids" (2) "If the choice was for restitution or help for the kid, I would go for the betterment of the kid" (3) "Fairness is consequences. Those who make mistakes should get the help they need so that they stop doing it"	(1) "I didn't want any vindictiveness, all I wanted was restitution" (2) "It's only fair that I should get what was wrongfully taken from me returned" (3) "Restitution is the major thing, they need to personally make restitution—strong connection between their actions/consequences"	(1) "The punishment isn't harsh enough—it was too lenient" (2) "It's been a slap on the wrist, he should serve time in a prison" (3) "A good-sized deterrent is the only thing that is going to make these people take notice"

Note: Each category in this typology is not mutually exclusive. Rather, each group represents the dominant or primary characteristics expressed by victims of burglary in this study. For example, although the primary concern of most victims fits Type A, these same individuals may also be concerned about some of the characteristics in Type B or Type C, but at a more secondary and less intense level.
Source: Umbreit (1989:54)

in communities. Community justice programs, sometimes considered under the title "restorative justice," seek to achieve a balance between offenders and victims. This balance is expected to reflect community values and restore order, not just determine who is guilty and impose punishment. Such programs involve mediation, restitution, and similar practices. One difficulty with such programs, of course, is that not all offenders (or victims) are well suited to participate. Presser and Lowenkamp (1999) urge the development of a mechanism for screening offenders to ensure that they will be able to participate effectively in restorative justice programs, including victim/offender mediation. Community justice programs seek to empower communities to solve disputes and problems without recourse to the formal system of criminal justice (Robinson, 1996; Stone, 1996). Karp and Clear (2000:324) defined community justice, writing, "Community justice broadly refers to all variants of crime prevention and justice activities that explicitly include the community in their processes and set the enhancement of community quality of life as a goal." Box 15.3 describes the priorities of community justice.

The growth and development in restitution also reflects an increasing emphasis on the private wrongs that accompany crime. In restitution programs, the offender is directed to repay the victim for losses incurred because of the crime (Galaway & Hudson, 1978). Although restitution had always been a traditional practice (Schwartz, Clear, & Travis, 1980), in the mid-1970s, several jurisdictions began experimenting with restitution as an official part of a criminal sanction (Galaway, 1977). The age-old practice of the offender paying restitution or reparation to erase or minimize the crime before sentencing became a part of the official sentence itself.

In addition to ordering that the offender make restitution to the crime victim, most states operate victim compensation programs for those who suffer a violent crime (McCormack, 1991). **Victim compensation** programs are designed so that the state can pay crime victims for the loss they experienced. However, relatively few victims of violent crime receive any compensation for the harm they have suffered. In fact, many victims are unaware of the funds and are often never informed of their eligibility (Davis & Mulford, 2008)

Perhaps the clearest indication of a movement toward private justice today is the development of programs for crime victims. Until very recently, the criminal justice system generally ignored the victim of crime. At best, the victim was an important witness; at worst, the system treated the victim almost as if he or she were the offender. In the 1980s, the separate threads of restitution, dispute resolution, and victim/offender mediation programs came together in comprehensive crime victim legislation (Walker, 1994).

Davis (1987) wrote that future historians might declare the 1980s as the period when crime victims were finally recognized by the justice system. He reported that

BOX 15.3 PRIORITIES OF COMMUNITY JUSTICE

Community justice recognizes that each neighborhood is different. The neighborhood that a person lives in influences their lives in many ways. Further, some neighborhoods experience far greater levels of crime (and response from the criminal justice system) than others. Thus, community justice has three priorities:

1. Focus on high-impact neighborhoods with high levels of crime
2. Strengthen the selected area's capacity for informal social control
3. Develop partnerships with residents, businesses, and other social services

Source: Clear et al. (2011)

more than 30 states had passed victims' rights legislation. This legislation recognizes the plight of the victim and tries to attend to victim concerns through providing compensation and requiring that victims be notified of the progress of their cases. Programs for crime victims run the gamut from counseling to compensation. Once again, the victims of crime have come to be defined as the injured parties in criminal acts. Technically, the offense may still be against the state, but today, the state is beginning to accept a responsibility to protect the individual interests of the victim. The Office for Victims of Crime reported that "the nation has witnessed dramatic progress in the expansion of crime victims' rights, protection, and services—empowering victims to participate in the criminal, civil, and juvenile justice systems, and to be heard at last" (Office for Victims of Crime, 2013:10).

In many jurisdictions, legislation allows the victim to address the court at sentencing, or the parole authority at release determinations (Erez & Tontodonato, 1992). It is increasingly common for presentence investigation reports to include a **victim impact statement**, which explains the loss incurred by the victim because of the crime. One of the most far-reaching laws providing for victim input is the California Victim's Bill of Rights, passed in 1982. This law allows the victim to appear before the court and parole authorities. Other states have adopted similar procedures that allow victims to speak at critical decision points in the justice process. Walker (1985:183) observed, however, that "[t]he great danger is that the presence of the victim would add a note of vengeance to the criminal process, or at least a greater one than presently exists."

Villmoare and Neto (1987) reported that the California legislation appeared to have little impact on criminal justice processing. Fewer than 3% of victims actually exercised their right to speak at sentencing. Of those who spoke at sentencing, less than one-half thought their comments had any effect on the disposition of the case. Villmoare and Neto concluded that such victim rights could not be successful if simply added on to the existing justice system. They concluded that one reason for the lack of impact of victim statements was the fact that so many cases had already been decided through plea bargaining. To give the victim of crime a real voice in case processing, they suggested it would be necessary to make profound changes throughout the justice system. In short, decision-making authority in the criminal justice system, from bail through sentencing, would need to be shared between the official agents and the victims of crime. Davis and Smith (1994a, 1994b) reported that victim impact statements appeared to have no effect on criminal justice agent considerations of harm caused to victims, and no impact on the severity of sentences imposed.

DUE PROCESS, CRIME CONTROL, AND PRIVATE JUSTICE

As is true whenever we attempt to predict the future, it is unclear where we are headed with our current privatization of justice. In many ways, we can dismiss current trends as a natural reaction to the due process revolution of the 1960s, which, according to many observers, "handcuffed the police." It is quite possible that what we see today is an effort to return the justice process to a point of equilibrium. Perhaps one result of the Supreme Court's decisions on criminal matters in the 1960s was to tip the scales too far in favor of offenders, and the contemporary focus on the victim is an effort to restore the previous balance. From the perspective of criminal justice agents, introduction of the crime victim creates an identified individual whose interests compete with those of the offender. The role of the crime victim may be most influential as a check on concerns for the liberty and rights of offenders.

It also may be that those who proclaimed the 1980s to be the "me generation" were correct. A fundamental shift in our perceptions of government and its duty to the citizenry may be reflected in criminal justice processes. Paradoxically, government today is expected to leave us alone as much as possible, yet it is supposed to protect our interests to the maximum. Insured loans to businesses and banks are an expected function of government, yet government is not expected to tax too greatly or regulate too strictly. Perhaps, then, we feel that the justice system should not control our behavior too closely, yet should serve our individual needs if we become victims.

The implications of increased citizen participation in crime control, especially through such practices as Neighborhood Watch and crime-stopper programs, may extend the scope of government control (Pfuhl, 1992). With our neighbors watching and willing to call the police anonymously, we may lose our privacy— and thus our liberty to do things in our private lives. With so many extra eyes and ears, the surveillance capability of the government expands greatly, at a cost to individual liberty (Welsh & Farrington, 2009). On the other hand, to the degree that fear of crime keeps people from doing the things they like (such as going out in the evenings), increased citizen surveillance may enhance our personal freedom by increasing our level of perceived safety. Fears of terrorist attack have led to unprecedented government power to monitor communications and citizens and have added to travel delays as airline passengers undergo security checks.

One can predict that the next several years will be a period of adjustment. Evidence thus far indicates that most victims of crime do not seem to want a direct voice in criminal justice processing. Reviews of the exercise of rights by victims of crime indicate that most victims make (or file) a victim impact statement at sentencing, but few still exercise the right to make recommendations at bail or parole hearings (Kilpatrick, Beatty, & Howley, 1998). In the end, it appears that the results of the privatization of criminal justice will be mixed. Victims may receive treatment that is more humane, services, and compensation to reduce the traumatic effects of victimization, but decisions about the handling of offenders will likely revert to the detached, professional judgments of criminal justice agents and officers. Citizens may engage in surveillance and reporting of criminality, but will probably focus their attention on more serious, traditional crimes by strangers. Agencies of the justice system encourage victim participation that helps "balance" concern for offender rights by introducing the competing concern for victims' interests. Still, these same agencies are not well suited to the provision of direct services to victims (Bryant & Brown, 2002). In short, over a span of years, it is likely that we will learn the limits to privatization, both practical and philosophical, and adjust the system accordingly.

TECHNOLOGICAL JUSTICE

In all aspects of life, technological changes have caused adjustments in behavior. We take for granted such advances as household electricity, indoor plumbing, telephones, automobiles, and other commonplace technological conveniences. By the end of 2014, the number of mobile-connected devices will exceed the number of people on earth (Cisco, 2014). Yet, as recently as 50 years ago, these technologies were unavailable to large segments of our population. The effects of technological advances on criminal justice have been staggering, as they have been on other areas of life. The telephone and the automobile changed the nature of policing. No longer did the neighborhood cop walk a beat and know everyone. Now a simple telephone call to an impersonal dispatcher results in the arrival, by automobile, of an equally impersonal police officer. In the past, offenders could simply give the police an alias or cross a state line to avoid prosecution. Today, computerized criminal records and fingerprint checks can lead to quick identifications. A simple traffic stop may lead to a felony arrest when a computer check yields outstanding warrants.

Warehouses full of paper documents have been reduced to a few boxes of microfiche. Crime records and court documents are now stored on computer files. The availability of electronic databases and powerful search engines has made the police, courts, and correctional agencies more effective in identifying and tracking known and/or wanted offenders. Television, videotapes, and computer simulations can be used to great effect in investigations and at trial to present and test evidence and to reduce delays and costs. Teleconferencing can be used to replace on-site hearings for parole or probation revocation, or even for parole release hearings; this advance reduces costs and increases efficiency.

Scientific advances (including genetic testing) have been adapted to criminal justice uses. Currently, investigators use DNA "fingerprinting" to help identify offenders conclusively, as well as to help identify innocent suspects (Rau, 1991). DNA evidence has been used in trials in most states. Although there are still some problems with this technology (Perry & Banks, 2011), including improper evidence collection by police, it would appear that the technique is firmly established. Other investigatory aids include computer-generated offender profiles to assist police in identifying likely suspects, and a variety of drug detection tests to both locate contraband and establish drug use among criminal suspects.

Modern prisons and jails are making use of a variety of technological innovations to improve custody and services. Electronic perimeter security (microwave, electric eye, and vibration sensors, which are increasingly replacing towers and walls) has reduced construction costs and accelerated construction schedules for new prisons (Camp & Camp, 1987; Donohoe & Greloch, 1997; Latessa, Travis,

Oldendick, McDermott, & Noonan, 1988). Closed-circuit television, automatic locking devices, and careful planning have reduced the need for custodial staff in prisons and jails. Joseph (2005) described cutting-edge correctional technologies including heartbeat monitors that can detect the heartbeat of those hiding in cars or cargo. Some states are experimenting with "smart cards" that contain inmate information on microchips to expedite processing of inmates in need of medication. Additional uses of these cards include identification and access control (Joseph, 2005). Automated video surveillance has enhanced the ability of correctional personnel to monitor inmate behavior and prison safety (Turner, 2007). Prisons can also monitor inmates by fitting them with a wristband or ankle bracelet equipped with active radio-frequency software, similar to the systems widely used by community corrections departments (Hickman, Davis, Wells, & Eisman, 2010). This technology allows for real-time monitoring of inmates from a central location and is currently in use by approximately 14 U.S. correctional facilities. See Box 15.4.

With technological development, the justice system now is able to detect, apprehend, and process offenders more quickly and economically. The technologies have allowed us to conduct business as usual but in a more efficient manner. Advances in medical science have also affected crime. Giacopassi, Sparger, and Stein (1992) note that improved emergency medical care may have suppressed the homicide rate. Many of today's felonious assaults would have been homicides but for the fact that medical care has been improved. Saving the life of the crime victim reduces the seriousness of the crime. Indeed, Hanke and Gundlach (1995) suggested that differences in access to quality emergency medical care may explain the observed differences in seriousness of crime between Caucasian and African American offenders. They provide evidence that lack of access to quality emergency medical care in minority, inner-city neighborhoods may help account for higher rates of homicide and more serious injuries to victims of violent crime. Other technologies have arisen that may alter the conduct of criminal justice business in more significant ways.

New technologies have affected the types of crimes that will be the focus of criminal justice efforts. Table 15.2 describes "cybercrimes" reported by a sample

---

BOX 15.4 EXPECTED BENEFITS FOR RADIO-FREQUENCY IDENTIFICATION SYSTEMS IN CORRECTIONAL ENVIRONMENTS

- Improved monitoring and control of inmates
- Reduction in violence and injuries
- Reduction in escapes
- Improved investigative capabilities
- Reduction in inmate grievances, lawsuits, and disciplinary actions

Source: Hickman et al. (2010)

Table 15.2	Prevalence of Computer Security Incidents		
	Percent of Businesses by Type of Incident		
Characteristic	**All Incidents (%)**	**Cyber Attack (%)**	**Cyber Theft (%)**
All businesses reporting	67	58	11
Industries with the highest prevalence of cybercrime:			
Telecommunications	82	74	17
Computer system design	79	72	15
Manufacturing, durable goods	75	68	15
Suspected offender was an:			
Insider	40	27	74
Outsider	71	74	32
Incidents were reported:			
Within the business	80	81	46
To another organization	15	14	9
To law enforcement officials	15	6	56

Source: Rantala (2008:1)

of businesses. New technologies also have affected the delicate balance between the rights of individuals and those of the community. For example, there has been an increased interest in the use of license plate–reading cameras. Mounted on patrol cars or fixed locations, license plate readers can capture images of every passing license plate. As Baker (2011) observed, the readers are increasingly being used to identify stolen cars, unregistered vehicles, and those with stolen license plates. In essence, the license plate readers have the capability to track the location of a vehicle's movement over a period of time. Civil liberties groups have expressed concern that few protections are in place to prevent the license plate readers' use in abusive or discriminatory targeting based on an individual's religion or ethnicity (ACLU, 2013). The Department of Homeland Security has expressed interest in creating a national database that would compile the information from license plate readers across the country (Nakashima & Hicks, 2014). The future of crime seems more easily predictable than does the outcome of the balance of state and individual interests (see Box 15.5).

Johnson (1981) explained that changes in police organization and operation were partly owing to the changes in the nature and extent of crime. Similarly, Lundman (1980) explained the development of police, in part as a result of changes in the rates and images of crime. That is, the police (and, by extension, the entire criminal justice system) must be responsive to those acts that we view as seriously threatening public order and safety. Technological change also changes crime.

Willie Sutton, a famous bank robber, is credited with a witty response to a question about his actions. When asked why he committed bank robberies, Sutton is said to have replied, "Because that's where the money is." If we look at crimes

BOX 15.5 DRONE USE BY LAW ENFORCEMENT

On January 14, 2014, a North Dakota farmer was convicted in an incident involving his failure to return three cows from a neighboring property that had strayed onto his property (Peck, 2014). This case is significant not because of the crime committed, but because the conviction represents the first time in American history that a U.S. citizen has been sentenced to prison with the assistance of an unmanned drone (without a search warrant). Some commenters argue that the use of unmanned drones is an appropriate and desirable tool for domestic law enforcement (Straub, 2014). However, privacy advocates suggest that strict regulations be placed on the use of these devices (Stanley & Crump, 2011). Drones can carry sophisticated surveillance technologies, such as:

- High-power zoom lenses
- Night vision
- See-through imaging
- Video analytics with capabilities to recognize specific people, events, and objects

Source: Stanley and Crump (2011)

throughout American history, we see that, very often, they take place "where the money is." Criminals such as Jesse James robbed stagecoaches because these coaches carried large sums of money (corporate payments, payrolls, etc.). These men became train robbers when cash began to be transported by rail. Bank robberies became more common when checks and fund transfers replaced cash transactions. Today's offender might well be described as a "lineman," that is, he or she often steals by computer. Fraud with computerized banking, already a problem, is likely to become more significant in the future. Counterfeiting is on the rise as more and more people gain access to sophisticated copiers, printers, and digital printing resources (Morris, Copes, & Perry-Mullis, 2009).

Not only is money itself at risk in an increasingly computerized commercial system, but information is also more often the target of theft. Trade secrets, customer lists, business records, and all sorts of other information (including national defense secrets) are stored in computer databases. Theft of such information often is more damaging (and more profitable for the thief) than fraudulent fund transfers. Detection of computer crime (and enforcement of laws against it) will require a different type of law enforcement response than that required by traditional street crime. The systems analyst at the terminal may replace the officer in the patrol car. This does not mean that street crime will disappear; it means that computer-related offenses will increase in frequency and importance, which will lead to justice system adaptations to combat them. Harris (1995) reported that there is growing recognition of the need for law enforcement officers with computer skills. She quoted one respondent who noted, "We need to begin recruiting people with technological skills, or at least basic computer system operation skills." The knowledge and skills required for effective search and seizure of computers are lacking in most law enforcement agencies (Harris, 1995).

A survey of law enforcement officials by Burns, Whitworth, and Thompson (2004) revealed that while most believe Internet fraud is being investigated by police at all levels, it would be better pursued by federal agencies. A lack of resources and inadequate organizational structure hamper local law enforcement efforts to respond to Internet fraud and similar computer crimes. We can only expect that all sorts of computer crime will increase in the future. Table 15.3 describes the types of computer crimes prosecuted by state court prosecutors in 2005. There is great interest in **identity theft**, the theft or misuse of personal information, similar to fraud or forgery. Common forms of the crime involve "posing" as someone else to use their credit cards or access their financial records or accounts. The federal government and some states have taken repeated steps to enhance penalties for identity theft in hopes of deterring offenders (Copes & Vieraitis, 2009). Box 15.6 describes the most common forms of computer offenses identified in state statutes.

During the 1970s, especially during the Carter administration, a shift toward increased efforts against corporate and white-collar crime could be detected in changes in federal law enforcement. In that time period, the FBI sought agents with the skills required to track white-collar crime, and recruits were trained in accounting, computers, or law. These backgrounds were to prepare the agents for the shifting emphasis of federal law enforcement to corporate and white-collar crimes. Since then, however, a reemergence of drug-related crimes and an increased concern about terrorism resulted, at least partially, in a return of federal law enforcement to more traditional practices during the Reagan administration. Of course, scandals such as the Enron fraud case and the obstruction-

Table 15.3	Computer Crimes Prosecuted by State Court Prosecutors, 2006	
Type of Crime	**Percentage of Offices Prosecuting**	
Prosecuted any cases as computer crime	60	
Credit card fraud	80	
Bank card fraud	71	
Identity theft	69	
Transmitting child pornography	67	
Computer forgery	40	
Cyberstalking	36	
Unauthorized access	23	
Computer sabotage	5	
Theft of intellectual property	5	
Unauthorized copying	4	
Other	11	

Source: Perry (2006:5)

BOX 15.6 CATEGORIES OF BEHAVIOR ADDRESSED BY STATE COMPUTER CRIME STATUTES

- *Intellectual property*—Expanded the idea that computer programs, computer data, and computer services are property or intellectual property.
- *Computer tampering*—Made illegal "knowingly or recklessly" degrading or disrupting computer services to the extent that such actions impair the ability of authorized users to obtain full use of their computer systems.
- *Computer trespass*—Made illegal the unauthorized access of a computer and its contents, including using the contents of a computer to aid and abet the commission of a crime.
- *Unlawful duplication/disclosure*—Made illegal copying and distributing the contents of a computer without authorization.
- *Defenses*—Allowed some defenses to restrict unauthorized access.
- *Venues/sites of offense*—Specified the jurisdiction for purposes of prosecuting the theft of computer information.

Source: Brown (2000)

of-justice conviction of Martha Stewart served to heighten again the interest in corporate and white-collar crime. High-profile cases of corporate misconduct in the accounting, mortgage, and health care industries have significantly impacted the American economy, leading to increased legal regulation (Edwards & Braswell, 2015).

Technology affects the types of crimes that can be (and are) committed. In response, the qualifications of justice system officials, the nature of cases in the criminal justice process, and responses to offenders will change. There is little doubt that, similar to the shift from stagecoach robbery to bank robbery, the practices of criminal justice will be required to adapt to high-technology crimes of computer fraud. These changes, however, do not appear likely to change the criminal justice system in any fundamental way.

Computer crimes may pit justice system investigators skilled in system analysis against offenders skilled in programming. Evidence at trials may come to be comprised of documents and disks more often than of hairs and weapons, but the process itself can continue in its present form. In this case, the type of crime and criminal may be different, but the basic response to crime remains. Schroeder and White (2009) reported that DNA evidence was used rarely in homicide investigations in New York City, largely because it was not needed. Other effects of technology, however, pose a greater likelihood of altering the way in which criminal justice is accomplished.

In addition to the opportunities for crime that computers offer, computerized record keeping can aid the efforts of criminal justice officials. Tremendous amounts of information about almost every citizen are kept somewhere on computer records. If a suspected offender has ever applied for credit, or if he or she operates a motor vehicle, police can garner much information, quickly and easily, by requesting computer records. Credit applications generate data about employment, earnings, savings, debts, addresses, dependents, references, demographic characteristics (such as age, sex, race, education, and marital status), and even height and weight. Access to a person's credit report can provide a tremendous amount of personal information about him or her. Operation of a motor vehicle provides similar background data, important identifying numbers (e.g., Social Security numbers), as well as information about possible criminal record. It is possible to conduct a relatively thorough background check on the average citizen without ever leaving a computer terminal.

Credit card purchase records allow investigators to track travel patterns of individuals. Credit card purchasing and payment information exists on computer records that do not require a check on access (other than perhaps knowledge of a correct password). This means that personal data are potentially available to anyone. Consider what information about your private life someone could learn with access to computer records. If someone had unlimited access, could that person discover your name, address, telephone number, income, age, sex, race, general whereabouts over the past month, courses you are taking, and your grade point average? How difficult would it be for such a person to identify your friends, family, or taste in clothes or music? Even though much of this information is freely available on various social media sites, we would consider much of the available information to be personal. Our right to be protected from unreasonable "searches and seizures" is increasingly at risk, and we are frequently unaware of the risk. The sheer availability of information about suspects, witnesses, and offenders could lead to increased surveillance by the justice system. There is no doubt that much of this information would prove useful in not only criminal investigations, but also for what is called "intelligence gathering."

Intelligence gathering relates to the compilation of information that may be helpful in solving crimes, but with no specific probable cause to believe the information will lead to solving a particular crime. As the emphasis on proactive, preventive efforts of criminal justice agencies increases, with a complementary focus on problem solving, we can expect justice agencies to compile and use larger and more diverse sets of information. Crime mapping and geographic analysis have become important planning tools for law enforcement agencies (Rich, 1995), and their use has spread to courts and to correctional agencies (Harries, 2003). In most applications, the criminal justice analyst ties a variety of data sources to a known location and then seeks relationships that help explain the presence or absence of crime to develop policy directed at reducing the likelihood of crime or other problems.

A contemporary development in policing relates to "intelligence-led" policing, where police agencies use sophisticated analyses and modeling to predict crimes and assign officers in anticipation of these problems. Although a number of police agencies are working toward intelligence-led policing, it is a difficult transition. Boba, Weisburd, and Meeker (2009) reported on a regional effort to develop shared data for problem-solving efforts. They recognized that the tradition of policing is to focus on a specific problem, and this tradition limits the ability and willingness of police departments to develop and maintain databases useful to "intelligence" operations. More recently, budgetary constraints seem to have hindered the development of intelligence-led policing (Chermak, Carter, Carter, McGarrell, & Drew, 2013).

Yet another computer-generated technological change promises to alter the way in which criminal justice decisions are made. It is increasingly common for justice agencies to employ statistical models to assist in the determination of resource allocation and case processing decisions. Spelman and Eck (1987) reported on "smart policing," in which police reactions to crime problems (in the form of changing patterns of patrol, enlisting community assistance, and selecting police problems for enforcement attention) are "incident driven." Crime reports and computer-generated patterns of police problems guide the deployment of police resources. In the latter part of the 1990s, police agencies began using computerized crime mapping and geographic analysis of crime to inform decisions about where and how to allocate police resources (Dabney, 2010).

Some commentators call for increasing use of such models for making police decisions. They suggest that criminal complaints should be ranked according to solvability, and that detective and patrol officers should be assigned to respond to cases based on the likelihood that the case can be solved. Therefore, the lower the probability that the case will be solved, the less the urgency for police to respond to the complaint.

Many prosecutors' offices differentiate cases based on factors associated with successful prosecution, or on other models of case importance. Cases receive special attention when an analysis of factors present in the case (witnesses, physical evidence, etc.) indicates a high probability of conviction. That is, prosecutorial resources focus on those cases for which there is the greatest probability of successful prosecution.

The courts and parole authorities rely on various analyses to assist in the determination of criminal sanctions. The tradition of research-generated guidelines for criminal justice decision making is longest in parole and sentencing (Travis & O'Leary, 1979). Block and Rhodes (1987) assessed the federal sentencing guidelines, noting that the Federal Sentencing Commission (which authored the guidelines) did not expect federal judges to deviate from guideline sentences very often. Wilkins (1987:8), chairman of the commission, predicted that "if this effort at the Federal level is generally found to be successful, these guidelines will foster the development of guidelines by many States that do not already have them." As we have seen, many states have implemented guidelines and/or sentencing commissions.

Probation and parole supervision levels in many states are determined with reference to risk and needs assessment measures. Gettinger (1981) described the California system for assigning levels of supervision, referring to the system as "doing parole by the numbers." In that system, each case was assessed for risk and determined to be either a "control case" or a "service case." Control cases received close supervision and an emphasis on crime prevention; service cases received counseling and assistance in receiving community services. Like the parolees, the parole officers were broken into classes of minimum-supervision agents, who administered large caseloads of parolees requiring little attention; control officers, who served as "personal police" for dangerous parolees; and service agents, who arranged social services for parolees needing them.

Partially an outgrowth of research over the past 3 decades that identified inefficiencies in criminal justice processing, the use of these classification technologies is expected to ensure that criminal justice resources are wisely expended on those cases for which they are most needed. The use of "problem-oriented policing," setting prosecution priorities, sentencing guidelines, and correctional classification also reflects the contemporary emphasis on career criminals (see Chapter 3).

The problem posed by this new decision-making technology for criminal justice revolves around the question of who makes the decisions. To the extent that all these classification and prediction technologies provide information and guidance to decision makers, they do not significantly alter justice system processing. These devices simply become another factor in the equation that produces criminal justice outcomes. The problem is that these technologies may actually alter the decisions themselves.

At least in community supervision, there is evidence that many jurisdictions simply adopted the National Institute of Corrections case management models, and that they did so without adjusting the models for local characteristics. Indeed, an evaluation of the application of the model system to several local departments indicated that the risk-assessment instruments did not work very well at predicting risk in some places (Wright, Clear, & Dickson, 1984). Nonetheless, classification decisions were based on an existing (albeit inappropriate) model; one could say that the model made the decisions.

Regarding prosecutorial guidelines, Weimer (1980) found that focusing resources on cases with lower probabilities of conviction produces more effective use of prosecution resources. After all, cases with high probabilities of conviction do not need as much special attention. Further, lacking an effort to deal strongly with lower-probability cases, and lacking continual evaluation of case decision making and outcomes, the model becomes self-perpetuating. Nothing will change, because there will be no new information generated that will lead to change.

For sentencing decisions, guidelines are often stifling. Convicted offenders receive predetermined sentences because of factors that often are beyond their control. When prior criminal record influences criminal sentences there is nothing the offender can do to alter his or her sentence. The prior record never gets better. When one considers that parole and sentencing guidelines are often based on past experience (what kinds of sentences were imposed in the past), the problem is more apparent. Arguably, one reason for the development of these models is to improve decision making, but the models are based on the very decisions they are expected to improve (Gottfredson, Cosgrove, Wilkins, Wallerstein, & Rauh, 1978).

For the near future, the tendency to adopt and use decision-making aids will probably continue and spread throughout the justice system. The effects of these models are presently unknown. By relieving decision makers of responsibility for decisions, the guidelines allow them to claim that they were forced to make a certain decision. As a result, there will probably be a tendency toward uniformity in decisions. This uniformity would have the effect of masking differences between individual cases, which could result in less humane treatment of offenders. Further, we can expect that such guidelines will further strengthen the justice system's ability to resist change. One long-range result may well be a call for greater individualization in criminal justice case processing, which would return us, full cycle, to where these guidelines began.

Technology and Criminal Justice in the Total System

Technological advances in all areas of society continue at an accelerated pace. The effects of these changes for society are both positive and negative. Increased communication capability, for example, applies to both good news and bad. Having voicemail means the phone will be answered, but the chance of speaking with a living person is greatly decreased. Changes in technology affect the environment of the criminal justice system, and thus we can expect them to produce changes in criminal justice processing.

As illustrated in the previous discussion, most of the effects of technological change have occurred in the material environment. Types of crimes and methods of detection and investigation have changed. The relative frequency of homicide as compared to assault, or white-collar crimes as compared with street crimes, may have changed. Similarly, the characteristics of criminal justice personnel, and the equipment they need to do their jobs, may change in response to technological innovation.

The impact of technology on the operations of criminal justice indicates the open-system nature of the justice process. These changes occur in the means of criminal justice operations but probably have little impact on the ends of processing. Other technological advances, such as decision-making aids, are more subtle, but may have more far-reaching effects because they alter the ends of criminal justice operations. To the extent that information technology assists criminal justice actors to achieve effective and fair decisions, the impact of technological change in the environment will be positive. To the degree that these alterations produce unintended consequences, such as institutionalizing discrimination, their effects may be negative. Whatever the effect on the means and ends of criminal justice, one factor to be considered in assessing the future of criminal justice remains the future environment of the system.

CRIMINAL JUSTICE IN THE EARLY TWENTY-FIRST CENTURY

What will the structure and practice of criminal justice in the United States be like as the twenty-first century progresses? If current developments continue on their present course, we can expect some changes. Three related developments promise to alter the fundamental nature of American criminal justice from its most recent tradition. There is a growing emphasis on crime prevention (Sherman et al., 1997) resulting in an expansion of the role of criminal justice in our society. We increasingly hold the justice system accountable for a broader quality of life than simply crime control. In part, this expansion of the role of criminal justice is a function of information suggesting that if we wish to reduce crime, we must attack problems of social order. Focusing on problems of social order has meant that the community has become an identified client and partner in criminal justice policymaking. Concern about the costs of justice system operation has risen at the same time that the criminal justice system is experiencing role expansion. This has meant that cost considerations have gained new prominence in criminal justice policy. Thus, concern about social order beyond crime has produced an expanded role for agents of the criminal justice system. This expanded role has increased costs, but also opened new avenues of funding for criminal justice operations. Finally, current assessments of criminal justice practices place greater emphasis on effectiveness than on democracy. In terms of our themes, contemporary criminal justice practices stress crime control over due process more than in the recent past.

Allen (1964) voiced concern about the role of the criminal justice system in dealing with social problems such as alcoholism. Allen suggested that many problems of social order lie on the borderland of the criminal justice system. His solution was that we limit the kinds of behaviors that should be the focus of criminal justice operations. Failing to limit the criminal justice system to the control of crime, Allen feared, would have negative consequences for both the system and society. More than 50 years later, the border of criminal justice has become less distinct.

As of the end of 2013, 20 states have legalized the medical use of marijuana. In 2012, Washington and Colorado became the first two states to legalize marijuana for recreational use (see Figure 15.4). These state-led initiatives are in direct conflict with federal law, which lists marijuana as a schedule 1 drug, subject to harsh punishments. However, the Justice Department in recent years has sent mixed messages regarding its enforcement of federal marijuana laws in states that have legalized marijuana (Kamin, 2013). There is an obvious lack of consensus in the United States regarding the appropriate regulation of marijuana.

Throughout the book we have explored community policing, community prosecution, community courts, community corrections, and community justice. All of these developments assume the existence of an identifiable community. What happens when there are no (or few) agreed-on community values? What happens if some members of the community are concerned about marijuana, but others are not? To whom do justice system officials listen?

FIGURE 15.4
Employees work behind the sales counter inside the Medicine Man marijuana retail store, which opened as a legal recreational retail outlet in Denver. State revenue officials reported that Colorado made roughly $2 million in marijuana taxes in January 2014.
AP Photo/Brennan Linsley, File

The tradition in American criminal justice has been to let the community decide what issues were important and communicate this by their complaints to the police. Increasingly, justice system agents are becoming involved in community-organizing activities in which they bring neighborhood residents together and help them to define problems and select solutions. To the extent that it is criminal justice agents who create these communities, the justice system is being proactive. A proactive justice system, you will recall, is associated with a less democratic society.

People, in general, may be more willing to use the law—and the criminal law in particular—to resolve disputes and conflicts (Miethe, 1995). Therefore, the range of issues that reach the attention of police, court, and correctional authorities has expanded. So, too, have the range of solutions. Justice system officials increasingly employ noncriminal justice solutions to problems of crime and disorder. Prosecutors use civil court processes such as eviction and license revocation to remove offenders from communities, and to close problem businesses (Finn, 1995). "Zero-tolerance" policing, which seeks to minimize disorderly behavior, can produce negative police–community relations, as some parts of the community experience repressive policing (National Institute of Justice, 2000). Asset forfeiture, in which justice agents seize the property of criminal offenders, provides a profit motive for criminal justice and may alter the selection of enforcement targets and the establishment of enforcement priorities in justice agencies (Holden, 1993; Miller & Selva, 1994). Rather than working for us, justice agents may be working for themselves.

The emphasis on crime prevention that is characteristic of recent changes in criminal justice operations is qualitatively different from an emphasis on crime control. In crime control, the justice system can be reactive and respond to instances of crime or potential crime. The system is effective to the extent that criminals are arrested and processed. A potential benefit may be that crime control efforts have preventive effects, such as deterrence and education. The emphasis on crime prevention, however, means that the justice system works to stop crimes that might happen, or that are predicted to happen. The difference is that these crimes have not yet occurred, and the offenders who might commit these crimes have yet to do anything wrong. What is the basis on which justice system authorities intervene in the lives of citizens who have not yet committed a crime?

At present, the balance between due process and crime control seems to have shifted in the direction of a greater emphasis on crime control. This can occur only at a cost to due process. In the foreseeable future, at least, we can expect increased criminal justice system efforts at crime prevention, accompanied by less concern about individual liberty and due process. We can expect that at some time in the future the balance will shift again to give primacy to individual liberty, due process, and the control of government power.

CRIMINAL JUSTICE THEORY REVISITED

How can we explain criminal justice? As we explored the criminal justice process in the United States, we reviewed a great deal of the research (and theory) about how the American criminal justice process works. We saw that some things influence all criminal justice decisions. Police, court, and correctional decisions reflect the seriousness of the offense and, whenever applicable, the availability of evidence. Beyond this, a number of other factors also prove to be influential in these decisions. The characteristics of criminal justice organizations, including size, rules, and supervision of personnel, seem to constrain decisions. The characteristics of individual decision makers (police officers, prosecutors, judges, etc.) are also important.

We can think of a number of theories or classes of theories of criminal justice. There is quite a bit of solid evidence for a legal theory of criminal justice. The law, both substantive and procedural, influences the operations of the criminal justice system. One explanation for what happens in criminal justice can be found in looking at the law.

There is also evidence for organizational theories of criminal justice. Police decisions vary, in part, based on the police department. Large police departments and departments with certain kinds of rules and supervision produce different outcomes than other departments. Courts and correctional agencies also reflect organizational characteristics including size, rules, and traditions.

The research supports group theories as well. In courts, in particular, the evidence indicates that group processes and shared understandings among prosecutors, defense attorneys, and judges explain rates and types of guilty pleas and sentences. Within police departments, different squads or units may behave differently. Probation and parole supervision outcomes reflect group beliefs shared among officers working in a particular office.

Individual characteristics of criminal justice officials also influence decisions. It seems the characteristics of individual police officers, prosecutors, judges, and the like are important, but that individual choices tend to be limited by legal, organizational, and group influences. The more independent the criminal justice official, the more likely the official's characteristics will explain decisions.

A large number of factors influence or explain criminal justice decisions and processes. It is probably most accurate to recognize that there are multiple "causes" of criminal justice outcomes. The most accurate theories of criminal justice are likely to be those that recognize that legal, organizational, group, and individual factors combine, often with other influences, to explain criminal justice outcomes. It is incumbent on us to work to develop and understand theories of criminal justice so we can refine and strengthen our understanding of the system.

CRIMINAL JUSTICE: A FINAL THOUGHT

The term "criminal justice" is paradoxical. Does it mean that justice is criminal, or that crime is just? We now know that it refers to how we define, detect, and react to behaviors that we deem criminal. We should also have an appreciation for how complex a topic it really is.

We have seen how present practices reflect various mixes of historical, political, economic, social, philosophical, and individual traits and factors. We can appreciate how the justice system, in balancing these many demands, is highly resistant to reform. There are so many places where reforms can be made, and so many levels at which reform can be stymied, that the justice process seems immune to change. Still, we have seen that changes have indeed occurred in criminal justice over the years. Some changes have been more fundamental than others. Some appear to have been more long lasting. Others are not yet complete.

Through our examination of criminal justice, we have come to see that no single purpose does (or can) predominate the system. The central dilemma is that of controlling behavior in a free society. The tension is between individual liberty and the need for an orderly and predictable society. The pendulum shifts over the decades from an emphasis on one to an emphasis on the other. The result is the appearance that no change has occurred. Criminal justice seems to proceed in a circular fashion, continually returning to earlier points. The effect is enough to make us despair in our hopes to achieve progress, but that is not the intent of the study of criminal justice.

An understanding of criminal justice promotes an understanding of our society and culture. Similarly, it is not possible to grasp the intricacies of the justice system without understanding its larger context. The failure of past reforms often can be traced to either or both of two mistakes. First, we must be reasonable in our expectations for change. It is probably not possible to eliminate injustice or inefficiency, and it may not even be desirable to do so. Second, change in the justice process is accomplished only by thorough planning and careful execution. As a system (or collection of separate systems), criminal justice is elastic and resists alteration. The would-be reformer must anticipate and prepare for reactions to change.

One thing that we can predict with confidence is that there will be a criminal justice process in the future. It is incumbent on us to try to understand it, and to work to improve it.

REVIEW QUESTIONS

1. Identify two ways in which an offender can receive a discharge from criminal justice custody.
2. What are collateral consequences of conviction? Identify five such consequences.
3. Describe a process by which an ex-offender may have his or her constitutional rights restored.
4. What are some of the problems in arriving at a definition of recidivism?
5. What are the implications of the concept of recidivism for criminal justice policy?
6. Some commentators argue there is a trend toward privatizing criminal justice. Summarize this argument, and discuss whether you agree with it.
7. One recent trend in criminal justice has been the development and use of decision-making guidelines. Give three examples of such guidelines, and discuss their possible effects.
8. Has the justice system moved more toward an emphasis on crime control than due process?

References

Allen, F. (1964). *The borderland of criminal justice.* Chicago: University of Chicago Press.

American Civil Liberties Union (ACLU) (2013). *You are being tracked: How license plate readers are being used to record Americans' movements.* New York, NY: American Civil Liberties Union.

Baker, A. (2011, April 11). Camera scans of car plates are reshaping police inquires. *The New York Times.* Retrieved from: http://www.nytimes.com/2011/04/12/nyregion/12plates.html?pagewanted=all.

Bennett, G. (1987). *Crime-warps: The future of crime in America.* New York: Doubleday.

Block, M. & Rhodes, W. (1987). *The impact of federal sentencing guidelines.* Washington, DC: National Institute of Justice.

Blumstein, A., & Nakamura, K. (2009). Redemption in the presence of widespread criminal background checks. *Criminology, 47*(2), 327–360.

Boba, R., Weisburd, D., & Meeker, J. (2009). The limits of regional data sharing and regional problem solving: Observations from the East Valley, CA COMPASS Initiative. *Police Quarterly, 12*(1), 22–41.

Braly, M. (1977). *False starts: A Memoir of San Quentin and other prisons.* New York: Penguin Books.

Brienza, L. (1998). New York Community Court honored for innovation. *Justice Technology Monitor*, *1*(1), 1–2 18.

Brown, M. (2000). Criminal justice discovers information technology. In G. LaFree (Ed.), *Criminal Justice 2000: The Nature of Crime: Continuity and Change: Vol. 1.* (pp. 219–259). Washington, DC: National Institute of Justice.

Bryant, K., & Brown, N. (2002). Victim service delivery at the federal level: A case study. *Journal of Crime and Justice, 25*(2), 121–128.

Buckler, K., & Travis, L. (2003). Reanalyzing the prevalence and social context of collateral consequence statutes. *Journal of Criminal Justice, 31*(5), 435–453.

Bureau of Justice Assistance (1997). *National Citizen's Crime Prevention Campaign.* Washington, DC: Bureau of Justice Assistance.

Burns, R., Whitworth, K., & Thompson, C. (2004). Assessing law enforcement preparedness to address Internet fraud. *Journal of Criminal Justice, 32*(6), 477–493.

Burton, V., Cullen, F., Travis, L. F., III (1987). The collateral consequences of a felony conviction: A national study of state statutes. *Federal Probation, 51*(3), 52–60.

Camp, G. M., & Camp, C. C. (1987). *Stopping escapes: Perimeter security.* Washington, DC: U.S. Department of Justice.

Carson, E. A., & Golinelli, D. (2013). *Prisoners in 2012: Trends in admissions and releases, 1991–2012.* Washington, DC: Bureau of Justice Statistics.

Chermak, S., Carter, J., Carter, D., McGarrell, E. F., & Drew, J. (2013). Law enforcement's information sharing infrastructure: A national assessment. *Police Quarterly, 16*(2), 211–244.

Chung, J. (2013). *Felony disenfranchisement: A primer.* Washington, DC: The Sentencing Project.

Cisco (2014). *Cisco visual networking index: Global mobile data traffic forecast update, 2013–2018.* San Jose, CA. Retrieved from http://www.cisco.com/c/en/us/solutions/collateral/service-provider/visual-networking-index-vni/white_paper_c11-520862.html.

Clear, T. R., Hamilton, J. R., & Cadora, E. (2011). *Community justice.* New York, NY: Routledge.

Cooper, A. D. (2012a). *Justice Assistance Grant (JAG) program 2011.* Washington, DC: Bureau of Justice Statistics.

Cooper, A. D. (2012b). *Justice Assistance Grant (JAG) program 2012.* Washington, DC: Bureau of Justice Statistics.

Cooper, A. D. (2013). *Justice Assistance Grant (JAG) program 2013.* Washington, DC: Bureau of Justice Statistics.

Cooper, A. D., & Reaves, B. A. (2011). *Justice Assistance Grant (JAG) program 2010.* Washington, DC: Bureau of Justice Statistics.

Copes, H., & Vieraitis, L. (2009). Bounded rationality of identity thieves: Using offender-based research to inform policy. *Criminology & Public Policy, 8*(2), 237–262.

Cunningham, W. S., Renauer, B., & Khalifa, C. (2006). Sharing the keys to the courthouse: Adoption of community prosecution by state court prosecutors. *Journal of Contemporary Criminal Justice, 22*(3), 202–219.

Dabney, D. (2010). Observations regarding key operational realities in a Compstat model of policing. *Justice Quarterly, 27*(1), 28–51.

Davidenas, J. (1983). The professional license: An ex-offender's illusion. *Criminal Justice Journal, 7*(1), 61–96.

Davis, R. (1987). *Crime victims: Learning how to help them.* Washington, DC: National Institution of Justice.

Davis, R., & Mulford, C. (2008). Victim rights and new remedies: Finally getting victims their due. *Journal of Contemporary Criminal Justice, 24*(2), 198–208.

Davis, R., & Smith, B. (1994a). Victim impact statements and victim satisfaction: An unfulfilled promise? *Journal of Criminal Justice, 22*(1), 1–12.

Davis, R., & Smith, B. (1994b). The effects of victim impact statements on sentencing decisions: A test in an urban setting. *Justice Quarterly, 11*(3), 453–469.

Donohoe, S., & Greloch, A. (1997). Keeping it simple: Design techniques can enhance security. *Corrections Today, 59*, 90–92.

Duwe, G., & Kerschner, D. (2008). Removing a nail from the boot camp coffin: An outcome evaluation of Minnesota's challenge incarceration program. *Crime & Delinquency, 54*(4), 614–643.

Edwards, B., & Braswell, M. (2015). Corporate misconduct and ethics. In M. Braswell, B. McCarthy, & B. McCarthy (Eds.), *Justice, crime, and ethics* (8th ed.). Boston: Elsevier (Anderson Publishing).

Einhorn, M. (2003). *Fighting urban crime: The evolution of federal–local collaboration.* Washington, DC: National Institute of Justice.

Eisinger, P. (2006). Imperfect federalism: The intergovernmental partnership for homeland security. *Public Administration Review, 66*(4), 537–545.

Erez, E., & Tontodonato, P. (1992). Victim participation in sentencing and satisfaction with justice. *Justice Quarterly, 9*(3), 393–417.

Finegan, S. (2013). Watching the watchers: The growing privatization of criminal law enforcement and the need for limits on Neighborhood Watch associations. *UMASS Law Review, 8*, 88–134.

Finn, P. (1995). *The Manhattan District Attorney's Narcotics Eviction Program.* Washington, DC: National Institute of Justice.

Finn, R., & Fontaine, P. (1985). The association between selected characteristics and perceived employability of offenders. *Criminal Justice & Behavior, 12*(3), 353–365.

Finn, P., & Lee, B. (1988). *Establishing and expanding victim-witness assistance programs.* Washington, DC: U.S. Department of Justice.

Friel, C. (2000). A century of boundary changes. In C. Friel (Ed.), *Criminal justice 2000: Boundary changes in criminal justice organizations: Vol. 2.* (pp. 1–17). Washington, DC: National Institute of Justice.

Galaway, B. (1977). The use of restitution. *Crime & Delinquency, 23*(1), 57–67.

Galaway, B., & Hudson, J. (Eds.) (1978). *Offender restitution in theory and action.* Lexington, MA: Lexington Books.

GAO (2013). *Sex Offender Registration and Notification Act: Jurisdictions face challenges to implementing the act, and stakeholders report positive and negative effects.* Washington, DC: United States Government Accountability Office.

Gettinger, S. (1981). Separating the cop from the counselor. *Corrections Magazine, 7*(2), 34–38.

Giacopassi, D., Sparger, J., & Stein, P. (1992). The effects of emergency medical care on the homicide rate: Some additional evidence. *Journal of Criminal Justice, 20*(3), 249–259.

Giblin, M. J., Burruss, G. W., Corsaro, N., & Schafer, J. A. (2011). Self-protection in rural America: A risk interpretation model of household protective measures. *Criminal Justice Policy Review, 23*(4), 493–517.

Gottfredson, D., Cosgrove, C., Wilkins, L., Wallerstein, J., & Rauh, C. (1978). *Classification for parole decision policy.* Washington, DC: U.S. Government Printing Office.

Gottfredson, M., Mitchell-Herzfeld, S., & Flanagan, T. (1982). Another look at the effectiveness of parole supervision. *Journal of Research in Crime and Delinquency, 18*(2), 277–298.

Hakim, S., Rengert, G., & Shachmurove, Y. (1996). Estimation of net social benefits of electronic security. *Justice Quarterly, 13*(1), 153–170.

Hanke, P., & Gundlach, J. (1995). Damned on arrival: A preliminary study of the relationship between homicide, emergency medical care, and race. *Journal of Criminal Justice, 23*(4), 313–323.

Hanna, J. (2008, Fall). Mediation in criminal matters. *Dispute Resolution Magazine, 15*(1), 4–8, 29.

Harries, K. (2003). Using geographic analysis in probation and parole. *National Institute of Justice Journal, 249*, 32–33 (July).

Harris, K. (1995). *Computer crime: An overview.* Sacramento: SEARCH, p. 5.

Harris, P. W., Lockwood, B., & Mengers, L. (2009). *A CJCA white paper: Defining and measuring recidivism.* Braintree, MA: Council of Juvenile Correctional Administrators.

Healy, G. (2002). *Policy analysis: "There goes the neighborhood: The Bush-Ashcroft Plan to 'help' localities fight gun crime".* Washington, DC: CATO Institute.

Helms, R., & Gutierrez, R. (2007). Federal subsidies and evidence of progressive change: A quantitative assessment of the effects of targeted grants on manpower and innovation in large U.S. police agencies. *Police Quarterly, 10*(1), 87–107.

Hickman, M. (2005). *Justice Assistance Grant (JAG) program, 2005.* Washington, DC: Bureau of Justice Statistics.

Hickman, L. J., Davis, L. M., Wells, E., & Eisman, M. (2010). *Tracking inmates and locating staff with active radio-frequency identification (RFID): Early lessons learned in one U.S. correctional facility.* Santa Monica, CA: RAND.

Hickman, M., & Reaves, B. (2006). *Local police departments, 2003.* Washington, DC: Bureau of Justice Statistics.

Holden, R. (1993). Police and the profit motive: A new look at asset forfeiture. *ACJS Today, 12,* 2.

Hughes, L., & Burchfield, K. (2008). Sex offender residence restrictions in Chicago: An environmental injustice? *Justice Quarterly, 25*(1), 647–673.

Hughes, L., & Kadleck, C. (2008). Sex offender community notification and community stratification. *Justice Quarterly, 25*(3), 469–495.

Hurst, H. (1999). *Workload measurement for juvenile justice system personnel: Practices and needs.* Washington, DC: Office of Juvenile Justice and Delinquency Prevention.

International Association of Chiefs of Police (2004). *Executive summary: National criminal intelligence sharing plan.* Gaithersburg, MD: International Association of Chiefs of Police.

Johnson, D. (1981). *American law enforcement: A history.* St. Louis, MO: Forum Press.

Joseph, J. (2005). Technoprison: Technology and prisons. In L. Moriarty (Ed.), *Criminal justice technology in the 21st century* (2nd ed.). Springfield, IL: Charles C. Thomas.

Jung, H., Spjeldnes, S., & Yamatani, H. (2010). Recidivism and survival time: Racial disparity among jail ex-inmates. *Social Work Research, 34*(3), 181–189.

Kamin, S. (2013). Medical marijuana in Colorado and the future of marijuana in the United States. *McGeorge Law Review, 43,* 147–167.

Karlamangla, S. (2013, November 2). City where Trayvon Martin was killed changes Neighborhood Watch rules. *Los Angeles Times.* Retrieved from http://articles.latimes.com/2013/nov/02/nation/la-na-sanford-neighborhood-watch-20131103.

Karp, D., & Clear, T. (2000). Community justice: A conceptual framework. In C. Friel (Ed.), *Criminal justice 2000: Boundary changes in criminal justice organizations: Vol. 2.* (pp. 323–369). Washington, DC: National Institute of Justice.

Kilpatrick, D., Beatty, D., & Howley, S. (1998). *The rights of crime victims—Does legal protection make a difference?* Washington, DC: National Institute of Justice.

Kurlychek, M., Brame, R., & Bushway, S. (2006). Scarlet letters and recidivism: Does an old criminal record predict future offending? *Criminology & Public Policy, 5*(3), 483–504.

Lab, S. (1990). Citizen crime prevention: Domains and participation. *Justice Quarterly, 7*(3), 467–491.

Latessa, E., Travis, L. F., III (1987). Citizen crime prevention: Problems and prospectives in reducing crime. *Journal of Security Management, 10*(1), 38–51.

Latessa, E., & Travis, L. F., III. Oldendick, R., McDermott, B., & Noonan, S. (1988). *The impact of technology in prisons: Final report.* Washington, DC: National Institute of Corrections.

Lundman, R. (1980). *Police and policing: An introduction.* New York: Holt, Rinehart & Winston.

Malsch, M., & Carriere, R. (1999). Victim's wishes for compensation: The immaterial aspect. *Journal of Criminal Justice, 27*(3), 239–247.

Maruschak, L., & Bonczar, T. (2013). *Probation and parole in the United States, 2012*. Washington, DC: Bureau of Justice Statistics.

McCormack, R. (1991). Compensating victims of violent crime. *Justice Quarterly, 8*(3), 329–346.

McGarrell, E. F. (2001). *Restorative justice conferences as an early response to young offenders*. Washington, DC: Office of Juvenile Justice and Delinquency Prevention.

Miethe, T. (1995). Predicting future litigiousness. *Justice Quarterly, 12*(3), 563–581.

Miller, J., & Selva, L. (1994). Drug enforcement's double-edged sword: An assessment of asset forfeiture programs. *Justice Quarterly, 11*(2), 313–335.

Mitchell, O., Wilson, D. B., Eggers, A., & Mackenzie, D. L. (2012). Assessing the effectiveness of drug courts on recidivism: A meta-analytic review of traditional and non-traditional drug courts. *Journal of Criminal Justice, 40*, 60–71.

Morris, R., Copes, H., & Perry-Mullis, K. (2009). Correlates of currency counterfeiting. *Journal of Criminal Justice, 37*(5), 472–477.

Nakashima, E. & Hicks, J. (2014, February 18). Homeland Security is seeking a national license plate tracking system. *The Washington Post*. Retrieved from: http://www.washingtonpost.com/world/national-security/homeland-security-is-seeking-a-national-license-plate-tracking-system/2014/02/18/56474ae8-9816-11e3-9616-d367fa6ea99b_story.html.

National Institute of Justice (2000). At-a-glance: Recent research findings—Effective police management affects citizen perceptions. *National Institute of Justice Journal, 244*, 24–25 (July).

Nobles, M. R., Levenson, J. S., & Youstin, T. J. (2012). Effectiveness of residence restrictions in preventing sex offense recidivism. *Crime & Delinquency, 58*(4), 491–513.

Office for Victims of Crime (2013). *Vision 21: Transforming victim services*. Washington, DC: Office for Victims of Crime.

Peck, M. (2014, January 27). Predator drone sends North Dakota man to jail. *Forbes*. Retrieved from http://www.forbes.com/sites/michaelpeck/2014/01/27/predator-drone-sends-north-dakota-man-to-jail/.

Perry, S. (2006). *Prosecutors in state courts, 2005*. Washington, DC: Bureau of Justice Statistics.

Perry, S. W., & Banks, D. (2011). *Prosecutors in state courts, 2007*. Washington, DC: Bureau of Justice Statistics.

Pew Center on the States (2012). *Time served: The high cost, low return of longer prison terms*. Washington, DC: Pew Center on the States.

Pfuhl, E. (1992). Crime stoppers: The legitimation of snitching. *Justice Quarterly, 9*(3), 505–528.

Porter, N. D. (2010). *Expanding the vote: State felony disenfranchisement reform, 1997–2010*. Washington, DC: The Sentencing Project.

Presser, L., & Lowenkamp, C. (1999). Restorative justice and offender screening. *Journal of Criminal Justice, 27*(4), 333–343.

Rantala, R. R. (2008). *Cybercrime against businesses, 2005*. Washington, DC: Bureau of Justice Statistics.

Rau, R. (1991). Forensic science and criminal justice technology: High-tech tools for the 90's. *National Institute of Justice Reports, 224*, 6–10, June.

Rich, T. (1995). *The use of computerized mapping in crime control and prevention programs*. Washington, DC: National Institute of Justice.

Robinson, L. (1996). Linking community-based initiatives and community justice: The Office of Justice programs. *National Institute of Justice Journal, 231*, 4–7.

Rosenbaum, D., Lurigio, A., & Lavrakas, P. (1986). *Crime stoppers—A national evaluation*. Washington, DC: U.S. Department of Justice.

Rottman, D., & Strickland, S. (2006). *State court organization, 2005*. Washington, DC: Bureau of Justice Statistics.

Schroeder, D., & White, M. (2009). Exploring the use of DNA evidence in homicide investigations: Implications for detective work and case clearance. *Police Quarterly, 12*(3), 319–342.

Schwartz, M., Clear, T., & Travis, L. F., III. (1980). *Corrections: An issues approach.* Cincinnati, OH: Anderson.

Sherman, L., Gottfredson, D., Mackenzie, D., Eck, J., Reuter, P., & Bushway, S. (1997). *Preventing crime: What works, what doesn't, what's promising?* Washington, DC: National Institute of Justice.

Simon, J. (1993). *Poor discipline.* Chicago: University of Chicago Press.

Socia, K. M., & Stamatel, J. P. (2012). Neighborhood characteristics and the social control of registered sex offenders. *Crime & Delinquency, 58*(4), 565–587.

Spelman, W. & Eck, J. (1987). *Newport new tests problem-solving policing.* Washington, DC: National Institute of Justice.

Stanley, J., & Crump, C. (2011). *Protecting privacy from aerial surveillance: Recommendation for government use of drone aircraft.* New York, NY: American Civil Liberties Union.

Stoll, M., & Bushway, S. (2008). The effect of criminal background checks on hiring ex-offenders. *Criminology & Public Policy, 7*(3), 371–404.

Stone, C. (1996). Community defense and the challenge of community justice. *National Institute of Justice Journal, 231,* 41–45 (August).

Straub, J. (2014, in press). Unmanned aerial systems: Consideration of the use of force for law enforcement applications. *Technology in Society.* Retrieved from http://www.sciencedirect.com/science/article/pii/S0160791X13000900.

Travis, L. F., III, & O'Leary, V. (1979). *Changes in sentencing and parole decision making: 1976–78.* Hackensack, NJ: National Council on Crime and Delinquency.

Turner, A. (2007). Automated video surveillance: Improving CCTV to detect and prevent incidents. *Corrections Today, 69,* 44–45 (June).

Uggen, C., Shannon, S., & Manza, J. (2012). *State-level estimates of felon disenfranchisement in the United States, 2010.* Washington, DC: The Sentencing Project.

Umbreit, M. (1989). Crime victims seeking fairness, not revenge: Toward restorative justice. *Federal Probation, 53*(3), 52–57.

Umbreit, M., & Greenwood, J. (2000). *National survey of victim-offender mediation programs in the United States.* Rockville, MD: Office for Victims of Crime.

Vile, J. (1981). The right to vote as applied to ex-felons. *Federal Probation, 45*(1), 12–16.

Villmoare, E., & Neto, V. (1987). *Victim appearances at sentencing under California's Victims' Bill of Rights.* Washington, DC: U.S. Department of Justice.

Wagner, A. (1997). A study of traffic pattern modifications in an urban crime prevention program. *Journal of Criminal Justice, 25*(1), 19–30.

Walker, S. (1985). *Sense and nonsense about crime: A policy guide.* Monterey, CA: Brooks/Cole.

Walker, S. (1994). *Sense and nonsense about crime and drugs: A policy guide* (3rd ed.). Belmont, CA: Wadsworth.

Ward, C. (1997). Community crime prevention: Addressing background and foreground causes of criminal behavior. *Journal of Criminal Justice, 25*(1), 1–18.

Weimer, D. (1980). Vertical prosecution and career criminal bureaus: How many and who? *Journal of Criminal Justice, 8*(6), 369–378.

Welsh, B., & Farrington, D. (2009). Public area CCTV and crime prevention: An updated systematic review and meta-analysis. *Justice Quarterly, 26*(4), 716–745.

Western, B. (2008). Criminal background checks and employment among workers with criminal records. *Criminology and Public Policy, 7*(3), 413–418.

Wilkins, W. (1987). *Sentencing commission chairman Wilkins answers questions on the guidelines.* Washington, DC: National Institute of Justice.

Worrall, J., & Kovandzic, T. (2007). COPS grants and crime revisited. *Criminology, 45*(1), 159–190.

Wright, K., Clear, T. R., & Dickson, P. (1984). Universal applicability of probation risk-assessment instruments: A critique. *Criminology, 22*(1), 113–134.

Zahm, D. (2007). *Using crime prevention through environmental design in problem-solving.* Washington, DC: Center for Problem-Oriented Policing.

Zgoba, K. M., & Levenson, J. (2012). Failure to register as a predictor of sex offense recidivism: The big bad wolf or a red herring? *Sexual Abuse, 24*(4), 328–349.

Zhao, S., Gibson, C., Lovrich, N., & Gaffney, M. (2002). Participation in community crime prevention: Are volunteers more or less fearful of crime than other citizens? *Journal of Crime and Justice, 25*(1), 41–61.

Glossary

A

abandonment a way of disposing unwanted or burdensome children, which gained prominence after the fourth century; the desertion of an infant or child by her or his parents.

absconders offenders who fail to submit to supervision (do not report as directed, change jobs or addresses without notifying their supervising officer, etc.).

actuarial prediction a method of forecasting that focuses on the characteristics of the group to which the individual belongs. Like insurance company life-expectancy tables, it presents the odds of a future event.

actus reus the behavioral or action element of a criminal offense.

adjudication the determination of the facts in a case by a judicial body. Specifically in the juvenile justice system, it refers to the fact-finding process that is similar to the trial in the adult system.

appellate courts tribunals authorized to hear and settle questions of law that arise from lower courts. In most cases, appellate courts do not hear factual matters, and most often the appellate court comprises panels of judges or justices.

apprenticeship a system of education or training in which a youth learned a trade by working as an assistant to a craftsperson. An apprenticeship typically had a set term of training.

arraignment a formal stage of the criminal justice process at which the accused is informed of the criminal charges against her or him, and asked to plead to those charges.

arrest taking a person into custody; one of the decision points of the criminal justice system.

assigned counsel a system for providing criminal defense services for the indigent in which attorneys are assigned or appointed to the case of a defendant from a list of candidates maintained by the court.

B

back door strategies a demand reduction solution aiming to reduce the amount of time inmates remain in prison (e.g., earlier release of inmates).

bail a monetary surety required of a defendant prior to release from custody to assure the defendant's appearance at later court hearings.

bench trial a criminal trial held before a judge alone, without a jury. The judge in a bench trial both presides over the trial and serves as the finder of fact.

benefit of clergy a forerunner to contemporary practices such as probation; the practice of excusing members of the clergy from state criminal responsibility in English courts, the benefit was later extended to all literate citizens.

blended sentencing a practice that allows either the juvenile court or the adult court to impose a sentence on a juvenile offender that can involve either the juvenile or the adult correctional system, or both.

booking the point in the criminal justice process at which the arrest of a criminal suspect is officially recorded (written in the police logbook).

boot camp a specialized prison program in which offenders (typically young) are subjected to a regimen of physical training and strict discipline, but are granted release earlier than more traditional incarceration.

C

career criminal a label given to repeat offenders, generally those who have a lengthy and involved history of criminality.

casework model a model of organizing service delivery in probation, parole, and other settings in which the criminal justice official is assigned subjects (cases) and is responsible for generally serving all of their needs.

charging the process by which the prosecutor (or state's attorney or district attorney) applies the criminal law to the facts of the case and identifies which provisions of the criminal code have been violated.

circuits districts or territories assigned to courts in the federal system; 11 circuits cover the United States; the District of Columbia comprises an additional circuit.

civil death loss or restriction of civil rights so that for legal purposes, the individual is "dead." Often a consequence of conviction in felony cases.

classification the testing and assessment of inmates to determine inmate treatment needs and prison custody and security needs.

clear and present danger conditions or behavior that pose an immediate threat to safety or order and relates to controls on the activities of inmates that pose a direct threat to the smooth operation of the facility.

clinical prediction a method of forecasting that focuses on the characteristics of an individual and estimates the likelihood of that specific person engaging in certain behavior in the future.

closed system a system or collection of interrelated parts that are relatively isolated or insulated from their environment.

cohort studies research based on the longitudinal study of an identifiable group of individuals. The identified group is the cohort about which the study seeks information.

cold case squads teams of detectives dedicated to pursuing cases (usually homicide cases) that have not been solved and lack significant leads.

collateral consequences effects or products of a criminal conviction that are in addition to any criminal penalty, for example, the loss of civil rights.

community corrections legislation statutes that create, and often encourage, the development of sentencing alternatives to imprisonment that involve dealing with the offender in her or his community.

community courts courts that attempt to resolve problems and disputes by addressing all concerned, including the community at large. Such courts are usually linked to community resources.

community justice the empowerment of communities for solving problems and disputes without recourse to the formal system of criminal justice.

community prosecution a type of prosecution in which the prosecutor is assigned to the case from initial appearance through disposition and works with the police, community, and other agencies not just to secure conviction, but to solve the problems that led to the criminal behavior.

community-oriented policing an approach to policing that relies on community definitions of police functions and a partnership between the police and the community in the production of public safety.

community service orders a command by the court that a convicted offender work, without compensation, at some task or job of benefit to the community.

compelling state interest a legal criterion used to judge the reasonableness of a practice or condition. In general, the state must justify its use of intrusive practices or conditions by showing that the practice accomplishes an objective that the state must achieve.

concurrent term a sentence for a criminal conviction that is executed ("runs") at the same time as another sentence.

conditional release permission for an offender to remain in the community if he or she abides by certain conditions, such as reporting regularly to a supervising officer, refraining from consuming alcohol, or other.

congregate system the silent or Auburn model of prison discipline in which inmates ate, worked, recreated, and worshipped together, but were housed in separate cells at night and prohibited from talking with each other.

consecutive term a sentence for a criminal conviction that is delayed in execution until after the sentence for another conviction has expired.

consent decrees decrees whereby the court and the state enter into a voluntary agreement about issues raised in court.

constable a court office in Norman England that had many administrative and public safety duties; a forerunner to the police.

contract systems the practice of leasing to the highest bidder inmate labor and the use of prison work areas and shops.

corporate gang a group of individuals that has a well-organized formal structure and whose purpose is to make money.

cottage reformatories institutions for juvenile offenders established in the mid- to late 1800s that attempted to parallel a family setting.

count a specific criminal charge in an indictment so that, for example, three counts of robbery means three separate charges of robbery.

courtroom work group the people who comprise the major actors in the court process and who generally develop common understandings and norms for how the business of the court will be conducted.

CPTED Crime Prevention Through Environmental Design (pronounced "sep-ted"); programs that change environmental conditions to reduce the likelihood of crime; for instance, by increased lighting and other security devices.

crackdown usually short-term, an intensive police response to a perceived problem. For example, strict enforcement of traffic or parking laws, saturation patrol, and other intensive police efforts focused at specific problem areas.

crime an act or omission in violation of a law, which is punishable by the state.

crime control model an analytic device developed by Herbert Packer that describes how the criminal justice process would operate if the control of crime were the only (or the predominant) goal served by the system.

Crime Index the total number of eight specific types of offenses that are known to the police in any given year, as reported by the Federal Bureau of Investigation.

crime rate a standardized measure of the amount of crime per unit of population. Typically, the number of crimes known to the police per 100,000 members of the population.

crime-stopper programs programs that offer citizens anonymity and rewards for providing information about crimes and criminals to the police.

crime-warps a term coined by Georgette Bennett to describe changes in the nature and definition of crime and criminal justice in America in the future.

criminal justice the formal social institution designed to respond to deviance defined as crime.

crystallized gang a group that has achieved recognition as a gang, has a leadership hierarchy, specialized roles and statuses, and is active in criminal activity.

cynicism in terms of police, the perception or belief that citizens, department leaders, politicians, and other criminal justice officials are not truthful and honest in their dealings with police officers.

D

"dark figure" of crime the amount of criminal activity that is unreported and undetected; specifically, the amount of crime that is not included in official statistics such as the Uniform Crime Reports.

day reporting a community corrections program in which convicted offenders are required to check in with (or at) a supervising center each day, but are allowed to remain in their homes at night and to engage in approved activities (i.e., work or school) during the day.

decoy operation an investigative technique in which police officers act as potential crime victims to attract the attention of criminals. The officers serve as decoys to lure offenders into a trap.

defounding the practice of reducing the seriousness of a crime alleged by a victim or complainant, such as recording a reported felony as if it were a misdemeanor.

deinstitutionalization the practice of refraining from confining juvenile status offenders in state institutions.

delinquent a juvenile who violates the criminal laws of the jurisdiction.

deprivation model a model that explains the development of prisoner subculture as a reaction to the loss of freedom, goods, services, and ties to life outside the prison.

design capacity the number of inmates that a prison was designed to house or hold.

detached workers workers placed in the environment of a gang to provide input geared toward more acceptable activities for the gang.

detection the decision point in the criminal justice process at which police officers come to believe that a crime has occurred.

detention decision the decision whether to keep a juvenile in custody or to allow the youth to go home with parents or guardians to await further court action.

determinate sentencing a sentencing to incarceration in which the exact length and nature of punishment is known at the time it is imposed.

deterrence a reason for criminal punishment based on the idea that punishment of the individual offender produces benefits for the future by making the idea of criminal behavior less attractive.

deviance behavior that violates socially accepted standards of proper conduct.

discharge release from sentence and custody or control by the criminal justice system.

disparity inequality; especially in sentencing when two similarly situated offenders receive different penalties.

disposition outcome; in the juvenile justice system and with probation and parole revocation, a specific hearing stage during which penalty/sentence is decided.

dispute resolution less formal mechanisms for reducing conflicts and resolving criminal complaints between individuals, including mediation, arbitration, and other alternatives to criminal justice processing.

diversion preventing cases from entering the criminal justice system or reducing how far cases progress into the system; avoiding criminal justice processing.

divestiture the elimination of juvenile court jurisdiction over status offenders.

drug courts special courts dedicated to the processing and supervision of drug cases.

drug testing chemical testing for the presence of drugs in the urine, blood, hair, and more of the test subject. A relatively common practice for suspected drug users in criminal justice populations, and often a requirement of employment in criminal justice agencies.

dual system a term used to describe the existence of two sets of courts in the United States, one federal and the other state.

due process model an analytic device created by Herbert Packer to describe a criminal justice system in which the most important goal is the protection of individual liberty.

E

electronic monitoring any of several systems in which criminal offenders are tracked and supervised, at least in part, by radio and or telephone contact.

emergency release programs mechanisms for legally releasing inmates in order to control prison crowding.

emergent gang a group of individuals that has some degree of structure and that engages in some minor offenses but lacks much formalized structure and a commitment to group criminality.

entrapment a defense to criminal charges that applies when the idea for the crime and the motivation to commit the crime are produced by the police and did not arise with the offender.

exclusionary rule created by the appellate courts as protection of constitutional rights and a sanction against police misbehavior, this rule prohibits the use of illegally obtained evidence in criminal prosecutions.

exculpatory evidence evidence that tends to establish the innocence of the accused or defendant.

executive clemency the authority of the executive officer of a jurisdiction to grant mercy or forgiveness to those accused or convicted of a crime. Clemency includes pardon, commutation, and reprieve.

F

false negative in criminal justice prediction, someone who is predicted to be safe, not to pose a threat of future criminality, but who is, in fact, dangerous and commits additional crimes.

false positive in criminal justice prediction, someone who is predicted to be dangerous, to pose a threat of future criminality, but who is, in fact, safe and would not commit additional crimes.

family model an analytic device developed by John Griffiths (in opposition to Packer's due process and crime control models) that contends that the criminal justice system should operate under the assumption that the interests of society and the interests of the offender are the same.

federalism the structure of government in the United States that distinguishes between federal, state, and local governmental interests, duties, responsibilities, and powers.

felony serious criminal offense defined by statute; usually punishable by a term of one year or longer in a state or federal prison.

forays attacks in which one or two gang members attack a single rival gang member, usually using a firearm from a moving vehicle, resulting in an ongoing series of small, isolated attacks between gangs.

forgetting in regard to victim surveys, the possibility that a respondent will forget a crime that occurred during a specific time period.

formal charges the official accusation of criminal conduct that the prosecutor must prove beyond a reasonable doubt if the case goes to trial; established by indictment or the filing of an information in court.

formal social control sanctions that are applied by some authorized body after a public finding of fault.

formalized gang a group of individuals that has a formal structure and organization, owns a meeting place, is committed to criminality as a group, and claims a wide territory.

frisk a limited search (pat down) of the outer clothing of a suspect for the purpose of self-protection through the discovery of any weapons.

front door strategies a demand reduction solution aiming to reduce the number of offenders sent to prison by increasing diversion programs and the use of community-based alternative sentences.

functions the purposes or goals served by social institutions or practices. They can be both manifest (stated, expressed) purposes and latent (hidden) purposes.

funnel effect the effect by which the criminal justice system operates like a giant sieve, continuously filtering the huge volume of crimes and criminals to the relatively small number of offenders who are incarcerated in the nation's prisons.

furlough temporary release from custody; programs of short-term release of prison inmates for specific purposes such as seeking employment and housing prior to release, attending to a personal or family emergency, and the like.

G

general deterrence a subtype of deterrence based on the notion that punishing a specific offender will frighten or warn the general population to avoid criminal behavior.

general jurisdiction a term used to describe the authority of some trial courts that indicates that the court is empowered to settle questions of fact in almost all civil and criminal matters arising within its geographical area.

Global positioning system a technology used in electronic monitoring which can provide real-time tracking of an offender's location using a satellite system.

good faith exception the tenet that if the police conduct a search believing in good faith that the search is permissible, then the evidence can be used at trial.

good time reductions in the length of sentence granted to inmates as a reward for good behavior in the institution.

grand jury a panel of citizens (usually 23, with a quorum of 16) that reviews evidence in criminal cases to determine whether sufficient evidence exists to justify trial of an individual.

H

habitual offender statutes legislative statutes that allow for increased penalties for repeat offenders.

halfway houses a generic term describing residential programs operating in the community in which criminal offenders are housed and provided various treatments. The term indicates that this option is "halfway" between incarceration in prison or jail and release to the community under supervision.

hands-off doctrine phrase describing the reluctance of appellate courts to intervene in the operation of prisons, jails, and other correctional facilities. The term implies that courts grant wide latitude to correctional administrators by keeping their (the court's) hands off of questions of facility administration.

home incarceration a sanction of incarceration that is served in the offender's home, essentially a restriction on liberty that requires the offender to remain in his or her residence during specified hours for a set term, and typically enforced by the use of electronic monitoring.

hot pursuit a circumstance in which the police are closely chasing a crime suspect. Officers engaged in a hot pursuit are not required to seek a warrant to search the area in which the suspect is caught or trapped.

hot spots of crime a term coined by Sherman, Gartin, and Buerger to refer to locations where much more crime can be found than at other places.

Houses of Refuge institutions established in the early 1800s for youthful offenders; they were designed to use education, skills training, hard work, and apprenticeships to produce productive members of society.

hung jury a jury that cannot reach consensus about the verdict.

I

importation model a model that explains the existence of a prisoner subculture as the result of inmates bringing criminal and anti-authority values with them from their lives in the community.

incapacitation a reason for criminal punishment based on the notion that the penalty will prevent the offender from having the chance to commit a crime in the future.

incarceration rate the number of persons incarcerated per 100,000 population eligible for incarceration.

indeterminate sentencing a sentencing to incarceration that is stated as a range of time between some minimum and some maximum term and in which, at the point of sentencing, the exact length of confinement is unknown.

indictment a true bill issued by a grand jury that establishes that the jury found probable cause to have a defendant respond to criminal charges in court. A mechanism of filing formal criminal charges against a defendant.

indigent poor; a criminal defendant or convict who is unable to afford the cost of defense counsel and for whom counsel will be provided at state expense.

infanticide literally, the killing of an infant; the practice in history of killing unwanted or burdensome children shortly after birth.

informal social control mechanisms that influence behavior without the need for a public finding of fault or the use of group-authorized sanctions.

information process a process occurring in open court in which the defendant and his or her attorney are present and are allowed to examine witnesses.

initial appearance the criminal suspect's first appearance in a court hearing, at which the question of pretrial release is decided.

innocence projects coordinated efforts to investigate claims of innocence maintained by persons convicted of criminal offenses.

institutionalization the tendency for residents of "total institutions" (e.g., prison inmates) to become habituated to and dependent on the institutional routine so that they lose the ability to make independent decisions.

intake decision a screening point in the juvenile justice system at which a court official, often a probation officer, decides whether a juvenile's case will be processed through the court or handled outside the formal court process.

intelligence gathering the compilation of information that may be helpful in solving crimes, but with no specific probable cause to believe the information will lead to solving a particular crime.

intensive supervision a form of probation and parole supervision in which offenders receive an increased level of attention from supervision officers that usually includes more in-person contact and closer monitoring by the officer.

intermediate sanctions the term given to describe a range of criminal penalties developed as alternatives to traditional probation or incarceration. These include intensive supervision, house arrest, community service, and other penalties.

interrogation questioning; specifically, the in-custody questioning of crime suspects by the police.

inventory search the routine check of seized property to establish what has been taken by the police. The term specifically applies to inventorying the contents of seized automobiles.

investigation the search for and accumulation of evidence that links a particular crime to a particular person or persons.

involuntary servitude slavery, the requirement that someone work for another; a practice once common for moving children from the family home by placing them in indentureships or apprenticeships.

J

jails relatively short-term custodial facilities, typically operated at the municipal (county) level, used to house a variety of offenders and criminal suspects.

jailhouse lawyers inmates who assist others in the preparation of court documents.

judicial reprieve a practice in early English courts that served as a forerunner to probation. It was essentially a suspended sentence ordered by the judge.

jurisdiction the limits of authority or interest placed on a criminal justice agent or agency and comprised generally of geographic boundaries and the identification of case or offender characteristics.

jury a panel of citizens selected to hear evidence and render a decision in a criminal matter. Grand juries make charging decisions; petit juries render conviction decisions.

jury nullification the power and practice of a petit jury rendering a not guilty verdict despite overwhelming evidence of wrong; this is a statement that the law involved is inappropriate, thus the jury nullifies the law by nonenforcement.

jury trial the determination of guilt by adjudication before a jury at which the state must prove, in open court, all elements of the offense beyond a reasonable doubt, and the jury members make the final determination concerning guilt.

just deserts a justification for criminal penalties based on the notion that criminals, by virtue of breaking the law, have earned their punishment, and noncriminals have earned the right to have criminals punished; therefore, crime deserves punishment.

juvenile a person who by virtue of age, as defined in applicable statute, has not yet reached majority and thus is subject to different treatment than adults. The age limits for juvenile status vary among the states.

L

latent functions the unstated or hidden goals of an institution.

lease system a model of prison labor in which the state rented the labor of convicts and the use of prison shops to the highest bidder.

least restrictive alternative the principle that requires the state use the least intrusive or least controlling practice or regulation to achieve its legitimate aims.

legalistic style coined by James Q. Wilson, this label is attached to those police organizations in which the normal practice is to intervene frequently and formally with citizens and in which the police role and activities are more narrowly defined by law and law enforcement obligations.

level of abstraction with reference to the systems approach or systems theory, the degree of complexity of the topic under study. For example, the social control system is at a higher level of abstraction than the criminal justice system.

lifecourse criminality a person's involvement in crime over his or her entire lifetime, including both childhood and adulthood.

limited jurisdiction used to describe courts or other judicial offices, this phrase generally refers to circumstances in which the court is authorized to hear only the early stages of serious cases, or only to hear less serious or specific types of cases.

lineups an investigatory practice in which the crime suspect, in the company of a group of similar persons, is brought before the witness for identification.

local autonomy a component of federalism, the freedom of local governmental units to define and respond to problems in their own way.

low visibility lacking review; as used by Joseph Goldstein, discretionary decisions by police not to invoke the criminal law. These decisions would not be reviewed by courts or others in the police administration and thus would have "low visibility."

M

mala in se "bad in itself," a term used to describe certain traditional crimes about which there is general agreement that the behavior is wrong.

mala prohibita "bad because prohibited," a term used to describe those crimes about which there is more general disagreement among people concerning whether the behavior is wrong. Often applied to vice and regulatory offenses.

mandatory minimum sentences sentences that reflect a required period of incarceration defined by statute that must be imposed as a sanction if the offender is convicted of a particular crime.

mandatory release release based on earned good time or other statutory sentence-reduction measures; usually does not depend on the discretionary decision of a parole board.

manifest functions the stated purposes of an institution.

mark system the "token economy" of Alexander Maconochie at Norfolk Island by which inmates could earn marks by good behavior and labor. These marks then allowed inmates to progress to increasingly less strict conditions of confinement.

mens rea "mental things," the mental element of a crime such as intention, voluntariness, and other cognitive conditions required by the law.

Miranda **warnings** notification of rights (to remain silent and to have an attorney present) that are required to be given to suspects prior to interrogation; named for the 1966 Supreme Court case *Miranda v. Arizona*, which established these rights.

misdemeanor a crime that is generally considered to be less serious than a felony and that is usually punishable by a term of no more than one year in a local jail.

Missouri Plan a method of judicial selection by which judges are appointed from a slate of qualified candidates and are periodically reviewed by means of a retention election in which citizens decide if the judge, running unopposed, should continue to serve.

model case management system a process for classifying offenders on probation and parole based on both risk of further crime as well as the service needs of the offender, using this information to structure and direct the activities of officers and entire field supervision agencies. The model system was developed and disseminated by the National Institute of Corrections beginning in the early 1980s.

multijurisdictional jails jails that serve more than one municipality or jurisdiction.

N

National Crime Victimization Survey (NCVS) an annual survey of a representative sample of Americans asking their experiences as crime victims. The NCVS is the primary source of victimization data concerning crime in America.

Neighborhood Watch citizen crime prevention programs involving the mobilization of residents to serve as the "eyes and ears" of the police and to watch for and report any crimes or suspicious activities.

net-widening the term used to describe the phenomenon of increasing the number of persons touched by some aspect of the justice system. In particular, it is applied to cases where a new program or service results in more people being subjected to criminal justice intervention because the new program is seen as appropriate to them.

nolle prosequie Latin term meaning "I do not prosecute"; a prosecutor may choose to refuse to prosecute, or "nol pros," a case.

nolo contendere Latin term meaning "no contest," or "I do not contest the charges"; a plea available to criminal defendants, with the consent of the court, in most jurisdictions. The effect of the *nolo contendere* plea is similar to that of a plea of guilty, except the defendant is not "proven" to have broken the law and thus is better able to defend against a civil suit.

O

observations as used here, a type of research that relies upon the on-site, in-person observations of criminal justice practice or the behavior of criminals by the research staff; more generally, "field research."

official statistics any data routinely collected and reported by official agencies of criminal justice. The best known example is the Uniform Crime Reports.

on paper serving a term of probation or parole supervision. The phrase refers to the supervision agreement or conditions of supervision that govern the behavior of the offender as the "paper" the offender is "on."

open system a system that is relatively sensitive to its environment and thus adapts and reacts to changes in the environment.

operational capacity a method of rating the size of a population appropriate for a given correctional institution, based on the facility's staff, existing programs, and services.

order maintenance functions of the police that serve to maintain order, including settling disputes, dispersing crowds, keeping traffic flowing smoothly, and the like.

organized/corporate gang a well-organized group that exists and functions for the purpose of making money through criminal activities.

P

pains of imprisonment a term originated by Gresham Sykes to refer to the social psychological deprivations experienced by prison inmates that combine to make the experience of incarceration personally painful to inmates.

panel attorneys assigned counsel in the federal system, named as such because defense counsel are assigned from a list or panel of approved lawyers.

paramilitary structure military-like structure; having the characteristics of a military organization such as formal ranks, a chain of command, pyramidal organizational structure, and more.

parens patriae "the state as parent"; a doctrine that suggests that the state or government has a parental interest in the welfare of children and can act as a parent when needed. The doctrine underlies the concept of the juvenile court as a nonadversarial, nonpunitive solution of juvenile offending.

parole from the French term meaning "word of honor," it refers to the release of prison inmates, prior to expiration of term, on the condition that they agree to abide by certain restrictions. It also describes the process of conditional liberty, which includes supervision by a state official. Parole can mean either the decision to release, or supervised release in the community.

parole eligibility established by the legislature, this defines which types of inmates can be paroled at what points in their sentence.

partial disclosure when the judge summarizes the facts and the reasons for sentence, allowing the defense to contest any errors.

penitentiary prison; although no longer commonly used in the names of correctional institutions, early prisons were considered to be places in which convicted offenders could "pay" for their crimes and "do penance." Thus, they were call penitentiaries.

peremptory challenges authorization to exclude someone from a particular trial jury without the requirement that a cause for exclusion be shown.

piece price system a method of organizing prison labor that was common in the earliest years of prison, in which the private contractor supplied raw materials and agreed to buy finished products made by inmates at fixed price for each piece of finished product.

plain view doctrine a doctrine that states that police do not need to obtain a warrant to seize contraband or criminal evidence that is plainly visible and requires no search.

plea bargaining the practice of exchange between the prosecution and defense in which the defendant agrees to plead guilty to criminal charges in return for some concession from the prosecution.

pre-gang a loose-knit group of individuals who regularly congregate but rarely engage in criminal activity.

preliminary hearing a hearing in open court at which the prosecution introduces evidence to establish probable cause to have a defendant bound over for trial on criminal charges.

presentence investigation (PSI) a background report on a convicted criminal offender designed to provide the judge with information about the offender's social and criminal history and current status, for use in making a sentencing decision.

presumptive sentencing suggested sanction for conviction of a particular offense, the expected or "presumed" sentence can be modified by the judge for cause.

preventive detention a practice by which defendants suspected to be dangerous are denied bail until their cases are tried.

priority prosecution a prosecutorial style in which offenders are selected to receive increased attention to ensure conviction. Rather than treating each case as unique, cases are classified into types that typically receive different treatments.

prisons typically larger institutions used to house convicted adult felons for terms of 1 year or longer.

Prison Litigation Reform Act a 1995 law requiring inmates to exhaust all administrative remedies (appeals through the prison administration and department of corrections) before they can file a suit in federal court.

Prison Rape Elimination Act a 2003 law providing for the development of better information about the nature and incidence of rape and sexual assault in prisons, and providing funding to correctional authorities to reduce and control sexual violence in prisons.

prisonization the term describing the process by which prison inmates come to learn and accept the values and norms of the inmate subculture.

private court offices or commissions for dispute resolution that divert cases away from the formal courts, usually staffed by volunteers or paid staff whose salaries are lower than that of a judge.

privately retained counsel counsel or attorney for the defense in a criminal matter, who is hired and paid privately by the defendant.

privatization the movement to turn government functions over to operation by private sector (profit or not-for-profit) organizations.

pro se **defense** "defense for self"; the provision of defense services in court proceedings by the defendant acting on his or her own behalf rather than by relying on a representative.

proactive self-motivated or self-initiated; specifically as related to policing, efforts to detect or respond to crimes that are motivated by the police themselves without reliance upon a formal complaint.

probable cause evidence that leads a reasonable person to conclude that a crime has occurred and evidence of the crime may be found to support the search.

probation a sentence of conditional and revocable release into the community, generally under supervision, usually imposed in lieu of incarceration. The process of supervising and enforcing conditions of release in lieu of incarceration.

Probation Subsidy Act an early form of community corrections legislation in California that provided financial incentives to counties to retain convicted offenders at the local level under probation supervision as an alternative to incarceration in state prisons.

prosecutorial case management a system for assigning, managing, and conducting the work of a prosecutor's office, generally involving case classification and the establishment of priorities for the expenditure of prosecutorial resources.

protective custody a method for protecting inmates from attacks by other inmates, usually a housing unit kept separate from the general inmate population.

public account system a model of prison industry in which prison labor is used in the production of goods for sale on the open market, and the prison industry, as a public agency, operates like a private business.

public defender common in larger and busier criminal jurisdictions, a model for the provision of defense counsel to the indigent that relies on a public office organized similarly to that of the prosecutor.

public works system a model of prison industry in which inmate labor is used in the completion of public works such as road construction and maintenance, the building or repair of public buildings, and similar public projects.

Q

quality-of-life policing a style in which the police focus on minor crimes as a means of preventing serious crime. Improving the quality of life in the neighborhood is seen to lead to effective informal social control and, ultimately, less serious crime.

R

Radio-frequency a technology used in electronic monitoring which confirms that an offender is at approved locations by sending a radio signal to an offender's land-line telephone or a receiver located in their home

rated capacity a method for determining the size of a population that is appropriate for a specific correctional institution, based on a judgment or rating of some official such as a health inspector or fire marshal.

reactive responsive; specifically as it relates to policing, efforts of the police to detect or prevent crime, which are initiated by or in reaction to a formal complaint.

recidivism the commission of criminal behavior by a person after release or discharge from the criminal justice process.

reentry the return of former inmates to life in the community.

reentry courts courts in which services for and supervision of parolees are coordinated and monitored in a court environment.

reformatory a prison typically reserved for youthful adult felony offenders.

rehabilitation a justification for the imposition of a criminal sentence based on the idea that crime is symptomatic of problems an offender has with regard to living within society. The punishment is imposed "for the offender's own good," and is intended to change the offender's need or proclivity to engage in crime.

release on recognizance (ROR) generally used at the pretrial stage of the process, the order allowing a defendant to remain at liberty in the community pending further court actions without posting any bond or surety.

restitution repayment for the harm caused by criminal behavior; an increasingly common part of criminal sanctions that requires convicted offenders to repay their victims.

restorative justice efforts to repair the harm to victims and/or communities caused by crime through interventions with the offender.

retribution a justification for criminal penalties that is based on the principle that wrong deserves to be punished, regardless of whether the punishment produces any benefit.

revocation recall; the cancellation of conditional liberty (usually probation or parole) upon a finding that the offender has violated the conditions of release.

routine activities theory a theory suggesting that crime occurs when a motivated offender and a suitable target (victim or property) come together in time and space in the absence of an effective guardian.

rumble the traditional image of the gang fight involving two groups of youths in a prearranged fight.

S

scavenger gang a group that exists without particular goals or organizational structure but serves to give members a sense of belonging.

search an investigatory technique in which police or other officials seek physical evidence of criminality or contraband.

segregate system an early form of prison discipline, practiced in the Pennsylvania penitentiaries, in which inmates were kept isolated from each other for the duration of their confinement.

self-report studies surveys that attempt to measure the amount of crime committed and describe the characteristics of offenders by asking people if they have committed offenses.

sentencing the imposition of a sanction upon conviction of a crime; the decision and process of deciding upon an appropriate penalty for a specific criminal act or acts.

sentencing commissions formal bodies assigned to assess and oversee criminal sentencing and recommend reforms.

separation of powers the reservation of specific functions and authority to particular branches of government that enables the system of "checks and balances" to operate.

service style coined by James Q. Wilson, the term refers to a method of policing in which officers intervene frequently, but informally, in the lives of citizens.

shire reeve an early Saxon political office representing the head of a large group of families (shire); forerunner to the contemporary office of sheriff.

shock incarceration short-term prison programs in which the conditions of incarceration are much more severe but limited in duration (e.g., boot camps).

shock parole early release to parole supervision after a comparatively brief period of incarceration. The purpose is to "shock" the offender with a small period of incarceration followed by an unexpected early release to supervision.

shock probation see shock parole; a grant of probation to an offender previously sentenced to prison after serving a relatively small portion of the prison term.

situational crime prevention an approach to controlling crime through efforts to change the context in which crime happens, including changing the physical, organizational, and social environment.

smug hack a brutal, calloused, authoritarian correctional officer; a prison guard who behaves as a petty tyrant.

social control the process of directing and limiting the behavior of individual members of a social group or society.

special conditions requirements for release and/or supervision written into the supervision agreement for probation or parole. These are not generally imposed on all probationers or parolees.

special jurisdiction a nontraditional authorization; for example, in policing, special jurisdiction agencies may have full police powers within a park, on transportation routes or on waterways but lack general police powers throughout the municipality.

special prosecutor an attorney appointed by a governmental authority for the purpose of conducting investigations and pursuing criminal cases arising from particularly complex or politically sensitive circumstances.

specific deterrence a subtype of deterrence in which the purpose of the penalty is to frighten the individual offender into conformity, regardless of the effect of the sanction on the broader, general public.

split sentences sentences combining a period of incarceration with a period of community supervision as part of the sentence order; splitting the total sentence between incarceration and community supervision.

standard conditions requirements for release and/or supervision that are imposed on everyone under supervision in a given jurisdiction.

state-use system a model of prison industry in which prison labor and prison factories are operated to produce goods solely for the use of governmental entities and not for sale on the open market; for example, using prison factories to produce state-issued automobile license plates.

status offenses regarding juvenile offenders, acts prohibited by law or justifying juvenile justice system intervention that apply to youth solely by virtue of their status as juveniles (e.g., truancy, running away, etc.).

sting operation a police decoy operation in which officers pretend to be involved in a criminal operation such as a stolen automobile "chop shop" or a fencing operation and in which criminal offenders who sell the proceeds of their crimes are "stung" or caught by these decoy officers.

street sense intuition based on experience that enables police officers to detect criminality; a phrase describing how police officers develop hunches and suspicions in circumstances that would not attract a second thought from civilians.

strict liability an offense in which the mental state or *mens rea* is presumed to be present so that mere behavior constitutes the elements of the crime regardless of intention.

supervision fees costs charged to offenders on probation and parole supervision that are used to offset the expenses of operating the supervision process. These fees are typically billed in monthly installments for the length of the supervision period.

suretyship the practice of a person of good standing in the community taking responsibility for guaranteeing the lawful behavior of another person; the forerunner to modern parole.

system a collection of interrelated parts working together toward a common goal.

T

team supervision a model of organizing probation or parole offices in which a group or "team" of personnel are assigned to provide service and surveillance to offenders. In theory, this model allows officers to specialize, thus improving the efficiency of the supervision process.

technical violations infractions of the rules of supervision that do not involve any new criminality (e.g., violating curfew).

telescoping in regard to victim surveys, the possibility that a respondent will erroneously include an earlier event in reporting on criminal victimizations during a specific time period.

territorial gang a group having a clear identity and leadership that is organized around specific, identifiable geographic areas.

theory a logical explanation for reality; a statement of how things work.

third-party policing a policing style in which the police work with outside parties to exert control over offenders or criminal contexts. For example, the police might pressure a landlord to evict a tenant who is selling drugs from his apartment.

three-strikes laws laws that increase prison terms for offenders having been convicted of a serious criminal offense on three or more separate occasions.

throw-downs a process of criminal suspect identification in which a set of photographs, including a picture of the suspect, is presented (thrown down) before a witness who is asked to pick out the photograph of the person who committed the crime.

ticket of leave a practice of early release developed by Sir Walter Crofton by which prisoners could be released early by issuance of a ticket of leave from the prison. A forerunner to modern parole.

tort a civil action; an offense against an individual settled in a civil court.

total institution a concept developed by Irving Goffman to refer to settings, such as prisons and mental hospitals, in which residents are completely dependent on facility staff and where virtually all decisions are made by staff rather than by the individuals.

TPC Model A parole case management model that approaches offender reentry as a process which begins at sentencing and continuing until discharge from community supervision.

transportation a practice of England in the eighteenth and nineteenth centuries in which offenders convicted of several types of crimes were banished to English colonies. Convicted offenders were "transported" to these distant locations as a punishment for crime. This practice was a forerunner to modern parole.

treatment see rehabilitation; a justification for sentencing based on the belief that criminal offenders can be helped to prevent them from committing future crimes; the delivery of services—and the services themselves—provided to criminal offenders as a means to reduce future criminality.

trial the fact-finding point in the criminal justice process; the court stage at which the state must present evidence sufficient to convince the judge or jury beyond a reasonable doubt that the defendant committed the crimes charged, or else the defendant is released from further processing.

trial courts those courts in which criminal (and often civil) cases are heard to determine the facts of the case.

truth in sentencing the concept that offenders should actually serve at least 85 percent of the term they receive; legislation requiring truth in sentencing has been passed in many states.

U

undetected crime crime that is not known to the criminal justice system or the victim; crimes that are not recognized as crimes.

unfounding the process that takes place when police decide that a citizen's complaint of a crime is not supported by available evidence. The unfounding of a complaint essentially "erases" the event as a crime known to the police.

unified court system a system that combines general-jurisdiction and limited-jurisdiction courts into one.

Uniform Crime Reports (UCR) published annually by the Federal Bureau of Investigation, the most well-known source of official statistics on crime. Among other things, the report includes a count of all crimes known to police participating in the UCR program, as well as a description of the characteristics of persons arrested for crimes.

unofficial statistics in regard to crime and criminal justice, statistics and data concerning the amount and distribution of crime and the activities of criminal justice agents and agencies that are collected and reported by persons who are not themselves involved in the official criminal justice processing of cases.

unreported crime crime that victims recognize as law-breaking behavior, but is not brought to the attention of authorities.

unsolved an adjective used to describe criminal cases in which the police have been unable to identify an individual or group as the offender.

unsupervised parole a practice used in some jurisdictions in which active supervision of a parolee is terminated before the expiration of sentence and the discharge of the parolee from criminal justice custody.

V

venire the panel of citizens from which a jury can be chosen.

vertical prosecution the practice of assigning the responsibility of a case to a single prosecutor who then follows that same case throughout the entire court process.

victim compensation the payment of damages to victims of crime to compensate them for the losses experienced by virtue of being a crime victim. The program by which states establish funds and procedures for the payment of claims by crime victims.

victim impact statement an official statement by a victim that explains the loss incurred by the victim as a result of the crime.

victim/offender mediation an alternative to criminal justice processing in which the crime victim and criminal offender are brought together to negotiate a "settlement" of the criminal complaint without full criminal justice processing.

victimization data estimates of the rate and distribution of crime derived from survey respondents' reports of experiences of being the victims of crime.

victims' rights a term referring to the status of crime victims in the criminal justice system and to summarize a movement designed to increase concern for crime victims and change criminal justice processing to be more sympathetic to the needs and concerns of crime victims.

violation a minor criminal offense typically punishable by a fine or restriction of privileges such as speeding, overtime parking, or the like. The breaking of a condition of supervision by a probationer or parolee.

voir dire "speak the truth"; the jury selection process in which members of a venire are interrogated by both sides (prosecution and defense, in criminal trials) to determine their suitability for service on the jury.

W

waiver decision the decision to transfer a juvenile offender to the adult court; a determination that, though a juvenile in terms of age, an offender should be tried and punished as an adult by virtue of the seriousness of the crime or the characteristics of the offender.

watchman style coined by James Q. Wilson, the term refers to police agencies in which officers only infrequently intervene in the lives of citizens.

wrongful conviction the result when innocent persons are convicted of criminal acts.

Author Index

Note: Page numbers followed by *b* indicate boxes, and *t* indicate tables.

Lauritsen, J., 34, 114–115
Lavrakas, P., 497
Lawton, B., 180–181, 253
Laycock, G., 77
LeBeau, J., 182
LeClair, D., 282–283, 399
Lee, B., 497
Lee, J., 142–143
Lee, M., 115–116
Lee, R., 342
Leffingwell, T.R., 436
Leifker, D., 292
Leigh, D., 47
Leo, R., 168, 175
Leone, M., 223–224
Lero, C., 376
Lersch, K., 190, 191
Levenson, J.S., 488
Levick, M., 470
Levinson, R.B., 354–355
Ley, B., 177–178
Liberty, H., 110–111
Lichbach, M., 106–107
Lichtstein, B., 360–361
Liederbach, J., 128–129, 141–142, 150
Liedka, R., 142–143, 351–352
Lilley, D., 98
Lilly, J.R., 70
Lin, J., 465
Lindquist, C., 392–393
Lindsey, E., 391
Link, B.G., 67
Linnemann, T., 100
Lipsey, M.W., 284, 477–478
Listwan, S., 322–323, 376
Litras, M., 244
Lo, C., 73–74
Lockwood, B., 491
Lockwood, D., 335, 371–372
Logan, C.H., 322, 352, 354, 356
Loges, W., 259–260, 262
Lombardo, L.X., 336, 367
Lommel, J., 353–354
Longmire, D., 219
Longshore, D., 217–218
Lonski, P.D., 364
Lonsway, K., 153
Lopes, G., 253
Lord, V., 155–156
Lotke, E., 84–85
Lovrich, N., 353–354, 498
Lowenkamp, C., 419, 425, 500–502
Lucas, W., 406–407
Luczak, S., 436

Lukoff, I.F., 102
Luna, E., 16, 69, 71
Lundahl, B., 357
Lundberg, J.C., 253
Lundman, R., 119, 130–132, 153, 507
Lundman, R.A., 17
Luongo, A., 180–181
Lurigio, A., 128, 304, 497
Lutze, F., 301, 333, 423, 439
Lynch, J., 34, 108–110, 114–115, 351–352
Lynch, T., 19, 186, 228, 229

M

Maahs, J., 54, 357
MacDonald, J., 194
MacIntosh, R., 257–258, 408
MacKenzie, D.L., 87, 284, 423, 424–425, 492, 515
MacKenzie, L.R., 474
Maddan, S., 299–300
Madensen, T., 87
Maguire, E., 146–147
Maguire, K., 366
Mahan, S., 374
Mahanna, P., 38
Maher, T., 190
Mahoney, A.R., 473
Major, A.K., 456t
Makarios, M., 166, 425
Malega, R., 249–250
Malsch, M., 500
Maltz, M., 102
Mann, C.R., 119–120
Mann, K., 427–428
Manning, P.K., 128–129, 152, 197
Manza, J., 489
Marcus, S., 183–184
Marenin, D., 10
Markowitz, F., 4
Marlowe, D., 217–218, 262–263
Marquart, J.W., 115, 338, 356–357, 368, 371, 374, 375
Marshall, F.H., 433
Martin, J., 360–361, 404
Martin, S., 80
Martinson, R.M., 283
Martinussen, M., 153
Maruschak, L., 61, 325–326, 353, 394, 395–396, 485
Marvell, T., 361
Marx, G., 426
Mason, M., 115–116
Mastrofski, S.D., 46, 115, 128–129, 146, 155, 183, 194

Matejkowski, J., 421
Mateu-Gelabert, P., 199–200
Matheson, D., 269–270
Mawhorr, T., 393
Maxson, C.L., 458
Maxwell, C.D., 50, 194
Maxwell, S., 224–225, 226–227, 236–237, 403
May, D., 404–405
Mayer, J., 190
Mayo-Wilson, E., 427–428
Mays, G.L., 210–211, 327
Mayzer, R., 403
Mazerolle, L., 180
McCall, K., 49–50
McCampbell, M.S., 146
McCarthy, B.R., 254, 304–305, 465
McCluskey, J., 194
McCorkle, R., 368–369
McCormack, R., 502
McCoy, C., 34, 120
McDermott, B., 505–506
McDevitt, J., 429
McDonald, D., 353, 358, 398
McDonald, J., 331
McElrath, K., 110–111
McEwen, T., 360–361
McGaha, J., 417
McGarrell, E.F., 9, 82–84, 90, 139, 143–144, 500, 511–512
McGee, R., 327
McGloin, J., 141–142
McIntyre, D.M., 165
McLearen, A., 149
McMahon, M., 354
McMillan, J., 257
McNulty, T., 116, 458
McSparron, J., 401–402
Meares, T., 352
Meehan, A., 118–119, 121
Meeker, J., 511–512
Mellow, J., 353, 397
Mellowa, J., 437–438
Menard, S., 102
Mendelsohn, R., 10–11
Mengers, L., 491
Menke, B., 353–354
Merritt, N., 98
Messner, S., 34
Metchik, E., 152
Meyer, J., 45, 118–119
Meyers, A., 46
Mieczkowski, T., 191
Miethe, T.D., 67, 516
Miggans, K., 141–142

Subject Index

Note: Page numbers followed by *b* indicate boxes, *f* indicate figures, and *t* indicate tables.